Why Sams Publishing's *Teach Yourself Oracle8 in 21 Days* Beats Oracle Press's *Oracle8 Beginner's Guide* for Beginners and DBAs:

	TY Oracle8	Beginner's Guide
Learning method used:	Uses both graphical tools and command-line code	Text-heavy, fewer GUIs used
Better coverage of Oracle tools:		
Enterprise Manager	Extensive coverage throughout the book	Half a chapter/nine figures
Schema Manager	Explore objects with figures and examples	Definition only
Jobs Manager	Learn jobs scheduling with examples and figures	No coverage
Replication Manager	Step-by-step guide with figures	No coverage
Web Publishing Assistant	Publish to the Web with easy-to-follow guide	No coverage
Database Assistant	Use the DA for installation	No coverage
Better coverage of new capabilities:		
Nested tables	Example with code	Definition only
Large object data types	Learn the various associated types	No discussion of LOB, CLOB, and so on

Teach
Yourself
ORACLE8™

in 21 days

Teach Yourself
ORACLE8™
in 21 days

Edward Whalen

Steve Adrien DeLuca

SAMS
PUBLISHING

201 West 103rd Street
Indianapolis, Indiana 46290

International Standard Book Number: 0-672-31159-3

Library of Congress Catalog Card Number: 97-67506

2000   99   4   3

Interpretation of the printing code: the rightmost double-digit number is the year of the book's printing; the rightmost single-digit, the number of the book's printing. For example, a printing code of 97-1 shows that the first printing of the book occurred in 1997.

Composed in AGaramond and MCPdigital by Macmillan Computer Publishing

Printed in the United States of America

Trademarks

President Richard K. Swadley
Publisher Joseph B. Wickert
Executive Editor Rosemarie Graham
Managing Editor Kitty Wilson Jarrett
Indexing Manager Johnna L. VanHoose
Director of Marketing Kelli S. Spencer
Product Marketing Manager Wendy Gilbride
Marketing Coordinator Linda B. Beckwith

Acquisitions Editor
Steve Straiger

Development Editor
Marla Reece-Hall

Production Editor
Kate Shoup Welsh

Copy Editor
Kimberly K. Hannel

Indexer
Erika Millen

Technical Reviewer
Kelly Leigh

Editorial Coordinators
Mandie Rowell
Katie Wise

Technical Edit Coordinator
Lorraine E. Schaffer

Editorial Assistants
Carol Ackerman
Andi Richter
Rhonda Tinch-Mize
Karen Williams

Cover Designer
Aren Howell

Book Designer
Gary Adair

Copy Writer
David Reichwein

Production Team Supervisors
Brad Chinn
Andrew Stone

Production
Mike Henry
Polly Lavrick
Mary Ellen Stephenson
Becky Stutzman

Overview

Week 3 in Review

Contents

Foreword

"Enabling the information age" is the slogan upon which Oracle is founded, but it is more than a slogan to engineers who dedicate their knowledge and experience to the task of delivering this information with accuracy and speed. In this age of information, just getting the data is not enough. The data that is so vital to business must be dependable, accurate, and delivered as quickly as possible.

Two such engineers I have worked with in this endeavor are Edward T. Whalen and Steve Adrien DeLuca. Edward has won his mastery in the field of performance benchmarks and system tuning. A former employee of COMPAQ Computers and currently CEO of Performance Tuning Corp., Edward has held many benchmark records for the highest degree of performance from the Transaction Processing Performance Council, which is responsible for creating and maintaining industry-standard benchmarks. Edward has also published a book on Oracle tuning, which has given him well-deserved notoriety.

Steve is an Architect Engineer in the COMPAQ products division of Oracle Corporation. Steve holds the distinction of being the co-inventor of the Oracle System Sizer (patent pending), which has won him much acclaim in the field of sizing and capacity planning.

Together, Edward and Steve have delivered lectures in the field of performance tuning, sizing, and capacity planning to audiences over the world. They have also performed benchmarks for such customers as Boeing Aircraft with more than satisfactory results. It is only natural that they would collaborate on this book. I look forward to working with Edward and Steve for many years to come, breaking new ground in the field of performance.

Richard French
Vice President
Enterprise Platforms Division
Oracle Corporation

Acknowledgments

Edward Whalen

Writing the acknowledgments for a book is difficult; I owe my thanks not only to those who worked on the book itself, but to those friends and family who supported and encouraged me to move the book forward. I am always afraid I have missed someone; if I have, I apologize.

I would like to thank Rosemarie Graham, Steve Straiger, Marla Reece-Hall, Kim Hannel, and especially Kate Shoup Welsh at Sams Publishing for their help in the development of the book. The editorial staff at Sams is excellent and absolutely great to work with. Without their help, this book could not have been published. I would also like to thank Kelly Leigh for doing a great job of technical editing. Lastly I would like to thank Erika Millen for creating the index for this book.

I would especially like to thank my good friend Steve DeLuca for his participation in this book. I would also like to thank Richard French for contributing a foreword to this book.

I would like to thank not only the people who have directly influenced this book and helped make it a reality, but those who have indirectly influenced it as well. These people are Bob Nissen, Thomas Cox, Keith Yedlin, Mike Brey, and Eric Speed. I would also like to thank some of the people who have influenced me in my endeavors and have taught me over the years: Lorna Livingtree and Brent Schroeder. Some other people who have been inspired me are Marci Frohock and Bryon Georgson.

In my previous book I failed to mention someone without whom none of this would be possible: Larry Ellison. I apologize. Larry Ellison's hard work made Oracle what it is today.

Writing a book involves a lot of time and effort. I would like to thank my wife, Felicia, for putting up with the sacrifices necessary to write this book as well as for her help in finishing the book.

Steve Adrien DeLuca

I would like to take this opportunity to thank the great management staff at Oracle: people like Jerry Baker, Gary Bloom, Jerry Held, Richard French, Bonnie Crater, Sylvia Cummings, Charles Weiss, David Appelbaum, and of course, Larry Ellison, for letting me develop my ideas; talented database engineers such as Andrew Rist for co-inventing Oracle System Sizer (patent pending) with me; and Mike Brey, Bob Nissen, Ethan Berry, John Viguerie, Jose Sanchez, Jeff Plank, Theresa Burghgraef, Fred Dambrosio, Bryon Georgson, Tamar Sofer-Rothenberg, Vicky Owens, and others too numerous to mention for helping me prove the theories.

What can one say about close friends such as Edward Whalen, who invited me to contribute to this writing, or family like my wife, Jean, and daughter Tina, who have always been there to support me. A special thanks to the folks at COMPAQ Computer such as Ronnie Ward, Keith Carlson, Douglas Mackbee, and Mike Nikolaiev, for letting me tinker around their labs.

About the Authors

Lead Author

Edward Whalen is president and CEO of Performance Tuning Corporation (www.perftuning.com), a consulting company specializing in database performance, administration, and backup/recovery solutions. He has had extensive experience in database system design and tuning for optimal performance. Mr. Whalen has also written another Sams book, *Oracle Performance Tuning and Optimization*. He is recognized as a leader in Oracle performance tuning and optimization.

He is a representative on the Transaction Processing Performance Council, which is responsible for creating and maintaining industry-standard database benchmarks. As part of this council, he has participated in the development of several TPC benchmarks.

Mr. Whalen currently resides in Cypress, Texas, with his wife, Felicia; their Border collies, Pierce (Dash), Chip, Teller, and Ty; their Great Pyrenees, Shasta; and their cats. He is active in many dog-related activities, including dog agility. He is also a certified EMT and volunteers with the local emergency ambulance service, Cypress Creek EMS, where he is a regular on Medic-53, Medic-54, and Medic-55.

Contributing Author

Steve Adrien DeLuca has been an architect engineer developing performance tools at Oracle Corporation since 1994. Mr. DeLuca co-invented the Oracle System Sizer (patent pending) and has been developing performance tools and lecturing about them around the world since 1984. Prior to working at Oracle Corporation, Mr. DeLuca served as a performance engineer specializing in sizing and capacity planning for companies such as DEC, Tandem, and Apple, and for organizations such as the U.S. Air Force.

Tell Us What You Think!

As a reader, you are the most important critic of and commentator on our books. We value your opinion and want to know what we're doing right, what we could do better, what areas you'd like to see us publish in, and any other words of wisdom you're willing to pass our way. You can help us make strong books that meet your needs and give you the computer guidance you require.

Do you have access to the World Wide Web? Then check out our site at http://www.mcp.com.

NOTE

If you have a technical question about this book, call the technical-support line at 317-581-3833 or send e-mail to support@mcp.com.

As the team leader of the group that created this book, I welcome your comments. You can fax, e-mail, or write me directly to let me know what you did or didn't like about this book—as well as what we can do to make our books stronger. Here's the information:

Fax: 317-581-4669

E-mail: enterprise_mgr@sams.mcp.com

Mail: Rosemarie Graham
            Comments Department
            Sams Publishing
            201 W. 103rd Street
            Indianapolis, IN 46290

Introduction

I have worked with Oracle for many years. Every time a new version is released or a new problem crops up, I am rejuvenated; I become excited about working with Oracle again. I want to share this enthusiasm with you, and I hope that after you become familiar with Oracle, more and more aspects of the Oracle RDBMS will interest you. The most important thing is that you enjoy what you are doing; I hope that you enjoy working with Oracle as much as I do.

The Oracle RDBMS is an enormous environment with unlimited potential. When you start working with Oracle, you might find it overwhelming. Don't give up; you will see how the different components work together as you learn about the Oracle RDBMS. Rarely do I undertake a project without learning something new about Oracle.

Who Should Read This Book?

This book is designed for inexperienced Oracle users. Experienced Oracle DBAs will likely find this book too elementary. Most of the lessons are designed to step the reader through specific administrative and user tasks.

Required Software

To be able to work through the examples in this book, you must have the following software:

- [ ] Oracle 8.0.3 or later
- [ ] Oracle Enterprise Manager
- [ ] Microsoft Windows NT 4.0 or other OS

Although many of the examples and exercises in this book are geared toward Microsoft Windows NT, you need not run NT. If your system runs UNIX, you will be fine.

How to Use This Book

The best way to use this book is to read each lesson, then practice the techniques and tasks outlined in that lesson. Each lesson covers a single topic, so some lessons might be longer than others. If you complete one lesson per day, you can easily complete the full course in three weeks.

At the end of each lesson, you'll find a series of questions and answers. These questions are designed to point out some of the key concepts that were covered in the lesson. Following the Q&A section, you'll find a series of quiz questions that focus on techniques and tasks covered in the lesson. Each lesson also includes a series of exercises that are intended to familiarize you with some of the key tasks covered in that lesson.

Conventions Used in This Book

 New terms appear in italic, and are accompanied by a new term icon.

Notes explain interesting or important points that can help you understand concepts and techniques.

Tips are pieces of information that help you in real-world situations. Tips often provide shortcuts or information to make a task easier or faster.

Warnings provide information about detrimental performance issues or dangerous errors. Pay careful attention to warnings.

Working with Code and Code Conventions

INPUT The input icon indicates code that you type.

OUTPUT The output icon indicates the result of running a piece of code.

All code in the listings appears in monospace. Many code-related terms within the text also appear in monospace. Placeholders in code or in text appear in *italic monospace*.

When a line of code is too long to fit on one line of this book, it is broken at a convenient place and continued to the next line. A code continuation character (➥) precedes the continuation of a line of code. (You should type a line of code that has this character as one long line without breaking it.)

ANALYSIS Paragraphs that begin with the analysis icon explain the preceding code example.

 The syntax icon identifies syntax statements.

Throughout this book there will be references to SQL statements and Oracle administration statements. These will be distinguished in the following manner:

☐ Any Oracle or SQL keyword that must be typed exactly will be displayed in uppercase letters, as in SELECT. This syntax does not necessarily require uppercase characters in its execution, but will be displayed that way for consistency.

☐ Statements that can be or need to be altered for your own particular configuration are indicated by italics, as in SELECT * FROM *table_name*. This would indicate that *table_name* should be substituted with your own table's name.

☐ The use of braces indicates a choice of several optional variables. An example of this would be the following SQL statement: SELECT [USER_NAME or USER_ID] FROM *table_name*;. This would indicate that the keywords USER_NAME or USER_ID must be used in that SQL query.

☐ The use of brackets indicates a choice of various optional parameters. In this case, the parameter may be used or omitted as necessary. An example of this is the SQL statement SELECT USER_NAME, GROUP_NAME FROM *table_name* [ORDER BY GROUP_NAME];.

Author's Note

Most of this book was written before the production version of Oracle8 was available. I have tried to change any example or explanation of a task that has changed since Oracle8 beta 2. I believe I have made all of these corrections, but if you see a figure or an explanation of a task that is not quite correct, it is because the original section was based on that beta release.

WEEK 1

1
2
3
4
5
6
7

At a Glance

You will spend Days 1–3 in the introductory section of the book, where the foundation for all subsequent lessons is built. This section begins with an introduction to Oracle and database concepts. Here you will learn a bit of Oracle history as well as read an explanation of terms and concepts. Subsequent lessons contain an introduction to the Oracle8 architecture. Understanding the architecture and operation of Oracle8 can offer great insight into why many DBA actions are taken. A tutorial on how to install Oracle8 will also be provided in this section. Finally, my good friend Steve DeLuca, world-renowned capacity planning expert from Oracle, will teach you how to size a system and plan for future growth.

Managing Database Storage

Days 4–7 cover topics concerning management of the Oracle database (including extensive use of Enterprise Manager), databases and datafiles, and tablespaces. Coverage regarding managing database storage continues into week 2.

Day 1

Starting Out with Oracle

Being an Oracle database operator or administrator can be a demanding but rewarding career that carries with it a great deal of responsibility as well as authority. This book is intended to help you embark on this exciting path. I hope that within the pages of this book I can convey some of the enthusiasm and excitement I feel when working with state-of-the-art hardware and software such as Oracle8.

I think the best way to grasp a concept is to fully understand why actions are taken and the consequences of those actions. If you understand how Oracle works and its interactions with the operating system and hardware, you can more easily predict and anticipate the result of actions you take. In this book, I attempt to fully explain the workings of Oracle and the supporting software and hardware.

A Brief History of Oracle

In 1977, Larry Ellison, Bob Miner, and Ed Oates formed a company called Relational Software Incorporated (RSI). This company built an RDBMS called *Oracle*. Ellison, Miner, and Oates made a key decision: to develop their RDBMS using C and the SQL interface. Soon after, they came out with version 1, a prototype. In 1979, RSI delivered its first product to customers. The Oracle RDBMS version 2 worked on the Digital PDP-11 running the RSX-11 operating system and was soon ported to the DEC VAX system.

1983 heralded the release of version 3, which touted changes in the SQL language as well as performance enhancements and other improvements. Unlike earlier versions, version 3 was written almost entirely in C. At this point, RSI changed its name to Oracle Corporation.

Oracle version 4 was released in 1984. This version supported both the VAX system and the IBM VM operating system. Version 4 was the first version to incorporate read consistency. Version 5, introduced in 1985, was a milestone because it introduced client/server computing to the market with the use of SQL*Net. Version 5 was also the first MS-DOS product to break through the 640KB barrier.

In 1988, Oracle presented version 6, which introduced low-level locking as well as a variety of performance improvements and functionality enhancements, including sequence generation and deferred writes. I was introduced to Oracle6 back in the days when we ran the TP1, TPC-A, and TPC-B benchmarks. At this point, Oracle was running on a large variety of different platforms and operating systems. In 1991, Oracle introduced the Oracle Parallel Server option on version 6.1 of the Oracle RDBMS on the DEC VAX platform. Soon the Parallel Server option was available on a variety of platforms.

Oracle7, released in 1992, included many architectural changes in the area of memory, CPU, and I/O utilization. Oracle7 is the full-featured RDBMS to which you are accustomed, the one you've been using for many years. Oracle7 introduced many advances in the area of ease of use, such as the SQL*DBA tools and database roles.

Finally, in 1997 Oracle introduced Oracle8, which added object extensions as well as a host of new features and administrative tools.

For more information about the history of Oracle (specifically about the Oracle server), check out the two-part article by Ken Jacobs in the January/February and March/April 1995 issues of *Oracle Magazine*.

For more information about the Oracle corporation, its products, and about working with Oracle, check out www.oracle.com. This Web site contains a wealth of information about Oracle parterships and products as well as information about the Oracle Developer Program, which specifically assists developers.

Introduction to Terms

Many different terms and concepts will be used throughout this book. I've introduced them here to make it easier for you to grasp many of the concepts and lessons to follow. If you encounter other terms with which you are unfamiliar, check out Appendix D, "Glossary."

Ad-Hoc Query

This use of the Latin term means an impromptu, simple query.

Block

A block is the smallest unit of storage in an Oracle database. The database block contains header information concerning the block itself as well as the data or PL/SQL code. The Oracle block size is configurable with the minimum size being 2KB and the maximum size being 16KB.

Bottleneck

In computer terms, a bottleneck is a system component that limits the performance of the system.

Buffer

This term refers to an amount of memory used to store data. A buffer stores data that is about to be used or that has just been used. In many cases, buffers are in-memory copies of data that is also on disk. Buffers can be used as a copy of data for quick read access, they can be modified and written to disk, or they can be created in memory as temporary storage.

In Oracle, database buffers of the SGA store the most recently used blocks of database data. The set of database block buffers is known as the *database buffer cache*. The buffers used to temporarily store redo entries until they can be written to disk are known as *redo log buffers*.

Cache

A cache is a storage area used to provide fast access to data. In hardware terms, the cache is a small (relative to main RAM) amount of memory that is much faster than main memory. This memory is used to reduce the time it takes to reload frequently used data or instructions into the CPU. CPU chips themselves contain small amounts of memory built in as cache.

In Oracle, the block buffers and shared pool are considered caches because they are used to store data and instructions for quick access. Caching is very effective in reducing the time it takes to retrieve frequently used data.

Caching usually works using a least recently used algorithm. Data that has not been used for a while is eventually released from the cache to make room for new data. If data is requested and is in the cache (a phenomenon called a *cache hit*), the data is retrieved from the cache, preventing it from having to be retrieved from memory or disk. After the data has been accessed again, it is marked as recently used and put on the top of the cache list.

Checkpoint

A checkpoint is an operation that forces all changed, in-memory data blocks to be written out to disk. This is a key factor in how long the database takes to recover in the event of a failure. This concept is discussed in depth on Day 2, "Exploring the Oracle Architecture."

Clean Buffer

A *clean buffer* is a buffer that has not been modified. Because this buffer has not been changed, it is not necessary for the DBWR to write this buffer to disk.

Concurrency

This term refers to the capability to perform many functions at the same time. Oracle provides for concurrency by allowing many users to access the database simultaneously.

Database

A database is a set of data, organized for easy access. The database is the actual data. It is the database that you will be accessing when you need to retrieve data.

Data Dictionary

The data dictionary is a set of tables Oracle uses to maintain information about the database. The data dictionary contains information about tables, indexes, clusters, and so on.

DBA (Database Administrator)

The DBA is the person responsible for the operation, configuration, and performance of the database. The DBA is charged with keeping the database operating smoothly, ensuring that backups are done on a regular basis (and that the backups work), and installing new software. Other responsibilities might include planning for future expansion and disk space needs, creating databases and tablespaces, adding users and maintaining security, and monitoring the database and retuning it as necessary. Large installations might have teams of DBAs to keep the system running smoothly; alternatively, the tasks might be segmented among the DBAs.

DBMS or RDBMS

The Database Management System is the software and collection of tools that manages the database. Oracle software is the DBMS. A Relational Database Management System is a DBMS that is relational in nature. This means that the internal workings access data in a relational manner. Oracle is an RDBMS.

DDL (Data Definition Language) Commands

These commands are used in the creation and modification of schema objects. These commands provide the ability to create, alter, and drop objects; grant and revoke privileges and roles; establish auditing options; and add comments to the data dictionary. These commands are related to the management and administration of the Oracle database. Before and after each DDL statement, Oracle implicitly commits the current transaction.

Dirty Buffer

A *dirty buffer* is a buffer that has been modified. It is the job of the DBWR to eventually write all dirty block buffers out to disk.

DML (Data Manipulation Language) Commands

These commands allow you to query and modify data within existing schema objects. Unlike the DDL commands, a commit is not implicit. DML statements consist of DELETE, INSERT, SELECT, and UPDATE statements; EXPLAIN PLAN statements; and LOCK TABLE statements.

Dynamic Performance Tables

These tables are created at instance startup and used to store information about the performance of the instance. This information includes connection information, I/Os, initialization parameter values, and so on.

Function

A function is a set of SQL or PL/SQL statements used together to execute a particular function. Procedures and functions are identical except that functions always return a value (procedures do not). By processing the SQL code on the database server, you can reduce the number of instructions sent across the network and returned from the SQL statements.

IM (Information Management)

This term is usually used to describe the department that handles your corporate data.

IS (Information Systems)

This term is also used to describe the department that handles your corporate data.

IT (Information Technology)

This term is used to describe the business of managing information.

Network Computing Architecture (NCA)

The Network Computing Architecture is a standard for computing over the network. The NCA was developed in conjunction with Oracle.

Physical Memory

This term refers to the actual hardware RAM (Random Access Memory) available in the computer for use by the operating system and applications.

Procedure

A procedure is a set of SQL or PL/SQL statements used together to execute a particular function. Procedures and functions are identical except that functions always return a value (procedures do not). By processing the SQL code on the database server, you can reduce the number of instructions sent across the network and returned from the SQL statements.

Program Unit

In Oracle, program unit is used to describe a package, a stored procedure, or a sequence.

Query

A query is a read-only transaction against a database. A query is generated using the SELECT statement. Users generally distinguish between queries and other transaction types because a query does not the change data in the database.

Schema

A schema is a collection of objects associated with the database.

Schema Objects

Schema objects are abstractions or logical structures that refer to database objects or structures. Schema objects consist of such things as clusters, indexes, packages, sequences, stored procedures, synonyms, tables, views, and so on.

System Global Area (SGA)

The SGA is a shared-memory region that Oracle uses to store data and control information for one Oracle instance. The SGA is allocated when the Oracle instance starts; it is deallocated when the Oracle instance shuts down. Each Oracle instance that starts has its own SGA. The information in the SGA is made up of the database buffers, the redo log buffer, and the shared pool; each has a fixed size and is created at instance startup.

Transaction

A transaction is a logical unit of work consisting of one or more SQL statements, ending in a commit or a rollback. Performance measurements often use the number of transactions per second or per minute as the performance metric.

Trigger

A trigger is a mechanism that allows you to write procedures that are automatically executed whenever an INSERT, UPDATE, or DELETE statement is executed on a table or view. Triggers can be used to enforce integrity constraints or automate some other custom function.

Virtual Memory

This term refers to the memory that can be used for programs in the operating system. To overcome the limitations associated with insufficient physical memory, virtual memory allows programs to run that are larger than the amount of physical memory in the system. When there is not enough physical memory in the system, these programs are copied from RAM to a disk file called a *paging* or *swap file*. This arrangement allows small systems to run many programs. You pay a performance penalty when the computer pages or swaps.

Storage Units

Data is stored in the computer in a binary form. The units used to refer to this binary data are as follows:

Term	Definition	Comment
bit	The smallest unit of data storage	A bit is either a 1 or a 0.
nibble	4 bits	This term is not commonly used.
byte	8 bits	The most commonly used storage unit.
word	This term is architecture dependent	On some systems, a word is 16 bits; on others, a word is 32 or 64 bits.
kilobyte (KB)		Even though *kilo* usually means 1,000, a kilobyte in computer terms is actually 1,024 bytes (because we like powers of 2).
megabyte (MB)		The term megabyte denotes 1,024KB or 1,048,576 bytes.
gigabyte (GB)		A gigabyte is 1,024 megabytes or 1,073,741,824 bytes.
terabyte (TB)		A terabyte is 1,024 gigabytes or 1,099,511,627,776 bytes.

It is not uncommon to hear large data warehousing sites talk in terms of terabytes. In the next few years, you will probably hear of systems using storage in the tens and hundreds of terabytes.

Oracle Configurations

There are many different types of Oracle configurations and uses. Let's look at some of these different types of systems and analyze their usage and characteristics.

OLTP

The Online Transaction Processing (OLTP) system is probably the most common of the RDBMS configurations. OLTP systems have online users that access the system. These systems are typically used for order-entry purposes, such as for retail sales, credit-card validation, ATM transactions, and so on.

Characteristics of OLTP Systems

OLTP systems typically support large numbers of online users simultaneously accessing the RDBMS. Because users are waiting for data to be returned to them, any excessive response time is immediately noticeable. OLTP systems are characteristically read and write intensive. Depending on the specific application, this read/write ratio might vary.

DSS

The Decision Support System (DSS) is used to assist with the decision-making process. These decisions might be based on information such as how sales in a particular region are doing, what cross-section of customers is buying a particular product, or to whom to send a mailing. The DSS system is used to help make decisions by providing good data.

Characteristics of a DSS

The DSS is characterized by long-running queries against a large set of data. Unlike the OLTP system, where users are waiting for data to return to them online, here users expect the queries to take minutes, hours, or days to complete. The data is typically generated from a different source and loaded onto the DSS computer in bulk. Except for during the load, the DSS system is characterized by being read intensive (with very few writes).

Data Warehouse

A data warehouse is typically considered to be a large-scale system that consists of both DSS and OLTP components. These systems are typically hundreds of gigabytes in size and support many users.

Characteristics of a Data Warehouse

Data warehouses have some of the attributes of a DSS system, such as long-running queries and a possible online component. In many cases, this component is the source of the data used in the DSS queries.

Data Mart

A data mart, which is a smaller-scale version of a data warehouse, serves many of the same functions as a data warehouse.

Characteristics of a Data Mart

A data mart is typically 100GB or less in size. As with a data warehouse, a data mart supports many online users as well as a decision-support function.

Video Server

A video server can support large numbers of video data streams. These video streams can be used for purposes such as video on demand for entertainment as well as training functions.

Characteristics of a Video Server

The video server system must support a high network bandwidth in order to support multiple data streams. The video server must also be able to support a high I/O bandwidth. These disk accesses are typically of a very large block size and sequential in nature.

Web Server

The Oracle Web server is designed to support both static and dynamic Web pages. These pages can be simple Web pages or complex database-generated pages. Oracle Web server systems are also typically used in Web commerce applications. These installations can allow

1

the customer to browse online catalogs, which might feature graphics or even video. The customer can then purchase items online.

Characteristics of an Oracle Web Server

The Oracle Web server typically supports many online users. There is typically a large amount of data that has been accessed frequently and other data that is less frequently accessed. A large amount of memory can help improve performance in this type of configuration.

OLAP

The term OLAP (Online Analytical Processing) is usually used in relation with multidimensional data. OLAP users might be financial analysts or marketing personnel looking at global data.

Characteristics of an OLAP System

An OLAP system typically involves a large amount of disk space with heavy I/O and memory requirements. An OLAP system might support only a few or many users. This depends on your type of configuration.

Roles and Responsibilities of an Oracle DBA

If you want to become an Oracle DBA, you should first understand what an Oracle DBA's job is. The basic roles of the DBA are fairly consistent among different companies, but these duties might be expanded based on the size of the company and the experience of the DBA. In fact, the DBA is considered the main resource for DBMS experience and knowledge in many companies.

Let's look at these roles and responsibilities and determine what skills are necessary to fulfill these duties. Here the roles and responsibilities are divided into two categories: basic duties and additional duties. The dividing line between these is not clear; there is significant overlap.

Basic Duties of the DBA

Here are some of the basic roles of the Oracle DBA. This is not an all-inclusive list. Depending on your installation and staff, your duties might not include all of these, or might include many more items. This section is simply intended as a general guide.

☐ Installation of new software—It is primarily the job of the DBA to install new versions of Oracle software, application software, and other software related to DBMS administration. It is important that the DBA or other IS staff members test this new software before it is moved into a production environment.

☐ Configuration of hardware and software with the system administrator— In many cases the system software can only be accessed by the system administrator. In this case, the DBA must work closely with the system administrator to perform software installations, and to configure hardware and software so that it functions optimally with the DBMS.

☐ Security administration—One of the main duties of the DBA is to monitor and administer DBMS security. This involves adding and removing users, administering quotas, auditing, and checking for security problems.

☐ Performance tuning and monitoring—The DBA must continually monitor system performance and be prepared to retune the system as necessary. Even a well-tuned system must be constantly monitored and adjusted. Sometimes this involves changing tuning parameters, other times this involves rebuilding an index or restructuring a table.

☐ Backup and recovery—Perhaps the most important responsibility of the DBA is protecting the data in the system. To effectively do this, you must develop an effective backup and recovery strategy and make sure it is carried out. A DBA's chief responsibility is to maintain the integrity of the database. It is important that the backup and recovery process be periodically tested.

☐ Routine scheduled maintenance—It is the job of the DBA to schedule routine DBMS maintenance and carry out this maintenance. This maintenance is regularly carried out in the early hours of the morning or on weekends when this maintenance causes the least inconvenience to the user community.

☐ Troubleshooting —In the event of a system or DBMS failure, it is the job of the DBA to troubleshoot or assist in the troubleshooting of the problem. The DBA might also participate in or lead the effort to find and eliminate problems or potential problems.

☐ Failure recovery—Because a system failure can mean that the users do not have access to their data, it can be the job of the DBA to lead efforts to recover from system failures. The well-prepared DBA has contingency plans for system outages and can soon have the DBMS running again.

Additional Duties of the DBA

Some of the more advanced duties of the Oracle DBA might include the following:

☐ Data analysis—The DBA will frequently be called on to analyze the data stored in the database and to make recommendations relating to performance and efficiency of that data storage. This might relate to the more effective use of indexes or the use of some feature such as the Parallel Query option.

☐ Database design (preliminary)—The DBA is often involved at the preliminary database-design stages. Through the involvement of the DBA, many problems that might occur can be eliminated. The DBA knows the DBMS and system, can point out potential problems, and can help the development team with special performance considerations.

☐ Data modeling and optimization—By modeling the data, it is possible to optimize the system layout to take the most advantage of your I/O subsystem.

☐ Assisting developers with SQL and stored procedure development—The DBA should be prepared to be a resource for developers and users. The DBA is often called on to help with SQL problems as well as to design and write stored procedures.

☐ Enterprise standards and naming conventions—Because many different groups might perform different roles in developing and deploying applications, it is often the DBA who is called on to help define enterprise standards and naming conventions as well as to ensure that new applications are conforming to these standards.

☐ Development of production migration procedures—Because the DBA is responsible for the availability and reliability of the DBMS and applications using that DBMS, it is up to the DBA to develop and maintain procedures for rolling out new applications and DBMS software. This involves evaluating new software or patches as well as testing them. It is up to the DBA to guarantee the stability and robustness of the system.

☐ Environmental documentation—The DBA should document every aspect of the DBMS environment, including hardware configuration and maintenance records, software updates, changes to the applications and DBMS, and all other items related to changes made to the system. The DBA should be able to access these records and fully reproduce the current system as necessary.

☐ Consult with development team and end users—The DBA is often called on to act as a consultant to the development team as well as to the user community. This might involve personally assisting a single user or developing training courses for the user community as a whole.

☐ Evaluation of new software—The DBA might be called on to evaluate new software and make recommendations based on that evaluation. This might be related to a software purchase or a scheduled rollout of a new version of software. This evaluation must be done in the context of the stability of the system. It is your responsibility to maintain system stability and reliability.

☐ Evaluation of new hardware and software purchases—There is much consideration involved in purchasing new hardware and software. Much of this consideration involves the functionality and compatibility of the software or hardware as well as the cost of these components. Although the cost of the item is not usually a concern of the DBA, the functionality and compatibility is. The DBA might be asked to make recommendations based on whether these purchases make sense.

    ☐ Capacity planning and sizing—Determining whether it is necessary to purchase new hardware or software to meet increased loads is often a job for the DBA. Capacity planning and sizing is important to provide the level of service your users require. By anticipating the future needs of your users, you can provide an excellent level of service with no interruptions.

Summary

This lesson introduces some of the topics you will see in the rest of the book. First you saw a brief history of how Oracle got where it is today. Then you examined number of terms that you will see throughout the book. These terms are important; you will use them every day in your job as a DBA. Finally, you were presented with some of your tasks and responsibilities as a DBA.

What's Next?

Tomorrow's lesson examines the structure and operation of Oracle. By having an understanding of how Oracle works, you can better understand how to administer it. You will look at some of the new features in Oracle8, as well as receive an overview of Oracle performance.

Q&A

Q What units of measurement are typically used in databases?

A With Oracle systems you usually discuss size in terms of megabytes and gigabytes, but some systems are growing into the terabyte range.

Q Are the duties of the DBA the same for all companies?

A No, far from it. No two sites are the same. Although the basic duties and responsibilities might be similar, the extended duties are always different.

Q Why is it important to document?

A If you document the system configuration and logging changes, you will have a much easier time reproducing the system in the event of a failure. By having configuration information in a log book you can save numerous hours of trial and error in reconfiguring the system.

Workshop

The workshop provides quiz questions to help you solidify your understanding of the material covered. For answers to quiz questions, see Appendix A, "Answers."

Quiz

1. How is a DBMS different from a database?
2. What is a DDL statement?
3. What is a DML statement?
4. What are some of the characteristics of an OLTP system?
5. What are some of the characteristics of a DSS system?
6. State five duties of an Oracle DBA.
7. What is the most important duty of an Oracle DBA?

Week 1

Day 2

Exploring the Oracle Architecture

NEW TERM   The Oracle Relational Database Management System, or *RDBMS*, is designed to allow simultaneous access to large amounts of stored information. The RDBMS consists of the database (the information) and the instance (the embodiment of the system). The database contains the physical files that reside on the system and the logical pieces such as the database schema. These database files take various forms, as described in the following section. The instance is the method used to access the data and consists of processes and system memory.

> Object extensions have been added to the RDBMS with Oracle8. The object extension to tables is covered in detail on Day 12, "Working with Tables, Views, and Synonyms." Oracle refers to Oracle8 as an O-RDBMS (Object-Relational Database Management System). In this book, I refer to Oracle as an RDBMS for clarity.

The Database

The Oracle database has a logical layer and a physical layer. The physical layer consists of the files that reside on the disk; the components of the logical layer map the data to these physical components.

The Physical Layer

The physical layer of the database consists of three types of files:

☐ One or more datafiles—Datafiles store the information contained in the database. You can have as few as one datafile or as many as hundreds of datafiles. The information for a single table can span many datafiles or many tables can share a set of datafiles. Spreading tablespaces over many datafiles can have a significant positive effect on performance. The number of datafiles that can be configured is limited by the Oracle parameter MAXDATAFILES.

☐ Two or more redo log files—Redo log files hold information used for recovery in the event of a system failure. Redo log files, known as the redo log, store a log of all changes made to the database. This information is used in the event of a system failure to reapply changes that have been made and committed but that might not have been made to the datafiles. The redo log files must perform well and be protected against hardware failures (through software or hardware fault tolerance). If redo log information is lost, you cannot recover the system.

☐ One or more control files—Control files contain information used to start an instance, such as the location of datafiles and redo log files; Oracle needs this information to start the database instance. Control files must be protected. Oracle provides a mechanism for storing multiple copies of control files.

The Logical Layer

The logical layer of the database consists of the following elements:

☐ One or more tablespaces.

☐ The database schema, which consists of items such as tables, clusters, indexes, views, stored procedures, database triggers, sequences, and so on.

Tablespaces and Datafiles

NEW TERM The database is divided into one or more logical pieces known as *tablespaces*. A tablespace is used to logically group data together. For example, you can create one tablespace for accounting and a separate tablespace for purchasing. Segmenting groups into different tablespaces simplifies the administration of these groups (see Figure 2.1). Tablespaces consist of one or more datafiles. By using more than one datafile per tablespace, you can spread data over many different disks to distribute the I/O load and improve performance.

Figure 2.1.

The relationship between the database, tablespaces, and datafiles.

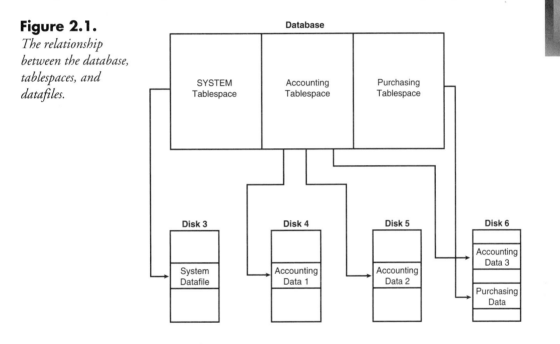

As part of the process of creating the database, Oracle automatically creates the SYSTEM tablespace for you. Although a small database can fit within the SYSTEM tablespace, it's recommended that you create a separate tablespace for user data. The SYSTEM tablespace is where the data dictionary is kept. The data dictionary contains information about tables, indexes, clusters, and so on.

Datafiles can be operating system files or, in the case of some operating systems, RAW devices. Datafiles and data access methods are described in detail on Day 12.

The Database Schema

NEW TERM The database schema is a collection of logical-structure objects, known as *schema objects*, that define how you see the database's data. These schema objects consist of structures such as tables, clusters, indexes, views, stored procedures, database triggers, and sequences.

☐ Table—A table, which consists of a tablename and rows and columns of data, is the basic logical storage unit in the Oracle database. Columns are defined by name and data type. A table is stored within a tablespace; often, many tables share a tablespace.

☐ Cluster—A cluster is a set of tables physically stored together as one table that shares a common column. If data in two or more tables is frequently retrieved together based on data in the common column, using a clustered table can be quite efficient. Tables can be accessed separately even though they are part of a clustered table. Because of the structure of the cluster, related data requires much less I/O overhead if accessed simultaneously.

☐ Index—An index is a structure created to help retrieve data more quickly and efficiently (just as the index in this book allows you to find a particular section more quickly). An index is declared on a column or set of columns. Access to the table based on the value of the indexed column(s) (as in a WHERE clause) will use the index to locate the table data.

NOTE

A new feature in Oracle8 is the index-only table. In an index-only table, the data and index are stored together. This is discussed in detail on Day 13, "Using Indexes and Sequences."

☐ View—A view is a window into one or more tables. A view does not store any data; it presents table data. A view can be queried, updated, and deleted as a table without restriction. Views are typically used to simplify the user's perception of data access by providing limited information from one table, or a set of information from several tables transparently. Views can also be used to prevent some data from being accessed by the user or to create a join from multiple tables.

☐ Stored procedure—A stored procedure is a predefined SQL query that is stored in the data dictionary. Stored procedures are designed to allow more efficient queries. Using stored procedures, you can reduce the amount of information that must be passed to the RDBMS and thus reduce network traffic and improve performance.

☐ Database trigger—A database trigger is a procedure that is run automatically when an event occurs. This procedure, which is defined by the administrator or developer, triggers, or is run whenever this event occurs. This procedure could be an insert, a deletion, or even a selection of data from a table.

☐ Sequence—The Oracle sequence generator is used to automatically generate a unique sequence of numbers in cache. By using the sequence generator you can avoid the steps necessary to create this sequence on your own such as locking the record that has the last value of the sequence, generating a new value, and then unlocking the record.

Segments, Extents, and Data Blocks

Within Oracle, the space used to store data is controlled by the use of logical structures. These structures consist of the following:

☐ Data blocks—A block is the smallest unit of storage in an Oracle database. The database block contains header information concerning the block itself as well as the data.

☐ Extents—Extents consist of data blocks.

☐ Segments—A segment is a set of extents used to store a particular type of data, as shown in Figure 2.2.

Figure 2.2.

Segments, extents, and data blocks.

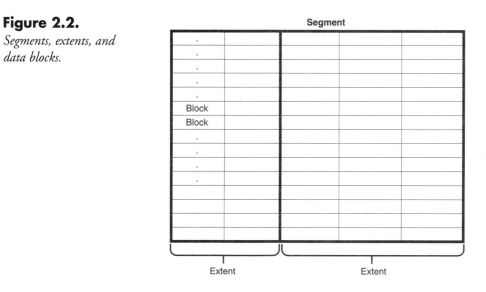

Note: Within an extent, the data blocks are contiguous.

Segments

An Oracle database can use four types of segments:

☐ Data segment—Stores user data within the database.

☐ Index segment—Stores indexes.

☐ Rollback segment—Stores rollback information used when data must be rolled back.

☐ Temporary segment—Created when a SQL statement needs a temporary work area; these segments are destroyed when the SQL statement is finished. These segments are used during various database operations, such as sorts.

Extents

Extents are the building blocks of segments; in turn, they consist of data blocks. An extent is used to minimize the amount of wasted (empty) storage. As more and more data is entered into tablespaces in your database, the extents used to store that data can grow or shrink as necessary. In this manner, many tablespaces can share the same storage space without preallocating the divisions between those tablespaces.

At tablespace-creation time, you can specify the minimum number of extents to allocate as well as the number of extents to add at a time when that allocation has been used. This arrangement gives you efficient control over the space used in your database.

Data Blocks

Data blocks are the smallest pieces of an Oracle database; they are physically stored on disk. Although the data block in most systems is 2KB (2,048 bytes), you can change this size for efficiency depending on your application or operating system.

NOTE

Oracle blocks do not need to be, and may not be the same as, operating system data blocks. In fact, in most cases they are not.

The Oracle Instance

The Oracle instance consists of the Oracle processes and shared memory necessary to access information in the database. The instance is made up of the user processes, the Oracle background processes, and the shared memory used by these processes (see Figure 2.3).

The Oracle Memory Structure

NEW TERM   Oracle uses shared memory for several purposes, including caching of data and indexes as well as storing shared program code. This shared memory is broken into various pieces, or *memory structures*. The basic memory structures associated with Oracle are the System Global Area (SGA) and the Program Global Area (PGA).

Figure 2.3.

The Oracle instance.

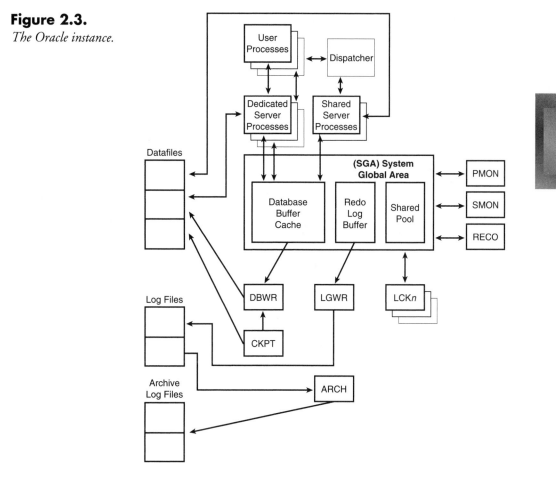

The System Global Area (SGA)

The SGA is a shared memory region that Oracle uses to store data and control information for one Oracle instance. The SGA is allocated when the Oracle instance starts and deallocated when the Oracle instance shuts down. Each Oracle instance that starts has its own SGA. The information in the SGA consists of the following elements, each of which has a fixed size and is created at instance startup:

☐ The database buffer cache—This stores the most recently used data blocks. These blocks can contain modified data that has not yet been written to disk (sometimes known as *dirty blocks*), blocks that have not been modified, or blocks that have been written to disk since modification (sometimes known as *clean blocks*). Because the buffer cache keeps blocks based on a most recently used algorithm, the most active buffers stay in memory to reduce I/O and improve performance.

☐ The redo log buffer—This stores redo entries, or a log of changes made to the database. The redo log buffers are written to the redo log as quickly and efficiently as possible. Remember that the redo log is used for instance recovery in the event of a system failure.

☐ The shared pool—This is the area of the SGA that stores shared memory structures such as shared SQL areas in the library cache and internal information in the data dictionary. The shared pool is important because an insufficient amount of memory allocated to the shared pool can cause performance degradation. The shared pool consists of the library cache and the data-dictionary cache.

The Library Cache

The library cache is used to store shared SQL. Here the parse tree and the execution plan for every unique SQL statement are cached. If multiple applications issue the same SQL statement, the shared SQL area can be accessed by each to reduce the amount of memory needed and to reduce the processing time used for parsing and execution planning.

The Data-Dictionary Cache

The data dictionary contains a set of tables and views that Oracle uses as a reference to the database. Oracle stores information here about the logical and physical structure of the database. The data dictionary contains information such as the following:

☐ User information, such as user privileges

☐ Integrity constraints defined for tables in the database

☐ Names and data types of all columns in database tables

☐ Information on space allocated and used for schema objects

The data dictionary is frequently accessed by Oracle for the parsing of SQL statements. This access is essential to the operation of Oracle; performance bottlenecks in the data dictionary affect all Oracle users. Because of this, you should make sure that the data-dictionary cache is large enough to cache this data. If you do not have enough memory for the data-dictionary cache, you see a severe performance degradation. If you ensure that you have allocated sufficient memory to the shared pool where the data-dictionary cache resides, you should see no performance problems.

The Program Global Area (PGA)

The PGA is a memory area that contains data and control information for the Oracle server processes. The size and content of the PGA depends on the Oracle server options you have installed. This area consists of the following components:

☐ Stack space—This is the memory that holds the session's variables, arrays, and so on.

☐ Session information—If you are not running the multithreaded server, the session information is stored in the PGA. If you are running the multithreaded server, the session information is stored in the SGA.

☐ Private SQL area—This is an area in the PGA where information such as binding variables and runtime buffers is kept.

Processes

NEW TERM In many operating systems, traditional processes have been replaced by *threads* or *lightweight processes*. The term *process* is used in this book to describe a thread of execution, or a mechanism that can execute a set of code; *process* refers to the mechanism of execution and can refer to a traditional process or a thread.

The Oracle RDBMS uses two types of processes: user processes and Oracle processes (also known as background processes). In some operating systems (such as Windows NT), these processes are actually threads; for the sake of consistency, I will refer to them as *processes*.

User Processes

User, or client, processes are the user's connections to the RDBMS system. The user process manipulates the user's input and communicates with the Oracle server process through the Oracle program interface. The user process is also used to display the information requested by the user and, if necessary, can process this information into a more useful form.

Oracle Processes

Oracle processes perform functions for users. Oracle processes can be split into two groups: server processes (which perform functions for the invoking process) and background processes (which perform functions on behalf of the entire RDBMS).

Server Processes (Shadow Processes)

Server processes, also known as shadow processes, communicate with the user and interact with Oracle to carry out the user's requests. For example, if the user process requests a piece of data not already in the SGA, the shadow process is responsible for reading the data blocks from the datafiles into the SGA. There can be a one-to-one correlation between user processes and shadow processes (as in a dedicated server configuration); although one shadow process can connect to multiple user processes (as in a multithreaded server configuration), doing so reduces the utilization of system resources.

Background Processes

Background processes are used to perform various tasks within the RDBMS system. These tasks vary from communicating with other Oracle instances and performing system maintenance and cleanup to writing dirty blocks to disk. Following are brief descriptions of the nine Oracle background processes:

☐ DBWR (Database Writer)—DBWR is responsible for writing dirty data blocks from the database block buffers to disk. When a transaction changes data in a data block, that data block need not be immediately written to disk. Therefore, the DBWR can write this data to disk in a manner that is more efficient than writing when each transaction completes. The DBWR usually writes only when the database block buffers are needed for data to be read. Data is written in a least recently used fashion. For systems in which asynchronous I/O (AIO) is available, there should be only one DBWR process. For systems in which AIO is not available, performance can be greatly enhanced by adding more DBWR processes.

☐ LGWR (Log Writer)—The LGWR process is responsible for writing data from the log buffer to the redo log.

☐ CKPT (Checkpoint)—The CKPT process is responsible for signaling the DBWR process to perform a checkpoint and to update all the datafiles and control files for the database to indicate the most recent checkpoint. A checkpoint is an event in which all modified database buffers are written to the datafiles by the DBWR. The CKPT process is optional. If the CKPT process is not present, the LGWR assumes these responsibilities.

☐ PMON (Process Monitor)—PMON is responsible for keeping track of database processes and cleaning up if a process prematurely dies (PMON cleans up the cache and frees resources that might still be allocated). PMON is also responsible for restarting any dispatcher processes that might have failed.

☐ SMON (System Monitor)—SMON performs instance recovery at instance startup. This includes cleaning temporary segments and recovering transactions that have died because of a system crash. The SMON also defragments the database by coalescing free extents within the database.

☐ RECO (Recovery)—RECO is used to clean transactions that were pending in a distributed database. RECO is responsible for committing or rolling back the local portion of the disputed transactions.

☐ ARCH (Archiver)—ARCH is responsible for copying the online redo log files to archival storage when they become full. ARCH is active only when the RDBMS is operated in ARCHIVELOG mode. When a system is not operated in ARCHIVELOG mode, it might not be possible to recover after a system failure. It is possible to run in NOARCHIVELOG mode under certain circumstances, but typically should operate in ARCHIVELOG mode.

☐ LCK*n* (Parallel Server Lock)—Up to 10 LCK processes are used for interinstance locking when the Oracle Parallel Server option is used.

☐ D*nnn* (Dispatcher)—When the Multithreaded Server option is used, at least one Dispatcher process is used for every communications protocol in use. The Dispatcher process is responsible for routing requests from the user processes to available shared server processes and back.

How Transactions Work

NEW TERM To give you a better idea how Oracle operates, this section analyzes a sample transaction. Throughout this book, the term *transaction* is used to describe a logical group of work that can consist of one or many SQL statements and must end with a commit or a rollback. Because this example is of a client/server application, SQL*Net is necessary. The following steps are executed to complete the transaction:

1. The application processes the user input and creates a connection to the server via SQL*Net.

2. The server picks up the connection request and creates a server process on behalf of the user.

3. The user executes a SQL statement or statements. In this example, the user changes the value of a row in a table.

4. The server process checks the shared pool to see whether there is a shared SQL area that has this identical SQL statement. If it finds an identical shared SQL area, the server process checks whether the user has access privileges to the data. If so, the server process uses the shared SQL area to process the request. If a shared SQL area is not found, a new shared SQL area is allocated, and the statement is parsed and executed.

5. The server process finds the data in the SGA (if it is present there) or reads the data from the datafile into the SGA.

6. The server process modifies the data in the SGA. Remember that the server processes can read only from the datafiles. At some later time, the DBWR process writes the modified blocks to permanent storage.

7. The user executes either the COMMIT or ROLLBACK statement. A COMMIT will finalize the transaction, a ROLLBACK will undo the changes. If the transaction is being committed, the LGWR process immediately records the transaction in the redo log file.

8. If the transaction is successful, a completion code is returned across the network to the client process. If a failure has occurred, an error message is returned.

> **NOTE**
>
> A transaction is not considered committed until the write to the redo log file is complete. This arrangement ensures that in the event of a system failure, a committed transaction can be recovered. If a transaction has been committed, it is set in stone.

While transactions occur, the Oracle background processes do their jobs, keeping the system running smoothly. While this process occurs, hundreds of other users might be performing similar tasks. Oracle's job is to keep the system in a consistent state, to manage contention and locking, and to perform at the necessary rate.

This overview is intended to give you an understanding of the complexity and amount of interaction involved in the Oracle RDBMS. As you look in detail at the tuning of the server processes and applications later in this book, you can use this overview as a reference to the basics of how the Oracle RDBMS operates. Because of the differences in operating systems, minor variances in different environments will be discussed individually.

RDBMS Functionality

If the RDBMS is to operate, you must provide for certain functions, including data integrity, recovery from failure, error handling, and so on. This is accomplished via events such as checkpointing, logging, and archiving. The following sections list and describe some of these functions.

Checkpointing

You know that Oracle uses either the CKPT background process or the LGWR process to signal a checkpoint; but what is a checkpoint and why is it necessary?

Because all modifications to data blocks are done on the block buffers, some changes to data in memory are not necessarily reflected in the blocks on disk. Because caching is done using a least recently used algorithm, a buffer that is constantly modified is always marked as recently used and is therefore unlikely to be written by the DBWR. A checkpoint is used to ensure that these buffers are written to disk by forcing all dirty buffers to be written out on a regular basis. This does not mean that all work stops during a checkpoint; the checkpoint process has two methods of operation: the normal checkpoint and the fast checkpoint.

In the normal checkpoint, the DBWR merely writes a few more buffers every time it is active. This type of checkpoint takes much longer but affects the system less than the fast checkpoint. In the fast checkpoint, the DBWR writes a large number of buffers at the request of the checkpoint each time it is active. This type of checkpoint completes much quicker and is more efficient in terms of I/Os generated, but it has a greater effect on system performance at the time of the checkpoint.

You can use the time between checkpoints to improve instance recovery. Frequent checkpoints reduce the time required to recover in the event of a system failure. A checkpoint automatically occurs at a log switch.

Logging and Archiving

The redo log records all changes made to the Oracle database. The purpose of the redo log is to ensure that in the event of the loss of a datafile as a result of some sort of system failure, the database can be recovered. By restoring the datafiles back to a known good state from backups, the redo log files (including the archive log files) can replay all the transactions to the restored datafile, thus recovering the database to the point of failure.

When a redo log file is filled in normal operation, a log switch occurs and the LGWR process starts writing to a different redo log file. When this switch occurs, the ARCH process copies the filled redo log file to an archive log file. When this archive process has finished copying the entire redo log file to the archive log file, the redo log file is marked as available. It's critical that this archive log file be safely stored because it might be needed for recovery.

NOTE

Remember that a transaction has not been committed until the redo log file has been written. Slow I/Os to the redo log files can slow down the entire system.

What Affects Oracle Performance?

Because one of the roles of the DBA is to anticipate, find, and fix performance problems, you must know what types of things affect performance. To understand why these things affect performance, you must first review the basics of how a computer system works.

Overview of Computer Architecture

Your computer system consists of thousands of individual components that work in harmony to process data. Each of these components has its own job to perform, and each has its own performance characteristics.

The brainpower of the system is the Central Processing Unit (CPU), which processes all the calculations and instructions that run on the computer. The job of the rest of the system is to keep the CPU busy with instructions to process. A well-tuned system runs at maximum performance if the CPU or CPUs are busy 100% of the time.

So how does the system keep the CPUs busy? In general, the system consists of different layers, or tiers, of progressively slower components. Because faster components are typically the most expensive, you must perform a balancing act between speed and cost efficiency.

CPU and Cache

NEW TERM The CPU and the CPU's cache are the fastest components of the system. The cache is high-speed memory used to store recently used data and instructions so that it can provide quick access if this data is used again in a short time. Most CPU hardware designs have a cache built into the CPU chip. This internal cache is known as a *Level 1* (or *L1*) *cache*. Typically, an L1 cache is quite small—8–16KB.

When a certain piece of data is wanted, the hardware looks first in the L1 cache. If the data is there, it's processed immediately. If the data is not available in the L1 cache, the hardware looks in the L2 cache, which is external to the CPU chip but located close to it. The L2 cache is connected to the CPU chip(s) on the same side of the memory bus as the CPU. To get to main memory, you must use the memory bus, which affects the speed of the memory access.

Although the L2 cache is twice as slow as the L1 cache, it's usually much larger. Its larger size means you have a better chance of getting a cache hit. Typical L2 caches range in size from 128KB to 4MB.

Slower yet is the speed of the system memory—it's probably five times slower than the L2 cache. The size of system memory can range from 4MB for a small desktop PC to 2–4GB for large server machines. Some supercomputers have even more system memory than that.

As you can see from the timeline shown in Figure 2.4, there is an enormous difference between retrieving data from the L1 cache and retrieving data from the disk. This is why you spend so much time trying to take advantage of the SGA in memory. This is also why hardware vendors spend so much time designing CPU caches and fast memory buses.

Figure 2.4.

Component speed comparison.

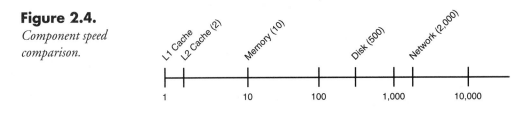

CPU Design

Most instruction processing occurs in the CPU. Although certain intelligent devices, such as disk controllers, can process some instructions, the instructions these devices can handle are limited to the control of data moving to and from the devices. The CPU works from the system clock and executes instructions based on clock signals. The clock rate and type of CPU determine how quickly these instructions are executed.

The CPU usually falls into one of two groups of processors: Complex Instruction Set Computer (CISC) or Reduced Instruction Set Computer (RISC).

CISC Processors

CISC processors (like the ones Intel builds) are by far the most popular processors. They are more traditional and offer a large instruction set to the program developer. Some of these instructions can be quite complicated; most instructions require several clock cycles to complete.

CISC processors are complex and difficult to build. Because these chips contain millions of internal components, the components are extremely close together. The physical closeness causes problems because there is no room for error. Each year, technology allows more complex and faster chips to be built, but eventually, physics will limit what can be done.

CISC processors carry out a wide range of tasks and can sometimes perform two or more instructions at a time in parallel. CISC processors perform most tasks, such as RDBMS processing, very well.

RISC Processors

RISC processors are based on the principle that if you can reduce the number of instructions processed by the CPU, the CPU can be simpler to build and can run faster. By putting fewer internal components inside the chip, the speed of the chip can be accelerated. One of the most popular RISC chips on the market is the DEC Alpha.

The system compiler determines what instructions are executed on the CPU chips. When the number of instructions was reduced, compilers were written to exploit this and to compensate for the missing instructions.

By reducing the instruction set, RISC manufacturers have been able to increase the clock speed to many times that of CISC chips. Although the faster clock speed is beneficial in some cases, it offers little improvement in others. One effect of a faster CPU is that the surrounding components such as L2 cache and memory must also run faster at an increase in cost.

One goal of some RISC manufacturers is to design the chip so that the majority of instructions complete within one clock cycle. Some RISC chips can already do this. But because some operations that require a single instruction for a CISC chip might require many instructions for a RISC chip, a speed-to-speed comparison cannot be made.

CISC versus RISC

Both CISC and RISC processors have their advantages and disadvantages; it's up to you to determine whether a RISC processor or a CISC processor will work best for you. When comparing the two types of processors, be sure to look at performance data and not just clock speed. Although the RISC chips have a much faster clock speed, they do less work per instruction. The performance of the system cannot be determined by clock speed alone.

Multiprocessor Systems

Multiprocessor systems can provide significant performance with very good value. With such a system, you can start with one or two processors and add more as needed. Multiprocessors fall into several categories; two of the main types of multiprocessor systems are the Symmetric Multiprocessor (SMP) system and the Massively Parallel Processing (MPP) system.

SMP Systems

SMP systems usually consist of a standard computer architecture with two or more CPUs that share the system memory, I/O bus, and disks. The CPUs are called *symmetric* because each processor is identical to any other processor in terms of function. Because the processors share system memory, each processor looks at the same data and the same operating system. In fact, the SMP architecture is sometimes called *tightly coupled* because the CPUs can even share the operating system.

In the typical SMP system, only one copy of the operating system runs. Each processor works independently by taking the next available job. Because the Oracle architecture is based on many processes working independently, you can see great improvement by adding processors.

The SMP system has these advantages:

☐ It's cost effective—The addition of a CPU or CPU board is much less expensive than adding another entire system.

☐ It's high performing—Under most applications, additional CPUs provide an incremental performance improvement.

☐ It's easily upgradable—Simply add a CPU to the system to instantly and significantly increase performance.

A typical SMP system supports between four and eight CPUs. Because the SMP system shares the system bus and memory, only a certain amount of activity can occur before the bandwidth of the bus is saturated. To add more processors, you must go to an MPP architecture.

MPP Systems

MPP systems are based on many independent units. Each processor in an MPP system typically has its own resources (such as its own local memory and I/O system). Each processor in an MPP system runs an independent copy of the operating system and its own independent copy of Oracle. An MPP system is sometimes called *loosely coupled.*

Think of an MPP system as a large cluster of independent units that communicate through a high-speed interconnect. As with SMP systems, you will eventually hit the bandwidth limitations of the interconnect as you add processors. However, the number of processors with which you hit this limit is typically much larger than with SMP systems.

If you can divide the application among the nodes in the cluster, MPP systems can achieve quite high scalability. Although MPP systems can achieve much higher performance than SMP systems, they are less economical: MPP systems are typically much higher in cost than SMP systems.

CPU Cache

Regardless of whether you use a single-processor system, an SMP system, or an MPP system, the basic architecture of the CPUs is similar. In fact, you can find the same Intel processors in both SMP and MPP systems.

As you learned earlier today, the system cache is important to the system. The cache allows quick access to recently used instructions or data. A cache is always used to store and retrieve data more quickly than the next level of storage (the L1 cache is faster than the L2 cache, the L2 cache is faster than main memory, and so on).

By caching frequently used instructions and data, you increase the likelihood of a cache hit. This can save precious clock cycles that would otherwise have been spent retrieving data from memory or disk.

System Memory Architecture

The system memory is basically a set of memory chips, either protected or not protected, that stores data and instructions used by the system. System memory can be protected by parity or by a more sophisticated advanced ECC correction method. Data parity will detect an incorrect value in memory and flag it to the system. An advanced ECC correction method will not only detect an incorrect value in memory, but in many cases can correct it. The system memory can range in size from 4MB on a small PC to 4GB on a large SMP server.

Typically, the more memory available to Oracle, the better your performance. Allocation of a large SGA allows Oracle to cache more data, thus speeding access to that data.

NEW TERM System memory is accessed by the CPUs through a high-speed bus that allows large amounts of data and instructions to be quickly moved from the CPU to L2 cache. Data and instructions are typically read from memory in large chunks and put into the cache. Because the CPU expects that memory will be read sequentially, in most cases it will read ahead the data or instruction that it thinks will be needed next. Sometimes this works, so the data that is needed next is already in cache; sometimes the CPU has guessed incorrectly and other data needs to be retrieved. This process of prereading the data is known as *prefetching*.

Depending on the specific implementation of an SMP system, the memory bus might be shared by all system processors; alternatively, each processor might have a private bus to memory.

Virtual Memory System

NEW TERM   In a virtual memory system, the OS and hardware allow programs and users to use more memory than is actually available in the system hardware. This memory, known as *virtual memory*, can be mapped to physical memory. Code or data that is being run by the CPU must reside in physical memory. If a program or data that is larger than physical memory is being accessed, the parts of code and data that are not immediately needed by the program can reside in virtual memory, not physical memory. As that bit of code or data is needed, it can be copied into physical memory, and parts no longer needed can be copied to disk. The process of mapping virtual memory onto physical memory by copying the memory to and from disk is called *paging* or *swapping* (depending on the OS architecture).

Both paging and swapping serve the same purpose, but each operates slightly differently from the other. In a swapping system, an entire process is swapped out (moved from memory to disk) or swapped in (moved from disk to memory). In a paging system, the movement of data to and from the secondary storage occurs on a memory page basis; when more memory is needed, one or more pages is paged out (moved from memory to disk) to make room. A memory page is the smallest unit of memory that is used in the operating system. A typical memory page size is 4KB. If data is requested from virtual memory and is not in physical memory, that data is paged in (moved from disk to memory) as needed. The rest of this section uses the term *paging* to describe both paging and swapping.

Suppose you have a computer system with 16MB of physical memory. If you have a program that needs to access 20MB of data, it obviously won't fit in physical memory. In a virtual memory system, the data is read until little memory remains (the OS reserves some for itself), then the OS copies some of the data pages to disk with the paging mechanism. This is usually done using a least recently used algorithm in which the oldest data is moved out. When some memory has been freed, the program can read more data into memory. As far as the program is concerned, all the data is still in memory; in fact, it is—in virtual memory. As the program begins to reread some of the data and manipulate it, different pieces might be paged in (from disk to physical memory) and paged out (from physical memory to disk).

As you can imagine, paging in or out can be time consuming and uses a lot of system resources. This is why I warn you several times in this book to avoid using so much memory that you cause paging or swapping. Access to disk is approximately 50 times slower than access to memory.

Bus Design

NEW TERM   Simply put, *bus* is a connection path used by the system to move data from one place to another. Buses get complicated when you look at them from a performance perspective: Capacity, or bandwidth, becomes an issue. Over the years, the term *bandwidth*, which was originally used to describe the electronic characteristics of a circuit, has been adopted by computer designers. In this case, *bandwidth* refers to the amount of data that can be transmitted across a bus in a certain time.

Several bus designs have been introduced in the last few years, all with the same goal: increased capacity. As processors, network hardware, disk controllers, and disks become increasingly fast, buses must develop to support the load generated by these devices. Thankfully, as computers have increased in performance, computer designers have improved bus designs to accommodate these changes. The system bus should not be a bottleneck in your system.

Oracle Resources

The Oracle DBMS allocates different resources for various different functions, including the allocation of system memory. The memory might be allocated for database caching or for the data dictionary or library cache. The careful balance of this precious resource is very important in tuning the Oracle RDBMS.

As much data as possible must be cached to avoid the additional cost of going to disk. If you allocate a large Oracle data cache, a higher cache-hit rate can be achieved. A high cache-hit rate indicates that a large percentage of requested data is found in the Oracle cache rather than retrieved from disk.

Application Design

Application design can affect performance more than any other factor. In most cases, performance can be severely degraded by an application that does not have well-tuned SQL statements or does not use indexes. A good application design can also significantly improve performance. The application is typically the first place to look when you experience system performance problems.

If a database is built with indexes on a certain set of columns but those columns are not specified in the WHERE clause of the SQL statement, the index probably won't be used. It's not enough to create the correct index on tables; you must ensure that the indexes are used.

> **TIP**
>
> It's wise to create a specification identifying the tables and indexes in your database. That way, the application developers and the team that creates the database have a crystal-clear document that identifies which columns are indexed. This can help avoid confusion and allow the application code to fully exploit the indexes.

Oracle Features

Another way to improve Oracle performance is to enable Oracle performance features. Among the most important of these features (and my personal favorite) is the Oracle Parallel Query option. Other Oracle performance features include partitioned tables and the Oracle index-only table, both new in Oracle8.

The Oracle Parallel Query Option

The Oracle Parallel Query option allows parallelism of many different operations, which greatly enhances performance. The Oracle Parallel Query option consists of several different components, including

- ☐ Parallel query
- ☐ Parallel index creation
- ☐ Parallel recovery
- ☐ Parallel table creation
- ☐ Parallel index tables

Parallel Query

The Oracle parallel query allows a single query to be divided into components and run in parallel. Because a query spends much of its time waiting for I/O operations to complete, parallelizing queries can greatly improve performance. In a well-tuned system where I/O is not a problem, parallel queries can run many times faster than normal queries. Statements that can be parallelized include

- ☐ Table scans
- ☐ Sorts
- ☐ Joins

NOTE

You might be wondering why parallelizing operations would help performance; after all, the work must still be done. In a typical Oracle operation (for example, a SELECT statement), the following steps occur:

1. Oracle performs some CPU processing to determine what data is needed.

2. Oracle submits an I/O request to disk (assuming that the data is not already in the SGA) and then waits for that I/O to complete.

3. This operation is repeated until all data is retrieved.

In the case of a parallel query, these steps would be adjusted like so:

1. Oracle performs some CPU processing to determine the query operation.

2. Different Oracle processes or threads receive their instructions on what data is needed.

3. Oracle thread 1 submits an I/O request to disk (if that data is not already in the SGA) and waits for that I/O to complete.

4. Oracle thread 2 submits an I/O request to disk (if that data is not already in the SGA) and waits for that I/O to complete.

5. Oracle thread 3 submits an I/O request to disk (if that data is not already in the SGA) and waits for that I/O to complete.

As shown here, that the time-consuming job of retrieving data from disk is duplicated, thus improving performance. This parallelism allows the CPU(s) to be utilized while other threads are waiting for I/Os.

Retrieving data from disk is a slow process compared to the activity of the CPU, and your goal is to keep the CPUs busy. Because a significant part of any Oracle operation involves CPU processing and I/Os, it is possible and desirable to keep the CPUs busy while many I/Os are being processed simultaneously. This is the main goal of the Parallel Query option.

Parallel Index Creation

Index creation involves reading from data tables and then writing to the index tables. Because the parallel query allows reading of tables to be accelerated, the index-creation process is sped up. Index creations can be quite time consuming, so this can be a real advantage.

Parallel Recovery

Recovery from a system failure can be quite time consuming. During recovery, users must usually wait for the system to come back online, so any improvement in performance is an advantage. Parallel recovery can speed the recovery process by parallelizing the read from the redo log files, and the roll forward and rollback process.

Parallel Table Creation

Although the Oracle Parallel Query option does not generally allow table creations to occur, it is often the case when a table is created as a subset of other tables. Data is often reduced from several large tables into a smaller subset, and this parallelism can be beneficial. In such instances, the following statement allows for parallelism:

```
CREATE TABLE table_name AS SELECT...
```

Oracle Index Tables

New to Oracle8, the index table allows indexes and tables to be stored together; this saves space and improves performance by reducing disk I/O. If you reduce the number of required disk I/Os, data can be accessed much faster.

OS Resources

 NEW TERM In most systems, few resources can be allocated in the operating system. Most OS parameters are changed only to allocate sufficient resources to Oracle; additional resources usually do not improve performance. A lack of resources, however, can decrease performance. *OS resources* often refers to system memory or, in the case of UNIX, shared memory. Other OS resources and tunables include network buffers and disk I/O tunables.

> **TIP**
>
> Windows NT is fairly self tunable, but there are a few things, relating primarily to configuration, to look out for:
>
> ☐ Remove unnecessary network protocols—Depending on how the system is configured, several network protocols that you do not use might be configured into your system. These extra protocols use CPU and memory resources.
>
> ☐ Configure the protocols you use in order from most-often used to least-often used—This reduces some of the overhead associated with traversing the infrequently used protocols.
>
> ☐ Keep a close eye on paging—Windows NT treats all memory as virtual. The best way to determine whether your system is paging is to watch Pages/Sec in NT's perfmon. If paging occurs, lower the amount of memory allocated to Oracle.

Hardware

Several hardware factors can affect your system's performance. These factors include

☐ Memory capacity
☐ Number of CPUs
☐ CPU cache
☐ Memory-bus bandwidth
☐ I/O capacity

Memory Capacity

Earlier today you saw an overview of how the system hardware operates. Clearly, any operation that must access slower components, such as a disk or network, will slow down processing. Therefore, it is important that you have sufficient memory in your system.

NEW TERM Most hardware architectures are limited to 4GB of physical memory, but some architectures on the market support much more. These architectures are said to support a *VLM*, or *Very Large Memory*, architecture. Soon it will be possible to support hundreds of gigabytes of physical memory in a system, allowing for very fast RDBMS operations.

System memory is allocated to Oracle and used for database caching, user memory, and the shared pool, which is used for both the data dictionary and the library cache. You must have enough memory for the shared pool because an insufficient shared pool can hurt performance. When the shared pool is satisfied, the more database buffers you can allocate to the DBMS the better. Be careful, though, to avoid starving the PGA memory needed by your processes, and avoid paging at all costs. You can never have too much memory in your system. Anything that can be cached will reduce system I/O, improving performance.

Number of CPUs

Oracle typically scales well with additional CPUs. By adding CPUs you can see significant performance improvement with little additional cost. Some factors that determine how much improvement you will see by adding more processors are the CPU cache and memory-bus bandwidth.

CPU Cache

A large CPU cache allows more data and executable code to be stored on the local processor than in memory. This reduces the number of times the CPU must access main memory. Whenever the CPU accesses memory, a slowdown occurs while the CPU waits for that data or code to be retrieved. It is especially bad when the memory bus is busy; the CPU waits even longer until the bus becomes free.

Memory-Bus Bandwidth

The memory-bus bandwidth determines how quickly data can be transferred between CPU to memory. If the memory bus is busy when data or code is needed, a CPU stalls waiting for the bus to free. This can severely degrade performance in a multiprocessor computer. A fast memory bus can reduce this problem. A large CPU cache can also reduce this problem by allowing more data and code to be cached.

I/O Capacity

I/O is typically one of the biggest factors limiting system performance. Because most DBMS operations involve retrieving data from disk, I/O can be a limiting factor if you do not have adequate capacity for your system load. Fortunately, you can usually solve this problem by carefully configuring your system for proper I/O distribution and by having sufficient I/O capacity. Simply having adequate disk space is insufficient; you must also have enough disk drives to support the number of disk I/Os that the system requires.

Oracle8 New Features

Oracle8 has introduced many new features, and I would like to focus on a few key features for the Oracle8 DBA:

- ☐ Partitioned objects
- ☐ Improved parallelism
- ☐ New index types
- ☐ Enhanced recovery features

Partitioned Objects

Partitioned objects allow Oracle objects, such as tables and indexes, to be broken into smaller, more manageable pieces. Partitioning these objects allows many operations that could normally be performed on only a table or an index to be divided into operations on a partition. By dividing these operations, you can often increase the parallelism of those operations, thus improving performance and minimizing system downtime.

Partitions are enabled via the PARTITION BY RANGE parameter of the CREATE TABLE statement. In this manner, ranges of data are assigned to each individual partition like so:

```
CREATE TABLE emp
(
name CHAR(30),
address CHAR(40),
region INTEGER
)
PARTITION BY RANGE ( region)
(
PARTITION VALUES LESS THAN (10) TABLESPACE tbl0,
PARTITION VALUES LESS THAN (20) TABLESPACE tbl1,
PARTITION VALUES LESS THAN (30) TABLESPACE tbl2
);
```

This creates a table with partitioning, as shown in Figure 2.5.

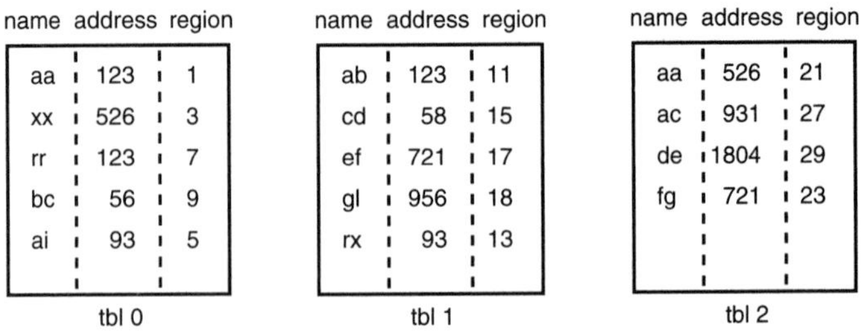

Figure 2.5.

Table partitioning.

name	address	region
aa	123	1
xx	526	3
rr	123	7
bc	56	9
ai	93	5

tbl 0

name	address	region
ab	123	11
cd	58	15
ef	721	17
gl	956	18
rx	93	13

tbl 1

name	address	region
aa	526	21
ac	931	27
de	1804	29
fg	721	23

tbl 2

Partitioning is recommended for large tables because it makes them much more manageable. Oracle does not currently support partitioning of clusters. By partitioning a table, you can break that large table into several much smaller pieces. A partitioned table can take advantage of some of the following features:

- ☐ Partitioned DML
- ☐ Exporting/importing by partition
- ☐ Range partitioning
- ☐ Local and global indexing
- ☐ Parallel loading by partition

Partitioned DML

Parallel INSERT, DELETE, and UPDATE operations can occur on a partition basis. Using partitions allows these operations to be conducted either globally or locally within a partition.

Exporting/Importing by Partition

Partitioning allows operations such as exports and imports to be performed on a partition basis. This can reduce the time required by some maintenance operations, such as reorganization of data or reclustering. This also allows you to change the physical layout of your database on a partition basis. If you limit the scope of export and import operations, they can benefit from a large degree of parallelism.

Range Partitioning

Range partitioning is a method whereby the partitioning of data is done based on the value of the data itself. This allows for tremendous flexibility in distributing data based on ranges of data values. Range partitioning allows you to partition high-volume data separately from low-volume data or to separate current from old data.

Local and Global Indexing

NEW TERM   A *local index* indexes data that resides in only one partition. A *global index* indexes data that resides on more than one partition. This allows for great flexibility in terms of adding new indexes, reducing index sizes, and allowing for partition independence.

An example of where local indexing might be beneficial is a table where sales records are stored. Using table and index partitioning, you can store data and indexes separately based on calendar months; doing this allows reduced index size and faster index lookups for entries of a particular month. If you partition these entries you can add new months and delete outdated entries without reindexing the entire table. You could keep 12 months of partitions and indexes online in this manner.

Parallel Loading by Partition

With a partitioned table, SQL*Loader can either load an entire table in parallel by partition or simply load a single partition. Either method provides great flexibility.

If you use the conventional path load, the loader automatically distributes the data to the correct partition and updates the local and global indexes. You can also use the loader to load a partitioned table or a partition of a table. Again, indexes are built automatically. It is also possible to direct-load a partition in parallel provided that no global indexes exist, but you must rebuild the local indexes yourself.

Improved Parallelism

The arrival of Oracle8 has heralded tremendous improvement in the area of parallelization. In addition to the new parallel features listed previously, some existing parallel operations have been extended.

Parallel recovery has been improved by allowing rollbacks of parallel DML operations that have failed to be performed in parallel. This parallel transaction recovery is supported on transaction and process failures but not during instance recovery.

New parallel hints have been added for parallel insert operations. The APPEND hint tells the optimizer to append the insert data beyond the high water mark of the segment.

New Index Types

The index-only table is new in Oracle8. With traditional indexes and tables, data and indexes are stored separately. With an index-only table, the data to which the index refers is stored in the leaf block or lowest level block of the index, so the data and indexes are stored together. Depending on your application, this can be an advantage.

Applications that access data primarily via a key value can see an advantage from the use of index-only tables. Because the data is stored within the index, the data is immediately available when the index has reached its lowest level. This can speed data retrieval.

Applications that do not access data primarily via a key value will see no improvement; indeed, performance will likely be degraded in these applications. Any application that involves table scans or requires multiple indexes will not benefit from the index table. The index table is covered in much more detail on Day 13.

Enhanced Recovery Features

Oracle has made tremendous improvements in the areas of backup and recovery. Most of these new features revolve around the Recovery Manager. Another recovery feature in Oracle8 is the image copy backup, which can improve recovery time in the event of a failure.

Recovery Manager

 Recovery Manager is an online utility designed to assist the DBA with all backup and recovery operations. Not only does it perform the backup and recovery, it maintains a database called the *recovery catalog* that stores information about these operations.

Image Copy Backup

An image copy backup essentially allows you to copy a datafile to another place on disk or to another disk on your system. In the event of a failure, no recovery is necessary from the image copy; you must simply switch to that backup copy. You must, however, perform a recovery to make that copy current. In the event of a failure, this might be the fastest way to recover.

NOTE

Days 16–18 cover backup and recovery techniques in greater detail.

Oracle Products

As part of the overview of the Oracle system, I would like to briefly cover the optional available Oracle products. Although many of these products are covered elsewhere in this book, you should at least aware of their existence. The Oracle product line is divided into three areas:

- [ ] The Oracle server
- [ ] Development tools
- [ ] Applications

The Oracle Server

The Oracle server is the DBMS itself, and includes many options and features such as the Parallel Query option, network protocols, and advanced system administration options. Some of the key options available to the Oracle server include

- [ ] Enterprise Manager—This option is fairly new to Oracle, and consists of the management console and intelligent agents. The management console, which is the core element in Oracle's new graphical administrative package, runs only on Windows NT, but can manage any Oracle server. The console allows the DBA to graphically control one or more Oracle systems. The console can be used to configure and manage Oracle instances as well as to diagnose problems and can be configured to alert the DBA in the event of a problem. The keys to Enterprise Manager are the intelligent agents, which run on the Oracle server and provide the communication layer necessary for the console to communicate with these systems. The intelligent agents use industry-standard SNMP (Simple Network Management Protocols) to communicate with the console, thus allowing for future expansion.

NOTE

Throughout this book, Enterprise Manager is referenced as the primary method for administering the system. Nonetheless, command-line management is also covered.

☐ ConText—When integrated with any text system, Oracle ConText can analyze, filter, and reduce text for speed reading and summary viewing. Oracle ConText returns detailed assessments of the text it processes, checking for grammatical errors and rating the quality and style of the writing.

☐ Media Server—Oracle Media Server provides high-performance, scalable, and reliable multimedia library functions on a wide variety of general-purpose systems. Media Server handles the storage, retrieval, and management of movies, music, photographs, and text articles.

☐ The Spatial Data option—The Oracle Spatial Data option can be used to manage a database that contains spatial data. This option allows for the storage of spatial or geographical data. If you store the spatial data within the database, the complexity of managing the storage is reduced and the performance is increased.

☐ The Oracle Web server—The Oracle Web server is designed to provide front-end services to allow World Wide Web access to an Oracle database. This product allows Web users to retrieve information directly from an Oracle database rather than from traditional flat files. This product can be used to enhance the performance and functionality of your Web server via the use of indexes and data caching. With the flexibility of the Oracle RDBMS, the functionality of your Web server can be enhanced via the use of language-sensitive context and other features.

☐ The Internet Commerce server—The Internet Commerce server is a complete set of tools designed to help you create, run, and administer an Oracle system that is used for Web commerce. Because it is based on the proven technology of the Oracle server, the system can provide these services in a robust and secure fashion.

Development Tools

One of Oracle's strongest points has been its development tools. Not only are these tools robust and full featured, they are flexible as well. When client/server systems became popular in the early 1990s, the Oracle tools quickly adapted. When HTML and Java applications became popular in the mid-1990s, the Oracle development tools quickly adapted yet again. The adaptability of these tools guarantees that applications developed with them can be quickly adjusted for new uses and technologies. Oracle provides the following tools:

- [ ] Designer/2000—This set of modeling tools reduces some of the pain associated with designing systems. These tools, which help with process and data modeling, can be used to provide input into the Developer/2000 system and to develop the fundamental models that are the foundation for your business processes.

- [ ] Developer/2000—This set of tools allows you to create an application and roll it out in Windows, Macintosh, Motif, and character mode. Developer/2000 incorporates graphics and images as well as support for multimedia objects such as video and sound in a variety of standard formats.

- [ ] Discoverer/2000—This data-analysis tool supports querying, reporting, and the graphical multidimensional analysis of the data warehouse. Its key features include graphical-representation and drill-down features.

- [ ] Power Objects—This lightweight, GUI development tool, which is available for Windows, Macintosh, and OS/2, allows the quick development of applications that use relatively small system resources. Power Objects is conceptually similar to Developer/2000, but lacks many of Developer/2000's features.

- [ ] Objects for OLE—This set of tools allows you to link OLE-compliant applications to an Oracle RDBMS. This tool provides a quick and easy way to exploit the power of applications such as spreadsheets. Objects for OLE also allows easy linking of database tables into word-processing documents.

- [ ] Programmer/2000—This suite of tools helps with the development of SQL, PL/SQL, and stored procedures. These tools can be helpful for application developers.

- [ ] Media Objects—Oracle's lightweight tool for developing multimedia applications, Media Objects supports client/server, CD-ROM, and interactive television processes.

- [ ] Database Designer—This lightweight version of the Oracle Designer/2000 product can assist in the design and creation of databases. Database Designer, a single-user tool, graphically designs the database tables and generates SQL that can be used to create this database.

Applications

Oracle's application software falls into two main categories: traditional applications and newer OLAP (Online Analytical Processing) applications.

Traditional Oracle Applications

Oracle's suite of traditional applications is used to perform basic and essential business tasks. These applications are used by many of the world's largest companies. The suite provides support for the following areas:

- [ ] Financial
- [ ] Human resources

☐ Project management

☐ Sales

☐ Manufacturing

OLAP Applications

The OLAP applications provide a graphical interface for DSS and data-warehousing applications. These tools lend a multidimensional model to the database, providing analysis, forecasting, and statistical operations.

Other Products

Oracle offers many other products that are not mentioned here. These products handle various tasks such as networking, office automation, workgrouping, and so on. Although these products and services are too numerous to cover here, rest assured that Oracle's full line can handle most (if not all) of your database and communication needs.

Summary

Today's lesson presents an overview of the Oracle architecture, including the physical structure (consisting of datafiles, redo log files, and control files) and the Oracle instance (consisting of processes and memory). Next you saw how a computer system works and how it depends on components such as cache memory to improve performance. Finally, you reviewed some of Oracle's products to get an idea of the different areas in which the Oracle server is used. This lesson set the foundation for many of the later lessons in this book. By having an understanding of the inner workings of Oracle, you will be better able to administer the Oracle DBMS.

What's Next?

You'll spend tomorrow installing the Oracle8 server. The key to the installation process is understanding what components you are installing and why you are installing them.

Q&A

Q What are the main hardware components that affect performance?

A The main hardware components that affect performance are the speed of the CPU(s), the amount of memory, and the I/O subsystem.

Q What happens if a failure corrupts the redo log files?

A If redo log files are lost, you cannot recover the database. All changes made since the last backup will be lost. This is why redo log files should be on protected or fault-tolerant disk drives.

Q What happens if a failure corrupts the datafiles?

A When a datafile is lost, the corrupted file can be restored from a backup. After the datafile is restored, the redo log files and archive log files can reapply any changes made before the time of the failure. No data is lost.

Q Why does parallelizing a query make things faster?

A Most of the realtime or clock-time processing a query operation is spent waiting for I/Os to complete. Parallelizing a query enables you to keep the CPUs busy while you are waiting.

Workshop

This workshop provides quiz questions to help you solidify your understanding of the material covered. Answers to quiz questions can be found in Appendix A, "Answers."

Quiz

1. What are the three types of files that make up an Oracle database?

2. What makes up the Oracle instance?

3. Which is faster—memory or disk?

4. Name two new features of Oracle8.

Week 1

Day 3

Installing Oracle Software

Today you will see the steps involved in installing Oracle8 software. You'll find numerous examples of installing Oracle8 on Windows NT 4.0, and other operating systems are not significantly different. Throughout this book I will be using Windows NT as the primary OS for examples and instruction, and where necessary, I will point out the differences for other operating systems.

Installing Oracle software is much less complicated than in the old days of Oracle6 and early Oracle7. Oracle has made tremendous progress in streamlining and improving the installation process. It is fairly straightforward to install Oracle8 server, client, and administrator systems. There is also an option to install individual components, which is a little bit more complex. Today you will see all four of these methods.

What You Need to Know Before You Begin

There is very little you need to know before you begin the installation process:

☐ What language do you want to use to run Oracle8? A large selection of different languages is available. You must decide which language you want to use before you begin the installation.

☐ Where do you want the Oracle8 binaries to reside? You will be asked to provide a path to where the binaries will be copied during the installation process.

☐ What Oracle8 products to you want to install? A number of different products can be installed based on the type of system that you are installing. There are four different types of installations.

The installation type that you choose will be based on the function of the system that you will be installing. Types of installations include the server, client, Programmer/2000, and custom installations. Each installs a different set of programs.

Server Installation

In the server installation, the components necessary for an Oracle8 server system will be installed. These components include

☐ Oracle8 server—The Oracle8 server is really the guts of the system. This is the Oracle8 RDBMS.

☐ Server networking components—These include the TNS listener program and the SQL*Net programs as well as the administrative tools necessary to manage them.

☐ Oracle Enterprise Manager—This component is the key to Oracle's new administrative system. The Enterprise Manager provides a graphical interface to administer the Oracle8 server.

☐ Oracle intelligent agents—These are the programs that allow the Oracle Enterprise Manager to communicate with the Oracle8 server and utilities. The Oracle intelligent agents use SMTP (Simple Management Transport Protocol) to allow this communication to occur.

☐ Oracle8 documentation (optional)—You can install the Oracle8 documentation locally or configure it so that you can access the documentation via CD-ROM.

☐ Miscellaneous utilities—Other utilities include SQL*Plus, the Oracle installer, SQL*Loader, ODBC, and so on.

Client Installation

The client installation gives you a choice of the DBA client or the application user clients. The DBA installation gives you the components needed to remotely administer an Oracle system. These products include

- ☐ Oracle Enterprise Manager—As mentioned previously, this component is the key to Oracle's new administrative system. The Enterprise Manager provides a graphical interface to administer the Oracle8 server.

- ☐ SQL*Plus—This is the primary interface into Oracle for ad-hoc access. SQL*Plus can be used for administrative purposes if desired.

- ☐ The Oracle8 toolbar—The toolbar provides a quick way to access the Oracle Enterprise Manager applications.

- ☐ SQL*Net—The SQL*Net components include the client-side networking components and administrative tools.

- ☐ Oracle8 documentation (optional).

- ☐ Miscellaneous tools and utilities—Items such as OCI, Oracle Installer, and so on are installed.

The application user client installation gives you the components needed to connect to Oracle as an end user. These products include

- ☐ SQL*Plus
- ☐ SQL*Net
- ☐ Oracle8 documentation (optional)

Programmer/2000 Installation

The Programmer/2000 installation provides the necessary client components to connect to the Oracle8 RDBMS, as well as a choice of the following development packages:

- ☐ Oracle Pro*C/C++—This is the method whereby database object types can be used within C/C++ programs. Pro*C/C++ is essentially a preprocessor that converts these objects into C/C++ objects.

- ☐ Pro*COBOL—This is Oracle's COBOL interface.

- ☐ ODBC—The Open Database Connectivity software and development libraries needed by the application developer.

- ☐ OCI—The Oracle Object Call Interface provides a method whereby Oracle can be accessed from a C program.

Custom Installation

The custom installation allows any or all products on the Oracle8 installation CD-ROM to be installed. Using the custom installation option, you simply choose which options you want to install.

The Installation Process

Now that you've decided where you want the Oracle8 installer to put the Oracle binaries and you've determined which language to install and which installation method to use, it's a simple matter of installing the Oracle products. In this part of the day you will see step-by-step how this installation process works.

This section is divided into four parts, each looking at a different installation type. First, the initial installation process is covered, then the Oracle8 Server, followed by the two types of client installations. Finally, the Developer/2000 and custom installation types are shown. Each is covered in detail, and each of the options is explained.

Basic Installation

The initial installation process begins when you place the Oracle8 CD into your CD-ROM drive. If your system has autorun configured, you will be prompted by the Oracle8 installation procedure; from here, decide whether you want to begin installing Oracle8, to browse information about Oracle8, or explore the CD-ROM (see Figure 3.1).

Figure 3.1.

The Oracle8 installation autorun message.

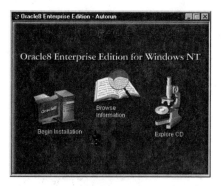

If you are ready to install Oracle8 at this time, simply click Begin Installation and the Oracle8 installation process will commence. If you are not ready to install, is possible to return at a later time and restart the installation process. Simply use NT Explorer and, from the CD-ROM drive, double-click the program `setup.exe`. This will also invoke the installation program.

After the installation process has begun, you will see the initial install screen (shown in Figure 3.2). This screen asks you which language you want to use to run the Oracle products. Choose OK to select the default language as English, or select a different language.

Figure 3.2.

The initial installa-tion screen.

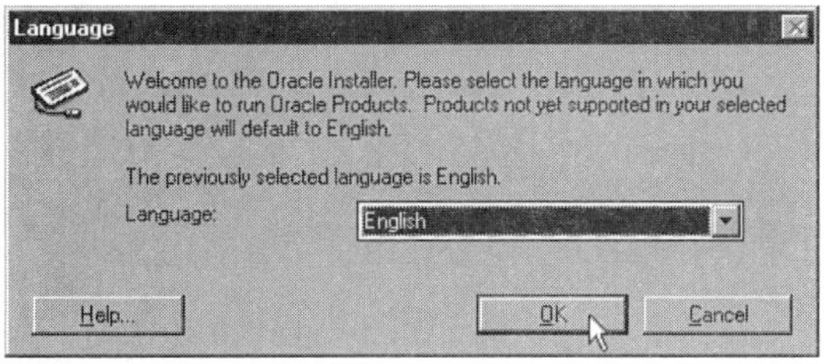

Next, you will be asked for some installation settings, as shown in Figure 3.3. These questions relate to your particular installation. The first screen simply asks for the name of your company and for the OS directory where the Oracle8 binaries will be installed. Before you choose a directory, be sure the selected disk volume has adequate disk space; a full installation can require more than 100MB.

Figure 3.3.

Installation settings.

After you decide on the installation language and location, you might be informed that certain path variables have been adjusted for the Oracle installation process and the Oracle programs to work properly. This is shown in Figure 3.4.

Figure 3.4.

The Oracle path changes.

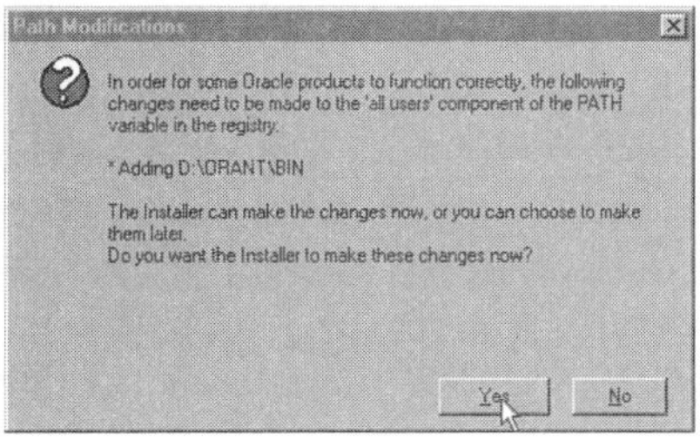

If you click the OK button, the path of the Oracle binary files will be added to your environment. Unlike earlier versions of the Oracle installation process, a reboot the system is not required at this time to continue the installation. After you have completed these steps, you will be presented with a screen asking you which type of installation you want to perform, as shown in Figure 3.5.

Figure 3.5.

Select the type of installation you want to perform.

At this point, the installation will be different based on your answer. These installations are covered separately in the following sections.

Installing the Oracle8 Server

The following is split into two sections. The first section describes the actual process of installing the software. The second section describes the system after the installation has occurred. Specifically, this section provides information about what products and services have been installed, and how the Registry has been modified.

The Installation Process

If you've chosen to install the Oracle8 server by clicking OK on the menu shown in Figure 3.5, the server installation process will begin. At this point, a few dependencies will be determined and you will be queried as to the Oracle data cartridges that you are licensed to install (see Figure 3.6). Oracle data cartridges are described on Day 21, "Exploring the Web Publishing Assistant and Network Computing Architecture."

Figure 3.6.

Installing additional cartridges.

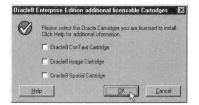

A short time into the installation process, you will be queried as to whether you want a typical database installation or whether you want to customize your database with the Database Assistant (see Figure 3.7).

Figure 3.7.

The Starter Database Installation Options dialog box.

The three selections are

- ☐ Typical—The typical starter database is 30MB in size and includes a small set of tables and tablespaces as a starter set. In most situations, this is probably the correct selection.

- ☐ Custom—Checking this option invokes the Oracle Database Assistant, which helps you create a custom Oracle database. Choose this option if you will be using this database as a replication system, if you want to install other options, or if you want to choose the name of your database. This option provides the most flexibility. Creating a custom database with the Database Assistant is described in detail on Day 6, "Administering Databases and Datafiles."

- ☐ None—If you are planning to immediately build a new database on this system, consider not building a starter database. This will save on space and time.

The final question that you will be asked is the location of the online documentation. You can either access the documentation via CD-ROM or install it on your local hard drive, as shown in Figure 3.8.

Figure 3.8.

Installing the documentation.

Installing the documentation on the hard disk requires approximately 66MB of disk space, but it's well worth the space (if available). There is nothing worse than not having the documentation immediately available when you need it. The Oracle8 documentation set is available in HTML format with hyperlinks, which makes it very convenient.

As the installation proceeds, you can watch its progress on the status bar. As the installation gets further along, the bar on the bottom increases in length. When the installation is complete, you will be so notified.

What Has Been Installed?

The installation of the Oracle8 server has instated the following components:

- ☐ The Oracle8 RDBMS
- ☐ Oracle Enterprise Manager
- ☐ Oracle intelligent agents
- ☐ The Oracle Administrators toolbar
- ☐ Online documentation
- ☐ Networking components
- ☐ Oracle utilities, including SQL*Plus

A few specifics should be mentioned here. The Oracle8 installation processes has registered Oracle as a service. Specifically, seven services have been registered (see Figure 3.9):

- ☐ OracleAgent—This service is the Oracle intelligent agent for the Oracle Enterprise Manager. This agent can communicate with multiple Oracle instances on the same system; therefore, only one agent service exists.

- ☐ OracleClientCache80—This service is manual. Once started, it stores in cache all information received from an Oracle names server.

- ☐ OracleNamesService80—Use this service, which is also manual, if you configure this system as a names server.

- ☐ OracleServiceORCL—This service is associated with the instance for Oracle SID=ORCL (default). This is not the actual Oracle instance, but a bootstrap instance. The service starting up does not start up the Oracle instance at boot time.

  If new databases are created with a different SID, a new service must be created with the new SID in the name. This is described in detail on Day 5, "Managing the Oracle RDBMS."

- ☐ OracleStartORCL—The OracleStartORCL service starts the Oracle service named ORCL (default) each time the system is rebooted.

- ☐ OracleTNSListener30—This is the TNS listener service. There is a TNS listener service for each network listener that you define. Typically, there is one listener per defined protocol.

- ☐ OracleWebAssistant. This service enables queries from the Oracle database to be published to a Web page.

Figure 3.9.

*These are the installed
Oracle services.*

If you decide you don't want a particular service to automatically start each time the system is booted, you can change this by modifying the Oracle service properties (see Figure 3.10). By changing the service startup from automatic to manual, the service will only start manually (you must modify the service through NT).

Figure 3.10.

*Use this dialog to
modify the Oracle
service properties.*

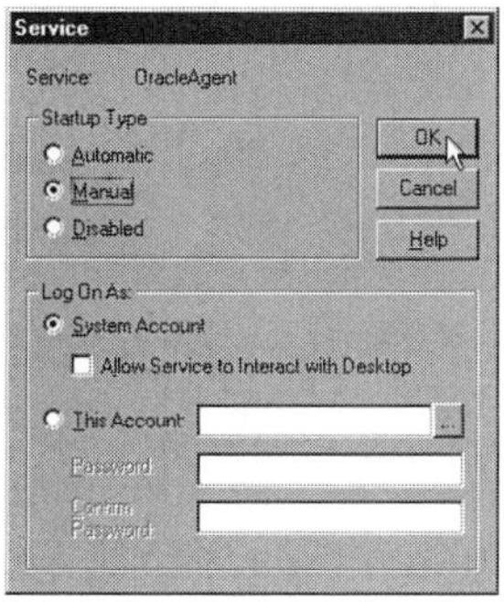

TIP

This can be useful on a development machine where you do not always need the ability to start up Oracle and want to save on system resources.

Also as part of the installation process, new program groups have been created and appear as part of the taskbar. The first of these groups is the Enterprise Manager group. This group contains icons for the following Oracle products:

- ☐ Enterprise Manager
- ☐ Backup Manager
- ☐ Instance Manager
- ☐ Network Topology Generator

☐ Schema Manager

☐ Security Manager

☐ Storage Manager

The second of these program groups is the Oracle for NT group. This group contains icons for the following Oracle products:

☐ Oracle ODBC Administrator

☐ Oracle Instance Manager

☐ Oracle Installer

☐ Oracle Network Configuration wizard

☐ SQL*Plus

The third program group created is the Oracle Replication Manager program group. One other feature of the Oracle Server installation is the Oracle Administrators toolbar. This toolbar is installed as part of the server installation as well as the administrators installation, and is shown in Figure 3.11.

Figure 3.11.

*The Oracle Adminis-
trators toolbar.*

| ORACLE | | 🔒 Security | 🔼 Schema | 🔼 Storage | 🔷 WorkSheet | 🔼 Instance | 🔼 Net8 Assistant |

This toolbar allows instant access to many of the applications that are part of the Oracle Enterprise Manager system.

Installing the Oracle8 Client Products

The following is split into two sections. The first section describes the actual process of installing the software. The second section provides a description of the system after the installation has occurred. Specifically, this section provides information on what products have been installed, what services have been installed, and how the Registry has been modified.

The Installation Process

You can choose to install the Oracle8 client products by clicking the Oracle8 Client Products button and then clicking the OK button. The client installation process immediately asks whether you want to proceed with the database administrator or application user installation. To install the database administrator client, click OK (see Figure 3.12).

Figure 3.12.

Installing the database administrator client.

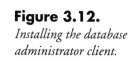

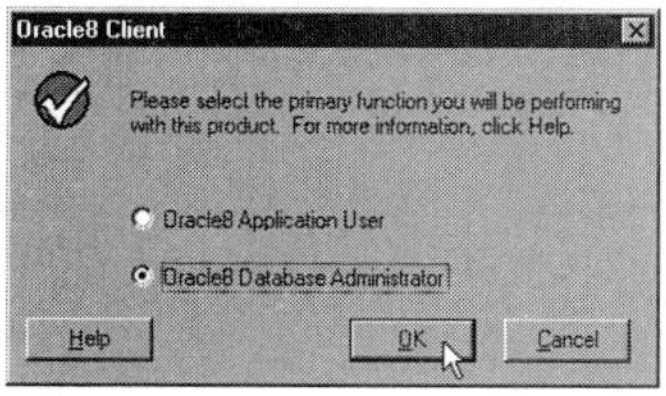

Oracle immediately begins installing the database administrator client components. As with the server installation, you will be asked whether you want to install the Oracle documentation on hard disk or whether you want to access the documentation via CD-ROM.

If your installation is for an end-user system, you will choose the application user installation. To install the application user client, click the Application User button, then click OK.

Oracle immediately begins installing the application user client components. As with the server installation, you will be asked whether you want to install the Oracle documentation on hard disk or whether you want to access the documentation via CD-ROM.

What Has Been Installed?

The database administrator client installation instates the following components:

- ☐ Oracle Enterprise Manager
- ☐ The Oracle Administrators toolbar
- ☐ Online documentation
- ☐ Networking components
- ☐ Oracle utilities, including SQL*Plus
- ☐ OCI

The application user client installation instates the following components:

- ☐ Networking components
- ☐ SQL*Plus
- ☐ Online documentation

At the end of today's lesson is an in-depth description of each of the products installed and how they are used.

Installing the Programmer/2000 System

The following is split into two sections. The first section describes the actual process of installing the software. The second section provides a description of the system after the installation has occurred. Specifically, this section provides information on what products and services have been installed, and how the Registry has been modified.

Installing the Oracle8 Custom Configuration

The following is split into two sections. The first section describes the actual process of installing the software. The second section provides a description of the system after the installation has occurred. Specifically, this section provides information on what products and services have been installed, and how the Registry has been modified.

The Installation Process

You can choose to install the custom installation path by clicking the Custom button and then clicking OK. This begins the custom installation procedure. The custom system is for those users who do not fit into the other catagories. You will be presented with the Software Asset Manager screen, where you select any components available on the Oracle8 CD-ROM (see Figure 3.13).

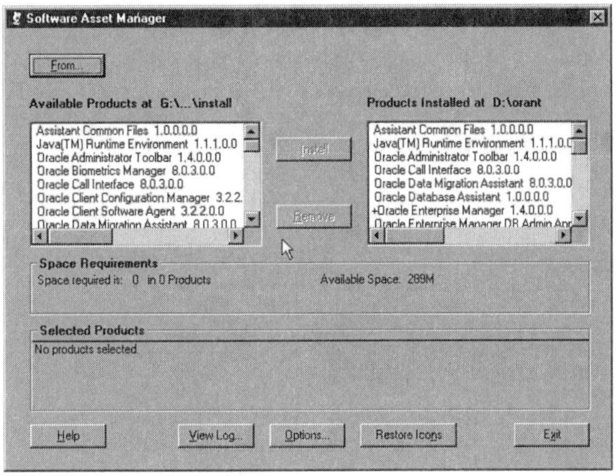

Figure 3.13.

The Software Asset Manager screen.

Simply choose any components you want by either selecting an entire group (Shift+click) or clicking a number of individual components (Ctrl+click) and then clicking the Install button. These components will be installed as requested.

If you choose the Oracle Documentation option, you will be asked whether you want to install the Oracle documentation on hard disk or whether you want to access the documentation via CD-ROM.

WARNING

The custom installation procedure should only be used after you've used the installation procedure several times, and only if you need specific components. It is much better to run both server and Programmer/2000 if you need components of both.

3

What Has Been Installed?

With the custom installation procedure, you will have installed whatever components you requested. The installation procedure will check for dependencies and some additional components might have been installed.

I do not recommend using the custom installation procedure in most cases. The other installation methods are usually perfectly adequate. In the next section, you will see how to remove unneeded components.

Removing Components

To remove any unnecessary or unwanted components, simply invoke the Oracle Installer through the Oracle for Windows NT group. Select any components you want to remove, as shown in Figure 3.14, and then click the Remove button. These components will be removed from the system.

Figure 3.14.

The Software Asset Manager screen with components selected for removal.

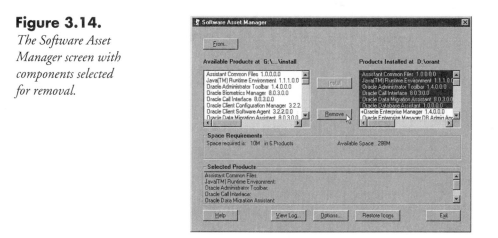

When you finish removing components, simply click the Exit button to exit the Oracle Installer.

Product Descriptions

The various products and components installed based on your selections were shown previously. Following is a brief description of what these products and components actually are.

Oracle8 Server

The Oracle8 server is the RDBMS itself. Within the RDBMS package are all the standard Oracle features, including the following options:

- ☐ Distributed—This allows the database to be distributed across different systems.
- ☐ Replication—This allows for the replication or copying of data to multiple different systems. This can be used for the performance increase provided by having local copies, or for protection in the event of a system failure.
- ☐ Parallel Query—This option is my favorite, and allows for several different types of operations to be split into many individual operations, thus improving performance of long-running tasks.
- ☐ PL/SQL—The Oracle procedural language option allows for procedural SQL commands to be written.

Enterprise Manager

Oracle Enterprise Manager is the graphical administration tool recently introduced by Oracle. The Enterprise Manager helps the DBA by simplifying some of the necessary tasks. The Enterprise Manager comes with a suite of tools, including

- ☐ Backup Manager—This option assists the administrator in backup and recovery operations.
- ☐ Instance Manager—This handles startup, shutdown, configuration, and so on.
- ☐ Schema Manager—This is used to view and modify tables, views, clusters, and so on.
- ☐ Security Manager—This is used to manage the user community. It allows you to add users, assign roles, and so on.
- ☐ Storage Manager—This is used to view and modify tablespaces, datafiles, and so on.

Intelligent Agents

Oracle intelligent agents are the programs that allow the Oracle Enterprise Manager to communicate with the Oracle8 server and utilities. The Oracle intelligent agents use SMTP (Simple Management Transport Protocol) to allow this communication to occur. The Oracle intelligent agents are implemented as a service under Windows NT and are started and stopped by the NT Service Manager.

Oracle Installer

The Oracle Installer is the application that is used to install and remove Oracle software. The Installer itself is installed on the system and can be used to install and remove additional components even after the initial installation.

Networking Components

The Oracle8 networking components consist of the programs and utilities necessary to connect to the Oracle8 server via a network. The networking components consist of the network server and network protocol adapters. These protocol adapters support various network protocols, such as

- [ ] TCP/IP
- [ ] SPX/IPX
- [ ] Named pipes
- [ ] DECNet
- [ ] Various other networking protocols, depending on your operating system

The networking components also include the administrative tools necessary to administer the Oracle networking components.

SQL*Plus

SQL*Plus is the ad-hoc user interface tool for the Oracle RDBMS. With SQL*Plus, you can connect into the RDBMS and run SQL commands and PL/SQL programs. This is the primary nonapplication interface into the Oracle RDBMS.

Utilities

These are miscellaneous utilities that are used to administer and modify the Oracle RDBMS. These Oracle utilities include

- [ ] SQL*Loader—This is used to load the database from input files. There are various methods of using the SQL*Loader, which are covered on Day 9, "Managing Data."
- [ ] Export—This program stores Oracle data and table definitions externally in an Oracle-specific binary format. Export is covered in depth on Day 9.
- [ ] Import—This program loads data into the database from an Oracle export file.

Server Manager

Server Manager is a character-based utility that can be used to perform administrative tasks on the Oracle RDBMS. Server Manager provides an interface for performing ad-hoc or scripted administrative tasks.

Instance Manager

The Oracle Instance Manager is part of the Enterprise Manager toolset and is used to graphically perform tasks such as starting and stopping the Oracle instance.

Recovery Manager

Recovery Manager is used to back up and restore the Oracle database. Recovery Manager not only performs the backup but also maintains backup and recovery information.

Summary

Today you learned how to install Oracle8 software. The various types of installations include

- ☐ Server installation
- ☐ Administrative client installation
- ☐ Application user client installation
- ☐ Programmer/2000 installation
- ☐ Custom installation

You were also presented with an overview of what was installed. As you can see, the new Oracle installation procedure is quite straightforward in most cases. This is quite an improvement from the Oracle6 and early Oracle7 installation procedures.

What's Next?

Tomorrow you will see how to properly size an Oracle system and how to plan for future growth. This is a very exciting area of Oracle administration and can be extremely important to the operation of the system. By anticipating growth and determining when your system will run out of resources, you can plan ahead, thus avoiding costly downtime and quick hardware purchases.

Q&A

Q What is the Oracle Enterprise Manager?

A The Oracle Enterprise Manager is the new graphical administration tool designed to help the DBA manage one or more Oracle systems.

Q What is SQL*Net?

A SQL*Net is Oracle's communication protocol. SQL*Net uses various network communication protocols such as TCP/IP, DECNet, and SPX/IPX, and provides a common programming layer for the Oracle developer.

Q What kind of user needs the Programmer/2000 installation?

A A software developer would use the development tools that come with the Programmer/2000 installation.

Q What is the Recovery Manager used for?

A The Recovery Manager is used for backup and recovery. This product performs these operations and maintains a catalog of previous backups.

Workshop

The workshop provides quiz questions to help you solidify your understanding of the material covered. See Appendix A, "Answers," for answers to the quiz questions you see here.

Quiz

1. What is the main component of an Oracle8 server?
2. What do the intelligent agents do?
3. Name three Oracle utilities.
4. Name several network protocols supported by Oracle SQL*Net.

Week 1

Day 4

Properly Sizing Your Database and Planning for Growth

by Steve Adrien DeLuca

Welcome to Day 4. Today you consider the size of the machine in your database system in terms of hardware resources necessary to process your workload. In this lesson you are introduced to *sizing* and *capacity planning*. These are the first two of three main topics under the heading *performance*. The third topic, *tuning*, the most well-known performance activity, refers to the adjustments made to the hardware and software after the machine has been sized, built, and loaded with the necessary software. Sizing and tuning are related more closely, though: One of the first principles of sizing is that the system you design will be tuned and as free from bottlenecks as possible. Tuning suggestions relevant to sizing are included in this chapter. Day 20, "Effectively Tuning and Optimizing the Database," gives you a complete view of the tuning part of performance.

NEW TERM The exact definition of *computer sizing* is the estimation of the hardware requirements necessary to process a workload within specified parameters. These parameters (also known as *service level agreements*) usually deal with the maximum amount of time allocated to process each workload type. These service level agreements provide a clear set of working thresholds as to how the machine will operate. Things such as processor utilization, disk I/O rates, and transaction response times are decided upon by the management staff and the system administrators before the system is even built. These parameters are defined ahead of time because these thresholds can drastically change the size of the machine in question. A commitment to having a transaction complete within five seconds or fewer can cause you to buy more disks, or running the system at under 75% processor utilization can cause you to purchase more memory. These parameters are then tracked to make sure that transactions are completing within specified parameters and the machine is performing at an acceptable rate. When addressing computer size, you usually deal in terms of the CPU type, quantity, and speed, the amount of required memory, and the size, speed, and quantity of required disks.

Sizing

In the early years of multiuser computers, sizing , capacity planning, and indeed performance itself were not widely understood or developed. By the early 1970s, a sizing project consisted of finding customers who ran an application in the same manner as the target customer application. Finding these customers was difficult, and finding a match between companies or organizations and their application use was even more challenging.

Benchmarking

In the mid 1970s, customers and application suppliers developed a methodology of running a benchmark to determine the amount of hardware required to sustain good performance with a given workload. This process consisted of building an application like that of the customer in question and running it on several different variations and sizes of hardware to gather performance statistics. These statistics were then used to determine the best-sized machine for the intended purpose. One benefit of this process was that the user could enact what-if scenarios to determine what size machine would be required if more users, application processes, or data were added to the system. Nevertheless, the process was expensive. Although early benchmarks were developed to simulate a customer's usage, a shift occurred: Benchmarks began to be used primarily by system vendors to sell systems and to compare the relative performance of competing hardware offerings. These benchmarks lost sight of the sizing issue for which they were developed.

By the next decade, these early benchmark simulations had evolved into standard benchmark loads such as the following:

- ☐ ST1 (Standard Transaction 1)—A simple banking transaction that is very much like an automatic teller machine (ATM) transaction.
- ☐ ET1 (Estimated Transaction 1)—A variation of the ST1 transaction.
- ☐ Debit/credit benchmarks.

During this era it became more important to find the fastest performing hardware for promotional use than to develop a standard application workload that could be used to size systems. Customers could not use the benchmark offerings of the time for system hardware comparisons because these benchmarks were all slightly different in nature. Customer demand led to the formation of a computer industry consortium, the Transaction Processing Performance Council (TPC). The council specified agreed-on transaction loads for over 45 hardware and software manufacturers. These benchmarks could often show relative capabilities of hardware and database software. Unfortunately these workloads were not useful for the sizing of an application workload.

At the same time, client/server computing and the use of relational database technology was maturing. Most modern applications are based on this architecture. Servers are used as central, data-storage devices while new, local, and/or Web clients primarily run the user interface. This is a cost-effective strategy. Rather than using expensive server processing power to run the application, the client now runs the application on a low-cost, PC-type machine and takes advantage of the graphical user interfaces (GUIs) to which customers are already accustomed and which normally run on the PC interface. With heavy utilization of database servers presently in the industry, the server is now the focus for sizing projects.

To date, the application-simulation benchmark remains the most common method of sizing database servers. Although it is expensive and time consuming, customers can achieve a fairly significant degree of accuracy if they simulate the exact usage of the server. However, because large projects might require a multimillion dollar investment by the customer or vendor, only the largest customers can access systems for this kind of testing. Another method is clearly required to perform in-depth, accurate system sizing. With some easy calculations and a general knowledge of the system's usage, you can size a system to within ±10% accuracy.

Sizing Considerations for Database Servers

Many offerings currently inhabit the database server market. For the sake of simplicity, I will generically describe hardware and functionality. The models that dominate the market are usually multiprocessor types that can accommodate large disk storage and memory. These are the focus of this discussion.

When sizing any type of system, you must understand what that system will do. For your purposes, this has already been determined: A database server performs only database functions. In terms of workload, it performs only transactions. When a SELECT or UPDATE statement is executed, a database server interprets this as a series of reads and writes. Considering that the atomic level of anything is its smallest part, it could be said that the atomic level of a transaction consists of the reads and writes it generates. If broken down to this level, a database server processes I/Os. So the system in question should be selected for the type of transactions and the subsequent I/Os they will cause. There are two main transaction types:

- ☐ Online Transaction Processing (OLTP) transactions
- ☐ Decision Support transactions

OLTP Transactions

An OLTP transaction is a unit of work that is usually expected to run in a very short duration of time because it deals with the database in real time or *online* mode. In other words, these transactions constantly update the database based on the most current information available so the next user can rely on that information being the most current. An example of this kind of transaction system would be an order-entry system. In this case, all the information pertaining to the system is kept in tables spread across a disk system, and the database is online. Any user in the community will have access to that information. Tables such as Item_Table or Stock_Level_Table must have the most current information on the types and quantity of the items that are sold. When an order for a specific item comes up, the database must know how many (if any) of those items are in stock to prevent items from being oversold.

Factors that Affect Performance and Sizing in an OLTP System

A typical sizing scenario for an OLTP system involves gathering specific information during an interview process. This is probably the most important part of the sizing process; it reveals the following:

- ☐ The number of transactions expected to be processed
- ☐ In what time range these transactions are expected to be processed
- ☐ The number of concurrent users
- ☐ Whether this time range is your peak-operation period (peak-utilization period) or working day in hours

The Peak-Utilization Period

NEW TERM *Peak-utilization period* refers to the period in a day that causes the most stress to the system. For example, consider an automated teller machine (ATM). On most days, the peak-utilization period would be between 11:00 a.m. and 2:00 p.m., the time period when most people go to lunch. When sizing for peak utilization, you build the machine with enough capacity to accommodate this peak period.

Determining Steady-State Processing Utilization

NEW TERM   The other philosophy of sizing an OLTP or any other system is *steady-state processing*, and is generally used when you cannot define the peak-utilization period. In this case, you know the maximum number of transactions you expect to complete in a processing day, but you don't know at what arrival rate (the number of transactions that get to a system resource at a given period) they will occur. In a situation such as this, you would need to size with a reserve capacity built into the system. *Reserve capacity* refers to a certain portion of system processing power left in reserve to accommodate heavier workload periods.

Knee of the Curve

NEW TERM   There are other reasons to build a machine with reserve capacity, specifically because utilization has a direct effect on response time. This theory, known as the *knee of the curve* (the point at which you go from linear growth to exponential growth), explains this effect by noting that utilization has a direct effect on queues and that queues are directly related to response time (in fact, queue length is part of the response time equation). This theory specifies that at a certain utilization factor, any response time gains exponentially, not linearly, which has a devastating effect on overall performance. The phrase "knee of the curve" refers to the radical bend this trend displays when placed on a graph (see Figure 4.2).

For example, say you're driving down a highway at 3:00 a.m. and you come upon a toll booth. No one is in front of you at this time in the morning, so the toll booth is experiencing 0% utilization and the queue length is 0. Your response time will equal your service time because no one is in front of you. Your service time, in this case the time it takes you to pay the toll and get your change, is all the time it will take you to complete this task. Now consider this scenario at 5:00 p.m. on a Friday: You come upon the same toll booth, but 15 people are in front of you. Your response time now equals the sum of the service times of all the people in front of you plus your own service time. Utilization of the tool booth is much higher at 5:00 p.m. than at 3:00 a.m.; this has a direct effect on queues. This could be expressed as:

Response Time = Sum of others' service times + your own service time

Utilization's Effects on Queue Growth

Although you might expect regular linear growth between the percent of a system's resource utilization and the length of queues (as shown in Figure 4.1), a sharp "curve" upward in queue length occurs at 75% utilization. When a system's resources hit 75% utilization, queues begin to grow exponentially in length, thus exponentially slowing performance.

NEW TERM   The even, incremental growth shown in Figure 4.1 does not occur in CPUs past 75% utilization. *Exponential growth* is growth that doubles itself at regular intervals (which might be very short) until it reaches infinity. The point at which infinity is reached is also known as the point of going *asymptotic*. The graph shown in Figure 4.2 depicts this type of growth.

Figure 4.1.

This is a graph of linear growth.

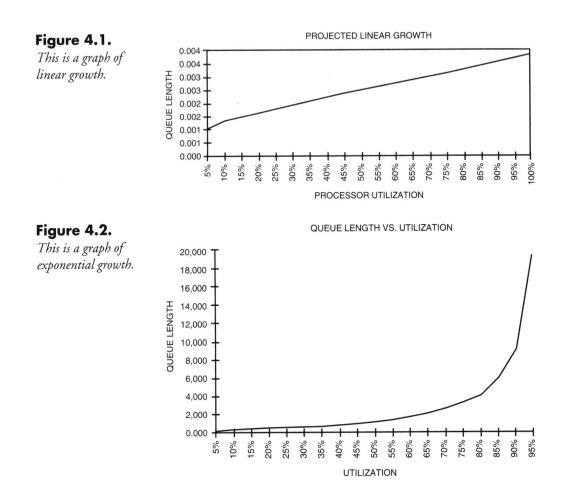

Figure 4.2.

This is a graph of exponential growth.

Notice on the graph shown in Figure 4.2 that at about 75% utilization, the growth of the queue length shifts from linear to asymptotic (or growth that appears on the graph to go straight up). The graph in Figure 4.3 shows how utilization has a direct effect on the response-time curve. This takes place because of the extreme likelihood of running into an object already using the resource that your transaction might need at utilizations past 75%. With the increase of each percentage point, this queue building radically increases the response time in a nonlinear fashion. The equation that calculates response time is

```
RESPONSE_TIME=Σ RESPONSE_TIMES=((QUEUE_LENGTH*SERVICE_TIME)+SERVICE_TIME)
```

This would indicate that if a transaction uses three resources to complete its task, you would add these resource response times together. These response times are equal to queue length multiplied by the service time for each object on the queue in front of you, plus the service time of your own task.

Figure 4.3.

This is a graph of response time growth versus utilization growth.

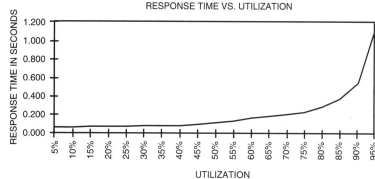

Notice that the curve in the queue-length graph also exists in the response-time graph. This is why you never want to run your CPUs in a steady state over 75%. This is not to say that you can never run your CPUs above 75%, but doing so at length negatively affects queues and response time.

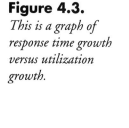

> **NOTE**
>
> The knee of the curve is one of the most important principles of sizing; you should consider it when selecting the number of CPUs your system will require. If you calculate that your system will produce 180% total processor utilization, it might be better to have three CPUs that run at 60% (keeping utilization 15% under the knee of the curve) than to have two CPUs running at about 90% (which pushes utilization 15% over the knee of the curve).

Maximum Utilization for Other Hardware

The knee of the curve principle also applies to other facets of your system, such as disks, that do not have the same knee of the curve as processors. The knee of the curve for disks tends to be at 85% as opposed to 75%. This percentage applies to the size and I/O capability of the disk drive in question. For example, a disk with a size capability of 9GB should not store more than 7.6GB of data at any given time. This allows for growth, but more importantly, it helps minimize response time factors; a disk at full capacity requires longer seek times, which adds to your overall response time. By the same token, if a disk drive has an I/O capability of 70/second, you would not want a constant I/O arrival rate of more than 60/second in a steady state of operation. By adhering to this principle, you can minimize your overall response times and get the most out of your system. This also gives your system a reserve capacity for peak-utilization periods.

Page Faulting

New Term   *Page faulting*, a normal system function for retrieving data from the disk, is as important to sizing memory as the knee of the curve is to sizing processors and disks. A system does all of its processing of requests in memory. If a user process needs a data record or a system needs a code page and it is found in memory, this is called a logical I/O (or memory read). A page fault occurs when the system determines that certain information that it must process, such as a code page, is not in memory. When this occurs, the system issues a page-fault interrupt. This instructs the system to retrieve the data from physical disk.

New Term   This is important because if the code sought by your system is not in memory, the system must retrieve the code from the disk. When a system or user function retrieves information from the disk, it is called *physical I/O*.

When a user transaction requests to read data, a simple data transfer from the disk to memory occurs if the data is not found in memory. This is usually handled by some sort of data-flow manager combined with disk-controller functions.

When a system requires a code page that is not in memory, it issues a page-fault interrupt. This prevents the system from running the process until the data it needs has been retrieved from disk. When the situation has been rectified, the process is placed on the ready list to be run again.

Either physical I/O condition prolongs response time because retrieval time for data found in memory is rated in microseconds (millionths of seconds) whereas physical I/Os are rated in milliseconds (thousandths of seconds). It takes much longer to process a physical I/O.

Types of Page Faults

New Term   Different types of page faulting can occur in your system; all page faults cause physical I/Os. For example, say your system is executing operating-system code and the next code address is not in memory. In such a case, the system issues a page-fault interrupt to retrieve the next code address; the system must go to the disk drive to get it. If this is a *code page fault*, the transfer of data goes only from disk to memory. This generates a one-way transfer through physical I/Os.

New Term   In the case of a data page that has been written to (known as a *dirty data page*), a two-step page fault known as a *page fault swap* will cause the system to retrieve the new data from disk as well as to write the data currently in memory to disk. This generates a two-way physical I/O transfer: from memory to disk to update the data, and from disk to memory to retrieve the data. The frequent occurrence of swaps can severely damage response time because two physical I/O sequences occur for each swap.

Remember that page-fault transfers occur in pages, not single-address transfers. The page-fault principle is used in the calculation of minimum memory. Minimum memory is defined as the least amount of memory you will require to process your workload without excessive page faulting. Note that you cannot remove all page faulting from your system, but you can minimize it.

NOTE

> *Single-address transfer* refers to the amount of data that is to be retrieved. For example, if I request a single, specific customer record, the retrieval of that single record can be thought of as a single-address transfer. This is because the request specifies a single record that is located at a single address. On the other hand, if the system requests a code page or a series of code pages, this transfer might involve many address transfers because the code might not be contiguous (in sequence) on the disk drive. The distinction is important because the single-address transfer will have a much shorter service time (because the system needs to find only one record) as compared to transfers required to find many pages of data or code scattered across many addresses on the disk. The seek time (the time it takes for a disk drive to locate data) will be much longer, and you will have a much longer service time.

DSS Transactions

A different type of application system that is currently in demand is the DSS, or Decision Support System. This type of system is generally used to provide information to management so decisions can be made about issues such as business growth, levels of stock on hand, and so on. For example, the United States Air Force uses such a system to inform high-level personnel about the current location and weaponry of jet fighters, bombers, and personnel.

In DSS systems, there is little writing to the database except when the database is being updated or loaded. With a DSS system, keeping processor utilization under 75% is less important than how long it will take to process requests. Indeed, most DSS queries utilize processors at 100% utilization until query completion, and that can take hours or even days to complete.

In the OLTP system, the rate of the throughput of transactions is commonly measured in transactions per second (TPS) or transactions per minute (TPM). With DSS, throughput is usually measured in queries per hour (QPH). QPH indicates that these queries are of extreme size and overwhelm the machine's resources until they are complete. In almost all cases, the ratio between OLTP and DSS transactions equals thousands (sometimes tens of thousands) of OLTP transactions to one DSS transaction. Nonetheless, the principles of disk configuration with DSS mirror those of OLTP: You don't want to overload the disks in terms of size or I/O. A system such as this would have to have certain qualities that are unique to this type such as massive processor power and usually a very large database capacity. An OLTP system, even a large one, is usually not much more than 300GB, whereas a large DSS system can be 1TB in size.

Sizing the Memory and Processor

When determining an adequate size for your processor and memory, you must have certain pieces of information:

- [ ] The number of users who will be on the system concurrently
- [ ] The transaction workload type
- [ ] The operating system type

The first step in sizing a system is to find out certain information pertaining to that system. This can be done via an interview process. When conducting this interview process you need access to three main persons:

- [ ] The database designer
- [ ] The application designer
- [ ] A representative of the management staff

Because you are sizing a database server, you already know that the application will run on various client machines; information pertaining to the memory usage and utilization of the application does not concern you when you size the database server.

The database server handles user requests that pertain to gathering information required to complete a transaction. To size a database server, you need such information as the number of concurrent user connections and the number of transaction I/Os (in the form of reads and writes) that will be generated because of the request. This is why you need the application designer at these proceedings: to explain the various transactions and the I/Os they will generate. When calculating the proper amount of memory for your system, the person performing the sizing must take into account things such as the desirable cache-hit rate (the rate at which information requested is found in the Oracle SGA memory cache) and any page faulting that might occur. The accepted standard cache-hit rate percentage is above 90%. The calculation for determining cache-hit rate percentage is defined later in this chapter. A typical scenario would be as follows:

1. Your first piece of information pertains to the system's usage type (any member of the interview team you assemble will know this). For example, this system will be used for an OLTP order-entry system.

2. Define the concurrent user community that will generate the workload. This piece of information will help you determine how much memory you need. For this example, you are using an Oracle8 database. Let's assume there will be 50 concurrent users on the system at any given time. Oracle 8 uses approximately 500KB for each user connected. For this system, you will need 25MB of memory for the user community alone.

3. Determine what operating system will be used. Most operating systems, including Windows NT, use roughly 18MB in size; this means you are up to 43MB of memory.

4. Establish the size of the database executable you plan to use. In this case, you are using the Oracle8 version of the Oracle database. The Oracle8 database executable is 5.5MB in size. This brings your total to 48.5MB of memory.

5. Another piece of information required is the size of the System Global Area (SGA). This area is indicative to Oracle databases only. The SGA provides for variable cache sizes, allowing for high cache-hit rates and high-speed processing.

Calculating the Size of the SGA

The SGA has three main facets:

- ☐ The shared pool size
- ☐ The log buffer size
- ☐ The database buffer size

The shared pool area contains such things as the stored procedures, and consists of two main areas:

- ☐ The library cache—This is where procedures are commonly used by the system and are in internal format (parsed). The effect that you, the system administrator or performance technician, want is a single parse accompanied by multiple uses. A shared pool that is too small causes undesirable effects such as prolonged response times because a parsed request will probably not be in a shared pool long enough to use multiple times, so when the same request is called again it will have to be parsed again.

- ☐ The dictionary cache—This area consists of the most frequent requests pertaining to the database. An example of this type of request would be a validation of access privileges.

The recommended size for the shared pool relates to the number of concurrent users. Table 4.1 shows the numbers to use when calculating shared pool size.

Table 4.1. Calculating the shared pool size.

Number in user community	Shared pool size
<44	3.5MB
44–95	6MB
>95	9MB

The log buffer area, the second part of the SGA that determines the size of memory, holds information about the write activity taking place. Like the calculation for shared pool size, the calculation for log buffer size relates to the size of the concurrent user community (see Table 4.2).

> **NOTE**
>
> The log buffer contains information showing the changes that have been made to the database. When this buffer fills up, a process known as the log writer (LGWR) writes the contents of the buffer to the redo log files associated with the database. If this buffer is too small, the LGWR process activates more often, thus slowing the performance of your system because of the write activity to the files.

Table 4.2. Calculating the size of the log buffer area.

Number in user community	Log buffer size
<44	8,192 bytes
44–95	32,768 bytes
>95	163,840 bytes

> **NOTE**
>
> These values are a recommended starting point for these parameters, and are suggested within the `initorcl.ora` file. After you load the Oracle database system, it's a good idea to read this file and review the suggested settings. These settings are a good starting point, but in most cases must be fine tuned for better performance.

The final part of the SGA that is pertinent to memory size is the database buffer size. The parameter name within the `initorcl.ora` file is `DB_BLOCK_BUFFERS`. This area is the cache area of your system. All the data that is processed by your system will pass through this area. The next section shows you how to calculate the size you'll need.

Calculating the Size of the Database Buffer

The larger this area is, the greater your cache-hit rate will be. Obviously you want the best cache-hit rate you can get. As in the case of the page fault, a cache area that is too small causes the occurrence of physical I/Os, thus increasing the response time of the transaction. My own studies show that the number of transaction completions distinctly increases relative to how high you set the parameter in the initorcl.ora file known as DB_BLOCK_BUFFERS. Table 4.3 shows this increase in transactions.

NOTE

DB_BLOCK_BUFFERS refers to the quantity of database buffers that this system will have. DB_BLOCK_SIZE refers to the size that each block will be. If you specify in the initorcl.ora file that DB_BLOCK_BUFFERS has a value of 1,000 and that DB_BLOCK_SIZE has a value of 2,048, you will have 1,000 database buffers at a size of 2,048 bytes each.

Table 4.3. Transaction differentials.

Run #	Number of users	Trans. completions	DB buffers
31	10	1,935	550
32	10	2,356	3,200
33	10	3,092	24,131
34	20	2,375	550
35	20	3,215	3,200
36	20	5,892	22,881
37	30	1,561	550
38	30	3,423	3,200
39	30	6,210	21,631
40	40	1,485	550
41	40	3,267	3,200
42	40	5,473	20,381
43	50	952	550
44	50	2,998	3,200
45	50	4,885	19,131
46	60	984	550
47	60	1,805	3,200
48	60	2,654	17,881

4

This table illustrates the dramatic effect of having a cache area that is too small. For example, examine run #31, which was performed with a simulated user community of 10 (as indicated in the Num Users column) and had a DB_BLOCK_BUFFERS setting of 550 (as indicated in the Database Buffers column). The Trans. completions column indicates that this run completed 1,935 transactions. Now examine run #32, which was performed with a simulated user community of 10, but with a DB_BLOCK_BUFFERS setting of 3,200. The Trans. completions column for this run indicates that the run completed 2,356 transactions. Finally, examine run #33, which, like the other two tests, was performed with a simulated user community of 10. However, this run was performed with a DB_BLOCK_BUFFERS setting of 24,131. The Trans. completions column indicates that 3,092 transactions per minute were completed.

NOTE

> The database block size used for these tests was 2,048 bytes.

Now that you know how important it is to an OLTP system to properly set DB_BLOCK_BUFFERS, you will need to know what the various settings to this parameter will cost in terms of memory size. Calculate this with the following equation:

```
DB_BUFFER_SIZE=DB_BLOCK_SIZE*DB_BLOCK_BUFFERS,
where
DB_BLOCK_SIZE=Block sizes ranging from 2,048 to 16,384
and
DB_BLOCK_BUFFERS=The parameter setting to the initorcl.ora file ranging from 100 to
the amount of memory you have.
```

This means that in the three test scenarios, each having a DB_BLOCK_SIZE of 2,048, run #31 had a total cache area of 1,126,400 bytes, run #32 had a total cache area of 6,553,600 bytes, and run #33 had a total cache area of 49,420,288 bytes. The target cache-hit rate for your system should be as close to 90% as you can get it.

Calculating the Total Memory Requirements

From the information provided by the interview so far, you can calculate the minimum amount of memory you require. You know there will be 50 users on this system and that it is an OLTP application. You would generally use a smaller block size for this type of application because you are going for transaction speed and short response time; use 2,048 bytes. An OLTP transaction will typically retrieve a few records at a time in random order for a read and possibly a few writes, so you need not have a large block size to fit these records. A small block size wastes less space and takes slightly less time to read into memory from the disk in a physical I/O than a large one, so it will not add to the response time.

Next you need to account for the operating system, the Oracle database executable, and the SGA. In this case, you will start with 4,500 DB_BLOCK_BUFFERS. You must also take into account any other software you have on the server. Keep in mind that this is a database server and you should restrict activities to that realm. A simple rule of thumb is to never mix development functions with the processing of your business system. Development functions, in particular compilations of code, will devastate the processing of your workload in terms of response times.

At this point, simple mathematics can be used to calculate the minimum amount of memory required for this system. You need 25MB for the user population, 18MB for the operating system, 5.5MB for the Oracle database executable, 32KB for the log buffers, 6MB for the shared pool, and finally, you need 9.22MB for the database buffer size. This comes out to 45,748,768 bytes of memory. It's always a good idea to add 5–10% to the minimum memory size for future growth.

In most cases, you cannot purchase the exact amount of memory you need because of the size of the manufactured memory chip. If this is the case, go to the next-highest quantity, 48MB, which would give you just over 5% additional memory for future growth. A formula to use when calculating minimum memory could be expressed as:

```
MINIMUM_MEMORY=Σ SYSTEM, USER_MEMORY, SYSTEM_GLOBAL_AREA,
where
SYSTEM=(OPERATING SYSTEM+ORACLE DATABASE SYSTEM),
USER_MEMORY=(CONCURRENT_USER_COUNT*MEMORY_PER_USER),
SYSTEM_GLOBAL_AREA=Σ SHARED_POOL, LOG_BUFFER, DB_BUFFER_SIZE,
and
DB_BUFFER_SIZE=DB_BLOCK_SIZE*DB_BLOCK_BUFFERS
```

NOTE

> The notation Σ denotes the summation or addition function within mathematics and is known as *sigma*.

This relatively simple equation can be used for calculating both OLTP and DSS application usage. The difference between the two application systems is that with a DSS system, you would select a larger block size because a DSS application does full-table scans in sequential-read mode. This allows more records to be read per physical I/O and cuts down on the number of physical reads performed. This helps response times because fewer physical reads take place. In the case of DSS, full-table scans are typically being used and cache will not be used because all the I/Os will be physical. My own studies show that cache has no effect on the processing times, as shown in Table 4.4.

Table 4.4. The effects of cache on DSS applications.

Run #	Trans. name	DB block buffers	Phys. reads	DB gets	Consis. gets	Log reads	Cache hit
21	q1	1,000	151,504	1,016	152,048	153,064	1.02%
22	q1	10,000	151,517	1,016	152,048	153,064	1.01%
23	q1	100,000	151,491	122	152,024	152,146	0.43%
24	q1	10,000	151,514	131	152,500	152,631	0.73%
25	q1	10,000	151,517	1,048	152,312	153,360	1.20%

In runs #21–#25, DB_BLOCK_BUFFER settings (under the DB block buffers column) ranged from 1,000 (in run #21) to 100,000 (in #23) and the cache-hit rate (under the Cache hit column) never exceeded 1.20%. You will also notice that the physical reads (under the Phys. reads column) for all the test runs were close to each other.

TIP

> If the application system is a DSS with many full-table–scan queries, it is a good idea to set the DB_BLOCK_BUFFER parameter low and increase the DB_BLOCK_SIZE to a much larger number or to the maximum, which is 16,384. This allows more records to be read per physical I/O and cuts down on the number of physical reads performed. This helps response times because fewer physical reads take place.

In the case of the OLTP application system, it is a good idea to check the cache-hit rate when the system is installed. The target cache-hit rate for your system should be as close to 100% as possible, but not less than 90%. You will need some additional information to calculate this; the installed Oracle database comes with scripts to retrieve this information. UTLBSTAT.sql, which is executed before you perform the test run, and UTLESTAT.sql, which is executed after the test run is completed, will provide this information for you. The information you will need from the UTLESTAT output is CONSISTENT_GETS, DB_GETS, and PHYSICAL_READS. You will then put these values in an equation that is set up as follows:

```
CACHE_HIT_RATE=(LOGICAL_READS–PHYSICAL_READS)/LOGICAL_READS,
where
LOGICAL_READS=CONSISTENT_GETS+DB_GETS
```

Remember: In the case of an OLTP application, you want a cache-hit rate of at least 90%. This will ensure that your system has the best possible response time and performance.

Sizing the Processor

You have sized the memory for your system; now it's time to size the processor. The following assumptions about the system must be made:

- ☐ The application and database design schema is complete.
- ☐ The target steady-state CPU utilization is less than 75%.
- ☐ The expected cache-hit rate is at least 90%.
- ☐ No disk drive will exceed 85% usage of space or I/O activity.
- ☐ The server is running only an Oracle database.
- ☐ The distribution of disk I/Os is even across all drives.

Some of these assumptions, such as the ones pertaining to the cache-hit rate and the target steady-state CPU utilization, serve as guidelines for determining the number of CPUs you require. But when sizing for the processor or CPU, you need additional information; this information can be provided by the database and application designers.

Sizing a CPU on a database server is not as complex as it might appear. A database server only processes transactions; the application runs on a client machine, so application sizing is immaterial. The server's role—processing requests from the user community in the form of retrieving data and writing data—amounts to nothing more than processing I/Os. The application designer will have pertinent information about what the transactions are doing. The database designer will have information pertaining to tables and indexes that will be affected by these transactions. The task at hand is to determine how many I/Os will be generated by the transactions and in what time frame they must be completed. So the following additional information is required to complete this task:

- ☐ You need to know how many transactions must be processed through the system and the definition of the system's working day in terms of hours or the peak-load period. As per our earlier discussion, it is better to size for peak periods because you can build the machine to accommodate the worst-case period. Information about the peak-load period will not be available in most cases if you are sizing a machine for a new business.
- ☐ You need a deeper understanding of the transactions that will be processed, so you must know the transaction anatomy. The transaction anatomy will help you determine the number of reads and writes (I/Os) that will be generated and calculate the anticipated CPU utilization. For this information, you must interview the database engineer and the application designer to determine the following:
  - ☐ The number of transactions of each type that will go through the system
  - ☐ The I/Os that will be generated by this in the form of reads and writes

☐ You need to examine the block diagram of the transactions in question (see Figure 4.4). If a block diagram of the transaction does not exist, one can be drawn fairly quickly.

Figure 4.4.

This is a block diagram of a transaction.

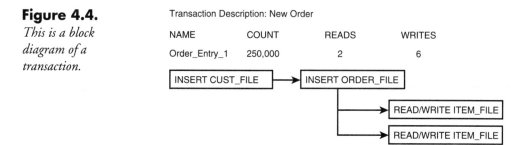

This diagram shows that 250,000 new order transactions are expected, and each one will generate two reads and six writes. How was this determined?

1. The new order transaction involves two inserts: one to CUST_FILE and one to ORDER_FILE.

2. Each insert involves two writes: one to insert the record and one to write to it. So far, there are four writes.

3. In this case, the customer orders two items. This involves one read from ITEM_FILE for each item being ordered, amounting to two reads.

4. After the item is ordered, ITEM_FILE must be updated to reflect that there is now one less of each item in stock; this amounts to two more writes.

Fault Tolerance

NEW TERM   Here the fault-tolerance factor comes into view. *Fault tolerance* is the method used to protect your database from hardware snafus such as disk-drive failures. Fault tolerance is important because hardware failures profoundly affect the performance of your machine; indeed, without fault tolerance, you can lose your database altogether in the event of a disk-drive failure. Most computers support fault tolerance through the support of the RAID (Redundant Array of Inexpensive Drives) factors:

☐ RAID 0—No data integrity (no fault tolerance). With RAID 0, the user does not specify a method of data recovery. Therefore, if a failure takes place (for example, if a disk drive becomes disabled), you lose the data on that disk drive. That means the odds of losing the entire database are high.

☐ RAID 1—Mirrored disk drive. With RAID 1, you have double the number of disk drives. Each disk drive in a volume has a mirrored image of its information.

Figure 4.5 shows the difference between the quantity of disk drives required for the RAID 0 factor and the RAID 1 factor.

Figure 4.5.

This is a diagram of the RAID 0 factor and the RAID 1 factor.

Notice that the RAID 0 factor requires a single disk; along with this comes a single point of failure, meaning that if the disk drive fails, you lose the data on that disk drive and therefore the entire database. In the RAID 1 factor, there is a mirror image of that database disk drive. In the eventuality of a disk drive failure, you have a backup data drive complete with all the data that was on that disk drive.

 If RAID 1 is the selected method of data integrity, users receive the added benefit of *split seeks*. Split seeks allows the system to split the access of the mirrored drives in two, greatly accelerating the location of the desired data and thereby reducing transaction response time. This means that if you are seeking a specific record (for example, record L), the two disk drives can split the seek load between them because both drives have the same data. Disk 1 might search records A–M, and disk 2 might search records N–Z. The choice of RAID factor directly affects the number of disk I/Os because different RAID factors change the number of writes to the disk. For example, RAID 1 increases the number of writes to two times that of RAID 0. If the user describes a transaction as having 50 reads and 10 writes and wants to use RAID 1, the number of writes increases to 20. This is because the data must be written to both disks at once.

RAID 5: Distributed Parity

RAID 5, also known as *distributed parity*, is the second type of fault tolerance I will discuss. RAID 5 operates by distributing parity pertaining to a disk drive to other disk drives in that volume. This parity (information about the data on that disk drive in internal format) is placed on other disks so that the other disks in that volume can continue to process requests in the event of a failure. For example, say you have four disk drives in a RAID 5 volume. Any three disks in that volume can continue to process requests because they contain the information about the disk drive that is disabled. If an online spare disk drive is declared, the disks will not only continue to process requests, they (along with the disk controller) will be able to rebuild the disabled disk drive on the online spare. Figure 4.6 depicts a typical RAID 5 configuration.

Figure 4.6.

This is a comparative diagram of a RAID 0 and a RAID 5 configuration.

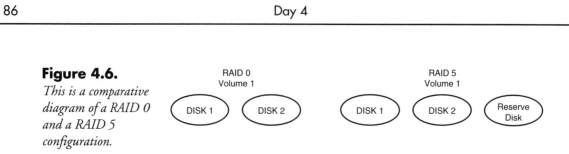

Notice that the RAID 0 configuration has two designated disk drives, and that the RAID 5 configuration has three (referred to as DISK 1, DISK 2, and Reserve Disk). The Reserve Disk data volume allows the continued transaction processing and rebuilding of a failed disk drive because in a RAID 5 configuration, each disk has enough information about the other disk drives' data to process requests and rebuild on the online spare disk drive. That is, DISK 1 has enough information to process requests and rebuild DISK 2 on the online spare labeled Reserve Disk if the need arises. Nonetheless, this configuration is expensive in terms of price and performance. Each write under RAID 5 generates as many as four times that number of I/Os (two reads and two writes for every write under RAID 5) for each transaction processed. This slightly prolongs the transaction response time. The following calculations should be used when determining your total I/O count:

☐ RAID 0 Trans I/O=(READS_PER_TRANS+WRITES_PER_TRANS)

If transaction 1 has 50 reads and 10 writes, the total number of I/Os is 60.

☐ RAID 1 Trans I/O=(READS_PER_TRANS+(WRITES_PER_TRANS*2))

If transaction 1 has 50 reads and 10 writes, the total number of I/Os is 70.

☐ RAID 5 Trans I/O=(READS_PER_TRANS+(WRITES_PER_TRANS*2 for reads, and *2 for writes))

If transaction 1 has 50 reads and 10 writes at RAID 0, you would multiply the writes by two for additional RAID 5 reads, and then multiply the writes again by two for the total writes. In this example, you would have 70 reads and 20 writes for a total number of 90 I/Os.

This could be expressed as:

```
RAID_5_TRANSACTION_I/O=RAID_5_READS+RAID_5_WRITES,
where
RAID_5_READS=ORIGINAL_READS+ADDITIONAL_RAID_5_READS,
ORIGINAL_READS=The number of reads the transaction had at RAID 0,
ADDITIONAL_RAID_5_READS=The number of writes at RAID 0 * 2,
and
RAID_5_WRITES=ORIGINAL_WRITES * 2,
ORIGINAL_WRITES=The number of writes the transaction had at RAID 0
```

This increase of writes is a function of the disk controller, and is transparent to the user, who does not need to make adjustments to the application. Remember that your RAID selection directly affects how many I/Os are processed. This increase of writes affects the utilization factors of the CPUs and the quantity of disks chosen by the sizing effort.

If you look at the example of the new order transaction, you can see that there will be a substantial change in the number of generated I/Os. The number of writes increases from six under RAID 0 to 12 under RAID 1. That makes the total writes for this transaction 3,000,000, causing the total I/O count to increase to 3,500,000 for 250,000 of these new order transactions. Under RAID 5, the number of writes increases fourfold: from six under RAID 0 to 24 under RAID 5. This makes the total number of writes for the new order transaction 6,000,000, causing the total I/O count to increase to 6,500,000 for 250,000 of these new order transactions.

There are standards for applying fault tolerance to a system. The operating system disks and log file disks are usually set up with a RAID 1 configuration, allowing the fastest possible recovery. The database disk drives are usually set up with a RAID 5 configuration. This is the most cost-effective way to ensure that your database will be fault tolerant. With RAID 5, if a disk-drive failure occurs, your system can still process I/O requests while the system rebuilds your failed disk drive.

Now that you have the information you need, let's calculate what the CPU utilization will be for your proposed system processing 250,000 new order transactions. A formula used to determine the CPU utilization of a proposed system is as follows:

```
CPU_UTILIZATION=THROUGHPUT*SERVICE_TIME,
```
where
```
THROUGHPUT=NUMBER_I/O,
```
and
```
SERVICE_TIME=AMOUNT_CPU_TIME_PER_I/O
```

If you carefully follow this formula, you can accurately predict the anticipated CPU. First you must calculate the total number of reads. This example boasts 500,000 total reads. Remember that you need a 90% cache-hit rate to minimize CPU utilization due to excessive physical reads, so out of the 500,000 reads, 450,000 of them will be found in memory and 50,000 will be physical reads.

This distinction is important because memory reads or logical reads involve much less intervention by the CPUs than physical reads. In this case, you are looking at 16% for the logical reads and 35% for the physical reads. Add these together to see a utilization factor for the reads of 51%, based on an eight-hour working day.

Finally, add in the total write time for these transactions. To do this, you must decide on a fault-tolerance level or a RAID factor. I recommend that a RAID 5 be used on the database; however, this causes the number of writes to increase from 1,500,000 reads (under RAID 0) to 6,000,000 writes (under RAID 5). After you perform the calculation, you find that you have 20.83% utilization based on the eight-hour working day. This gives you an expected 20.99% utilization just from the new order transaction. The following formula steps should be performed on every transaction that will be processed as part of this workload set:

1. Using the following formula, calculate the total number of reads that will be going through the system:

   `TOTAL_READS=NUMBER_READS_PER_TRANS*TOTAL_TRANS_TYPE`

2. Using the following formula, determine how many of these reads will be physical and how many will be logical:

   `TOTAL_LOGICAL_READS=TOTAL_READS*CACHE_HIT_RATE,`

   `TOTAL_PHYSICAL_READS=TOTAL_READS—LOGICAL_READS`

3. Using the following functions, convert the total number of each read type to reads per second:

   `LOG_READS_PER_SEC=TOTAL_LOGICAL_READS/WORK_PERIOD)/60/60,`

   `PHYS_READS_PER_SEC=TOTAL_PHYSICAL_READS/WORK_PERIOD/60/60`

4. Using the following method, calculate the amount of CPU time used for each of the read functions:

   `LOG_READ_TIME=LOG_READS_PER_SEC*LOG_READ_CPU_TIME,`

   `PHYS_READ_TIME=PHYS_READS_PER_SEC*PHYS_READ_CPU_TIME`

TIP

My own studies show that an average of 2 milliseconds (.002) are required to read a block into memory (physical read), and .1 millisecond (.0001) is used to read a block from memory. Use .002 seconds for the value in the variable PHYS_READ_CPU_TIME and .0001 seconds for the variable LOG_READ_CPU_TIME.

5. Calculate the CPU utilization for the various read functions using a variation of the equation `CPU_UTILIZATION=THROUGHPUT*SERVICE_TIME`:

   `LOG_READ_UTIL=LOG_READS_PER_SEC*LOG_READ_TIME,`

   `PHYS_READ_UTIL=PHYS_READS_PER_SEC*PHYS_READ_TIME`

6. Using the following formula, calculate the total number of writes that will be going through the system:

```
TOTAL_WRITES=TRANSACTION_WRITES*RAID_FACTOR_INCREASE,
where
TRANSACTIONS_WRITES=WRITES*TOTAL_TRANS_TYPE
```

7. By performing the following calculation, determine the writes per second that will be going through the system:

```
WRITES_PER_SEC=TOTAL_WRITES/WORK_PERIOD)/60/60
```

8. By performing the following calculation, determine the total CPU time used to process the writes:

```
CPU_WRITE_TIME=WRITES_PER_SEC*WRITE_CPU_TIME
```

9. Using the following formula, calculate the write utilization:

```
WRITE_UTIL=WRITES_PER_SEC*CPU_WRITE_TIME
```

TIP   Additional studies of mine show that an average of 1 millisecond (.001) is used to write a block from memory (write) to disk. Use .001 second for the value in the variable CPU_WRITE_TIME.

4

10. Using the following formula, calculate the total CPU utilization for the transaction type:

```
TRANS_UTILIZATION=Σ LOG_READ_UTIL, PHYS_READ_UTIL, WRITE_UTIL
```

NOTE   These calculations must be performed on each transaction type to accurately size the CPUs for your system.

11. Using the following formula, calculate the total processor utilization:

```
TOTAL_CPU_UTILIZATION=Σ TRANS_UTILIZATION,
if TOTAL_CPU_UTILIZATION>75%,
then TOTAL_CPU_UTILIZATION/NUMBER_CPU,
where
NUMBER_CPU=a number that will bring the total below 75%
```

For example, if `TOTAL_CPU_UTILIZATION` = 180, you would start off providing the variable `NUMBER_CPU` with the value 3 (three being the number of proposed CPUs). After the equation `TOTAL_CPU_UTILIZATION` / `NUMBER_CPU` was applied, you would have a recommendation of three CPUs running at about 60%.

When sizing for the number of CPUs in a DSS system, it's better to use multiple CPUs. This way, the user can take advantage of the Parallel Query option offered by the Oracle database. In short, this allows a large query to be broken into segments based on the Parallel Query option value (for example, if a Parallel Query option value of 4 is selected, the query is broken into four sections) and to hit the database simultaneously, thus expediting processing. This process performs best when multiple CPUs are used. Most DSS systems are large and contain multiple CPUs. A rule of thumb: The more CPUs and disks you have for a DSS system, the better your processing times will be.

Sizing the Disk Subsystem

Now that you have sized the memory and the processor, it's time to size the disk subsystem. This is the easiest section of the system to size because you already have most of the information you need to do this sizing:

- [ ] First you need the total number of I/Os that will be processing through the system. You already have this information from the processor sizing.
- [ ] Second you need the size of the database. This could easily be provided by the database designer.

When sizing the disk subsystem, you must understand that you're sizing relative to the size of the database or the I/Os per second, whichever is greater. One commonly asked question pertaining to disk subsystem sizing is, "If my database is only 10GB in size, why do I need so many disk drives for it?" The answer is that although the database is relatively small in size and could probably fit on two 9.1GB disk drives, you want more drives than that to give more access points to the data. In this case, if all the data was on two disk drives, you would probably run into a bottleneck situation on either or both disk drives.

You might also generate many I/Os per second and require more disks to accommodate the I/O load than necessary for the database size. For example, say you have a database system that is 10GB in size and generates 3,500 I/Os per second. You would need three 4.3GB drives to accommodate the size of the database; if these disk drives were rated at 70 I/Os per second, you would need 59 disk drives to accommodate the number of I/Os per second (based on 85% utilization). When sizing the disk subsystem, always use the 85% usage rule (remember the knee of the curve?) for the size of the database or for the I/Os per second generated by users, and always remember that too many I/Os per second to the disk drives in question will cause bottlenecks and, therefore, problems with prolonged response times.

Here are some simple calculations that you can perform to determine the proper number of disk drives you will need for your system. First, you need disk drives to support your operating system and the Oracle database executable. You will usually want these disk drives to be a separate volume set to RAID 1 (mirrored disk drives) for the fastest possible recovery. You want the fastest possible recovery on the operating system because everything will slow down *drastically* if you do not have this. The number of disk drives might vary depending on size, but the operating system and the Oracle database executable can usually fit on a single disk. A simple calculation for this would be

OPERATING_SYSTEM_DISKS=OS_ORACLE_DISK*RAID_FACTOR,
where
OS_ORACLE_DISK=disk drive for operating system and Oracle,
and
RAID_FACTOR=number of disks for RAID drives (disks that will be required for a desired RAID factor). For example you will need twice the number of disks for RAID 1.

This case would be for two mirrored disk drives. It is not recommended to set the operating system volume to RAID 5 or RAID 0. You must have at least two initial disk drives to use RAID 5 and you will want the fastest possible recovery for the operating system and the Oracle executable.

Next you need to determine how many log disk drives you will need for your system. This depends heavily on the total number of writes per second your transactions will cause. Remember that the information on these disks is most important; these are the audit trails, or the before images, and will be needed if anything happens to your database. These audit trails allow you to back out of partially complete transactions due to disk failure.

Do this by calculating the number of writes that will occur (this was done earlier in this lesson in the section titled "Sizing the Processor"). Using the values from the new order transaction, you initially calculated 1,500,000 writes under RAID 0. If the RAID 1 factor should be used for the log disk drives, you are looking at 3,000,000 reads over an eight-hour period, or 104.16 writes per second. If you use the 85% ceiling for the number of writes allowed on a disk drive that has a capacity of 70 I/Os per second, you need 1.73 (round up to two) disk drives. A good calculation to use for this is

LOG_DISK=((WRITES_PER_SEC/MAX_DISK_I/O) ROUNDUP)*RAID_FACTOR,
where
WRITES_PER_SEC=((TOTAL_WRITES/WORK_PERIOD)/60)/60,
MAX_DISK_I/O =MAXIMUM_I/O_PER_DISK −15%,
and
ROUNDUP=that value rounded to the next whole integer

Finally, you must determine the number of disk drives required for the database. First, determine the number of disk drives required for the database size like so:

```
DISKS_FOR_SIZE=(DB_SIZE/(MAX_DISK_SIZE-15%)+RAID_FACTOR),
```
where
`DB_SIZE`=database size in bytes,
`MAX_DISK_SIZE`=maximum disk size in bytes (−15%),
and
`RAID_FACTOR`=number of extra disk drives to support fault tolerance

TIP

> It is recommended that a RAID 5 be used for database drives.

The number of disk drives for I/Os can drastically change the disk recommendation as compared to the recommendation pertaining to database size. The required calculations are as follows:

1. Using the following formula, calculate the total number of reads that will go through the system:

   ```
   TOTAL_READS=NUMBER_READS_PER_TRANS*TOTAL_TRANS_TYPE
   ```

2. Using the following formula, determine how many of these reads will be physical and how many will be logical:

   ```
   TOTAL_LOGICAL_READS=TOTAL_READS*CACHE_HIT_RATE,
   TOTAL_PHYSICAL_READS=TOTAL_READS--LOGICAL_READS
   ```

3. By performing the following function, convert the total number of physical reads to reads per second:

   ```
   PHYS_READS_PER_SEC=TOTAL_PHYSICAL_READS/WORK_PERIOD/60/60
   ```

4. Using the following formula, calculate the total number of writes that will be going through the system:

   ```
   TOTAL_WRITES=TRANSACTION_WRITES*RAID_FACTOR_INCREASE,
   ```
   where
   ```
   TRANSACTIONS_WRITES=WRITES*TOTAL_TRANS_TYPE
   ```

5. Using the following calculation, determine the total number of physical I/Os:

   ```
   TOTAL_PHYS_I/O=TOTAL_PHYS_READS+TOTAL_WRITES
   ```

6. Calculate the total number of database disk drives as follows:

`NUM_DB_DISKS=(TOTAL_PHYS_I/O/(MAX_DISK_SIZE-15%)+RAID_FACTOR`

where

`MAX_DISK_SIZE`=maximum disk size in bytes (−15%),

and

`RAID_FACTOR`=number of extra disk drives to support fault tolerance

Capacity Planning

NEW TERM *Capacity planning* refers to a complex, ongoing performance study of hardware and software resource consumption on an existing system to prepare for the growth of that system's workload. These studies are established primarily to maintain the *service level agreements* on the operation of the system in question. These agreements are set up to ensure that response times (how long it takes for an activity or transaction to complete) of certain functions are maintained, and that a certain amount of reserve capacity (the amount of free space left in reserve for CPU processing power or the amount of free space available on a disk drive) is available to maintain the response times of these activities under peak-load conditions.

Capacity planning studies offer another outstanding feature: the capability to project what-if scenarios on workloads. In a typical capacity-planning study, the technician performing the task will have historic performance data stored in a database and will be able to project trends in the following:

☐ Normal growth of CPU utilization (the amount a time a CPU is busy during an observation period)

☐ Disk usage

☐ Memory usage

This technician will also be able to project sudden rises in CPU, disk, and memory utilization caused by the addition of new users to the system.

These studies can be extremely detailed and can involve profiling the activities of specific users. This is valuable information because not only can you add hypothetical users to the system in a generic method to project rises in the usage of CPU, memory, and disk, you can add specific users (such as people who perform general-ledger functions) to the system workload scenario to predict exactly what kind of resource consumption will occur in the event of the addition of similar users or workloads. This gives the system manager ample time to obtain the necessary hardware before the new users are added to the system, thus averting the degradation of system performance or response time.

4

Tuning information can also be obtained by capacity-planning studies. Using the case of the general-ledger users, information pertaining to the tables being hit due to the additional load can be useful in determining whether the relocation of some of these tables might prevent a bottleneck in the disk subsystem.

Summary

Sizing a system is an involved piece of work. Whoever performs such a study will obtain a wealth of knowledge about that system and will know all aspects of the proposed system. Remember that any sizing result is only as good as the information on which it is based. Make sure the information you get is accurate; if it is, the sizing results should be accurate within ±15%.

What's Next?

On Day 5, "Managing the Oracle RDBMS," you will learn the techniques necessary to manage Oracle. In this lesson you will learn about the Oracle administration accounts and the Oracle SID (System Identifier). You will also learn how to use Oracle Enterprise Manager, the graphical administration tool. Finally, you will learn about the Oracle instance and how to administer Oracle networking.

Q&A

Q What is the "knee of the curve" and why is it important when sizing or when performing capacity-planning studies?

A The knee-of-the-curve principle states that queues build exponentially if utilization is higher than 75%. This drastically degrades the response times of transactions because a large queue will always be at any resource required by the transaction.

Q What type of situation is better to size for, steady state or peak period? Why?

A It is always better to size for peak period. If you size for steady state, you do not know when the arrival rate of the transactions will be at its highest level; you must guess how much reserve capacity you will need. This leaves you open to accidental undersizing. If you size for peak period, you know the worst-case scenario and can better prepare for it.

Q What are the differences between OLTP transactions and DSS transactions? Name examples of each type of transaction.

A OLTP, or Online Transaction Processing, queries demand short response times because they update the database online. Slow response times hold up other users that require the resources you are using. DSS, or Decision Support System, queries are of long duration and do little or no updating. An example of an OLTP system would be an order-entry system; an example of a DSS workload would be an archive-retrieval system.

Q **What is a page fault and why is it detrimental to performance?**

A A page fault is a situation where either a code or data page address is required and is not found in memory. This causes a page-fault interrupt, which prevents the system from getting what it needs from the disk drive. When these code or data pages are found in memory, they take much less time to access. When sizing, you should try to leave enough memory for things such as the operating system so page faulting will not occur.

Workshop

The workshop provides quiz questions to help you solidify your understanding of the material covered and exercises to provide you with experience in using what you've learned. Find answers to quiz questions in Appendix A, "Answers."

Quiz

1. How much memory is required for each concurrent user on the system you are sizing?
2. What individuals are required for any sizing effort?
3. What would be a good database block size for an OLTP-type system?
4. What is a desirable cache-hit percentage? Why?
5. When calculating RAID factors into your total number of writes, what factor would RAID 1 use? What factor would RAID 5 use?
6. When sizing the disk subsystem, what information will you need to calculate the number of disk drives for your system?
7. What method of sizing can you use to eradicate all page faulting?
8. What is the maximum CPU utilization you would want to have in a steady-state situation?
9. What is the maximum disk utilization you would want to have in a steady-state situation?
10. How much memory should be allocated for the Oracle8 executable?

Exercises

1. At a sizing effort, you have calculated that a workload will generate 422,300 reads and 28,000 writes at RAID 0. Calculate the total number of I/Os per second this will generate at RAID 5 if the workload process time is two hours. *Note*: All the reads generated will be physical reads.

2. Based on the preceding information, calculate the anticipated number of processors (and their utilizations) needed to process this workload with a 50% cache-hit rate, and again at a 90% cache-hit rate.

Day 5

Managing the Oracle RDBMS

Today you will look at the basics. Here you will see some of the objects that must be set up by the DBA (including the Oracle DBA login account, the DBA roles, and the Oracle SID) as well as some of the tasks that the DBA must perform, including

- ☐ Setting up Enterprise Manager
- ☐ Using Enterprise Manager
- ☐ Using Server Manager
- ☐ Starting up and shutting down the Oracle instance

All these are basic functions that need to be covered before you move on to topics such as creating a database. This day lays a foundation for many of the days to come. It is important that you completely understand these concepts.

The Oracle DBA

On Day 1, "Starting Out with Oracle," you were presented with a list of the duties and responsibilities of the Oracle DBA. Let's refresh your memory with some of the key duties and responsibilities:

☐ Installing and upgrading Oracle products

☐ Installing and maintaining your company's applications

☐ Creating databases, tablespaces, tables, views, and indexes to the specification of the application developers

☐ Creating user accounts and monitoring system security

☐ Monitoring space used in the database and planning for future growth

☐ Monitoring system performance and making changes as necessary to maintain the required performance levels

☐ Maintaining the integrity of the data in the database

☐ Planning and implementing a sound backup and recovery strategy

All these duties are part of being an Oracle DBA.

The DBA Account

To accomplish these tasks, the DBA must be given special privileges. These privileges allow the DBA to run commands that other Oracle users are not allowed to perform. These privileges are maintained within Oracle itself. As part of the installation of the Oracle RDBMS, several accounts are created with these special privileges. These accounts and their privileges are described here.

INTERNAL

The INTERNAL account is provided mainly for backward compatibility with earlier versions of Oracle, but is still used for key functions such as starting up and shutting down the instance. The INTERNAL account appears as user SYS if you look at the connected sessions, but the INTERNAL account has additional key features: It can start up or shut down the instance. The INTERNAL account is available even when a database has not been created and when no instances are started up.

SYS

The SYS account is automatically created whenever a database is created. This account is used primarily to administer the data dictionary. This account is granted the DBA role, as well as CONNECT and RESOURCE roles.

5

SYSTEM

The SYSTEM account is also automatically created whenever a database is created. This account is used primarily to create tables and views important to the operation of the RDBMS. This account has been granted the DBA role.

Administrative Users

I recommend that you create individual user accounts and grant the DBA role to those users who will be acting as the DBA. In this way, fewer people access the same account, thus avoiding confusion. Also, if auditing is enabled, there is a record of who made these system changes.

TIP

> Avoid using the default administrative accounts. If DBAs are authorized with the proper roles, they can perform the tasks they need to do and maintain their individual accounts. This allows you to determine which DBA or DBAs modified the system and who is currently active on it.

The DBA Roles

Several roles are available and are assigned to the DBAs. As you will see on Day 10, "Administering User Accounts," these roles are sets of privileges assigned to a particular Oracle role. Each role can then be assigned to a user, thus giving that user all the privileges needed for that particular task. The use of roles is covered in detail on Day 10, but it is appropriate to go over the roles and privileges assigned to the Oracle DBA here.

5

DBA

The DBA role consists of most of the other Oracle roles and privileges. By assigning the DBA role to a user, there is virtually no task that user cannot do. This role should be assigned to trusted users who are active DBAs for this system.

OSOPER

The OSOPER role is one of two special operating system roles. These roles are assigned to special accounts that need OS authentication. It is necessary to have OS authentication for some accounts because Oracle authentication can be done only when the database is open. If the database is shut down, Oracle cannot validate the user permissions.

The OSOPER role allows the user to perform the following operations:

- [ ] STARTUP and SHUTDOWN
- [ ] ALTER DATABASE MOUNT

☐ ALTER DATABASE OPEN

☐ ALTER DATABASE BACKUP

☐ ALTER DATABASE RECOVER

☐ ALTER DATABASE ARCHIVE LOG

After the database is up and running, other users can be authenticated through Oracle security. These operations require a special authentication method because the database is not available.

OSDBA

The OSDBA role includes the permissions granted to the OSOPER role with some additional permissions. These additional permissions include the CREATE DATABASE command and all system privileges with the ADMIN OPTION. The ADMIN OPTION allows the user to grant these permissions to other roles or users. Without the ADMIN OPTION, you cannot propagate these permissions and roles.

Administrator Authentication

Authenticating the user can be done either through OS authentication using OS accounts and groups or through the use of Oracle password files. Which of these is right for your installation is up to you. These methods are covered in detail on Day 10; until then, all examples are done using Oracle password files.

The SID

As you learned on Day 2, "Exploring the Oracle Architecture," an Oracle instance is an Oracle database, the Oracle processes or threads, and the memory it uses. The instance is the logical term that refers to the components necessary to access the data in the database.

Each Oracle instance is identified by a SID (system identifier), which uniquely identifies this instance and is used by the Oracle utilities and networking components to connect you to the correct instance.

A SID is up to four alphanumeric characters in length and is required in order to connect to an Oracle instance. The SID is set by the ORACLE_SID environment variable. From the NT command line, you can set the SID with the following syntax:

```
Set ORACLE_SID=ORCL
```

The default SID value is set in the NT Registry. If you do not set the SID using the environment variable, the Registry entry is used. The TNSNAMES.ORA file also resolves the SID with a service name. As you will see tomorrow, when you create a network entry using a utility such as the Oracle Network Configuration wizard, you will be prompted for a service name that you pick, a network type and address, and an Oracle SID. This service name is used to resolve both the network and the SID. Even the Oracle service name includes the SID as an identifier.

You will be seeing more of the use of the Oracle SID in the next few days; for now, it is enough to think of the SID as a unique identifier and a way to connect to an Oracle instance.

The Oracle Enterprise Manager

The Oracle Enterprise Manager is a new tool from Oracle that allows the DBA to graphically administer one or more Oracle instances. By allowing many operations to be performed graphically, the presentation of data can be simplified and more meaningful.

Enterprise Manager allows the administrator to manage one or more Oracle instances either locally or via the network. Enterprise Manager consists of two main components: the graphical console and the intelligent agents.

The Enterprise Manager console is the graphical tool that allows you to graphically administer the Oracle instances. This console communicates to the various systems it administers via the intelligent agents that run on these systems. These intelligent agents allow the console to communicate with the instances. The agents use the SNMP (Simple Network Management Protocol) to take requests from the console and communicate those requests to the Oracle system running on these systems.

Enterprise Manager allows the DBA to perform the following tasks from a central location:

- ☐ Tune and administer one or more Oracle databases.
- ☐ Distribute software to both clients and servers.
- ☐ Monitor events from multiple instances.
- ☐ Perform backup and recovery operations from a single location.
- ☐ Perform standard DBA tasks such as user administration.

The Oracle Enterprise Manager is a very powerful and flexible tool that can help in many of your daily DBA duties.

NOTE

In many cases I prefer to graphically administer the Oracle system, but in some cases, I still prefer the character-based commands that can be run via the Oracle Server Manager. Throughout this book, both the graphical and character-based administrative methods are shown. I will point out where I feel one tool is more appropriate than another and why, but it is your preference that is important. You will have to decide which tool or set of tools is right for you.

In this section, you will learn how to configure Enterprise Manager and how to invoke its major functions. The individual tools that comprise Enterprise Manager, such as the Instance Manager, the Storage Manager, the Schema Manager, and so on, are presented separately in the lesson where most appropriate.

Configuring Enterprise Manager

The Oracle Enterprise Manager is installed as part of the Oracle server installation process or can be installed as part of the administrator client installation. After Enterprise Manager is installed, you can connect to it by using the NT toolbar and selecting Enterprise Manager from Enterprise Manager program group.

If this is the first time you've invoked Enterprise Manager, you will probably see a screen indicating that the repositories for Enterprise Manager and Software Manager are not installed (see Figure 5.1).

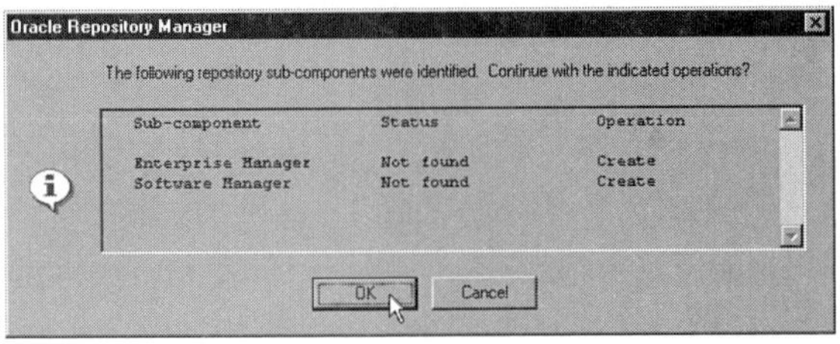

Figure 5.1.

Enterprise Manager and Software Manager repositories are not installed.

In this case, click OK and allow Enterprise Manager to create the repositories. This operation will take some time. During this period you will see indications that the repositories are being created, as shown in Figure 5.2.

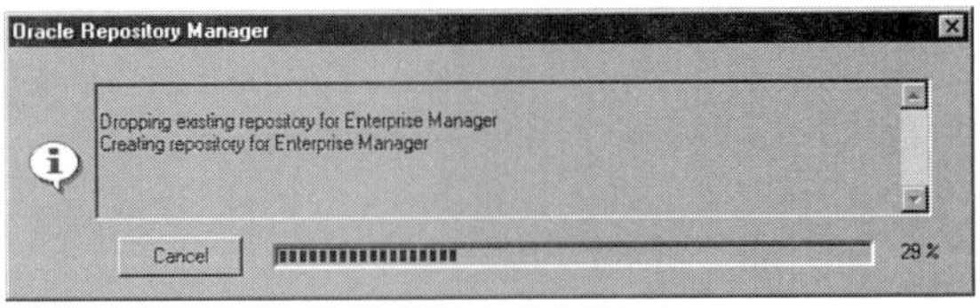

Figure 5.2.

The Oracle Repository Manager screen.

When the creation operation is complete, Enterprise Manager will start; you will see the four default panes shown in Figure 5.3.

Figure 5.3.

*The Enterprise
Manager.*

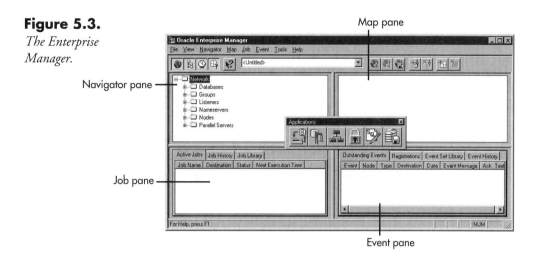

Map pane

Navigator pane

Job pane

Event pane

The four panes displayed are

☐ The Navigator pane—This pane provides a tree-type listing of the various objects available to Enterprise Manager. Through this list, you can launch various administrative operations (described later today).

☐ The Map pane—Though blank at startup, the Map pane allows you to create a geographical representation of the systems to be administered. This graphical display allows you to drill down into various sites and administer systems worldwide.

☐ The Job pane—This pane allows you to view and administer various jobs that are running in the system. Through this pane, you can schedule jobs to run on various nodes in the system at various times. This provides you with a way of scheduling routine operations from a single console.

☐ The Event pane—This pane is used to view system events that occur on any node that you are administering from this console. *Events* are occurrences that trigger some kind of action. This action can be a simple alert or can be some type of action.

NOTE

When Enterprise Manager is invoked, the Administrator toolbar is also invoked (as seen in the center of the Enterprise Manager). This toolbar allows quick access to the Enterprise Manager utilities. Some administrators like to move the toolbar or remove it altogether. This is up to you. I like to use it on occasion, but usually I remove it.

5

Using the Enterprise Manager

The Enterprise Manager is distinguished from Enterprise Manager applications in this book in that the applications are presented in the section that applies to that application's function. For example, the Schema Manager is covered in the chapter that covers the Oracle schema, the Backup Manager is covered in the chapters covering backup and recovery, and so on. Today's focus is on configuring Enterprise Manager and using the functions associated with the Navigator, Map, Job, and Event panes.

General

A few general setup parameters can be modified with Enterprise Manager. These pertain primarily to how Enterprise Manager looks and acts.

The View Menu

The View drop-down menu can be used to modify the display. Select the View menu as shown in Figure 5.4.

Figure 5.4.

The View menu.

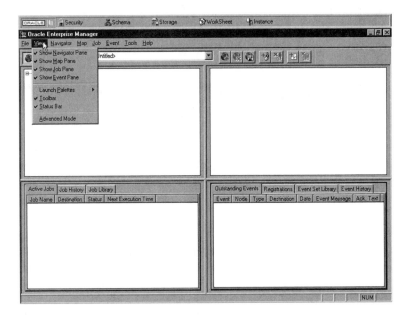

From here you can uncheck the various panes that you do not want to view. For example, if you unselect the Show Map Pane button, the Map pane will be removed from the screen.

The Navigator Menu

The Navigator drop-down menu can be used to invoke the Discover New Services wizard. To access the wizard, select Navigator | Discovery, as shown in Figure 5.5.

Figure 5.5.

The Navigator menu.

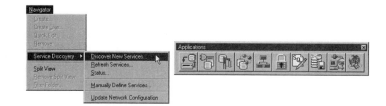

Depending on whether a database is selected in the Navigator pane, you will see several available options. One of the options is for the Discover New Services wizard. This wizard finds the available services on specified systems. To use this wizard for this purpose, do the following:

1. Select Discover New Services Wizard, and you will see the first screen of the Discover New Services wizard, as shown in Figure 5.6.

Figure 5.6.

The first screen of the Discover New Services wizard.

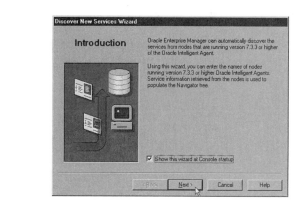

2. Click Next to move to the next screen. This screen allows you to specify node names for the discovery process to run on. After the discovery process has run, Enterprise Manager can communicate with that node and manage the various instances available on that node.

3. Type the node name, then click Add. This node will then be ready to be discovered when you click the Finish button (see Figure 5.7).

4. After you click the Next button, you are asked for the time interval at which you want discovery to occur. You can retrieve this information immediately or on a regular basis.

5. Finally, you are presented with a summary of your choices. If you are satisfied that everything is correct, you can proceed with the discovery by clicking Finish.

5

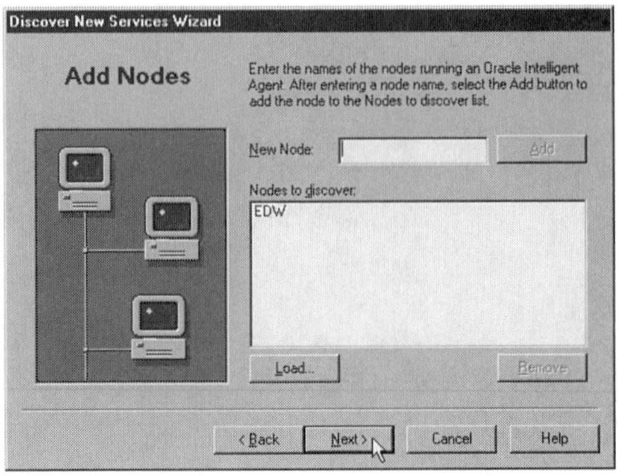

Figure 5.7.

The Discover New Services wizard Add Nodes screen allows you to add nodes to be discovered.

6. After you click the Finish button, the Discover New Services wizard proceeds to discover that node. When it has completed, you will see the discovered status in the Service Discovery Status screen, shown in Figure 5.8.

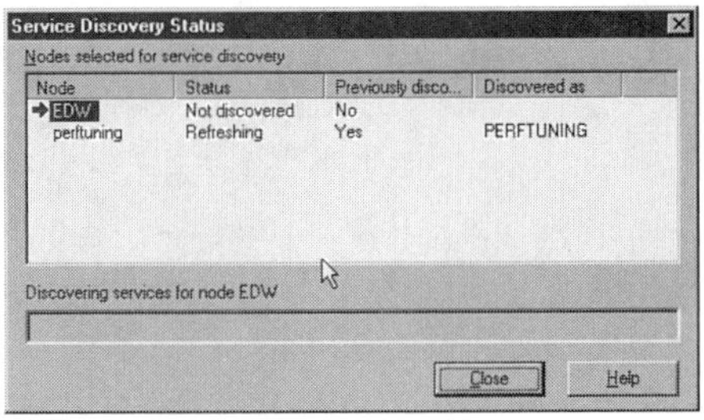

Figure 5.8.

The Service Discovery Status screen shows you the discovery process in action.

NOTE

Using the Discover New Services wizard is the best way to configure the Enterprise network topology. Enterprise Manager uses a combination of the discovery feature, the Oracle intelligent agents, and the TOPOLOGY.ORA file described later today.

File Menu

The File menu is important to the configuration in that it is where the user preferences setup is found. When you select the user preferences setup, you will see a screen that displays the services found in the discovery process (see Figure 5.9).

Figure 5.9.

The User Preferences screen.

The User Preferences screen allows you to configure the username, password, and role assigned to the connection that the Enterprise Manager will use to that service. This allows you to keep separate passwords and DBA accounts for each system on your network, but still administer all of them from a common console.

Setting the user preferences now will save you a lot of time and aggravation later. It will allow you to connect directly to these services without having to go through the entire login procedure.

Using the Navigator Pane

The Navigator pane is probably where you will do most of your work. As I mentioned, the Navigator pane provides a tree-like presentation with the following top-level branches:

- Databases—This branch shows all the databases known by Enterprise Manager (either by discovery or with the TOPOLOGY.ORA file).
- Groups—These allow you to arrange objects with similar functions together, thus allowing you to administer these objects together.
- Listeners—The known listeners to which Enterprise Manager can connect.
- Nameservers—The nameservers of which Enterprise Manager is aware.
- Nodes—The nodes known to Enterprise Manager.
- Parallel servers—The parallel-server systems known to Enterprise Manager.

An example of the Navigator pane with the first-level trees expanded is shown in Figure 5.10. Note that all the other panes except the Navigator pane are closed in this figure. Most of the objects here are the default database objects from the installation procedure.

Figure 5.10.

The Navigator pane.

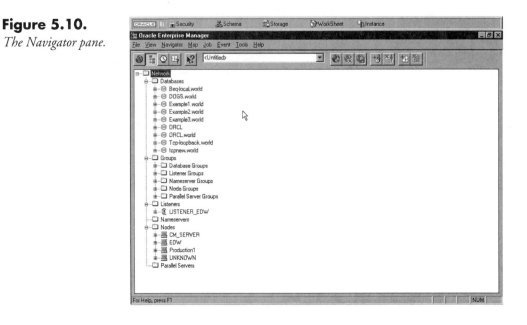

Using the Map Pane

The Map pane is designed to facilitate the administration of systems located worldwide. The Map pane allows you to create groups of systems that can be administered by drilling down on the map. After Enterprise Manager groups are set up, you can drill down into a group by simply clicking the map location.

To create a map, perform the following steps:

1. Select the Map pane from the View | Map Pane menu.
2. Select Map | Create Map.
3. At this point, you will see the Create a New Map screen, shown in Figure 5.11. Fill in the name of the map, choose a bitmap file for the map, and click OK.

After the map is created, you will see a picture of the map (see Figure 5.12). By creating a group, you can then move the icon of the group to the location on the map where those systems reside.

The map can be very useful if you are administering a large number of systems that are geographically disparate. You can even draw your own graphics that depict a building or a floor in a building where these systems reside. Take some time and play around with the Map pane. Most of the features are fairly self-explanatory and easy to use.

Figure 5.11.
Creating a map.

Figure 5.12.
The map.

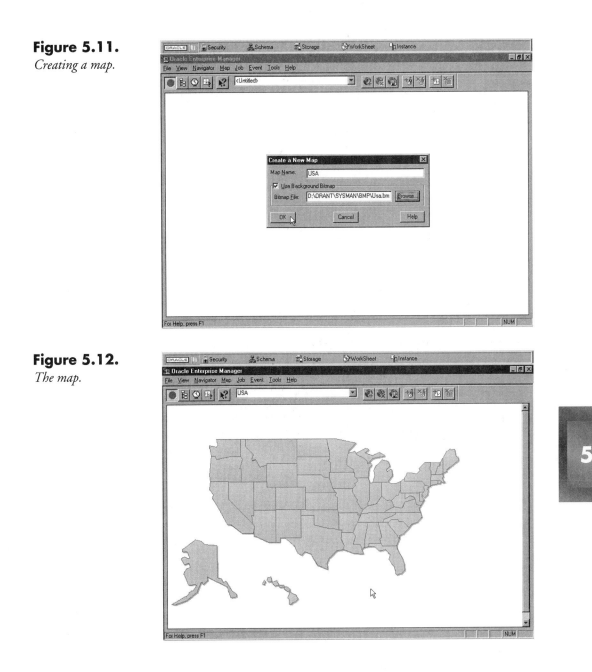

TIP

> Play around with the Map pane. See what kind of configurations you can put together. Using the Navigator pane, you can drag and drop databases into the groups you have created, and they will show up in the Map pane.

Using the Job Pane

The Job pane allows you to create and monitor jobs you have scheduled for one or more systems. This pane can be very useful in scheduling regular activities such as coalescing tablespaces, gathering statistics, or any other type of job that you would like to schedule.

The Job pane allows you to schedule all types of jobs, including

- ☐ SQL scripts
- ☐ SQL commands
- ☐ DBA commands, such as DDL statements
- ☐ OS commands and scripts
- ☐ Administrative tasks
- ☐ Software distribution

The Job pane is described in much more detail on Day 15, "Managing Job Queues and Using Oracle Auditing."

Using the Event Pane

The Event pane is used for monitoring events anywhere under the administration of Enterprise Manager. Enterprise Manager uses SNMP (Simple Network Management Protocol) to allow the intelligent agents to signal the console if an event has occurred.

Enterprise Manager allows you to configure the system to monitor whatever you want, and to alert you if anything it is monitoring has passed a threshold. Enterprise Manager can be configured to alert you via the console itself, e-mail, pager, and so on.

This allows you to set up Enterprise Manager to monitor your installation even when you are not there.

Using Server Manager

Server Manager provides a character-based interface into the Oracle instance. Invoke Server Manager by running it directly from the NT command line or by clicking the executable from NT Explorer. Server Manager is available under all operating systems in one form or another.

You can invoke Server Manager from the command prompt by typing the program name as shown here:

```
D> Svrmgr30
```

After Server Manager has been invoked, you will see the initial connection information, as shown in Figure 5.13.

Figure 5.13.

Server Manager.

As you can see, Server Manager provides a command-line interface that can be used to directly input SQL statements. Because Server Manager is designed as an administrative tool, it supports a superset of the SQL commands that are accepted through other SQL interfaces such as SQL*Plus. An example of some of these additional commands is the show parameter command, which can be used to show the current value of the Oracle initialization parameter that is requested. Listing 5.1 contains an example of this.

INPUT

Listing 5.1. Using Enterprise Manager to display some tunable parameters.

```
D:\>svrmgr30

Oracle Server Manager Release 3.0.3.0.0 - Production

(c) Copyright 1997, Oracle Corporation.  All Rights Reserved.

Oracle8 Enterprise Edition Release 8.0.3.0.0 - Production
With the Partitioning and Objects options
PL/SQL Release 8.0.3.0.0 - Production

SVRMGR> connect internal
Password:
Connected.
SVRMGR> show parameter block
```

OUTPUT

```
NAME                                      TYPE     VALUE
----------------------------------        ------   ----------------------------
db_block_buffers                          integer  100
db_block_checkpoint_batch                 integer  8
db_block_checksum                         boolean  FALSE
db_block_lru_extended_statistics          integer  0
db_block_lru_latches                      integer  1
db_block_lru_statistics                   boolean  FALSE
db_block_size                             integer  2048
db_file_multiblock_read_count             integer  8
delayed_logging_block_cleanouts           boolean  TRUE
hash_multiblock_io_count                  integer  8
log_block_checksum                        boolean  FALSE
SVRMGR>
```

ANALYSIS   In this example, I requested the value of all of the parameters that had the word *block* in them. As you can see, I got back a number of parameters with *block* in their names.

This is useful for determining the default values of all the Oracle parameters on your system. By using the command SHOW PARAMETERS with no qualifiers, you will see a listing of all the Oracle tunable parameters (see Listing 5.2).

INPUT   ### Listing 5.2. See a listing of the Oracle tunable parameters.

```
D:\>svrmgr30

Oracle Server Manager Release 3.0.3.0.0 - Production

(c) Copyright 1997, Oracle Corporation.  All Rights Reserved.

Oracle8 Enterprise Edition Release 8.0.3.0.0 - Production
With the Partitioning and Objects options
PL/SQL Release 8.0.3.0.0 - Production

SVRMGR> connect internal
Password:
Connected.
SVRMGR> show parameters
```

OUTPUT

```
NAME                                      TYPE     VALUE
----------------------------------        ------   ----------------------------
07_DICTIONARY_ACCESSIBILITY               boolean  TRUE
allow_partial_sn_results                  boolean  FALSE
always_anti_join                          string   NESTED_LOOPS
aq_tm_processes                           integer  0
arch_io_slaves                            integer  0
audit_trail                               string   NONE
     .
     . Parameters Omitted due to length
     .
```

```
      timed_os_statistics                    string  off
      timed_statistics                       boolean FALSE
      transaction_auditing                   boolean TRUE
      transactions                           integer 66
      transactions_per_rollback_segment      integer 11
      user_dump_dest                         string  %RDBMS80%\trace
      utl_file_dir                           string
      SVRMGR>
```

ANALYSIS This represents all the Oracle tunable parameters. Throughout this book, you will see most of these parameters again, and a full listing of all these parameters appears in Appendix B, "Oracle Tuning Parameters."

When this book shows an operation done with a SQL statement, it is being done via Server Manager. Server Manager provides the flexibility to use SQL commands with all the available options. These commands can be put into a script file, with the extension .SQL and can be run from within Server Manager. Simply put an @ before the filename of the SQL script and it will be run. It is not necessary to add the .SQL extension to the name when running it. For example, to run a SQL script called build.sql in the c:\database directory, you can use the syntax shown in Listing 5.3 within Server Manager.

**INPUT/
OUTPUT**   **Listing 5.3. Using Server Manager to invoke a SQL script.**

```
D:\>svrmgr30

Oracle Server Manager Release 3.0.3.0.0 - Production

(c) Copyright 1997, Oracle Corporation.  All Rights Reserved.

Oracle8 Enterprise Edition Release 8.0.3.0.0 - Production
With the Partitioning and Objects options
PL/SQL Release 8.0.3.0.0 - Production


SVRMGR> connect internal
Password:
Connected.
SVRMGR> @c:\database\build
...
... Data Returned
...
SVRMGR>
```

As you will see throughout the book, there are certain operations that I prefer to do within a SQL script. By scripting these operations, I have certain advantages, including the following:

5

☐ A permanent record of exactly how the operation was done.

☐ A template for future work. After I have scripted a database build, I can modify that script for use on other databases.

☐ This script can be used to re-create the database in the event of some sort of failure.

TIP

> By keeping your build scripts, you will be able to quickly rebuild your database in the event of a catastrophic failure.

Throughout this book, you will see numerous examples in which Server Manager is needed for some operations.

Managing a Bootstrap Instance Under NT

With the NT operating system, the Oracle bootstrap instance must be created before the database can be created. Because it is a service, the instance is a little different from the Oracle instance on other operating systems. A service called `OracleServiceSID` (where `SID` is the system identifier) is created when the instance is created. This service or instance service is used to bootstrap the more traditional Oracle instance. Because the Oracle server is a service under NT, you cannot connect to Oracle or create the database without this service's being started. The instance is created via the NT Instance Manager. This utility should not be confused with the Enterprise Manager's Instance Manager; they are separate utilities.

Creating an Instance with the Oracle Database Assistant

When you invoke the Database Assistant from the Oracle for Windows NT workgroup, you will see the Database Assistant Welcome screen. This will remain until the Database Assistant has loaded. After the Database Assistant has loaded, you will be prompted with the initial choice as to the function you want to perform (see Figure 5.14).

You have the choice of creating or deleting a database. For the sake of example, let's create a database. To do so, perform the following steps:

1. You can perform either a typical or a custom database creation, as shown in Figure 5.15. A typical database creation creates the standard starter database, whereas the custom installation lets you change parameters such as instance and datafile names. In this example, let's perform the typical database creation. The custom database creation is shown oon Day 6, "Administering Databases and Datafiles."

Figure 5.14.

Database Assistant.

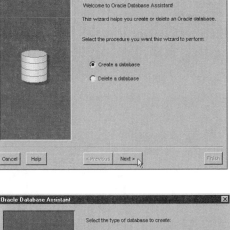

Figure 5.15.

Performing a typical database creation with Database Assistant.

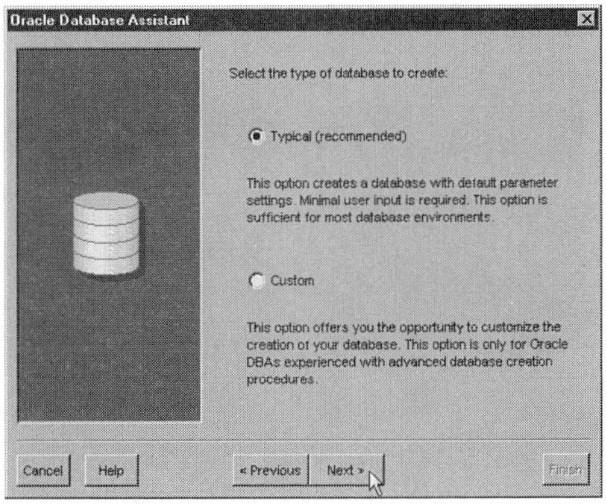

2. As shown in Figure 5.16, you will be asked whether you want to add replication support to this database. If you will be using advanced replication, select the Advanced Replication button. This adds the extra stored-procedure packages used by advanced replication. Replication is covered in detail on Day 18, "Administering Oracle Replication."

3. You will be asked whether you can take advantage of the timesaving feature of copying database files from your CD-ROM rather than creating them, as shown in Figure 5.17. If you do not have the CD-ROM available, you need to create the files.

Figure 5.16.

Select Advanced Replication if you want to add replication support to this database.

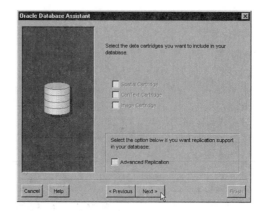

Figure 5.17.

Create new database files using Database Assistant.

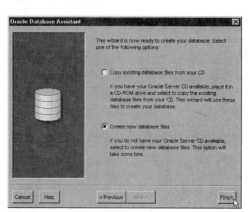

4. Click the Finish button; the database will be created for you. As usual, you have one last chance to change your mind, as shown in Figure 5.18. If the directory looks correct, click Yes; the database will be created.

Figure 5.18.

Confirm that you want to proceed with the database-creation process.

5. One final screen asks for input and informs you that the database named oracle will be created with the SID orc1. If this is suitable, click OK (see Figure 5.19).

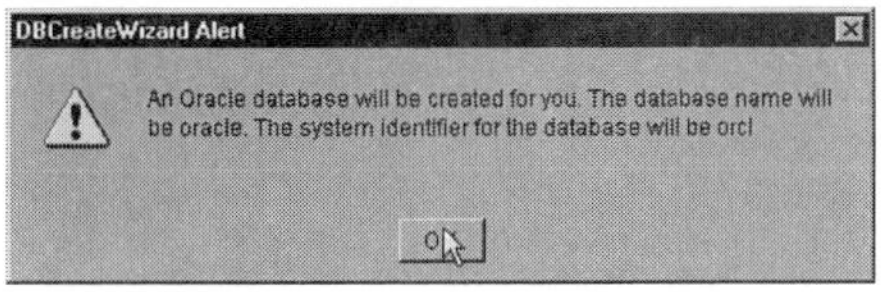

Figure 5.19.
This dialog identifies the new database's name and SID.

Creating the Instance from the Command Line

Creating the instance from the command line uses the same program as the GUI version, but with command-line arguments. The Instance Manager is actually the program named ORADIM80.EXE. To obtain help on the various parameters of ORADIM80, use the command ORADIM80 -?.

Creating the Instance

To create an instance using ORADIM80.EXE, run it with the following arguments:

```
ORADIM80 -NEW -SID SID -INTPWD password [-MAXUSERS number]
➥[-STARTMODE AUTO or MANUAL] [-PFILE pfile_name]
```

The values for SID and password are mandatory, whereas the values for MAXUSERS, STARTMODE, and PFILE have defaults. Here is an example of creating an instance called dogs:

```
ORADIM80 -NEW -SID dogs -INTPWD oracle
```

This will create the instance dogs with a default PFILE of initDOGS.ora and manual startup.

Starting and Stopping the Instance

The instance can be started or stopped from the command line through the use of the following arguments to ORADIM80.EXE:

```
ORADIM80 -STARTUP -SID SID -PFILE pfile_name
➥[-USRPWD password] -STARTTYPE SRVC or INST
```

or

```
ORADIM80 -SHUTDOWN -SID SID -PFILE pfile_name
➥[-USRPWD password] -SHUTTYPE SRVC or INST -SHUTMODE a,i,n
```

where the shutdown modes are a=abort, i=immediate, and n=normal.

Modifying the Instance

At times, it becomes necessary to modify the instance you have created. This can be done with the NT Instance Manager or with the ORADIM80.EXE program. Both methods use the executable ORADIM80.EXE. If you do not provide command-line options, the graphical tool will be invoked.

5

> The Oracle Database Assistant can be used only to create and delete a
> database, not to modify one.

Modifying an Instance with the GUI

You can edit an instance by selecting the instance name and then clicking the Edit button
(see Figure 5.20).

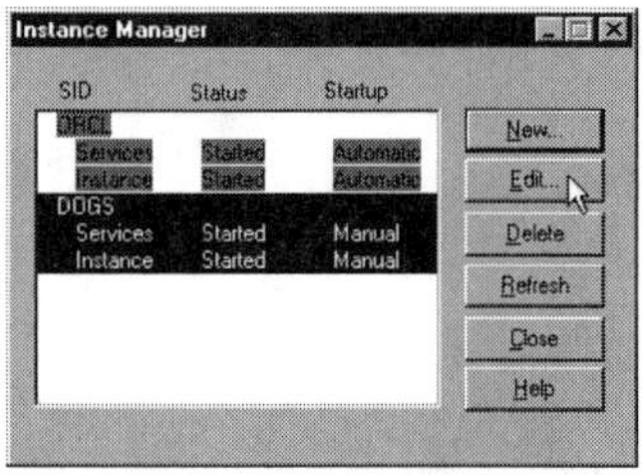

Figure 5.20.
Select Edit in the
Instance Manager.

This will take you to the Edit Instance screen. You have several options available from the
Edit screen; from here, you can change the administrative password or the startup mode by
clicking a button or typing a value.

Editing the Instance with ORADIM80.EXE

To edit an instance, use the same command with the -EDIT flag like so:

```
ORADIM80 -EDIT -SID SID -INTPWD password [-MAXUSERS number]
➥[-STARTMODE AUTO or MANUAL] [-PFILE pfile_name]
```

The parameters are the same.

Deleting an Instance Under NT

It is occasionally necessary to delete an instance under Windows NT. This can be accomplished via the NT Instance Manager or with the ORADIM80 command, as demonstrated
previously.

Deleting an Instance

To delete an instance, select the instance you want to delete and click OK. This deletes the
instance and its services from the system.

Deleting the Instance with ORADIM80.EXE

Using ORADIM80.EXE, you can delete an instance or a service. This is done using the -DELETE
option like so:

```
ORADIM80 -DELETE -SID SID
```

or

```
ORADIM80 -DELETE -SRVC service
```

Starting Up the Instance

The Oracle instance can be started manually, automatically, through a graphical tool, or from the command line. In this section, you will look at all the different ways the Oracle instance can be started.

Starting the Instance Automatically

The Oracle instance can be configured to start automatically when NT Server is booted. Configure the instance to start this way by specifying the automatic startup option when the instance is created, as shown in the section called "Creating an Instance with the Oracle Database Assistant." After the instance has been created, you can edit the service OracleStartSID by editing the service properties from the NT Service Manager program.

After you select the service with NT Service Manager, click the Startup button. Here you can change the startup type from Automatic to Manual, as shown in Figure 5.21.

Figure 5.21.

Changing the startup type to Manual.

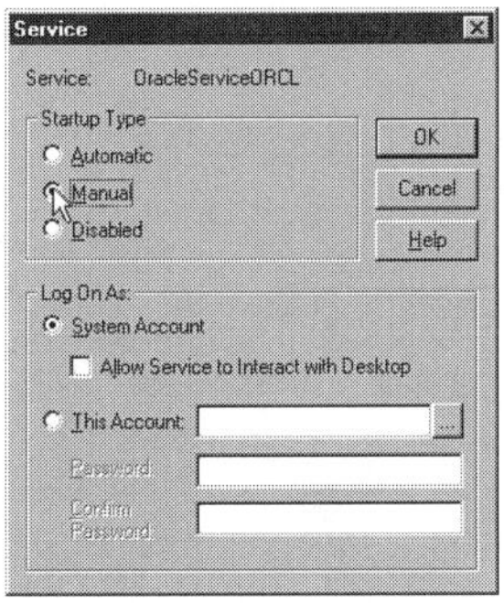

This invokes the Oracle bootstrap instance at startup, but does not start the main Oracle instance. This can be accomplished as shown in the next section.

Starting the Instance with Enterprise Manager

After the bootstrap instance has been created, you can use Enterprise Manager's Instance Manager to start up and shut down the instance. Invoke the Instance Manager by clicking the Instance tab on the Oracle Enterprise Manager toolbar or through the Enterprise Manager program group, or by using Enterprise Manager. You will be presented with the Instance Manager user information screen shown in Figure 5.22.

Figure 5.22.

The Instance Manager Login Information screen.

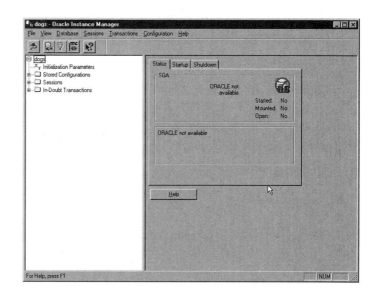

Here you need to log on with the `internal` username and the appropriate password. If you are connecting to an instance that is not the default instance as assigned in the NT Registry, you should specify the service that connects to the desired Oracle instance.

After you connect, you will see the Instance Manager startup screen on the right side and database information screen on the left side, as shown in Figure 5.23. In this example, you will see that the Oracle instance is currently not up.

Figure 5.23.

The Instance Manager main screen provides information about the state of the instance.

To get to the Startup screen, click the Startup tab on the right side of the screen; you will then see the Startup screen, shown in Figure 5.24.

From this screen, you can specify the startup options. The available options are

☐ No Mount—Starts the instance but does not mount a database.

☐ Mount—Starts the instance and mounts the database, but does not open the database.

☐ Mount and Open (default)—Starts, mounts, and opens the database.

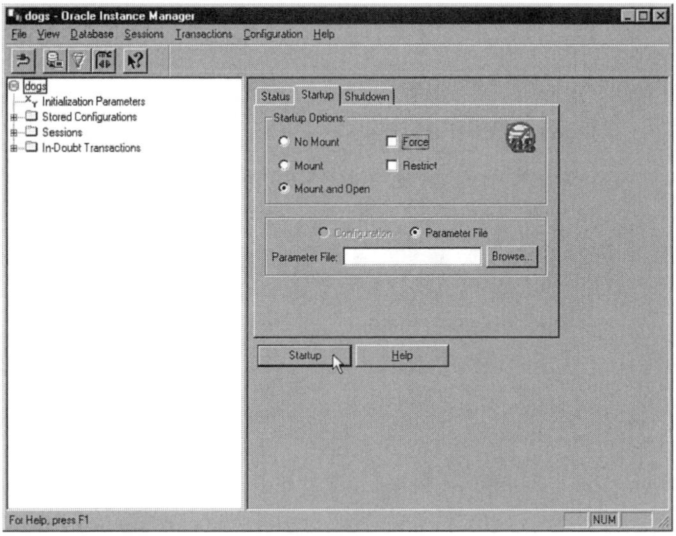

Figure 5.24.

The Startup screen.

☐ Force—Forces the startup, even if there are problems.

☐ Restrict—Starts the database in restricted mode. Only users with RESTRICT SESSION privilege can access the database.

You also have the option of accessing an internally saved configuration file (available only if the instance is started), or specifying a parameter file. Specifying the parameter file allows you to use the parameter file you created for this instance. This is covered in more detail on Day 6.

Clicking the Startup button starts the Oracle instance with the options you have specified.

Starting the Instance with Server Manager

From Server Manager or from a SQL script, you can use the command STARTUP.

The Syntax for STARTUP

The STARTUP command is used to start an Oracle instance and has the following syntax:

```
STARTUP
[PFILE=parameter_file]
[MOUNT or NOMOUNT]
[PEN]
[EXCLUSIVE]
[RESTRICT]
[FORCE]
[RECOVER]
```

These options, which are approximately the same as with the Instance Manager described previously, are

- ☐ PFILE=*parameter_file*—This specifies which parameter file to use. This file is often referred to as the init.ora file.
- ☐ NOMOUNT—Starts the instance but does not mount a database.
- ☐ MOUNT [*database*]—Starts the instance and mounts the database named *database*, but does not open the database.
- ☐ OPEN [*database*]—Starts, mounts, and opens the database named *database*. This is the default parameter.
- ☐ FORCE—Forces the startup, even if there are problems.
- ☐ RESTRICT—Starts the database in restricted mode. Only users with RESTRICT SESSION privilege can access the database.
- ☐ EXCLUSIVE—Allows only one instance to mount the database.
- ☐ PARALLEL/SHARED —These parameters are synonymous. They allow multiple instances to mount the database in a parallel-server environment. This parameter has an additional qualifier, RETRY, which specifies that if a database is busy being recovered by another instance, this instance will try to open the database every five seconds.

As you can see, the startup options are the same whether you are using the Instance Manager or the character-based Server Manager. The advantage of using Server Manager is that this can be scripted into the same file as the database-creation scripts.

Shutting Down the Instance

Because much of the data that has been changed in the Oracle database might still be residing in the database buffer cache, a disorderly database shutdown can result in a significant recovery period when the database is started up again. To avoid this, an orderly shutdown should always be performed. Four different types of shutdowns can be performed by Oracle:

- ☐ Normal—This type of shutdown is by far the most highly recommended way to shut down the instance. Once a normal shutdown has been initiated, no new users can log on to the database and the instance will wait until all users have disconnected before the instance is terminated.
- ☐ Immediate—With an immediate shutdown, all currently active transactions are terminated and any uncommitted transactions are rolled back. All connected users are simultaneously disconnected from the instance. Upon completion of these tasks, the Oracle instance is terminated.

☐ Transactional—The transactional option allows currently running transactions to complete. As soon as a transaction has completed or aborted, the connection is terminated. During this time, no new connections are allowed.

☐ Abort—The abort shutdown essentially aborts the instance. All activity is terminated, and the instance aborted. The result of an abort shutdown is a database recovery on startup.

The abort shutdown should be used only as a last resort when no other options are available. The immediate shutdown should be used only when it is critical that the instance be shut down as soon as possible. You will typically use the normal shutdown option.

Similar to the instance startup, the instance shutdown can be done graphically (through Enterprise Manager's tools) or via the character-based Server Manager. Both options are presented here.

Shutting Down the Instance Automatically

The Oracle instance can be configured to start automatically when the NT Server is booted, as shown previously. When the instance is configured this way, NT automatically shuts down services that were automatically started. In this way, you might see quite a delay when shutting down NT, but an orderly database shutdown is occurring.

Shutting Down the Instance with the Instance Manager

From the Instance Manager, click the Shutdown tab on the right side of the screen. This invokes the Shutdown screen shown in Figure 5.25.

Figure 5.25.
The Shutdown screen.

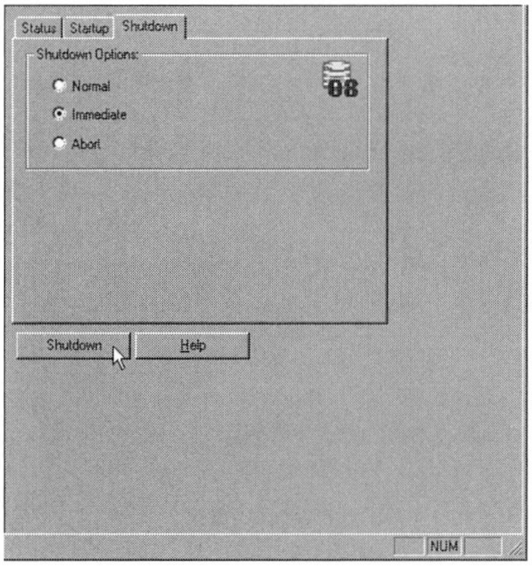

Here you can choose Normal, Immediate, or Abort. Normal is the preferred option, although in the event of an urgent shutdown, the Immediate option should be selected. SHUTDOWN ABORT should be used only as a last resort.

Shutting Down the Instance with Server Manager

Shutting down the database with Server Manager can be accomplished through the use of the SHUTDOWN command. This can be useful when you want to shut down the instance from within a script.

The Syntax for SHUTDOWN

The SHUTDOWN command is used to shut down an Oracle instance and has the following syntax:

```
SHUTDOWN
[NORMAL]
or [IMMEDIATE]
or [TRANSACTIONAL]
or [ABORT]
```

These options, approximately the same as with the Instance Manager, are

- ☐ NORMAL—The default option. Shuts down the instance normally.
- ☐ IMMEDIATE—Shuts down the instance immediately, as described previously.
- ☐ TRANSACTIONAL—Allows currently running transactions to complete and shuts down the instance, as described previously.
- ☐ ABORT—Aborts the instance, as described previously.

I like using the SHUTDOWN command from Server Manager when I am scripting an operation such as a database creation. In this way, the entire procedure can be scripted.

Configuring the Network

After the instance has been created, you must configure the network so you can connect to it. The network configuration serves two purposes:

- ☐ To allow a remote process to connect to the database. This is done via the LISTENER.ORA configuration. This is essentially the server side of your network configuration.
- ☐ To allow a connection into the instance via an alias. In this manner, you can connect to various databases with different SID values by connecting to the service that points to that SID. There are two ways to configure the network service: through the Network Topology Generator that comes with Enterprise Manager, or through the Oracle Network Configuration wizard that comes with Oracle for NT.

Let's look at the LISTENER.ORA configuration, then at the client-side configuration.

LISTENER.ORA **Configuration**

The LISTENER.ORA file is created for each network protocol at installation time. This file defines not only the network protocols, but the Oracle SIDs that can be accessed through the listener. By default, the SID defined in the LISTENER.ORA file is ORAC (from the starter database). The initial LISTENER.ORA file looks like this:

```
 1: ###############
 2: # Filename......: listener.ora
 3: # Node.........: local.world
 4: # Date.........: 24-MAY-94 13:23:20
 5: ###############
 6: LISTENER =
 7:   (ADDRESS_LIST =
 8:         (ADDRESS=
 9:           (PROTOCOL= IPC)
10:           (KEY= oracle.world)
11:         )
12:         (ADDRESS=
13:           (PROTOCOL= IPC)
14:           (KEY= ORCL)
15:         )
16:         (ADDRESS=
17:           (COMMUNITY= NMP.world)
18:           (PROTOCOL= NMP)
19:           (SERVER= EDW)
20:           (PIPE= ORAPIPE)
21:         )
22:         (ADDRESS=
23:           (COMMUNITY= TCP.world)
24:           (PROTOCOL= TCP)
25:           (Host= edw)
26:           (Port= 1521)
27:         )
28:         (ADDRESS=
29:           (COMMUNITY= TCP.world)
30:           (PROTOCOL= TCP)
31:           (Host= edw)
32:           (Port= 1526)
33:         )
34:   )
35: STARTUP_WAIT_TIME_LISTENER = 0
36: CONNECT_TIMEOUT_LISTENER = 10
37: TRACE_LEVEL_LISTENER = ADMIN
38: SID_LIST_LISTENER =
39:   (SID_LIST =
40:     (SID_DESC =
41:       (SID_NAME = ORCL)
42:     )
43:   )
44: PASSWORDS_LISTENER = (oracle)
```

5

To add an additional SID onto the SID list, simply copy the section of the `LISTENER.ORA` that describes the SID as shown here and paste it to the `LISTENER.ORA` file after the `ORCL` SID definition. The following should be placed on line 43:

```
(SID_DESC =
     (SID_NAME = ORCL)
    )
```

Be sure to keep the parentheses correct. Change the SID value to the value of the SID that you have added to your system.

Oracle Net8 Easy Config

In order to administer the `TNSNAMES.ORA` file, you can use the Oracle Net8 Easy Config utility found in the Oracle for NT tools:

1. When you invoke the Net8 Easy Config utility, you will be greeted with the main screen of the Oracle Service Name wizard. From here you can choose to create a new service or to modify, delete, or test an existing configuration. If you are adding a new service, type the service name and click Next (see Figure 5.26).

Figure 5.26.

Choose to modify, delete, or test a configuration.

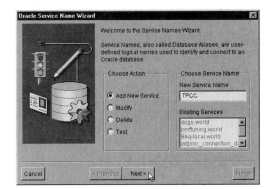

2. You will be prompted for the network protocol for this service, as shown in Figure 5.27. Highlight the protocol that you want and click Next.
3. The next screen, shown in Figure 5.28, prompts you for the hostname (if you chose TCP/IP protocol). Enter the hostname of the system. You can change the port number if you want, but that is not recommended.
4. The next screen, shown in Figure 5.29, prompts you for the SID of the instance being configured. If the instance name is correct, click Next.

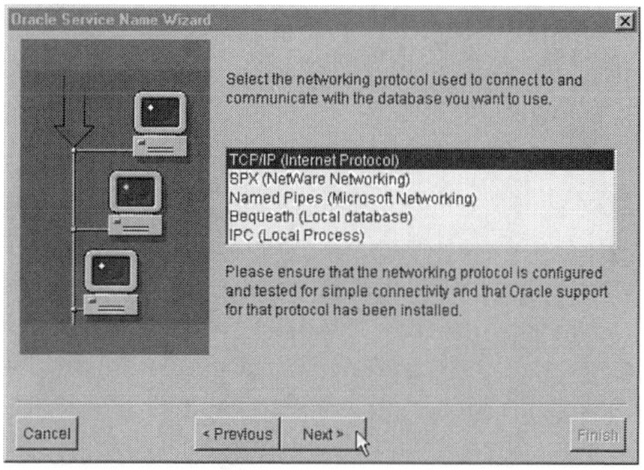

Figure 5.27.

The Oracle Service Name wizard allows you to choose a network protocol to use for this service.

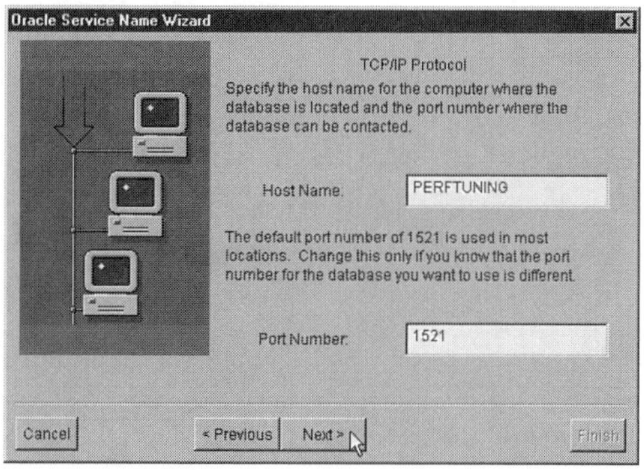

Figure 5.28.

The Oracle Service Name wizard allows you to change the hostname and port number.

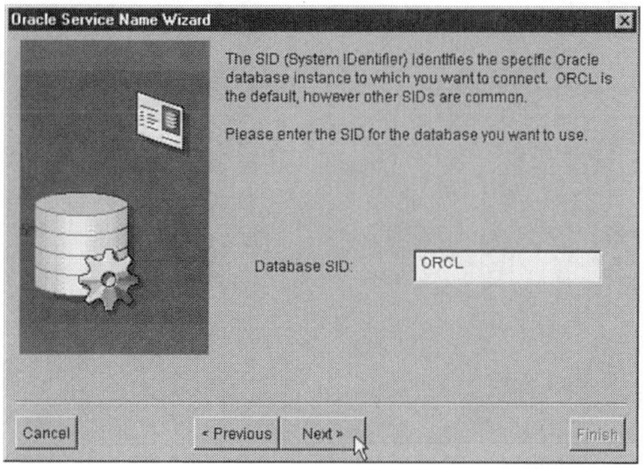

Figure 5.29.

The Oracle Service Name wizard allows you to specify the SID.

5

5. In the screen shown in Figure 5.30, you can test the newly created service. Although you can skip this step, I don't recommend it. Just click the Test Service button.

Figure 5.30.

The Oracle Service Name wizard lets you decide whether you want to test the connection.

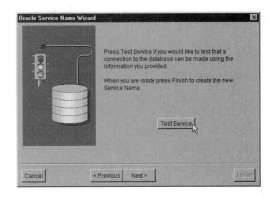

6. Test the connection in the Connection Test screen. If the test is successful, you will be duly informed (see Figure 5.31).

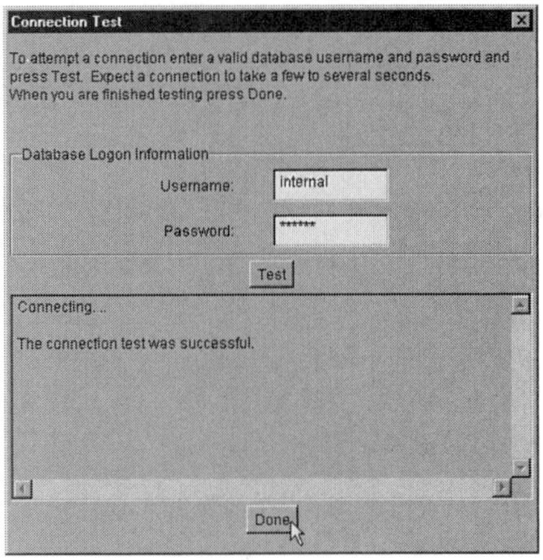

Figure 5.31.

The Connection Test screen allows you to test the connection before saving it.

7. After you finish testing the service, return to the previous screen and click Next to see the final screen of the wizard (see Figure 5.32). If everything was successful, click the Finish button to save the configuration.

Figure 5.32.

Finishing with the Oracle Service Name wizard.

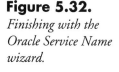

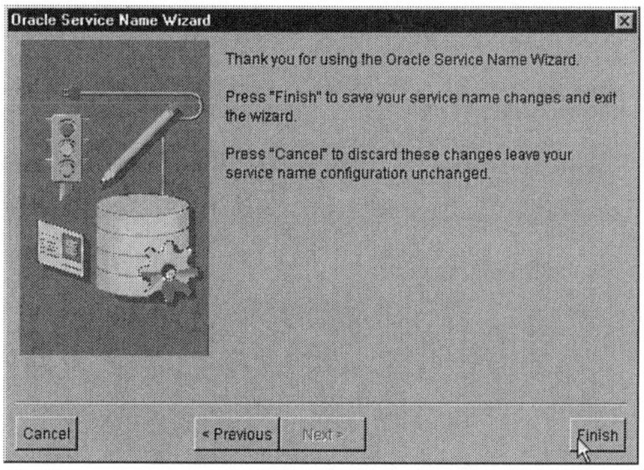

After you click Finish, the application will exit. Your new network configuration is ready to use. You can also manage the network through the Oracle Net8 Assistant.

Modifying the State of the System

During the normal operation of the RDBMS, it is often necessary to modify the state of the instance. These operations actually modify the state of the instance or cause events to occur in the Oracle instance.

Modifying the instance can be done only using the ALTER SYSTEM command. There is currently no way to run these commands via a graphical utility.

Modifying the System using the ALTER SYSTEM Command

Using the ALTER SYSTEM command, you can alter the state of the system or cause some event to occur in the Oracle instance.

The Syntax for ALTER SYSTEM

The ALTER SYSTEM command is run with the following syntax:

```
ALTER SYSTEM
[ENABLE RESTRICTED SESSION]
[DISABLE RESTRICTED SESSION]
[FLUSH SHARED_POOL]
[CHECPOINT [GLOBAL or LOCAL]]
[CHECK DATAFILES [GLOBAL or LOCAL]]
[SWITCH LOGFILE]
[ENABLE DISTRIBUTED RECOVERY]
[DISABLE DISTRIBUTED RECOVERY]
[ARCHIVE LOG archive_log_clause]
[KILL SESSION 'SID, serial_no']
[SET ??]
```

SYNTAX

5

where the options that can be used by the set parameter are

```
SET
[RESOURCE_LIMIT = TRUE or FALSE]
[GLOBAL_NAMES = TRUE or FALSE]
[SCAN_INSTANCES = number]
[CACHE_INSTANCES = number]
[MTS_SERVERS = number]
[MTS_DISPATCHERS = 'protocol' , 'number']
[LICENSE_MAX_SESSIONS = number]
[LICENSE_SESSIONS_WARNING = number]
[LICENSE_MAX_USERS = number]
[REMOTE_DEPENDENCIES_MODE = TIMESTAMP]
or  [REMOTE_DEPENDENCIES_MODE = SIGNATURE]
```

The parameters used to alter the system are defined as follows:

- ENABLE RESTRICTED SESSION —Sets the mode of the instance so that only users with the RESTRICTED SESSION permission can log on.

- DISABLE RESTRICTED SESSION —Disables the restricted session, allowing all users to log on.

> **TIP**
>
> This can be very useful for temporarily restricting new users from logging onto the system if you think there might be some sort of problem or a load issue. By restricting the sessions, you are not causing problems to current users; you are simply preventing new users from logging on. You can reverse this without shutting down the instance.

- FLUSH SHARED_POOL —Clears all data from the shared pool.

- CHECKPOINT [GLOBAL or LOCAL]—Initiates a checkpoint. In a parallel-server environment, CHECKPOINT LOCAL checks only its own log group, whereas CHECKPOINT GLOBAL checks all log groups.

> **TIP**
>
> If you anticipate that the system might need to be shut down or you feel you might be in danger of losing power, you can checkpoint the system, thus shortening any recovery time you might need in the event of a failure.

- CHECK DATAFILES—Verifies that your instance can access all online datafiles. In the parallel-server environment, the GLOBAL qualifier additionally verifies that all instances can access all online datafiles. The LOCAL qualifier specifies only your instance.

- ☐ SWITCH LOGFILE—Initiates a log switch; a log switch automatically triggers a checkpoint.

- ☐ ENABLE DISTRIBUTED RECOVERY —Enables distributed recovery in a single-process environment.

- ☐ DISABLE DISTRIBUTED RECOVERY —Disables distributed recovery.

- ☐ ARCHIVE LOG *archive_log_clause*—The ARCHIVE LOG clause is described in detail in Days 16, "Understanding Effective Backup Techniques," and 17, "Recovering the Database," which cover backup and recovery.

- ☐ KILL SESSION '*SID, serial_no*'—Kills a session. Values of both *SID* and *serial_no* must be provided. These are obtained from the V$SESSION view.

TIP

> This can be useful for stuck or nonresponding sessions. This can also be done through the Instance Manager.

- ☐ SET ??—The SET parameter is used to set a number of Oracle parameter values. These values as shown in the ALTER SYSTEM syntax are described in detail in the Oracle documentation.

Summary

This lesson covers quite a bit of material that introduces the Oracle administrative duties and tools. The day begins by looking at the various duties of the DBA. It later presents the various default accounts used by the DBA to connect to the Oracle instance and how they are used.

A major part of this chapter looks at the tools of the trade. I am really happy with the work Oracle has done to create Enterprise Manager and the applications that go with it. Along with Enterprise Manager are tools such as Instance Manager, Storage Manager, Schema Manager, Security Manager, and Backup Manager. You will see these in more detail later on in this book.

You saw how to invoke Enterprise Manager and how to configure the different panes, as well as how to use the Discover New Services wizard to determine the services available for administration by Enterprise Manager.

For those of you running on the Windows NT platform, this chapter demonstrates how to create the Oracle bootstrap instance. Because Oracle is a service under NT, it needs this bootstrap instance to allow you to connect, and to start up and shut down the Oracle instance.

You also learned how to use the various network tools to configure the TOPOLOGY.ORA and TNSNAMES.ORA files, as well as how to configure the LISTENER.ORA file. These are the key components to the Oracle networking system.

5

Finally, you learned how to alter the instance. This is not typically done, but is occasionally necessary to initiate a checkpoint by hand or to manually archive a redo log file. In any case, it is good to know how to perform these operations when necessary.

What's Next?

Tomorrow you will learn how to create an Oracle database. This is the first of two days that take you through the process of creating redo log files, control files, and datafiles, and building the initial database. In the second of these days, you will learn how to build on that initial starter database and add your own tablespaces and datafiles. After you finish Days 6 and 7, "Administering Tablespaces," you will be able to create your own database.

Q&A

Q What is the primary duty of the DBA?

A The primary duty of the DBA is to protect the database and provide continuous (if required) access to that data for the user community.

Q Should all DBAs use the SYS account?

A A lot of installations have their DBAs use the SYS account, but I think it is better to provide all the DBAs with accounts that have the proper level of permissions. User permissions are discussed on Day 10.

Q Is it better to use the graphical tools or Server Manager?

A Both tools have their place. The Enterprise Manger tools are absolutely great. I really like using them, but there are times when I just can't get the job done without using Server Manager.

Q Why does an instance need to be created before the database can be created?

A This is unique to Windows NT. The Windows NT system uses services to run the Oracle instance. The bootstrap instance must be created so Instance Manager or Server Manager can connect to it to start up the full instance.

Workshop

The workshop provides quiz questions to help you solidify your understanding of the material covered and exercises to provide you with experience in using what you've learned. Find the answers to quiz questions in Appendix A, "Answers."

Quiz

1. What two accounts are created by default when a database is created?
2. What are some duties of the DBA?
3. How can you protect the system against data loss?
4. What two OS roles are created by default when a database is created?
5. What is the bootstrap instance?
6. What is the TNSNAMES.ORA file for?
7. How do you administer the TNSNAMES.ORA file?
8. What tool is used to modify the state of the system (that is, cause a checkpoint to occur, and so on)?

Exercises

1. Create a new Oracle instance using the NT Instance Manager.
2. Create a new Oracle instance using the ORADIM80 command.
3. Add this instance to the TNSNAMES.ORA file using the Oracle Network Configuration wizard.
4. Add this instance to the TOPOLOGY.ORA file using the Network Topology Generator.

Day 6

Administering Data-
bases and Datafiles

Today you will begin to look at some of the basic tasks the Oracle DBA must perform. Specifically, you will look at the database-creation procedure as well as some of the tuning parameters that must be set.

The database-creation operation is split into the tasks of the DBA and the tasks of the end user or application developer. These tasks are split based on what level they access the DBMS.

The Oracle DBA is responsible for all tasks that relate to the DBMS at the low level. Operations that involve the management of datafiles, redo log files, control files, tablespaces, extents, and segments are the responsibility of the DBA, as are the tasks of creating the tables, indexes, clusters, and views (with certain installations, some of these tasks might be performed by or in conjunction with the application development team). In any case, these responsibilities are addressed separately.

Tasks Involved in Creating a Database

Creating a database involves one Oracle DDL statement, and perhaps weeks or months of preparation to be ready for that one step. To create a database, you must know a lot about the data that will be put into the database, the data-access patterns, and the database's volume of activity. All these factors are used to determine the layout of the datafiles and redo log files. These are the responsibility of the Oracle DBA.

Under Windows NT, you must create the instance before you create the database. Because Oracle runs as a service under NT, the instance is necessary for the database-creation phase. An instance can be created, modified, or deleted through the NT Instance Manager. This should not be confused with the Enterprise Manager instance-management tool. Procedures on how to create this bootstrap instance were covered yesterday.

Creating the database actually occurs in two separate—but related—steps. The first step involves the actual database-creation command. This command creates the redo log files, the control files, and the datafiles necessary to create the SYSTEM tablespace. The SYSTEM tablespace contains the SYSTEM rollback segment, the data dictionary, stored procedures, and other structures necessary to run the Oracle instance.

The second phase involves adding tablespaces, tables, indexes, and so on that are used to store your specific data. The first phase described here is covered today; the remaining tasks necessary to finish creating your database will be described tomorrow. It is only when these additional tablespaces are added and your tables are created that your database is complete.

It is important that the DBA and end user work together in defining the database, because the physical layout and the actual data should be configured in an optimal manner. If you underconfigure the hardware or create a poor database layout, you will see a severe degradation in performance.

Tasks of the DBA

The DBA is responsible for all the low-level formatting of the database. I refer to this as *formatting* because that is basically what these steps do. When you format a disk, it is checked and zeroed out; likewise, when you create a tablespace and datafile, Oracle essentially checks out the disk space and lays down its internal format on the physical disk.

The DBA is responsible for creating the database, adding datafiles, and managing the control files and redo log files necessary for the proper function of the Oracle RDBMS. The DBA is also responsible for allocating these resources to the end user so that he or she can properly use them. The DBA or developer must then build tables, indexes, and clusters on these tablespaces. After the tables have been built and loaded, the user can then access this data.

Tasks of the User or Developer

It is the responsibility of the developer to relay to the DBA what the structure of the data should be and how it will be accessed. In this way, the DBA can have all of the information necessary to properly lay out the database. It is the responsibility of both the DBA and the application developer to work together to provide a stable and usable environment for the end user.

Designing the Database

Designing the database can be quite complex and time consuming, but well worth the effort. Any mistakes at this point can be very costly in terms of performance and stability of the system in the long run. A well-designed system takes into account the following factors:

- ☐ Performance—The database that has been designed for performance from the very beginning will outperform any system that has not. Many critical performance items can only be configured in the design stage, as you will soon see.

- ☐ Backup—Often, the DBA is given only a short time to accomplish the required backup operations. By planning the data layout at the very beginning with this criterion in mind, these operations can more easily be accomplished.

- ☐ Recovery—Nobody plans for his system to crash, but it is an unfortunate fact of life that hardware and software components sometimes fail. Planning can facilitate the recovery process and can sometimes be the difference between recovering and not recovering.

- ☐ Function—The database layout has to take into account its ultimate function. Depending on what type of applications are being run and what the data looks like, there might be different design considerations.

Physical Database Layout

As part of the design considerations mentioned previously, the physical layout of the database is very important. You should consider several factors when designing the physical layout, including

- ☐ Database size—You must be able to support the amount of data you will be loading into the database.

- ☐ Performance—A physical disk drive can support only a certain number of I/Os before performance begins to suffer.

- ☐ Function—You might decide to lay out tablespaces based on their function. This allows different departments to have different backup schedules, and so on.

☐ Data protection—It is very important that some types of files be protected against media failure. Primarily, the redo log files and the archive log files need to be protected.

☐ Partitioning—Depending on what type and amount of partitioning you will be doing, the physical layout might vary.

So you gain a complete understanding of how and why the physical database design might vary based on function, let's review a few basic factors.

Database Size

The size of the database is a key factor in how the physical layout is designed. For very small databases, this might not be much of an issue, but for very large databases it can be a major issue. You must make sure that you have not only enough space for the datafiles themselves, but also for associated indexes. In some cases, you might need to have a large temporary area to copy input files to before they are loaded into the database. Oracle has a few restrictions on the size of the components of the database:

☐ The maximum size of a datafile is 32GB (gigabytes).

☐ The maximum number of datafiles per tablespace is 1,022.

☐ The maximum size of a tablespace is 32TB (terabytes).

As you can see, Oracle allows you to create and maintain very large databases. You might think this is an incredible size for a database and no system will ever achieve this size. Well, I can remember when a 10MB disk drive was huge for a PC. If industry trends continue the way they've been going, I would not be surprised to see systems with 32TB tablespaces in the near future.

As you saw on Day 4, "Properly Sizing Your Database and Planning for Growth," it is not only necessary to build your system with today's requirements in mind, but also to plan for the future. Systems can increase in size at incredible rates, and you must be ready for it.

Performance

An important factor to remember when designing the physical layout of your database is the performance of the various components in the system. The load on the system caused by numerous users requesting data will generate a certain amount of disk I/O.

The disk drives that comprise the system can service only so many I/Os per second before the service time (the time it takes for an I/O to complete) starts increasing. In fact, it is recommended that for a standard 7200 RPM SCSI disk drive, you run it at only the following rates:

☐ Random I/O—60–70 I/Os per second per disk drive.

☐ Sequential I/O—100 I/Os per second per disk drive.

NOTE

With a sequential I/O, the data that is requested is either on the same track as the last data accessed or on an adjacent track.

With a random I/O, the data that is requested is on another track on the disk drive, which requires the disk arm to move, thus causing a seek. This track seek takes much more time to complete than the actual reading of the data.

Taking these factors into account, you should isolate the sequentially accessed data and spread out the randomly accessed data as much as possible. A hardware or software disk array is a good way to spread out these randomly accessed I/Os. By determining the amount of I/O traffic that will be generated, you can decide how many disk drives are required. A lack of disk drives can cause severe performance problems. In many cases, you will find that you are required to use many more disk drives for performance reasons than you would for size requirements.

TIP

The redo log files are sequentially accessed, as are the archive log files. These files should be isolated from randomly accessed files in order to increase performance.

Function

You might also find that you want to separate your database into different tablespaces based on function. That way, maintenance operations and backups can be done on a per-department basis. For example, you can put accounting and sales on different tablespaces so they can be backed up separately.

You will also find that different types of operations have different characteristics. For example, an OLTP system that has a large number of updates is very sensitive to the placement of the redo logs due to performance considerations. This type of system might also be continuously creating archive log files that need to be protected and backed up. This requires some planning.

On the other hand, a decision support system (DSS) that primarily queries might not need a high-performance redo log volume, and archiving might occur only once per day. In that case, you might want to design your database layout to favor the datafiles.

Data Protection

The primary job of the DBA is to protect the data in the system. As part of this job, you the DBA must determine how to protect that data. As you saw on Day 2, "Exploring the Oracle

6

Architecture," every change that Oracle makes to the database is written to the redo log files and, in turn, these redo log files are archived. These redo log files and archive log files can be used, in conjunction with a recent backup, to recover the database to the point of system failure. This is, of course, assuming that the redo log files and archive log files are intact.

It is therefore necessary to protect the redo log files and archive log files from media failure. This can be accomplished either via hardware or software fault tolerance. I prefer hardware fault tolerance in the form of a RAID (redundant array of inexpensive disks) subsystem, but software fault tolerance is also very good.

There are several options available with RAID controllers; the most popular are RAID-1 and RAID-5. Each has advantages and disadvantages, as shown here:

☐ RAID-1—Also known as *mirroring*. The entire contents of a disk drive are duplicated on another disk drive. This is the fastest fault-tolerant method and offers the most protection. It is, however, the most costly because you must double your disk-space requirements.

☐ RAID-5—Also known as *data guarding*. In this method of fault tolerance, a distributed parity is written across all the disk drives. The system can survive the failure of one disk drive. RAID-5 is very fast for reading, but write performance is degraded. RAID-5 is typically too slow for the redo log files, which need fast write access. RAID-5 can be acceptable for datafiles and possibly for the archive log files.

 TIP

It is a good idea to put your operating system and redo log files on separate RAID-1 volumes. This provides the best level of protection and performance.

Typically, the archive log files can reside on a RAID-5 volume because performance is not critical. If you find that you are having trouble keeping up on the archive log writes, you might need to move them to RAID-1.

Your datafiles can reside on a non-fault-tolerant disk volume if you are limited on budget and can afford to have your system down in the event of a disk failure. As long as you have a good backup, you lose no data.

Partitioning

You might also decide to adjust the physical layout of your database based on the partitioning method you have chosen. Oracle has introduced a new partitioning method with Oracle8. Various partitions can be allocated to Oracle tables based on ranges of data. Because the partitioning is actually done at the tablespace level and the tablespaces are made up of datafiles, it is important to plan your partitioning before you build your datafiles.

Because Oracle supports only range partitioning, whether you partition your data is dependent on your application and data. If you can take advantage of partitioning, you will definitely see some advantages in terms of reduced downtime and increased performance.

Creating the Instance

As you saw yesterday, before you can create the Oracle database under Windows NT or even start up the Oracle instance, you must create an instance. Follow the steps in the previous chapter to create the Oracle instance; start up the instance, and then you can create the database. Because Oracle functions as a service under NT, you cannot create a database without creating the instance.

Creating the Database

When you create a database, you are primarily creating the redo log files, the control files, and the SYSTEM tablespace. This SYSTEM tablespace is where important structures such as the data dictionary are kept. The data dictionary keeps track of all of the datafiles, the database schema, and all other pertinent database information. After you create this initial database, you will create more tablespaces and assign your schema to those tablespaces. So let's continue creating the initial database.

After the instance has been created, you can create the database. Creating the database is done either through Enterprise Manager or with the CREATE DATABASE DDL command. Although Enterprise Manager is quite convenient and easy to use, I prefer to script the creation procedure into a SQL file. By doing this, you can easily run this creation procedure over and over again and modify it for other purposes. This also provides you with a record of how this procedure was done.

Setup

There are a few initial setup steps that should be completed before you begin the actual creation process. These steps are designed to help you create the right configuration as well as to protect yourself from potential future problems. These steps involve the following:

1. Backing up any existing databases on the system
2. Creating the init.ora file
3. Starting up the Oracle instance

If you follow these steps, you should be ready to successfully create an Oracle database. Let's look at these steps.

Backing Up Existing Databases

This is purely a precautionary step. It is always a good idea to back up all your databases on a regular basis. It is also recommended that you back up your databases prior to any major system changes, such as the creation of a new database.

No matter how careful you are in preparing for the database creation, there is always some danger in making major changes to the system. Because it is possible that a mistake could affect existing control files, redo log files, or datafiles, this precaution might save you quite a bit of work.

If some unforeseen event causes data loss in an existing database, the recovery process will be facilitated by having a fresh backup. This is just a precaution, and one that is well worth the time and effort.

Creating the `init.ora` File

It is necessary to create a new parameter file for each new database. The parameter file, also known as the `init.ora` file, contains important information concerning the structure of your database. All the Oracle tuning parameters are described in Appendix B, "Oracle Tuning Parameters," but a few parameters are critical to the creation of the database:

- ☐ `DB_NAME`—This parameter specifies the name of the database. The `DB_NAME` parameter is a string of eight or fewer characters. This name is typically the same as your Oracle SID (system identifier). The default database was built with `DB_NAME = oracle`.

- ☐ `DB_DOMAIN`—This parameter specifies the network domain where your server resides. This parameter, in conjunction with the `DB_NAME` parameter, is used to identify your database over the network. The default database was built with `DB_DOMAIN = WORLD`.

- ☐ `CONTROL_FILES`—This parameter specifies one or more control files to be used for this database. It is a very good idea to specify multiple control files, in case of disk or other failures.

- ☐ `DB_BLOCK_SIZE`—This parameter specifies the size of the Oracle data block. The data block is the smallest unit of space within the datafiles, or in memory. The `DB_BLOCK_SIZE` can make a difference in performance, depending on your application. The default size is 2,048 bytes, or 2KB. After the database is built, the block size cannot change.

- ☐ `DB_BLOCK_BUFFERS`—This parameter specifies the number of blocks to be allocated in memory for database caching. This is very important for performance. Too few buffers causes a low cache-hit rate; too many buffers can take up too much memory and cause paging. This parameter can be changed after the database has been built.

☐ PROCESSES—This parameter specifies the maximum number of OS processes or threads that can be connected to Oracle. Remember that this must include five extra processes to account for the background processes.

☐ ROLLBACK_SEGMENTS—This parameter specifies a list of rollback segments that is acquired at instance startup. These segments are in addition to the system rollback segment. This should be set after you create the rollback segments for your database.

The following parameters should also be set, based on your licensing agreement with Oracle:

☐ LICENSE_MAX_SESSIONS—This parameter specifies the maximum number of concurrent sessions that can connect into the Oracle instance.

☐ LICENSE_SESSION_WARNING—This is similar to LICENSE_MAX_SESSIONS in that it relates to the maximum number of sessions that can be connected into the instance. After LICENSE_SESSION_WARNING sessions have connected into the instance, you can continue to connect more sessions until LICENSE_MAX_SESSIONS has been reached, but you will receive a warning from Oracle that you are reaching your limit.

☐ LICENSE_MAX_USERS—This parameter specifies the maximum number of unique users that can be created in the database.

After these parameters are set, you can move on to the next phase: starting up the Oracle instance.

Starting Up the Oracle Instance with NOMOUNT

Before you start up the Oracle instance, check your SID. This will indicate which database you will connect to. You should typically set your SID to the same name as in the DB_NAME parameter. When your application connects into Oracle, it uses the SID to determine which database (if there is more than one) to connect to. Depending on the application and your network, the SID might be used to connect you to a particular database on a particular system via SQL*Net.

This is similar to starting up the instance as shown yesterday, except that to create a database, the instance be must be started with the NOMOUNT option (this is because no database associated with that instance is available to mount). After the SID has been checked, you can then start the Oracle instance. This can be accomplished in two ways: by using the Oracle Instance Manager or by using Server Manager. Both methods are presented here.

Starting the Instance with the Instance Manager

The first phase is to start up the Oracle Instance Manager. In this example, you will be using the instance named DOGS that you created yesterday:

6

1. Log in to the Instance Manager with the INTERNAL user, the password that you gave it, and the DOGS service name. The Instance Manager starts with the status screen visible.

2. Switch to the Startup screen by clicking the Startup tab. The Startup screen is shown in Figure 6.1.

Figure 6.1.

The Startup screen.

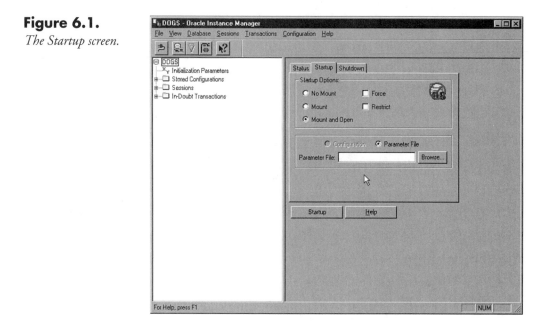

3. When the Startup screen is visible, click the No Mount option.

4. Specify a parameter file by typing its name or by clicking the Browse button and finding the parameter file you just created (see Figure 6.2).

Figure 6.2.

Browsing for the parameter file.

5. Click the Startup button. This starts the Oracle instance without mounting or opening a database. After the instance starts, you will move on to the next step: creating the database.

NOTE   It is possible to modify the parameter file within the Instance Manager by clicking the Initialization Parameters entry on the left side of the Instance Manager screen, shown in Figure 6.3. After you've selected the parameter you want to modify, double-click it; a change screen will be displayed (see Figure 6.4). Be sure to save your changes to a parameter file.

Figure 6.3.

Modifying initialization parameters within the Instance Manager.

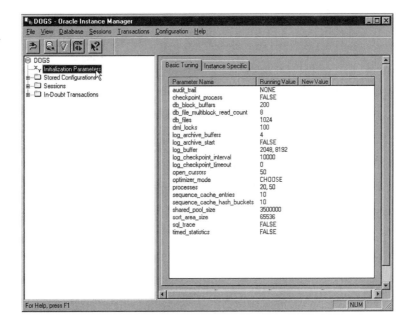

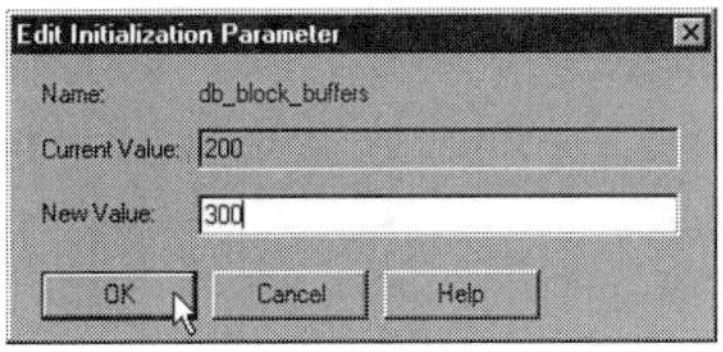

Figure 6.4.

Modifying a parameter.

Starting the Instance with Server Manager

The way I prefer to build a database is by scripting it into a command file. That way, I will have a permanent record of what I have done to create the database. The first command in my script will be to start the Oracle instance in NOMOUNT mode as follows:

```
connect internal/oracle

startup [pfile=c:\orant\database\initORCL.ora] NOMOUNT;
```

NOTE   The brackets indicate an optional parameter. If the pfile parameter is not specified, c:\orant\database\initSID.ora will be used (where SID is the value of your SID environment variable).

By scripting, you can reuse this in the event you need to re-create the database or as a template for other database creations.

Creating the Database

After you have created the instance, you can move on to the next stage: creating the database itself. As with the instance, it is possible to create the database both from a graphical tool (in this case, the NT Instance Manager) or from the command line or script using the Oracle Server Manager. Here you will look at both methods. I prefer character-based creation because it can be scripted and thus re-used.

Creating the Database with the NT Instance Manager

As shown yesterday, when you create the instance with the GUI version of the Database Assistant, a database can be created for you. When you create a database with the Database Assistant, the NT bootstrap instance, database, and SYSTEM tablespace are created, and the CATALOG.SQL and CATPROC.SQL scripts are automatically executed.

NOTE   The Database Assistant is new with Oracle8 for NT. This is a nice tool that can really help you create and delete databases.

So you can have more influence over the creation of the database, I will show you the Custom configuration (see Figure 6.5).

1. As with the Typical option, the first decision you are asked to make is whether you will use advanced replication (see Figure 6.6). If you choose to add the replication option, default users and stored procedure packages will be added.

Figure 6.5.
Using the Custom option on the Oracle Database Assistant.

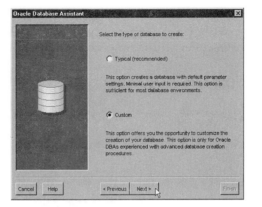

Figure 6.6.
You can select advanced replication support.

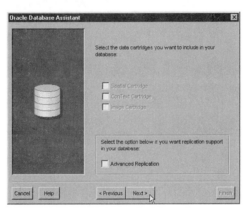

2. In the next screen, you can choose the size of the database (you get an option to modify this) and can change the character set and compatability parameter, as shown in Figure 6.7.

Figure 6.7.
Choosing the relative database size.

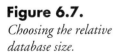

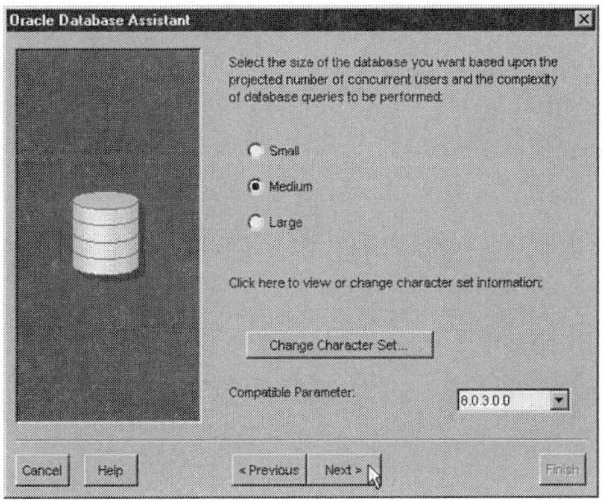

6

3. The next screen, shown in Figure 6.8, allows you to select the database name, SID, initialization parameter filename, and internal password. For this example, I am creating the dogs database with the SID name dogs.

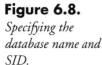

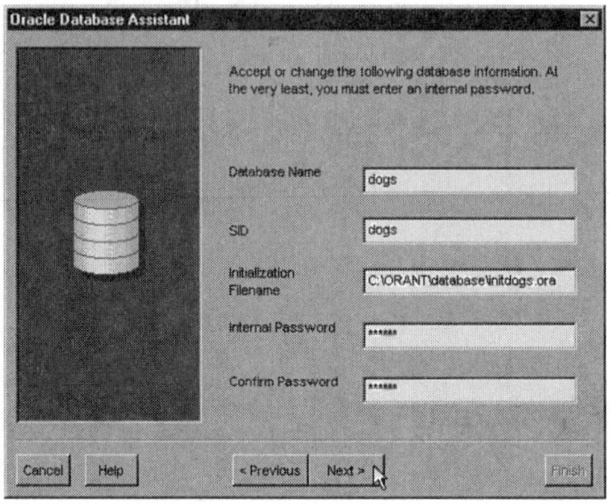

Figure 6.8.

Specifying the database name and SID.

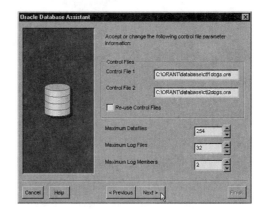

4. After you set the database name and SID, the other screens will have defaults set with those names being used. In the next screen, shown in Figure 6.9, you are asked to set the control filenames (dogs is used by default) and some maximum parameters.

Figure 6.9.

Setting maximums and control files.

5. The next screen provides five tabs that allow you to change various datafile sizes and attributes for the following tablespaces:

- [ ] SYSTEM
- [ ] USER
- [ ] ROLLBACK

☐ INDEX

☐ TEMPORARY

The SYSTEM tablespace screen is shown in Figure 6.10.

Figure 6.10.
The SYSTEM tab with SYSTEM tablespace information.

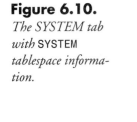

6. The other tabs have the same or similar options for you to set the name of the tablespace, its location and size, the extents for percent increase, whether to turn on auto extent, and the minimum and maximum settings.

7. When you are satisfied with the configuration of these tablespaces, click Next. This invokes the log file creation screen, where you can set up your redo log files (see Figure 6.11).

Figure 6.11.
The redo log file parameters.

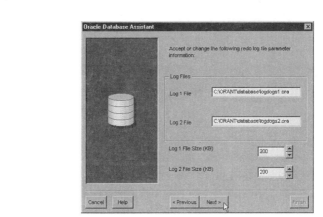

8. The next screen, shown in Figure 6.12, sets up the checkpoint interval and archiving.

Figure 6.12.

Setting up the archive log and archive information.

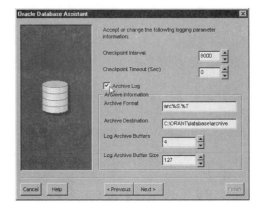

 NOTE

> I highly recommend that you set up your database to archive. You have the option of setting up the archive destination in the screen shown in Figure 6.12.

9. The next screen, shown in Figure 6.13, lets you specify inititialization parameters that affect the SGA, including the following

   ☐ Shared pool size, in bytes (`SHARED_POOL_SIZE`)

   ☐ Block buffers (`DB_BLOCK_BUFFERS`)

   ☐ Log buffer, in bytes (`LOG_BUFFER`)

   ☐ Processes (`PROCESSES`)

   ☐ Block size, in bytes (`DB_BLOCK_SIZE`)

 TIP

> For OLTP, a block size of 2,048 is usually very good. For DSS applications, a larger block size might improve performance.

10. The next screen, shown in Figure 6.14, allows you to specify where trace files for user and background processes will be written.

11. In the last screen (see Figure 6.15), you are asked whether you want to execute the commands necessary to create the database that you specified or write them to a file. If you write them to a file, you will have a permanent record of the actions taken. If you simply want to create the database, click Finish.

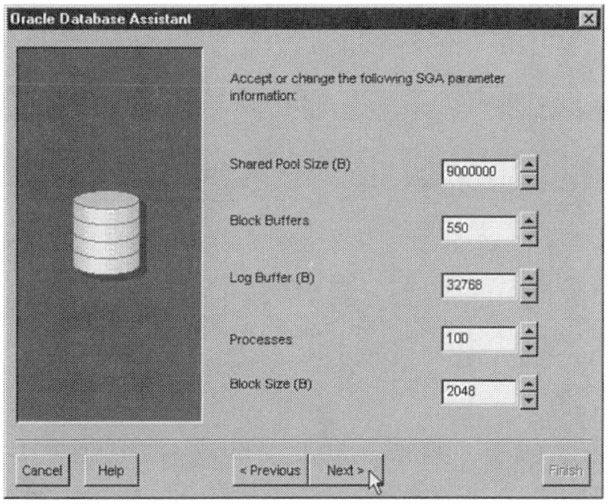

Figure 6.13.

Setting SGA parameter information.

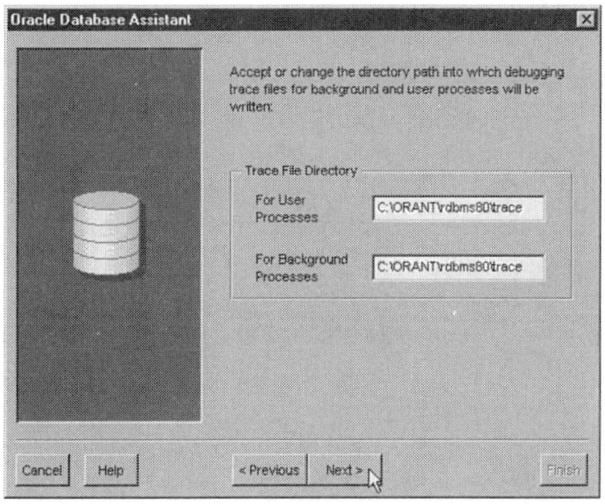

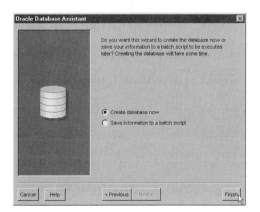

Figure 6.14.

Setting the locations of trace files.

Figure 6.15.

Create the database or save the information to a batch script.

6

12. After you click Finish, you are given one last chance to confirm the database creation, as shown in Figure 6.16.

Figure 6.16.

Setting the database creation in motion.

13. Finally you'll see a confirmation screen, as shown in Figure 6.17.

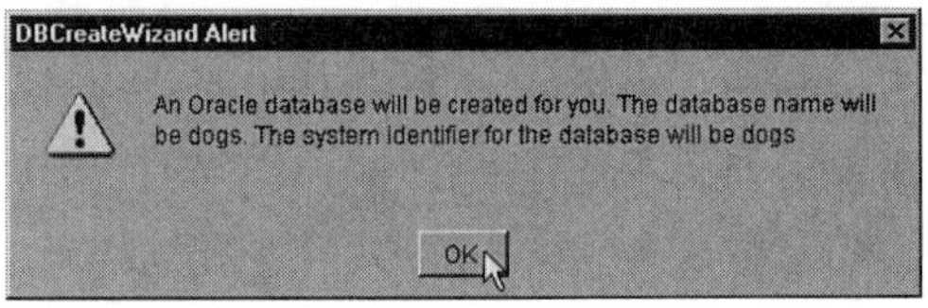

Figure 6.17.

The Oracle Database Assistant confirmation screen.

14. After you click OK, database creation begins. The progress of the process is shown in a Progress dialog.

I tend to prefer command-line database creation because it allows more flexibility and the additional feature of saving your creation scripts. This allows you to use these scripts again or as a template for new database creations.

Creating the Database with Server Manager

To create the database with Server Manager, you must type it manually or, as I prefer, use a SQL script. The database is created with the CREATE DATABASE command.

The Syntax for CREATE DATABASE

The syntax for this command is as follows:

```
CREATE DATABASE [[database]
[CONTROLFILE REUSE]]
LOGFILE [GROUP group_number] logfile
[, [GROUP group_number] logfile] ...
[MAXLOGFILES number]
[MAXLOGMEMBERS number]
[MAXLOGHISTORY number]
[MAXDATAFILES number]
[MAXINSTANCES number]
[ARCHIVELOG or NOARCHIVELOG]
[EXCLUSIVE]
[CHARACTER SET charset]
[NATIONAL CHARACTER SET charset]
DATAFILE file_specification [AUTOEXTEND OFF ¦ ON
➥[NEXT number K ¦ M] [MAXSIZE UNLIMITED ¦ number K ¦ M]
[, DATAFILE file_specification [AUTOEXTEND OFF ¦ ON
➥[NEXT number K ¦ M] [MAXSIZE UNLIMITED ¦ number K ¦ M]]
```

The various parameters and variables are

- [ ] *database*—The name of the database to be created. This is up to eight characters long.
- [ ] CONTROLFILE REUSE—This optional parameter specifies that any existing control files be overwritten with this new information. Without this parameter, the CREATE DATABASE command would fail if the control files exist.
- [ ] LOGFILE—This parameter is followed by the log-file name. This specifies the name of the redo log file. You can specify the log-file group with the optional GROUP parameter, or a log-file group number will be assigned automatically.
- [ ] MAXLOGFILES—This parameter specifies a maximum number of log-file groups that can be created for this database.
- [ ] MAXLOGMEMBERS—This parameter specifies a maximum number of log-file members in a log-file group.
- [ ] MAXLOGHISTORY—This is a parallel-server parameter that specifies a maximum number of archive log files to be used in recovery in a parallel-server environment.
- [ ] MAXDATAFILES—This parameter specifies the maximum number of files that can be added to a database before the control file automatically expands.
- [ ] MAXINSTANCES—This parameter specifies a maximum number of instances that the database can have open simultaneously.
- [ ] ARCHIVELOG—This parameter specifies that the database will be run in ARCHIVELOG mode. In ARCHIVELOG mode, a redo log group must be archived before it can be reused. ARCHIVELOG mode is necessary for recovery.
- [ ] NOARCHIVELOG—This parameter specifies that the database will be run in NOARCHIVELOG mode. In NOARCHIVELOG mode, the redo log groups are not archived. This is the default setting.
- [ ] EXCLUSIVE—This parameter specifies that the database is mounted in EXCLUSIVE mode after it has been created. In EXCLUSIVE mode, only one instance can mount the database.
- [ ] CHARACTER SET—This parameter specifies that the data in the database will be stored in the *charset* character set.
- [ ] NATIONAL CHARACTER SET—This parameter specifies that the National Character Set used to store data in the NCHAR, NCLOB, and NVARCHAR2 columns will use the *charset* character set.
- [ ] DATAFILE—This parameter specifies that the file identified by *file_specification* will be used as a datafile.

6

File specification is made up of the following:

- ☐ `'filename'` `SIZE` `number` (`K` or `M`)—The file specification is used to define the name and the initial size in `K` (kilobytes) or `M` (megabytes) of the datafile.

- ☐ `[REUSE]`—This parameter allows you to use the name of an existing file.

The following options are available to the `DATAFILE` parameter:

- ☐ `AUTOEXTEND OFF`—Specifies that the autoextend feature is not enabled.

- ☐ `AUTOEXTEND ON`—Specifies that the autoextend feature is enabled.

The following options are available to the `AUTOEXTEND ON` parameter:

- ☐ `NEXT`—Specifies the number `K` (kilobytes) or `M` (megabytes) automatically added to the datafile each time it autoextends.

- ☐ `MAXSIZE UNLIMITED`—Specifies that the maximum size of the extended datafile is unlimited. It continues to grow until it runs out of disk space or reaches the maximum file size.

- ☐ `MAXSIZE` `number` (`K` or `M`)—Specifies that the maximum size that the datafile can autoextend to is `number` `K` (kilobytes) or `M` (megabytes).

The `CREATE DATABASE` command might seem to be quite complex, but it is not really that difficult. It is not necessary to use all the optional parameters, but as you gain experience, you might decide to use them. An example of creating a database is shown here:

```
CREATE DATABASE dogs CONTROLFILE REUSE
LOGFILE
GROUP 1 ( 'd:\database\log1a.dbf', 'e:\database\log1b.dbf') SIZE 100K,
GROUP 2 ( 'd:\database\log2a.dbf', 'e:\database\log2b.dbf') SIZE 100K
DATAFILE 'd:\database\data1.dbf' SIZE 10M,
'd:\database\data2.dbf' SIZE 10M AUTOEXTEND ON NEXT 10M MAXSIZE 50M;
```

It is not necessary to create all the datafiles at database-creation time. In fact, if you are creating a large number of datafiles, it is more efficient to create the datafiles in parallel using `ALTER TABLESPACE ADD DATAFILE`.

The `CREATE DATABASE` command serializes its operations. So if you specify two datafiles, the second will not be created and initialized until the first one has completed. The operation of adding datafiles can, however, be accomplished in parallel. This will reduce the time necessary to create the database.

Creating the Catalogs

After the database has been created, two scripts (`CATALOG.SQL` and `CATPROC.SQL`) should be run to create the data dictionary views. These views are important to the operation of the system as well as for the DBA. These catalog scripts can be run within the Server Manager by using the @ character to indicate that you are running a SQL script, as shown here:

```
@D:\ORANT\RDBMS80\ADMIN\CATALOG;
...
Much data returned
...
@D:\ORANT\RDBMS80\ADMIN\CATPROC;
...
Much data returned
...
```

You will see the SQL script text as it is running. This process is quite time consuming and will display a very large amount of data.

NOTE

Running the CATALOG.SQL and CATPROC.SQL scripts will take a significant amount of time; don't worry if it seems like it is taking forever.

CATALOG.SQL

The Oracle SQL script CATALOG.SQL creates many of the views used by the system and by the DBA. These include the V$ tables that are referenced throughout the book. Also created by this script are the DBA_, USER_, and SYS_ views. Synonyms are also created, and many grants are done by this script. All these views, synonyms, and permissions are very important to the operation of the system.

CATPROC.SQL

The CATPROC.SQL script is also extremely important to the function of the system. This script sets up the database for the procedural option. The CATPROC.SQL script runs many other SQL scripts, including ones that set up permissions, insert stored procedures into the system, and load a number of packages into the database.

If you run the CATALOG.SQL and CATPROC.SQL scripts, your system will be configured and ready to create tables and load the database. Nonetheless, there might be other options you want to set or parameters you want to alter. These can be accomplished through the use of the ALTER DATABASE command, as shown in the next section.

Modifying the Database

Many of the tasks involved in modifying the Oracle database, tablespaces, and datafiles can be done via the Oracle Enterprise Manager tools or through the use of DDL statements via the Oracle Server Manager. Both methods are described in this section. As you will see, the Oracle Enterprise Manager simplifies the task by providing you with choices, but is somewhat limited in functionality.

Modifying the Database with Enterprise Manager

Modifying the Database with Enterprise Manager cannot be done with the current Enterprise Manager. Thankfully, the ALTER DATABASE command is quite flexible and offers several options that cannot be performed with a graphical tool. It is because of the large number of different parameters that are available with the ALTER DATABASE command that the Server Manager is still such a valuable and powerful tool.

Modifying the Database with the ALTER DATABASE Command

Modifying the database from Server Manager is accomplished via the ALTER DATABASE command. This command is used to alter various parameters and specifications on the database itself, and can be typed into Server Manager or run as a SQL script. The syntax of the ALTER DATABASE command is as follows.

```
ALTER DATABASE [database]
[MOUNT [STANDBY DATABASE] [EXCLUSIVE ¦ PARALLEL]]
[CONVERT]
[OPEN [RESETLOGS ¦ NORESETLOGS]]
[ACTIVATE STANDBY DATABASE]
[ARCHIVELOG ¦ NOARCHIVELOG]
[RECOVER recover_parameters]
[ADD LOGFILE [THREAD number] [GROUP number] logfile
[, [GROUP number] logfile] ...]
[ADD LOGFILE MEMBER 'filename' [REUSE]
➥[, 'filename' [REUSE] ...][TO GROUP number] or
➥['filename' [, 'filename'] ...]
[, 'filename' [REUSE] [, 'filename' [REUSE] ...
[TO GROUP number] or ['filename' [, 'filename'] ...]]
[DROP LOGFILE [GROUP number] or ['filename' [, 'filename'] ...]
[, GROUP number] or ['filename' [, 'filename'] ...]]
[DROP LOGFILE MEMBER 'filename' [, 'filename'] ...]
[CLEAR [UNARCHIVED] LOGFILE
[GROUP number] or ['filename' [, 'filename'] ...]
[, GROUP number] or ['filename' [, 'filename'] ...]
[UNRECOVERABLE DATAFILE]]
[RENAME FILE 'filename' [, 'filename'] ... TO 'filename' [, 'filename'] ...
[CREATE STANDBY CONTROLFILE AS 'control_file_name' [REUSE]]
[BACKUP CONTROLFILE
[TO 'filename' [REUSE]] or [TO TRACE [RESETLOGS or NORESETLOGS]]]
[RENAME GLOBAL NAME TO database[.domain] ...]
[RESET COMPATABILITY]
[SET [DBLOW = value] or [DBHIGH = value] or [DBMAC ON or OFF]]
[ENABLE [PUBLIC] THREAD number]
[DISABLE THREAD number]
[CREATE DATAFILE 'filename' [, 'filename'] ...
AS filespec [, filespec] ...]
DATAFILE 'filename' [, 'filename'] ...
ONLINE or OFFLINE [DROP] or RESIZE number (K or M)
or AUTOEXTEND OFF or ON [NEXT number (K or M)] [MAXSIZE UNLIMITED or number
➥ (K or M)]
or END BACKUP]
```

The various parameters and variables for the ALTER DATABASE command are as follows:

- ☐ *database*—This specifies the name of the database to be created and is a character string up to eight characters in length.
- ☐ MOUNT—This parameter is used to mount an unmounted database.

The various options to the ALTER DATABASE *database* MOUNT command are as follows:

- ☐ MOUNT STANDBY DATABASE—This is used to mount a standby database. The standby database will be described in detail on Days 16, "Understanding Effective Backup Techniques," and 17, "Recovering the Database."
- ☐ MOUNT EXCLUSIVE—This is used to mount the database in EXCLUSIVE mode. EXCLUSIVE mode specifies that only one instance can mount the database. This is the default mode for the ALTER DATABASE MOUNT command.
- ☐ MOUNT PARALLEL—This is used to mount the database in PARALLEL mode. PARALLEL mode allows other instances to mount the database in a parallel-server environment.

Other optional parameters to the ALTER DATABASE command are

- ☐ CONVERT —This option is used to convert an Oracle7 data dictionary to the Oracle8 data dictionary.
- ☐ OPEN—This parameter opens the database for normal use. Optionally, you can specify the additional parameter RESETLOGS or NORESETLOGS.

The options to the ALTER DATABASE *database* OPEN command are as follows:

- ☐ OPEN RESETLOGS—With the RESETLOG parameter set, the redo logs are essentially reset to sequence number 1. This basically discards all information in the redo logs, thus starting over. The RESETLOGS command is required after an incomplete recovery done with the RECOVER UNTIL option of media recovery or after a backup control file. A backup should be taken immediately after an ALTER DATABASE RESETLOGS command. This is described in more detail on Days 16 and 17.
- ☐ OPEN NORESETLOGS—This is the default operation of the ALTER DATABASE OPEN command, specifying not to reset the redo logs.

Other optional parameters to the ALTER DATABASE command are

- ☐ ACTIVATE STANDBY DATABASE —This parameter is used to make a standby database into the current active database. The standby database is described in detail on Days 16 and 17.
- ☐ ARCHIVELOG —This specifies that this database is running in ARCHIVELOG mode. In ARCHIVELOG mode, each redo log group is archived to an archive log file before it can be reused. ARCHIVELOG mode is essential for data recovery in the event of media failure.

- NOARCHIVELOG—This specifies that the database is not running in ARCHIVELOG mode. Running in NOARCHIVELOG mode is very dangerous because media recovery might not be possible. See Days 16 and 17 for more details.

- RECOVER—The recovery parameters are shown immediately after this section.

- ADD LOGFILE 'logfile'—This parameter is used to specify the addition of log files named 'logfile' to the database. By specifying the THREAD option, you can add this log file to a specific parallel server thread; omitting the THREAD parameter will cause the redo log group to be added to your current instance. You can also specify the value of the GROUP parameter. If you omit the GROUP value, one is assigned automatically. You can specify one or more log-file groups with this parameter.

- ADD LOGFILE MEMBER 'filename'—This parameter adds members named 'filename' to existing log-file groups. The optional parameter REUSE must be included if the file 'filename' already exists. You specify the group that you are adding to in one of several different ways.

The various options to the ALTER DATABASE database ADD LOGFILE MEMBER command are as follows:

- TO GROUP number—This can be used if you know the log-file group identification parameter.

- TO GROUP 'filename'—You can also add to the log-file group by specifying the name or names of all members of the existing log-file group.

Other optional parameters to the ALTER DATABASE command include

- DROP LOGFILE —This parameter drops all members of a log-file group. You specify the group that you are dropping in one of two ways: by specifying the GROUP or by specifying members of the group as described here.

The various options to the ALTER DATABASE database DROP LOGFILE command are as follows:

- GROUP number—If you know the group identifier, you can drop the log-file group by specifying it.

- 'filename'—You can add to the log-file group by specifying the name or names of all members of the existing log-file group.

Other optional parameters to the ALTER DATABASE command are

- DROP LOGFILE MEMBER 'filename'—This command is used to drop a member or members of a log-file group. The member to be dropped is specified by the log-file member's filename. One or more members can be specified.

- CLEAR LOGFILE —This command is used to drop and re-create a log file. This can be used in the event of a problem with an existing log file. By using the optional

UNARCHIVED qualifier, you can clear a log file that has logging information in it without having to first archive that logging information. If you use the UNARCHIVED qualifier, you will probably make your database unrecoverable in the event of media failure. You specify the log files that you are clearing in one of two ways: by specifying the GROUP or by specifying members of the group as described here.

The various options to the ALTER DATABASE *database* CLEAR LOGFILE command are as follows:

- [ ] GROUP *number*—If you know the group identifier, you can drop the log-file group by specifying it.
- [ ] '*filename*'—You can add to the log-file group by specifying the name or names of all members of the existing log-file group.
- [ ] UNRECOVERABLE DATAFILE—This option to CLEAR LOGFILES is used if the tablespace has a datafile that is offline. This requires that the tablespace and the datafile be dropped after the CLEAR LOGFILES operation has finished.

Other optional parameters to the ALTER DATABASE command are

- [ ] RENAME FILE '*filename*' TO '*filename*'—This command is used to rename datafiles or log files. This only changes the name in the control file, not on disk.
- [ ] CREATE STANDBY CONTROLFILE AS '*control_file_name*'—This command is used to create a standby control file called *control_file_name*. The optional REUSE qualifier allows you to specify the name of an existing file that will be reused.
- [ ] BACKUP CONTROLFILE —This command is used to create a backup of the control file. This can be accomplished in the following two ways.

The various options to the ALTER DATABASE *database* CLEAR LOGFILE command are as follows:

- [ ] TO '*filename*'—By assigning the backup control file to a filename, the control file will be backed up to this file. If the file already exists, the optional REUSE qualifier must be used.
- [ ] TO TRACE—This optional parameter writes SQL to a trace file that can be used to re-create the control files. You can specify the qualifiers RESETLOGS or NORESETLOGS, which will add SQL to open the database with these options. The SQL statements are complete enough to start up the database, re-create the control files, and recover and open the database appropriately.

TIP

> By running the ALTER DATABASE *database* BACKUP CONTROLFILE TO TRACE command after your database has been altered in any way, you will have a method of re-creating the control files if necessary. This is part of a good recovery plan.

6

Other optional parameters to the ALTER DATABASE command are

- [ ] RENAME GLOBAL NAME TO—This command allows you to rename the database name, domain name, or both.

- [ ] RESET COMPATABILITY—This command resets the compatability level of the database to an earlier version of Oracle after the instance is restarted.

- [ ] SET—The following trusted Oracle parameters are modified via the SET command SET DBLOW = *value*, SET DBHIGH = *value*, SET DBMAC ON or OFF. Trusted Oracle is not covered in this book. See the *Trusted Oracle Administration Guide* from Oracle for more information.

- [ ] ENABLE [PUBLIC] THREAD *number*—This parallel-server command is used to enable a thread of redo log groups identified by *number*. The addition of the PUBLIC qualifier allows this log file thread to be used by any instance.

- [ ] DISABLE THREAD *number*—This command disables a log file thread group identified by *number*, making it unavailable to any instance.

- [ ] CREATE DATAFILE '*filename*'—This parameter is used to create a datafile that was lost due to media failure and was not backed up.

- [ ] AS *filespec*—This option of the CREATE DATAFILE command is used to specify the *filespec* specification parameters.

- [ ] DATAFILE '*filename*'—The ALTER DATABASE *database* DATAFILE command has several different functions that allow you to change the state of database datafiles.

The various options to the ALTER DATABASE *database* DATAFILE '*filename*' command are as follows:

- [ ] ONLINE—Brings the datafile online.

- [ ] OFFLINE [DROP]—Takes the datafile offline. When the database is running in NOARCHIVELOG mode, the drop command takes it offline.

- [ ] RESIZE number (K or M)—This is used to resize a datafile to number K (kilobytes) or M (megabytes).

- [ ] AUTOEXTEND OFF or ON—This command is used to alter a datafile to have autoextend either on or off. With autoextend on, the file will increase in size based on the AUTOEXTEND parameters.

The various options to the ALTER DATABASE *database* DATAFILE '*filename*' AUTOEXTEND ON command are as follows:

- [ ] NEXT *number* (K or M)—This option specifies that the database will grow in increments of *number* K (kilobytes) or M (megabytes) whenever space requirements force the datafile to grow.

- ☐ MAXSIZE UNLIMITED—This parameter specifies that the maximum size of the datafile is governed only by disk space and OS datafile limitations. On NT, a datafile can grow to 32GB in size.

- ☐ MAXSIZE *number* (K or M)—This option specifies that the maximum size a datafile will grow to is *number* K (kilobytes) or M (megabytes).

Another optional parameter to the ALTER DATABASE command is

- ☐ END BACKUP —This option specifies that media recovery should not be done when an online backup was interrupted by an instance failure.

The parameters and options to the RECOVER clause are

```
RECOVER [AUTOMATIC] [FROM 'path']
[[STANDBY] DATABASE]
[UNTIL CANCEL] or [UNTIL TIME 'time']
➥or [UNTIL CHANGE number] or [USING BACKUP CONTROLFILE] ...]
[TABLESPACE tablespace [,tablespace] ....]
[DATAFILE 'filename' [, 'filename'] ....]
[LOGFILE 'filename']
[CONTINUE [DEFAULT]]
[CANCEL]
[PARALLEL parallel_definition]
```

The various parameters and variables for the RECOVER option are

- ☐ AUTOMATIC—This qualifier specifies that the recovery process automatically figures out the names of the redo log files that it needs to apply in order to perform media recovery.

- ☐ FROM '*path*'—This qualifier allows you to specify the location of archive log files. This is useful because you do not always keep the archive log files in the directory where they were originally generated.

- ☐ STANDBY—This recovers the standby database.

- ☐ DATABASE—This is the default option. It indicates that the database should be recovered.

- ☐ UNTIL ??—The UNTIL parameters are very important to the recovery of the database if you are recovering from a software or operator problem. These parameters allow you to recover up until a specific point.

The various options to the ALTER DATABASE *database* RECOVER UNTIL ?? command are as follows:

- ☐ UNTIL CANCEL—The database will be recovered until you submit an ALTER DATABASE *database* RECOVER CANCEL command.

- ☐ UNTIL TIME '*time*'—This command performs a time-based recovery. It recovers all transactions that have finished until '*time*'. The qualifier is given in the form

`'YYYY-MM-DD:HH24:MI:SS'`. This can be quite useful if you know when the suspected SQL statement that caused the failure occurred.

☐ `UNTIL CHANGE` *number*—This performs a recovery up until the last transaction before the system change number.

Other optional parameters to the `ALTER DATABASE` *database* `RECOVER` command are

☐ `USING BACKUP CONTROLFILE`—This specifies that the recovery should be done using a backup control file.

☐ `TABLESPACE` *tablespace*—This performs recovery only on the specified tablespace(s).

☐ `DATAFILE` *'filename'*—This performs recovery only on the specified datafile.

☐ `LOGFILE` *'filename'*—This performs recovery using the specified log file.

☐ `CONTINUE [DEFAULT]`—This continues recovery after it has been interrupted. `CONTINUE DEFAULT` is similar, but uses Oracle-generated default values.

☐ `CANCEL`—This cancels the `UNTIL CANCEL`-based recovery.

☐ `PARALLEL (DEGREE` *number*)—This specifies the degree of parallelism to use during the recovery process. The number of parallel processes is determined by the value of *number*.

The recovery process is key to the stability of Oracle and your database. This topic is covered in much more detail on Days 16 and 17.

Let's look at a few examples of using the `ALTER DATABASE` command to perform regular maintenance tasks.

Changing to Use `ARCHIVELOG` Mode

If you are not running in `ARCHIVELOG` mode, you are in danger of losing data in the event of a system failure. To alter the database to run in `ARCHIVELOG` mode, use the following syntax:

```
ALTER DATABASE dogs ARCHIVELOG;
```

Performing a Timed Recovery

It is sometimes necessary to perform a timed recovery. If a certain SQL statement caused a system failure, you should recover until just before that statement was issued. If a SQL statement that caused data loss was inadvertently run, you can recover until just before that statement was issued. Here is an example of how to perform a timed recovery:

```
ALTER DATABASE dogs RECOVER UNTIL TIME '1999-07-04:15:03:00';
```

This statement recovers the database until 3:03 p.m. on July 4, 1999.

Open a Closed Database

Databases are often brought up and mounted but not opened for maintenance. To open a closed database, use the following syntax:

```
ALTER DATABASE dogs OPEN;
```

Backing Up a Control File

Backing up control files is an important operation. Here is an example of how to use ALTER DATABASE to back up your control files:

```
ALTER DATABASE dogs BACKUP CONTROLFILE TO 'C:\backup\cntrlDOGS.dbf;
```

Backing Up a Control File to Trace

Backing up your control file to trace generates a SQL script that can be used to re-create the control file in the event of an emergency recovery. Use this syntax:

```
ALTER DATABASE dogs BACKUP CONTROLFILE TO TRACE;
```

Followup

Even after the database and datafiles have been created, your job is not over. You must watch the system carefully to make sure that you don't run out of space or other resources. As you saw on Day 4, capacity planning and sizing are not easy jobs. By anticipating and solving problems before they become critical, you will avoid costly setbacks. You must periodically monitor the system from the OS and the Oracle perspectives to avoid these types of problems.

Monitoring the Datafiles

To make sure you are not running out of space, you can use Enterprise Manager's Storage Manager utility. If you click the Datafiles icon on the left, you will see a list of datafiles, the size of each file, and how much it is used on the right. This is a quick and easy way of determining whether you are running out of space in your datafiles. You can manually check this by looking at several different system views and by adding up individual free spaces. The Oracle Storage Manager simplifies this task.

Load Balancing

It is important that you not overdrive any of the disk drives or disk arrays in your system. This can severely hurt your performance. The I/O rates at which your system is running can be monitored with the NT Performance Monitor. I will not spend much time on the Performance Monitor, but I do want to mention a few points that you should watch out for:

☐ Use diskperf—Turn on diskperf by using the NT command diskperf -y. By turning on diskperf, you will see much more information about your disk I/O rates when you run perfmon.

☐ Monitor I/O—Use perfmon to look at PhysicalDisk. Of great importance is the reads and writes per second (throughput) and the seconds/read and seconds/write (latency).

If you see a disk drive or disk array (a disk array looks like a big disk drive to the OS) that has many more I/Os per second per disk than the others, you might have a balance problem.

TIP

> The I/Os per disk drive per second should not exceed 60–79 on the data volumes. On an array, divide the number of I/Os by the number of drives to get the I/Os per drive.
>
> A typical disk drive should take about 20–30 milliseconds to read or write to the drive. If your seconds/read or seconds/write is much higher, you are probably overloading your disks.

Summary

Today you learned how to create a database on the server. This procedure involves creating an instance to be able to connect into Oracle and then creating the database itself. You also learned how to configure the network components to connect to this database. Finally, you learned how to modify that database as necessary.

You have seen how to accomplish all these steps with the graphical administration tools that are part of Oracle for NT and part of the Oracle Enterprise Manager. As I have recommended throughout this chapter, there are some tasks for which I prefer to employ the graphical tools, and others that I prefer to script (so I can reuse the SQL statements). You will have to determine which ones you prefer.

What's Next?

Tomorrow, you will see how to create tablespaces using the database and datafiles you created today. The tablespace is the building block upon which tables, clusters, and indexes are built. Tablespaces are also key to the new Oracle8 partitioned tables and indexes.

Q&A

Q Can I use the Oracle Enterprise Manager to create an instance?

A Unfortunately, the Oracle Enterprise Manager does not have that facility because it is necessary primarily on the NT system (since Oracle is a service). On other operating systems, it is not necessary to create an instance before creating the database.

Q What is a log-file group?

A A log-file group is a set of log files that is used to store system redo information. By having a group of log files, Oracle will automatically mirror redo information to the log files in the groups.

Q What tasks are involved in creating a database?

A Under Windows NT, the first step is to create an Oracle instance using the NT Instance Manager. The second step is to create the database itself. The third step is to create the entry in the LISTENER.ORA file.

Workshop

The workshop provides quiz questions to help you solidify your understanding of the material covered and exercises to provide you with experience in using what you've learned. Find the answers to the quiz questions in Appendix A, "Answers."

Quiz

1. How many I/Os per second per disk drive can a standard disk drive service?
2. What is an SID?
3. Is the size of a datafile permanently fixed?
4. Can you have more than one instance on a system?
5. How many databases can you create with one SID?
6. How many databases can you create on one system?

Exercises

1. Create a database using the CREATE DATABASE command.
2. Repeat Exercise 1 using three separate datafiles.

6

Day 7

Administering Tablespaces

Yesterday you learned the first part of how to create a database. Using the CREATE DATABASE statement, you will create by default the SYSTEM tablespace. This tablespace will be created on the datafiles that you specify in the CREATE DATABASE statement. This SYSTEM tablespace is used to store important internal structures such as the data dictionary, the system stored procedures, and the system rollback segments.

Unless you specify otherwise, the SYSTEM tablespace will be used as the default for all database users. This is not desirable, so it is important to create additional tablespaces as soon as possible. The creation of the additional tablespaces, where you place your own tables, indexes, and so on, is really the second part of creating your own database.

WARNING

> The SYSTEM tablespace is used to hold important system schema objects. It is a good idea not to create user objects on the SYSTEM tablespace. If the SYSTEM tablespace runs out of space, this could disrupt the entire operation of the RDBMS.

Today you will learn how to create tablespaces, what they are used for, and how to properly configure the tablespaces for optimal performance using Oracle8 partitioning.

Review of Tablespaces

Day 2, "Exploring the Oracle Architecture," presented you with an overview of the Oracle architecture and briefly outlined Oracle tablespaces. This section reviews the Oracle tablespace in more detail.

The Oracle tablespace is the lowest logical layer of the Oracle data structure. The tablespace consists of one or more datafiles; these can be files on the operating system filesystem or raw devices. Until recently the size of a datafile was fixed, but now datafiles can be extended automatically or manually.

The tablespace is important in that it provides the finest granularity for laying out data across datafiles. After the tablespace is created, you don't have much control over how the actual tables are distributed within the tablespace. By carefully configuring the tablespace, you have some coarse configuration options (you will see these later today), but for the most part, the internal layout of schema objects on tablespaces is done automatically.

As you will see later, if you take advantage of the range partitioning feature of Oracle8, the partition configuration is very important. In fact, how and where your tablespaces are created is crucial to the optimization of range partitioning.

Every Oracle database must have at least one tablespace. When you create a database, the SYSTEM tablespace is created by default. This is where the data dictionary is kept. By default, a user is assigned to the SYSTEM tablespace, but this is not recommended. As you will see on Day 10, "Administering User Accounts," users can and should be assigned tablespaces based on the function they are to perform. Quotas can also be placed on these users, specifying how much space they can use.

Tablespaces can hold any one of four types of segments:

☐ Data segments—This type of segment, which is the basic type, can be used to hold tables and clusters.

☐ Index segments—This type of segment is used to hold indexes.

☐ Rollback segments—This special type of segment is used to store undo information. Rollback segments are covered in more detail tomorrow.

☐ Temporary segments—This type of segment is used for storing temporary data.

Tablespaces are made read-write by default, but can be altered to become read-only as shown later today. Read-only tablespaces can be very useful in a number of situations.

Creating Tablespaces

Creating a tablespace consists of specifying one or more datafiles and storage parameters. The datafiles can be either filesystem files or raw devices. The storage parameters specify how the tablespace is used. The storage parameters are important and are discussed later today.

As with most of the operations you have seen so far, the tablespace can be created both graphically with the Oracle Enterprise Manager or with a SQL script using the Server Manager. Both methods are described here.

 NOTE

Under Windows NT, each datafile can be 4MB blocks in size. For a 2KB block size, this is 8GB; for an 8KB block size, this is 32GB in size. A tablespace can consist of a maximum of 1,022 datafiles. Therefore, a tablespace under Windows NT can be a maximum size of 32TB (terabytes).

Creating Tablespaces with Enterprise Manager

You can create tablespaces using either Enterprise Manager or Storage Manager. Either method performs essentially the same task; in fact, the screens used to perform the creation are identical.

For this example, I have shut down all Enterprise Manager panes except the Navigator pane. I did this by unchecking all panes in the View drop-down menu that I did not want displayed. By unchecking the Map, Job, and Event panes, I removed them from the screen. From here you will work through an example of how to create a tablespace using Enterprise Manager.

Drill down to the DOGS.world database by clicking the Database option and then clicking the DOGS.world option.

If you click the Tablespace option, you will see that there is already (by default) one tablespace present in the system: the SYSTEM tablespace.

By drilling down into the SYSTEM tablespace option, you can see that it is also possible to administer datafiles and rollback segments from here.

With Enterprise Manager, it is simply necessary to right-click the Tablespace option in the tree structure, as shown in Figure 7.1. This will present you with a number of tasks that you can perform on tablespaces. From here you can create a tablespace.

Figure 7.1.

Tablespace options.

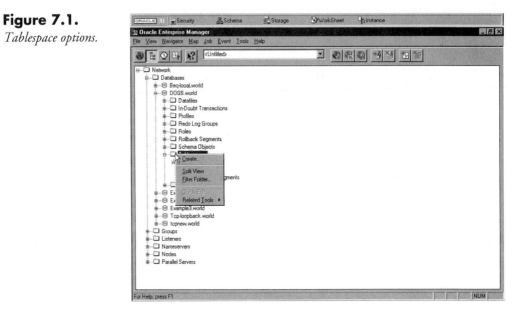

As you can see, the first option available is the Create option. Clicking this option will invoke the Create Tablespace dialog box, shown in Figure 7.2. From this dialog box, you can create additional tablespaces.

Figure 7.2.

The Create Tablespace dialog box.

Available options include

☐ Online—This option specifies that the tablespace is brought online after creation.
This is the normal operation, so you can have immediate access to this tablespace
after creation.

☐ Offline—This specifies that the tablespace is left offline after creation. If you want
to leave the tablespace unavailable until you perform other operations on it, you
should select this option.

☐ Read Only—This specifies that the tablespace is read-only. There is not much
point in making a tablespace read-only at creation time. Typically you will create
tables and populate them, then make the tablespace read-only (if desired).

☐ Permanent—This specifies that the tablespace is for permanent objects. This is the
default parameter. This option is used for all schema objects except for temporary
tablespaces.

☐ Temporary—This specifies that the tablespace is for temporary objects.

If you click the Add button, a new datafile will be created. The Create Datafile dialog box
is shown in Figure 7.3.

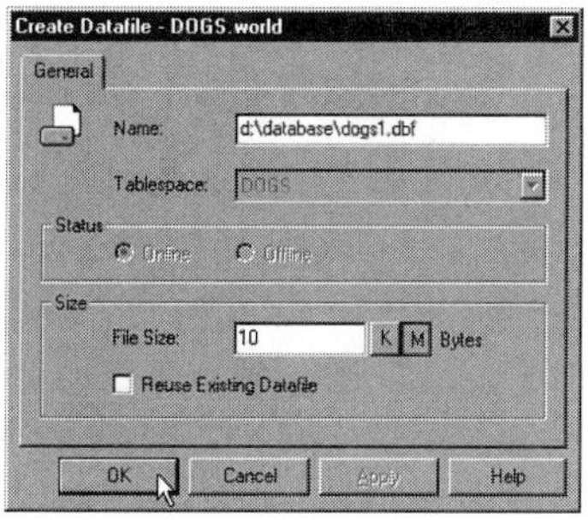

Figure 7.3.
*The Create Datafile
dialog box.*

In the Create Datafile dialog box, provide a datafile name and a size. Click M if you want the
size to appear in megabytes; K (kilobytes) is the default. After you have filled in the Create
Datafile dialog box, you are returned to the Create Tablespace dialog box. To finish, click
the OK button.

Enterprise Manager provides you with the ability to view the SQL used to create the
tablespace. If you click the Show SQL button, you will see the SQL statement used to create
the tablespace (see Figure 7.4). As you can see, after you click the Show SQL button, that
button changes to a Hide SQL button. If you click the Hide SQL button, the SQL statement
will no longer be displayed.

Figure 7.4.

Option to view the SQL statement.

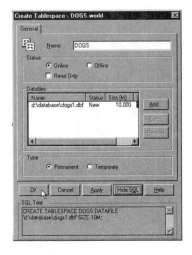

Viewing the SQL statements created by the graphical tools can be a very nice learning tool. By trying various options, you can see the different SQL statements that are created and how they change. Following these procedures, you can create new tablespaces directly from the Oracle Enterprise Manager.

Creating Tablespaces with Storage Manager

Tablespaces can also be created through the use of the Storage Manager application that is part of Enterprise Manager. Storage Manager is used to manage storage objects such as tablespaces and datafiles on a particular instance. Unlike Enterprise Manager, where multiple databases are displayed, Storage Manager is concerned only with the instance you log in to it with. After you log in to Storage Manager, you will see the main dialog box (see Figure 7.5).

As with Enterprise Manager, you can drill down to the tablespace level in Storage Manager by clicking the Tablespace option (shown in Figure 7.6).

Again you see the SYSTEM option, but with Storage Manager, you see a detail screen on the right-hand side that shows the following:

☐ Name—The tablespace name.

☐ Status—Whether the tablespace is offline or online.

☐ Size—The allocated size of the tablespace.

☐ Used—How much of the tablespace is currently being used. The display also shows the approximate percentage of space that is used.

From this point, you can look at the tablespaces and datafiles that are currently in use, or you can create new tablespaces. If you right-click the Tablespace option, you will see a menu

similar to the one shown in Figure 7.1. From this menu you can click the Create button to
invoke the Create Tablespace dialog box (refer to Figure 7.2).

Figure 7.5.

*The Storage Manager
main screen.*

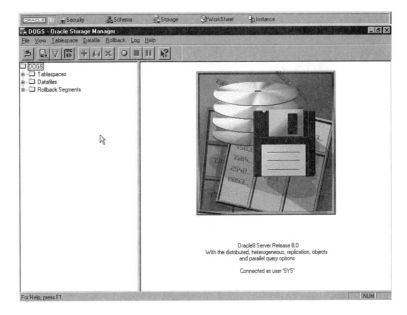

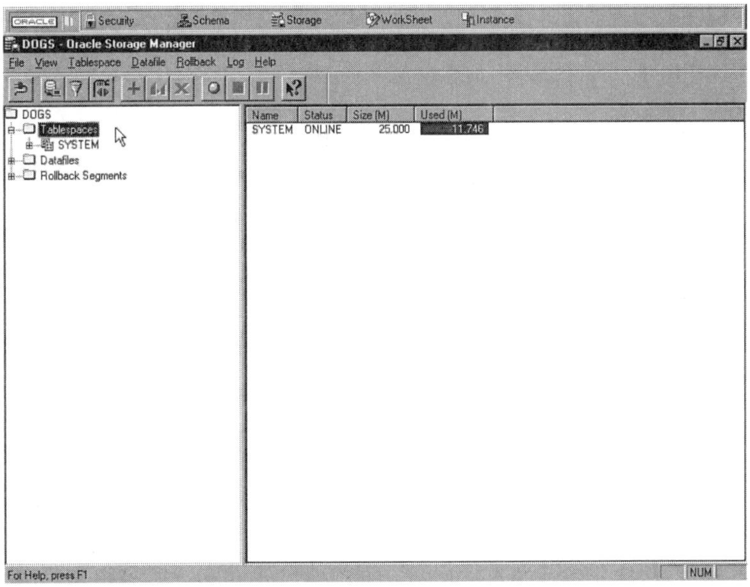

Figure 7.6.

The Tablespace view.

If you use Storage Manager, you will see that the screens and operation are identical to those used in Enterprise Manager. The basic differences are in the main screen (refer to Figure 7.5), which gives you more information than Enterprise Manager. The same options are used and the same procedures are followed to create a tablespace using Storage Manager.

Creating Tablespaces with the CREATE TABLESPACE Command

You can create a tablespace with the Server Manager using the CREATE TABLESPACE command. This command can be run either interactively within Server Manager or from a SQL script. As with the CREATE DATABASE command, I prefer to use a SQL script because it can be reused or used as a template for further tablespace creations. This SQL script is also a good record of the operations necessary to re-create the database in case of a catastrophic failure. The following command is used to create a tablespace:

```
CREATE TABLESPACE
DATAFILE file_specification
[AUTOEXTEND OFF]
or [AUTOEXTEND ON [NEXT number K or M]
    [MAXSIZE UNLIMITED or MAXSIZE number K or M]
[NOLOGGING or LOGGING]
[, file_specification
[AUTOEXTEND OFF]
or [AUTOEXTEND ON [NEXT number K or M]
    [MAXSIZE UNLIMITED or MAXSIZE number K or M]
[NOLOGGING or LOGGING]]
[MINIMUM EXTENT number K or M]
[DEFAULT STORAGE storage_clause]
[ONLINE or OFFLINE]
[PERMANENT or TEMPORARY]
```

DATAFILE

DATAFILE file_specification specifies the filename or filenames of the datafiles that make up the tablespace. File specification is made up of the 'filename' SIZE number (K or M) [REUSE] component. The file specification is used to define the name and the initial size in kilobytes (K) or megabytes (M) of the datafile. The REUSE parameter allows you to use the name of an existing file.

Additional qualifiers to the DATAFILE parameter are

☐ AUTOEXTEND OFF—This parameter specifies that the autoextend feature is disabled on this datafile.

☐ AUTOEXTEND ON—This parameter specifies that that autoextend feature is enabled. Additional qualifiers to the AUTOEXTEND ON parameter are

☐ NEXT number K or M—When a datafile autoextends itself, it extends by number K (kilobytes) or number M (megabytes).

☐ `MAXSIZE UNLIMITED`—This specifies that the maximum size of the datafile is limited only by disk space and OS-specific maximum sizes.

☐ `MAXSIZE` *number* `K or M`—This specifies that the maximum size that autoextend will grow this datafile to is *number*. This size is either specified in K (kilobytes) or M (megabytes).

Other parameters available with the `CREATE TABLESPACE` command are

☐ `LOGGING`—This specifies that redo log information is kept on table, index, and partition operations. This is the default. Logging can be disabled by using the `NOLOGGING` option on these operations.

☐ `NOLOGGING`—This specifies that logging is not done on operations that support the `NOLOGGING` option.

☐ `MINIMUM EXTENT` *number* `K or M`—This specifies the minimum extent size for extents created in this tablespace.

☐ `DEFAULT STORAGE` *storage_clause*—Specifies the default storage parameters for this tablespace.

☐ `ONLINE`—Specifies that the state of the tablespace is available immediately after creation.

☐ `OFFLINE`—Specifies that the state of the tablespace is unavailable immediately after creation.

☐ `TEMPORARY`—Specifies that this tablespace will be used only to hold temporary objects.

☐ `PERMANENT`—Specifies that this tablespace will be used to hold permanent objects. This is the default.

As you can see, there are many options available in the creation of the tablespace. Among these are the storage parameters that are shown later in this lesson. These storage parameters define the characteristics of the tablespace and how it grows.

Modifying Tablespaces

It is often necessary to modify a tablespace that has already been created. This can be accomplished in several ways, either using Enterprise Manager or Server Manager. Before I go into the syntax of operations that are available to modify the tablespace parameters and state, I would like to go through the various options and why you would perform these operations. At the end of this section you will see how to operationally change the tablespace properties and state.

7

Bring a Tablespace Offline

Bringing the tablespace offline can occur in several different ways. These methods normally take the tablespace offline either with the Temporary option or with the Immediate option. Each of these options has different purposes and consequences.

Normal Tablespace Offline

Bringing a tablespace offline normally involves Oracle checkpointing all the datafiles used by the tablespace and then bringing the tablespace offline. Bringing a tablespace offline normally requires all the datafiles to be available and functioning properly. Bringing a tablespace back online from a normal offline operation does not require recovery.

Temporary Tablespace Offline

Bringing a tablespace offline with the Temporary option will allow the tablespace to be brought offline even if a datafile is unavailable. So even if you are having a problem with a datafile, you can bring the tablespace offline with the Temporary option. All the available datafiles will be checkpointed. Bringing the tablespace back online might require some recovery.

Immediate Tablespace Offline

Using the Immediate option to take a tablespace offline does just what you'd think: The tablespace is immediately taken offline without the datafiles being checkpointed, so recovery is required when the tablespace is brought back online. This should be done only as a last resort under emergency conditions.

Bring a Tablespace Online

Any tablespace that has been taken offline for any reason can be brought back online either through Enterprise Manager or Server Manager. Bringing a tablespace online alters the state of that tablespace so that it can be accessed by users. Depending on how the tablespace was taken offline, there might be recovery involved in bringing it back online.

Modifying the Tablespace for Backup

When performing an online backup operation using traditional methods not involving the new Recovery Manager, use the following procedure:

1. The tablespace is altered for backup. This guarantees that the datafile will not be written to during the backup.
2. The datafiles are backed up using OS or third-party utilities.
3. The tablespace is brought back online and any unwritten changes are updated on the datafiles.

This has been the traditional method for the Oracle backup operation. Backup and recovery are covered in detail on Days 16, "Understanding Effective Backup Techniques," and 17, "Recovering the Database."

Coalescing the Tablespace

Because the tablespace allocates space to schema objects in extents of various sizes, it is possible that over time this space will become fragmented. As extents are allocated, Oracle looks for free space that is closest in size to the space needed for the new extent. As the tablespace ages and extents are added and freed, you might find many small free extents located next to each other, as illustrated in Figure 7.7.

Figure 7.7.
A fragmented tablespace.

f	x	f	f	f	x	f	x	f	f	x	f	f

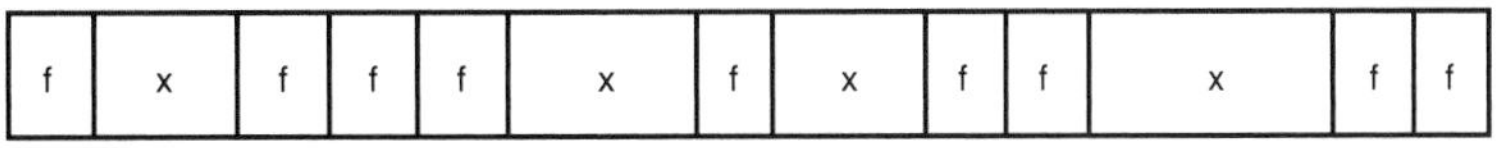

By coalescing the tablespace, you coalesce the adjacent free extents into larger free extents, thus making the free space more flexible to new extent allocations. Compare the fragmented tablespace shown in Figure 7.7 with the same tablespace after it is coalesced (see Figure 7.8).

Figure 7.8.
A coalesced tablespace.

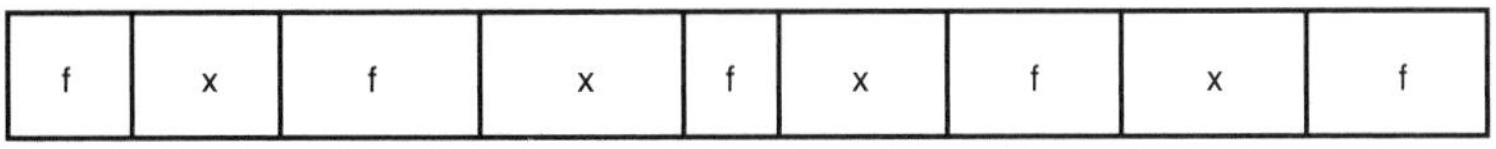

f	x	f	x	f	x	f	x	f

The SMON process automatically coalesces tablespaces unless the process has been disabled. It is rarely necessary to coalesce a tablespace by hand, but it is necessary to know how and why this operation is performed.

Adding Datafiles

It is often necessary to add more datafiles to a tablespace if you need more space or want to spread out I/Os among more disk drives. It is also faster to add datafiles to a tablespace than to create them at database-creation time. The CREATE TABLESPACE command works serially. That is, it creates one datafile at a time. By adding datafiles, this operation can be parallelized, so multiple datafiles can be added to a tablespace at once.

TIP

It can be faster to add datafiles to a tablespace than to specify them at tablespace creation because adding datafiles can be done in parallel. Datafile creation at tablespace-creation time is done in serial, one at a time. For creation of a large tablespace, this can save significant time.

7

Altering Tablespace Properties

The tablespace can be altered with Storage Manager and with the ALTER TABLESPACE command that can be run from Server Manager.

Modifying Tablespaces with Enterprise Manger

There is some limited ability to modify the tablespace from within Enterprise Manager itself. Drill down to the Tablespace option and right-click the tablespace you want to modify. In this case, I have right-clicked the DOGS tablespace. Selecting Quick Edit will invoke the Quick Edit Tablespace dialog box, shown in Figure 7.9.

Figure 7.9.

The Quick Edit Tablespace dialog box.

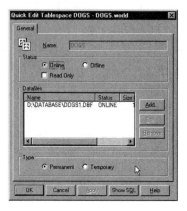

As you can see, the options available from the Quick Edit Tablespace dialog box are quite limited:

- [ ] Online—Enabling this radio button puts the tablespace online.
- [ ] Offline—Enabling this radio button takes the tablespace offline.
- [ ] Read Only—Checking this option makes the tablespace read-only.
- [ ] Add—Clicking this invokes the Create Datafile dialog box, where you can add a datafile to the tablespace.
- [ ] Permanent—Enabling this radio button changes a temporary tablespace to a permanent one.
- [ ] Temporary—Enabling this radio button changes a permanent tablespace to a temporary one.

The options to modify a tablespace via Enterprise Manager are quite limited compared to the various tablespace options that are available.

Modifying Tablespaces with Storage Manger

To modify the database through a graphical utility, you can use Enterprise Manager or Enterprise Manager's application, Storage Manager. Storage Manager is invoked either through Enterprise Manager or from the Oracle Administrators toolbar.

On the left side of the Enterprise Manager screen, you see the Navigator pane, where a tree-like structure displays the SID as the top level and branches out to tablespaces, datafiles, and rollback segments. If you drill down to the tablespace level, you will see the detail screen of the tablespaces, as shown in Figure 7.10.

Figure 7.10.

The Storage Manager Tablespace view.

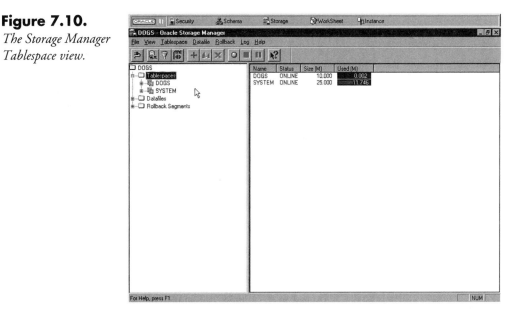

An extremely useful feature of this screen is the capability to show how much of your space is used in the tablespaces. On the far-right side, you can see both the size of the tablespaces and the amount of space that each tablespace has used.

You can drill down to the Tablespace screen and right-click to invoke a list of options, as shown in Figure 7.11. As you can see, the options available to modify the tablespaces are as limited as within Enterprise Manager. You do, however, get a few more features within Storage Manager.

An extremely useful feature of this screen is the capability to show how much of your space is used within each object. If you click the Datafile option, you can view each of the datafiles and the space available in each, as shown in Figure 7.12.

As with the tablespace and datafile screens, you can view the space used in the rollback segments by clicking the Rollback Segments option. You will see more on how to use Storage Manager with rollback segments tomorrow.

Figure 7.11.

The Storage Manager Tablespace options.

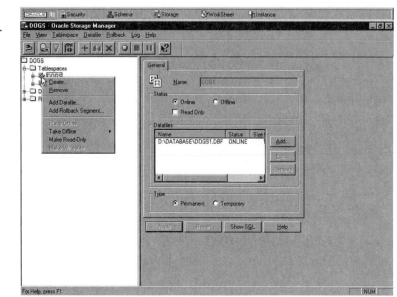

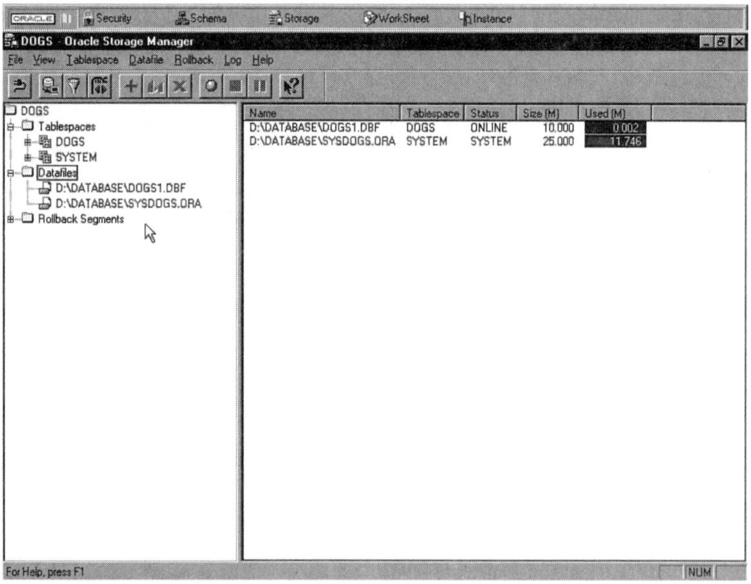

Figure 7.12.

Datafile view.

Modifying the Tablespace with the ALTER TABLESPACE Command

As you can see, Enterprise Manager and Storage Manager are quite limited when it comes to modifying tablespaces. Only a few options are available. All the tablespace options can be modified with the ALTER TABLESPACE command. This command can be used to modify the tablespace parameters that are set when the tablespace is created, to alter the state of the tablespace, or to add datafiles.

The Syntax for ALTER TABLESPACE

The ALTER TABLESPACE command is run with the following syntax:

```
ALTER TABLESPACE tablespace
[LOGGING or NOLOGGING]
[ADD DATAFILE file_specification
[AUTOEXTEND OFF]
or [AUTOEXTEND ON [NEXT number K or M]
     [MAXSIZE UNLIMITED or MAXSIZE number K or M]]
[, file_specification
[AUTOEXTEND OFF]
or [AUTOEXTEND ON [NEXT number K or M]
     [MAXSIZE UNLIMITED or MAXSIZE number K or M]]
[RENAME DATAFILE 'filename' [, 'filename]...
     TO 'filename' [, 'filename']...]
[COALESCE]
[DEFAULT STORAGE storage_clause]
[MINIMUM EXTENT number [K or M]]
[ONLINE]
[OFFLINE NORMAL or OFFLINE TEMPORARY or OFFLINE IMMEDIATE]
[BEGIN BACKUP or END BACKUP]
[READ ONLY or READ WRITE]
[PERMANENT or TEMPORARY]
```

The parameters used to alter the tablespace are defined as follows:

- ☐ LOGGING—This parameter specifies that redo log information is kept on table, index, and partition operations. This is the default. You can disable logging by using the NOLOGGING option on these operations.

- ☐ NOLOGGING—This parameter specifies that logging not be done on operations that support the NOLOGGING option.

- ☐ ADD DATAFILE file_specification—This parameter specifies that a datafile or datafiles specified by file_specification will be added to the tablespace.

file_specification consists of the 'filename' SIZE number (K or M) [REUSE] component. file_specification is used to define the name, and the initial size in kilobytes (K) or megabytes (M) of the datafile. The REUSE parameter allows you to use the name of an existing file.

Additional qualifiers to the ADD DATAFILE parameter are

☐ AUTOEXTEND OFF—This parameter specifies that the autoextend feature is disabled on this datafile.

☐ AUTOEXTEND ON—This parameter specifies that that autoextend feature is enabled. Additional qualifiers to the AUTOEXTEND ON parameter are

    ☐ NEXT *number* K or M—When a datafile autoextends itself, it extends by *number* K (kilobytes) or *number* M (megabytes).

    ☐ MAXSIZE UNLIMITED—This specifies that the maximum size of the datafile is limited only by disk space and OS-specific maximum sizes.

    ☐ MAXSIZE *number* K or M—This specifies that the maximum size autoextend will grow this datafile to is *number*. This size is either specified in kilobytes (K) or megabytes (M).

Other parameters available with the ALTER TABLESPACE command are

☐ RENAME DATAFILE 'filename' [, 'filename]... TO 'filename'—This command is used to rename one or more datafiles in the [, 'filename']... tablespace.

☐ COALESCE—This command is used to coalesce the tablespace as described previously.

☐ DEFAULT STORAGE storage_clause—This command is used to change the default storage parameters for the tablespace. These default storage parameters are used when schema objects are created unless a storage parameter is specified.

☐ MINIMUM EXTENT *number* [K or M]—This specifies the minimum size of an extent that is created on the tablespace. The minimum extent size will be *number* K (kilobytes) or *number* M (megabytes).

☐ ONLINE—This is used to bring the tablespace online.

☐ OFFLINE NORMAL—This is used to bring the tablespace offline normally as described previously.

☐ OFFLINE TEMPORARY—This is used to bring the tablespace offline temporarily, as described previously.

☐ OFFLINE IMMEDIATE—This is used to force the tablespace offline with the IMMEDIATE option.

☐ BEGIN BACKUP—This takes the tablespace offline and defers all writes to the datafiles while the backup is taking place.

☐ END BACKUP—This brings the tablespace back online and writes out all changes that have occurred since the BEGIN BACKUP.

☐ READ ONLY—This modifies the tablespace to be read-only. The read-only tablespace is described later today.

☐ READ WRITE—This modifies a read-only tablespace to be read-write.

☐ PERMANENT—This converts the tablespace from temporary to permanent status.

☐ TEMPORARY—This converts the tablespace from permanent to temporary status.

As you have seen, the ALTER TABLESPACE command allows many changes to be made to the tablespace. Changes to tablespaces should always be logged when they occur. If the database ever needs to be re-created, this information is critical.

The STORAGE Clause

The STORAGE clause is very important because it is used to specify the initial size and characteristics of the tablespace as well as the future growth of that tablespace.

The Syntax for the STORAGE Clause

The STORAGE clause has the following syntax:

```
STORAGE
(
[INITIAL number K or M]
[NEXT number K or M]
[MINEXTENTS number]
[MAXEXTENTS number or MAXEXTENTS UNLIMITED]
[PCTINCREASE number]
[FREELISTS number]
[FREELIST GROUPS number]
[OPTIMAL [number K or M] or [NULL]]
)
```

The parameters used in the STORAGE clause are defined as follows:

☐ INITIAL number K or M—This parameter specifies the initial size of the extents. These extents are created when the schema object is created. This parameter specifies the size to be number K (kilobytes) or number M (megabytes). The default is 5 data blocks. The size is rounded up to the nearest multiple of 5 blocks.

☐ NEXT number K or M—The NEXT parameter specifies the size of subsequent extents to be number K (kilobytes) or number M (megabytes). This number is also rounded up to the nearest multiple of 5 data blocks, and defaults to 5 data blocks.

☐ MINEXTENTS number—This specifies the minimum number of extents created when the schema object is created. Each of these extents is the size of the INITIAL extent, and Oracle uses NEXT and PCTINCREASE to calculate the size of subsequent extents. The default value is 1 except for rollback segments, where the default is 2.

☐ MAXEXTENTS number—This specifies the maximum number of extents that can be created for a schema object. This includes the first extent.

☐ MAXEXTENTS UNLIMITED—This specifies that the maximum number of extents that can be created for a schema object is unlimited. Oracle does not recommend that you use this option with any schema objects except for rollback segments.

- □ PCTINCREASE *number*—This specifies the size of extents after the second extent (that is, from the third extent on). The initial extents are sized via the INITIAL parameter. The next extent is sized via the NEXT parameter. If the PCTINCREASE parameter is nonzero, all subsequent extents are sized as NEXT multiplied by PCTINCREASE *number*. This product is a percentage, so 40 means 40% larger, and so on. A value of 0 specifies that all subsequent extents are the same size as specified in the NEXT parameter. The default value is 50, except for rollback segments, which can only have a PCTINCREASE of 0.

- □ FREELISTS *number*—The FREELISTS parameter specifies the number of sets of freelists for each of the freelist groups of tables, indexes, partitions and clusters. A freelist is a linked list of available data blocks in the extent that have free space greater than PCTFREE. These are essentially lists of blocks that are available for inserts. By having more than one freelist, you can reduce contention on inserts.

- □ FREELIST GROUPS *number*—FREELISTS GROUPS specifies the number of groups of freelists in a parallel-server environment. This allows each instance to have its own set of freelists. FREELIST GROUPS is a parallel-server–only parameter.

- □ OPTIMAL [*number* K or M]—This parameter applies only to rollback segments. It specifies the ideal size of the rollback segment. Because the rollback segment grows as described tomorrow, this parameter describes what size Oracle should attempt to keep them.

- □ OPTIMAL [NULL]—This parameter specifies that the rollback segments never shrink, as they can with the OPTIMAL parameter set to a value. This is described in detail tomorrow.

These storage parameters can be used not only in the creation of tablespaces, but also in the creation of schema objects, as you will see later in the book. The size and characteristics of the tablespaces can be very important to the performance of the system.

NOTE

> For tablespaces, you specify the DEFAULT STORAGE options. These are used as the default values for the schema objects that you will be creating. Your schema object creation options override the default storage parameters.

Using the STORAGE Clause

By using the STORAGE clause, you can be very efficient with how the schema objects are stored. If you know you will be loading a large amount of data that will be stored in a certain table, it is much more efficient to have a few large extents rather than many small extents. This is typically be done using the STORAGE clause on the schema objects like so:

```
CREATE TABLESPACE ts_1
DATAFILE 'D:\database\ts_1_a.dbf' SIZE 20M,
E:\database\ts_1_b.dbf SIZE 20M
DEFAULT STORAGE
(
INITIAL 2M NEXT 2M PCTINCREASE 0 MINEXTENTS 2
);
```

This creates the tablespace ts_1 with two datafiles and two initial extents. To create the same tablespace but allow the second datafile to autoextend, you can affix the additional parameters as follows:

```
CREATE TABLESPACE ts_1
DATAFILE 'D:\database\ts_1_a.dbf' SIZE 20M,
E:\database\ts_1_b.dbf SIZE 20M AUTOEXTEND ON NEXT 1M MAXSIZE 30M
DEFAULT STORAGE
(
INITIAL 2M NEXT 2M PCTINCREASE 0 MINEXTENTS 2
);
```

Remember that the DEFAULT STORAGE clause is used for the creation of extents. Extents are used to hold schema objects. When the schema objects are created and grow, the default storage parameters are used. These parameters are simply defaults for the schema objects that are created on these tablespaces. Schema objects created with their own storage parameters override the tablespace defaults.

Read-Only Tablespaces

As described previously, it is possible to alter a tablespace to make it read-only. Read-only tablespaces are similar to read-write tablespaces except that no changes can be made to the schema objects residing on those tablespaces. When a tablespace is read-only, the need to back up this tablespace is eliminated.

Because the data is guaranteed not to change, it is unnecessary to perform regular backups on the read-only data. If a backup has been performed at some time, that backup should be good for the life of the tablespace.

Because the read-only tablespace is not modified by Oracle, it is possible to place the tablespace on a read-only medium such as a CD-ROM or a WORM drive. If this data is archival in nature but must be available, a CD-ROM is an excellent choice.

Creating Read-Only Tablespaces

All tablespaces are created as read-write tablespaces and must be populated with data before they are useful. After the data and indexes have been created to your specifications, the tablespace can be made read-only. This can happen in several ways.

Enterprise Manager or Storage Manager can be used to modify a tablespace to be read-only, as described in the previous section. Simply go to the Tablespace Modification screen, shown in Figure 7.13, and click the Read Only box.

7

Figure 7.13.

Making a tablespace read-only.

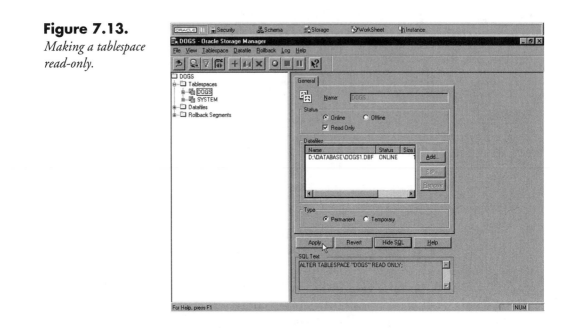

I enjoy Enterprise Manager's capability to show the SQL used to perform the command. I encourage you to use this feature to become familiar with the DDL statements that are used in these operations.

The tablespace can also be made read-only through the use of the ALTER TABLESPACE command. The syntax looks something like this:

```
ALTER TABLESPACE DOGS READONLY;
```

There are several uses for the read-only tablespace, but they are fairly specific. Whether you can take advantage of it depends on your applications.

If you have a large amount of static data that can be put on slower media, the read-only tablespace might be advantageous for you. A read-only tablespace might also be advantageous if you want to guarantee that archival data is not modified.

Temporary Tablespaces

Temporary tablespaces are used to perform sort operations that cannot fit into memory. If you allocate a tablespace specifically for sorting, it is unnecessary to allocate and deallocate space in tablespaces that are used for other purposes (doing so causes fragmentation).

When a sort operation cannot fit in memory, it must create and use a temporary segment. This temporary segment allocates extents and continues to do so until it has enough room to perform the sort. With large DSS queries, these temporary segments can become quite large. By having tablespaces specifically for this type of operation, not only will the sorts be more efficient, there will be less temporary usage on your data tablespaces.

Creating Temporary Tablespaces

A tablespace can be made temporary when it is created with Enterprise Manager, with Storage Manager, or with the CREATE TABLESPACE command. You can change an existing tablespace from a permanent one to a temporary one using the GUI tools or the ALTER TABLESPACE command. This syntax looks something like this:

```
ALTER TABLESPACE DOGS TEMPORARY;
```

It is rare that you will change a permanent tablespace to a temporary one, or vice versa. A temporary tablespace is typically created as such, and will remain so for the duration of its existence.

Tablespace Tricks and Tips

The tablespace is the resource from which the schema objects obtain their space. Think of a tablespace as a filesystem on a set of disk drives. The space is there and allocated, but is not used until somebody creates a file or saves some data. This is also true of the Oracle tablespace.

As schema objects are created, extents are allocated from the tablespace. These extents are allocated based on the storage parameters of the schema creation or the tablespace's default storage parameters.

As objects are created, the space is taken from the front of the tablespace; as more and more objects are created, the space is allocated from where the last object was created. This can cause some problems.

NOTE

Here is an example of where the tablespaces can work counter to your intent: The system has two disk drives, each 4GB in size. You create a tablespace that uses two datafiles, one on each drive of 4GB each.

In this case, only the first disk drive will be used until you use up 4GB of space in the tablespace, as shown in Figure 7.14. Only then it will start using space on the second datafile. Unfortunately, this does little to balance the I/O load.

Instead, create eight, 1GB datafiles, four on each disk drive in an alternating pattern (see Figure 7.15). This will more evenly spread the load.

7

Figure 7.14.
Unbalanced tablespaces.

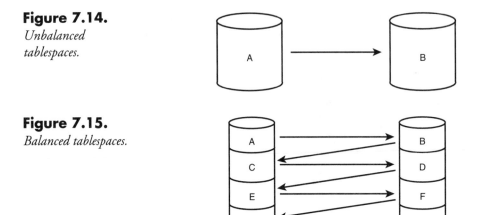

Figure 7.15.
Balanced tablespaces.

Other ways to balance the I/O load are to use hardware features or OS features such as disk striping. If you stripe your disk drives with a disk array or with software striping, the load will be fairly well balanced among all the disk drives in the stripe.

TIP | Disk striping can be an easy way to balance the I/O load between disk drives. A hardware or software disk array will evenly distribute the data among all the disk drives in the stripe.

Configuring and managing the tablespaces can be a time-consuming task requiring much up-front planning. This planning is well worth it. More time spent planning now means less time spent fixing problems later.

Followup

Even after the tablespaces have been created, your job is not over. You must monitor the space used and the load balancing of your tablespaces. As you recall from Day 4, "Properly Sizing Your Database and Planning for Growth," capacity planning and sizing are very important duties. By anticipating problems and solving them before they become critical, you can avoid costly mishaps. By monitoring the system and planning for the future, you can avoid costly downtime.

Monitoring the Tablespaces

As described previously, you can use Storage Manager to view both the tablespaces and the datafiles for space utilization. The information provided by Storage Manager is quite useful.

From the Tablespace view, you can see both the space allocated to the tablespace and the amount of space used in the tablespace (refer to Figure 7.6). The SYSTEM tablespace has used approximately 11.7MB of its available 25MB. The colored bar shows this to be about 45% used.

This feature is also available from the Datafiles option (refer to Figure 7.12). This shows approximately the same view as in the Tablespace view since both tablespaces, SYSTEM and DOGS, have one associated datafile. In situations where more datafiles exist, you might be able to determine whether balancing of space is an issue. You must use the NT Performance Monitor to determine whether I/O balancing is a problem.

Load Balancing

As detailed yesterday, you should use diskperf to determine whether you are overloading your I/O system. Periodically look at the physical disk statistics during peak and nonpeak usage periods. If you see one or two disk drives that have more activity than others, you may have an I/O problem. Don't rely on things staying the same. Performance characteristics of your system are constantly changing and must be monitored.

TIP

Try scheduling several days during the month to monitor system performance. Put it on your calendar at the beginning of the month. Monitor several different days of the week and times of day to get some different samples.

Summary

Yesterday you looked at the database-creation operation that creates the database, the redo log files, the control files, and the SYSTEM tablespace. This tablespace is populated with stored procedures and structures necessary to run the Oracle RDBMS. But this does not leave room for your data.

Today you looked at the second step of creating your own database: creating tablespaces. After the database has been created, you must create additional tablespaces for your own data. These tablespaces are where your specific schema objects will reside, and where your data will be loaded. This is why I refer to tablespace creation as the second step in creating your database.

These tablespaces are very important because your data and the performance of your system rely on how well you design these tablespaces. The tablespaces are the key to data partitioning and load balancing. It is very important to plan the layout of your tablespaces and datafiles

with performance and functionality in mind. In subsequent lessons you will see how important this is.

What's Next?

Tomorrow you will see the importance of the redo log files, the control files, and the rollback segments. After finishing tomorrow's lesson, you will be familiar with all operations that involve physical datafiles. The four types of files that exist in the Oracle database are datafiles, control files, redo log files, and parameter files. All other Oracle structures reside within the datafiles.

As you learned on Day 2, "Exploring the Oracle Architecture," the Oracle instance consists of the Oracle datafiles (all types), the Oracle memory structures, and the Oracle processes. By the end of Day 8, "Administering Redo Logs, Control Files, and Rollback Segments," you will have seen all the physical files used in normal operations (don't forget backups and archiving, which you will see later).

Q&A

Q What utilities can be used to create a tablespace?

A You can use Enterprise Manager, Storage Manager, or the CREATE TABLESPACE command to create a tablespace.

Q What is a tablespace used for?

A The tablespace is used to create schema objects. Tables, indexes, views, and clusters all are created within tablespaces.

Q Is using Enterprise Manger better than using SQL commands?

A Neither is better or worse. You should learn how to use both of them. I really like Enterprise Manager, but there are still lots of things I use Server Manager for.

Workshop

The workshop provides quiz questions to help you solidify your understanding of the material covered and exercises to provide you with experience in using what you've learned. For answers to quiz questions, see Appendix A, "Answers."

Quiz

1. What is an extent?
2. How big can a tablespace be?
3. Is the size of a tablespace permanently fixed?

4. What states can a tablespace be in?

5. How many tablespaces can you have in a database?

6. Name the four types of segments.

Exercises

1. Create a tablespace using Storage Manager.

2. Create a tablespace using the CREATE TABLESPACE command.

3. Take the tablespace offline.

4. Alter the tablespace to be read-only using Storage Manger and the ALTER TABLESPACE command.

7

WEEK

1

1

2

3

4

5

6

7

In Review

You spent Days 1–4 in the introductory section of this book. These chapters are designed to give you an idea of how Oracle works and how to work with Oracle. On Days 1–3, you learned the basics of how Oracle works as well as some of the history of Oracle, and you did a tutorial on how to install Oracle8 on NT. On Day 4, you learned about sizing and capacity planing from Steve DeLuca of Oracle. The end of this week and the beginning of the second week were spent learning about Oracle data storage.

Managing Database Storage

You spent the last three days of week 1 and the first two days of week 2 learning about advanced topics such as database creation, tablespace creation, the Oracle redo logs, checkpointing, and rollback segments. This section covers some of the core concepts of the Oracle DBMS.

On Day 5 you learned about managing the Oracle RDBMS using both the Enterprise Manager and the more traditional command-line utilities. Finishing up the week, you learned about managing databases and datafiles on Day 6 and tablespaces on Day 7. The remainder of the discussion about managing database storage continued into week 2.

At a Glance

Week 2 begins by finishing up topics related to managing database storage. On Days 8 and 9, you learn how to create and manage the Oracle redo log files, control files, and rollback files. You also finish the topic of Oracle storage by learning how to manage data by using the SQL*Loader, Export and Import utilities.

Managing Users and Processes

Days 10 and 11 teach you how to create and alter user accounts in the Oracle database as well as how to manage the various Oracle processes. You will also learn how to manage the Oracle job queues and how to schedule jobs for later execution.

8

9

10

11

12

13

14

Managing the Database Schema

Days 12–14 cover topics that are typically outside of the responsibilities of the Oracle administrator. The database schema is typically the responsibility of the application developer. It is, however, very important that the Oracle DBA be familiar with these concepts and able to assist the application developer when required. These topics include table and index creation as well as clusters and views.

Day 8

Administering Redo Logs, Control Files, and Rollback Segments

In the last few days you saw how to create a database and how to add datafiles and tablespaces to customize that database for your own use. Remember, the instance is made up of the files used by Oracle, the processes or threads, and the memory used by Oracle. The files used by the database are made up of the following:

- [ ] The datafiles. These are the actual files that are used to store tablespaces.

- [ ] The redo log files (sometimes just known as the *redo log*). This is where all redo information is kept. Without the redo log files you would not be able to recover from a system failure.

- [ ] The control files. These files contain information vital to the Oracle database. The information that is used to tell the instance where the datafiles and log files reside is stored in the control file.

□ The parameter file. This file contains tuning information that is used by Oracle at startup. This is commonly referred to as the init.ora file.

There are also the RDBMS binaries and other files such as backup files, archive log files, and so on, but they are not really part of the database itself, even though they are essential to the RDBMS.

As you saw on Day 7, "Administering Tablespaces," a tablespace can hold four different types of segments:

□ Data segment—Used to hold tables and clusters

□ Index segment—Used to hold indexes

□ Rollback segment—Special types of segments that are used to store undo information

□ Temporary segment—Used for storing temporary data

Today you will look at the rollback segments. Data segments, index segments, and temporary segments are covered on Days 12–15. The rollback segment is not only important to the basic function of the Oracle RDBMS, but it has performance implications as well.

Redo Log Files

The redo log files are used to store redo information. Each time data is changed in the database, a log record is written describing the change(s). With this information the database can be recovered in the event of a system failure.

If a catastrophic system failure occurs, such as a power failure, component failure, or similar occurrence, the Oracle instance will be aborted. The instance will be cut off immediately or, in the event of a disk failure, the instance might crash. If this occurs, all changed data in the buffer cache will be lost; only changes that have been written out to disk will be saved.

New Term When Oracle is restarted, the information in the redo log file will be used to reproduce changes that have been made to the database, thus saving as much work as possible. All previously committed transactions will be recovered; this is also known as being *rolled forward*. All transactions that had modified data but had not been committed will be backed out; this is known as *rolling back*.

The redo log file is necessary for proper recovery. If this file is lost due to a disk failure, you will not be able to recover in the event of a system failure; therefore, you must protect the redo log file against this kind of failure. I recommend you use disk mirroring or RAID-1 on all redo log files.

Because the redo log files are so critical to the recoverability of the system, it is recommended that you do not use a caching disk controller with write-caching unless that cache is backed up with a battery. In the event of a power failure, you must make sure that no redo information is lost. It is often recommended that write-caching not be used at all on the redo log, but I feel that if you have a battery back-up your risk is reduced.

WARNING

> If you use a write-caching on the controller that has the redo log files and it is not backed up with a battery, you are in danger of losing data. In the event of a power failure, you will lose redo information and might not be able to recover.

How Does the Redo Log Work?

Each change to the database is logged into the redo log. Because of this, in the event of a failure all changes made since the last backup can be recovered with the use of these redo log files. If the instance should fail due to a power failure or other system failure, the redo log files can recover all changes done since the last checkpoint.

NOTE

> A checkpoint causes all in-cache data blocks that have not been written out to disk to be written out to disk. These unwritten, changed buffers are called *dirty buffers*. These dirty buffers are what cause the system to need to be recovered. If there are no dirty buffers when the system fails, recovery time will be instantaneous.

When a COMMIT operation is performed, the redo information is written into the redo log buffers. The LGWR process writes the redo log files with the information in the redo log buffer. The COMMIT operation is not completed until the redo log has been written. After that has occurred, that transaction is irrevocable and will be recovered in the event of a system failure. You can see how important the redo log file really is.

The redo log is made up of two or more redo log files or log file groups. A *log file group* is a set of files that Oracle automatically mirrors. In this manner the redo log is protected against disk failure. A redo log group is made up of one or more redo log files and must be protected against disk failure. If you are using disk mirroring to protect the redo log, it is not necessary to use log file groups; because the disk is protected, single log files are sufficient.

NEW TERM   The redo log has two or more log files or log file groups that are used in an alternating fashion. When the first log file has filled up, the logging operation moves to the next redo log file in the chain. If archiving is enabled, when it fills up and the log switch occurs, this file is copied to an *archive log file*. These archive log files are very important for the recoverability of the system in the event of a catastrophic failure.

Operations on the redo log files are done with the ALTER DATABASE command that was described on Day 6, "Administering Databases and Datafiles." Using the ALTER DATABASE command you can add redo log groups, add redo log files, rename redo log files, and so on.

Log Switches and Checkpoints

NEW TERM   Each time a redo log file or log file group fills up, it switches to the next redo log file in the sequence. This switch, called the *log switch*, causes several automatic events to occur:

☐ Checkpointing—A log switch always causes a checkpoint to occur. The checkpoint flushes all dirty buffers from the Oracle buffer cache. This reduces the amount of time a recovery will take, if needed.

☐ Archiving—If archiving is turned on (and it should be), the log switch causes the redo log file that was just active to copy its contents to an *archive log file*. This archive log file is used in recovery if needed.

☐ Log Sequence Number—Each time a redo log file is reused, it is given a *log sequence number*. This log sequence number is also given to the associated archive log file. By having this number, the RDBMS can keep track of which log file and archive log files have been used.

Archiving and checkpointing are covered on Days 16 and 17, "Understanding Effective Backup Techniques" and "Recovering the Database," where backup and recovery are covered in detail.

Log Switch and Checkpoint Intervals

You can use the LOG_CHECKPOINT_INTERVAL and LOG_CHECKPOINT_TIMEOUT initialization parameters to control the checkpoint interval.

LOG_CHECKPOINT_INTERVAL

The LOG_CHECKPOINT_INTERVAL parameter is set by the administrator to a number of operating system blocks that are used before the log switch occurs. For most operating systems, the size of the operating system block size is 512 bytes, so this parameter will define the number of 512-byte blocks that are used in the redo log before a checkpoint occurs.

If your redo log files are 10MB in size and you want the checkpoint interval to be one tenth of the redo log file or 1MB, use the following formula to determine the value of LOG_CHECKPOINT_INTERVAL:

LOG_CHECKPOINT_INTERVAL = 1MB / 512 (bytes/block) = 2,048 blocks

To accomplish this, set LOG_CHECKPOINT_INTERVAL = 2048 in the parameter file. To have the checkpoint occur only at log switches, set the value of LOG_CHECKPOINT_INTERVAL to be larger than the size of your redo log files.

LOG_CHECKPOINT_TIMEOUT

The parameter LOG_CHECKPOINT_TIMEOUT specifies a time interval, in seconds, at which the checkpoint will occur. This will automatically run the checkpoint process at this interval. To set the checkpoint to occur every 10 minutes, for example, set LOG_CHECKPOINT_TIMEOUT = 600. By setting the checkpoint interval on a timer, you can be assured that checkpoints will happen regularly, even if there is not much activity at the time.

Forcing a Checkpoint

A checkpoint can be forced by hand. If you want to force a checkpoint, you can do it with the following command:

```
ALTER SYSTEM CHECKPOINT;
```

You might want to do this if you think that your system is at risk of some sort of failure, such as from a thunderstorm or other phenomenon that might cause a power outage or similar situation.

Forcing a Log Switch

As with the checkpoint, a log switch can be forced by hand. If you want to force a log switch, you can do it with the following command:

```
ALTER SYSTEM SWITCH LOGFILE;
```

It is only in rare circumstances where you will need to switch log files. This may happen when you want to force an archive before some system maintenance or other occurrence where the system may be at risk, or you may want to do this before your regular backup of archive log files.

Sizing the Redo Log Files

Typically the size of the redo log file is based on the capability of the medium that will contain the archive log files. If the archive log files will be written out to cartridge tape that can hold 525MB, you should consider making the redo log files 520MB. This will allow you to copy one archive log file to tape and have a little space left over for a margin of error.

If you do not have a particular medium in mind for archiving, or if the space is unlimited, you should make the redo log file a manageable size. A very large redo log file, say 2GB in size, might be a little unmanageable. Copying such a file can take quite some time.

There is no rule of thumb for the size of the redo log files. Your own preference should help you decide on it. Remember, if you make them too big you could potentially go all day without performing a checkpoint. This can be dangerous because the longer you go without checkpointing, the longer the recovery interval would be in the event of a system failure.

Archiving the Redo Logs

When a log switch occurs, the log records in the filled redo log file are copied to an archive log file if archiving is enabled. This archiving is usually done automatically. Because the redo log file cannot be reused until the archive process has completed, you should make sure that you will not try to reuse that log file before the operation is complete. There are several ways to make sure that the archiving process happens quickly:

☐ Archive to disk. You can archive to disk and then copy those archive log files to tape later. This will prevent the archiving process from waiting for a tape drive or other, slower medium to complete.

☐ Use multiple log files. By having more than two redo log files, you can simultaneously archive two or more log files while a third is being used for logging.

Archiving is very important to maintain recoverability in the database. Archiving and backups are covered in more detail on Day 16.

Adding Redo Log Files and Groups

As with many of the functions that you have seen in this book, there are several ways to add to the redo log. Most of these utilities have the option of using either a graphical or a command-line utility.

Using the Enterprise Manager

If you choose, you can add log files to the redo log via the Enterprise Manager. To do so, drill down into the database that you want to modify using the Navigator pane and right-click the Redo Log Groups icon. You will see the Create option. Select the Create option and you will see the Create Redo Log Group screen (see Figure 8.1). From here you fill in the size of the new redo log file that you want to create, specify a name under the New Members label, and click Add to add the redo log member. After you have clicked Add, that member will appear in the Current Members list, as shown in Figure 8.2.

NOTE

> In this example I have closed all panes except for the Navigator pane.

After you have entered all the filenames for the redo log group members, click OK to create the log group. To add a member to an already existing group, right-click on the Redo Log Group icon. This will bring up the Create Redo Log Member screen, as shown in Figure 8.3.

Figure 8.1.

The Create Redo Log Group screen.

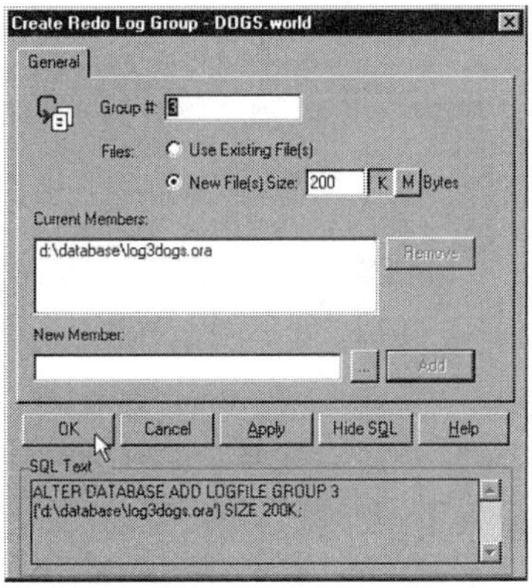

Figure 8.2.

The name of the new member of the redo log group appears in the Current Members list after you add it.

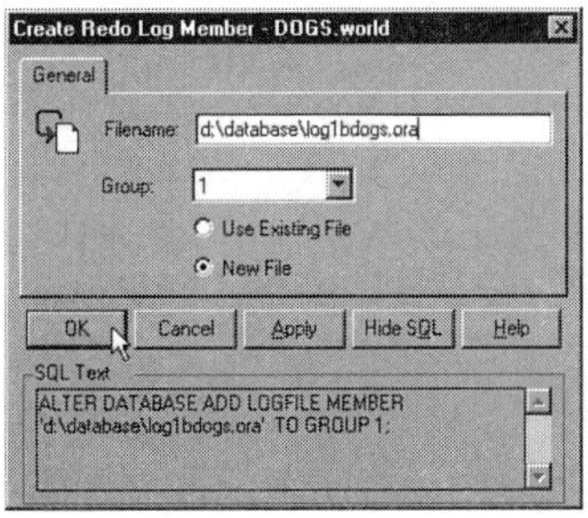

Figure 8.3.

The Create Redo Log Member screen.

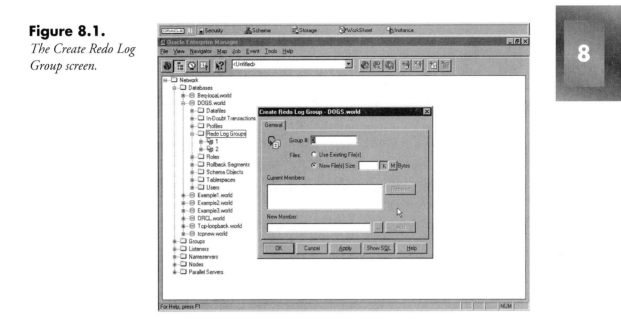

Here you type the name of the redo log group member and click OK to create that member. To create a redo log group member with the same characteristics as an existing redo log group member, right-click the redo log group member that you want to duplicate and select the Create Like option. You will then see the Create Log Group Member screen, as shown in Figure 8.4. Simply type the new log group member's name and click the OK button to create the redo log group member.

Figure 8.4.

You can base a new log group member on an existing member after clicking Create Like.

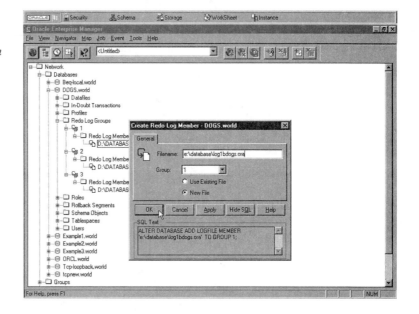

The options for the redo log group creation is somewhat limited in the Enterprise Manager. It is not possible to add redo log group members and groups from the Storage Manager.

Using the ALTER DATABASE Command

Log files or log file groups can be added or modified with the ALTER DATABASE command, as shown on Day 6. I prefer the command-line utilities because they can be scripted, and as such are a permanent record that can be used over and over again. An example of how to use the ALTER DATABASE command to add a log file is shown here:

```
ALTER DATABASE database
ADD LOGFILE ( 'log3a', 'log3b' ) SIZE 10M;
```

To add a new log file to an already existing group, you can use this command:

```
ALTER DATABASE database
ADD LOGFILE MEMBER 'log3c' TO GROUP 3;
```

If you don't know the group name, you can use the same command and specify the other members of the log file group, as in

```
ALTER DATABASE database
ADD LOGFILE MEMBER 'log3c' TO GROUP ( 'log3a', 'log3b');
```

As I have said before, by using a SQL script and the `ALTER DATABASE` command, you can preserve a permanent record of the change and then use the file as a template for other, similar operations.

Modifying Redo Log Files and Groups

As with many functions you have seen in this book, there are several ways to add to the redo log. Most of these utilities have an option of using either a graphical or a command-line utility.

Using the Enterprise Manager

To modify a redo log group member, right-click that member via the Enterprise Manager's Navigator pane and choose the Quick Edit option. From here you will see the Quick Edit Redo Log Member screen, as shown in Figure 8.5. In this screen you can change the name of the redo log group member, thus causing the `ALTER DATABASE RENAME FILE` command to be run. As you can see here, the options for modifying the redo log via the Enterprise Manager are very limited. I prefer to use the `ALTER DATABASE` command because of its flexibility and options.

Figure 8.5.

The Quick Edit Redo Log Member screen.

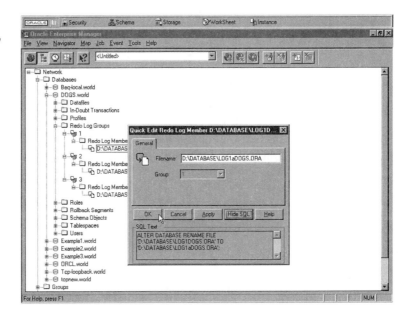

Using the ALTER DATABASE **Command**

You can modify log files or log file groups with the ALTER DATABASE command, as shown earlier today and on Day 6. Again, I really prefer the command-line utilities because they can be scripted, and as such are a permanent record that can be used over and over again. For example, a redo log file can be renamed with the command

```
ALTER DATABASE database
RENAME LOGFILE 'log1' TO 'log2';
```

Or you can delete a rollback segment with this command:

```
ALTER DATABASE database
DROP LOGFILE 'log1';
```

You can drop an entire log file group with the following command:

```
ALTER DATABASE database
DROP LOGFILE GROUP 3;
```

If you don't know the number of the log file group, you can drop it by specifying the names of the log file group members:

```
ALTER DATABASE database
DROP LOGFILE GROUP ('log3a', 'log3b');
```

If necessary, you can drop just a log file group member with this syntax:

```
ALTER DATABASE database
DROP LOGFILE GROUP MEMBER 'log3b';
```

Characteristics of the Log Files

The redo log files are one of the few files in the Oracle database that are always written to in a sequential manner. Because redo records are only read during recovery, they are write-only files during normal operations.

Because of the sequential nature of the redo log files, by isolating these files onto separate disk volumes you can take advantage of the fact that sequential I/O is much faster than random I/O. Keep in mind that the archival operation reads from the redo log file, so if you have two redo log files on the same disk volume, the archive process in conjunction with the redo log operation will cause random I/O.

NOTE

I use the term *disk volume* to refer to either a disk drive or set of disk drives in a RAID array.

In most cases, the performance of the redo log operation is not usually a problem. If you are running in a high transaction rate environment, you might need to separate each redo log file on its own disk volume.

TIP

> The redo log files should be protected, either by using log file groups or with a RAID array. When using a RAID array (either hardware or software), use RAID-1 for the redo log files. RAID-1 offers the most protection and the fastest write performance.

The performance of the archive log volume is not as important as that of the redo log volume, but it is still fairly important. It is necessary that the archival operation be completed before you need to reuse the redo log file.

In many cases, archival information can be kept on another system and restored when necessary. If you are doing this, or are keeping your archive log files on tape, you might want to archive to disk first and then copy to tape or to the network so you can restore the data more quickly. If you are copying your data to a backup system, you can use RAID-5, which is slower but less costly. In any case, by archiving to a temporary area first, you free up the redo log file in the fastest possible time. This is covered in more detail on Day 16.

Control Files

Control files are used to keep information critical to the operation of the RDBMS. The control file (or files) resides on the operating system file system. These files are used in the startup of the instance to identify where the datafiles and redo log files are in the system. The loss of a control file can be devastating to the operation of the RDBMS. It is always a good idea to have multiple control files on different disk volumes so that a failure does not cause the loss of all the control files. You can add an additional control file after the database has been created by following these steps:

1. Shut down the Oracle instance.
2. Copy the control file to another location on another disk volume.
3. Edit the parameter file to include the new file name in the CONTROL_FILES parameter.
4. Restart the Oracle instance.

The control file can also be created using the CREATE CONTROLFILE command. This creation of the control file should be done only in extreme situations, such as when you need to rename a database or reproduce a control file because all control files are damaged and you don't have backups.

The best way to save and protect your control files is to use the ALTER DATABASE *database* BACKUP CONTROLFILE command. The options to the ALTER DATABASE *database* BACKUP CONTROLFILE command are as follows:

- [ ] TO '*filename*'—Creates a new control file with the name specified as *filename*. If the file already exists, the optional REUSE qualifier must be used.

- [ ] TO TRACE—This optional parameter writes SQL to a trace file that can be used to re-create the control files. Optionally you can specify the qualifiers RESETLOGS or NORESETLOGS, which will add additional SQL to open the database with these options. The SQL statements are complete enough to start the database, re-create the control files, and recover and open the database appropriately.

> **TIP**
>
> Any time you make changes to the structure of the database by adding datafiles, redo log files, and so on, run the command ALTER DATABASE *database* BACKUP CONTROLFILE TO TRACE. By doing this you will have a method of re-creating the control files if necessary. This will save you a lot of work if you have to recover the entire system.

The control files are an important part of your system, although they rarely require any maintenance. As long as you do a backup after you make any major changes, you should be in pretty good shape.

Rollback Segments

NEW TERM   *Rollback segments* record transactional information that will be used in the event that the transaction is rolled back. They also provide read consistency and are used for database recovery. Rollback segments keep the undo information that is used in rollback operations.

Remember, a transaction can be finished by issuing either a COMMIT or a ROLLBACK statement. These statements perform completely opposite operations. A commit operation finishes a transaction by finalizing all the changes that have been made. When the commit operation has finished, the changes cannot be undone. In the event of a system failure, all changes made in this transaction will be recovered. A rollback operation causes all the changes made during the transaction to be undone. When the rollback operation has finished, you must resubmit the transaction to reproduce the changes that were made. After a rollback, it is as if the transaction never occurred.

NEW TERM   *Read consistency* allows a long-running transaction to always obtain the same data within the query. During the transaction, the data is consistent to a single point in time and does not change. Even though the data might have been changed by another user and the DBWR might even have written it out, other transactions do not see those changes until a COMMIT has occurred. In fact, only transactions that start after this transaction has been committed see those changes.

8

Rollback segments can be either public or private. A private rollback segment can be used only by the instance that opened the database, and a public rollback segment can be used by any instance. If you are not running Oracle Parallel server, the private and public rollback segments are identical. Rollback segments must be carefully watched and can be tuned in several ways. It is important not only to size the rollback segments correctly but also to create the proper number of rollback segments and properly distribute them according to the number of user processes that require them.

Understanding How Rollback Segments Work

As a transaction is being processed, information relating to changes made to the datafiles by that transaction is constantly being written to the rollback segments. It is important that this information be saved because a rollback would require that all data be restored to its original condition.

The information written by the transaction to the rollback segments is held in *rollback entries*. Depending on the length of the transaction and the number of changes to data, there might be more than one rollback entry for each transaction. These entries are linked together so that they can easily be used in the event of a rollback.

This information stored in the rollback segments include block information about what blocks have been modified and the data as it was before the change occurred. Remember that the redo log also records information about changes in the database. The redo log, along with the rollback segments, can restore your data up to the point of failure.

Rollback segments are used concurrently by one or more transactions. You can tune the rollback segments to provide for optimal efficiency and space usage. Having more transactions sharing rollback segments causes more contention and uses space more efficiently. Having fewer transactions per rollback segment causes less contention and wastes more space.

NEW TERM
Oracle maintains what is called a *transaction table* for each rollback segment. The transaction table stores information about what transactions use that rollback segment and the rollback entries for each change done by those transactions.

Each time a new transaction begins, it is assigned to a rollback segment. This can happen in one of two ways:

- ☐ Automatically—Oracle automatically assigns the transaction a rollback segment. The assignment takes place when the first DDL or DML statement is issued. Queries are never assigned rollback segments.

- ☐ Manually—The application can manually specify a rollback segment by using the SET TRANSACTION command with the USE ROLLBACK SEGMENT parameter. This allows the developer to choose the correct size of rollback segment for a particular task. The rollback segment is assigned for the duration of the transaction.

At the end of each transaction, when the commit operation has occurred, the rollback information is released from the rollback segment but is not deleted so as to maintain read-consistent views for other queries that started before the transaction was committed. To retain this information as long as possible, the rollback segments are written as a circular buffer.

You can think of rollback segments as a sort of *circular buffer*. A rollback segment must have at least two extents (usually more). When a transaction fills up one extent, it starts using the next extent in sequence. When it gets to the last extent, the transaction continues with extent 1 again if it is available, as shown in Figure 8.6.

Figure 8.6.

A logical representation of a rollback segment.

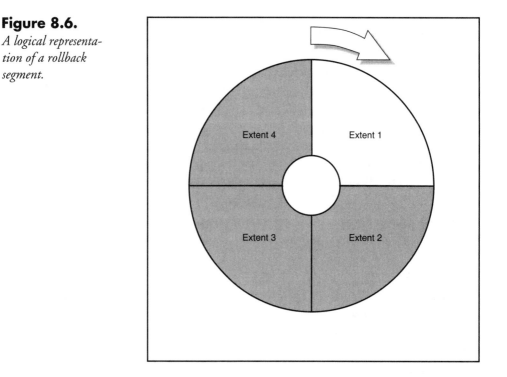

If the transaction uses the last extent in the segment, it looks to see whether the first extent is available. If it is not, another extent is created, as shown in Figures 8.7 and 8.8. The number of extents used for rollback segments is determined in the definitions of the rollback segments when you create them.

Figure 8.7.

A rollback segment with all extents used.

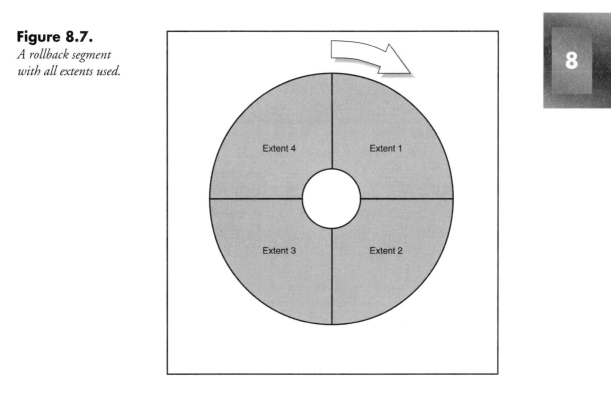

Figure 8.8.

A rollback segment showing dynamic growth.

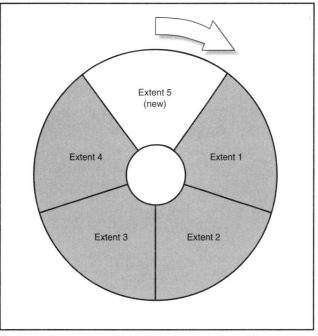

Creating Rollback Segments

Rollback segments are created graphically with Enterprise Manager or Storage Manager or on the command line with the CREATE ROLLBACK SEGMENT command. Although all three of these are functional, some have more functionality than others, as you will learn in the following sections.

Using the Enterprise Manager

To create a rollback segment with Enterprise Manager, drill down through the database that you will be operating on until you get to the Rollback Segment entry. When you right-click this icon you are given a list of options.

NOTE

> For this example I have chosen to display only the Navigator pane.

After you have selected Create from the options you will see the Create Rollback Segment screen. Type a name for the rollback segment and choose a tablespace in which you want to create the rollback segment.

TIP

> I have clicked the Show SQL button to display the SQL used to create the rollback segment.

If you click the Online button, the SQL statement will be altered to put the rollback segment online after it is created, as shown in Figure 8.9. As you can see, there are not a whole lot of options available when creating rollback segments with the Enterprise Manager. It is also possible to create rollback segments with the Storage Manager, which gives you more flexibility and options.

Using the Storage Manager

The left side of the Storage Manager is similar to the Enterprise Manager, as shown in Figure 8.10.

Click on the Rollback Segment icon, and the tree in the left side of the Storage Manager will expand to show the existing rollback segments. The right side of the Storage Manager shows the name, tablespace name, status, size, and high water mark of the rollback segments. (The *high water mark* indicates how much rollback data can be used in that extent before a new one is allocated.)

Figure 8.9.

Clicking the Online button puts the rollback segment online after you create it.

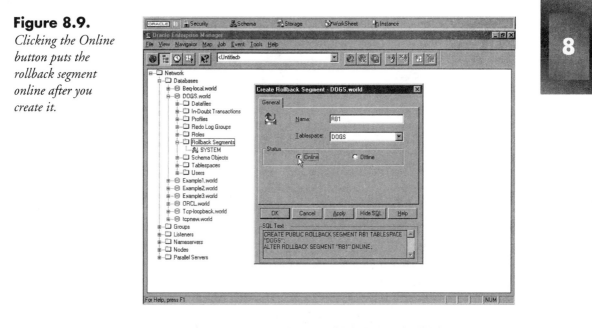

Figure 8.10.

The Storage Manager.

By right-clicking on the Rollback Segment icon you will see a menu that includes an option to create a rollback segment. By clicking the Create button you will see a screen that is identical to the Create Rollback Segment screen used by the Enterprise Manager. This is shown in Figure 8.11.

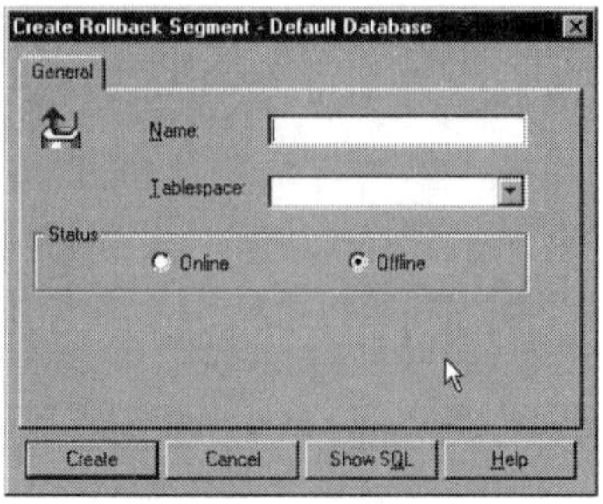

Figure 8.11.

*The Create Rollback
Segment dialog box in
the Storage Manager.*

As you can see, with both the Enterprise Manager and the Storage Manager, the options available when creating rollback segments are very limited. To create rollback segments with more options, use the CREATE ROLLBACK SEGMENT command.

Using the CREATE ROLLBACK SEGMENT Command

If you create a rollback segment with the CREATE ROLLBACK SEGMENT command, you have two advantages: the ability to create the rollback segments with more options and the advantage of using cut and paste in your editor to create multiple rollback segments. If you are adding 50 or 100 rollback segments, using Enterprise Manager and Schema Manager can become quite tedious. By using cut and paste in your editor and just changing the rollback segment name, you can more easily create a large number of rollback segments. An example of creating a rollback segment with the CREATE ROLLBACK SEGMENT command is shown here:

```
CREATE [ PUBLIC or PRIVATE ] ROLLBACK SEGMENT rsname
TABLESPACE tsname
STORAGE (
INITIAL number K or M
NEXT number K or M
OPTIMAL number K or M
MINEXTENTS number
MAXEXTENTS number
);
```

The parameters of CREATE PUBLIC ROLLBACK SEGMENT are as follows:

☐ *rsname*—The name of the rollback segment you are creating.

☐ TABLESPACE *tsname*—Specifies the name of the tablespace where that rollback segment will be created.

☐ INITIAL *number* K or M—The initial extent size in K (kilobytes) or M (megabytes).

☐ NEXT *number* K or M—The size of the second extent in K (kilobytes) or M (megabytes). With rollback segments, it is always a good idea to make all extents the same size because there is no distinction between different extents.

☐ OPTIMAL *number* K or M—Specifies the size that you would like the rollback segment to try to stay, in K (kilobytes) or M (megabytes). When extents are no longer needed, they are eliminated until this size is reached.

8

☐ MINEXTENTS *number*—The minimum number of extents. This is also the number allocated when the segment is created.

☐ MAXEXTENTS *number*—The maximum number of extents that can be dynamically allocated.

Initially, there are MINEXTENTS number of extents in the rollback segment. As extents fill up, they are used in a circular fashion, returning to the first extent when all others are filled. If a rollback segment has used all the space in all the extents and MAXEXTENTS has not been reached, another extent is created. If the size of the rollback segment is larger than OPTIMAL and there are unused extents, the unused extents are dropped from the rollback segment.

Both the creation and destruction of a rollback segment extents cause overhead in the system. In addition to the overhead created by the addition of extents to a rollback segment, the transaction needing to write into that rollback segment must wait for the extent to be created before it can continue. The following sections explain how to tune your rollback segments.

Tuning Rollback Segments

To properly configure a system's rollback segments, you must create enough rollback segments, and they must be of a sufficient size. That seems fairly simple, but it is not. You can observe how the rollback segments are being used, and from that determine what needs to be done.

Determining the Number of Rollback Segments

The number of rollback segments should be determined by the number of concurrent transactions in the database. Remember—the fewer transactions per rollback segment, the less contention. A good rule of thumb is to create about one rollback segment for every four concurrent transactions.

Rollback contention occurs when too many transactions try to use the same rollback segment at the same time, and some of them have to wait. You can tell whether you are seeing contention on rollback segments by looking at the dynamic performance table, V$WAITSTAT. Following is the data contained by V$WAITSTAT that is related to rollback segments:

☐ UNDO HEADER—The number of waits for buffers containing rollback header blocks.

☐ UNDO BLOCK—The number of waits for buffers containing rollback blocks other than header blocks.

☐ SYSTEM UNDO HEADER—Same as UNDO HEADER for the SYSTEM rollback segment.

☐ SYSTEM UNDO BLOCK—Same as UNDO BLOCK for the SYSTEM rollback segment.

The system rollback segment is the original rollback segment that was created when the database was created. This rollback segment is used primarily for special system functions but is sometimes used when no other rollback segment is available. Typically the SYSTEM rollback segment is not used, and you do not need to be concerned about it.

You can view these values with the SQL statement shown in Listing 8.1.

INPUT   **Listing 8.1. Rollback segment waits.**

```
SQL> SELECT class, count
  2  FROM V$WAITSTAT
  3  WHERE class IN
  4  ('undo header', 'undo block', 'system undo header', 'system undo block');
```

OUTPUT

```
CLASS                      COUNT
------------------ --------
system undo header             0
system undo block              0
undo header                    0
undo block                     0
```

Compare these values with the total number of requests for data. Remember (from earlier in the chapter) that the number of requests for data is equal to the sum of DB BUFFER GETS and CONSISTENT GETS from V$SYSSTAT. Also remember that you can extract that information with the query shown in Listing 8.2.

INPUT   **Listing 8.2. Total number of rollback requests.**

```
SQL> SELECT SUM(value) "Data Requests"
  2  FROM v$sysstat
  3  WHERE name IN ('db block gets', 'consistent gets');
```

OUTPUT

```
Data Requests
-----------
       5105
```

ANALYSIS   If the number of waits for any of the rollback segment blocks or headers exceeds more than 1% of the total number of requests, you should reduce the contention by adding more rollback segments.

In this example the total number of requests is 5,105, as shown in Listing 8.2, whereas the number of waits were all 0, as indicated in Listing 8.1. This indicates that there was no contention.

Determining the Size of Rollback Segments

The advantage of small rollback segments is that they tend to remain cached, but rollback segments that are too small will grow and shrink unnecessarily. Long-running transactions tend to like larger rollback segments because they usually generate more rollback information.

It is possible to create several different sizes of rollback segments. Each type of rollback segment should be used by the application developer based on the type and length of the transaction (see the following).

☐ OLTP—OLTP transactions are characterized by many concurrent transactions, each modifying perhaps only a small amount of data. These types of transactions benefit from a reduction of contention and quick access from cached rollback segments. Try to create many small rollback segments of perhaps 10KB to 20KB in size, each with 2 to 4 extents (optimally with a rollback segment available for each transaction).

☐ The small size of the rollback segments provides for a better chance of being cached in the SGA. There is probably very little dynamic growth of the extents.

☐ Long Queries—For long queries where read consistency calls for quite a bit of rollback information to be accessed, use a larger rollback segment. A good rule of thumb is to create rollback segments approximately 10% the size of the largest table (most SQL statements affect only about 10% of the data in a table).

☐ Large Updates—For transactions that update large amounts of data, you should also use a larger rollback segment. As is the case with the long queries, it is appropriate to create rollback segments approximately 10% the size of the largest table.

Determining the Size and Number of Extents

In general, the best performance of rollback I/O performance can be obtained when there are approximately 10 to 20 extents of equal size per rollback segment. To determine the size and number of extents, use the following formula:

Rollback segment size = Rsize = Size of largest table / 10
Number of extents = NE = 10
Size of extents = Esize = Rsize / NE

When creating the rollback segments, use the value of Esize for INITIAL and NEXT; use the value of NE for MINEXTENTS. Even when using these rules, you might not achieve the most effective size for your rollback segments. If dynamic growth is occurring, you might be losing performance.

Avoiding Dynamic Growth

As stated earlier, you want to avoid the dynamic space management that causes additional overhead and transactional delays. To determine whether rollback segments are a problem, look in the dynamic performance table, V$ROLLSTAT. The following columns are of particular interest:

☐ EXTENTS—Number of rollback extents.

☐ RSSIZE—The size (in bytes) of the rollback segment.

☐ OPTSIZE—The size to which OPTIMAL was set.

☐ AVEACTIVE—The current average size of active extents. *Active extents* are defined as extents with uncommitted transaction data.

☐ AVESHRINK—The total size of free extents divided by the number of *shrinks* (see the second item following).

☐ EXTENDS—The number of times the rollback segment added an extent.

☐ SHRINKS—The number of times the rollback segment shrank. Each shrink may be one or more extents at a time.

☐ HWMSIZE—The high water mark of rollback segment size. This is the largest that the segment size ever grew to be.

You can look at these statistics by using a SQL statement like the one shown in Listing 8.3.

INPUT | **Listing 8.3. Check statistics.**

```
SQL> SELECT substr(name,1,40), extents, rssize, aveactive,
➥aveshrink, extends, shrinks
  2  FROM v$rollname rn, v$rollstat rs
  3  WHERE rn.usn = rs.usn;
```

OUTPUT

SUBSTR(NAME,1,40)	EXTENTS	RSSIZE	AVEACTIVE	AVESHRINK	EXTENDS	SHRINKS
SYSTEM	4	202752	0	0	0	0
RB_TEMP	53	540672	23929	0	0	0
RB1	2	202752	0	0	0	0
RB2	2	202752	55193	0	0	0

If the average size is close to the size set for OPTIMAL, OPTIMAL is set correctly. If either extends or shrinks is high, you must increase the value for OPTIMAL.

Summary

You have now seen all the basic files that are used by Oracle. The Oracle instance is made up of the Oracle files, the processes, and the memory used by Oracle. The Oracle files are made up of the datafiles, the redo log files, the control files, and the parameter file. There are more files used in your day-to-day operations such as archive log files, export files, and so on, but they are not critical to the operation of the Oracle instance.

This chapter covers the redo log files, control files, and rollback segments. The redo log files are used to store system redo information, which is used to recover the database in the event of a catastrophic system failure. The redo log, in conjunction with the archive log files, enables Oracle to recover transactions that were committed before the failure.

The control file is used to keep internal Oracle control information. This file is used to tell Oracle where the data and redo log files are in the operating system. The control files are critical to the operation of the instance.

Finally, you learned about rollback segments. Rollback segments keep undo information that is used to roll back transactions and for read consistency. The rollback segments have a lot of tuning options, which you learned about in this chapter.

What's Next?

In tomorrow's lesson, "Managing Data," you will learn how to use several of the data-manipulation tools that come with your server: Export, Import, and the SQL*Loader. Export and Import are used to move data in and out of the database. The SQL*Loader utility is just used for loading data into the database.

Q&A

Q What files are used in the Oracle instance?

A There are several different files used in the Oracle instance. There are one or more datafiles, two or more redo log files, the control files, and the parameter file.

Q What Oracle object is used for recovery operations?

A The redo log files and the archive log files are used for database recovery.

Q What Oracle object is used for read consistency?

A The rollback segments are used for read consistency.

Q What is read consistency?

A Read consistency allows a long-running transaction to always obtain the same data within the query.

Workshop

The workshop provides quiz questions to help you solidify your understanding of the material covered and exercises to provide you with experience in using what you've learned. For answers to quiz questions, see Appendix A, "Answers."

Quiz

1. How many redo log files do you need?
2. What is a log group?
3. What is a control file used for?

4. Can you have more than one control file?

5. Can the instance be started without a control file?

6. What can you do to help re-create the control file?

7. Does a log switch force a checkpoint?

8. Does a checkpoint force a log switch?

9. What is a rollback segment used for?

10. How big is a rollback segment?

Exercises

1. Back up your control file to trace.

2. Use the Storage Manager to determine how much space your rollback segments use.

3. Add another control file to your system.

Week 2

Day 9

Managing Data

An important aspect of Oracle8 administration is getting data into and out of the database. There are several different ways of performing both of these tasks:

- [ ] Export—Put a database's content and structure into a binary export file. Export files can be read only by the Oracle Import utility.

- [ ] Import—Use data from an import file to re-create the database's content and structure.

- [ ] SQL*Loader—This is a very flexible tool that is used to load ASCII or *flat-file* data into an Oracle database. The SQL*Loader utility offers many options, as you will see later today.

- [ ] Backup/recovery—The backup and recovery features have their own way of loading and restoring data. Because this is covered on Days 17, "Recovering the Database," and 18, "Administering Oracle Replication," I do not go into it here.

Using Export and Import

 The Oracle Export utility is designed to write Oracle object definitions and data to an Oracle-specific binary file. This file is known as the *export file*. An export file is Oracle specific and can be read only by the Oracle Import utility, which you will learn about today. The Export utility can be used for several different purposes, including

- To back up the database—Export can be used to create a backup of the Oracle database, but is not the most efficient backup mechanism. Backup and recovery are covered on Days 16–18.
- To move data between databases—You can export data to an export file and then import this data back into a different database. This is a great way to transfer tables from one database to another.
- To rebuild a database—If you have a database whose tablespaces are fragmented, you can use Export and Import to defragment the database. This could improve performance if fragmentation is slowing you down.
- To reorganize a database—If you want to reorganize the locations of datafiles and so on, you can use Export and Import. In this manner, you can create new tablespaces and use Import to reload this data.

As you can see, there are several different reasons for using Export and Import.

Export

The Oracle Export utility provides a straightforward and simple service. Export writes object definitions and table data to an Oracle-format binary file. This information can be used to transfer data between databases on different machines or to supplement the normal backup process.

The export file first contains the object data followed by the related objects. For example, if tables have indexes on them, first the table data is written to the export file, then the object's indexes.

NOTE

> The binary files written by the Oracle Export utility can be read only by the Oracle Import utility. If you want to transfer data to another RDBMS or read it with another utility, do not use Export.

The export file is also used to reorganize data within the database. The normal backup process copies an image of the datafile; if recovery is needed, it can only write back the same image. Because Export organizes the data as it is written to the export file, importing that data does not necessarily place the data in the exact same place on disk. This provides a great advantage because it can reduce fragmentation and row chaining.

NOTE

Before you can run Export and Import, the administrative SQL script `CATEXP.SQL` must have been run once on the database. The administrative SQL script `CATALOG.SQL`, which is typically run at database-creation time, automatically runs `CATEXP.SQL`.

As with almost every Oracle utility, the export function can be accomplished graphically via Data Manager or by using the EXP80 program.

Export Using Data Manager

To perform an export graphically, you must first invoke Data Manager. For Data Manager to work, the Oracle agent and Enterprise Manager must be running.

NOTE

Data Manager must be run by a user with DBA privileges if a full export is to be performed.

1. When you invoke Data Manager, you will see the initial screen (shown in Figure 9.1).

Figure 9.1.
Data Manager.

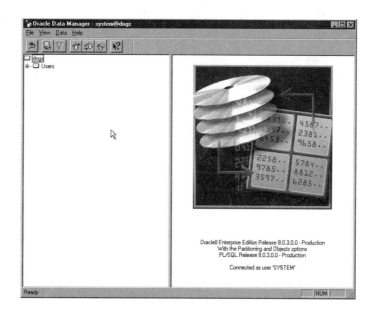

2. From Data Manager, you can invoke the export operation by selecting Data | Export. This invokes the Data Manager Export wizard. This wizard asks a number of questions concerning the export operation. As shown in Figure 9.2, the first screen involves the location of the export file.

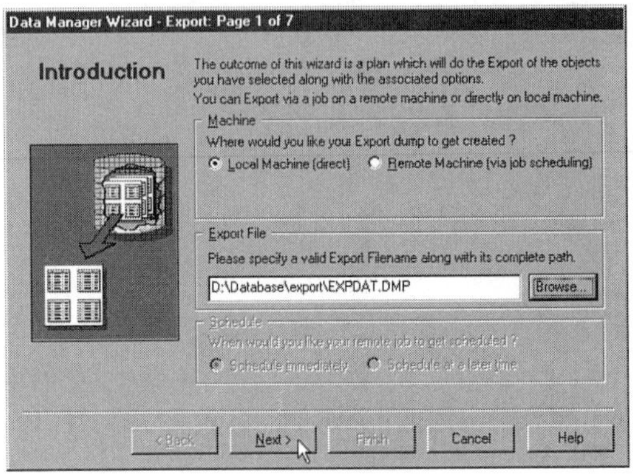

Figure 9.2.

Screen one of the Data Manager Export wizard.

TIP | Instead of creating the export file in the default directory, I prefer to create a directory specifically for export files. You can easily change the location where the export file will be created in the Data Manager.

3. Screen two of the Data Manager Export wizard lets you choose the objects to be exported. By default, the entire database is selected, as shown in Figure 9.3.

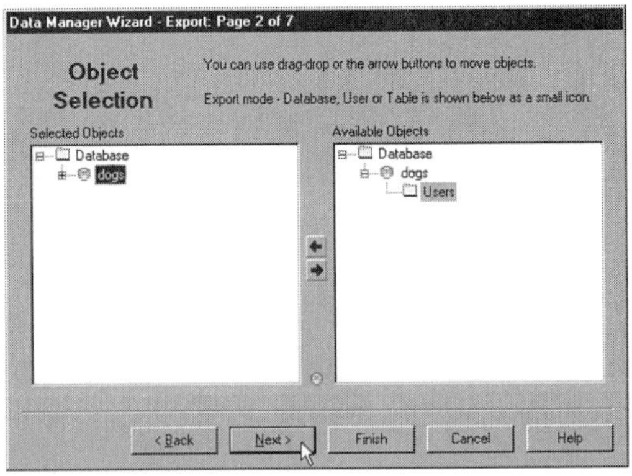

Figure 9.3.

Screen two of the Data Manager Export wizard.

4. In screen three, you can select the objects you want to export, including grants, indexes, table rows, and constraints. To perform an export in full mode, leave all of the boxes checked. At this point you can also choose the Direct Export option, which is not the default.

5. Screen four allows you to select the record length (this is necessary if you are transferring an export file to another OS), buffer size, and log file. I find that the default settings are usually sufficient.

6. Screen five allows you to select whether you are performing a complete or incremental export. Statistics modes are also selected here. These indicate whether estimated or calculated statistics will be gathered for the optimizer when this data is imported. Finally, you can configure the consistency mode and the extent merging options here. This screen is shown in Figure 9.4.

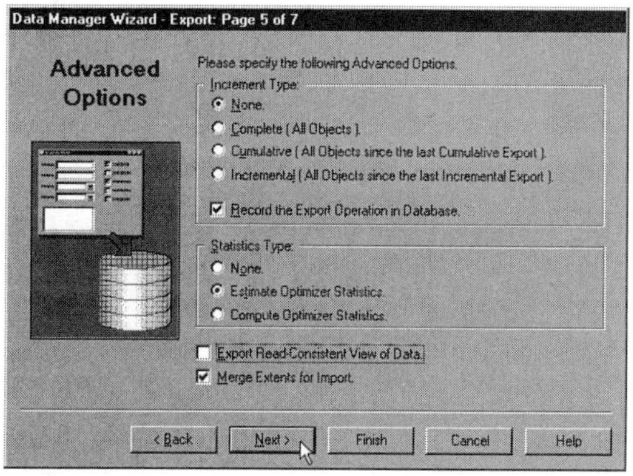

Figure 9.4.

Screen five of the Data Manager Export wizard.

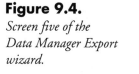

7. Screen seven summarizes the export actions that will be taken when the Finish button is clicked, as shown in Figure 9.5.

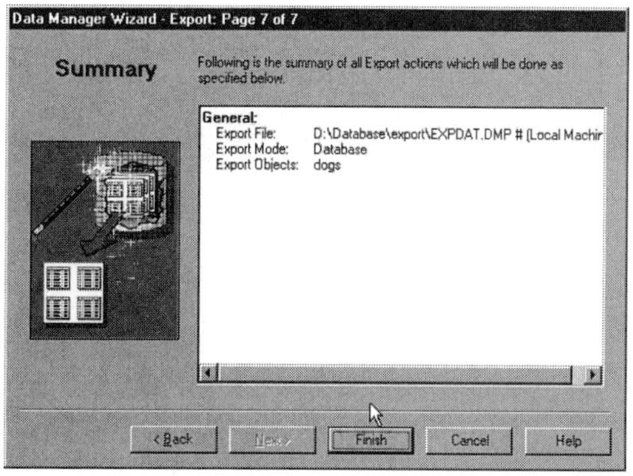

Figure 9.5.

Screen seven of the Data Manager Export wizard.

8. If you selected to schedule the export rather than perform this operation immediately, you are presented with screen six, which is shown in Figure 9.6. If you did not select the schedule option, the Data Manager Export wizard jumps from screen five to screen seven.

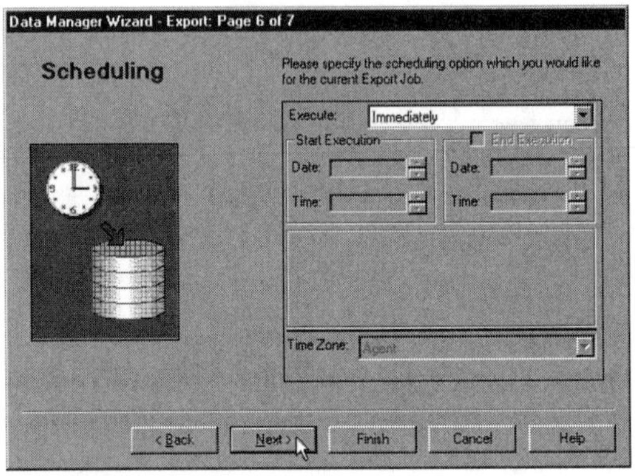

Figure 9.6.

Screen six of the Data Manager Export wizard.

9. The status of the export is displayed in the Export Status screen. Errors and successful completion messages are displayed here.

Export Using the EXP80 Utility

Exports can be performed via the graphical utilities, as well as with a command-line option. When you run the Export utility via the NT command prompt, a program called EXP80 is run.

> **NOTE**
>
> Under Windows NT, the export program is called EXP80. Under other operating systems, it may be known simply as EXP.

Export has several options and modes of operation:

☐ Full—Operating Export in full mode causes all database objects not in the SYS schema to be exported. Because the SYS schema and schema objects are created at database-creation time, the SYS schema and schema objects are excluded.

> **NOTE**
>
> That the SYS schema objects are not exported in the full mode is another good reason not to create objects under the SYS schema.

☐ Table—Operating Export in table mode allows you to specify which schema objects to export.

☐ User—Operating Export in user mode exports all objects belonging to the specified user. These objects include tables, data, grants, and indexes.

Export can also be used to export partitions in a partitioned table. This is accomplished by exporting in table mode and specifying the table partition.

Using Export

Export is invoked from the command line and supports a variety of options. Because of the importance of the Export and Import commands, these options are described here. For more detailed information, refer to the Oracle8 documentation.

The Syntax for Export

Export is invoked with the following syntax:

```
EXP80 username/password [ options ... ]
```

To simplify the usage of Export and to allow for the standard use of options, you can use a parameter file and store the export parameters. I recommend this for consistency, reusability, and error reduction. To invoke Export with the parameter file, use this syntax:

```
EXP80 username/password  PARFILE=filename [ options ... ]
```

If you use the parameter file, it is not necessary to use command-line options, but you can if you want. The parameter file contains a list of parameters, one per line. An example of a parameter file is included at the end of this section. The available Export parameters use the following format:

```
PARAMETER=value
```

The Export parameters are

☐ BUFFER=number—This parameter specifies the size of the copy buffer (in bytes) used by Export. If this is zero, one row at a time will be fetched.

☐ COMPRESS=[Y or N]—This parameter specifies how the initial extent is treated. If this parameter is set to Y, Export consolidates all table data into one extent. If this parameter is set to N, Export uses the current storage parameters to create the extents. The default is Y.

☐ CONSISTENT=[Y or N]—This parameter specifies whether the export will be performed in a manner that causes data to be consistent to a single point in time. A value of Y causes the export to be consistent but can consume significant rollback space and can fail if there is significant update activity. The default is N.

☐ CONSTRAINTS=[Y or N]—This parameter specifies whether to export table constraints. The default is Y.

☐ DIRECT=[Y or N]—This parameter specifies whether the direct path export option is used, thus bypassing the SQL command-processing layer. Direct path export cannot be used on some schema objects. The default is N.

☐ FEEDBACK=*number*—This parameter specifies that a dot be displayed for every *number* exported rows. For example, if FEEDBACK=100, you see a dot for every 100 exported rows to indicate the progress of the export operation. The default is 0.

☐ FILE=*filename*—This parameter specifies the name of the export file. The default is EXPDAT.DMP.

☐ FULL=[Y or N]—This parameter specifies whether a full database export is performed. Specifying FULL=Y exports in full mode. The default is N.

☐ GRANTS=[Y or N]—This parameter specifies that grants are exported. The default is Y.

☐ HELP=[Y or N]—If this parameter is set to Y, a list of export parameters is displayed. The default is N.

☐ INCTYPE=*type*—This parameter specifies an incremental export. The values available are COMPLETE, CUMULATIVE, and INCREMENTAL.

    ☐ INCTYPE=COMPLETE—This parameter serves as the baseline for CUMULATIVE and INCREMENTAL exports. It is the same as FULL=Y with additional information updated for incremental exports.

    ☐ INCTYPE=CUMULATIVE—This parameter exports tables that have changed since the last COMPLETE or CUMULATIVE export.

    ☐ INCTYPE=INCREMENTAL—This parameter exports tables that have changed since the last COMPLETE, CUMULATIVE, or INCREMENTAL export.

☐ INDEXES=[Y or N]—This parameter specifies that indexes should be exported. The default is Y.

☐ LOG=*logfile*—This parameter specifies the name of a log file in which to write error and status messages. Even when this parameter is set, messages are still displayed on the screen.

☐ OWNER=*owner_name(s)*—This parameter specifies a list of users whose objects will be exported in user mode.

☐ PARFILE=*param_file*—This parameter specifies the parameter filename.

☐ POINT_IN_TIME_RECOVER=[Y or N]—This parameter specifies whether a point-in-time recovery will be performed on import.

☐ RECORD=[Y or N]—This flag specifies that the system tables SYS.INCVID, SYS.INCFIL, and SYS.INCEXP record a cumulative or incremental export. The default is Y.

- [ ] RECORDLENGTH=*number*—This parameter specifies the size in bytes of the file record. This is used if you are going to transfer the export file to another operating system.
- [ ] RECOVERY_TABLESPACE=*ts_name*—This parameter specifies the names of the tablespaces to be used in the point-in-time recovery.
- [ ] ROWS=[Y or N]—This parameter specifies that the rows of table data should be exported. The default is Y.
- [ ] STATISTICS=*type*—Available values are ESTIMATE, COMPUTE, and NONE. The default is ESTIMATE.
  - [ ] STATISTICS=ESTIMATE—This parameter specifies that statistics are generated on the tables using the ESTIMATE method when the data is imported.
  - [ ] STATISTICS=COMPUTE—This parameter specifies that statistics are generated on the tables using the COMPUTE method when the data is imported.
  - [ ] STATISTICS=NONE—This parameter specifies that statistics are not generated on the tables when the data is imported.
- [ ] TABLES=*tables*—This parameter specifies a list of tables to export when using Export in table mode.
- [ ] USERID=*username/password*—This parameter specifies the username and password of the Oracle user performing the export.

Here is an example of a parameter file:

```
FULL=Y
BUFFER=8192
FILE=D:\database\export\EXPDAT.DMP
STATISTICS=COMPUTE
```

If no parameters are specified, the Export utility prompts you for values. Most prompted items come with a default value. An example of using Export interactively is shown in Listing 9.1.

Listing 9.1. Example of EXP80.

```
D:\>exp80

Export: Release 8.0.2.0.2 - Beta on Thu Jul 17 18:15:20 1997

Copyright (c) Oracle Corporation 1979, 1994, 1996.  All rights reserved.


Username: internal
Password:

Connected to: Oracle8 Server Release 8.0.2.0.2 - Beta
With the distributed, heterogeneous, replication, objects
```

continues

Listing 9.1. continued

```
and parallel query options
PL/SQL Release 3.0.2.0.2 - Beta
Enter array fetch buffer size: 4096 >

Export file: EXPDAT.DMP >

(2)U(sers), or (3)T(ables): (2)U >

Export grants (yes/no): yes >

Export table data (yes/no): yes >

Compress extents (yes/no): yes >
```

Both methods export the data in the same way. There exists the possibility of certain error conditions that may or may not cause Export to fail. These error conditions are described in the Oracle documentation.

Import

The Oracle Import utility has one function: to load data that has been exported into an Oracle database. The Import utility can read only exported data. If you want to load other data into an Oracle database, you must use another utility such as SQL*Loader, which is discussed later today.

As described earlier today, Export and Import can be used for several different functions:

☐ For backup/recovery—Backup and recovery are covered on Days 16–18.

☐ To move data between databases on different systems.

☐ To rebuild a database—This is useful to eliminate fragmentation and chained rows.

☐ To reorganize a database—If you want to reorganize the locations of datafiles and so on, you can use Export and Import.

There are several different reasons for using Export and Import. As with the Export utility, imports can be performed via Data Manager or via a command-line program.

Import Using Data Manager

Data Manager can be used to export, import, or load data. The import operation is much less complicated than the export operation because the export file contains information about the options used during the export process.

1. To invoke the import operation, select Data | Import in Data Manager. The initial screen in the Data Manager Import wizard allows you to select the export file from which you want to import. This filename can be typed, or it can be selected via the Browse function (see Figure 9.7).

Figure 9.7.

Screen one of the Data Manager Import wizard.

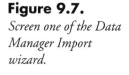

2. Select the objects to be imported in screen two. By default, no objects are selected. You must select at least one object for the import to work. This is shown in Figure 9.8.

Figure 9.8.

Screen two of the Data Manager Import wizard.

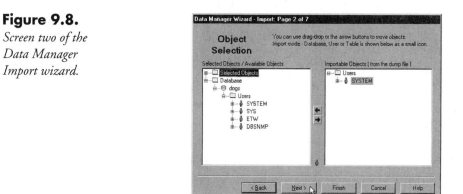

3. In screen three, the objects that were exported are selected. If you do not want to import a schema object (such as grants and the like), it can be deselected at this point.

4. Screen four allows you to select the record length (this is necessary if you are importing an export file from another OS), buffer size, and log file. I find that the default settings are usually sufficient.

5. Screen five contains advanced options such as the import type and whether to import all data or only recent data. From this screen you can also write index-creation commands to a file to allow you to re-create the indexes rather than import them. You'll also find the Commit after each array insert and the Overwrite existing data files checkboxes here. This screen is shown in Figure 9.9.

Figure 9.9.

Screen five of the Data Manager Import wizard.

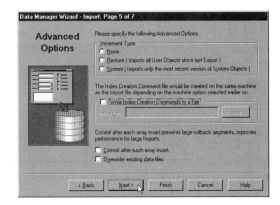

6. As with the Export wizard, the final screen shows a list of the selected items for final approval before the import operation proceeds. Screen six is displayed only if you have chosen to schedule the import operation to occur at a later time.

7. Like the Export utility, the Import utility shows a status screen and logs status information to a log file. For example, Figure 9.10 contains numerous error messages, which are due to the fact that I tried to import data over existing tables and did not select to overwrite existing data in screen five. This offers you some protection from accidentally destroying your own data by unintentionally overwriting good data.

Figure 9.10.

The Data Manager Import wizard's Import Status screen.

Import Using the IMP80 Utility

As with the Export utility, the Import utility features a command-line utility for performing imports. The Import utility's command-line utility is called IMP80 under Windows NT. Under certain other operating systems, it is known simply as IMP.

IMP80 supports a variety of options, many very similar to the export options. Because of the importance of the Export and Import commands, these options are described here. For more detailed information, refer to the Oracle8 documentation.

The Syntax for Import

Import is invoked with the following syntax:

```
IMP80 username/password [ options ... ]
```

As with Export, you can store the Import parameters in a parameter file in Import. I recommend this for consistency, reusability, and error reduction. To invoke Import with the parameter file, use this syntax:

```
IMP80 username/password  PARFILE=filename [ options ... ]
```

If you use the parameter file, it is not necessary to use command-line options, but you can if you want. The parameter file contains a list of parameters, one per line. An example of a parameter file is included at the end of this section. The available Import parameters use the following format:

```
PARAMETER=value
```

The Import parameters are

- [ ] ANALYZE=[Y or N]—This parameter specifies that the SQL ANALYZE command be run. The default is Y.

- [ ] BUFFER=number—This parameter specifies the size of the copy buffer (in bytes) used by Import. If this is zero, one row at a time will be fetched.

- [ ] CHARSET=character_set—This parameter specifies the character set used for the export if it was an Oracle6 export. From Oracle7 forward, the character-set information is written to the export file. Import will use this value to verify that the export file was written with this character set. It is usually not necessary to use this option.

- [ ] COMMIT=[Y or N]—This parameter specifies that a commit should occur after each array insert. By default, the commit occurs after each table is imported. The default is N.

- [ ] DESTROY=[Y or N]—This parameter specifies that the original datafiles should be reused. This essentially adds the reuse option to the CREATE TABLESPACE operation. The default is N.

- [ ] FEEDBACK=number—This parameter specifies that a dot be displayed for every number of imported rows. For example, if FEEDBACK=100, you will see a dot for every 100 rows, indicating the progress of the import operation. The default is 0.

- [ ] FILE=filename—This parameter specifies the name of the export file. The default is EXPDAT.DMP.

- [ ] FROMUSER=username—This parameter specifies a schema to import the data for. If no schema is identified, the entire export file will be imported.

☐ FULL=[Y or N]—This parameter specifies whether a full database import is performed. Specifying FULL=Y imports in full mode. The default is N.

☐ GRANTS=[Y or N]—This parameter specifies that grants should be exported. The default is Y.

☐ HELP=[Y or N]—If this parameter is set to Y, a list of Export parameters will be displayed. The default is N.

☐ IGNORE=[Y or N]—This parameter describes how the system will operate if table-creation errors occur. If IGNORE=Y, the import will continue without reporting an error if an error occurs. If IGNORE=N, an error will be reported before the import continues. The default is N.

☐ INCTYPE=type—This parameter specifies the type of import. Available options are SYSTEM and RESTORE.

    ☐ INCTYPE=SYSTEM—This parameter restores the most recent copy of the SYSTEM objects.

    ☐ INCTYPE=RESTORE—This parameter restores all user and database objects that are in the export file.

☐ INDEXES=[Y or N]—This parameter specifies that indexes should be imported. The default is Y.

☐ INDEXFILE=filename—This parameter specifies that index-creation syntax should be written to filename. This allows you to easily re-create the indexes rather than restore them.

☐ LOG=logfile—This parameter specifies the name of a log file in which to write error and status messages. Even with this parameter set, messages are still displayed on the screen.

☐ PARFILE=param_file—This parameter specifies the parameter filename.

☐ POINT_IN_TIME_RECOVER=[Y or N]—This parameter specifies that you want to recover to a particular point in time. The default is N.

☐ RECORDLENGTH=number—This parameter specifies the size in bytes of the file record.

☐ ROWS=[Y or N]—This parameter specifies that the rows of table data should be exported. The default is Y.

☐ SHOW=[Y or N]—This parameter specifies that the contents of the export file are displayed on the screen rather than imported into the database. This can be useful in debugging situations. The default is N.

☐ SKIP_UNUSABLE_INDEXES=[Y or N]—If set to Y, this parameter specifies that unusable indexes are not immediately rebuilt, thus allowing you to rebuild them after the import has completed. The default is N.

□ TABLES=*tables*—This parameter specifies a list of tables to import when using Import in table mode.

□ TOUSER=*username*—This parameter specifies a list of users whose schema will be used on the import. If you want to import one schema's data to another schema, use FROMUSER and TOUSER.

□ USERID=*username/passwd*—This parameter specifies the username and password of the Oracle user performing the export.

Here is an example of a parameter file:

```
FULL=Y
BUFFER=8192
FILE=D:\database\export\EXPDAT.DMP
STATISTICS=ESTIMATE
```

If no parameters are specified, the Import utility will prompt you for values. Most prompted items come with a default value. An example of using Import interactively is shown in Listing 9.2.

Listing 9.2. Example of IMP80.

```
D:\>imp80

Import: Release 8.0.3.0.0 - Production on Sat Jul 19 12:24:53 1997

(c) Copyright 1997 Oracle Corporation.  All rights reserved.

Username: system
Password:

Connected to: Oracle8 Enterprise Edition Release 8.0.3.0.0 - Production
With the Partitioning and Objects options
PL/SQL Release 8.0.3.0.0 - Production

Import file: EXPDAT.DMP > d:\database\export\EXPDAT.DMP

Enter insert buffer size (minimum is 4096) 30720>

Export file created by EXPORT:V08.00.03 via conventional path
List contents of import file only (yes/no): no >

Ignore create error due to object existence (yes/no): no >

Import grants (yes/no): yes >

Import table data (yes/no): yes >

Import entire export file (yes/no): no >
Username: ETW

Enter table(T) or partition(T:P) names. Null list means all tables for user
Enter table(T) or partition(T:P) name or . if done:
```

Whether you use Import via Data Manager or with the IMP80 utility, the outcome will be the same. As mentioned earlier, Import can be used only with data generated from Export. If you want to load ASCII data or other data into a database, you must use the SQL*Loader utility.

Using SQL*Loader

SQL*Loader is another Oracle utility that is used for loading data into an Oracle database. Where the Import utility is designed to accept data in a specific format, SQL*Loader is designed to be flexible and to accept data in a variety of formats.

SQL*Loader accepts two input file types: the actual input datafile and a loader control file. The control file is used to specify the format of the datafile(s). The control file is also used to specify such things as the column data types, field delimiters, and various other data-specific information.

Like Export and Import, SQL*Loader can be invoked from within Data Manager or from the command line. Regardless of which method you use, you are still required to specify a control file.

The Control File

The control file is used to specify information about the data to be loaded. The format of the control file contains control information and can also contain the data itself.

The control file can contain multiple lines for each statement and is not case sensitive except for characters within single or double quotes. The control file can also include comments that are indicated by double hyphens (- -).

The control file has more than 90 keywords that can be used to specify the format of the data and how it is to be loaded. Because of the large number of options, I cover only the key topics here. The entire list of keywords can be found in the Oracle documentation.

The basics of the control file involve control statements that tell SQL*Loader the following:

- ☐ What operation to perform
- ☐ Where to find the input datafile
- ☐ Where to load the data to
- ☐ The format of the data

The data can be of fixed length or delimited.

Fixed Record Format

When loading data that has a fixed record format (each field is the same length), you must specify the length of the fields in the control file. Here is an example of a fixed record control file:

```
LOAD DATA
INFILE 'D:\database\load\dogs.dat'
INTO TABLE "ETW".dogs2 (
Id    POSITION(01:02) INTEGER EXTERNAL,
Name  POSITION(05:08) CHAR,
OWNER_ID    POSITION(11:11) INTEGER EXTERNAL,
BREED_ID    POSITION(13:13) INTEGER EXTERNAL,
RANK    POSITION(15:16) INTEGER EXTERNAL,
NOTES    POSITION(18:20) CHAR)
```

The various components consist of

- ☐ A load directive
- ☐ The input file specification
- ☐ A table definition
- ☐ A data format definition

This is enough information to define the load operation.

Variable Record Format

To load a variable record format datafile (all columns are not the same size), you must specify a column delimiter. This column delimiter indicates to SQL*Loader where one column finishes and another picks up. Here is an example of a variable record control file:

```
LOAD DATA
INFILE 'D:\database\load\dogs2.dat'
INTO TABLE "ETW".dogs2
FIELDS TERMINATED BY "," OPTIONALLY ENCLOSED BY '"'
(id, name CHAR, owner_id, breed_id, rank, notes CHAR)
```

The various components consist of

- ☐ A load directive
- ☐ The input file specification
- ☐ A table definition
- ☐ A data format definition

This provides SQL*Loader with enough information to load the data. There are a few more optional parameters, which you will see next.

Optional Parameters in the Control File

There are numerous options available to SQL*Loader via the control file or at the command line. Here are some useful options available to the loader:

- ☐ BAD=*filename*—The bad file filename. This is where bad data is logged.
- ☐ CONTROL=*filename*—The name of the control file.
- ☐ DATA=*filename*—The name of the input datafile.
- ☐ DIRECT=(TRUE or FALSE)—This specifies whether the direct path loader is used. The direct path loader is described in the next section.
- ☐ PARALLEL=(TRUE or FALSE)—This specifies a parallel load.
- ☐ LOAD=*n*—The number of records to load. The default is all.
- ☐ LOG=*filename*—The log file filename.
- ☐ ROWS=*n*—The number of rows in each array insert.
- ☐ SKIP=*n*—The number of logical records to skip.
- ☐ UNRECOVERABLE=(TRUE or FALSE)—Available only with the direct path load. This parameter specifies that the load data operation does not log to the redo log files. This makes the loading operation faster but data cannot be recovered if the load fails.

Using the Direct Path Loader

The conventional loading technique uses SQL INSERT statements to load the data into the database. Each insert goes through all the logic and steps performed in a standard INSERT statement. To improve performance, another option is available: the direct path loader.

When you use the direct path loader, data is inserted directly into the datafiles, thus bypassing much of the logic involved in the conventional path load. The direct path loader is faster and more efficient, but there are a few restrictions on it:

- ☐ You cannot direct path load a clustered table.
- ☐ You cannot direct path load a table when active transactions are pending.

The advantages of using the direct path loader include the capacity to bypass many of the steps taken by the conventional loader and the capability to load in parallel. Another advantage is the capability to use the UNRECOVERABLE option.

With the UNRECOVERABLE option set, the load is not logged; thus, performance is enhanced. Nonetheless, there is an inherent danger in using the UNRECOVERABLE option: Because it is not logged, it is unrecoverable. Be sure to perform a backup soon after using the UNRECOVERABLE option.

Loading Using Data Manager

To use the loader from Data Manager, select Data | Load. This invokes the Data Manager Load wizard. The first screen, shown in Figure 9.11, prompts you to select a control file, and you cannot proceed until you do so. Either type the name of the control file or use the Browse function.

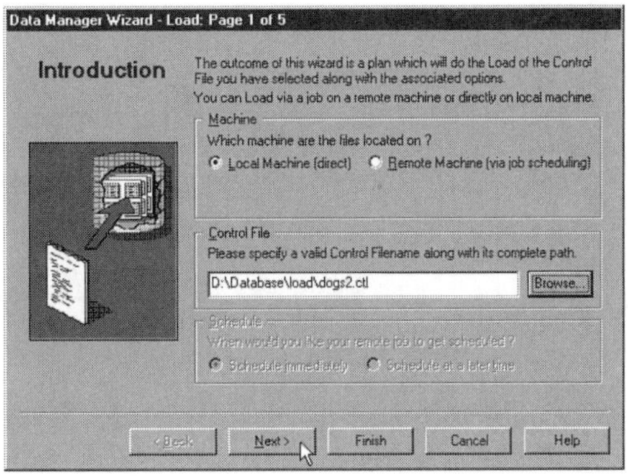

Figure 9.11.

Screen one of the Data Manager Load wizard.

After you select the control file, proceed to screen two (shown in Figure 9.12). Here you can fill out the following file descriptors:

☐ Data File—Enter the name of the datafile.

☐ Log File—Specify where the logging information is to be stored.

☐ Bad File—Specify where records that have errors should be stored.

☐ Discard File—Specify where rejected and uninserted records should be stored.

☐ Parallel File—Specify whether direct loads can perform concurrent sessions.

These files will be used in the load if not already specified in the control file.

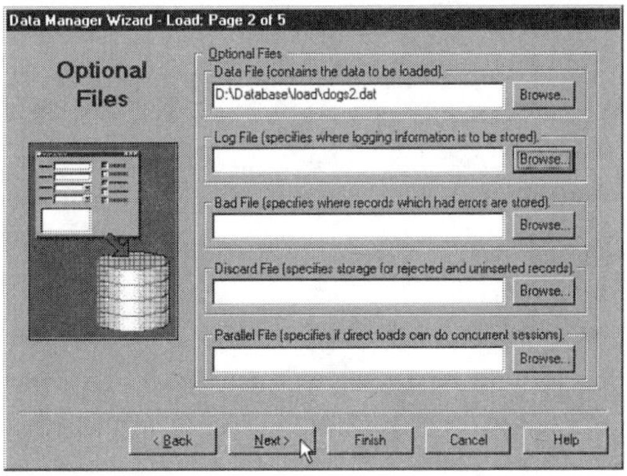

Figure 9.12.

Screen two of the Data Manager Load wizard.

Screen three, shown in Figure 9.13, allows you to select advanced options such as direct path loading, skipped records, records to load, and so on.

Figure 9.13.

Screen three of the Data Manager Load wizard.

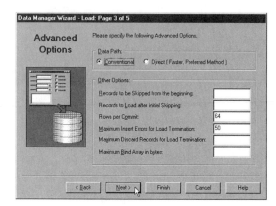

After you select from these options, you jump to screen five, the summary page, which allows you to review your selections before you proceed. Screen four is displayed only if you have chosen to schedule the load.

The Data Manager wizard makes it quite convenient to perform operations such as exports, imports, and loads. But as with the other utilities, SQL*Loader can also be run from the command line, as shown in the next section.

Loading Using the SQLLDR80 Utility

Invoke SQL*Loader on the command line by using the program SQLLDR80. This is the Windows NT filename; under other operating systems, it may be known simply as SQLLDR. All the options mentioned in the section about control files are available to SQL*Loader from the command line.

Because most of the options can be placed in the control file, only a few command-line options are necessary:

☐ USERNAME=*username*/*password*—This parameter specifies the username under which to run the loader.

☐ PARFILE=*parameter_file*—This parameter optionally specifies the name of a parameter file that contains additional parameters.

☐ BAD=*filename*—This parameter specifies the bad file filename. This is where bad data is logged.

9

- ☐ CONTROL=*filename*—This parameter specifies the name of the control file.
- ☐ DATA=*filename*—This parameter specifies the name of the input datafile.
- ☐ DIRECT=(TRUE or FALSE)—This parameter specifies whether the direct path loader is used.
- ☐ PARALLEL=(TRUE or FALSE)—This parameter specifies whether a parallel load can occur.
- ☐ LOAD=*n*—This parameter specifies the number of records to load. The default is all.
- ☐ LOG=*filename*—This parameter specifies the log file filename.
- ☐ ROWS=*n*—This parameter specifies the number of rows in each array insert.
- ☐ SKIP=*n*—This parameter specifies the number of logical records to skip.

These parameters are also available for use in the control file. If you are specifying multiple parameters and running the loader frequently, I recommend putting the parameters in the control file or in a parameter file.

Summary

Today you learned the various methods for moving data in and out of the Oracle database. The utilities described here are very useful and are frequently used.

I have included the Export and Import utilities here rather than in the backup and recovery lessons because they have significantly more uses than just for backup and recovery. The Export and Import utilities can be used to move data between systems or to help reorganize a database, whereas the backup and recovery process has only one use.

SQL*Loader can be used to load both fixed and variable length records into the database. You saw both methods today.

Both a graphical and a command-line option are available with all these utilities. The graphical option is available through the Enterprise Manager's Data Manager utility. Command-line options are available through various utilities.

What's Next?

On Day 10, "Administering User Accounts," you will learn how to administer user accounts in the Oracle RDBMS. You will see how users are defined and modified, as well as profiles and roles. Administering user accounts is probably the most common job of the Oracle DBA because new users are constantly being added or modified. You will learn tomorrow how this task is simplified by using roles and profiles.

Q&A

Q Why would I use the Export/Import utilities?

A The Export/Import utilities can be used for several purposes, including backups, movement of data between systems, database rebuilds, and database reorganization.

Q How is the loader different from Import?

A SQL*Loader is designed to load formatted datafiles of various formats, whereas the Import utility can only load export files.

Q What kind of data can be loaded with SQL*Loader?

A Any data can be loaded with SQL*Loader.

Q What is the difference between the conventional path loader and the direct path loader?

A The conventional path loader essentially loads the data by using INSERT statements, whereas the direct path loader bypasses much of the logic involved with that and loads directly into the datafiles.

Workshop

The workshop provides quiz questions to help you solidify your understanding of the material covered and exercises to provide you with experience in using what you've learned. Find answers to the quiz questions in Appendix A, "Answers."

Quiz

1. What is Export used for?
2. What is Import used for?
3. What is SQL*Loader used for?
4. What Oracle utilities can be used to load export files?
5. Name two uses of Export/Import.
6. What is the name of the Windows NT version of the Export utility?
7. What is the name of the Windows NT version of the Import utility?
8. What is the name of the Windows NT version of SQL*Loader?
9. What is the different between a fixed and a variable record load file?
10. What is the parameter file?

Exercises

1. Perform an export using Data Manager.
2. Perform an export using the EXP80 utility.
3. Import the data using Data Manager.
4. Import the data using the IMP80 utility.
5. Load a small dummy table using the load option in Data Manager.

9

Day 10

Administering User Accounts

Today you will learn how to administer user accounts in the Oracle RDBMS. You will see how user accounts, profiles, and roles are defined and modified. Administering user accounts is probably the most common job of the Oracle DBA because new user accounts are constantly being added or modified. You will see in this lesson how this task is simplified by using roles and profiles.

Oracle security is administered differently depending on what resource is needed. Access to the database is allowed or disallowed based on a user ID. This user ID has permissions associated with it. These permissions can be assigned either individually or via a role or profile.

NEW TERM Roles and profiles each control a different type of resource. A *role* is used to assign privileges that allow the user to access different objects and operations; a *profile* is used to control the amount of system resources that the user is allowed to consume.

A user can be assigned both a role and a profile as necessary. You will learn more about roles and profiles as the lesson continues.

Creating User Accounts

You can create user accounts with Enterprise Manager, Security Manager, or the `CREATE USER` command. You will essentially be doing the same job no matter which of these tools you use. I present all three of these methods in the following sections.

NOTE

> You must have the `CREATE USER` system privilege to create a new user.

Creating User Accounts with Enterprise Manager

To create user accounts with Enterprise Manager, go into Enterprise Manager and drill down into the database where you want to add a user or users. Below the Databases entry you will see a number of different symbols representing different objects. By right-clicking the Users entry, you will be presented with a menu. From this menu, click the Create button to invoke the Create User screen, shown in Figure 10.1.

Figure 10.1.
The Create User screen.

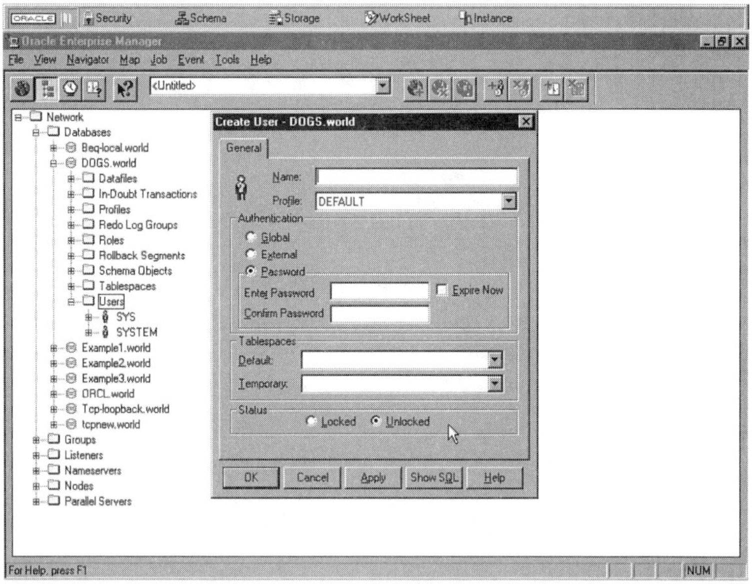

In this screen you need to fill out the username, the profile (if you aren't using `DEFAULT`), authentication information such as where the password is taken from and what that password is, and the default and temporary tablespaces that this user will use. You also need to specify whether the user account will be locked or unlocked when created. As always, I have clicked the Show SQL button to display the SQL statement that will create this user. A filled-in Create User screen is shown in Figure 10.2. As you can see, I've identified this user's name, profile (if not DEFAULT), default tablespace, and temporary space. I've also given this user an initial password for security.

Figure 10.2.

The Create User screen.

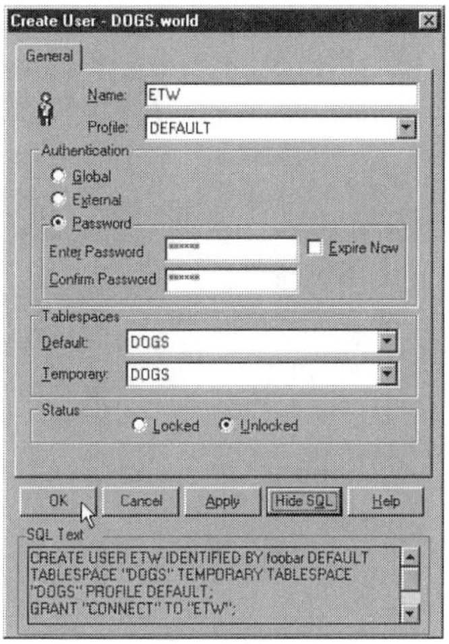

If you want to create a user account that is identical to another user account already defined in the system, you can right-click the user account you will be utilizing as a template and select the Create Like button.

This will again invoke the Create User screen, this time with the values used by the selected user SYS2 already in place, as shown in Figure 10.3.

Figure 10.3.

The Create User screen with the values of user SYS2 already in place.

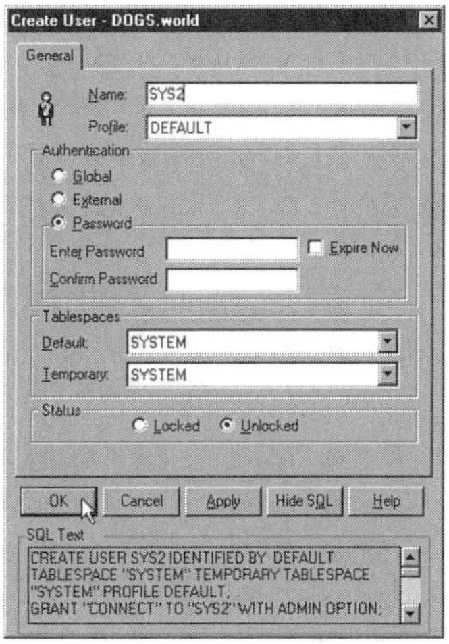

With this function, you can essentially clone user accounts to a new username. If you are adding a large number of user accounts that all require the same profile and tablespaces, this can be a real timesaver. It is also possible to add user accounts with Security Manager.

Creating User Accounts with Security Manager

As with Enterprise Manager, you can create user accounts with Security Manager. When you invoke Security Manager and click the Users icon, you will see the already-created user accounts on the left side of the screen and a wealth of information about the user accounts on the right side, as shown in Figure 10.4.

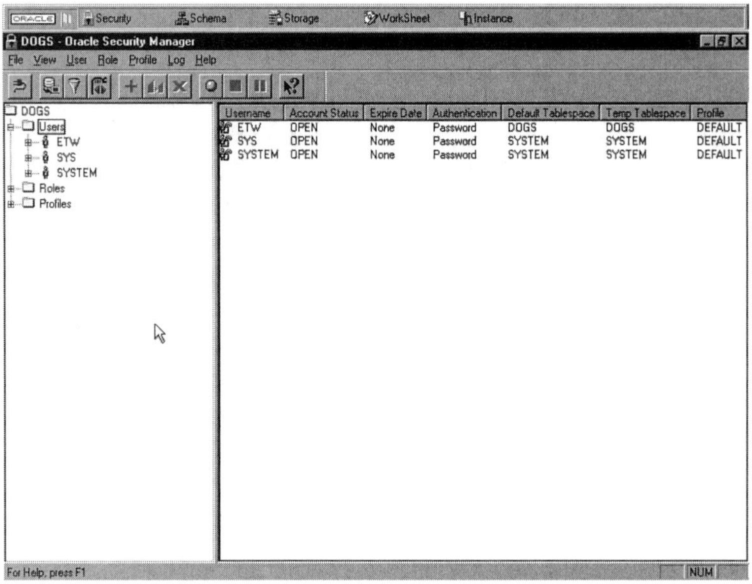

Figure 10.4.

The main screen of Security Manager.

This information includes the following for each user:

- ☐ Username.
- ☐ Account Status—Whether the account is online.
- ☐ Expire Date—When the password will expire.
- ☐ Authentication—Whether it's done by OS, by password file, and so on.
- ☐ Default Tablespace—Where the user's schema objects are, by default.
- ☐ Temporary Tablespace—Where the user's sorts will take place (if needed).
- ☐ Profile—The user's profile.

By right-clicking on the Users entry, you can invoke the Create User screen as shown in Figure 10.1. As you can see, this is the same Create User screen that you have seen with Enterprise Manager. The function is the same: Just fill in the boxes and click the OK button, and the new user will be created. As with Enterprise Manager, by right-clicking on a user's icon you will get the option to Create Like that user, as shown in Figure 10.5.

Figure 10.5.

You can choose Create Like from the right-click menu to base a new user on an existing user.

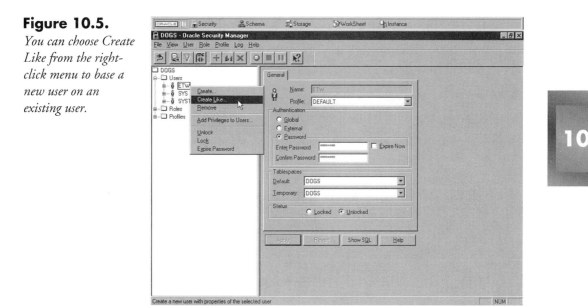

By filling out this screen, you will be able to create a user identical to an existing user but with a different username.

As you will see in the next section, there are many more options available with the command function CREATE USER than with Enterprise Manager or Security Manager.

Creating User Accounts with the CREATE USER Command

The new user account can also be created with the CREATE USER command. This command supports more options than Enterprise Manager or Security Manager.

The Syntax for the CREATE USER Command

The CREATE USER command is run with the following syntax:

```
CREATE USER user_name
IDENTIFIED BY password
     or IDENTIFIED EXTERNALLY
     or IDENTIFIED GLOBALLY
AS 'CN=user'
[ DEFAULT TABLESPACE ts_name ]
[ TEMPORARY TABLESPACE ts_name ]
[ QUOTA [ number K or M or UNLIMITED ] ON ts_name ]
[, QUOTA [ number K or M or UNLIMITED ] ON ts_name ]
[ PROFILE profile_name ]
[ PASSWORD EXPIRE ]
[ ACCOUNT LOCK or ACCOUNT UNLOCK ]
```

The parameters for this command are

- ☐ CREATE USER user_name—The CREATE USER command requires a username for the user you want to create.

- ☐ IDENTIFIED BY password—Oracle internally maintains a password for this user. This is the original password that is created.

- ☐ IDENTIFIED EXTERNALLY —The username is authenticated in the OS. The username must be identical to the username defined in the OS.

- ☐ IDENTIFIED GLOBALLY AS 'CN=user'—The username is authenticated by the Oracle security domain central server. The CN name identifies the external name of the user.

> **NOTE**
>
> One of the previous three qualifiers must be used in the CREATE USER command or the command will fail.

- ☐ DEFAULT TABLESPACE ts_name—The default tablespace to which the user is connected. If not specified, the SYSTEM tablespace will be used.

- ☐ TEMPORARY TABLESPACE ts_name—The temporary tablespace that the user will use by default. If not specified, the SYSTEM tablespace will be used.

- ☐ QUOTA number K or M ON ts_name—Specifies that the user has a quota of number K (kilobytes) or M (megabytes) on the identified tablespace.

- ☐ QUOTA UNLIMITED ON ts_name—Specifies that the user has an unlimited quota on the identified tablespace.

- ☐ PROFILE profile_name—The name of the profile that is used for this user.

- ☐ PASSWORD EXPIRE—Immediately sets the password to the expired state. The user must change his password before he can log on to the database.

☐ ACCOUNT LOCK—If this is set, the account is locked after creation.

☐ ACCOUNT UNLOCK—If this is set, the account is not locked after creation.

There is little you can do with the CREATE USER command that you cannot do with the graphical tools. The QUOTA option is the only additional feature you get with the command-line option.

Modifying User Accounts

Modifying a user is very similar to creating one. You can modify a user with either of the two graphical utilities or with the ALTER USER command. As with the process of user creation, there is only a slight difference between the functionality of the graphical utilities and the command-line utility. Let's look at these operations.

NOTE   You must have the ALTER USER system privilege to modify a user account.

Modifying User Accounts with Enterprise Manager

You can modify a user in Enterprise Manager by drilling down to the level of the users. When you see the user you want to modify, right-click the user's icon and choose the Quick Edit option from the pop-up menu. This will bring up the Quick Edit User screen, as shown in Figure 10.6.

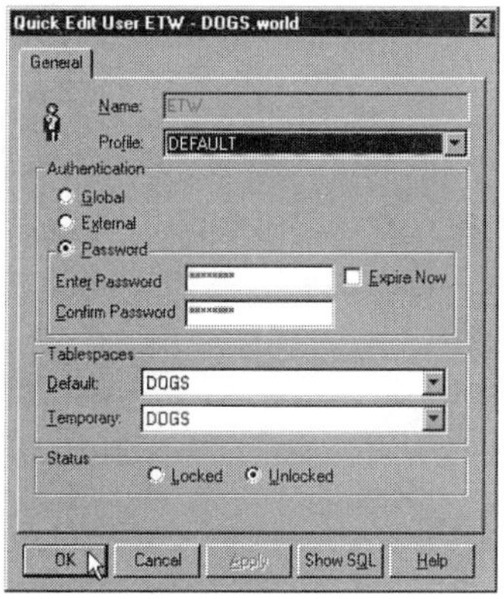

Figure 10.6.

You modify a user with the Quick Edit User screen.

From here you can change the profile, the password identification method, the tablespaces, the password, and whether the user is locked or unlocked. This is essentially the Create User screen without the option of specifying the username.

You can also remove the user from the same menu that invoked the Quick Edit option. This will permanently remove the user from the Oracle system.

Modifying User Accounts with Security Manager

You can also modify a user in the Security Manager utility. Specify the user you want to modify by clicking on that user's icon on the left side of Security Manager. On the right side you will see information about that user that you can modify.

You can alter all the data presented on the right side of the screen, except for the username. You can change the profile, the password identification method, the tablespaces, the password, and whether the user is locked or unlocked. Again, this is essentially the Create User screen without the option to specify the username.

Security Manager will also allow you to change permissions and remove users, and lock, unlock, and terminate the user's password, as shown in Figure 10.7.

Figure 10.7.

Use Security Manager options to modify the user's attributes.

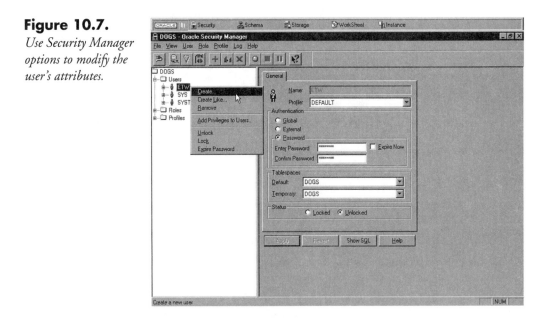

By choosing the Add Privileges to Users option, you can add user privileges. Selecting this option brings up the Add Privileges to Users screen, as shown in Figure 10.8.

Figure 10.8.
Use the Add Privileges to Users screen to modify the user's privileges.

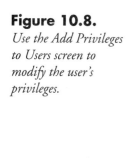

10

From here you can modify the user's privileges by selecting roles, system privileges, or object privileges with or without the ADMIN option. Remember, the ADMIN option allows you to pass that privilege to other user accounts.

Modifying User Accounts with the ALTER USER Command

You can also modify user accounts via the Oracle command ALTER USER. ALTER USER has similar functionality to Enterprise Manager and Security Manager, plus a few options not available with the graphical utilities. The ALTER USER command is used to alter various attributes of the user account.

The Syntax for the ALTER USER Command

SYNTAX

The ALTER USER command is run with the following syntax:

```
ALTER USER user_name
IDENTIFIED BY password
    or IDENTIFIED EXTERNALLY or IDENTIFIED GLOBALLY AS 'CN=user'
[ DEFAULT TABLESPACE ts_name ]
[ TEMPORARY TABLESPACE ts_name ]
[ QUOTA [ number K or M or UNLIMITED ] ON ts_name ]
[, QUOTA [ number K or M or UNLIMITED ] ON ts_name ]
[ PROFILE profile_name ]
[ PASSWORD EXPIRE ]
[ ACCOUNT LOCK or ACCOUNT UNLOCK ]
[ DEFAULT ROLE role [, role ]
    or [ DEFAULT ROLE ALL [ EXCEPT role [, role ] ] ] or [ DEFAULT ROLE NONE ]
```

NOTE With the exception of the DEFAULT ROLE option, the syntax of the ALTER USER command is identical to that of the CREATE USER command.

The parameters for this command are

- ☐ ALTER USER *user_name*—The ALTER USER command requires a username that is to be modified.
- ☐ IDENTIFIED BY *password*—Oracle internally maintains a password for this user. The password is changed to the one specified here.
- ☐ IDENTIFIED EXTERNALLY—The username is authenticated in the OS. The username must be identical in the username defined in the OS.
- ☐ IDENTIFIED GLOBALLY AS 'CN=*user*'—The username is authenticated by the Oracle security domain central server. The CN name identifies the external name of the user.

NOTE One of the previous three qualifiers must be used. If you do not specify an IDENTIFIED qualifier, the command will fail.

- ☐ DEFAULT TABLESPACE *ts_name*—The default tablespace to which the user is connected. If not specified, the SYSTEM tablespace is used as the default.
- ☐ TEMPORARY TABLESPACE *ts_name*—The temporary tablespace that the user will use by default. If not specified, the SYSTEM tablespace is used as the default.
- ☐ QUOTA *number* K or M ON *ts_name*—Specifies that the user has a quota of *number* K (kilobytes) or M (megabytes) on the identified tablespace.
- ☐ QUOTA UNLIMITED ON *ts_name*—Specifies that the user has an unlimited quota on the identified tablespace.
- ☐ PROFILE *profile_name*—The name of the profile that is used for this user.
- ☐ PASSWORD EXPIRE—Changes the password to the expired state. The password must be set before the user can log on to the database.
- ☐ ACCOUNT LOCK—If set, the account is locked after creation.
- ☐ ACCOUNT UNLOCK—If set, the account is not locked after creation.
- ☐ DEFAULT ROLE *role* [, *role*]—Specifies the default role or roles for this user.

☐ DEFAULT ROLE ALL—Specifies that all roles are enabled for this user. In conjunction with the EXCEPT *role* [,*role*] qualifier, all roles are enabled except for those specified.

☐ DEFAULT ROLE NONE—Specifies that no default roles are given.

As you can see, the privileges are mostly assigned to user accounts via the use of a role. Where privileges are given via the role, limitations on the user are typically assigned via the profile. In the next section of this lesson, you will look at the profiles and the roles, how to create them, and what they mean.

Managing Profiles

Profiles are created as an easier way of setting limitations on users. Instead of setting individual limits on users, you can set up a profile for each type of user. For example, you can set up the following types of users:

☐ Administrators—These users are given unlimited resources.

☐ Developers—These users have an unlimited number of sessions but a limited number of CPU cycles/sessions.

☐ Other—Perhaps you have other types of users with special needs. By defining your own set of special profiles, you can easily assign users with like attributes the same privileges.

By creating profiles for each type of user, you can simplify the security-management task. You can have as many profiles as you want, but a user can only be assigned one profile, unlike roles.

Profiles can be created, removed, and modified in several ways. You can manage profiles graphically with both Enterprise Manager and Security Manager and via scripts on the command line by using the CREATE PROFILE and ALTER PROFILE commands. I present all three ways in the following sections.

Managing Profiles with Enterprise Manager

Profiles can be created graphically with Enterprise Manager. After you have invoked Enterprise Manager and have drilled down into the database that you want to modify, right-click the Profiles entry and choose Create, as shown in Figure 10.9.

Another way to create a profile is by right-clicking a profile that already exists and choosing Create Like.

Figure 10.9.

Choosing Create to create a profile.

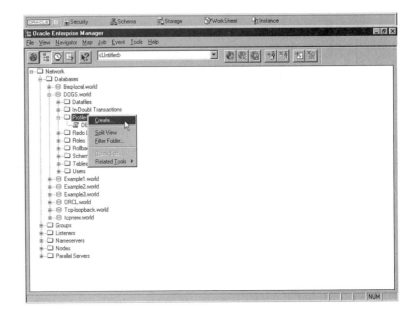

Depending on whether you're creating an all-new profile or basing a new one on an existing profile, you will be presented with either the Create Profile screen or the Create Like screen. These screens are identical, except that with Create Like, the values are already set to the values of the selected profile. The Create Like screen is shown in Figure 10.10.

Figure 10.10.

The Create Like screen.

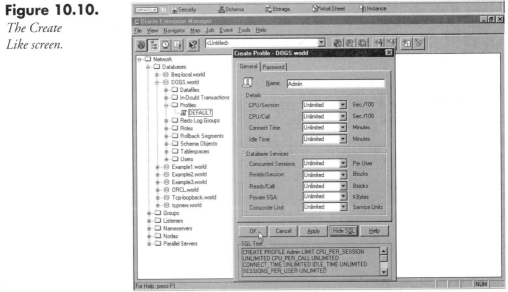

Through this screen you can enter or change a number of values for the profile in both the General and Password tabs. To switch to the Password screen, simply click the Password tab. The Password screen is shown in Figure 10.11.

Figure 10.11.

The Profile Password screen allows you to change password attributes.

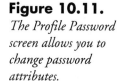

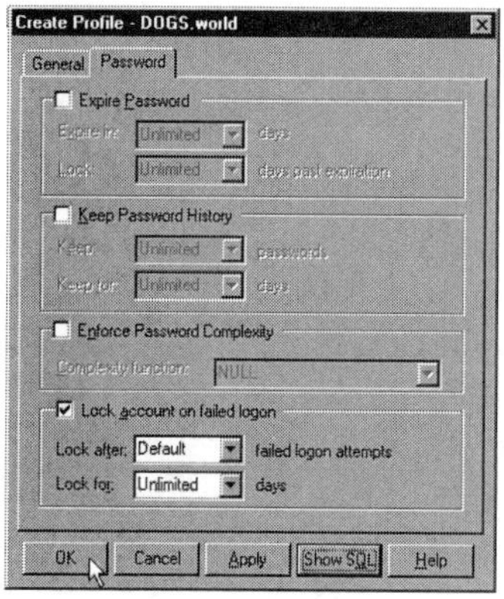

The General screen has quite a few options that can be set or changed. These options are split into Details and Database Services items. The parameters for the Details section are

- [ ] CPU/Session (Sec/100)—Specifies the amount of time, in hundredths of seconds, that a session can use.
- [ ] CPU/Call (Sec/100)—Specifies the amount of time, in hundredths of seconds, that a session can use per call.
- [ ] Connect Time (Min)—The total connect time allowed for a session.
- [ ] Idle Time (Min)—The total idle time allowed before the session is disconnected.

For the Database Services portion, the parameters are

- [ ] Concurrent Sessions (Per User)—The number of concurrent sessions allotted for this user ID.
- [ ] Reads/Session (Blocks)—The number of blocks that this session can read. This includes blocks both from disk and from the buffer cache.
- [ ] Reads/Call (Blocks)—The maximum number of blocks that can be read per call.
- [ ] Private SGA (KBytes)—The maximum size of the session's SGA.
- [ ] Composite Limit (Service Units)—A composite limit composed of the preceding limits.

On the Password tab, the parameters that can be set or changed are

☐ Expire Password—Specifies how long a password is valid before it must be changed.

☐ Keep Password History—Keeps a number of older passwords and does not let you reuse the past passwords.

☐ Enforce Password Complexity—Requires passwords to be complex.

☐ Lock Account on Failed Logon—Limits the number of failed logon attempts before the account is locked.

As you can see, you can change a lot of items in the profile. This can be quite useful for setting limits if necessary. The DEFAULT profile sets all these values to UNLIMITED as the default.

To modify a profile with Enterprise Manager, right-click the profile that you want to alter and select Quick Edit. This will bring up the Quick Edit Profile screen, as shown in Figure 10.12.

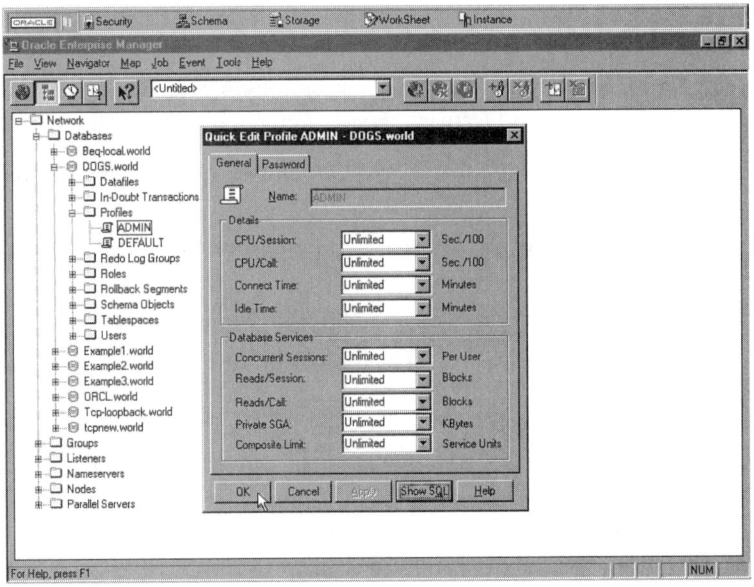

Figure 10.12.

The Quick Edit Profile screen allows you to change quota limits.

From this screen, you can edit the properties of that profile. To remove a profile, right-click the profile and select Remove from the pop-up menu. This will permanently remove the profile from the system.

Managing Profiles with Security Manager

With Security Manager you can essentially perform the same operations as with Enterprise Manager, but with a few more options. When you drill down into the profile using Security Manager, you will see not only the profiles but the users assigned to each of those profiles.

Right-click the Profile entry and you will be presented with a list of options, as shown in Figure 10.13.

Figure 10.13.

Use the Security Manager option to create a new profile.

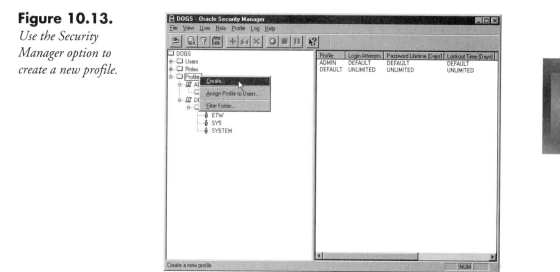

If you choose the Create option, you will be presented with the same Create Profile screen that you saw with Enterprise Manager, with the same options. Clicking one of the profiles causes the profile properties to appear on the right side of Security Manager screen, as shown in Figure 10.14.

You modify profiles under Security Manager by changing the parameters on the right side of the screen. As you can see, there is also a Password tab here. You can click this Password tab and see the same password parameters as with Enterprise Manager.

As will all the facilities available through Enterprise Manager and utilities such as Security Manager, you can also create and modify a profile via the Server Manager or scripts.

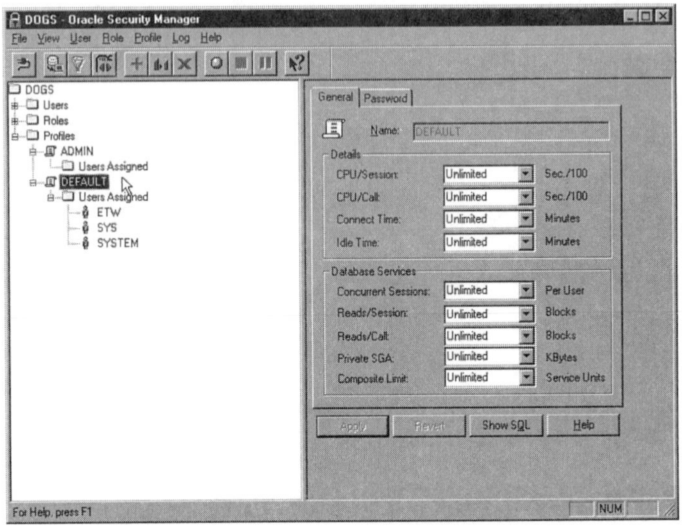

Figure 10.14.

The Edit Profile screen offers a detailed view of the default profile.

Managing Profiles with the CREATE PROFILE and ALTER PROFILE Commands

As with all the commands that you have seen so far, you can create and modify profiles via a command-line utility. For the profile, these utilities are the CREATE PROFILE, ALTER PROFILE, and DROP PROFILE commands. The syntax of the CREATE PROFILE and ALTER PROFILE commands is identical except that the first creates a profile and the other changes an already-existing profile.

The syntax of these commands is given in the Oracle8 documentation and really does not need to be repeated here. Look in the Oracle8 Server SQL Reference Manual for the exact syntax and how to use it. Another good way to learn some of the syntax used in these commands is to take advantage of the Show SQL option available in many Enterprise Manager utilities.

If you are setting up many different profiles and you find that the number you have is quite large, it is a good idea to start putting them in a SQL script. If you have it in a script, you can use it to rebuild the database if necessary, and if you ever need to create an additional database for the same user community, it will be much easier to set up the profiles.

Managing Roles

Roles are very important because they are the primary way of allocating system privileges to the user community. Privileges can be allocated to a user either via a role or directly, but directly can be quite time-consuming and tedious for the DBA. By creating a role for a certain type of user and allocating system privileges to that role, you can cut down on the amount of work that must be done and have an easier way of tracking privileges.

A complete list of Oracle default roles and system privileges is given in Appendix C, "Oracle Roles and Privileges." Please see that appendix for answers to questions on specific privileges.

You can create, modify, and assign roles to users via Enterprise Manager, Security Manager, or the CREATE ROLE, ALTER ROLE, DROP ROLE, and ALTER USER commands. In general, if you are just changing a few roles or users, the graphical tools are very nice. If you are modifying a large number of different roles or users, it might be better to use a script, where the SQL commands can be saved and used again if necessary.

Managing Roles with Enterprise Manager

You can create and modify roles graphically via the Enterprise Manager utility. Drill down into the database that you want to administer and right-click the Roles entry. This will bring up the Create Role screen, which is shown in Figure 10.15.

Figure 10.15.

The Create Role screen allows you to create a new role.

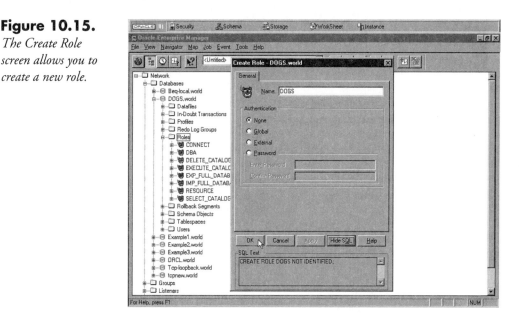

Here you can create a new role that, when created, will have no other roles or privileges associated with it. To populate the role with other roles, simply drag and drop a role onto the Granted Roles entry under the role that you have created (see Figure 10.16). This will add that selected role as one for which your newly created role has privileges. It is also possible to do this from system privileges.

Figure 10.16.

Drag and drop roles to populate a new role with them.

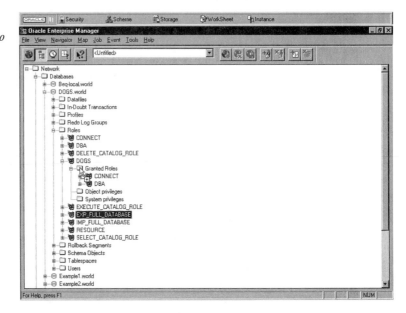

After you have created the role and populated it with other roles or system privileges, you might want to assign it to a user. With Enterprise Manager, it is possible simply to drag this role onto the Granted Roles entry under the user to whom you want to give it. This will automatically grant the role to the designated user. This drag-and-drop operation is shown in Figure 10.17.

Figure 10.17.

Dropping roles onto a user to assign that role to the user.

If you like the drag-and-drop features provided in Enterprise Manager, this may be the best method for you. Security Manager provides this functionality plus a little bit more, as you'll learn in the next section.

Managing Roles with Security Manager

Security Manager can also be used to create roles, grant them to users, and manage them. If you prefer using a graphical tool but need a bit more functionality than what is provided with Enterprise Manager, you will find Security Manager very useful.

To create a new role, use the same technique as with Enterprise Manager: Right-click the Roles icon and select Create. This will bring up the same Create Role screen that you saw earlier. It is shown here in Figure 10.18.

Figure 10.18.

The Create Role screen in Security Manager is the same as the one used in Enterprise Manager.

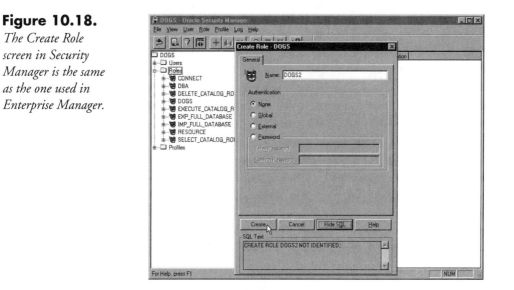

After you have created the role, right-click its name in the Security Manager screen and you will see the option to Add Privileges to Roles.

From this screen, you can modify the new role by adding new roles (as shown in Figure 10.19) or by adding system privileges (as shown in Figure 10.20). Both of these are accomplished by selecting the roles or privileges you want and adding them to the selected role or roles with the mouse.

Figure 10.19.

Adding roles to a role.

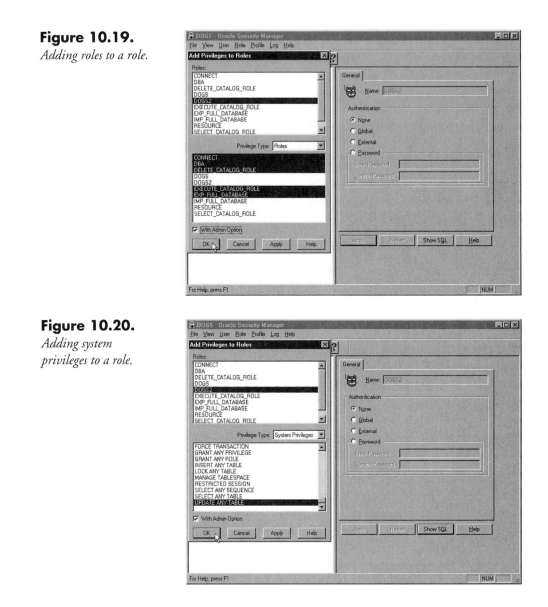

Figure 10.20.

Adding system privileges to a role.

Once nice benefit of Security Manager is the capability to expand the roles and privileges to see what is available. Simply drill down into the different parameters to see what is available or allocated. An example of this is shown in Figure 10.21.

Figure 10.21.

This Security Manager screen allows you to view the roles and privileges associated with the DOGS2 *role.*

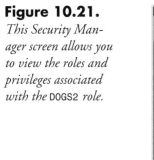

Managing Roles from the Command Line

Managing roles is a little different from working with some of the other commands you have seen throughout the book because managing a role takes more than just one command.

To create and maintain a role, you can use the CREATE ROLE, ALTER ROLE, and DROP ROLE commands. The CREATE ROLE and ALTER ROLE commands are used only to create the role and to manage the security on the role; privileges and other roles are not assigned to roles via the ALTER ROLE command. The CREATE ROLE and ALTER ROLE commands take the following options:

```
CREATE ROLE role
NOT IDENTIFIED
Or IDENTIFIED BY password
Or IDENTIFIED EXTERNALLY
Or IDENTIFIED GLOBALLY
```

These options simply have to do with the security of the role itself. To modify a role by adding other roles or system privileges to it, you must use the GRANT command.

Using GRANT and REVOKE

You use GRANT to assign roles or system privileges to roles or users. The same command works whether you are assigning these roles or system privileges to an individual user or to a role that in turn can be assigned to many users.

The Syntax for the GRANT Command

SYNTAX

The GRANT command takes the following syntax:

```
GRANT role or system privilege [, role or system privilege ]
TO user or role or PUBLIC [, user or role ]
[ WITH ADMIN OPTION ]
```

The GRANT command can take any number of system privileges and roles and assign them to any number of users or roles. By specifying that you want to grant a role or system privilege to PUBLIC, you are specifying that you want that role or privilege to be granted to all users in the system.

The REVOKE command is just the opposite of the GRANT command; it will take a role or system privilege away from a user or role:

```
REVOKE role or system privilege [, role or system privilege ]
FROM user or role or PUBLIC [, user or role ]
```

The DROP Command

Finally, you can use the DROP command to completely take away a role from the system. You should not have to be dropping roles very often if the roles that you create are planned out in advance.

The ADMIN Option

The ADMIN option specifies that the grantee has the right to pass this role or system privilege to any other user or role in the system. If the user is granted the role with the ADMIN option, that user may also alter or drop the role.

Summary

Today you learned how to manage users in your Oracle8 database. At the beginning of the lesson you saw how to create user accounts using both graphical and command-line utilities. This is the most basic building block of user administration.

After the user account has been created comes the task of administering that user account. This might consist of adding and/or removing roles and system privileges, or modifying some of the resource limitations placed on the user in the form of a profile.

You also learned how to administer profiles, which are used to limit certain system resources that the user session might be consuming. By using a profile, you can assign these limits to a profile and then assign the profile to a class of users.

Finally, you learned how and why to use roles. Roles are very powerful devices. By using roles, administrative tasks can be simplified by assigning a set of system privileges to a class of user, and then handling exceptions as they arise.

Roles are very important and should be well documented. By documenting roles, you can easily decide what role a new user should be assigned. As always, any changes to the system, such as adding or modifying roles, should be logged in the system journal.

What's Next?

In tomorrow's lesson, "Managing Processes," you will start to see more of how the Oracle processes work. You will learn how to find out what processes are active in the system, and how to kill runaway processes. You will also see how the Oracle multithreaded server works.

Q&A

Q What's the difference between a privilege and a role?

A A *privilege* is the authority to perform a certain act or command. A *role* is a collection of privileges and roles that can be assigned to a user.

Q What is the DEFAULT profile?

A The DEFAULT profile was created by the system when the database was created. By default, all users have unlimited access to the system.

Q Why do you use roles instead of just assigning system privileges?

A Assigning system privileges can be very time-consuming and complicated. By creating a role for each user type, such as accounting, finance, payroll, and so on, you can assign the privileges based on duties.

Q Can a user have more than one role?

A Certainly. A user can have multiple roles, depending on that user's job and duties.

Workshop

The workshop provides quiz questions to help you solidify your understanding of the material covered and exercises to provide you with experience in using what you've learned. Find the answers to the quiz questions in Appendix A, "Answers."

Quiz

1. Should more than one user share a user account?
2. How many accounts should each user have?
3. Where would you set the maximum amount of CPU per session?
4. Where would you set permissions to export data?
5. What is the ADMIN option?

6. How do you remove a role?

7. How do you remove a system privilege from a role?

8. Are quotas assigned via roles?

9. How are temporary tablespaces assigned?

10. What does the Create Like feature in Enterprise Manager or Security Manager do?

Exercises

1. Create a user using Enterprise Manager.

2. Modify that user using Security Manager.

3. Create a new profile.

4. Create a new role.

5. Add several roles and privileges to that new role.

Week 2

Day 11

Managing Processes

Today you'll learn about processes, or threads that are used in the NT instance. You'll see how to identify, monitor, and kill a process or thread.

NEW TERM The term *process* is used in this book to describe a thread of execution, or a mechanism that can execute a set of code. In many operating systems, *processes* has been replaced with *threads* or *lightweight processes*. To minimize confusion, the term *process* refers to the mechanism of execution and can refer to either a traditional process or a thread.

First you'll review how the Oracle processes work and what they do. You'll examine a bit of the terminology and the function of the Oracle8 instance. Later you'll see how to monitor the processes. You'll spend the remainder of this lesson on one of my favorite topics: the Oracle Parallel Query option.

Understanding the Oracle8 Processes

NEW TERM   The Oracle RDBMS uses two types of processes: the user processes (also known as the *shadow* or *server processes*) and the Oracle processes (also known as *background processes*). In some operating systems, such as Windows NT, these processes are actually threads; for consistency, I will refer to them as *processes*.

User, or client, processes are the user's connections into the RDBMS system. The user process manipulates the user's input and communicates with the Oracle server process through the Oracle program interface. The user process is also used to display the information requested by the user and, if necessary, can process this information into a more useful form.

Background Processes

Background processes are the Oracle processes used to perform various tasks within the RDBMS system. These tasks vary from communicating with other Oracle instances and performing system maintenance and cleanup to writing dirty blocks to disk. The nine Oracle processes are DBWR, LGWR, CKPT, PMON, SMON, RECO, ARCH, LCK*n*, and D*nnn*. Refer to Day 2, "Exploring the Oracle Architecture," for descriptions of these processes.

With Windows NT, these processes are implemented as threads. Because the Oracle threads are listed by number, you cannot readily distinguish which thread is which. So you can cross-reference them, the Oracle threads are listed in Table 11.1.

Table 11.1. Oracle service threads.

Thread number	Oracle process
0, 1	Oracle service
2	PMON
3	DBWR
4	LGWR
5	SMON
6	RECO

Server Processes (Shadow Processes)

The server, or shadow, processes communicate with the user and interact with Oracle to carry out the user's requests. For example, if the user process requests a piece of data not already in the SGA, the shadow process is responsible for reading the data blocks from the datafiles into the SGA.

There can be a one-to-one correlation between the user processes and the shadow processes (as in a dedicated server configuration). Although one shadow process can connect to multiple user processes (as in a multithreaded server configuration), doing so reduces the utilization of system resources.

Each shadow process or thread uses a certain amount of Oracle and OS resources. Specifically, each shadow process uses approximately 1MB of memory. This memory and the overhead of managing large numbers of processes create quite a load on the system. Therefore, you should reduce the number of user connections if possible.

Multiplexing Processes

Because the load incurred by large numbers of user processes can be quite heavy on the system, measures should be taken to reduce this number. Several different methods that involve multiplexing the connections into the Oracle instance can be used to reduce the user load.

Multiplexing involves reducing the number of connections. On one side of the multiplexor, each process or user might have its own connection On the other side, many processes or users might share the same connections. Let's look at a multiplexor as a gray box, as shown in Figure 11.1.

Figure 11.1.

The logical view of a multiplexor.

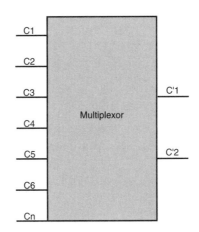

In its simplest form, the multiplexor reduces a large number of connections to a smaller number of connections. The multiplexing can be done on the server itself, but in general, the multiplexing is done on another server.

 A system that has a middle server to handle connection processing is typically called a *three-tier system*. If you are directly connecting all the users from client systems to the database server, this is known as a *two-tier system*.

An example of a two-tier system is shown in Figure 11.2. As you can see, a number of network client systems are connected to the database server via a LAN.

Figure 11.2.

The two-tier system.

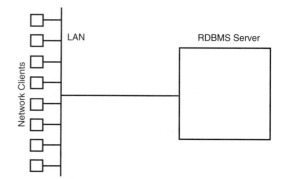

The two-tier system directly links the user connections (via a LAN) into the Oracle instance via the server processes. If you are using the multithreaded server, the server processes might be reduced but the LAN connections into the server are still there for all of the users. This is shown as a logical view in Figure 11.3.

Figure 11.3.

*The two-tier system
logical view.*

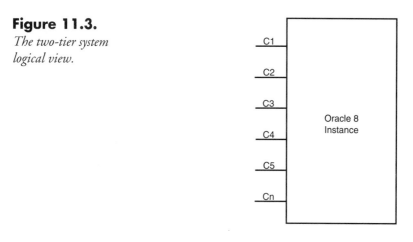

In the logical view, you can see more clearly that there is a one-to-one relationship between the users and the connections into the Oracle instance. As I mentioned earlier, these connections can be quite expensive.

NOTE

In computer system performance language, a process is said to be *expensive* if it consumes a relatively large amount of system resources.

11

NEW TERM In a three-tier system, a middleware system is used to handle much of the overhead involved in handling user connections and large numbers of processes. This *middleware* can be in the form of a transaction monitor (TM) or an application. An example of a three-tier system is shown in Figure 11.4.

Figure 11.4.

The three-tier system.

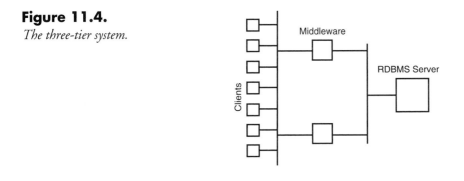

This looks very similar to the two-tier system when you look at the physical layer, but when you look at the logical picture of this system, as shown in Figure 11.5, you can see that the number of connections into the RDBMS has been greatly reduced. Because each connection is expensive in CPU and memory, this savings can improve the performance of your system.

11

Figure 11.5.

The three-tier system logical view.

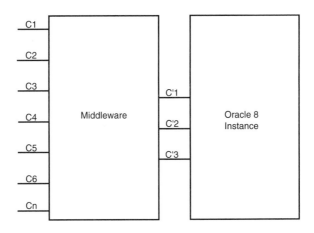

The three-tier system is becoming quite popular and will likely become more so. In fact, Microsoft released a middleware component in 1997 called the Microsoft Transaction Server. Other transaction monitors in use today include Tuxedo, Encina, and TopEnd. Many of these products have been around for years.

Transaction monitors have typically been used in mid-range to high-end systems, but with the popularity of PC servers, you'll see more and more multiplexing done in this area as well.

Dedicated Versus Multithreaded Server Processes

As mentioned previously, the user connection into the Oracle instance can occur via a dedicated server process or a multithreaded server process. In either case, they appear and act identically to the end user under most conditions.

There are a few situations when it is necessary to connect via the dedicated server process:

- [ ] To start up and shut down an instance
- [ ] To perform media recovery
- [ ] To run a batch job

Under these conditions, the system must use a dedicated server process. Forcing a dedicated server process under other conditions is described a bit later.

Dedicated Server

When a SQL request from a user is sent to the RDBMS, the server process executes that command. This mechanism protects Oracle from being directly manipulated by a user process. This actually increases the stability and robustness of the Oracle8 RDBMS. A diagram of the dedicated server process is shown in Figure 11.6.

Figure 11.6.

The dedicated server process.

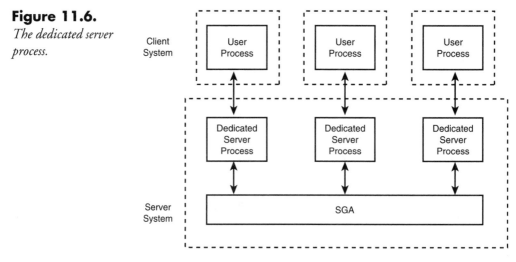

With a dedicated server process, there is a one-to-one correlation between the user process and the server process. Each server process is dedicated to one user process. To request a dedicated server process when the system is running with the multithreaded server enabled, include the parameter SRVR=DEDICATED in the connect string. This will create a dedicated server process for that user process.

Multithreaded Server

The multithreaded server process allows many user processes to share a number of shared server processes. This is diagrammed in Figure 11.7.

Figure 11.7.

The multithreaded server process.

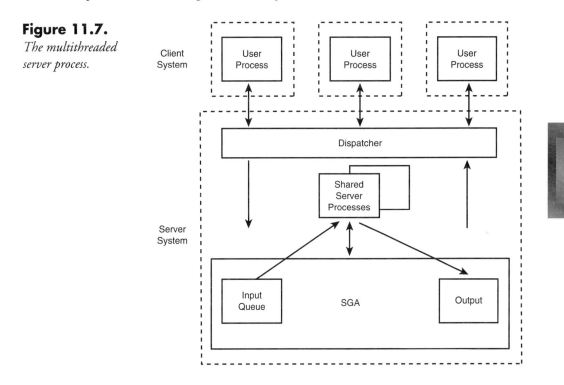

As you can see, all requests to the shared server processes must go through the dispatcher process, which in turn queues the request in the shared pool in the SGA. Once the request has been processed, it is returned to the dispatcher through the shared pool in the SGA.

WARNING

> Because the multithreaded server uses the shared pool for queuing requests and returning data, it is important that the shared pool be large enough.

The main advantage of using the multithreaded server is the reduction of server processes. This can greatly reduce CPU and memory usage. As you might guess, however, the multithreaded server does add overhead to the system. This is why a dedicated server process is recommended for long-running batch jobs.

Tuning the Multithreaded Server

To configure and tune the multithreaded server for use, you'll need to tune the following parameters in your parameter file. You should also monitor the shared pool very carefully to make sure you are not running out of space.

Try monitoring the shared session memory with a small number of users to determine how much memory they are using. You can then extrapolate how much memory all the sessions will require. This can be accomplished by using the following SQL statement:

```
SELECT SUM(value) || 'bytes' "Memory"
FROM v$sesstat, v$statname
WHERE name = 'session memory'
AND v$sesstat.statistic# = v$statname.statistic#;
```

This tells you how much memory you are using. Dividing this by the number of connections tells you the amount of memory per session. You can determine from this how much memory you'll need in the shared pool for all the sessions you'll be supporting.

If you think the shared-pool size might be too small, you can increase it by tuning the parameter SHARED_POOL_SIZE. Remember, the shared pool is also used for the library cache and the data dictionary. Learn to tune these on Day 20, "Effectively Tuning and Optimizing the Database."

The number of dispatchers per protocol is determined by the initialization parameter MTS_DISPATCHERS. If you increase this number, each session will potentially see greater performance because it will not have to wait on a dispatcher to become available. Here is an example of how you would set five dispatcher processes for the TCP/IP protocol:

```
MTS_DISPATCHERS = "TCP, 5"
```

Each network protocol is set separately. For protocols with fewer users, set the number lower. The more concurrent sessions per dispatcher, the greater the possibility you'll have to wait for a dispatcher when you need one.

Other parameters related to the multithreaded server are

- ☐ MTS_MAX_DISPATCHERS—The maximum number of dispatcher processes that can be created in the instance. This includes the dispatchers for all protocols combined.

- ☐ MTS_SERVERS—The initial number of shared server processes. If this value is set to 0, Oracle will not use shared server processes. The number of shared server processes will increase dynamically to meet the needs of the system.

☐ MTS_MAX_SERVERS—This value specifies the maximum number of shared server processes.

The number of dispatcher processes and the minimum number of shared server processes can be changed dynamically with the ALTER SYSTEM parameter.

The Oracle Parallel Query Option

The Oracle Parallel Query option is by far my favorite enhancement that Oracle has made in the last few years. By using the Parallel Query option, you can greatly improve the performance of some database operations.

The Oracle Parallel Query option makes it possible for some Oracle functions to be processed by multiple streams of execution. These functions include some queries, index creation, data loading, and recovery. In each of these functions, the general principle is the same: Keep the CPUs busy while Oracle is waiting for I/O.

For most queries, the time spent waiting for the data to be retrieved from disk usually overshadows the amount of time spent processing the results. With the Parallel Query option, you can compensate for this by using several server processes to execute the query. While one process is waiting for I/Os to complete, other processes can be executing.

Many processes working together can simultaneously process a single SQL statement, a situation known as parallel query processing. The other functions are known as parallel index creation, parallel loading, and parallel recovery, each of which is discussed in the following sections.

Parallel Query Processing

Parallel query processing allows certain Oracle statements to be run in parallel. The Oracle server can process the following statements in parallel:

☐ SELECT statements

☐ Subqueries in UPDATE and DELETE statements

☐ CREATE TABLE *tablename* as SELECT statements

☐ CREATE INDEX statements

Parallel queries are effective on large operations such as table scans and sorts.

Parallel Query Operation

With traditional queries such as table scans, the server process reads the data sequentially, as shown in Figure 11.8. Much of the time spent in this query is spent waiting for I/Os to complete.

Figure 11.8.

A table scan without parallel query.

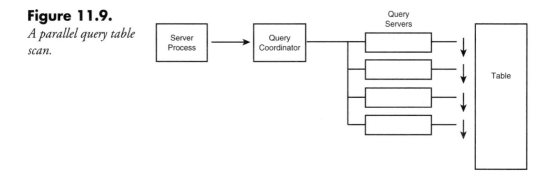

NEW TERM   A parallel query divides the query into several different pieces, each processed by a different server process. These processes are called *query servers.* The query servers are dispatched by a process known as the *query coordinator.* The query coordinator dispatches the query servers and coordinates the results from all the servers to send back to the user. The result of this arrangement is that many smaller table scans take place under the hood (transparent to the user). From the user's standpoint, it is simply a much faster table scan. Figure 11.9 shows a parallel query.

Figure 11.9.

A parallel query table scan.

The query coordinator is given a SQL statement and a degree of parallelism, and is responsible for dividing the query among the query servers and integrating the individual results into one result. The degree of parallelism is the number of query servers assigned to the particular query.

The Oracle server can make parallel the following operations:

- ☐ Joins
- ☐ Sorts
- ☐ Table scans

Each of these operations has requirements that determine how the query is parallelized. The performance achieved by the parallel query is determined by the amount of data to be accessed and the degree of parallelism achieved.

How the query is parallelized (if at all) is determined by the query coordinator. The decision is made in this order:

1. The optimizer determines the execution plan of the statement.
2. The query coordinator determines which operations can be performed in parallel.
3. The query coordinator determines how many query servers to enlist.
4. The query coordinator enlists query servers that perform the query.
5. The query coordinator reassembles the resulting data and passes it back to the user.

The degree of parallelism is determined using the following precedence:

1. Query hints—User-defined hints included in the SQL statement have the highest precedence.
2. Table definition—The default degree of parallelism defined for the table has second precedence.
3. Initialization parameters—The Oracle initialization parameters are used.

Regardless of how these values are set, the number of query servers cannot exceed the number of query servers available in the query server pool. This number is specified by the Oracle initialization parameter PARALLEL_MAX_SERVERS.

Hints for the degree of parallelism are set within a comment string in the SQL statement.

The Syntax for Parallelism in a Comment String

The syntax of this comment is as follows:

```
PARALLEL ( alias_or_tablename , [ integer/DEFAULT ] [ , integer/DEFAULT ] )
```

The parallel hint specifies the table or alias being scanned, followed by a value for the number of query servers to be used (or the default). The final optional value specifies how the table is to be split among different instances of a parallel server. Here is an example of using hints:

```
SELECT /*+ FULL(emp) PARALLEL(emp, 4) */
empno
FROM emp;
```

If you add the FULL and PARALLEL hints to this statement, the Oracle optimizer will create an execution plan that uses a full-table scan. Furthermore, this table scan will be executed with a parallel degree of 4 if the query servers are available. This statement overrides both the degree of parallelism specified in the table definition and the default Oracle initialization parameters.

The hint NOPARALLEL disables parallel scanning of a table and overrides the specified degree of parallelism.

The Syntax for the NOPARALLEL Hint

The NOPARALLEL hint has the following syntax:

```
NOPARALLEL ( alias_or_tablename )
```

Parallel Query Tuning

Parallel query operations can be very effective on multiprocessor or parallel-processing computers; they can also be effective on uniprocessor systems where much of the time is spent waiting for I/O operations to complete. Systems with sufficient I/O bandwidth—and especially systems with disk arrays—benefit from parallel query operations.

If your system is typically processing at 100% of its CPU utilization and you have a small number of disk drives, you probably won't benefit from parallel query operations. If your system is extremely memory limited, you also will probably not benefit from parallel query operations.

The two areas that can be tuned for parallel queries are I/O and parallel servers. By properly configuring your datafiles, you can help parallel queries be more effective.

I/O Configuration

The function of a parallel query is to split up query operations so they more effectively use the system. One of the ways a parallel query does this is by allowing the processing of the query to continue while pieces of the query operation are stalled waiting for I/Os to complete. Parallel queries are not effective if the entire table is limited to one disk drive.

By striping the table across many drives, I/Os can be distributed and a higher level of parallelism can occur. Striping can be done with OS striping, with Oracle striping, or (better yet) with a hardware disk array.

Large contiguous extents can also help performance in parallel query operations. During scan operations, the query coordinator splits contiguous ranges of blocks into large, medium, and small groups. Each query server is given a large group of blocks to start with, progressively working its way down to the small group of blocks until the scan is completed. This is done in an attempt to balance the load performed by each query server. If there are several large extents in a table, the query coordinator can find blocks to dispatch to the query servers much more easily.

 TIP

> Remember to compose your temporary tablespace of several large extents on a striped volume. This arrangement helps sorting performance.

Degree of Parallelism

Properly distributing I/Os and the degree of parallelism are the two most important things to tune in the Parallel Query option. Tuning the degree of parallelism is partially trial and error and partially analysis. It is very important to take notes when you are experimenting with the degree of parallelism. Your first iteration should be based on the following factors:

- ☐ The CPU capacity of your system—the number and capacity of CPUs has an effect on the number of query processes you should run.

- ☐ The capacity of the system to handle large numbers of processes—some operating systems can handle many simultaneous threads; others are more limited.

- ☐ The system load—if the system is already running at 100% capacity, the degree of parallelism doesn't have much effect. If you are running at 90%, too many query processes can overload the system.

- ☐ The amount of query processing on the system—if most operations are updates but there are a few critical queries, you might want many query processes.

- ☐ The I/O capacity of the system—if your disks are striped or if you are using a disk array, you should be able to handle a large number of parallel queries.

- ☐ The types of operations—are you performing a large number of full-table scans or sorts? These operations benefit greatly from parallel query servers.

All these parameters should have some influence on the degree of parallelism you set up for your system. Remember that the preceding points are just guidelines to help with your best attempt at a starting point. Here are a few other suggestions:

- ☐ CPU-intensive operations such as sorts should indicate a lower degree of parallelism. CPU-bound tasks are already taking advantage of the CPUs and tend not to be waiting on I/O.

- ☐ Disk-intensive operations such as full-table scans should indicate a higher degree of parallelism. The more operations waiting on I/O, the more the system can benefit from another query server.

- ☐ Table size is very important. A small table does not need parallel queries. Reserve this for larger tables.

- ☐ Many concurrent processes should indicate a lower degree of parallelism. Too many processes can overload the system.

Once you determine your starting point, you can monitor your system by querying the dynamic performance table, V$PQ_SYSSTAT. This can be done with the query shown in Listing 11.1.

11

INPUT   **Listing 11.1. Monitoring a parallel query from V$SYSSTAT.**

```
SQL> select * from v$pq_sysstat;
STATISTIC                             VALUE
-------------------------------- ----------
Servers Busy                              0
Servers Idle                             12
Servers Highwater                        16
Server Sessions                         380
Servers Started                           4
Servers Shutdown                          4
Servers Cleaned Up                        0
Queries Initiated                        21
DFO Trees                                77
Local Msgs Sent                     2459361
Distr Msgs Sent                           0
Local Msgs Recv'd                   2459318
Distr Msgs Recv'd                         0
```

OUTPUT   13 rows selected.

When looking at this query, the following statistics are quite useful.

☐ Servers Busy—This is the number of servers busy at any one time. Check this statistic several times to get a good idea of the average value. If the value is equal to the initialization parameter PARALLEL_MIN_SERVERS, you have probably configured too many query servers.

☐ Servers Idle—This is the number of servers idle at any one time. If you always have many idle servers, consider reducing PARALLEL_MIN_SERVERS.

☐ Servers Started—This is the number of query servers that have started up in this instance. If the value for Servers Busy is low but you see a large number in Servers Started, you might be using query servers sporadically.

☐ Servers Shutdown—This is the number of query servers that have been shut down because they are idle. This value is most likely similar to the Servers Started value.

After you determine your degree of parallelism, begin testing; evaluate the information you get from V$PQ_SYSSTAT and from your operating-system–monitoring facilities. Keep an eye out for CPU usage and excessive waiting on I/O. If the CPU usage is too high, try reducing the degree of parallelism. If the CPU usage is too low and there is significant waiting for I/O, try increasing the degree of parallelism.

Remember that the degree of parallelism is determined by SQL hints, table definitions, and initialization parameters. The total number of query servers is determined by the initialization parameter PARALLEL_MAX_SERVERS; the number started up initially is determined by the initialization parameter PARALLEL_MIN_SERVERS.

The total number of query servers in use is the number of queries executed in parallel multiplied by their degree of parallelism. If you try to use more than PARALLEL_MAX_SERVERS, you won't be able to parallelize your query.

Direct Write Sorts

You can use the Direct Write Sort option with the Parallel Query option and have the query servers each perform their own direct writes.

As you saw earlier, using direct writes causes the server processes to write the output of sort operations directly to disk, bypassing the buffer cache. The effect of direct writes is that for sort operations, large amounts of block buffers are not ejected from the buffer cache. This leaves the buffer cache available for normal queries and updates. When using direct write sorts with the Parallel Query option, each query server gets its own set of direct write buffers.

NOTE

Direct write sorts take more memory than normal sorts. The amount of memory they use with the Parallel Query option can be determined with the following formula:

Direct write sort memory =
(number of query servers) * (SORT_WRITE_BUFFERS) *
(SORT_WRITE_BUFFER_SIZE)

Only use direct write sorts if you have sufficient memory and temporary disk space. The temporary disk space should have a sufficient space and I/O bandwidth to handle the load.

Parallel Index Creation

Another feature of the Parallel Query option is its capability to create indexes in parallel. With the parallel index creation feature, the time it takes to create an index can be greatly reduced.

As in parallel query processing, a coordinator process dispatches two sets of query servers. One set scans the table to be indexed to obtain the ROWIDs and column values needed for the index. Another set performs the sorting on those values and passes the results to the coordinator process. The coordinator process then puts together the B*-tree index from these sorted items.

When creating an index, the degree of parallelism follows the same precedence as it does in parallel query processing. The first value is an optional PARALLEL clause in the CREATE INDEX statement, followed by the table definition and finally the initialization parameters.

11

Creating an index in parallel can be several times faster than creating an index by normal means. The same conditions apply for index creation as were given for parallel query processing. A system that has been configured to take advantage of parallel query processing will also see good performance from parallel index creation.

Parallel Data Loading

Loading can be done in parallel by having multiple concurrent sessions perform a direct path load into the same table. Depending on the configuration of the system, you can see excellent load performance by loading in parallel. Because loading is both CPU and I/O intensive, you should see good results in an SMP or MPP environment with a high-bandwidth, I/O subsystem.

Parallel loads are performed by multiple, direct-loader processes, each using the PARALLEL=TRUE and DIRECT=TRUE options. When you specify PARALLEL=TRUE, the loader does not place an exclusive lock on the table being loaded as it would otherwise. During the parallel load, the loader creates temporary segments for each of the concurrent processes and merges them together on completion.

Although parallel loading performs best when each temporary file is located on a separate disk, the increased performance of the load does not usually justify the complexity of the manual striping needed to do this. I still recommend striping the tables on an OS level or preferably on a hardware disk array. Performance can be improved by putting each of the input files on a separate volume to take advantage of the sequential nature of the reads.

Parallel loading can be beneficial, especially if load time is critical in your environment. By putting each of the input files on separate disk volumes, you can increase performance. Overall, the general tuning principles used in parallel query processing are valid in parallel loading also.

Parallel Recovery

Having multiple concurrent sessions perform a recovery is probably my favorite feature of the Parallel Query option. When benchmarking Oracle and testing hardware and software, it is often necessary to intentionally crash the system to prove recoverability. With the Parallel Recovery option, the time it takes to perform an instance recovery can be dramatically reduced.

Recovery time is significantly reduced when the system being recovered has many disks and supports asynchronous I/O. For a small system that has few drives or for an operating system that does not support asynchronous I/O, it might not be wise to enable parallel recovery.

In traditional recovery, one process reads from the redo log files and applies changes to the datafiles, as shown in Figure 11.10. This operation can take a significant amount of time because the recovery process must wait for disk I/Os to complete.

Figure 11.10.

Recovery without parallel recovery.

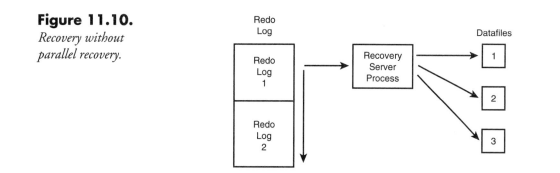

With the Parallel Recovery option, one process is responsible for reading and dispatching redo entries from the redo log files and passing those entries on to the recovery processes that apply the changes to the datafiles, as shown in Figure 11.11.

Figure 11.11.

Parallel recovery.

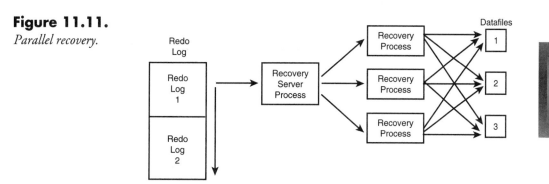

Because the recovery process reads sequentially from the redo log files, the I/O performance is much higher than that of the recovery processes that are writing random data throughout the datafiles. Because writing the data is very seek intensive, it is a good idea to have one or two recovery processes for each data disk in the system.

By having more recovery processes, you can have more outstanding I/Os and thus simultaneously use all the data drives. Because recovery is done at instance startup, this arrangement reduces dead time when no other database processing can be done.

The number of concurrent recovery processes is set with the initialization parameter RECOVERY_PARALLEL. The value of this parameter cannot exceed the value specified in the initialization parameter PARALLEL_MAX_SERVERS.

By specifying a sufficient number of recovery servers, you'll see an immediate improvement in instance recovery time. Do not use parallel recovery if your system does not support asynchronous I/O or if you are limited to a small number of disk drives. If your I/O subsystem is fast enough and your data is properly striped across these drives (either through software or hardware RAID), you should see very good improvement.

In summary, the Parallel Query option is useful in distributing processing loads so that CPUs are kept busy processing while other processes are waiting for I/Os to complete. With multiprocessor machines, the Parallel Query option can be quite beneficial; this is not to say that the option is not beneficial on uniprocessor machines as well.

NOTE

> As larger and larger disks are produced at lower and lower prices, many installations end up with I/O problems caused by not having the required I/O bandwidth. Two disk drives are faster than one disk drive if your I/O is balanced.
>
> The Parallel Query option can help only in systems where I/O is not a bottleneck. When I/O is not a problem, you'll see significant gains from parallel queries.

Monitoring Processes

The processes or threads used by Oracle can be monitored via the OS facilities of your operating system or from within the Oracle instance itself. Each of these has its own advantages and disadvantages. By looking at the processes from within Oracle, you can gain more insight as to what these processes are actually doing, but you cannot determine exactly how many resources they are currently consuming. It takes a combination of external and internal monitoring to get the complete picture. Let's look at some of the ways you can monitor these processes and resources.

Monitoring Processes from the NT Task Manager

The NT Task Manager is an ideal tool to get a quick view of what is happening in your system. It is not a very complex tool, nor does it give you a great deal of information, but for a quick look it is very useful. To invoke the Task Manager, right-click the NT 4.0 toolbar and select Task Manager, as shown in Figure 11.12.

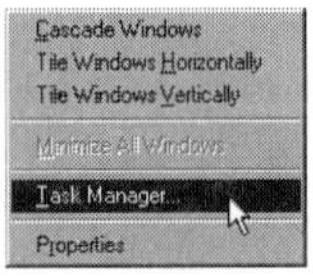

Figure 11.12.

Select Task Manager
from the context
menu.

Once the Task Manager is running, you'll see the performance screen (see Figure 11.13). This screen shows the CPU and memory usage in the system. In the lower part of the screen, you'll see numerical information relating to thread and process statistics and memory usage.

Figure 11.13.

Viewing performance.

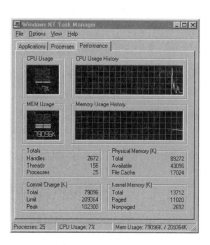

By clicking the Processes tab, you can view the Processes screen. From here you can see CPU, physical memory, and virtual memory used by the various processes in the system. The Processes screen is shown in Figure 11.14.

Figure 11.14.

Viewing processes.

This information is quite useful and easy to get to, but it is quite coarse. As you can see, Oracle shows up as one process named `oracle80.exe`. This monitor gives you no information on the individual threads that make up this process.

Monitoring Processes from perfmon

The NT Performance Monitor (*perfmon*) can also be used to monitor threads, but as with the Task Manager, not much useful information can be gleaned from this. Once the Performance Monitor is invoked, you can select thread information, as shown in Figure 11.15. This information can be in terms of CPU time, context switches per second, and so on. This information has some use, but without knowing what session it is, it is not worth much.

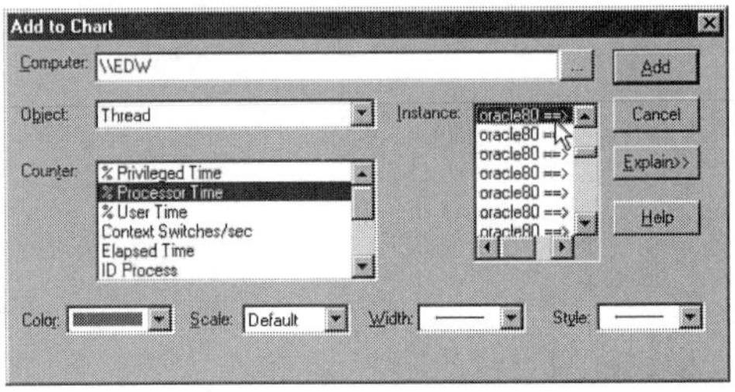

Figure 11.15.

An example of the perfmon.

For viewing process and thread information, I think the NT Performance Monitor is of little use. However, as you'll see on Day 20, the NT Performance Monitor is great for viewing I/O and CPU information.

Monitoring Sessions with the Instance Manager

The Instance Manager has some fundamental information that you can view about sessions. This information essentially concerns connections and activities. Open the Instance Manager and click the Sessions icon. Here you'll see the Sessions screen, which is shown in Figure 11.16.

You can glean a lot of information from this screen. The right portion of the screen provides the following session information:

- Session ID—The session's internal ID number
- Status—Whether the session is active
- Username—The Oracle user ID
- Schema Name—The schema to which the user is attached
- OS User—The OS user account that is connected
- Terminal—The connection name (if applicable)
- Machine Name—The machine on which this user is running
- Program—The program that is connected to the instance

Figure 11.16.

Viewing sessions with the Instance Manager.

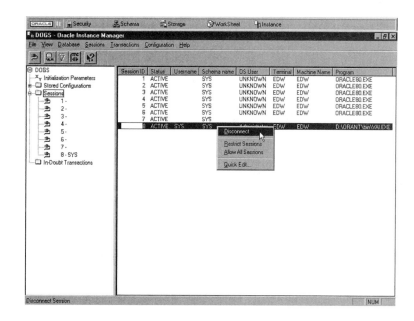

This information can be quite useful if you are looking for a particular session. It is also possible to disconnect a session from the instance using the Instance Manager. Right-click the session and select Disconnect, as shown in Figure 11.17. This disconnects that session from the Oracle instance.

Figure 11.17.

Disconnecting a session.

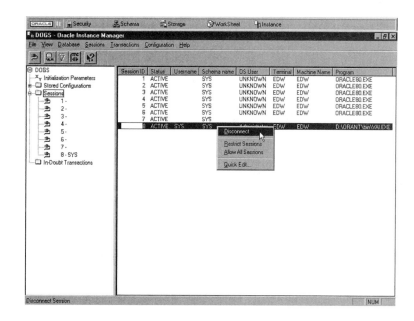

Monitoring Oracle Processes from the Command Line

You can gather a huge amount of information about the Oracle processes by querying the internal performance tables using the V$ views. These views, predefined by Oracle, look into the dynamic performance tables. This information can be quite useful. Some V$ views that are of most interest when you are monitoring processes are as follows:

- ☐ V$CIRCUIT—Contains information about virtual circuits that are created through the dispatcher and server processes
- ☐ V$DISPATCHER—Contains dispatcher information
- ☐ V$QUEUE—Contains information pertaining to the multithreaded message queues
- ☐ V$SESS_IO—Contains I/O information for each session
- ☐ V$SHARED_SERVER—Contains shared server information
- ☐ V$SYSSTAT—Contains miscellaneous system statistics

If you want more information about the dynamic performance tables or performance in general, I suggest you read my first book, *Oracle Performance Tuning and Optimization* (Sams Publishing), in which I go into this and more in great detail.

Summary

Today you were introduced to two types of processes: user processes (also known as the shadow or server processes) and Oracle processes (also known as background processes). In some operating systems, such as Windows NT, these processes are actually threads.

As you saw, it is only through the server or shadow processes that the user communicates with the database. The user process manipulates the user's input and communicates with the Oracle server process through the Oracle program interface. The user process is also used to display the information requested by the user and, if necessary, can process this information into a more useful form. As you saw, this can happen on a one-to-one basis with the dedicated server process, or on a shared basis with the multithreaded server.

What's Next?

Day 12, "Working with Tables, Views, and Synonyms," introduces the Oracle schema. The next three days cover the various schema objects such as tables, views, clusters, and indexes. The partitioned table, which is new in Oracle8, is covered tomorrow. Also new in Oracle8 is the index only table, which is covered in the next three lessons.

The Oracle schema is a very important concept to both the Oracle DBA and to the application developer. The next three chapters finish the basics on building an Oracle database.

Q&A

Q What are the server processes?

A The server processes are the background processes or threads that perform tasks on behalf of Oracle. They consist of the following: DBWR, LGWR, PMON, SMON, RECO, ARCH, CKPT, LCK*n*, and D*nnn*.

Q What is a dedicated server process?

A A dedicated server process has a one-to-one correlation between the user process and the server process. Each user process gets one server process.

Q What is a shared server process?

A The shared server process handles more than one user process. The dispatcher queues the job and the shared server process executes it.

Q What is the Parallel Query option?

A The Parallel Query option is an Oracle option that allows large database operations to be parallelized and run simultaneously.

Workshop

The workshop provides quiz questions to help you solidify your understanding of the material covered and exercises to provide you with experience in using what you've learned. Find the answers in Appendix A, "Answers."

Quiz

1. What is the DBWR process used for?
2. What is the LGWR process used for?
3. What is the CKPT process used for?
4. Under what circumstances will the LCK*n* process be used?
5. What type of system includes a Transaction Monitor (TM)?
6. What component is usually the limiting factor in your system?
7. What is the order of precedence (that is, parameters, hints, table definitions, and so on) for Oracle choosing the degree of parallelism?
8. Does the Parallel Query option help you only if you have multiple processors?
9. With Oracle on NT, does the Oracle server use processes or threads?
10. Where does the multithreaded server get its memory from?

11

Exercises

1. Use the Instance Manager to see how many sessions are active in your system.
2. Using perfmon, look at the Oracle8 threads.
3. Try running a table scan both with and without the Parallel Query option.
4. Compare the disk activity with and without the Parallel Query option.

Day 12

Working with Tables, Views, and Synonyms

NEW TERM Today you will begin to learn about the Oracle schema objects. The *schema objects* are the collection of objects associated with the database. They are an abstraction or logical structure that refers to database objects or structures. Schema objects consist of such things as clusters, indexes, packages, sequences, stored procedures, synonyms, tables, views, and so on.

Only tables, views, and synonyms are covered today. Tomorrow you will learn about indexes, and on Day 14, "Using Oracle Clusters, Stored Procedures, and Database Links," clusters will be presented. All these objects make up the Oracle schema.

Tables

NEW TERM A *table*, which is the most visible object in the Oracle RDBMS, is a structure that is used by Oracle to store data. Logically the table structure is referenced in terms of rows and columns. *Column* refers to the component of the record that is placed in the database. When you create an empty table, you define the columns. A *row* can also be referred to as a *record*. This is an individual piece of data that contains information that corresponds to the columns in the table. It is not necessary that each row have an entry for every column, but this is typically the case. An example of a table is shown in Figure 12.1.

Figure 12.1.

Example of a table.

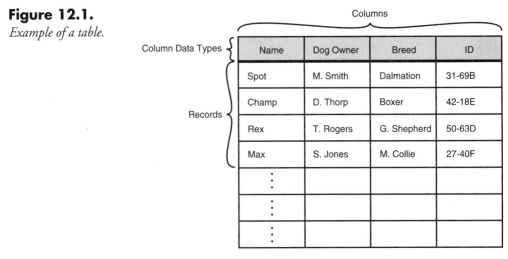

Because I have several dogs and participate in a number of dog-related activities, I like to use dog-related data in my examples. As you can see, the columns consist of particular data types and each row contains data that reflects those columns.

How Tables Work

A table is created in a table segment. The table segment in turn consists of one or more extents. If the table grows to fill the current extents, a new extent is created for that table. These extents grow in a manner specified by the STORAGE clause used to create the table.

If a STORAGE clause is not included at table creation, the default STORAGE clause defined on the tablespace is used. If no default STORAGE clause is defined on the tablespace, system defaults are used.

The data from the table is stored in database blocks. The number of rows put in one data block depends on the size of the row and the storage parameters. Depending on the type of data and how it will be accessed, you might want to consider how it is stored.

NOTE

Different database types might benefit from different storage parameters. The goal of storage management is to exploit the data cache as much as possible. Ideally, all data would be in cache when you need it, but this is not usually possible. To maximize the cache-hit rate, employ the table-storage parameters and database-creation options.

For example, if you know your data will be sequentially accessed most of the time, you can use a large block size and storage parameters that pack as many rows as possible into the data blocks. The advantage here is that when the first row in the block is requested, the entire block is loaded into memory. When subsequent rows are requested, they are already loaded into memory.

The opposite of this is a table whose data is randomly accessed with both reads and inserts. If you know you won't typically be requesting adjacent rows, use a small block size and pack the data less. Because there will be inserts, reserving some free space in the block will allow space for those inserts without causing chained rows (a *chained row* is a row that spans more than one block).

Table creation should be carefully planned. You should know what the data looks like as well as how it will be accessed. This information should help you in the database-creation phase.

Table Columns

Table columns are the individual components of a row. They can be of fixed or variable size, depending on the data type of that column. A row of a database record consists of one or more columns that hold the data. Each column is assigned a data type.

Table Rows

NEW TERM Although it is desirable to store one or more rows in a data block, this is not always possible. If the block has inadequate room, a row is split and referred to as a *chained row*. Chained rows consist of multiple *row pieces*. Even if the entire row is stored in the same block, it is sometimes referred to as a row piece.

12

The row piece is effectively a row of data. Each row piece consists of the row header and the row data. The row header stores information about the row and contains the following information:

- [ ] Information about the row piece
- [ ] Information about chaining (if applicable)
- [ ] Cluster keys (if applicable)
- [ ] Column definitions

This information is necessary for Oracle to properly process this row. For a typical nonclustered row, the row header is about three bytes in length.

Oracle Data Types

NEW TERM   Oracle8 has evolved from an RDBMS to an ORDBMS (object-relational database management system). With the new object extensions come several new Oracle data types. The traditional data types to which you are accustomed are now referred to as *scalar* data types. Other new data types include VARRAYS, REFs, and LOBs, as described later today.

Scalar Data Types

The following scalar data types are available in Oracle:

- [ ] CHAR—Fixed-length character. This can be any length between 1 and 255 bytes.
- [ ] DATE—Stores Year, Month, Day, Hour, Minute, and Second values.
- [ ] LONG—Variable-length character data up to 2GB in size.
- [ ] LONG RAW—Similar to long except it is not converted via Oracle utilities the way LONG data is.
- [ ] MLSLABEL—For use with Trusted Oracle, this data type stores the binary format of the system label.
- [ ] NUMBER—Stores fixed and floating-point numbers. Its definition includes the precision and scale.
- [ ] ROWID—Stores a triplet that consists of the data block, the row, and the datafile. Every row in a nonclustered table has a ROWID.
- [ ] VARCHAR—A variable-length character data type. The VARCHAR data type is not guaranteed to remain the same, so VARCHAR2 is recommended. Today these two data types are identical.
- [ ] VARCHAR2—A variable-length character data type that stores 1–2,000 characters. Anything larger requires LONG or LONG RAW.

The data type you choose for each column is defined at table-creation time. Other data types, such as ANSI data types, are available but are simply converted to Oracle data types. These are illustrated in Table 12.1.

Table 12.1. Oracle data types.

Non-Oracle data type	Converted to this Oracle data type
DECIMAL	NUMBER
INTEGER, INT	NUMBER(38)
SMALLINT	NUMBER(38)
FLOAT	NUMBER
REAL	NUMBER
DOUBLE	NUMBER

For more specifics on these data types, see the Oracle documentation.

VARRAYS

The VARRAY data type consists of a set of built-in types or objects referred to as *elements* of the array. Each element has an index that corresponds to the position in the array. The number of elements in an array varies, which is why it is referred to as a VARRAY, or variable array. To create an array, you must declare its maximum size because it does vary. To create an array type, use this syntax:

```
CREATE TYPE cost AS VARRAY(20) OF NUMBER(12,2)
```

This will create an array of 20 elements, each being a floating-point number with a precision of 2. This essentially allows you to create an array of values that are actually stored in one column, which can be useful in a variety of situations.

REFS

REFs are also new in Oracle8. Think of the REF data type as a pointer to an object. A REF can also be used in a manner similar to a foreign key in an RDBMS. A REF is used primarily to store an object identifier, and to allow you to select that object.

```
SELECT d.name
FROM dogs d
WHERE d.owner_id = 1;
```

In this example, d acts as a reference to dogs in order to allow easier access to that table.

12

LOBs

LOB refers to large schema objects. Oracle recognizes several different types of LOBs, including the following:

- [ ] BLOB—An unstructured binary data field. A BLOB might be something like video or picture information.
- [ ] CLOB—A large field that consists of standard, single-byte characters. This might be something like a document.
- [ ] NCLOB—Similar to the CLOB type, but consists of single or multibyte characters from the National Character Set.
- [ ] BFILE—Essentially a pointer to an externally stored file.

All these types reference large pieces of data, such as video or text. Because they are large by definition, Oracle does not store the data inline with the other columns of the table. Instead, a LOB pointer is stored there, which points to the location of the LOB data. This makes scanning of that table much faster, thus improving access to the data.

Creating Tables

Tables can be defined and created with several different Oracle tools, including Enterprise Manager, Schema Manager, and the CREATE TABLE command. This command has many more features than the graphical utilities. If you are creating a simple, straightforward table, the graphical utilities are good and easy to use; If you are performing more complex tasks, you should use the CREATE TABLE command. Today you will see all three ways of creating a table.

Managing Tables with Enterprise Manager

It is possible to manage tables with Enterprise Manager, but I prefer to use Schema Manager or Server Manager for schema operations. If you prefer Enterprise Manager, you should use that tool.

With Enterprise Manager, you can drill down into the database. If you expand the Schema Objects icon, you will see a list of the schema objects that can be managed via Enterprise Manager (see Figure 12.2).

A number of schema objects can be managed here, including

- [ ] Clusters
- [ ] Database links
- [ ] Functions
- [ ] Indexes
- [ ] Package bodies
- [ ] Packages

- ☐ Procedures
- ☐ Refresh groups
- ☐ Sequences
- ☐ Snapshot logs
- ☐ Snapshots
- ☐ Synonyms
- ☐ Tables
- ☐ Triggers
- ☐ Views

Figure 12.2.

Enterprise Manager.

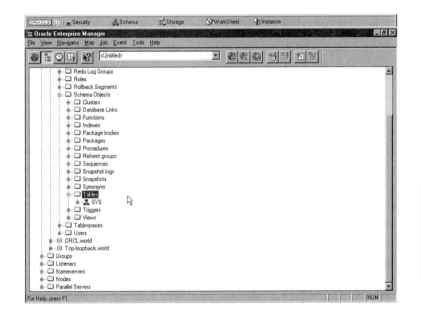

This shows only the SYS schema because I am logged into Enterprise Manager as SYS. The SYS schema objects are created by default when the database is created. If you expand the SYS icon (by clicking it), you will see a list of icons that represent the tables that currently exist in your system (see Figure 12.3).

The tables that you see in the SYS schema are the internal tables needed for the operation of Oracle. Managing and creating tables in Enterprise Manager is similar to the same operation under Schema Manager, as shown next.

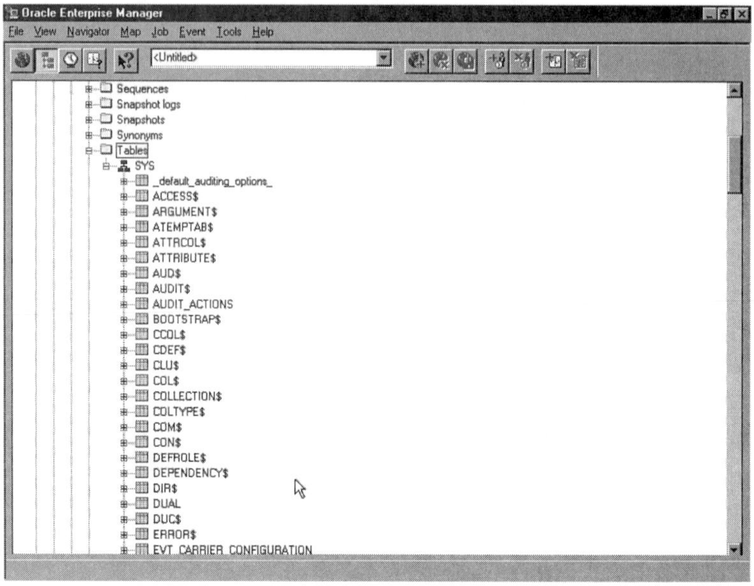

Figure 12.3.

*Icons that represent
the tables currently in
your system.*

Managing Tables with Schema Manager

Schema Manager is a nice tool for managing schema objects. When you invoke Schema Manager, you immediately see the list of schema objects similar to the one that you saw with Enterprise Manager.

If you expand the Tables icon, you will see a list of user schemas. When you expand the Tables icon with Schema Manager, you will see a list of the defined tables on the right side of the screen. This list contains the schema, the table name, and the name of the tablespace in which these tables exist (see Figure 12.4).

To create a new table with Schema Manager, right-click the Tables icon and select Create. The New Table dialog asks whether you want to use the Table wizard or create the table manually (see Figure 12.5).

Here I have selected the Use Table Wizard radio button. This wizard contains seven pages that must be completed. The first page asks for the table name, schema, and tablespace name. I have filled in these values appropriately, as shown in Figure 12.6.

When you finish entering values for these parameters, click the Next button to reach the next screen. Here you must assign a name and data type to each of the columns in the table. Do this by filling in the column name, column data type, and column size for each column, as shown in Figure 12.7.

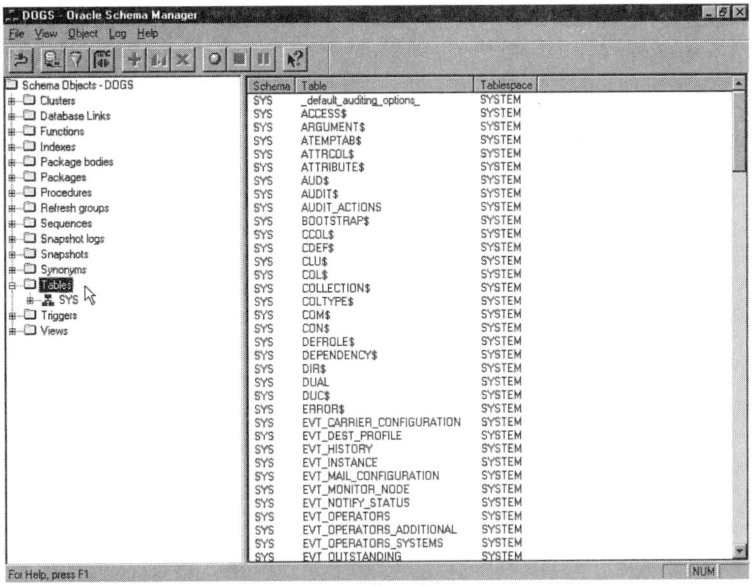

Figure 12.4.

Schema Manager showing tables.

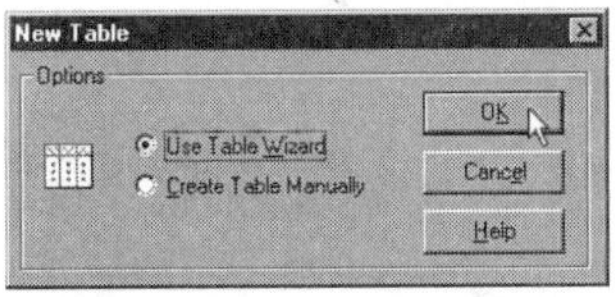

Figure 12.5.

The New Table dialog.

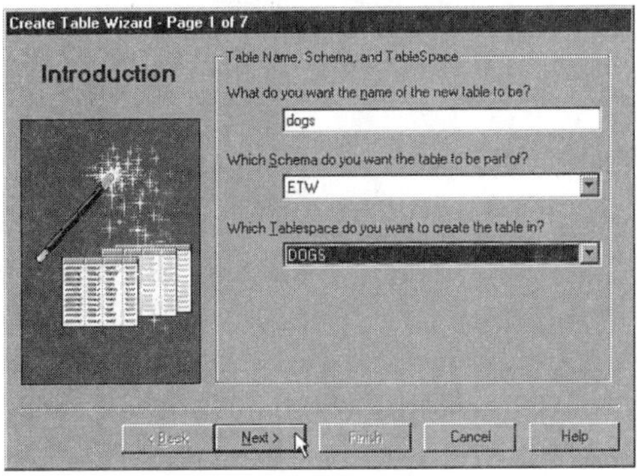

Figure 12.6.

Screen one of the Create Table wizard.

12

Figure 12.7.

*Screen two of the
Create Table wizard.*

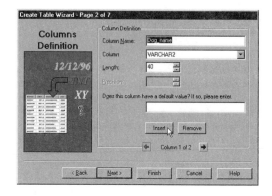

After you fill out the column information, click Insert and fill out the same information for all the columns in the table. After you fill out the information for all the columns, click the Next button to move to the third screen of the Table Creation wizard. From this screen, shown in Figure 12.8, you can set up the primary key definitions. If you desire a primary key, click the Yes I Want to Create a Primary Key button, then click the columns you want the key to be on. The order that you click the columns is the order in which the primary key is defined. Click Next to get to the next screen.

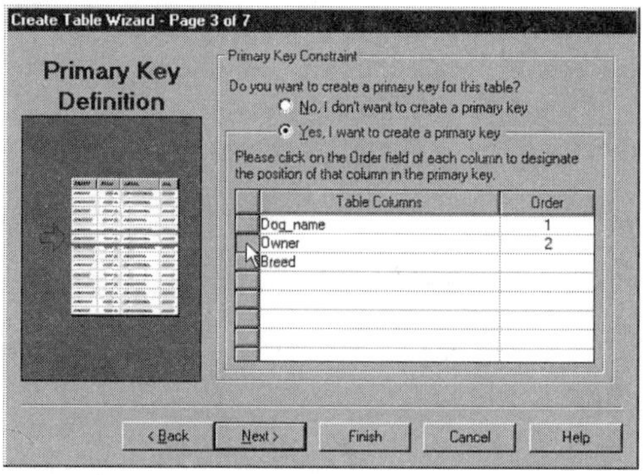

Figure 12.8.

*Screen three of the
Create Table wizard.*

The next screen, shown in Figure 12.9, takes you through the process of defining null and unique constraints. These constraints will be added to the table as configured here. Go through this screen for each column to which you want to apply null and unique constraints. Click Next when you finish.

The fifth screen, shown in Figure 12.10, is used to set up foreign key definitions. This will define constraints on your table. If defined here, an element in your table must reside in the table on which the foreign key constraint is defined. Click Next to move on.

Figure 12.9.

*Screen four of the
Create Table wizard.*

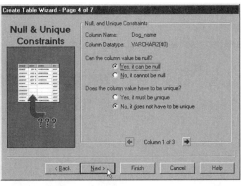

Figure 12.10.

*Screen five of the
Create Table wizard.*

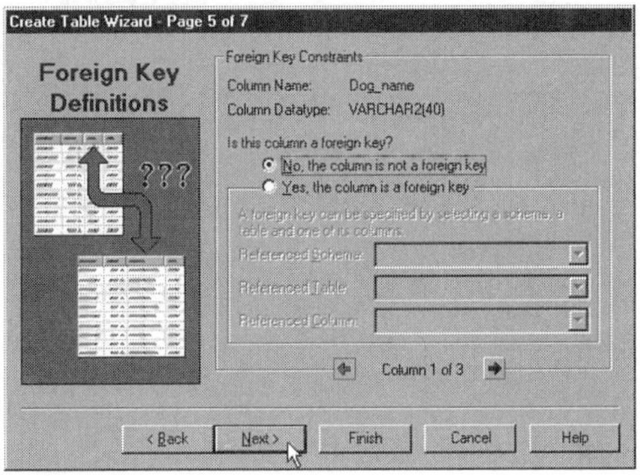

The sixth screen of the Create Table wizard, shown in Figure 12.11, is used to define any
check conditions on any of your columns. Simply select the column and enter the check
condition to which the column must adhere. Click Next to move to the next screen.

Figure 12.11.

*Screen six of the
Create Table wizard.*

12

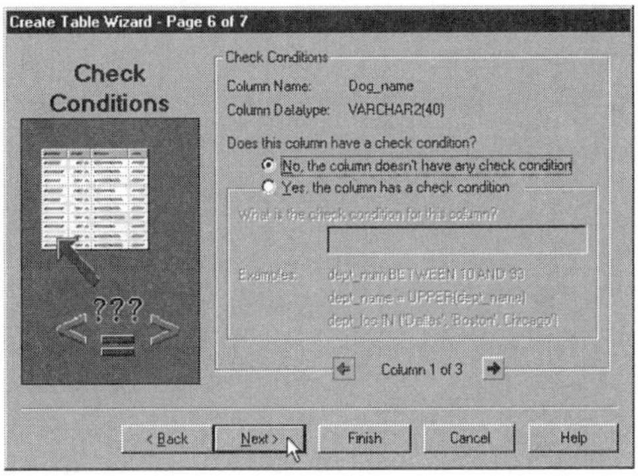

The final screen of the Create Table wizard, shown in Figure 12.12, reviews the columns, constraints, check conditions, and so on that you have defined for this table. After you complete the review screen, click the Finish button and the table will be created for you.

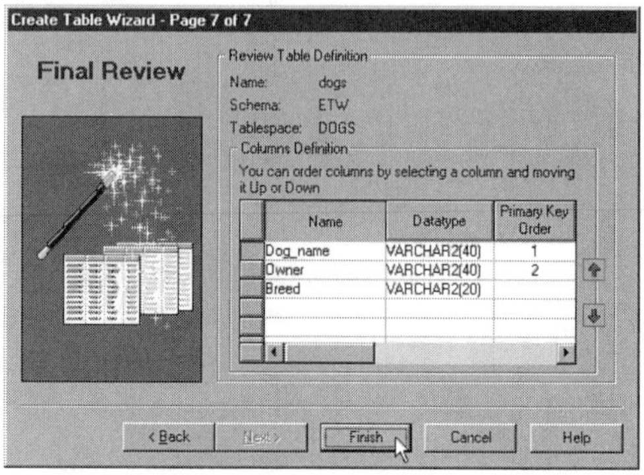

Figure 12.12.

Screen seven of the Create Table wizard.

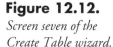

Earlier you were given the option of using the Table Creation wizard or manually creating the table. If you had chosen the manual path, you would see the Create Table screen (shown in Figure 12.13). From here it is a simple matter of entering the schema name, the table name, and various column definitions. The Create Table screen is easy to use but somewhat limited. For more control over the table-creation process, consider using the CREATE TABLE command.

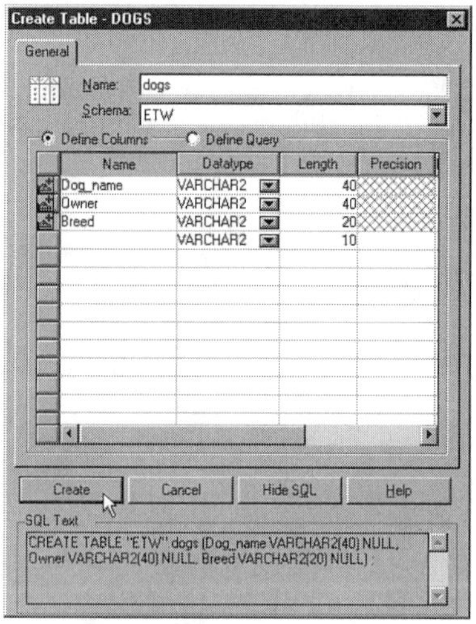

Figure 12.13.

The Create Table screen.

After the table has been created, you have several options. If you right-click the table's icon from Schema Manager, you can grant privileges, create synonyms, or index the table, as shown in Figure 12.14.

Figure 12.14.

Modify table attributes.

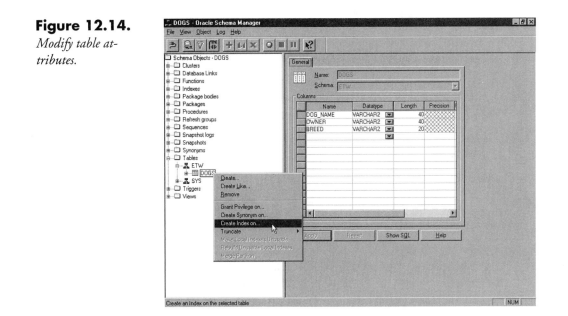

Managing Tables with the CREATE TABLE and ALTER TABLE Commands

The CREATE TABLE command can be used to create new tables, the ALTER TABLE command is used to change parameters on an already existing table, and the DROP TABLE command is used to delete an existing table. The CREATE TABLE and ALTER TABLE commands are very similar.

The CREATE TABLE command has many options and parameters, which are described in the Oracle server SQL reference manual. I won't show the syntax here, but I would like to cover some of the key parameters that are available in the CREATE TABLE and ALTER TABLE commands.

The STORAGE Clause

The primary advantage of using the CREATE TABLE and ALTER TABLE commands is your ability to include the STORAGE clause. As you saw on Day 7, "Administering Tablespaces," the STORAGE clause can be used to define how your space is created and grows. If you recall, Day 7 introduced you to the DEFAULT STORAGE clause; here it is the STORAGE clause.

The DEFAULT STORAGE clause is used to define the storage parameters on a tablespace. These DEFAULT STORAGE parameters will be used for any table created within that tablespace that does not have a STORAGE clause defined on it. A STORAGE clause will override the DEFAULT STORAGE definitions. The STORAGE clause always takes priority over the DEFAULT STORAGE clause.

12

The STORAGE clause is very important because it is used to specify the initial size and characteristics of the tablespace as well as the future growth of that tablespace. The STORAGE clause has the following syntax:

▼ SYNTAX

```
STORAGE
(
[ INITIAL number K or M ]
[ NEXT number K or M ]
[ MINEXTENTS number ]
[ MAXEXTENTS number or MAXEXTENTS UNLIMITED ]
[ PCTINCREASE number ]
[ FREELISTS number ]
[ FREELIST GROUPS number ]
[ OPTIMAL [ number K or M ] or [ NULL ] ]
)
```

▲

The parameters used in the STORAGE clause are defined as follows:

- [ ] INITIAL number K or M—This parameter specifies the initial size of the extents. These extents are created when the schema object is created. This parameter specifies the size to be number K (kilobytes) or M (megabytes). The default is about five data blocks. The size is rounded up to the nearest multiple of five blocks.

- [ ] NEXT number K or M—The NEXT parameter specifies the size of subsequent extents to be number K (kilobytes) or M (megabytes). This number is also rounded up to the nearest multiple of five data blocks, and defaults to five data blocks.

- [ ] MINEXTENTS number—This specifies the minimum number of extents that are created when the schema object is created. Each of these extents will be the size of the INITIAL extent and Oracle will use NEXT and PCTINCREASE to calculate the size of subsequent extents. The default value is 1 except for rollback segments, where the default is 2.

- [ ] MAXEXTENTS number—This parameter specifies the maximum number of extents that can be created for a schema object. This includes the first extent.

- [ ] MAXEXTENTS UNLIMITED—This parameter specifies that the maximum number of extents that can be created for a schema object is unlimited. Oracle does not recommend that you use this option with any schema objects except for rollback segments.

- [ ] PCTINCREASE number—This parameter specifies the size of extents after the second. The initial extents are sized via the INITIAL parameter. The next extent is sized via the NEXT parameter. If nonzero, all subsequent extents are sized to be NEXT multiplied by the PCTINCREASE number parameter. This number is the percentage, therefore 40 is 40% larger, and so on. A value of 0 specifies that all subsequent extents are the same size as specified in the NEXT parameter. The default value is 50, except for rollback segments which can only have a PCTINCREASE of 0.

- [ ] FREELISTS *number*—The FREELISTS parameter does not apply to tablespaces. This parameter specifies the number of groups of freelists for each of the freelist groups for tables, indexes, partitions, and clusters.

- [ ] FREELIST GROUPS *number*—The FREELIST GROUPS parameter does not apply to tablespaces. This parameter specifies the number of groups of freelists.

- [ ] OPTIMAL [*number* K or M]—This parameter applies only to rollback segments; it specifies the ideal size of the rollback segment. Because the rollback segment grows, as described tomorrow, this describes what size Oracle should attempt to keep them.

- [ ] OPTIMAL [NULL]—This parameter specifies that the rollback segments never shrink, as they can with the OPTIMAL parameter set to a value. This is described in detail tomorrow.

These storage parameters are defined on the schema object that is being created. Even though you may have defined a DEFAULT STORAGE parameter, you might define a different STORAGE parameter on each schema object.

Using the STORAGE Clause

By using the STORAGE clause, you can be very efficient with how the schema objects are stored. If you know you will be loading a large amount of data into a certain table, it is much more efficient to have a few large extents rather than many small extents. This will typically be done using the STORAGE clause on the schema objects.

In this example, I will create a table similar to the one that was created with Schema Manager. In this case, I will add the STORAGE clause to define how the table will grow and use space.

```
CREATE TABLE dogs
(
Dog_name VARCHAR2(40),
Owner VARCHAR2(40),
Breed VARCHAR2(20)
)
TABLESPACE dogs
STORAGE
(
INITIAL 2M NEXT 2M PCTINCREASE 0 MINEXTENTS 2
);
```

Remember that the STORAGE clause is used for the creation of extents. Extents are used to hold schema objects. When the schema objects are created and grow, the default storage parameters are used. These parameters are simply defaults for the schema objects that are created on these tablespaces. Schema objects that are created with their own storage parameters override the tablespace defaults.

12

Partitioned Tables

Traditionally, you have had very little control over where your table data physically resided in the database. A tablespace is created using one or more datafiles. Extents are then created on that tablespace using the datafiles, but you had no control over which datafiles your data resided on. This is usually not a problem for most systems, but it would occasionally cause an I/O imbalance.

With Oracle8, you have much more control over where your data will reside. This is accomplished through the use of the partitioned table. Oracle8 currently supports only *range partitioning* on tables, which assigns rows to different tablespaces or partitions based on the value of that data. Each partition is assigned a range of data based on column data. As data is loaded into the system, it is sent to particular partition based on that data. The partitioned table looks and feels the same to the end user, but there are many advantages:

☐ Smaller data segments, thus smaller table scans—Because the data can be divided into ranges such as month, year, and so on, if you select the data correctly (for example, by month), you can reduce a table scan to just use one partition.

☐ Smaller indexes—With range partitioning, you have the ability to create indexes individually on each partition. This cuts down on the size of each index, speeding up access to it.

☐ Easier backup and recovery—Because partitioned tables can be backed up and recovered on a partition basis, the backup operation can be split and run in parallel.

In many cases, the ability to partition your tables can be very effective and provide increased performance and ease of use. Partitioned tables are typically used when the table is very large and logically can be divided into reasonable pieces.

Creating Partitioned Tables

Partitioned tables are created with the following CREATE TABLE options:

```
CREATE TABLE [schema.] tablename
(column datatype)
PARTITION BY RANGE (column_list)
(PARTITION [partition_name] VALUES LESS THAN column_value
TABLESPACE ts_name
[, (PARTITION [partition_name] VALUES LESS THAN column_value
TABLESPACE ts_name])
```

By specifying the ranges, all rows with values less than the specified values will be placed in the specified tablespace. This partitions the data based on these columns. Using partitioning, you can better distribute I/O usage, thus improving performance by not overloading any specific components.

To create a partitioned table you must first determine which columns to partition. This is very important because the layout of your data depends on this partitioning. Key issues involved in determining the partitioning parameters include

☐ Data distribution for space—If you want to distribute data such that data is evenly distributed among tablespaces, you must know the data distribution and variance.

☐ Data distribution for I/O—If your goal is to distribute data based on I/O rates, you must know the I/O distribution of the data.

☐ Other—You might have other goals, such as keeping new information on certain disk volumes and distributing older data elsewhere.

Say you want to partition a table that keeps track of warehouse information around the country. There are 100 warehouses, with 25 in each of four districts. Information about these warehouses is retrieved for each district about 50% of the time and for the whole country about 50% of the time. This would be an ideal application for range partitioning. Let's partition this table by region.

The table should be partitioned on the column named region; because each region has a region number from 1 to 4, region is the perfect column to partition on. The table creation looks something like this:

```
CREATE TABLE warehouses
(region INTEGER,
column datatype,
.
.
.
column datatype)
PARTITION BY RANGE (region)
(PARTITION VALUES LESS THAN 2 TABLESPACE ts_r1
PARTITION VALUES LESS THAN 3 TABLESPACE ts_r2 )
PARTITION VALUES LESS THAN 4 TABLESPACE ts_r3 )
PARTITION VALUES LESS THAN MAXVALUE TABLESPACE ts_r4 )
```

This table will then partition the data so that data for each region will be on a separate tablespace. It is possible to index each partition separately or all of them together. For queries to a specific region, performance will be improved.

Object Tables

As mentioned previously, Oracle8 is an ORDBMS, or object-relational database management system. The Oracle server has additional object extensions that allow object models to be used.

12

NEW TERM   With object tables, instead of using data types, you use *object types*. These are similar to a data types in the way they are used but different in function. An object type consists of attributes and methods. An object attribute is the structure of the object type. Methods are functions or procedures that are used by that object type. For example, if I want to create an object used to categorize dogs by their owner, I could create an object type using the following SQL statement:

```
CREATE TYPE dog_info AS OBJECT
(
dog_breed varchar2(40),
dog_id NUMBER,
MEMBER FUNCTION get_id RETURN VARCHAR2
);
```

Here the attributes are dog_breed and dog_id, whereas the method is get_id. This is how an object is defined. Now that this object type is defined, it can be used in a table-creation statement. Any column in a table can now be an object type.

Now that you have created the type dog_info, you can create a table with one of the columns of type dog_info. This will use the type definition to define the column and this column will have both the attributes and the member function.

```
CREATE TABLE dogs (
Dog_name VARCHAR2(40),
dog_owner VARCHAR2(40),
dog_id dog_info );
```

This table can be populated by using a statement such as:

```
INSERT INTO dogs VALUES (
'Pierce',
'Whalen',
dog_info('Border Collie','U1234') );
```

Now you can retrieve the dog's ID number via the following SQL statement:

```
SELECT dog_id.get_id
FROM dogs
WHERE dog_name = 'Pierce' AND dog_owner = 'Whalen';
```

This allows me to track multiple dogs in one table. This data can be retrieved easily in a straightforward manner. Of course, if you use objects, you will probably use structures that are much more complex.

Index-Only Tables

Index-only tables are a new feature in Oracle8. The index-only table allows the table data to be stored within the leaf block of the index. The advantage of this is that when the leaf block of the index is reached, you have immediate access to the data rather than a reference. The index-only table is covered tomorrow.

Nested Tables

NEW TERM   A *nested table*, new with Oracle8, is a table that appears as a column in another table. This can be useful for the creation of information that is a subset of other information. A nested table can be created with this syntax:

```
CREATE TYPE dog_info_table (
Dog_id NUMBER,
Dog_breed VARCHAR2(40),
Dog_birthdate DATE);

CREATE TABLE dog_owners (
Name VARCHAR2(40),
Address VARCHAR2(60),
Dog_name VARCHAR2(40),
Dog_info dog_info_table);
```

Each item `dog_owners.dog_names` is a nested table. With this, each record in the `dog_names` table relates to a dog that is owned by the `dog_owner` referenced here. Data can be inserted into the table in the following manner:

```
INSERT INTO dog_owners VALUES (
'Whalen',
'12345 Main St., Houston, TX',
'Pierce'
Dog_info('U1234', 'Border Collie', '18-Nov-1988') );
```

An index can be created with the syntax:

```
CREATE INDEX dogs_index ON dogs_owners.dog_names(dog_id);
```

Views

NEW TERM   A *view* is a window into a table. Although a view is treated like a table in that you can select columns from it, a view is not a table; it is a logical structure that looks like a table but is actually a superset or subset of a table. A view derives its data from other tables, which are referred to as *base tables*. These base tables can be tables or even other views. Views are used to simplify the access of certain data and to hide certain pieces of data. Views are very powerful and can be quite useful in many situations.

By creating views, you can protect sensitive data within a table. For example, an employee record might contain sensitive information such as salary and job grade. If you create a view on that table that does not include those columns and allow users to access only the view, you can protect the sensitive information.

Managing Views

To create views with Enterprise Manager or Storage Manager, right-click the Views icon and select the Create option. This invokes the Create View screen. From here, you must build a query that will be used to create a view, as shown in Figure 12.15.

Figure 12.15.

The Create View screen.

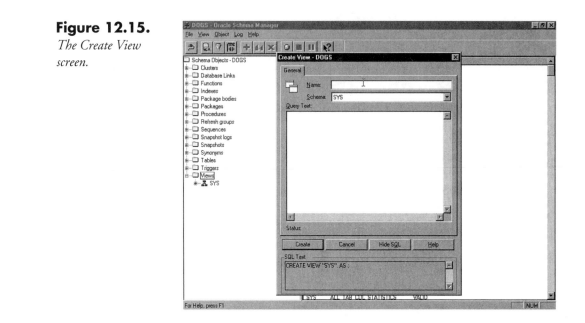

You create a view by entering a view name and schema at the top of the screen, then typing a query into the Query Text area. As you can see, the Show SQL option has been enabled. Similarly, a view can be created with the CREATE VIEW command like so:

```
CREATE VIEW executives AS
SELECT employee_name, employee_rank, employee_salary
FROM employee
WHERE employee_rank > 99;
```

Assume you have an employee table where each employee has a rank based on job grade. Executive job grades start at 100. This view selects employee information for only those employees who have a 100 or greater job grade.

Views can be built from simple queries that select a subset of a table or they can be built from joins from multiple tables. After a view is created, it cannot be modified but it can be replaced. If a view already exists, you can use the CREATE OR REPLACE VIEW syntax. This either creates or replaces a view, depending on the current status.

Synonyms

NEW TERM *Synonyms* are simply database objects that point to another object in the system; they are aliases for tables, views, sequences, or program units. Synonyms are typically used to hide certain details from the end user, such as object ownership or location of the distributed object. If you use synonyms, you can ensure that only the information you want seen will be seen.

12

Synonyms come in two forms: public and private. A public synonym is owned by the PUBLIC schema and is available to every user in the database. A private synonym is contained in the schema of the user who created it, and that user has control over who has access to it.

Synonyms can also be used to simplify the access to certain data in a distributed system. Instead of attaching system names to the object name, you can use a synonym. For example, the following SQL query

```
SELECT * FROM etw.dogs;
```

can be simplified to

```
SELECT * FROM dogs;
```

When you create a synonym the access path is simplified; because etw.dogs is defined as dogs, the user need not know the system name. To create this synonym via the graphical tools, right-click the Synonym icon and use the Create Synonym tool, shown in Figure 12.16.

Figure 12.16.

The Create Synonym tool.

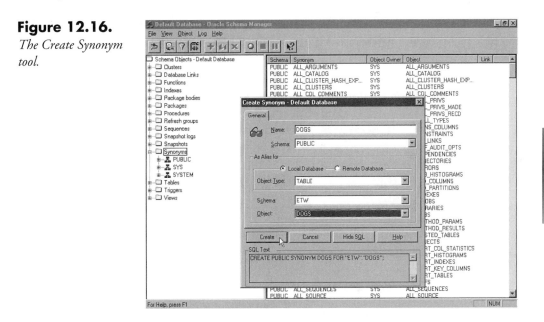

Here I have selected PUBLIC as the schema in which I want this synonym to exist. I have also configured this synonym to be an alias for the dogs table I created earlier. I used the Show SQL option. The SQL syntax used here (which can also be used with Server Manager) is

```
CREATE PUBLIC SYNONYM DOGS for "ETW"."DOGS";
```

Summary

Today's lesson introduced you to the Oracle schema objects. These consist of the logical database structures used to organize data within the database itself. The schema objects consist of tables, indexes, clusters, views, and so on.

You were introduced to the Oracle table; first you learned about the traditional Oracle table structure, then about the new features of Oracle8. These new schema objects consist of objects, partitioned tables, object tables, and nested tables.

You also learned about Oracle views. These views are used to simplify data access or to hide details from the user. With a view, you can allow users to see certain employee information while hiding more sensitive information such as salaries.

You were also introduced to the Oracle synonym, which is simply a pointer to another object in the database. Synonyms can hide certain details from the user just as views can hide certain columns from the user.

What's Next?

On Day 13, "Using Indexes and Sequences," you will learn about indexes, one of the most important performance features in the Oracle RDBMS. Indexes are used to speed up access to randomly selected data. You will learn how indexes work, how to create and modify indexes, and how to properly use indexes for enhanced performance. When used correctly, indexes are very powerful tools; however, they are easy to misuse. When indexes are misused, their potential is not fully realized.

On Day 14, you will finish learning about the basic building blocks in the Oracle schema. The main schema objects consist of tables, indexes, and clusters. By the time you finish Day 14's lesson, you will know about all of these.

Q&A

Q What are tables used for?

A A table is the Oracle object that actually holds the data that is entered into the database. A table consists of rows of data that are defined by table columns.

Q What is a partitioned table?

A A partitioned table uses the new Oracle feature, range partitioning. Data is stored in a location based on a range of data you have defined. This range can be numeric or a data format.

Q What can nested tables be used for?

A Nested tables can be used for many things. They are particularly useful for holding information of the same type, thus simplifying the access of that data. For example, if you were storing spatial data, you could use a nested table to hold compass and altitude information. This way, you could use a single column, location, in the main table.

Q Why would you use a view?

A Views can be useful to hide certain information from the end user. They can be used for security purposes (for example, to hide salary information from users) or to simplify access to a distributed table or complex join.

Workshop

The workshop provides quiz questions to help you solidify your understanding of the material covered and exercises to provide you with experience in using what you've learned. Answers to quiz questions can be found in Appendix A, "Answers."

Quiz

1. What is a table column?
2. What is a row in a table?
3. What two components are row pieces made of?
4. What makes up an object?
5. What is a nested table?
6. What is a partitioned table?
7. How are tables partitioned?
8. What is a view?
9. What is the STORAGE clause used for?
10. What is a synonym?

Exercises

1. Create a simple table.
2. Create a table with a nested column.
3. Create a view on that table.
4. Create a synonym to that view.

12

Day **13**

Using Indexes and Sequences

An index is an optional structure designed to help you gain faster access to data. Just like the index in this book, an Oracle index is logically and physically independent of the data in the associated table or cluster. You can use the index to speed access to the data or you can retrieve the data independently from the index by searching the tables for it. When optimally configured and used, indexes can significantly reduce I/O to the datafiles and greatly improve performance.

The presence of an index is transparent to the user or application and requires no application changes. However, if you are aware of an index, you should be able to design your applications to take better advantage of those indexes. The only indication of an index might be an improved access time to data.

The index itself should be created with some knowledge of the application and data-access patterns. If indexes are created on columns that are not used to access the data, the index is useless.

After an index has been created for a table, Oracle automatically maintains that index. Insertions, updates, and deletions of rows in the table automatically update the related indexes.

A table can have any number of indexes, but the more indexes there are, the more overhead is incurred during table updates, insertions, and deletions. This overhead is incurred because all associated indexes must be updated whenever table data is altered.

 TIP

> Indexes can be created with the Parallel Index Creation feature of the Parallel Query option. Using this feature greatly reduces index-creation time. Because all data must be read to create the index, a table scan is forced. This table scan is parallelized, greatly improving performance.

It is often necessary to create a sequence of numbers to be used as an identifier in your application. This number might be an account number, order number, or some other sort of ID number. Rather than generating these numbers manually, Oracle has a facility to generate these sequences of numbers automatically. To create a unique sequence of numbers on your own, you would have to lock the record that has the last value of the sequence, generate a new value, and then unlock the record. To avoid locking these records, Oracle provides a sequence generator that performs this service for you.

The Oracle sequence generator can generate sequential numbers of up to 38 digits, without having to manually lock records. When you define a sequence, you can specify the original values of the sequence, whether the sequence should be cached, and whether the sequence should be in ascending or descending order. Later today you will learn how to use the Oracle sequence generator to automatically generate sequences of numbers for you.

Index Types

There are several different types of indexes. An index can be limited to one column value or can consist of several columns. An index can be either unique or nonunique.

NEW TERM A *unique index* is an index value that has the additional constraint that the set of indexed columns defines a unique row. Although this constraint might be specified, it is usually better to associate this constraint with the table itself rather than with the index. Oracle enforces UNIQUE integrity constraints by automatically defining a unique index on the unique key.

NEW TERM A *nonunique index* does not impose the constraint that the index value be unique. Such an index can be quite useful when quick access is desired on a nonunique value.

13

NEW TERM Another type of index is a *composite index*, which indexes several columns in a table. These column values can be in any order and the columns do not have to be adjacent in the table.

A composite index is useful when SELECT statements have WHERE clauses that reference several values in the table. Because the index is accessed based on the order of the columns used in the definition, it is wise to base this order on the frequency of use. The most-referenced column should be defined first, and so on.

The index should be created based on the values accessed in the application; the application should be developed to take advantage of these indexes. Having knowledge of and influence over these indexes can be very useful to the application developer.

How the Oracle Index Works

NEW TERM When an index is created, an index segment is automatically allocated. This index segment contains information that speeds access to data by determining the location of indexed data with as few I/Os as possible. Oracle indexes data by using an index structure known as a *B*-tree index*. A B*-tree index is designed to balance the access time to any row. A B*-tree index is a tree of descending comparison values, as shown in Figure 13.1. As you traverse down the index, you compare the desired value with the values in the upper-level index blocks, called *branch blocks*. Based on the outcome of the comparison with the branch blocks, you compare the desired value with more branch blocks until you reach the lowest-level index blocks. The index blocks on the lowest level, called *leaf blocks*, contain every indexed data value and the associated ROWID of that data.

Figure 13.1.

The B*-tree index structure.

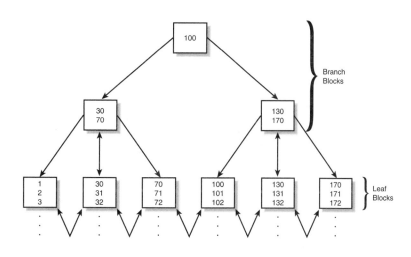

With a unique index, there is one ROWID per data value in the leaf block, as shown in Figure 13.2. With a nonunique index, there might be several values associated with the data value. In the case of the nonunique index, the data values are sorted first by the index key and then by the ROWID.

Figure 13.2.

The index block
structure.

Index Block

VALUE	ROWID
130	XXX
131	XXX
132	XXX
133	XXX
134	XXX

With a B*-tree index, all the leaf blocks are at the same level. Access of index data takes approximately the same time regardless of the value of the data. B*-tree indexes provide quick access to data whether it is an exact match or a range query. In addition, B*-tree indexes provide good performance regardless of the size of the table; performance does not degrade as the table grows.

Deciding What to Index

An index is effective only when it is used. The use of the index is determined primarily by the column values that are indexed. Remember that the more indexes you have on a table, the more overhead is incurred during updates, insertions, and deletions. Therefore, it is important to index selectively. Use the following guidelines for deciding which tables to index:

- Index tables when queries select only a small number of rows. Queries that select a large number of rows defeat the purpose of the index. Use indexes when queries access less than 5% of the rows in the table.

- Don't index tables that are frequently updated. Updates, insertions, and deletions incur extra overhead when indexed. Base your decision to index on the number of updates, insertions, and deletions relative to the number of queries to the table.

- Index tables that don't have duplicate values on the columns usually selected in WHERE clauses. Tables in which the selection is based on TRUE or FALSE values are not good candidates for indexing.

- Index tables that are queried with relatively simple WHERE clauses. Complex WHERE clauses might not take advantage of indexes.

If you decide to use an index, it is important to determine the columns on which you put the index. Depending on the table, you might choose to index one or more columns. Use the following guidelines for deciding which columns to index:

☐ Choose columns that are most frequently specified in WHERE clauses. Frequently accessed columns can benefit most from indexes.

☐ Don't index columns that do not have many unique values. Columns in which a good percentage of rows are duplicates cannot take advantage of indexing.

☐ Columns that have unique values are excellent candidates for indexing. Oracle automatically indexes columns that are unique or primary keys defined with constraints. These columns are most effectively optimized by indexes.

☐ Columns that are commonly used to join tables are good candidates for indexing.

☐ Frequently modified columns probably should not be index columns because of the overhead involved in updating the index.

In certain situations, the use of composite indexes might be more effective than individual indexes. Here are some examples of where composite indexes might be quite useful:

☐ When two columns are not unique individually but are unique together, composite indexes might work very well. For example, although columns A and B have few unique values, rows with a particular combination of columns A and B are mostly unique. Look for WHERE clauses with AND operators.

☐ If all values of a SELECT statement are in a composite index, Oracle does not query the table; the result is returned from the index.

☐ If several different queries select the same rows with different WHERE clauses based on different columns, consider creating a composite index with all the columns used in the WHERE statements.

Composite indexes can be quite useful when they are carefully designed. As with single-column indexes, they are most effective if applications are written with the indexes in mind.

After you create the index, you should periodically use the SQL Trace facility to determine whether your queries are taking advantage of the indexes. It might be worth the effort to try the query with and without indexes and then compare the results to see whether the index is worth the space it uses.

In summary, indexes can significantly improve performance in your system if they are used properly. You must first decide whether an index is appropriate for the data and access patterns in your particular system. After you decide to use an index, you must decide which columns to index. Indexing an inappropriate column or table can reduce performance. Indexing appropriately can greatly improve performance by reducing I/Os and speeding access times. Careful planning and periodic testing with the SQL Trace feature can lead to a very effective use of indexes, with optimal performance being the outcome.

13

Taking Advantage of Indexes

Because one or more columns are indexed, it is necessary to include the indexed column or columns in the WHERE clause of the SQL statement. Because the indexed column or columns are referenced in the WHERE clause, the optimizer will immediately know to use an index scan rather than a table scan to access the requested data. If you do not include the columns that are indexed in the WHERE clause of the SQL statement, the index will probably be bypassed, thus causing a table scan.

> **TIP**
>
> It takes the right application coding to take advantage of indexes. If one or more columns are indexed but are not referenced in the WHERE clause of the SQL statements accessing that table, the index will not be used. Coordination between the DBA and the application developers is required to take advantage of indexes.

You can tell whether you are taking advantage of indexes by using the Oracle EXPLAIN PLAN facility to show the query execution plan that the optimizer has chosen for your SQL statements. If you are using the index as expected, you will see an index scan in the execution plan.

How Indexes Improve Performance

NEW TERM If there are no indexes on your table, the only way Oracle can find the data you want is to search every piece of data in the table and compare it against the requested data. This is typically referred to as a *table scan* or *full-table scan*. A table scan is not very efficient in most cases because you typically want to select or update only a few rows.

Because I/Os are expensive operations on a computer system, table scans are very expensive. Reducing the amount of data that is read from the disk is desirable. By reducing the amount of data that is read, you reduce system overhead. An index improves your performance by knowing exactly where the data is on disk and avoiding costly table scans, thus reducing I/O overhead.

Creating Indexes

Indexes can be created either via the graphical utilities provided with Oracle Enterprise Manager or via the CREATE INDEX command. Because Enterprise Manager and Schema Manager provide essentially the same functionality, I will not discuss Enterprise Manager here. Schema Manager provides all the functionality of Enterprise Manager, but with additional features.

Creating Indexes with Schema Manager

Schema Manager is used to administer all Oracle schema objects. As you have seen, indexes and tables are schema objects. Schema Manager provides an easy way to create indexes graphically. To create an index with Schema Manager, drill down into the table on which you want to create the index. Right-click the Indexes option under the table's entry, as shown in Figure 13.3.

Figure 13.3.

Creating an index with Schema Manager.

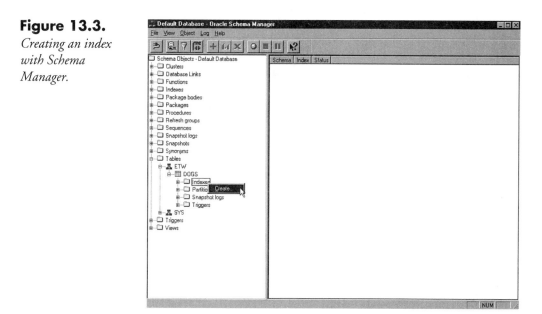

This invokes the Create Index screen, where you provide the information required to create the index on the selected table. The initial Create Index screen is shown in Figure 13.4. A number of options must be filled in before the index can be created:

- [ ] Name—The name of the index. Each index must have a unique identifier.
- [ ] Schema—The schema where the index resides. The index and the table need not be within the same schema.
- [ ] Type—This is used for partitioning. If this were a partitioned table, you would be able to choose whether your index was local or global.
- [ ] Index On—You can choose whether you are indexing a table or a cluster.
- [ ] Schema—The schema where the table resides.
- [ ] Table—The table to be indexed.

13

☐ Index Columns—After the table has been selected, a list of the table's columns is displayed. If you click the Order column in the order you want the index columns to be created, you will see a number appear. This indicates the index order.

☐ Options—Optional parameters define whether the index is unique, sorted, and whether the index creation is written to the log file. For large indexes, it might be beneficial to abstain from logging the index creation to save log space and improve performance.

Figure 13.4.

The Create Index screen.

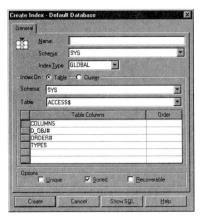

A completed Create Index screen is shown in Figure 13.5. Here I have selected to index the DOGS ID field. This will speed up access to the DOGS table whenever I am using the ID column in the WHERE clause. When I access a row in the database where the selection criteria are based on a value of the ID column, the index will be used.

Figure 13.5.

Creating an index for the DOGS table on the ID field.

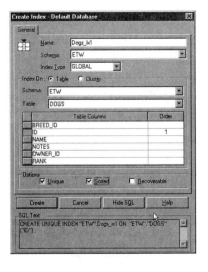

That is really all there is to creating an index using Schema Manager. The index will be automatically maintained by Oracle after the index has been created. If you use the CREATE INDEX command, you have more options available.

Creating Indexes with the CREATE INDEX Command

With this command you can specify all the options available with Schema Manager, as well as other options. Rather than go over all the options available with the CREATE INDEX command, I will highlight some of the optional parameters that are not available with the graphical tools. Please reference the Oracle SQL Reference Manual for the complete syntax of the CREATE INDEX command.

- ☐ BITMAP—This parameter is used to specify a bitmap index. The bitmap index is described in detail in the section titled "Bitmap Indexes."

- ☐ NOSORT—This specifies to the index-creation process that the rows are already in sorted order, thus skipping the sort process. This can save substantial time in creating the index.

- ☐ REVERSE—This parameter specifies that the blocks in the index are stored in reverse order.

- ☐ GLOBAL—This parameter specifies a global partitioned index, as described in the section titled "Global Indexes."

- ☐ PARTITION—This parameter is used for partitioned indexes, as described in the section titled "Partitioned Indexes."

- ☐ VALUES LESS THAN—This parameter is also used for partitioned indexes, as described in the section titled "Partitioned Indexes."

- ☐ PARALLEL—This parameter allows you to specify the degree of parallelism for the index-creation process. For large indexes, the time savings can be substantial.

- ☐ STORAGE clause—This parameter allows you to modify the storage parameters for the index. This is the same STORAGE clause you saw before.

In many cases, creating the index by hand with the CREATE INDEX command can be beneficial. In addition to allowing you more control over the storage and parallelism of the index creation, through scripting you have a saved record of the index-creation process. If you are creating indexes on large tables, the CREATE INDEX command might be the best way for you to create the index. An example of the CREATE INDEX procedure is shown in Listing 13.1.

13

Listing 13.1. Using the CREATE INDEX command.

```
CREATE INDEX "ETW".dogs_ix1
ON  "ETW"."DOGS" ("ID")
PARALLEL (DEGREE 10)
TABLESPACE DOGS;
```

ANALYSIS This creates the same index as shown with Schema Manager except that it uses a parallelism of 10. This allows 10 parallel processes to scan the table to retrieve the data necessary to create the index.

NOTE
> There is no limit to the number of indexes that you can create on a table. Remember that each time a column is updated or inserted, the index might need to be modified. This causes overhead on the system. For tables whose access pattern is mostly read, there is very little penalty for multiple indexes except in terms of the space they use. Even though indexes can take up considerable space, they are well worth it.

Partitioned Indexes

As you saw yesterday, a new feature of Oracle8 is range partitioning. Like tables, indexes can also be partitioned; but with indexes you have a few more options because the underlying table might or might not also be partitioned. There are essentially two different types of partitioned indexes available with Oracle8:

- ☐ Global indexes—These are created in a manner different from the underlying partitioning of the table that is indexed.
- ☐ Local indexes—These are partitioned in the same manner as the underlying table partitioning.

Global Indexes

NEW TERM A *global index* can be thought of as a single B*-tree index over the entire contents of the table. Even though this is one large index, it can be partitioned. This single index has information about all rows in all partitions in the table.

To create a global partitioned index, use the CREATE INDEX parameter GLOBAL. This specifies that the index will be a global index. Further partitioning of the index is accomplished by using the following parameters:

- ☐ GLOBAL—This parameter specifies a global partitioned index.

- [ ] PARTITION *part_name*—This parameter is used to identify the partition. If you do not specify the partition name, a default name will be provided. It is not usually necessary to provide the partition name.

- [ ] VALUES LESS THAN—This parameter is used to specify the range that is allocated for that particular partition in the same way as the partition was specified in the CREATE TABLE statement (discussed yesterday).

NOTE

The last partition should contain the keyword MAXVALUE for its range.

For example, to range-partition the index that was created earlier in this lesson, use the syntax that appears in Listing 13.2.

 Listing 13.2. Creating a partitioned index.

```
CREATE INDEX "ETW".dogs_ix1
ON  DOGS (ID)
PARTITION BY RANGE (ID)
PARTITION pt1 VALUES LESS THAN ('1000') TABLESPACE ts1,
PARTITION pt2 VALUES LESS THAN (MAXVALUE) TABLESPACE ts2);
```

ANALYSIS This create two partitions, the first holding values of ID that are less than 1,000, the second holding the remaining values of ID. If you do not specify the partition name, as is the case here, a default name will be provided.

Local Indexes

NEW TERM In contrast to the global index, a *local partitioned index* is individually created on each partition. If you specify a local partitioned index, Oracle automatically maintains the index's partitioning along with that of the underlying table.

Local partitioned indexes are created through the use of the LOCAL parameter with the CREATE INDEX statement. It is unnecessary to provide partitioning information because the underlying table partitioning will be used. A local index can be created with the following syntax:

```
CREATE INDEX "ETW".dogs_ix1
ON  DOGS (ID)
LOCAL;
```

Because the index is local, all partition changes to the table will be automatically reflected on the index partitions as well.

13

Local partitioned indexes have some inherent advantages that are similar to the advantages you get from partitioned tables. These advantages include the following:

- [ ] Because the index exists entirely on one partition, any maintenance operations affect only that one partition.
- [ ] The Oracle optimizer can use the local index to generate better query plans based on the fact that a local index is used.
- [ ] If a partition is lost and must be recovered, only the data and index for that particular partition needs to be recovered. With a global index, the entire index would need recovery.

As you can see, there are many advantages of using both global and local partitioned indexes.

Index-Only Tables

NEW TERM   An *index-only table* is a schema object introduced in Oracle8. An index-only table is similar to an index, but whereas an index contains the primary key value and a ROWID pointing to where the data is kept, the index-only table stores the column data in the leaf block of the index.

Because the leaf blocks of the Oracle index are traditionally very small and tightly packed, there can be some drawbacks to having large rows stored there. Oracle has developed a way to compensate for this: If rows become too large (by a set threshold), the row data is stored in an overflow area as specified in the CREATE TABLE statement. This creates storage more like the traditional index and table relationship.

An index-only table contains the same structure as the Oracle B*-tree index. Only the leaf blocks have changed. Index-only tables have many of the attributes of both indexes and tables, but there are a few exceptions:

- [ ] Because it is part index and part table, no other indexes can be added to the index-only table.
- [ ] The UNIQUE constraint is not allowed on an index-only table.
- [ ] A trigger can be added to the index-only table.
- [ ] An index-only table cannot be stored in a cluster.
- [ ] Replication is not supported at this time.

As you can see, there are some restrictions on index-only tables, but there are also a great deal of benefits.

When to Use Index-Only Tables

Index-only tables are very useful whenever data is always accessed via the primary key index. If this is the case with your data, the index-only table will cut down on the space used by both the index and the table (by combining them) and improve performance. Performance is improved because, by the time the ROWID would have been retrieved, you have the data.

Tables that are not accessed via the primary key value are not good candidates for index-only tables. Also, tables whose primary key values are updated and tables that have frequent insertions are not good candidates for index-only tables.

How to Create Index-Only Tables

Index-only tables are created with the CREATE TABLE command; the ORGANIZATION INDEXED qualifier is used to identify the table as index-only. The following qualifiers are used in creating index-only tables:

- ☐ ORGANIZATION INDEXED—This qualifier specifies an index-only table organization.
- ☐ OVERFLOW TABLESPACE *ts_name*—This qualifier specifies the overflow tablespace name.
- ☐ PCTTHRESHOLD *threshold*—This qualifier specifies the percent of a block that a row must be larger than in order to be offloaded to the overflow tablespace.

An example of how to create an index-only table is shown in Listing 13.3.

Listing 13.3. Creating an index-only table with the CREATE TABLE command.

```
CREATE TABLE "ETW".DOGS (
ID NUMBER,
NAME VARCHAR2(40),
OWNER_ID NUMBER,
BREED_ID NUMBER,
RANK NUMBER NULL,
NOTES VARCHAR2(80)
PRIMARY KEY(ID) )
ORGANIZATION INDEXED
PCTTHRESHOLD 40
OVERFLOW TABLESPACE "DOGS2"
TABLESPACE "DOGS";
```

ANALYSIS This specifies that the index-only tablespace be created on the DOGS tablespace, whereas the overflow tablespace used is DOGS2.

NOTE It is necessary to specify the PRIMARY KEY value when creating an index-only table. This is the value on which the index is created.

13

Bitmap Indexes

 Another type of index available in Oracle8 is the *bitmap index*. With the traditional index you saw earlier, Oracle uses a B*-tree method to traverse the index to find the leaf block. With a bitmap index, a bitmap of ROWIDs is kept; this bitmap indicates which rows correspond to the index item. If the bit is set, this indicates that the corresponding row contains the key value; if the bit is not set, the opposite is true.

As you can probably tell, bitmap indexes can probably be quite useful under the right circumstances, and useless overhead otherwise. An example of a bitmap index is shown in Figure 13.6.

Figure 13.6.

A bitmap index.

ID	Name	Sex		Bitmap on Index Sex M	F
1	Dash	M		1	0
2	Puff	F		0	1
3	Pierce	M		1	0
4	Chip	M		1	0
5	Teller	M		1	0
6	Jenny	F		0	1

When to Use Bitmap Indexes

As you can probably guess, the bitmap index works well on items with low cardinality. *Low cardinality* means there is a small amount of variance in the possible values stored in that column. For example, the column representing the sex of the dog is said to have low cardinality because only two values are possible. Other column types that might have low cardinality include

- ☐ Marital status
- ☐ Account status (good or bad)
- ☐ Sales region (if there are only a few)
- ☐ Rank (if there are only a few)
- ☐ Special notes (whether there is a note)

With columns that have low cardinality, the bitmap index can greatly improve performance. Columns with high cardinality are not candidates for bitmap indexes.

How to Create Bitmapped Indexes

A bitmap index is created with the CREATE INDEX command with the BITMAP qualifier. For example, the following will create a bitmap index:

```
CREATE BITMAP INDEX
```

To create a bitmap index on the SEX field in the DOGS table, you can use the following syntax:

```
CREATE BITMAP INDEX "ETW".dogs_bx1
ON  DOGS (SEX);
```

This simple statement will create the bitmap index on the column specified. At this time, bitmap indexes cannot be created with the graphical tools.

Table Sequences

It is frequently necessary to generate a sequence of numbers to use in your database. For example, you might need these numbers to identify a particular record. To create a unique sequence of numbers on your own, you would have to lock the record that has the last value of the sequence, generate a new value, and then unlock the record. To avoid locking these records, Oracle provides a sequence generator that performs this service for you.

The Oracle sequence generator can generate sequential numbers with as many as 38 digits without having to manually lock records. When you define a sequence, you can specify the original values of the sequence, whether the sequence should be cached, and whether the sequence should be in ascending or descending order.

Sequences can be created either with graphical tools, such as Schema Manager, or with the CREATE SEQUENCE command.

Creating Sequences with Schema Manager

To create a sequence with Schema Manager, select the Create option after right-clicking the Sequence icon. This invokes the Create Sequence screen. By filling in parameters such as Minimum, Maximum, Increment, and so on, you can specify how the sequence works. A filled-in Create Sequence screen is shown in Figure 13.7.

Figure 13.7.

The Create Sequence screen.

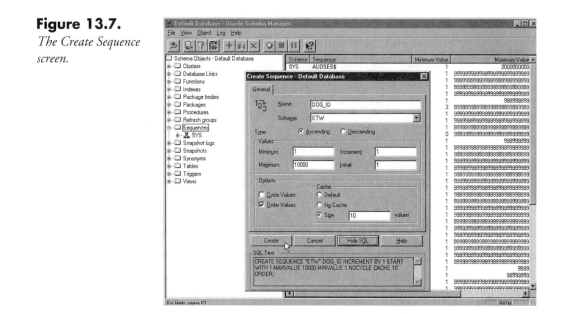

Creating Sequences with the CREATE SEQUENCE Command

Sequences can be created with the CREATE SEQUENCE command. This command has the following syntax:

```
CREATE SEQUENCE DOG_ID
   INCREMENT BY 1
   START WITH 1
   NOMAXVALUE
   NOCYCLE
   CACHE 4;
```

The following provides brief descriptions of each parameter:

☐ INCREMENT BY—This parameter specifies the amount by which to increment the sequence each time a value is obtained.

☐ START WITH—This parameter specifies the starting value.

☐ MAXVALUE *n*—This parameter specifies the maximum value that the sequence can obtain.

☐ NOMAXVALUE (Default)—This parameter specifies no maximum value for a sequence. The sequence can grow to 10^{27} for ascending sequences and –1 for descending sequences.

- ☐ MINVALUE *n*—This parameter specifies the minimum value of the sequence.
- ☐ NOMINVALUE (Default)—This parameter specifies no minimum value for a sequence. The sequence can have a minimum of 1 for ascending sequences and -10^{26} for descending sequences.
- ☐ CYCLE—This parameter specifies that a sequence will restart after reaching the maximum or minimum value.
- ☐ NOCYCLE (Default)—This parameter specifies that the sequence cannot recycle after reaching the maximum or minimum value.
- ☐ CACHE *n*—This parameter specifies the number of sequence entries to cache for quick access. (The default is 20 values.)
- ☐ NOCACHE—This parameter specifies that no sequence entries should be cached.
- ☐ ORDER—This parameter specifies that sequence entries are generated in the order in which they are requested. By default, this is not the case.
- ☐ NOORDER (Default)—This parameter specifies that sequence numbers are not necessarily generated in the order in which they are requested. This is usually fine for primary key values.

Tuning Sequences

To get the best performance out of sequences, you should cache as many sequences as you think you will have simultaneous requests for. By over-specifying the number of cached sequences, you use more memory than necessary. By under-specifying the number of cached entries, you cause undue waiting for the sequences.

Using the Oracle sequence generator is much more efficient than manually generating sequences. If you have a series of values that must be sequential, I recommend using the Oracle sequence generator.

Using Sequences

To generate a new sequence value, simply reference the value of *sequence_name*.NEXTVAL. To re-reference that number from within the same SQL block, reference the value of *sequence_name*.CURVAL. When you reference *sequence_name*.NEXTVAL, a new sequence number is generated.

Listing 13.4 contains the sequence created in the preceding section to generate a new value in the DOGS table. The result of this INSERT statement is to insert a dog with a sequentially growing value for the ID column. Remember, the ID column of the DOGS table is a sequential value for the dog's ID number.

13

Listing 13.4. Inserting a row using a sequence.

```
SQL> INSERT INTO dogs
  2  ( id, name)
  3  VALUES
  4  ( DOG_ID.NEXTVAL, 'Shasta');

1 row created.
```

Sequences are incremented as they are accessed, independent of rollback or commit. If a transaction generates a sequence and then rolls back, the sequence is not replaced. Therefore, there might be holes in your sequential values. This is usually not a problem.

NOTE

Because sequences are generated independently of commits or rollbacks, you might have gaps in the sequences. Although this is usually not an issue, you should make a note of it.

Using Cached Sequences for Primary Key Values

As shown in the preceding example, it can be efficient to use cached sequences to generate unique primary-key values. Not only is the performance of the cached sequence good, you are guaranteed a unique number (unless you have enabled CYCLE).

WARNING

If you use cached sequences to generate primary-key values, be sure to set the NOCYCLE parameter for the sequence and make sure the minimum and maximum values are sufficiently high. Cycling sequences causes integrity constraints to be violated.

Summary

Today you learned about indexes and sequences. An index is an optional structure designed to help you gain faster access to data. Just like the index in this book, an Oracle index is logically and physically independent of the data in the associated table or cluster. You can use the index to speed access to the data or you can retrieve the data independently from the index by searching the tables for it. When optimally configured and used, indexes can significantly reduce I/O to the datafiles and greatly improve performance.

The presence of an index is transparent to the user or application and requires no application changes. However, if you are aware of an index, you should be able to better design your applications to take advantage of it. The index itself should be created with some knowledge of the application and data-access patterns. If indexes are created on columns that are not used to access the data, the index is useless.

You also learned about the Oracle sequence generator. Using the sequence generator, you can generate a unique sequence of numbers quickly and without duplication. To create a unique sequence of numbers on your own, you would have to lock the record that has the last value of the sequence, generate a new value, and then unlock the record. To avoid locking these records, Oracle provides a sequence generator that performs this service for you.

The Oracle sequence generator can generate sequential numbers with as many as 38 digits, without having to manually lock records. When you define a sequence, you can specify the original values of that sequence, whether the sequence should be cached, and whether the sequence should be in ascending or descending order.

What's Next?

Tomorrow you will learn about Oracle clusters: the index cluster and the hash cluster. You will learn what these schema objects are and how to use them. You will also learn about another Oracle schema object, the stored procedure. Stored procedures are used to perform application functions within the Oracle instance itself. Finally, you will learn about database links, which are also Oracle schema objects. After you complete Day 14, "Using Oracle Clusters, Stored Procedures, and Database Links," you will be familiar with all the Oracle schema objects.

Q&A

Q How are indexes important to an RDBMS?

A Indexes are important mainly from a performance standpoint. Without indexes, every access to the database would have to be done based on a scan of all records in the table. An index provides a mechanism by which to find data quickly without having to read all records in a table.

Q What are some important factors involved in creating an index?

A Several factors should be kept in mind when creating an index. First, an index is only useful when it is accessed. If you do not access the table using the columns that you have indexed in the WHERE clause, the index will not be used. Second, if the table is used primarily for historical data (many insertions, few selections), it is not a good candidate for indexing.

13

Q What makes a column a good candidate to be used in an index?

A Columns that have many unique values are good candidates for indexing. If a combination of columns is unique, a complex index might be better.

Q How are sequences useful?

A Sequences are useful because they provide a mechanism to generate a unique sequence of numbers quickly with reduced locking on the database.

Workshop

The workshop provides quiz questions to help you solidify your understanding of the material covered and exercises to provide you with experience in using what you've learned. Answers to the question in the workshop can be found in Appendix A, "Answers."

Quiz

1. How many indexes can be created on a single table?
2. Can an index be created in parallel?
3. What is a B*-tree index?
4. Can indexes be partitioned?
5. What is an index-only table?
6. What is a bitmap index?
7. What is a sequence used for?
8. How big can a sequence be?
9. Does an index need to be based on unique values?
10. Can an index be used to enforce uniqueness?

Exercises

1. Create a simple index on one column using Schema Manager.
2. Create a compound index using Schema Manager.
3. Delete that index using Schema Manager.
4. Create and delete a sequence using Schema Manager.

Day 14

Using Oracle Clusters, Stored Procedures, and Database Links

In addition to the regular tables you've seen in previous lessons, Oracle has an object known as a cluster, which is used to modify the way table data is stored. In fact, there are two different types of clusters available within the Oracle RDBMS: the index cluster, sometimes just referred to as a cluster, and the hash cluster. In this lesson you will learn about both the index cluster and the hash cluster—what they are, how they work, and how to effectively use them.

NEW TERM Today you will also learn how to use Oracle *procedures* and *functions*. Procedures and functions are similar; in fact, they are so much alike that they are typically referred to indiscriminately as *stored procedures* when they are used in packages and stored in the database. Procedures and functions are subprograms made up of PL/SQL code that take a set of parameters given to them by the calling program and perform a set of actions. Both can modify and return data passed to them as a parameter. The difference between a procedure and a function is that a function will always return a single value to the caller, whereas a procedure does not. Usually, procedures are used unless only a single return value is needed. A procedure or function that has been stored in the library cache is referred to as a *stored procedure* or a *stored function*; typically both procedures and functions are collectively referred to as procedures.

Because these procedures and functions are stored in the library cache in an already-parsed form, the parsing stage of execution can be bypassed. Also, because the SQL statements are identical each time they are used, they will be taken from the shared SQL area in the SGA if they have been executed recently. These features of stored procedures, in conjunction with the fact that network traffic is reduced (because the SQL statements are not transmitted), greatly enhance performance.

This lesson also deals with *database links*, which are exactly what you would think—links from one database to another. Using database links greatly simplifies accessing these other databases, thus making it easier for users to take advantage of remote data.

Clusters

NEW TERM A *cluster*, sometimes called an *index cluster*, is an optional method of storing tables in an Oracle database. Within a cluster, multiple related tables are stored together to improve access time to the related items. Tables that share a common column can be clustered around this column, thus speeding access to those rows that are accessed based on that column. The existence of a cluster is transparent to users and to applications; the cluster affects only how data is stored.

Remember that when Oracle retrieves data from disk, that operation is done on data blocks, not rows; therefore, if the data is stored together it will be copied from disk to memory together in the same data block. When the data block is read, all data from the clustered tables in that data block is read. If you will be using both pieces of data most of the time, this can be a real advantage; in fact, this is a major reason why you would create a cluster. So if the data that is clustered is primarily used in your application with a join operation, a cluster is advantageous.

If you have two tables that have related data and are frequently accessed together, using clusters can improve performance by preloading the related data into the SGA. Because you frequently use the data together, having that data already in the SGA greatly reduces access time.

Clusters are beneficial in joins where the join occurs on the cluster data because the data is all retrieved in one I/O operation. For example, suppose you are keeping a database of information for a dog club. (Because I am a dog lover and have several dogs of my own, I can

14

easily relate to this.) In this database, you want to keep track of all the dogs and their owners as well as some information about each of the dogs. To do this, you must create several tables. First, you need a table of all the dogs who are members of the dog club. You also need a table of the dog owners, as shown in Figure 14.1. (This is the same table used in previous lessons.)

Figure 14.1.

The Dogs *and* Dog_Owners *tables.*

DOGS Table

ID	Name	Owner-ID
1	Dash	1
2	Chip	1
3	B.J.	3
4	Pierce	2
5	Teller	1
6	Piper	4
7	Jack	4
8	Ty	1
9	Lacy	5
10	Shasta	1

DOG_OWNERS Table

ID	Last_Name	First_Name
1	Whalen	Edward
2	Smith	Joe
3	Brown	Bob
4	Wilson	Sally
5	Jones	Jerry

By combining the two tables into a cluster, you can save time when retrieving the data (because the dog owner information for a particular dog is essentially read into the SGA when the information for that dog is read in). The common column(s) of the cluster is called the *cluster key*, and must be indexed.

Figure 14.2 shows what the tables look like as a cluster. Note that the cluster key is the owner identification number.

If the data from the two tables is frequently used together, this cluster arrangement is a performance win. It provides the ease of use of individual tables but the additional performance of a cluster.

If you do not typically use their information together, there is no performance benefit of putting tables into a cluster. There is even a slight disadvantage because more SGA space is taken up by the additional data when the cluster is read in.

14

Figure 14.2.

The cluster including
the Dogs *and*
Dog_Owners *tables.*

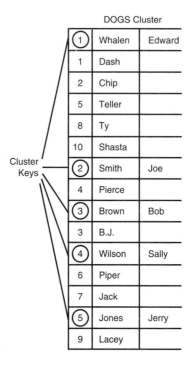

An additional disadvantage of clusters is a reduction of the performance of INSERT statements. This performance loss is caused by the fact that the data must be inserted based on the cluster key and the fact that there are multiple tables in the same block. The clustered table also spans more blocks than the individual tables, thus causing more data to be scanned.

In summary, a cluster can be useful for tables where data is primarily accessed together in a join. The reduced I/O needed to bring the additional data into the SGA and the fact that the data is already cached can be a big advantage.

If the tables have a large number of INSERT statements or if the data is not frequently accessed together, a cluster is not useful and should not be used.

WARNING

Do not cluster tables if full-table scans are often performed on only one of the tables in the cluster. The additional space required by the cluster and the additional I/O will reduce performance.

Hash Clusters

NEW TERM A *hash cluster* is similar to a cluster but uses a hash function rather than an index to reference the cluster key. A *hash function* is a numeric function that determines the data block in the cluster based on the value of the cluster key. A hash cluster stores the data based on the result of a hash function. Figure 14.3 shows a hash cluster.

Figure 14.3.

A hash cluster.

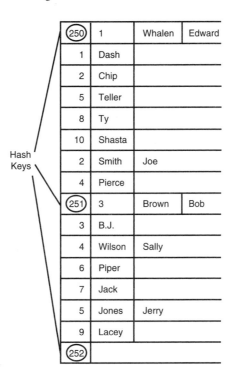

To find the data block in an index cluster, there must first be one or more I/Os to the cluster index to find the correct data block. In a hash cluster, the cluster key itself tells Oracle where the data block is, an arrangement that can reduce to one the number of I/Os needed to retrieve the row.

In contrast to the index cluster, which stores related data together based on the row's cluster-key value, the hash cluster stores related rows together based on their hash values.

The number of hash values is determined by the value of the HASHKEYS parameter of the CREATE CLUSTER command. The number and size of the cluster keys are very important and should be carefully calculated.

14

Do not use hash clusters on tables where table scans are often performed on only one of the tables in the cluster. The additional space required by the cluster and the additional I/O required can reduce performance.

Also, do not use a hash cluster on a table where the application frequently modifies the cluster key or when the table is constantly being modified. Because the cluster key is based on a calculation, significant overhead is involved in constantly recalculating the key.

When to Hash

Although hash clusters can be used in a similar fashion to index clusters, you do not have to cluster multiple tables. In fact, it is frequently useful to create a single table as a hash cluster to take advantage of the hashing feature. By using hashing, you might be able to retrieve your data with only one I/O rather than the multiple I/Os required to retrieve data using a B*-tree index.

Because hashing uses the value of the data to calculate the data block in which the desired data is located, hashing is best used on tables that have unique values for the cluster key and where the majority of queries are equality queries on the cluster key. For equality queries, the data is usually retrieved in one read operation; the cluster key does not have to be a single column. If the typical query uses an equality on a set of columns, use these columns to create a composite key. A composite key is one that is made up of more than one column.

Hashing is also most optimal when the table or tables are fairly static in size. If the table stays within its initial storage allocation, hashing usually does not cause a performance degradation. If the table grows out of its initial allocation, however, performance can degrade because overflow blocks are required.

Hashing might degrade the performance of table scans because the hashing process reads blocks that may not have much data in them. Because the table is originally created by laying out the data into the cluster based on the value of the cluster key, some blocks might have only a few rows.

Hashing can also degrade performance when the value of the cluster key changes. Because the location of the block in which the data resides is based on the cluster key's value, a change in that value can cause the row to migrate in order to maintain the cluster.

A good candidate for hashing has the following properties:

- ☐ The cluster-key value is unique.
- ☐ The majority of queries are equality queries on the cluster key.
- ☐ The size of the table is static; very little growth occurs.
- ☐ The value of the cluster key does not change.

An example of a good hashing candidate is a table used for storing parts information. By using a hash cluster keyed on the part number, access can be extremely efficient and fast. Any time you have a somewhat static table with a unique column value or set of column values, consider creating a hash cluster.

Just as with index clusters, there are both advantages and disadvantages in using hash clusters. Hash clusters are efficient in retrieving data based on equality queries on the cluster key. If you are not retrieving data based on that key, the query is not hashed. As with the index cluster, you see a performance decrease when executing INSERT statements in a hashed table.

With both index clusters and hash clusters, make a careful determination about whether a cluster can help performance based on the access patterns on the tables. As with many aspects of RDBMS, tuning based on a wrong decision can end up costing in performance.

If you can take advantage of hashing by meeting somewhat strict criteria, you can see very good performance. Hashing is extremely efficient if you can meet the criteria described in this section.

Managing Clusters

Once you have decided whether to use an index cluster or a hash cluster, you can start the cluster-creation process. As with almost all the operations you have seen thus far, this can also be accomplished via the Schema Manager or via the CREATE CLUSTER command.

Cluster creation can actually be thought of as a three-step process. These steps consist of the following operations:

1. Create the cluster. This first step involves using the Schema Manager or the CREATE CLUSTER command to create the actual cluster itself. This cluster is a logical structure that will hold the clustered tables.

2. Create the tables in the cluster. This can be accomplished using the CREATE TABLE command with the CLUSTER parameter.

3. Create the index on the cluster key. Before any rows can be inserted into the tables, the cluster index must be created.

The remainder of this section goes through the process of creating the cluster, the tables, and the index.

Creating Clusters

As stated, the cluster-creation process can be accomplished via the Schema Manager or the CREATE CLUSTER command. To create a cluster using the Schema Manager, right-click the Cluster icon.

From the options available from this menu, select the Create button. This will invoke the Create Cluster screen, a completed version of which is shown in Figure 14.4.

After you have invoked the Create Cluster screen you must fill in the values for the cluster name, the schema, the cluster size, whether it is an index cluster or a hash cluster, and the

14

cluster columns. The size value is important; it specifies the average size that you expect a cluster key and its associated rows to consume. This parameter will be used to reserve space for each key value and rows. This does not limit the amount of data that can be used by a cluster value, but will improve efficiency.

Figure 14.4.

The Create Cluster screen for the Dogs table.

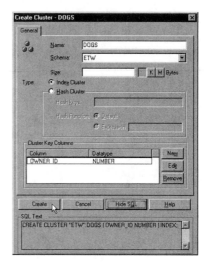

When you have completed this operation, the cluster will be created. You can also create a cluster with the CREATE CLUSTER command. Here is an example:

```
CREATE CLUSTER dogs (owner_id NUMBER(4))
TABLESPACE dogs;
```

The complete syntax for the CREATE CLUSTER command can be found in the Oracle documentation. Of course, you can add storage parameters to this command, such as the storage clause, parallelism, and so on. The next step involved is creating the clustered tables.

Creating Clustered Tables

You can create the cluster tables by using the CREATE TABLE command, as shown in earlier lessons in this book. The CREATE TABLE command must include the CLUSTER parameter. To create the two tables (here we'll use the tables Dogs and Dog_owners that you saw on Day 12, "Working with Tables, Views, and Synonyms") as a cluster, you can use SQL commands with the Server Manager (see Listings 14.1 and 14.2).

INPUT   **Listing 14.1. The SQL for the Dogs table.**

```
CREATE TABLE "ETW".Dogs (
ID NUMBER NULL,
NAME VARCHAR2(40) NULL,
```

14

```
OWNER_ID NUMBER NULL,
BREED_ID NUMBER NULL,
RANK NUMBER NULL,
NOTES VARCHAR2(80) NULL)
CLUSTER dogs(OWNER_ID);
```

INPUT **Listing 14.2. The SQL for the Dog_owners table.**

```
CREATE TABLE "ETW".Dog_owners (
ID NUMBER NOT NULL,
Last_Name VARCHAR2(40) NULL,
First_Name VARCHAR2(20) NULL,
Street VARCHAR2(40) NULL,
City VARCHAR2(20) NULL,
State CHAR(2) NULL,
Zip VARCHAR2(10) NULL,
Phone VARCHAR2(15) NULL,
Notes VARCHAR2(80) NULL)
CLUSTER dogs(ID);
```

Notice that the CLUSTER parameter specifies the cluster name and the cluster-key value. For more information on the CREATE TABLE command, refer to the Oracle documentation.

The final stage involved in creating a cluster is to create the index on the cluster key. This must be accomplished before any data can be loaded into the tables.

Creating the Cluster Index

Creating the cluster index can be accomplished either via the Schema Manager or the CREATE INDEX command. To create the cluster index using the Schema Manager, right-click the icon of the cluster on which you want to create the index and select the Create Index On option from the menu that pops up.

This will invoke the Create Index screen that you have seen in previous lessons. There are, however, a few differences this time. In this screen the Cluster button has already been selected for you, and you cannot select any columns for indexing. The cluster index is on the cluster key only. The filled-out Create Index screen is shown in Figure 14.5.

You can use the Schema Manager to easily create the cluster index. If, however, you want to use the CREATE INDEX command, you also have that option. It is often convenient to script the entire database-, table-, cluster-, and index-creation process so that it can be used again or as a template for other database creations. To create the cluster index using the CREATE INDEX command, use the following syntax:

```
CREATE INDEX "ETW".Dog_owners_IX1 ON CLUSTER  "ETW"."Dogs";
```

At this point your cluster is created and ready for use. In the next part of this lesson you will learn how to use procedures, functions, and packages (also known as stored procedures).

14

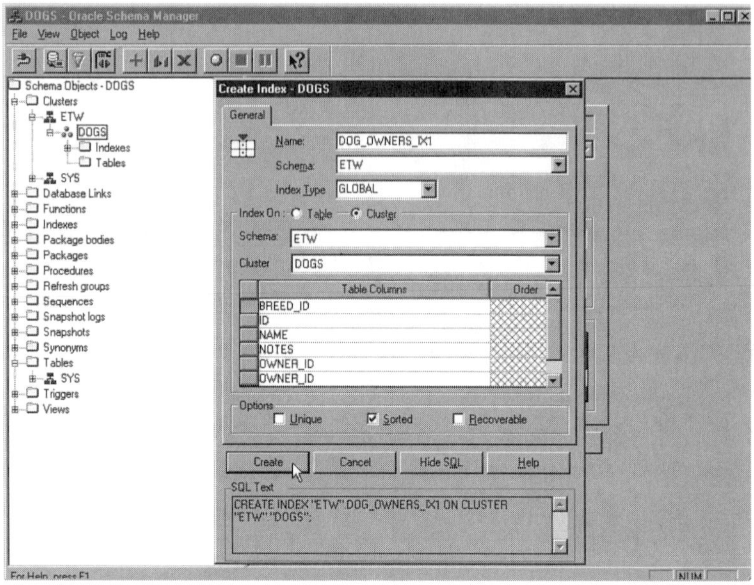

Figure 14.5.

The Create Index screen, with information for this example filled in.

Procedures, Functions, and Packages

NEW TERM   *Procedures* and *functions* are subprograms made up of PL/SQL code that take a set of parameters given to them by the calling program and perform a set of actions. The only real difference between a procedure and a function is that a function will include a single return value. Both functions and procedures can modify and return data passed to them as a parameter. Usually, procedures are used unless only one return value is needed.

A procedure or function that has been stored in the library cache is referred to as a *stored procedure* or a *stored function*. A stored procedure or stored function has the following characteristics:

- [ ] It has a name—This is the name by which the stored procedure or function is called and referenced.

- [ ] It takes parameters—These are the values sent to the stored procedure or function from the application.

- [ ] It returns values—A stored procedure or function can return one or more values based on the purpose of the procedure or function.

- [ ] It is stored in the data dictionary—The stored procedure or function is stored in a parsed form in the data dictionary.

14

Procedures

A *procedure* is a set of PL/SQL statements that form a subprogram. The subprogram is designed and created to perform a specific operation on data in your database. A procedure takes zero or more input parameters and returns zero or more output parameters. The syntax of a procedure is as follows:

```
PROCEDURE procedure_name [( parameter_declaration )] IS
    [local declarations]
BEGIN
    PL/SQL Statements
[EXCEPTION
    Optional Exception Handler(s)]
END [procedure_name];
```

In this syntax, the *parameter_declaration* has the following format:

```
parameter_name [IN ¦ OUT ¦ IN OUT] datatype
```

The parameter qualifiers have the following meanings:

- ☐ IN—This parameter is used as an input value only.

- ☐ OUT—This parameter is used as an output value only.

- ☐ IN OUT—This parameter is used as both an input and an output variable.

The procedure is made up of two parts: the declaration and the body of the procedure. The declaration begins with the keyword PROCEDURE and ends with the last parameter declaration. The body begins with the keyword IS and ends with the keyword END.

The declaration section is used to define which variables are passed to the procedure and which values are returned from the procedure back to the calling program. The body of the procedure is where the real work is done. The body is made up of the PL/SQL statements that perform the desired task.

Functions

A *function*, like a procedure, is a set of PL/SQL statements that form a subprogram. The subprogram is designed and created to perform a specific operation on data in your database. A function takes zero or more input parameters and returns just one output value. If more than one output value is required, a procedure should be used. The syntax of a function is as follows:

```
FUNCTION function_name [( parameter_declaration )] RETURN datatype IS
    [local declarations]
BEGIN
    PL/SQL Statements
[EXCEPTION
    Optional Exception Handler(s)]
END [function_name];
```

The *parameter_declaration* has the same format as it does with a procedure:

parameter_name [IN ¦ OUT ¦ IN OUT] *datatype*

The parameter qualifiers have the following meanings:

- ☐ IN—This parameter is used as an input value only.
- ☐ OUT—This parameter is used as an output value only.
- ☐ IN OUT—This parameter is used as both an input and an output variable.

As with a procedure, a function is made up of two parts: the declaration and the body. The declaration begins with the keyword FUNCTION and ends with RETURN statement. The body begins with the keyword IS and ends with the keyword END.

The declaration section is used to define which variables are passed to the function and which values are returned from the function back to the calling program. The body of the function is where the real work is done. The body is made up of the PL/SQL statements that perform the desired task.

The difference between a procedure and a function is the return value. A function has the return declaration as well as a RETURN function within the body of that function that returns a value. This RETURN function is used to pass a return value to the calling program. If you do not intend to return a value to the calling program, or you want to return more than one value, use a procedure.

NOTE

For the remainder of this lesson, the term *procedure* is used to refer to both procedures and functions because both are similar in nature and function.

How Procedures and Functions Operate

Procedures and functions use the same basic syntax in the program body with the exception of the RETURN keyword, which can only be used by functions. The body itself is made up of PL/SQL blocks that perform the desired function and return the desired data to the calling program. The goal of the body of the procedure is both to minimize the amount of data to be transmitted across the network (to and from the calling program) and to perform the PL/SQL statements in the most efficient manner possible.

The PL/SQL Language

PL/SQL is a block-structured language offered by Oracle to facilitate the use of the Oracle RDBMS. It has the following properties and features that can be used to aid in application development:

14

☐ Block structure—The block structure allows blocks to contain nested subblocks.

☐ Block declarations—Each block can have its own declarations, which means that you can logically separate functions.

☐ Variable declaration—Variables can be declared and used within a PL/SQL block.

☐ Constant declaration—Constants can be declared and referenced within a PL/SQL block.

☐ Conditional statements—PL/SQL allows for conditional processing with IF...THEN...ELSE, WHILE...LOOP, FOR...LOOP, EXIT...WHEN, and GOTO functions.

These features make PL/SQL a powerful SQL processing language. Using PL/SQL has several major advantages over using standard SQL statements (in addition to allowing the use of stored procedures and functions). Among these are ease of use, portability, and higher performance.

The primary performance difference between PL/SQL and SQL is the fact that PL/SQL statements are transmitted to Oracle as a block of statements rather than as individual statements. In a network application, the additional overhead needed to transmit individual statements can be quite high. It takes very little additional CPU and network resources to send a larger packet than it does to send a smaller one.

The RETURN Statement

In the declaration portion of a function, a RETURN *parameter* is used to declare the type of the return value. Later, in the body of the function, the RETURN *statement* is used to exit the function and return the specified value to the calling program. With a procedure, the RETURN statement can also be used, but not to return a value. In a procedure, the RETURN statement can be used only to exit the procedure. No values can be associated with the RETURN statement in a procedure.

The EXCEPTION Statement

In both procedures and functions, you can add optional exception handlers. These exception handlers allow you to return additional information based on certain conditions (such as no data found or some user-specified condition). By using exception handlers and allowing the stored procedure to notify you of some special conditions, you can minimize the amount of return-value checking that must be done in the application code. Because the work to determine that no data has been selected has already been done by the RDBMS engine, you can save on resources if you take advantage of this information.

The RDBMS_OUTPUT Package

To visually represent data selected within a stored procedure or function, you can use the RDBMS_OUTPUT package supplied by Oracle. To see data returned by RDBMS_OUTPUT in SQL*Plus or Server Manager, you must set the SERVEROUTPUT option by issuing the command SET SERVEROUTPUT ON. Also be sure to terminate the procedure with a slash (/) to invoke it.

14

When using the RDBMS_OUTPUT package, you can select several options for inputting or outputting data. The following procedures are available in the RDBMS_OUTPUT package:

- [ ] RDBMS_OUTPUT.ENABLE—Enables output processing.
- [ ] RDBMS_OUTPUT.DISABLE—Disables output processing.
- [ ] RDBMS_OUTPUT.PUT_LINE—Places a newline-terminated string in the buffer.
- [ ] RDBMS_OUTPUT.PUT—Places a string in the buffer (no newline).
- [ ] RDBMS_OUTPUT.GET_LINE—Gets one line from the buffer.
- [ ] RDBMS_OUTPUT.GET_LINES—Gets an array of lines from the buffer.

In this manner, you can use a stored procedure for ad-hoc functions that require data to be displayed in SQL*Plus. The typical stored procedure is used to return data that has been bound to variables in a program.

How to Create Stored Procedures and Stored Functions

NEW TERM There are advantages to using procedures and functions; however, the greatest advantage of using functions and procedures happens when the procedures and functions are stored in the database. Such procedures and functions are referred to as *stored procedures* and *stored functions*. A stored procedure or stored function has the advantage of being stored in the library cache in an already parsed form, thus reducing parsing time. In this section you will see how to parse the procedure and store it in the database.

To create a stored procedure or function, use the keywords CREATE PROCEDURE or CREATE FUNCTION with the same syntax as the PROCEDURE and FUNCTION commands shown earlier in this lesson. When creating a procedure or function, however, the IS keyword is replaced with the AS keyword. Listing 14.3 shows an example of how to create a stored procedure to retrieve some information from the Dogs table.

NOTE The typical stored procedure or function is called by an application program. In the following example, however, to better illustrate how a stored procedure is coded, I chose to use SQL*Plus.

INPUT **Listing 14.3. Creating the stored procedure old_dogs.**

```
SQL> CREATE OR REPLACE PROCEDURE
  2       old_dogs
  3  AS
  4       CURSOR dog_cursor IS
```

```
 5      SELECT
 6          dogname, age, owner
 7      FROM dogs
 8      WHERE age > 8;
 9  BEGIN
10      RDBMS_OUTPUT.PUT_LINE('Dogs older than 8 years old');
11      RDBMS_OUTPUT.PUT_LINE('Name  Age  Owner');
12      FOR dog IN dog_cursor LOOP
13      RDBMS_OUTPUT.PUT_LINE(dog.dogname¦¦'  '¦¦dog.age¦¦'  '¦¦dog.owner);
14      END LOOP;
15  END old_dogs;
16  /

Procedure created.
```

To view the output of this stored procedure from SQL*Plus, you must to enable the SERVEROUTPUT option, as follows:

INPUT SQL> set serveroutput on

INPUT SQL> execute old_dogs;

The resulting output of this procedure is

OUTPUT
```
Dogs older than 8 years old
Name  Age  Owner
Shasta  9  Jones
Jessy  10  Wilson
Ruff  9  King

PL/SQL procedure successfully completed.
```

ANALYSIS As you can see, to enable the stored procedure to return multiple rows selected from the Dogs table, it is necessary to declare a cursor. By looping through this cursor, you can output all the lines that were selected.

How to Replace Procedures and Functions

If the procedure or function is already stored in the library cache, you must *replace*, rather than *create*, the procedure or function. You do this by using the command CREATE OR REPLACE PROCEDURE or CREATE OR REPLACE FUNCTION. With this command, an already-present procedure or function is replaced; if it is not already present, it is created.

Packages

Packages are sets of related procedures or functions that are compiled and stored together in the data dictionary. They allow you to group together PL/SQL types, objects, and subprograms into a logical unit. When you link these logically related entities together, it can be easier to program and modify modules based on their function and relation. Performance

is enhanced because the entire package is loaded into memory when it is first called, thus increasing the chance for a cache hit on a related function or object that is likely to be called soon.

Packages are actually created in a statement with two different parts. The first is the declaration part, where the package is defined. Then there is the package body definition, where the body of the package is defined. The syntax of the statement used to create the package definition is as follows:

```
CREATE PACKAGE package_name AS package_specification
    public type and object declaration
    subprogram definition
END [package_name];
```

This definition part of the package creation declares the parts of the package available to the user. The rest of the package definition is used by the user, but is not visible to the user. This second part has the following syntax:

```
CREATE PACKAGE BODY package_name AS package_body
    private type and object declaration
    subprogram bodies
[BEGIN
    initialization statements]
END [package_name];
```

The user application must have knowledge of the package specification in order to call the package correctly. The arrangement of the package-creation process has several advantages:

☐ Portability—The body of the package can change without requiring any changes to the application—as long as the package specification does not change.

☐ Security—The package can access tables you might not want the user to see. Because the package body is hidden from the user, some security can be maintained.

☐ Modularity—With packages, modules can have specific functions that can be logically grouped and specified.

☐ Ease of design—The specification part of the package can be completed first, thus allowing different teams to work on the package body and the application. Once the specification is completed, both groups can write to that specified interface.

☐ Better performance—Because the entire package is loaded into memory when the first component is accessed, additional calls to the package do not invoke disk I/O.

Using Procedures, Functions, and Packages

Using procedures, functions, and packages can improve performance in several ways—for example, through a reduction in the amount of data that must be transmitted across the network and an increase in hits in the shared SQL cache.

New Term *Packages* are sets of related procedures or functions compiled and stored together in the data dictionary. Packages allow you to group PL/SQL types, objects, and subprograms into a logical unit. If you link these logically related entities together, it can be easier to program and modify modules based on their function and relation. You enhance performance because the entire package is loaded into memory when it is first called, increasing the chance for a cache hit on a related function or object that is likely to be called soon.

Because a procedure, function, or package is stored within the library cache, it is available for immediate use by your applications. Because these objects are stored in an already-parsed form, performance is also improved.

Procedures, functions, and packages are used to call certain SQL statements that are used over and over again. Any set of SQL statements that you use frequently in your application can benefit from being made into a stored procedure or function.

Stored Procedures' Use of the Library Cache

As you know, the library cache contains the shared SQL and PL/SQL areas. By increasing the cache-hit rate in the library cache, you increase performance. This increase comes from reducing the overhead needed to parse the SQL statements in the shared SQL area and from retrieving those statements from cache (reducing the need to retrieve those statements from disk).

A cache miss in the shared SQL area occurs either when a parse statement is called and the already-parsed statement does not exist in the shared SQL area or when an application tries to execute a SQL statement and the shared SQL area containing the parsed statement has been deallocated from the library cache.

Here is a review of the requirements necessary for a SQL statement to take advantage of the library cache. For a SQL statement to take advantage of SQL or PL/SQL statements that have already been parsed, the following criteria must be met:

- ☐ The text of the SQL statement must be identical to the SQL statement that has already been parsed. This includes whitespaces and case.
- ☐ References to schema objects in the SQL statements must resolve to the same object.
- ☐ Bind variables must match the same name and data type.
- ☐ The SQL statements must be optimized using the same approach and, in the case of the cost-based approach, the same optimization goal as the already parsed statement.

14

You might think that these conditions make it difficult to take advantage of the shared SQL areas, but by reusing application code you can quite easily meet these conditions. When writing applications, you should strive to use the same SQL statements to access the same data and ensure that these SQL statements can meet these criteria.

Use stored procedures and functions whenever possible to guarantee that the same shared PL/SQL area is used. Another advantage of using stored procedures is that they are stored in a parsed form, eliminating runtime parsing altogether.

Standardizing on naming conventions for bind variables and spacing conventions for SQL and PL/SQL statements can also increase the likelihood of reusing shared SQL statements.

Using Database Links

NEW TERM   A *database link* is simply a link within the local database to another database on the network. By setting up a database link, it is a simple matter for a user connected to a local database to access data in the remote database from the local instance. This access to the remote database is transparent to the user.

Let's say there is a database link called club. club is a link to the service named club_server. To access the dogs table on the club server, you would use the following SQL statement:

```
SELECT * FROM dogs@club;
```

Because the link is transparent, the data is retrieved from the server named club_server, which was accessed with the link named club.

To create a database link, right-click the Database Link icon in the Schema Manager or use the CREATE DATABASE LINK command. The Create Database Link screen is displayed, as shown in Figure 14.6.

Simply fill in the name, whether it is a public or private link, and what the service name is. You can set up the link to use an anonymous or a named link, where all access to this database uses the same username and password that was used to define the link. You can create a database link with a SQL statement; for this example, it would be

```
CREATE DATABASE LINK CLUB.WORLD  USING 'CLUB_SERVER';
```

Database links provide a transparent way for users to access data in remote databases very easily. The database link is very easy to use.

Figure 14.6.

*The Create Database
Link screen.*

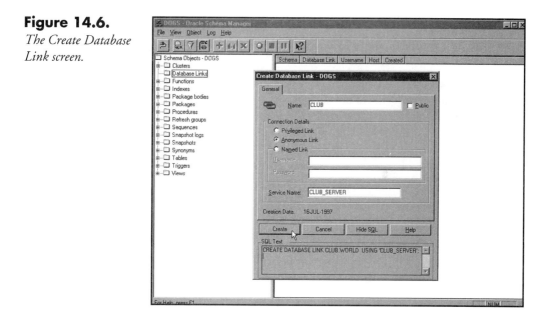

Summary

Clusters can be very useful under certain conditions, as you have seen in this lesson. A cluster enables you to store multiple tables in the same space. This allows data that is typically used together to be retrieved together, thus reducing I/O. A cluster can be either an index cluster or a hash cluster depending on which one suits your needs. An index cluster uses an index on the cluster key, whereas the hash cluster uses a hash function on the cluster key. Regardless of which type of cluster you use, the function is similar.

If you have two tables with related data that are frequently accessed together, using clusters can improve performance by preloading the related data into the SGA. Because you frequently use the data together, having that data already in the SGA greatly reduces access time. Clusters are beneficial in joins where the join occurs on the cluster data because the data is all retrieved in one I/O operation.

Also in this lesson you have seen the use of functions, procedures, and packages to improve performance. These performance enhancements include reduction in the amount of data that must be transmitted across the network and an increase in hits in the data dictionary cache.

Because a procedure, function, or package is stored within the data dictionary, it is available for immediate use by your applications. Because stored procedures and functions are stored

14

in the library cache in an already-parsed form, performance is improved. Any set of SQL statements that your application frequently uses can benefit from being made into a stored procedure or function.

There are very few SQL statements that cannot benefit from the use of procedures, functions, and packages. By storing these subprograms in the database, you reduce network traffic and increase performance in accessing these programs. Whenever possible, use stored procedures and packages; there is no disadvantage associated with their use.

What's Next?

In Day 15's lesson, "Managing Job Queues and Using Oracle Auditing," you will see how to enable the Oracle auditing feature, how to view the data, and how to interpret that data. The auditing feature is part of Oracle security and is very useful when that level of security is required.

Q&A

Q What is the difference between an index cluster and a hash cluster?

A An index cluster is a cluster that has an index on the cluster key, whereas the hash cluster uses a hashing function to access the cluster key.

Q How is table access different in a cluster?

A Table access is no different between a cluster and an ordinary table. There is a performance difference, however—if you are accessing multiple tables that are clustered, as in a join operation, you will see a significant performance improvement and reduction of I/O.

Q Why are stored procedures useful?

A Stored procedures not only cut down on network traffic, but improve the cache-hit rate in the shared SQL area by making sure that SQL statements are identical.

Q Why would I want to use a database link?

A Database links can simplify access to tables and hide details that you don't want users to know about.

Workshop

The workshop provides quiz questions to help you solidify your understanding of the material covered and exercises to provide you with experience in using what you've learned. Answers to the quiz questions appear in Appendix A, "Answers."

Quiz

1. What is the best criterion for creating a cluster?
2. Give two criteria for using hash clustering.
3. What benefit do you get from using a cluster?
4. What kind of criteria indicate that clustering is not a good idea? (Name two things.)
5. What is a stored procedure?
6. How do you benefit from stored procedures?
7. Can stored procedures perform programmatical operations?
8. What are database links used for?

Exercises

1. Create an indexed cluster using the Schema Manager.
2. Create two tables using the same cluster key using the CREATE TABLE command.
3. Create an index on the cluster using the Schema Manager.
4. Using the Schema Manager, create a database link to another server.

14

WEEK 2

8
9
10
11
12
13
14

In Review

Week 2 begins by addressing the remaining topics related to managing database storage, including the Oracle redo log files, control files, rollback segments (Day 8), and managing data (Day 9). Day 9 covers how to load data using SQL*Loader, Export, and Import.

Managing Users and Processes

Days 10 and 11 taught you how to create and alter user accounts in the Oracle database as well as how to manage the various Oracle processes. You also learned how to manage the Oracle job queues and how to schedule jobs for later execution.

Managing the Database Schema

Days 12–14 cover the database schema, including table and index creation as well as clusters and views.

WEEK 3

At a Glance

So far you have learned about the structure of the Oracle database from the standpoint of the data itself. By the end of week 3, you will know more about the tasks required of the Oracle administrator, including management of user accounts, Oracle processes, security, backup and recovery, and tuning. You also will have learned about the Oracle Network Computing Architecture (NCA) and the Oracle Web Publishing Assistant.

Oracle Security

Day 15 covers various topics relating to Oracle security matters, specifically auditing.

15

16

17

18

19

20

21

Backup and Recovery

Days 16–18 cover the most important responsibility of the Oracle DBA: the development and implementation of a backup and recovery plan. An effective plan can save your company millions of dollars in the event of a system failure. Also covered in this section are other methods of quick recovery, such as the Oracle standby database, the use of replication for quick recovery, and the use of backup images.

Advanced Topics

Days 19–21 cover more advanced topics such as the use of the Oracle parallel server. Also included is a lesson on Oracle optimization and performance tuning. The book concludes with a lesson covering the Oracle Web Publishing Assistant and the Oracle Network Computing Architecture (NCA).

Day **15**

Managing Job Queues and Using Oracle Auditing

Today you will learn about managing job queues and the Oracle auditing facility. Job queues are used to schedule jobs during off-peak hours or to schedule certain tasks on a recurring basis. The Oracle job queue facility allows you to schedule single or recurring tasks in an easy and reliable manner.

The Oracle auditing facility allows the administrator to monitor or audit the system usage. Auditing is important if one or more incident has occurred to make you suspicious of the activity of one or more users. Through auditing, a record is made of the suspicious activity and can be used to track down the party at fault. Think of auditing as a way of logging activity in the system.

Oracle job queues are used to divert the execution of an operation to a later time. This allows you to schedule jobs.

Managing Job Queues

NEW TERM   A *job queue* is a method whereby you can schedule a PL/SQL task to run at some time in the future, or even to run periodically. The job-scheduling task can be done either graphically through the Enterprise Manager or via the Oracle job-scheduling commands. As always, you will learn about both methods here.

Using the Oracle job-queuing facility, you can easily schedule jobs to be run at various times or on a regular schedule. Some examples of where this might be useful include

☐ Regularly scheduled jobs, such as end-of-day accounting—A job that must run every weekday can be scheduled to run unattended.

☐ Large jobs that need to be run during off-peak hours—If you schedule them, you need not be present at 3:00 a.m.

☐ A large number of jobs that must be run sequentially—In this case, the jobs might be so large that in order to reduce CPU usage, only one is run at a time.

NOTE An advantage of scheduling jobs is that you need not be present when the job runs. A disadvantage is that if the job fails during its operation, nobody is around to restart it. Therefore, you should thoroughly test your job before queuing it.

Let's look at how to schedule jobs using both the Enterprise Manager and the stored procedures in the DBMS_JOB package.

Scheduling Jobs Using the Enterprise Manager

As you recall from Day 5, "Managing the Oracle RDBMS," the Enterprise Manager has a pane called the Job pane. Within this pane you can manage jobs that are running on this or other systems managed by this Enterprise Manager. By default, the Job pane is located in the lower-left corner of the Enterprise Manager, as shown in Figure 15.1.

Because this lesson is concerned only with the job-queuing functions of the Enterprise Manager, I closed the other Enterprise Manager panes for the remaining figures in today's lesson by deselecting them in the View drop-down menu.

To create a job using the Enterprise Manager, select the Create option by pulling down the Job menu. This will invoke the Create Job dialog box, as shown in Figure 15.2. It is from this dialog that you create an Oracle job, as you will see in this section.

Figure 15.1.

The Oracle Enterprise Manager.

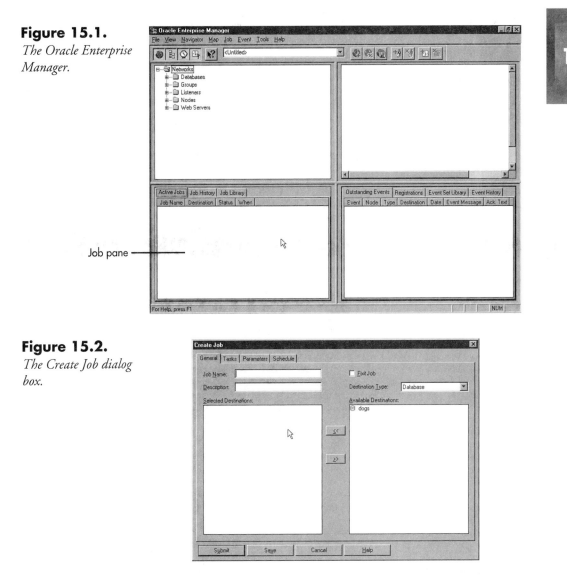

Job pane —

Figure 15.2.

The Create Job dialog box.

Say you're the president of a dog club that keeps track of a large number of dogs and their owners. Each week, an export image of this database is sent out to various other dog clubs. Therefore, you want to create a job that, on a weekly basis, will export the Dogs database. The first task is to invoke the Create Job dialog, as you saw in the previous figure. This dialog has four different tabs that invoke different screens, each of which has its own function. These tabs are

☐ General

☐ Tasks

☐ Parameters

☐ Schedule

These screens are very flexible and easy to use.

The General Screen

Use the General screen to uniquely define the job. Type the name of the job and provide a description of it as well as defining the database, node, or listener that the job will act on. The General screen, filled in for this example, is shown in Figure 15.3.

Figure 15.3.

Use the General screen to define the job.

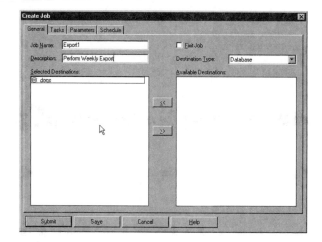

The Tasks Screen

You use the Tasks screen to define the task that the job will perform. There are a number of predefined tasks, or you can define your own, as shown in Figure 15.4.

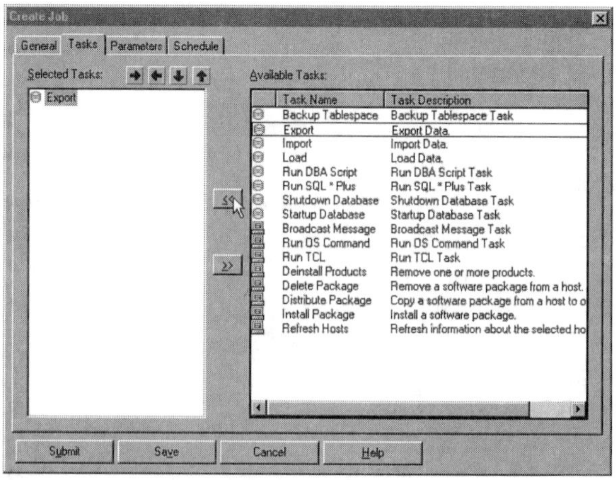

Figure 15.4.

The Tasks screen is where you define what the job will do.

Possible choices include the following administrative tasks:

- ☐ Backup Tablespace
- ☐ Export
- ☐ Import
- ☐ Load
- ☐ Run DBA Script
- ☐ Run SQL*Plus
- ☐ Shutdown Database
- ☐ Startup Database

There are also a number of predefined, non-database administrative tasks, such as

- ☐ Broadcast Message
- ☐ Run OS Command
- ☐ Others

The appearance of the Parameters screen will vary depending on what type of task is selected in the Tasks screen.

The Parameters Screen

The Parameters screen allows you to further define the parameters for the task that was selected. Because I selected an export task for this example, this screen allows me to define further export parameters, as shown in Figure 15.5.

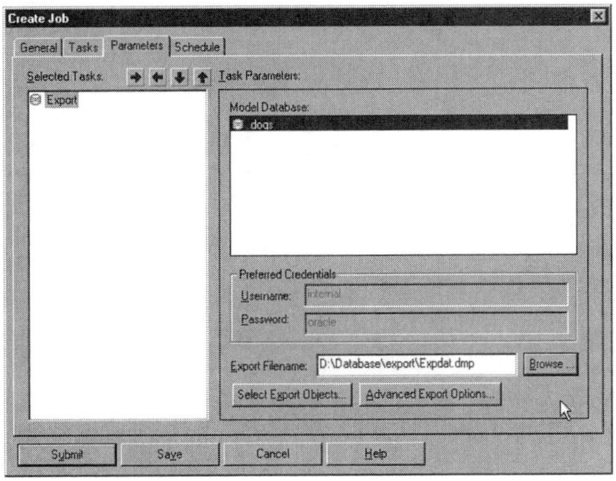

Figure 15.5.

You further define the task in the Parameters screen.

Here you can select the database to be exported as well as the export filename. You can also choose to select export objects or advanced export options. The advanced export options screen is shown in Figure 15.6.

Figure 15.6.

You can choose advanced options for exporting.

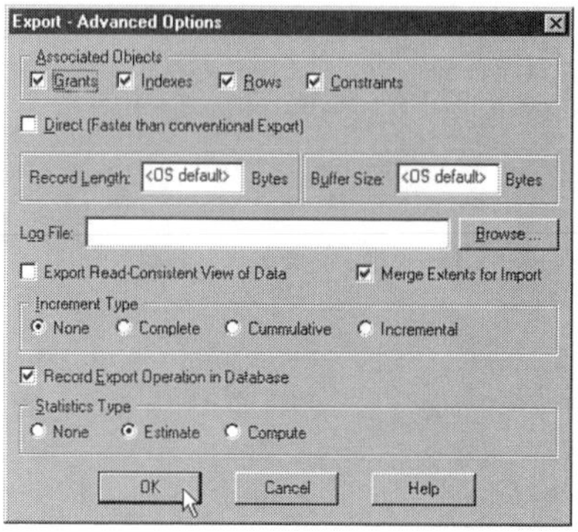

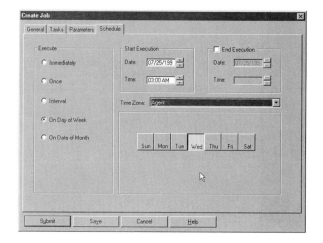

This gives you a wide range of options for the export operation. Similarly, other tasks have their own parameters you can set.

The Schedule Screen

The Schedule screen allows you to define how the job is to be run, as shown in Figure 15.7.

Figure 15.7.

You define the timing of the job in the Schedule screen.

Scheduling can be done at various rates, including

☐ Immediately

☐ Once

15

☐ Interval (for example, every *x* days)

☐ On Day of Week

☐ On Day of Month

Scheduling is very flexible and easy to set up and run. At this point, all that is necessary to schedule the job is to click the Submit button. You will see the scheduled job listed on the Active Jobs screen, as shown in Figure 15.8.

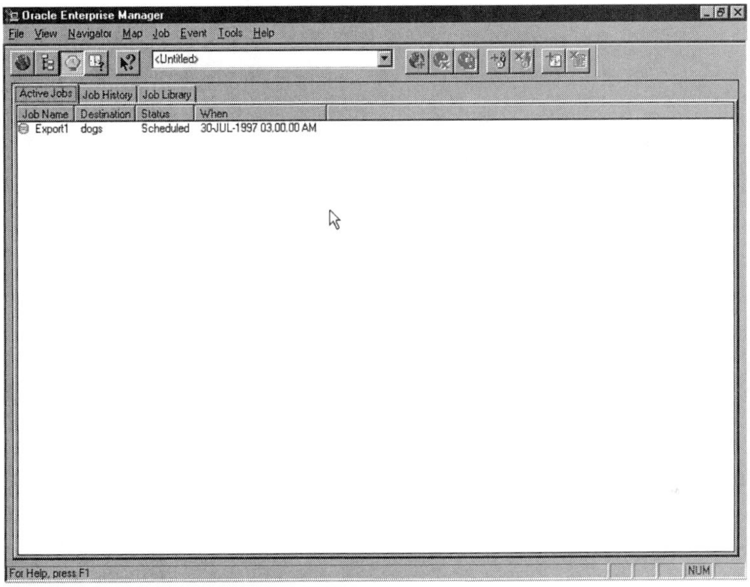

Figure 15.8.

The Active Jobs screen shows the status of active jobs.

NOTE

For job queuing to work properly, the user preferences must be set up correctly. The user for the database must be a valid database user with the system permissions necessary to perform the task required. The user for the node must be a valid NT user with "login as batch job" permission. This user must also have a password. Accounts with no passwords cannot be used. The preferences setup screen for the Enterprise Manager is shown in Figure 15.9. For my setup I created a batch account and added the proper privileges.

It is important for the Enterprise Manager to be properly configured for it to be able to submit jobs. After you have submitted the job, you can also modify it from the Enterprise Manager.

Figure 15.9.

Setting Enterprise Manager preferences.

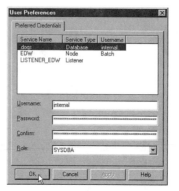

Administering Jobs

After the job has been scheduled, you can administer it from the Enterprise Manager. You can't do much here except monitor the status and delete the job; these tasks can be accomplished from the Jobs menu. Selecting the Show Details option shows you how the job was submitted. Selecting the Remove Job option deletes the selected job.

Scheduling Jobs Using the Command-Line Facilities

It is possible to manage the Oracle job queues through the Server Manager or SQL*Plus rather than use the Enterprise Manager. This is very useful because all users can use Oracle queuing, and typically only administrators have access to the Enterprise Manager console.

A job is administered by calling the DBMS_JOB package just as you would call any other package. The stored procedures that make up this package are the following:

- ☐ BROKEN—Disables job execution without removing the job.
- ☐ CHANGE—Can be used to alter the job description, when it will run, or the interval between runs.
- ☐ INTERVAL—Alters the interval between runs.
- ☐ NEXT_DATE—Alters the next execution time of the job.
- ☐ REMOVE—Removes a job from the job queue.
- ☐ RUN—Forces a job to run.
- ☐ SUBMIT—Submits a job to the job queue.
- ☐ WHAT—Alters the job description.

Each of these options has its own parameters that call it. The following sections outline the parameters for a few of them.

SUBMIT

The SUBMIT function can be executed by calling the package with a syntax such as

```
DBMS_JOB.SUBMIT(
Job
What
Next_date
Interval
No_parse )
```

where *Job* is an output parameter and the others are input parameters.

The SUBMIT procedure returns the job number. Here is an example:

```
SQL> VARIABLE job number;
SQL> begin
  2  DBMS_JOB.SUBMIT(
  3  :job,
  4  'DELETE FROM dogs2;',
  5  SYSDATE,
  6  NULL);
  7  COMMIT;
  8  end;
  9  /

PL/SQL procedure successfully completed.

SQL> PRINT job;

       JOB
----------
         1
```

REMOVE

The REMOVE function can be executed by calling the package with syntax such as

```
DBMS_JOB.REMOVE(Job)
```

where *Job* is the job number.

An example of using DBMS_JOB.REMOVE is as follows:

```
SQL> begin
  2  DBMS_JOB.REMOVE(1);
  3  COMMIT;
  4  end;
  5  /

PL/SQL procedure successfully completed.
```

If you don't know the job number, you can try to find it by using the following query:

```
SQL> select job, next_date, next_sec from user_jobs;

       JOB NEXT_DATE NEXT_SEC
---------- --------- --------
         1 25-JUL-97 16:55:28
         2 25-JUL-97 17:07:51
```

Other activities, such as DBMS_JOB.BROKEN, use a similar syntax. You can find more details in the Oracle documentation.

Using Oracle Auditing

The Oracle auditing facility is used to log information about database operations such as when they occurred and who performed them. Auditing is important primarily if one or more incidents have occurred to make you suspicious of the activity of one or more users. Through auditing, a record is made of this activity that can be used to track down the party at fault.

 TIP

> For auditing to be effective, it is necessary for each user (especially the DBAs) to have his own account and use it. It does no good to audit database activity and determine that the SYSTEM user is at fault if you have 15 DBAs who use the SYSTEM account.

Auditing is not only used when you think you have some sort of problem; it can also give you useful information about the usage of your system that might help you to determine a better system configuration in the future. By having information about the activities that are going on within the Oracle RDBMS, you will be better able to provide the proper services to the user community.

Auditing, although useful, is very expensive in terms of both CPU overhead and disk usage. As such, you should use auditing very carefully and selectively. Let's look at how to set up the auditing process.

Developing an Auditing Strategy

Before attempting to start auditing, you must first decide what needs to be audited. This not only involves the activity that is to be audited, but the user accounts that are to be audited as well. The first step in developing an auditing strategy is to determine the purpose of auditing.

There may be one or more reasons why you want to audit. By determining these reasons, you can better put together the audit plan. You might perform auditing for either of the following reasons:

- ☐ Informational purposes—It is common to use auditing to retain specific historical information about your system. This can provide valuable insights.
- ☐ Suspicious behavior—It is more common to use the audit trail to investigate suspicious activities that have occurred in the database.

 15

Depending on the reason for auditing, different guidelines should be followed. In this section you will learn how these different types of audits are handled.

Auditing for Informational Purposes

If you are auditing for historical information, you should determine which database activities will provide the most useful information for the audit. Because you are auditing for information only, decide which events are of interest to your audit and which events are not. Once you have compiled a list of pertinent activities, only those activities should be audited. Occasionally, you should extract the important information and purge the audit logs. In this way, you can keep down the size of the logs and still get the information you want.

Auditing for Suspicious Behavior

When auditing suspicious behavior, it is usually necessary to audit most database activity. If you limit the database activity that is being audited, you might miss some vital clue that can help you solve the mystery of the suspicious behavior. If you start out auditing all activity, you can reduce the auditing as you gather clues. When you have determined more information about the suspicious behavior, you can reduce the number of activities being audited.

Also, note that when auditing suspicious behavior it is necessary to protect the audit logs. If this undesirable behavior is intentional, the perpetrator might try to cover up his or her tracks by removing information from the audit trail. How to protect the audit trail is described later today in the section titled "Protecting the Audit Trail."

Creating the Audit Trail

To enable the audit trail, first you must run the administration SQL script CATAUDIT.SQL. This script is located in the directory Orant\Rdbms80\Admin. This administrative SQL script will create a number of views into the audit tables; each view shows a different perspective of the tables. The CATAUDIT.SQL script should be run by the SYS user.

To remove the audit trail views when they are no longer needed, use the administrative SQL script CATNOAUD.SQL. This will remove the views and disable auditing.

The Format of the Audit Trail

Each entry in the audit trail contains a wealth of information about the event in question:

- ☐ Username
- ☐ Session identifier
- ☐ Terminal identifier
- ☐ Object being accessed
- ☐ Operation performed or attempted
- ☐ Completion code
- ☐ Date and time stamp

For some auditing events, this might be all the information that is provided. Other auditing events might provide more information than this.

Enabling Auditing

The audit trail contains a variety of information depending on how the system is configured. Auditing of particular functions and users is enabled with the AUDIT statement. Auditing is disabled using the NOAUDIT statement. By default, some operations are automatically audited. These operations include

- [ ] Instance startup
- [ ] Instance shutdown
- [ ] All connections to Oracle with SYSOPER or SYSDBA privileges

All other auditing information is enabled by specifying them individually using the AUDIT command. Auditing can be set on three different levels:

- [ ] Statements—Audit on particular SQL statements.
- [ ] Privileges—Audit on SQL statements that require a particular system privilege.
- [ ] Objects—Audit on statements that involve a particular table or other schema object.

Auditing Statements and Privileges

To audit SQL statements you should use the following syntax with the AUDIT SQL statement:

```
AUDIT
SQL_STATEMENT_OPTIONS or PRIVILEGE
[, SQL_STATEMENT_OPTIONS or PRIVILEGE ...]
[BY user_name [, user_name]...]
[BY SESSION or BY ACCESS]
[WHENEVER SUCCESSFUL or WHENEVER NOT SUCCESSFUL]
```

This statement is all that is necessary to enable auditing. The explanations of the parameters are as follows:

- [ ] SQL_STATEMENT_OPTIONS—With the audit command there are certain keywords, called *statement options*, that are used to indicate auditing of associated SQL statements. For example, the statement option CLUSTER indicates auditing on the CREATE CLUSTER, ALTER CLUSTER, DROP CLUSTER, and TRUNCATE CLUSTER SQL statements. A complete list of the statement options is given in the Oracle documentation.

- [ ] PRIVILEGE—Indicates that SQL statements authorized by this system privilege are to be audited. A complete list of system privileges is given in Appendix C, "Oracle Roles and Privileges."

☐ BY *user_name*—Indicates that the SQL statements issued by this user or users will be audited. If omitted, the SQL statements for all users will be audited.

☐ BY SESSION—Causes Oracle auditing to write only one record for each SQL statement issued in a session, so duplicate SQL statements are not logged.

☐ BY ACCESS—The opposite of BY SESSION. Causes an audit record to be written for each SQL statement issued.

☐ WHENEVER SUCCESSFUL—Causes an audit record to be written only when the SQL statement was successful. If omitted, all SQL statements are audited regardless of success.

☐ WHENEVER NOT SUCCESSFUL —Causes an audit record to be written only when the SQL statement was unsuccessful. If omitted, all SQL statements are audited regardless of success.

Besides auditing particular SQL statements by statement or privilege, you may also audit schema objects, as shown in the next section.

Auditing Objects

Auditing schema objects is very similar to auditing SQL statements. You can also audit access to particular schema objects. The syntax used to audit objects is very similar to the syntax used to audit SQL statements, as shown here:

```
AUDIT
Object_Option [, Object_Option ...]
ON [schema.]object] or ON DIRECTORY dir_name or ON DEFAULT
[BY SESSION or BY ACCESS]
[WHENEVER SUCCESSFUL or WHENEVER NOT SUCCESSFUL]
```

This statement is all that is necessary to enable auditing. Following are the explanations of the parameters:

☐ *Object_Option*—Specifies the type of operation that is audited. These keywords are SQL commands such as ALTER, DELETE, SELECT, and so on, and are described in detail in the Oracle documentation. One of the object options is ALL, specifying that all operations are to be audited.

☐ ON [*schema.*]*object*—Specifies the schema or schema object that will be audited.

☐ ON DIRECTORY *dir_name*—Specifies the directory that is being audited.

☐ ON DEFAULT—Specifies that objects that have not even been created will be audited with the same auditing options as other objects.

☐ BY SESSION—Causes Oracle auditing to write only one record for each SQL statement issued in a session, so duplicate SQL statements are not logged.

☐ BY ACCESS—The opposite of BY SESSION. Causes an audit record to be written for each SQL statement issued.

- WHENEVER SUCCESSFUL—Causes an audit record to be written only when the SQL statement was successful. If omitted, all SQL statements are audited regardless of success.

- WHENEVER NOT SUCCESSFUL —Causes an audit record to be written only when the SQL statement was unsuccessful. If omitted, all SQL statements are audited regardless of whether it is successful or not.

This is the syntax necessary to perform auditing on schema objects.

| **Tip** | If you audit WHENEVER NOT SUCCESSFUL, a record is kept of unsuccessful attempts at various operations. If you suspect that a user is trying to tamper with the system, this information can be very useful. |

Protecting the Audit Trail

It is important that you protect the audit trail if you suspect unusual behavior. In this manner, if there is malicious behavior going on, the party or parties involved cannot cover their tracks. You protect the audit trail with the following two steps:

1. Limit the DELETE ANY TABLE system privilege to the database administrators only. This keeps other users from being able to delete the audit trail.

2. Enable auditing on the audit trail itself. You do this with the following SQL statement:

```
AUDIT INSERT, UPDATE, DELETE
ON sys.aud$
BY ACCESS;
```

This will cause all access to the audit trail to be audited, thus indicating whether someone is covering up something.

Viewing Audit Information

As mentioned in the beginning of this lesson, there are a number of views into the audit trail created by the CATAUDIT.SQL administrative script. You can select these views to provide useful auditing information. Here is a description of the most relevant of the views:

- [USER or DBA]_AUDIT_OBJECT—Audit trail entries for objects that are audited.

- [USER or DBA]_AUDIT_SESSION—Audit entries for CONNECT and DISCONNECT operations.

- [USER or DBA]_AUDIT_STATEMENT—The audit trail concerning GRANT, REVOKE, AUDIT, NOAUDIT, and ALTER SYSTEM commands.

- [USER or DBA]_AUDIT_TRAIL—All audit trail entries.

By selecting from these views, you can retrieve information about the audit trails. The specific information in the audit trails may vary, but all of them contain the same basic information:

- [ ] Username
- [ ] Session identifier
- [ ] Terminal identifier
- [ ] Object being accessed
- [ ] Operation performed or attempted
- [ ] Completion code
- [ ] Date and time stamp

The auditing information can be useful, but should be used with care to avoid consuming excess system resources. Using auditing as necessary and selectively can be very enlightening.

WARNING

> Because of the overhead auditing adds to the system, it should be used sparingly. Only audit the events that are necessary and only audit when necessary.

Summary

In today's lesson you have learned about managing job queues and the Oracle auditing facility. Oracle job queues are used to divert the execution of an operation to a later time, thus allowing you to schedule jobs. By using the Oracle job-queuing facility, you can easily schedule jobs to be run at various times or on a regular schedule. This allows you to automate many of the repetitive tasks that need to be done. You have learned how to schedule jobs using both the Enterprise Manager and the stored procedures in the DBMS_JOB package.

The Oracle auditing facility is used to log various database operations such as when they occurred and who performed that operation. Auditing is important if one or more incidences have occurred to make you suspicious of the activity of one or more users. Through auditing, a record will be made of this activity that can be used in tracking down the party at fault. Auditing is also useful to periodically monitor the activity of the system and to allow you to make adjustments to improve performance or usability of the system.

What's Next?

In tomorrow's lesson, "Understanding Effective Backup Techniques," you will begin to learn about one of the most important tasks the DBA is charged with: backup and recovery. In the next three days you will learn various techniques for putting together a backup and recovery plan and various methods of quick recovery and fault tolerance. This is one of my favorite topics, and I hope you will enjoy it too.

Q&A

Q What is the job queue used for?

A The Oracle job-queuing mechanism is used to defer the execution of database operations or to run operations in the background.

Q Who can use the job queues?

A Any user can use the job queues, but use of the Oracle Enterprise Manager is usually limited to the database administrators.

Q What is auditing used for?

A Auditing is used either to characterize database activity or to find the source of suspicious activity.

Q Who uses auditing?

A Auditing is limited to database administrators. There is no reason for users to need to use the auditing facilities.

Workshop

The workshop provides quiz questions to help you solidify your understanding of the material covered and exercises to provide you with experience in using what you've learned. Find answers to the quiz questions in Appendix A, "Answers."

Quiz

1. What is the job-scheduling facility used for?
2. What kind of jobs can be scheduled?
3. Can only database operations be scheduled?
4. Should a new user account be created for job queuing?
5. What NT user right needs to be created for this user account?
6. Can jobs be run on remote systems?
7. What kinds of scheduling can be done?
8. What needs to be configured in the Enterprise Manager?
9. Why might you need to enable auditing?
10. What do you need to watch out for with auditing?

Exercises

1. Invoke the Enterprise Manager and look for any running jobs.

2. Create a test job using the Enterprise Manager. This job can be a simple select operation.

3. Schedule this job to run every week.

4. Delete this job from the job queue.

15

Day 16

Understanding Effective Backup Techniques

In the next three days, you will learn about some of my favorite topics: backup and recovery and ways to engineer maximum uptime. This is one of my favorites because of the various ways you can design backup and recovery strategies and because of the enormous importance of this task.

Review of Oracle Procedures

Before you learn how backups work, I would like to review a little bit about how Oracle works. This section does not cover all the Oracle functions and processes, just those pertinent to the integrity of the data in the database.

If none of the data in the database ever changed, there would never be a need to back up that data more than once. Because the data never changed, any backup that occurred in the past could be used to restore the data to a useful state. Well, this is not the case in most systems, although by using read-only tablespaces it can be achieved.

Because most systems' data changes, the database is now a constantly changing system. It is of utmost importance that this data be protected. If a system failure should occur, it is unreasonable to think that all changes that are in progress should be recovered, but it is a reasonable expectation that all committed transactions be recovered.

 NEW TERM In fact, if you have a good backup-and-recovery plan, no committed transactions should ever be lost. In recovering the database from a failure, you have to determine which of the two types of failure occurred so you know which recovery mechanism to use. The two types of recovery are *instance recovery* and *data recovery*.

Instance Recovery

NEW TERM An *instance failure* can occur due to a system failure, such as a power outage or a hardware or software problem. When an instance failure occurs, the Oracle recovery process can completely recover the database on instance startup. All committed transactions will be recovered or rolled forward, and all noncommitted transactions will be rolled back.

 NOTE

> Instance recovery can be quite time consuming. How much time instance recovery takes depends on the number of dirty buffers in the SGA, and the number of dirty buffers depends on the amount of time since the last checkpoint. The time it takes for instance recovery also depends on the recovery parallelism. The recovery parallelism is the amount of parallelism used in the recovery process; this is part of the Parallel Query option's Parallel Recovery feature.

As you will see later today and tomorrow, instance recovery can and should be tuned to provide for the shortest possible recovery time.

TIP

> By tuning the checkpoint interval and recovery parallelism, you can shorten the recovery time.

Data Recovery

Data recovery is necessary when media failure has occurred—for example, when a datafile is damaged. If a datafile is damaged, you must first restore the damaged file from backup before recovery can occur. The Oracle recovery process will then apply archive log files and redo log files to restore the damaged datafile to the state that it was at prior to the failure. It may take as many as all the archive log files created since the backup to recover the restored datafile. This process can be quite time consuming.

 TIP

> By scheduling frequent backups, you can shorten the restoration and recovery time.

As you will see today and tomorrow, the goal is to have the shortest possible downtime in the event of a catastrophic system failure.

Log File Recovery

You cannot do anything to recover a lost log file. If a log file is damaged and the system is still functional, you can drop the log file, re-create it, and immediately perform a full backup. (The backup is necessary because you will not be able to use the archive log files and redo log files for any recovery on this database.) This is why I always recommend that log volumes be fault tolerant.

How Transactions Work

Remember, the term *transaction* is used to describe a logical group of work. This group of work can consist of one or many SQL statements and must end with a commit or a rollback. This definition assumes a client/server application, so SQL*Net is necessary. To review the steps required to execute a transaction, review Day 2, "Exploring the Oracle Architecture."

For today's lesson it is important to note that the transaction requires the redo log entry to be written out before the transaction has been committed. If a failure occurs before that entry has been written, the transaction will not be recovered.

Logging and Archiving

As mentioned on Day 2, the *redo log* records all changes made to the Oracle database. The purpose of the redo log is to ensure that, in the event of the loss of a datafile caused by some sort of system failure, the database can be recovered. By restoring the datafiles back to a known good state from backups, the redo log files (including the archive log files) can replay all the transactions to the restored datafile, thus recovering the database to the point of failure.

When a redo log file is filled in normal operation, a log switch occurs and the LGWR process starts writing to a different redo log file. When this switch occurs, the ARCH process copies the filled redo log file to an archive log file. When this archive is complete, the redo log file is marked as available. It is critical that this archive log file be safely stored, because it might be needed for recovery.

NOTE

Remember that a transaction has not been committed until the redo log file has been written. Slow I/Os to the redo log files can slow down the entire system.

ARCHIVELOG **Mode**

The Oracle RDBMS is not required to run in ARCHIVELOG mode, so the archiving mechanism can be disabled. However, if you do not run in ARCHIVELOG mode, it is impossible to recover any transactions that are not in the current redo log files.

WARNING

If you do not run in ARCHIVELOG mode, you will most likely lose valuable data in the event that a datafile is lost. I recommend that all production systems be run in ARCHIVELOG mode. You can run test systems without archiving.

If your data is important to you, you should always run your production systems in ARCHIVELOG mode.

Enabling Archiving

Archiving is enabled by running the ALTER DATABASE command with the parameter ARCHIVELOG. To enable archiving, use

```
ALTER DATABASE ARCHIVELOG;
```

Disabling Archiving

Archiving is disabled by running the ALTER DATABASE command with the parameter NOARCHIVELOG. To disable archiving, use

```
ALTER DATABASE NOARCHIVELOG;
```

If you are in ARCHIVELOG mode and want to disable it for a particular startup, you can set the Oracle parameter LOG_ARCHIVE_START=FALSE.

Setting the Archiving Destination

Use the Oracle parameter LOG_ARCHIVE_DEST to set the destination for Oracle archiving. Archive log files will be created in this directory with a different filename for each archive log file. This filename is defined by the Oracle parameter LOG_ARCHIVE_FORMAT. Both of these parameters are described in the Oracle documentation.

How to Configure Your System

In configuring your hardware system, it is important to plan for protecting your data. By carefully configuring your system for data integrity, you can optimally configure for both performance and protection. In this section, I give you a few tips on how to configure your system using RAID disk subsystems.

Review of Disk Arrays

NEW TERM A *disk array* is collection of disk drives configured to act as one larger disk drive. Both hardware and software disk arrays are available today. Hardware disk arrays consist of a disk array controller and a set of disk drives (typically SCSI). Software disk arrays are made up of a software layer that lies between the file system and the device driver layers.

Disk arrays usually support disk striping, disk mirroring, disk parity, and so on. Hardware disk arrays also support other features such as hot-swappable disks. An array with fault tolerance and hot-swappable disks allows you to replace a defective disk while the system is active. Depending on the manufacturer and model, the disk array controller can support several different types of RAID fault tolerance.

Disk arrays offer many benefits to the system administrator and the end users:

☐ Ease of management. A disk array can offer tens of gigabytes of disk space that appear to the administrator as one large disk. This arrangement simplifies some of the management tasks involved with managing large numbers of disks.

☐ I/O balancing. Because a disk array is made up of many individual disks with striped data, random I/O is automatically distributed among the disks.

☐ Fault tolerance. Disk arrays provide a wide range of RAID options with a wide variety of performance and economic choices.

NEW TERM A disk array is a set of disk drives that make up a larger logical disk, which is sometimes called a *logical volume.* The logical volume is made up of identical-sized pieces of the individual drives, called *stripes.* The data is said to be *striped* across the logical volume because the logical drive has pieces of all the individual drives striped within it, as shown in Figure 16.1. If you look at the logical volume, the physical drives seem to make stripes.

The stripes are all the same size and in sequence (that is, disk 1 holds the first stripe, disk 2 the second, and so on). The size of the stripe varies based on the manufacturer and model of the disk array controller. The stripe size also varies in a software array. The size of the stripe is called the *striping factor* and is given in number of blocks. A typical striping factor is 32. Given a size of 512 bytes per block, a striping factor of 32 makes the disk stripe 16KB in size.

16

Figure 16.1.

Disk stripes on a logical volume.

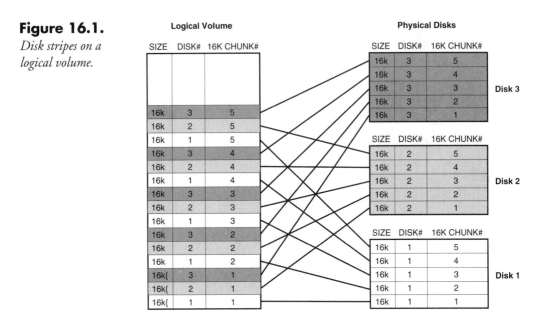

As far as the user and the RDBMS are concerned, there is only one large disk drive. It is up to the OS and the hardware to manage the individual disks within the array.

RAID Levels

The configuration of disks in an array is sometimes called a *Redundant Array of Inexpensive Disks* (RAID) configuration. RAID technology allows systems to maintain very large amounts of storage at relatively low cost. The inexpensive SCSI drives that make up the array have not only improved in performance and quality over the years, but they have significantly dropped in price.

NEW TERM The term *RAID* is also used to describe the type of striping you use. Striping methods vary in both performance and space overhead. The type of configuration used in your system depends on your individual needs. Different configurations of striping and fault-tolerant striping are identified by RAID levels.

The various RAID levels are determined by a body of computer vendors called the RAID Advisory Board. This standards body determines the basics of the various RAID levels but does not force any particular implementation, thus allowing vendors to differentiate themselves. Following are brief descriptions of the various RAID levels.

RAID-0

RAID-0 is the base RAID level and is used to describe disk striping with no fault tolerance. RAID-0 drives simply have data striped over all the drives, as shown in Figure 16.2.

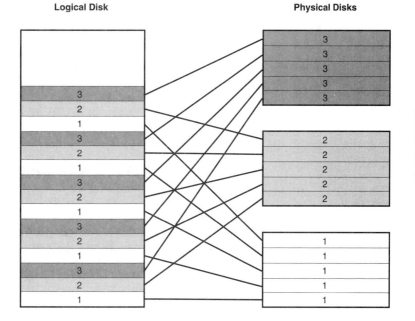

Figure 16.2.

RAID level 0 has no fault tolerance.

RAID-0 is the highest-performing and most economical of the RAID levels. The amount of data in the logical volume is equal to the sum of the amount of data on each disk drive. RAID-0 causes no additional I/O to be generated on behalf of the fault-tolerant method.

The downside of RAID-0 is that if a disk were to fail, the entire volume would become invalid. Because the data in the logical volume is striped across all the disks, the loss of a single disk causes a loss of data throughout the logical volume. If a 14-disk volume fails, you must restore the data for all 14 disk drives. There is no way to back up and restore data for a single drive in a disk array.

If you are looking for the highest performance and the best value possible and are not worried about fault tolerance, this is the RAID level you should use.

RAID-1

The RAID-1 level is also known as *disk mirroring*. In RAID-1, all the data stored on a disk drive is duplicated on another disk in the array. Each time a write occurs to the logical disk, the data must be written to *both* physical disks before the logical write is considered completed. With disk mirroring, a single disk is mirrored to another disk; these disks can also be striped with other disks to form a larger logical volume, as shown in Figure 16.3.

Figure 16.3.

RAID level 1 is also called disk mirroring.

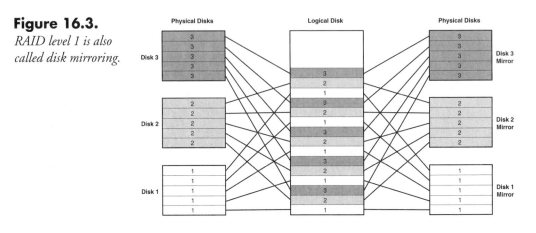

Because the mirroring is on a one-to-one basis, you can actually lose half the disks in your system (depending on which disks they are) and still be operational. With most disk array controllers, you can split the mirror across SCSI buses. This arrangement allows for the failure of an entire SCSI bus (for example, a cabinet failure) without affecting operation.

With disk mirroring, you can use only half the disks in the system (the other half are used for the mirrors). In other words, if you use disk mirroring with two, 2.1GB disks, you can use only 2.1GB of space. When writing, you get the benefit of only one disk in terms of performance, because a logical write invokes two physical writes.

Under certain conditions, you will see a benefit from reading from mirrored drives. Some disk array controllers support *split-reads*, in which reads can occur simultaneously on different mirrored drives to different data. The disk with the heads closest to the requested data retrieves the data. Depending on your data-access methods, this feature might or might not provide any benefits to you.

If you can afford the cost of disk mirroring, RAID-1 is the best choice when fault tolerance is required. With disk mirroring, you achieve the highest level of protection as well as the fastest disk access possible for a fault-tolerant volume.

RAID-2

RAID level 2 is data striping that is protected by a method known as *hamming code* that is similar to the method used in error detection and correction in RAM. Because of the difficulty in implementing RAID-2, it has not been widely accepted.

RAID-3

RAID level 3 uses a parallel-access parity RAID configuration. RAID-3 stores data and parity on a several disks using a bit-by-bit parity. RAID-3 uses a parallel access method to achieve high performance but requires that the individual disk rotations be synchronized, which may be difficult. RAID-3 is not widely used.

RAID-4

NEW TERM   RAID level 4 is known as *drive parity*, or *data guarding*. In RAID-4, one of four drives is used for data parity. If any one of the four disks fails, the other three continue running. Because the algorithms used in RAID-4 are considered obsolete, RAID-4 is not used much. RAID-4 has essentially been replaced by RAID-5.

When you use RAID-4, a lot of I/O is generated. To calculate the parity, RAID-4 reads data from all the drives in the set. As you can imagine, the overhead involved with RAID-4 is very high.

RAID-5

NEW TERM   RAID-5 is also known as *distributed data guarding*. In distributed data guarding, enough information is stored about each drive so that any one drive in the set can fail; the data is restored by using all the other drives. The space you get from RAID-5 is equal to the following:

Drive Space = (N–1) * Drive Size

In this equation, N is the number of drives in the logical volume. In other words, if you are running 12 disk drives with RAID-5, you get the space of 11 disk drives.

As with RAID-4, there is a penalty associated with RAID-5. For each write to disk, two reads take place, a calculation of the parity is done, and then two writes are done. Although a read generates only one I/O, a write generates four I/Os.

RAID-6

RAID-6 is almost identical to RAID-5 but with the addition of an independently computed data check. This makes the RAID-6 volume very secure, with extremely high data availability because of the addition of one extra disk for this additional fault tolerance. Thus, with RAID-6 the cost is

Drive Space = (N–2) * Drive Size

Other RAID Levels

You might see other RAID levels mentioned that are a combination of these RAID levels. Some vendors call a combination of RAID-0 (striping) and RAID-1 (mirroring) a RAID-10 or RAID-0+1 array.

Caching RAID Controllers

NEW TERM   Write caches are designed to cache the writes written to the controller and to post the I/O request to the disk driver. *Posting the request* means that the device driver believes the I/O is completed. Posting the write allows the overhead associated with queuing the request and writing it to the individual disk to be masked. All the OS and the RDBMS see is an incredibly fast write and can continue with their operations as though the data had been completely written out to disk.

Unless the write cache is protected, it is not usually recommended that write-caching be enabled on the redo log volume. If the RDBMS believes a write to have occurred to the redo log, and a controller failure occurs before that data has actually been written to the disk drives, you might not be able to recover the instance.

Some disk array controllers have incorporated both mirroring or parity and a battery backup into the write cache to ensure the data is protected even in the event of a power outage. Use your own judgment about running a write cache on the redo log volumes.

Protecting the System

If you use RAID technology, there are essentially three modes in which you can run your database:

☐ No data protection—Fault tolerance is not used on any of the logical volumes.

☐ Full data protection—Fault tolerance is used on all the volumes.

☐ Partial data protection—Fault tolerance is used on some of the volumes and not on others.

Although disk drives have become much more reliable in the past few years, they are still the component most likely to fail. Disk drives are susceptible to failure because they are mostly mechanical devices.

Disks are made up of sophisticated electronics and motors. Forces such as heat, dust, and friction can cause even the most well-built disk drive to fail. No matter how well you take care of your system, it is inevitable that you will one day see a disk failure.

TIP

Depending on the size and critical nature of your database, a failure of one disk can be devastating if you are not protected. When taking into account your budget for fault-tolerant components, keep in mind the cost of extended downtime that results from a failure.

No Data Protection

In No Data Protection mode, no fault tolerance is used and the data is completely unprotected. Any disk failure causes you to reload all the affected files from the last backup.

If the failure occurs on a data volume, you can restore the data (if you are running in ARCHIVELOG mode, you can use the archive log files to restore the database up to the point of failure). Even so, when a disk drive fails, you must restore the entire *volume*, which might mean tens of gigabytes of data.

If the failure occurs on the volume containing your redo log files, you can recover only up to the last good archived log file. At instance recovery, you can recover only up to the point at which the LGWR started writing to the damaged log file(s).

If the failure occurs on the volume containing the OS and Oracle binaries, you must restore from a backup or reinstall the operating system, reload Oracle, and then restart Oracle.

As you can see, in each of these unprotected situations, the recovery interval can be quite long. No failure of an unprotected system is easy to recover from.

Full Data Protection

Full Data Protection mode is by far the most secure option. If you have fault tolerance on every disk drive in the system, any single failure does not cause a system failure. Depending on the level of fault tolerance you run, many multidisk failures can be tolerated. The level of fault tolerance you run depends on the performance you require and the budget you have.

In the last few years, the cost of disk drives has dropped so dramatically that it is not unusual to see entire systems run with disk mirroring. The cost of the extra drives needed to support fault tolerance usually outweighs the cost incurred by extended downtime.

In assessing the level of fault tolerance, look at your required I/O rates. If possible, use RAID-1 because it gives the best performance. If RAID-1 is not in your budget, perhaps you can use it for at least your OS and redo log volumes. (The redo log volumes usually demand the highest protection available.)

Partial Data Protection

Another option for protecting your data is to apply fault tolerance to specific pieces of critical data. This might be the best option if you have a limited budget and require high performance.

Critical areas that should be protected are the OS, the redo logs, and the archive logs. If these areas are protected and a drive volume fails, you will not have to spend extra time restoring or reloading the operating system. If the redo log volumes are not protected and a drive fails, you might not be able to recover your database to the point of failure. If the archive files are not protected and a drive fails, you will not be able to recover from a data loss failure if that archive log file is needed for recovery.

By using partial fault tolerance, you might be able to reduce downtime in the event of a failure and still keep within your budget. Protecting areas such as the OS volumes and redo log volumes will help you reduce the amount of time needed to recover.

Fault Tolerance Summary

The component in your system most likely to fail is a disk drive because it is a heavily used mechanical device. To avoid extended downtime, it is wise to employ some type of fault tolerance. The extent to which you protect your data depends on your uptime requirements, performance requirements, and budget.

Depending on your needs, you might not have to completely protect all your data, but *some* fault tolerance is recommended. If it is too expensive to protect all your disks, protect at least the critical areas. Depending on your needs, you might want to use different data-protection modes on different volumes. Here are a few suggestions about fault tolerance for you to consider:

- ☐ Fully protect your OS and Oracle binaries using RAID-1 or RAID-5. This level of protection is worth the cost of the extra disks because you avoid reloading the OS and Oracle.

- ☐ Fully protect the redo log files. If possible, put each redo log file on a separate mirrored volume. By separating the redo log files, you maintain the sequential nature of the I/Os generated by the LGWR even when archiving.

- ☐ Fully protect the archive log files. This does not have to be high-performance fault tolerance as you have with the redo logs; it can be done using RAID-5.

- ☐ Use RAID-5 on read-intensive volumes. The performance degradation experienced when using RAID-5 occurs only on writes. If the volume is mainly used for reads, very good performance can be achieved with RAID-5.

The amount and type of fault tolerance you employ depends on your specific requirements. If you cannot permit any downtime, you must protect yourself against disk failures.

Configuration Recommendations

I would recommend that you employ some sort of fault tolerance on your system. At the very least, use mirroring on your OS volume as well as on the Oracle binaries, control files, and redo log files. This will allow you to reduce the amount of downtime that you would suffer in the event of a system failure. The worst-case scenario would be to have to reinstall an operating system, reinstall Oracle, rebuild the database, and then restore. This scenario calls for maximum downtime. By carefully configuring your system, downtime can be reduced.

Types of Backups

There are a variety of options available for backing up the Oracle database. Each option provides a different amount of protection and typically causes a different amount of downtime. The options are as follows:

- ☐ Archive log file backup—A backup of the archive log files.
- ☐ Control file backup—A backup of the control files.
- ☐ Datafile backup—A backup of a single datafile.
- ☐ Full backup—A backup of all datafiles and control files.
- ☐ Tablespace backup—A backup of a single tablespace.

In this section you will learn how these backup types differ, which you need to run, and how they complement each other.

Archive Log Backup

Because archive log files are continually being created, they are typically backed up to offline storage. Because the archive log information can be quite large, it is usually not feasible to keep this data online, but if possible you should keep the archive log files online until a complete database backup is performed.

Remember, once a datafile is restored from backup, the archive log files that were created since that backup was taken are applied to roll-forward transactions. Archive log files older than the last backup are needed only if the restore operation fails and an older backup needs to be used.

TIP

A good procedure would be to save archive log files until the next datafile backup, and then archive them to tape or other archival storage.

While online, these archive log files need to be protected. I recommend keeping your online archive log files on a RAID-protected disk volume or backing up the archive log files to tape as soon as they are created. The loss of an archive log file could mean that you can't recover your database in the event of a failure.

Another way to protect your archive log file is to use the Oracle archive log duplexing feature. If you set the Oracle parameter LOG_ARCHIVE_DUPLEX_DEST, a second copy of each archive log file will be created in this directory. This protects the archive log files against any single point of failure.

Control File Backup

The control files are very important to the operation of the Oracle RDBMS because they contain information about the physical construction of the database. If the control file is lost, it might still be possible to re-create it, but it will be very difficult.

On Day 8, "Administering Redo Logs, Control Files, and Rollback Segments," you learned how to back up control files using the ALTER DATABASE command. The two options for the ALTER DATABASE *database* BACKUP CONTROLFILE command are as follows:

- ☐ TO '*filename*' —This will create a new control file with the name specified by *filename*. If the file already exists, the optional REUSE qualifier must be used in order to overwrite it; otherwise you will get an error.

- ☐ TO TRACE—The TO TRACE parameter optionally writes SQL to a trace file that can be used to re-create the control files. The SQL statements are complete enough to start up the database, re-create the control files, and recover and open the database appropriately.

Another option is to simply back up the control file(s) when performing operating-system backups. If a control file is lost, it can be restored from that backup. The control file(s) needs to be backed up any time there is a structural change to the database, because such changes alter the control file.

Full Backup

A full backup occurs when the entire database and its associated control files are backed up. A full backup can occur either offline or online. The best type of backup to perform is the full offline backup because you get a consistent view of the entire database, but for many systems this is not an option because little or no downtime is allotted for backups.

Full Offline Backup

The full offline backup is sometimes called a *consistent whole database* backup. The full offline backup is done when the database instance has been shut down cleanly. With the database shut down, you back up the datafiles and control files using OS or third-party backup software and hardware. If you have the downtime available to you, the full offline backup is the best backup solution.

NOTE

Even though you have backed up the datafiles and the control files, you should only restore the control files if necessary. Never overwrite a newer control file with an older one unless there is no other alternative.

Full Online Backup

In many cases where systems need to be up and running 7 days a week, 24 hours a day, the offline backup is not an option. In this situation, the online backup is your only choice.

A full online backup is really just a combination of tablespace backups and control file backups. With the full online backup, the control files and, in turn, each tablespace are backed up using the online tablespace backup facility.

NOTE

> Online backups are valid only if you are running in ARCHIVELOG mode. If you are not running in ARCHIVELOG mode, your only choice is an offline backup.

16

Tablespace and Datafile Backups

The tablespace backup allows you to back up a single tablespace while the database is online and running. When the administrator signals the Oracle instance that a backup will be performed on that tablespace, special actions are taken. Once the tablespace has been marked for backup, one or more of the datafiles that make up the tablespace are backed up using OS or third-party utilities.

When you mark the tablespace for backup, the Oracle RDBMS will know that this online backup has occurred, and it will know how to recover the database if recovery is necessary. In the next section you will learn the actual mechanics of how to perform this type of backup.

How to Back Up the Database

With Oracle8 there are several different ways that the Oracle database can be backed up. You can use any of the following:

- [ ] Backup Manager/Recovery Manager
- [ ] OS facilities
- [ ] Export
- [ ] The NT Backup utility

NOTE

> The new Oracle8 utility for backup and recovery is called *Recovery Manager*. The graphical utility provided with Enterprise Manager that uses Recovery Manager is called *Backup Manager*. You will see references to both Backup Manager and Recovery Manager. Keep in mind that both are essentially the same utility.

Each of these utilities can perform an effective backup. It is usually your own personal preference that can help you decide which one to use.

Backing Up with Backup Manager

Backup Manager is invoked and runs through Enterprise Manager, and therefore can be run either locally or remotely. Backup Manager is a graphical utility and fairly easy to use.

Setting Up Backup Manager

Before Backup Manager can be used, the recovery catalog must be created. This catalog can be created by using the following SQL statements:

```
SPOOL recovery.log
CREATE USER rman IDENTIFIED BY rman
TEMPORARY TABLESPACE temporary
DEFAULT TABLESPACE rcvcat QUOTA unlimited ON rcvcat;
GRANT recovery_catalog_owner TO rman;
CONNECT rman/rman
@d:\orant\rdbms80\admin\catrman
```

NOTE

> The recovery catalog should be created in its own database. If the database you are backing up is damaged and contains the recovery catalog, the catalog will also be damaged.

The next step is to set up Oracle for remote administration so that Backup Manager can connect in. The following steps must be taken to allow this to happen:

1. Change directories to the `orant\dbs` directory.

2. Save your existing password file (if you have one). It will be named `orawpSID` (where *SID* is your SID name).

3. Create a new password file with the following syntax:

   ```
   ORAPWD80 file=orapwSID password=password entries=10
   ```

4. Change or add this line to your `init.ora` file:

   ```
   remote_login_passwordfile=exclusive
   ```

16

5. Create the remote user with this syntax:

```
CREATE USER remote IDENTIFIED BY remote
```

6. Grant the following to the remote user:

```
GRANT connect, resource TO remote;
GRANT sysdba TO remote;
```

After you have created the remote user, you must set up Backup Manager to use these accounts. The first step is to start up Backup Manager. From Enterprise Manager, select the Oracle Backup Manager. The first screen you will see is the Backup Manager—Subsystem screen, as shown in Figure 16.4.

Figure 16.4.

The Backup Manager—Subsystem screen allows you to choose which method of backup you prefer.

From this screen, choose Oracle8 Recovery Manager. This will bring up the Oracle Recovery Manager's graphical interface, known as Backup Manager (see Figure 16.5). This is Backup Manager's main screen. You might notice that this screen is similar to some of the other Enterprise Manager applications. Because of the nature of the backup-and-recovery process, this screen allows you to browse many of the Oracle schema objects, such as

- ☐ Control files
- ☐ Tablespaces
- ☐ Datafiles
- ☐ Redo log groups
- ☐ Archived logs
- ☐ Channels
- ☐ Jobs

Backup Manager also allows you to change the state of the instance. This is useful if you want to shut down the instance in order to perform an offline backup.

After you have invoked Backup Manager, you must change the database connection to use the remote user you have just set up. First, select Change Database Connection from the File menu. This will invoke the Target Database Login screen, shown in Figure 16.6. From here you should change the login to select the username, password, and service necessary to connect into the database you will be backing up.

Figure 16.5.

The main screen of Backup Manager.

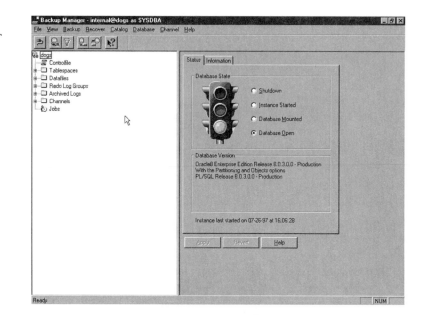

Figure 16.6.

Change the login in the Target Database Login screen to connect to the database you will be backing up.

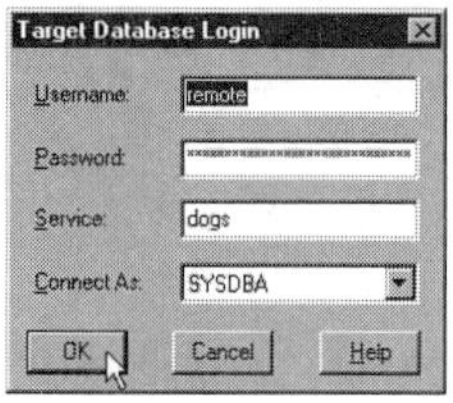

Be sure that you have selected to connect as SYSDBA.

It is also necessary to select the connection to the recovery catalog that you created earlier in this section. To do this, select the Catalog Connect String option from the Catalog menu. This will invoke the Recovery Catalog Login screen, which is very similar to its counterpart in Figure 16.6. This is where you select the username, password, and service for the recovery catalog database. Remember that in a production environment, the recovery catalog should be in a database other than the one you're backing up.

Once you have set up the connections for the database and the catalog, you should register the recovery catalog. You do this by selecting Register from the Catalog menu, which will invoke a job to register the recovery catalog. After you have registered the recovery catalog, you are ready to use Oracle Backup Manager.

Running Backup Manager

To invoke Backup Manager, use the procedures described in Figures 16.4 and 16.5. After you have invoked the Backup Manager, you should select the Backup Wizard option from the Backup menu.

If this is the first time you have run the Backup Manager, you will be informed that you do not have any channels defined, as shown in Figure 16.7.

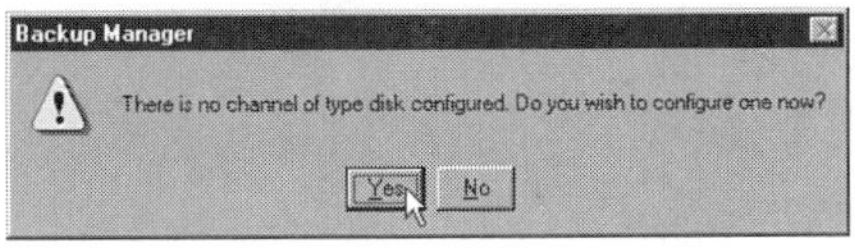

Figure 16.7.

You see this message if this is the first time you have used Backup Manager.

The channels are actually I/O channels. The more channels you have defined, the more parallelism you will achieve. In my case, because I am running on a small, single-processor system, I will create only one channel. Give the backup channel a name and a destination if you want the data to be backed up to disk. (See Figure 16.8.)

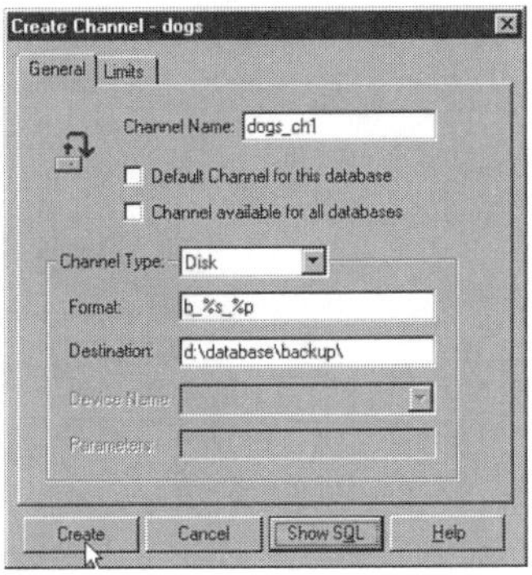

Figure 16.8.

The Create Channel screen is used to create a backup channel.

After you have created at least one channel, you can proceed with the Backup wizard. The first screen in the Backup wizard is the introduction (see Figure 16.9). Here you select what type of backup you want to perform. The options are

☐ Database backup

☐ Tablespace backup

☐ Datafiles backup

☐ Archived logs only backup

Figure 16.9.

You can select from several options in the Introduction screen of the Backup wizard.

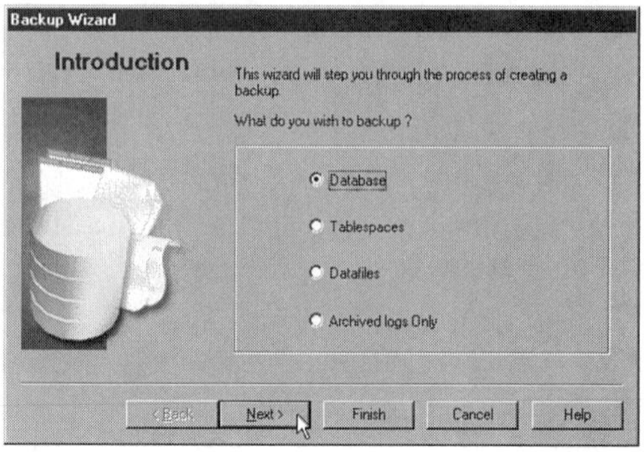

In the figure, I have selected to perform a database backup. The appearance of the next screen varies based on the selection of the backup type. If you have chosen Database, you will be asked whether you want to back up the archived logs. If you have chosen Tablespace, you will be presented with a list of tablespaces to select from, and if you have chosen Datafiles, you will be presented with a list of datafiles to choose from. If you have chosen Archived logs Only, you will be given a range of archived logs to back up.

For this illustration, the Database option has been selected. The Backup wizard then proceeds to the next screen, where you will be asked whether you want to back up the archived logs. I prefer to handle those separately, so I chose to back up none of the archived logs. This is shown in Figure 16.10.

Figure 16.10.

In the Archived logs screen of the Backup wizard, you choose whether you want to back up any of the archive log files.

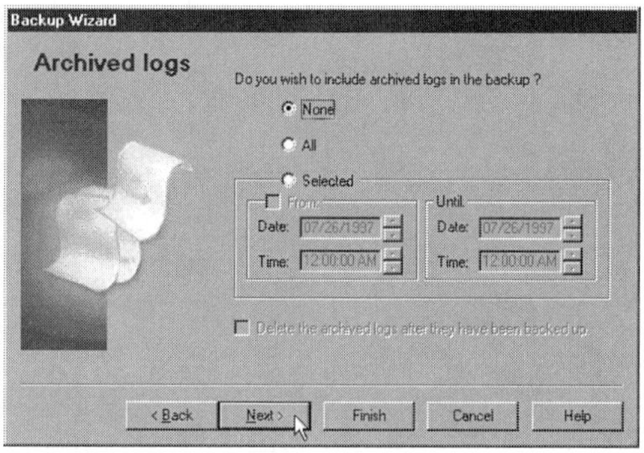

In the next screen of the Backup wizard, you will be prompted to select one or more channels to back up to. Using more than one channel will increase the parallelism of the backup. The Channels screen is shown in Figure 16.11.

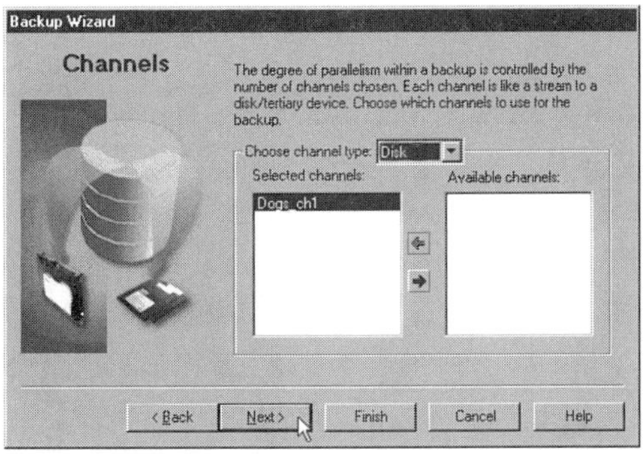

Figure 16.11.

Here you choose the channels to which you want to back up.

The next screen gives you some options that should be set. You should set the tag to a meaningful name for the backup. If you are doing an incremental backup, you can set the level of the backup here. This is shown in Figure 16.12.

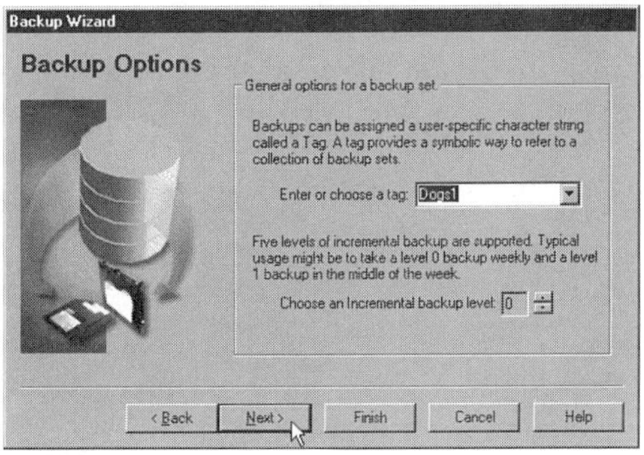

Figure 16.12.

Backup wizard—Backup Options. Here you select a tag to identify the backup set.

The next screen is the Parameters screen. Here you can set the maximum files per backup set, as shown in Figure 16.13. By setting this number, you force multiple channels to be used. The more files per backup set, the more channels that will be used.

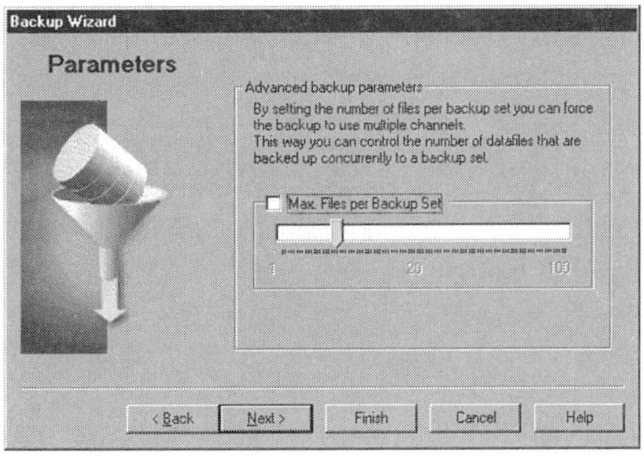

Figure 16.13.

The Backup wizard—Parameters screen allows you to set the maximum number of files per backup set.

The next screen is the Schedule screen, which is very similar to the one you saw in yesterday's lesson on job scheduling. You can set the backup to begin immediately or at some time in the future, as shown in Figure 16.14.

Figure 16.14.

In the Schedule screen of the Backup wizard, you specify whether you want the backup to begin immediately or at some later time.

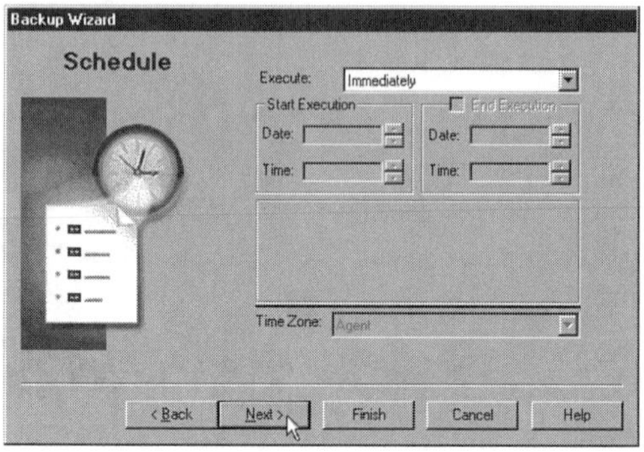

The last configuration screen for the Backup wizard is the Save/Submit screen. With this screen, you can select to submit the backup, to save these parameters to the library, or both, as shown in Figure 16.15. Typically you will submit at this point.

Figure 16.15.

The Backup wizard—Save/Submit screen allows you to either submit the job or save the settings for later use.

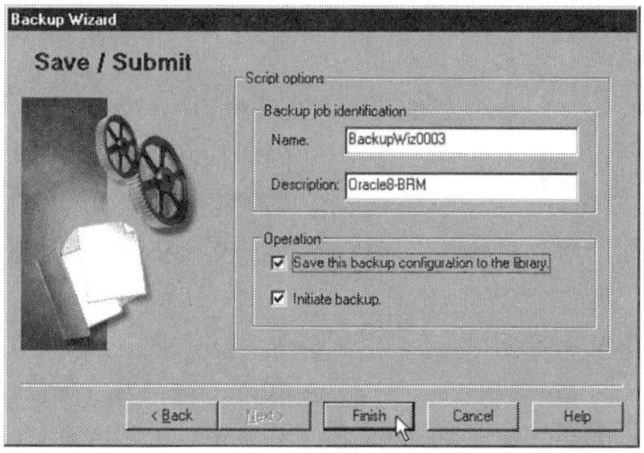

After you have completed all the screens of the Backup wizard and clicked the Finish button, you are presented with a summary of your selections, as shown in Figure 16.16.

Click OK to submit the backup job. Depending on the scheduling parameters you have set, the backup might begin to execute immediately. This screen allows you only to view the settings. No changes are allowed. If you find that the settings are in error, you can cancel the job and start the process over again.

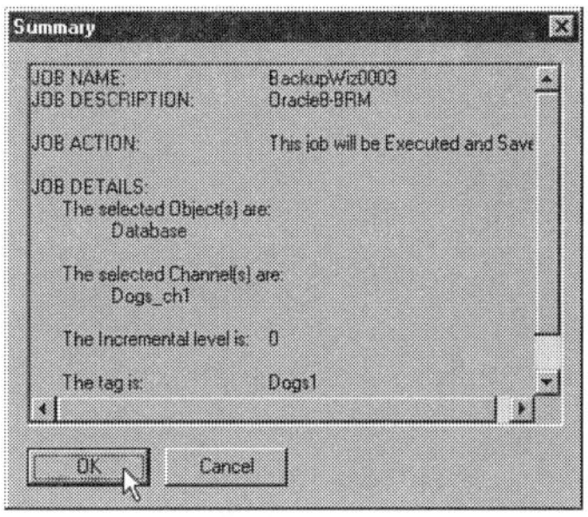

Figure 16.16.

The Backup wizard's Summary screen shows you the options you've chosen for your backup.

Summary	
JOB NAME:	BackupWiz0003
JOB DESCRIPTION:	OracleB-BRM
JOB ACTION:	This job will be Executed and Save
JOB DETAILS:	
The selected Object(s) are:	Database
The selected Channel(s) are:	Dogs_ch1
The Incremental level is:	0
The tag is:	Dogs1

OK   Cancel

NOTE

At this point the backup has been submitted and will be completed. You can click the Jobs icon (refer to Figure 16.5) if you want to view the current progress of the job. From the Jobs screen you can also view the status of previous jobs and look at the job library.

Backing Up with OS Facilities

Performing a backup with your OS facilities is a very straightforward process. As with Backup Manager, you can perform a full database backup or a tablespace backup. The basic process is different, depending on whether you will be performing an offline backup or an online backup.

Offline Backup

The offline backup is perhaps the most straightforward and simplest backup method. You perform an offline database backup by following these steps:

1. Shut down the database normally.
2. Back up all the datafiles, the control files, and the parameter file, using OS or third-party utilities.
3. Restart the database.

This is all there is to performing an offline database backup using OS facilities. You can do this using either OS or third-party facilities. There are a number of very good third-party backup utilities that include bar coding, catalog management, and other features.

Online Backup

The online backup is not actually a full backup because each tablespace is backed up separately. You can think of it as a set of online tablespace backups that make up the entire database. To perform an online tablespace backup, follow this procedure:

1. Mark the beginning of the tablespace backup using the SQL command

   `ALTER TABLESPACE tsname BEGIN BACKUP;`

2. Back up the datafiles that constitute that tablespace using OS or third-party utilities.

3. Mark the end of the tablespace backup using the SQL command

   `ALTER TABLESPACE tsname END BACKUP;`

When you mark the beginning of the backup, Oracle will divert writes from those datafiles to the SGA until the backup has completed and you have marked the end of the backup. This is all that is necessary to perform the online tablespace backup.

Backing Up with Export

The Export utility can also be used to perform system backups. Because this utility is covered in the lesson on Day 9, "Managing Data," it is not covered here.

Backing Up with the NT Backup Utility

Yet another way to back up the Oracle database (if you are running on an NT server) is via the NT Backup utility. This utility comes with the Oracle8 Server for NT and can only be used to back up the local database—you cannot use it to back up databases remotely. The NT Backup utility is very easy to use. It is invoked through the Oracle for NT program group.

Upon invoking the NT Backup Manager, you will be prompted to supply the INTERNAL password.

The internal account will be used to perform the backup. Specifying this password is all that is necessary to connect to the Oracle instance on your system. If you are running in NOARCHIVELOG mode (which is not recommended), you will see the screen shown in Figure 16.17, where a full offline backup is the only option. This is because the full offline backup is the only option for a system running in NOARCHIVELOG mode.

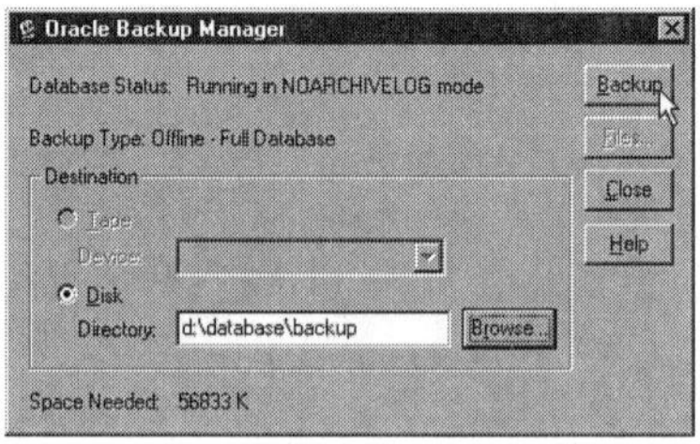

Figure 16.17.

NT Backup Manager with only the option for a full offline backup.

When running in NOARCHIVELOG mode, the only option is to specify the destination for the backup, either by typing it in or by using the Browse option. If you are running in ARCHIVELOG mode (which is recommended because it makes your system more recoverable), you will see the screen shown in Figure 16.18 where a full offline backup, online tablespace backup, and online control file backup are the available options.

Figure 16.18.

NT Backup Manager with multiple options, because the system is running in ARCHIVELOG *mode.*

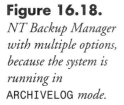

Again you have the option to specify the destination for the backup, either by typing it in or by using the Browse button. When you have selected the options you want, simply click the Backup button and the backup will be performed.

The NT Backup Manager does not have the flexibility and performance of the Recovery Manager and its graphical interface, Backup Manager, but for a small database it is the ideal utility because of its simplicity and ease of use.

So far in this lesson, you have seen how to back up your system. Equally as important is determining what to back up and how to schedule those backups. In the next section you will learn how to develop a backup strategy and how to implement it.

Backup Strategies

Knowing how to back up a system is only one part of the process. Putting together a backup-and-recovery plan or strategy is also very important. Many times you are limited in the time allotted for backups and must be very creative. Remember that your highest priority is to protect the data in your database.

In developing a backup-and-recovery strategy, you must first look at the parameters of your system. Many variables affect the backup strategy and the backup process, including

☐ Time allotted for the backup

☐ Amount of data to be backed up

☐ Speed of the backup device(s)

☐ System downtime allotted for backups (if any)

☐ Off hours (if no downtime allotted)

☐ Performance degradation allowed

These factors and others will affect the backup strategy. They must be measured against the main goals of the backup process, which include

☐ Protecting the database by having a current backup.

☐ Reducing the time necessary to recover.

☐ Affecting the performance of the system as little as possible.

By putting together all these factors, you should be able to come up with a backup strategy that meets as many of these requirements as possible.

NOTE

> It is unlikely that you will be able to meet all the goals of a backup strategy. Do your best to come up with the best compromises you can.

When and What to Back Up

Scheduling backups is usually not a very easy task. Backups should be taken often enough to protect the system's data from loss, yet should not interfere with normal business operations. Depending on the size of the data that needs to be backed up and the operational schedule of your business, you might choose different options. The options vary, depending on which type of operation your business runs:

☐ 5×8 Operation: This term designates a business whose corporate data must be available 5 days a week, 8 hours a day.

☐ 7×24 Operation: This term designates a business whose corporate data must be available 7 days a week, 24 hours a day. No downtime is allowed.

Each of these types of operation has different backup needs, depending on the type of data and the frequency of modifications to that data. Let's look at those cases.

Scheduling Backups in a 5×8 Shop

Scheduling backups is a little easier in a 5×8 shop because there is plenty of time when the system need not be available to the users and can be backed up without disturbing them. The frequency of the backups in this type of operation can depend in some part on the activity in the database. Here are some guidelines that might help you determine your backup schedule:

16

Type of database or operation	*When to back up*
Small database	For a small database, perform a full offline backup every night. This will offer the most protection possible for your data.
Large database	If the database is very large, perform a full offline backup every weekend and incremental backups during the week.
Active tablespaces	If certain tablespaces are very active, target them for tablespace backups as often as possible.
Structural changes	Any time a structural change is made to the database, you should perform a full offline backup.
Unrecoverable operations	Any time unrecoverable operations are performed on the database, a full offline backup should be done.
RESETLOGS	Anytime that you have to reset the redo logs with the RESETLOGS command, you should perform a full offline backup.
Recover until	Any time you have recovered with the Recover until option, you should perform a full offline backup.
Archive log files	Every night or every few nights, back up the archive log files. The frequency depends on the number of archive log files created every day.

Remember, these are just guidelines. Your specific situation will determine how to create an effective backup strategy for your system.

Scheduling Backups in a 7×24 Shop

It is much more difficult to plan a backup strategy in a 7×24 shop because there is never a time when the system is not in use. Whenever you perform the backups, there will be one or more people who might be inconvenienced by a performance drop. Remember, backups do tend to affect performance.

The frequency and type of backups will be influenced by the activity of the system. Here are some guidelines that might help you determine your backup schedule:

Type of database or operation	*When to back up*
Small database	If the database is small, perform a full online backup every night. This will offer the most protection possible for your data.
Large database	If the database is very large, perform a full online backup every weekend and incremental online backups during the week.

continues

Type of database or operation	*When to back up*
Very large database	It is frequently necessary to rotate the backup schedule such that a tablespace or set of tablespaces gets backed up every night. It might take several days to get a complete backup set, but this will shorten the time each night that the backup is active and therefore affecting performance.
Active tablespaces	If certain tablespaces are very active, target them for tablespace backups as often as possible.
Unrecoverable operations	Any time unrecoverable operations are performed on the database, a full offline backup should be done. If this is not acceptable, avoid performing unrecoverable operations.
RESETLOGS	Any time you have to reset the redo logs with the RESETLOGS command, you should perform a full offline backup. If this is not acceptable, avoid using the RESETLOGS operation.
Recover until	Any time you have recovered with the Recover until option, you should perform a full offline backup.
Archive log files	In a 7×24 shop it is a good idea to back up the archive log files at soon as they are created. Keep online and available as least as many as are needed to recover from the oldest tablespace backup.

Examples of Backup Strategies

This section provides a few examples for setting up a backup strategy. Your backup strategy might be more complicated, but I hope these examples can help you in setting it up.

Example of a Full Daily Backup

The scenario for this example is a small business that is open only during the day. There is fairly good activity on the database, and the data is very important. Perhaps in this case the database is small enough that a complete offline backup to tape can be run every night. The previous night's tape is archived to storage every day; after a month, the tapes can be reused, keeping one tape from each month permanently. If a problem occurs and a restore must be performed, a backup tape will always be available. Backup tapes should always be kept offsite to protect them in the event of a disaster, such as a fire. If the computer room and backup tape are destroyed, previous backup tapes are available in offsite storage.

Example of an Online Tablespace Backup

The scenario for this example is a large business that is open 24 hours a day, 7 days a week. There is high database activity, and no downtime is allowed. The data is extremely critical to the operation of the company. In this situation I would recommend some sort of standby system, but I discuss that on Day 18, "Administering Oracle Replication." For backups, I would suggest that a partial online backup be done every night on a rotational basis such that all of the tablespaces are backed up in three or four days, thus minimizing the impact on the users. To further reduce the effect on the users, these backups should be done to disk, perhaps across a network. These backup files on disk should in turn be backed up every night and archived offsite. The backup files should remain online for at least two backup cycles before being removed. The archive log files should also be backed up to disk, either locally or on a networked system, and backed up to tape and sent offsite. This will offer a good level of protection and provide for quick restoration if necessary. A fault-tolerant system should be a part of this solution as well.

Summary

In this chapter you have learned about one of the most important topics related to database operations. The database backup can make the difference between being able to effectively and quickly restore the system and suffering a total failure. Without an effective backup strategy, your system is completely unprotected against failure.

In this chapter you not only learned about how to develop a backup strategy and perform Oracle backups, but a little bit about fault tolerance as well. By carefully designing your system, you might be able to survive a disk failure that might otherwise have caused you to rebuild your entire system. Careful planning makes all the difference in this type of situation.

What's Next?

On Day 17, "Recovering the Database," you will learn how to recover from a failure using the backup strategy you created in this chapter. A backup without a recovery plan is not much better than having no backup at all. Tomorrow you will see how to develop a recovery solution and how to recover the database from a failure.

Q&A

Q What kind of failures require instance recovery?

A Any failure that causes the Oracle instance to terminate in an unorderly fashion will require an instance recovery to occur. This includes system failure, software failure, or a shutdown abort.

Q What kind of failure requires the application of archive log files?

A Any failure after which a datafile needs to be restored from backup requires the application of archive log files.

Q How can my OS and redo log files be protected against the loss of a disk drive?

A By using a RAID hardware disk controller or software RAID, you might be able to save yourself weeks of work trying to restore your system.

Q What different types of backup methods are available?

A Under Windows NT, you can back up your database by using Backup Manager, the NT Backup utility, OS or third-party utilities, or the Export utility.

Workshop

The workshop provides quiz questions to help you solidify your understanding of the material covered and exercises to provide you with experience in using what you've learned. For answers to quiz questions, see Appendix A, "Answers."

Quiz

1. What is an instance recovery?
2. Can you recover from the loss of a log file?
3. Can you recover from the loss of a datafile?
4. Can you recover if you are not running in ARCHIVELOG mode?
5. What different types of backups can you do?
6. What different types of files need to be backed up?
7. What is RAID?
8. Can the NT Backup Manager back up a remote system?
9. What are the archive log files used for?
10. What is the difference between an online backup and an offline backup?

Exercises

1. Design a database system using full fault tolerance.
2. Design a database system using partial fault tolerance.
3. Back up a tablespace using Backup Manager.
4. Back up a tablespace using NT Backup Manager.

Day 17

Recovering the Database

Yesterday you learned how to back up your database; today you will learn how to recover your database in the event of an emergency. Several types of failures can necessitate a recovery:

- [ ] An instance failure necessitates an instance recovery. As long as no permanent hardware failures have occurred, the instance recovery will be automatic and complete. Enabling parallel recovery improves performance.

- [ ] A hardware failure that results in the loss of a datafile necessitates a media recovery. This involves both recovering the lost data and performing an instance recovery (if necessary). This process will be explained in the section titled "Media Recovery."

- [ ] A user error that results in the loss of data might necessitate a point-in-time recovery, which allows you to recover up to a certain point before the failure occurred. This can be very useful, but very problematic. The point-in-time recovery is detailed in the section titled "The Point-in-Time Recovery."

No matter what type of recovery is required, the important task of recovery should be performed as quickly as possible. If a failure requiring recovery occurs, many users will have little to do until the recovery is complete. But even though the recovery operation must be completed quickly, you should not rush. Any mistakes during the recovery will only delay the resumption of normal operations.

Recovery Versus Restoration

Today you will learn about recovery and restoration operations. These two concepts might sometimes be thought of as the same, but they are actually quite different:

- *Recovery* is the act of bringing the database back to where it was an instant before the failure, and refers to the process whereby Oracle rolls forward committed transactions and rolls back noncommitted transactions. Recovery is automatic.

- *Restoration* is the act of replacing a datafile with a backup copy. You can restore a database only if it is not running in ARCHIVELOG mode and has overwritten redo log files. Restoration is a manual operation requiring operator intervention (either by hand or via the graphical administration tools).

Recovering Your Database

Despite how reliable hardware has become, there are still occasions when the system might fail (perhaps because of a component failure or a power failure). If the failure causes no data loss, Oracle can recover itself; this is referred to as an *instance recovery*. If data has been lost, data must be restored from a previous backup and recovered; this is referred to as *media recovery*. If some event, such as an accidental deletion of a table, has occurred, a *point-in-time recovery* must be performed to avoid recovering the table-drop statement and repeating the mistake.

Instance Recovery

NEW TERM When an instance failure occurs, the Oracle recovery process can completely recover the database upon instance startup. All transactions that were committed at the time of the failure will be recovered, or *rolled forward*, and all transactions that were in process (also known as *in-flight transactions*) will be *rolled back*.

NOTE

> Instance recovery can be quite time consuming. How much time instance recovery takes depends on the number of dirty buffers in the SGA. The number of dirty buffers depends on how much time has passed since the last checkpoint and the number of data modifications.

The instance-recovery process is automatic. When the instance is started, the startup process examines the datafiles and redo log files to determine whether the instance was properly shut down. At this point, the redo log is read and the affected transactions are rolled forward or back. If the checkpoint launched by the last log switch was completed, the transactions in fewer than one log file will require recovery.

TIP If you tune the checkpoint interval and recovery parallelism, you can shorten the recovery time.

Users cannot access the database during the recovery process; only after the instance recovery is complete can users access the database. For this reason, recovery time should be kept to a minimum. Using the parallel-recovery feature of the Parallel Query option can help you reduce the time it takes for instance recovery to be completed. As you will see on Day 19, "Advanced Oracle Options," the number of processes or threads that perform the instance recovery can be tuned. If you tune the number of recovery processes to run best with your system, you can optimize the recovery interval.

Media Recovery

In the event of a media failure (if, for example, a datafile is damaged), data recovery is necessary. If a datafile is damaged, you must restore it from backup before recovery can occur. The Oracle recovery process then applies archive log files and redo log files to restore the damaged datafile to its prior-to-failure state. This process might require the use of all archive log files created since the backup to recover the restored datafile, which can be quite time consuming.

TIP If you schedule frequent backups, you can shorten restoration and recovery time. Recovery time depends both on how much time has passed and how much data has been modified since the last backup.

By placing the latest backup files as well as any archive log files created since the last backup online, you can shorten the time it takes to start the recovery process. If you have a plan and have everything ready to go, things will run more smoothly.

In order to assist the recovery process, Oracle8 provides several different methods for database recovery:

- ☐ Backup Manager
- ☐ OS facilities
- ☐ The Import utility
- ☐ The NT Recovery utility

Each of these utilities can perform an effective backup; personal preference and your system needs dictate which one you use.

Backup Manager

As with the database-backup procedure, you can perform a recovery using Enterprise Manager's Backup Manager utility. To do so, follow these steps:

1. After you invoke Backup Manager, you can start the recovery process by selecting Recover | Restore Wizard.

2. The Restore wizard leads you through a series of screens that are similar to those of the Backup wizard. The first screen, shown in Figure 17.1, allows you to choose what type of restore you want to perform. Note that I have selected the Tablespaces radio button. After you decide what type of restore you want to perform, click Next.

Figure 17.1.

Screen one of the
Restore wizard.

 NOTE

> The available options in this case are Tablespaces and Datafiles. Because the instance is up and running in this example, the database recovery option is not available. If the instance was down, Database would be an option.

17

3. Because I chose the Tablespaces option, the Tablespaces screen (shown in Figure 17.2) appears. From here you select what tablespaces you want restored; you can choose as many or as few tablespaces as you want. Note that I have chosen to restore the DOGS tablespace. After you select a tablespace, click Next.

Figure 17.2.

The Tablespaces screen of the Restore wizard.

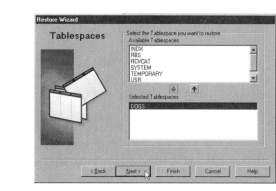

4. After you select the tablespace(s) you want recovered, the Restore wizard determines which datafiles will be restored. The Rename screen, shown in Figure 17.3, allows you to change the name of the datafile to be used in the restore. This is valuable because the volume that contains that datafile might not be available due to a hardware failure. If you want, you can change the name of the datafile. When you finish, click Next.

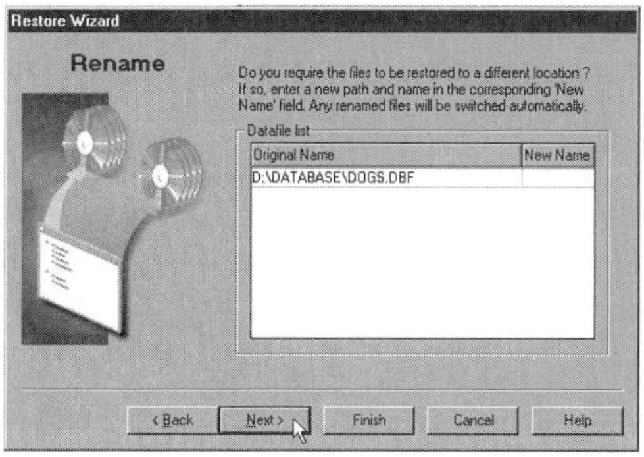

Figure 17.3.

The Rename screen of the Restore wizard.

5. The Channels screen, shown in Figure 17.4, allows you to select the channel(s) to be used during the recovery process. Depending on how many backup files and datafiles you are working with, a larger number of channels can improve performance by adding some parallelism. It might occasionally be necessary to change the channel from the one used in the backup operation. After you determine what channel to use, click Next.

Figure 17.4.

The Channels screen of the Restore wizard.

6. Finally, the Restore wizard presents the Summary screen, shown in Figure 17.5. If all is correct, start the restoration process by clicking OK.

Figure 17.5.

The Summary screen of the Restore wizard.

If you want to change the type of restore operation from an online to an offline restore, you can change the state of the instance from the main screen of the Backup Manager utility. To shut down the database, simply select the Shutdown radio button and click Apply (see Figure 17.6).

After you select the Shutdown option, you are asked what type of shutdown you want to perform. Your options are

☐ Normal—If you select the Normal option, the shutdown process waits for all users to disconnect and then continues. During this time, no new connections are allowed.

☐ Immediate—If you select the Immediate option, all idle connections are disconnected, current transactions are rolled back, and the instance is shut down.

☐ Abort—If you select the Abort option, the Oracle instance is immediately terminated. A shutdown with Abort causes media recovery to be necessary.

Figure 17.6.

Change the state of the database from the main screen of Backup Manager.

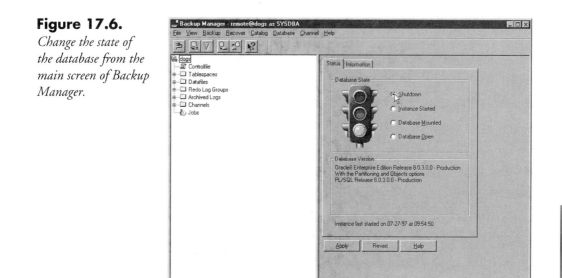

☐ Transactional—If you select the Transactional option, currently running transactions are allowed to complete. As soon as a transaction has finished or aborted, the connection is terminated. During this time, no new connections are allowed.

I recommend that you always use the Immediate or Normal option. The Abort option should be used only in the case of an emergency.

As you have seen, it is easy to back up and restore a database using Backup Manager. Nonetheless, it is still important to test the recovery process periodically to make sure it is working correctly.

OS Facilities

The method for restoring a datafile using OS facilities is as simple as the method used for creating the backup using OS facilities:

1. With the tablespace offline, copy the datafile from the backup to the original datafile.

2. After you bring the tablespace back online (via the ALTER TABLESPACE command or the restarting of the Oracle instance), Oracle will realize that the datafile has been replaced and prompt you to apply the archived log files.

Tablespace and datafile recovery can be performed only if the RDBMS is running in ARCHIVELOG mode. Otherwise, you must restore the entire database from the last full, offline backup. No roll forward or rollback occurs.

The Import Utility

You can use the Import utility to restore the database if and only if the Export utility was used to create the backup. For more information about the Import and Export utilities, see Day 9, "Managing Data."

The NT Recovery Utility

NT Recovery Manager is very similar to NT Backup Manager. NT Recovery Manager, provided with your Oracle for Windows NT software, is not part of Enterprise Manager. Because of this, NT Recovery Manager can recover only a local database—it cannot provide recovery over a network. To recover a local database with NT Recovery Manager, perform these steps:

1. As with NT Backup Manager, the first step in invoking NT Recovery Manager is to supply the password for the internal account.

2. After you supply the password for the internal account and connect with the instance, you will see NT Recovery Manager's first screen. This screen, shown in Figure 17.7, lists the following recovery options:

   - ☐ Automatic recovery
   - ☐ Restore from full database backup
   - ☐ Restore datafile, then do recovery (supply the name of the datafile)
   - ☐ Restore control file, then do recovery

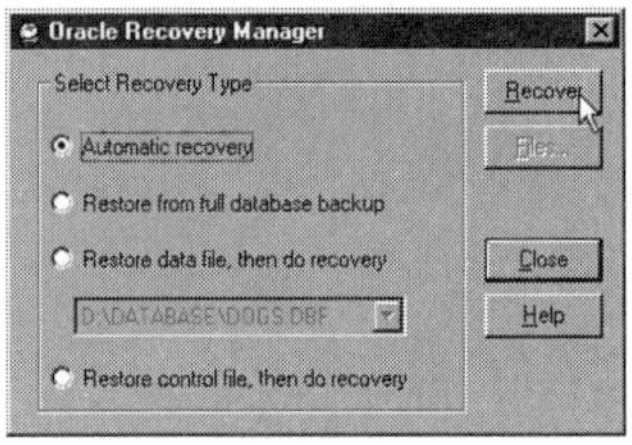

Figure 17.7.

Oracle Recovery Manager offers a variety of recovery options.

3. The screen you see after selecting an option and clicking Recover depends on what option you select. In this case, I have selected the Restore datafile option and specified the filename \DATABASE\DOGS\DBF. Consequently, I am presented with the Data File Recovery screen shown in Figure 17.8.

4. After you specify which datafiles to recover, NT Recovery Manager automatically recovers them for you. If instance recovery is necessary, it is performed as well.

17

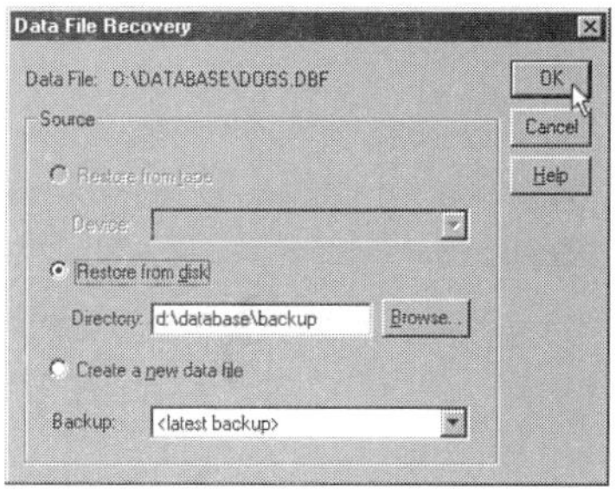

Figure 17.8.

The Data File Recovery screen of NT Recovery Manager.

The Log File Recovery

You cannot restore from the loss of a log file. If a log file is damaged and the system is still functional, you can drop the log file, re-create it, and immediately perform a full backup. The backup is necessary because you will not be able to use the archive and redo log files for any recovery on this database. That is why I always recommend that redo log files reside on fault-tolerant disk volumes.

NOTE

> I recommend using RAID mirroring on the redo log files to protect them in the event of a disk failure.

The Point-in-Time Recovery

The point-in-time recovery allows you to recover a database back to a specified point in time, allowing you to recover from user errors or software problems that caused a failure to occur. However, because of the potential side effects, the point-in-time recovery, a somewhat complex operation, should be performed only on rare occasions. When you recover back to a point in time, the entire database will be recovered to that point. If a table is deleted by accident and the point-in-time recovery is being used to recover to a point just before that deletion, you must keep in mind that all other work to other tables that occurred after that point will be lost.

WARNING

> The point-in-time recovery can be dangerous to use, because you are restoring to a point in time in the past. Always perform a full backup of your current database before attempting the point-in-time recovery. A point-in-time recovery recovers the entire database to that point in time. There is no way to recover a single tablespace or table, so all work done after that point to other tables will be lost.

NOTE

> I have mentioned the point-in-time recovery only so that you will know it exists. If you plan to use the point-in-time recovery, you should study the Oracle documentation and carefully plan a restore before you attempt it.

The point-in-time recovery can be performed via Recovery Manager or via the RECOVER administrative SQL command. In either case, the syntax for performing the point-in-time recovery is entered through the command-line interface; there is no GUI option for the point-in-time recovery.

What method you use to restore your data depends on what type of error necessitated the recovery. In the event of a media failure, you must restore the datafile, then perform the media recovery with the point-in-time recovery option. In the event of a user error, follow these steps:

1. Create a temporary copy of the database.
2. Restore this temporary database from a previous backup.
3. Specify a point in time immediately before the failure, then perform the point-in-time recovery on this temporary database.
4. Export the table that has been damaged, which now is in a state just before the damage.
5. Import that undamaged table to the real database.

This task can be time consuming and dangerous. If you confuse the temporary and real copies of the database, you might destroy valuable data.

Point-in-Time Recovery Using Recovery Manager

Recovery Manager can be used to perform a point-in-time recovery via its command-line syntax. Because of the complexity of the command-line interface to Recovery Manager and the rarity of its use, I will not go into great detail on how to use it here. You can find very complete documentation in the Oracle Backup and Recovery manual.

When using the command-line interface to Recovery Manager, you must specify this additional parameter:

```
SET UNTIL
```

This parameter takes the following qualifiers:

```
TIME date
LOG SEQ number THREAD number
SCN scn
```

With this syntax, you can specify the exact time you want the recovery to stop by specifying the time, the log sequence, or the system change number. By using the SET UNTIL parameter when performing a recovery via Recovery Manager, you restore until the specified time.

Point-in-Time Recovery Using the RECOVER Command

When you perform a recovery with the RECOVER command, you can restore to any point in time by using the RECOVER UNTIL syntax. The RECOVER command has a number of options, but the important ones for the point-in-time recovery are

- [ ] RECOVER UNTIL CANCEL
- [ ] RECOVER UNTIL TIME *date*
- [ ] RECOVER UNTIL CHANGE *scn*

Like Recovery Manager, the RECOVER command can be used to recover a database, a tablespace, or a datafile, and can include a parallel clause. If you increase the degree of parallelism, you might see a performance benefit.

Developing a Recovery Strategy

It is important that you plan your recovery strategy so that in the event of a system failure you will be ready. Several scenarios must be planned for, depending on the type of failure.

Instance Failure: Planning for Instance Recovery

Except for requiring you to set the degree of parallelism, the instance-recovery process is automatic; it requires no operator intervention. Therefore, your planning should concentrate on the parallel recovery option. Evaluate your system to determine the degree of parallelism for the recovery process. This is set as the Oracle initialization parameter RECOVERY_PARALLELISM.

The number of disk drives and CPUs typically determines the degree of parallelism in your system. My rule of thumb is to use one process (thread) for every two disk drives, up to 20. Try starting with a number like this, and adjust it to suit your system. Because every system is different, it is difficult to make across-the-board recommendations. If you set this number too high, you might cause additional overhead.

Hardware Failure: Planning for Media Recovery

When you plan for media recovery, you must consider not only the steps required to recover the damaged media, but the restoration of data as well. Some of the key items necessary for quick media recovery include

- [ ] Hardware availability—Most system vendors offer hot-swappable disk drives. A failed disk drive need only be replaced with the same type disk in order to start automatic recovery. For this reason, you should keep spares available.

☐ Backup files—Backup files should be kept until subsequent backups have been completed and verified. If you make these files available on the system or on a network drive, you can perform quick media recovery.

☐ Archived log files—Any archived log files created since the last backup should be kept available on the system itself or on a network server until the next backup occurs.

If downtime is not an option, consider using a fault-tolerant disk subsystem. You can avoid considerable downtime by protecting your disk drives with a RAID disk array.

 Tip

> The component in your system that is most likely to fail is probably a disk drive. The more disk drives you have in your system, the more likely one will fail. By protecting your disk drives with hardware or software RAID, you can avoid considerable downtime.

Planning for Operator Error Recovery

Recovering from operator error is similar to recovering from media failure, except with operator error recovery you might need a large amount of disk space to temporarily recover your database. Fortunately, users can typically continue working on the permanent database unless their duties require them to access the table(s) that was deleted or corrupted. To recover, you need the following components:

☐ Backup files
☐ Archived log files
☐ Large temporary space

Summary

Today you learned how to recover from various types of system failures. You learned how instance, media, and point-in-time recoveries work. You also learned how to recover from an operator error. You learned the importance of planning ahead to reduce downtime; in most businesses, downtime can be very expensive.

What's Next?

On Day 18, "Administering Oracle Replication," you will learn how to use Oracle replication to increase performance and quicken recovery. You will also learn about other Oracle options for quick recovery, including the standby database option. These features do not provide fault tolerance, but do help you to come back online quickly.

Q&A

Q What is the difference between restoring and recovering?

A Restoring involves copying a backup file to replace a damaged datafile, whereas recovery involves Oracle using the transaction log to roll forward transactions.

Q What is the difference between instance recovery and media recovery?

A With instance recovery, Oracle automatically rolls forward committed transactions to bring the database up to date; media recovery requires a damaged datafile to be replaced with a backup copy before commencing.

Q What is an in-flight transaction?

A This term is sometimes used to describe a transaction that was in the process of execution when a failure occurred.

Q What Oracle utility is needed to restore from an export file?

A An export file can only be restored with the Import utility.

Workshop

The workshop provides quiz questions to help you solidify your understanding of the material covered and exercises to provide you with experience in using what you've learned. See Appendix A, "Answers," for the answers to quiz questions.

Quiz

1. What types of recovery operations are there?
2. What transactions are recovered from an instance failure?
3. What transactions can be recovered from media failure?
4. What is ARCHIVELOG mode?
5. What is a dirty buffer?
6. What is a checkpoint?
7. What files are necessary for instance recovery?
8. What files are necessary for media recovery?
9. What is a point-in-time recovery?
10. What is a point-in-time recovery used for?

Exercises

1. Using Backup Manager, restore the tablespace you backed up yesterday.

2. Using NT Recovery Manager, restore the tablespace you backed up yesterday.

3. On a small test system, use the SHUTDOWN ABORT command to abort an Oracle instance. (Do not do this on a production system or one that others are using.)

4. Restart the instance and observe the recovery process; try this again with a larger degree of parallelism. (*Note:* You must perform some transactions for recovery to have activity.)

Day **18**

Administering Oracle Replication

Today's lesson completes the three-day section on maximizing uptime and securing your data. On Day 16, "Understanding Effective Backup Techniques," you learned how to back up your database; on Day 17, "Recovering the Database," you learned how to restore that data in the event of a system failure. Today you will learn how to use other techniques to maximize uptime and minimize recovery time.

Not all replication is used for maximizing uptime. It is convenient, however, to include all the benefits and uses of replication in this lesson. Replication can be used for many different purposes, such as read-only copies in satellite locations and multiple access points.

Today you will learn about replication and other methods for reducing downtime, such as the backup database and Oracle failover.

What Is Replication?

NEW TERM *Replication* is the facility that allows you to copy database data to multiple local and remote systems. This data can be accessed and modified in certain instances. In many cases, systems are designed so that the remote data is read-only and updates are processed on the master system. There are various options available.

A replicated database might consist of the entire database or of certain tables or tablespaces. This is completely up to you. With Oracle replication, you can configure a number of options to provide whatever features you want.

Replication Options

Oracle provides several replication options; the most basic of these is the *read-only table snapshot*. This basic method of replication allows you to copy a table to a remote site as a read-only table. Any updates to the table must be made on the master database. This method is described as a "snapshot" because it is a picture of the database at a certain point in time. Unlike other replication options, the read-only table snapshot refreshes the remote copy only on a periodic basis, which you control.

Another option for replication is Oracle *advanced replication*. With advanced replication it is possible for all replicated objects to be updated. Advanced replication is much more complex than the read-only table snapshot because conflict resolution must be programmed. The advanced replication option can be quite powerful, but it is more difficult to maintain.

Read-Only Table Snapshots

Read-only table snapshots are used when a read-only copy is all that is needed. You might think this method is quite limiting, but in reality it is very useful. Indeed, there are quite a few applications where the read-only table snapshot is sufficient, and even desirable:

- ☐ Retail—Retail stores typically maintain a master price list at a central location and download new prices on a regular basis. It does not make sense for each store to change its own prices. Of course, you would want to maintain the inventory database locally.

- ☐ Lookup tables—Lookup tables are also very good applications for read-only snapshots because they are not usually updated and you might want their data to be controlled by a central site.

- ☐ Data analysis—OLTP data can be periodically replicated to another system for analysis. This replicated system might be performing DSS tasks to analyze sales data and so on.

- ☐ Manufacturing—Component parts lists can be maintained at a central database and each assembly line gets a read-only copy of that data. If a part replacement is necessary, this should be done globally.

☐ Telemarketing—A list of clients should be maintained at a central location and downloaded periodically to each sales office. It is desirable for all offices to have the same client list.

These are just a few examples of places where a read-only replicated table is quite sufficient for the satellite location. With this type of replication, the data on the local or master database is periodically updated to the replicated sites, as shown in Figure 18.1.

Figure 18.1.
Read-only snapshots.

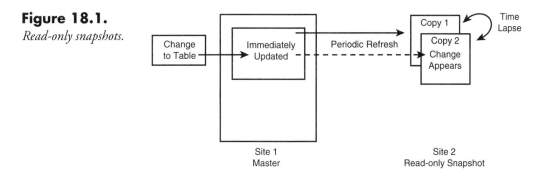

This snapshot can be an entire table or a selected view of that table. In this manner you can keep information in the master table that is not propagated to the replicated sites, such as item costs or sales figures. With replication you have many options for what data you want to replicate and when you want to replicate it.

In some cases you must update the data on each replicated site. This is where the advanced replication option is necessary.

Advanced (Symmetric) Replication

NEW TERM   The Oracle *advanced replication* option, sometimes known as *symmetric replication* or *updateable snapshots*, allows each of the replicated databases to be updated. The updates are typically batched and periodically sent to the other replicated objects. You can, however, configure Oracle to propagate updates immediately. This is known as *synchronous data propagation* or *realtime data replication*.

The updateable snapshot method is usually sufficient, but with certain applications it is necessary to use realtime data replication.

With the advanced replication option, the system is sometimes described as having multiple masters. These masters can each have read-only table snapshots if desired. An advanced replication system is shown in Figure 18.2.

Figure 18.2.
An advanced replica-tion system.

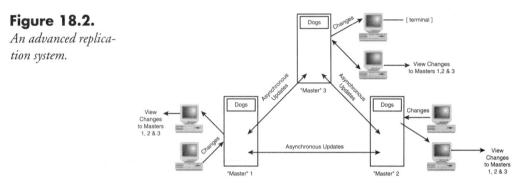

With the advanced replication option, you can have multiple sites throughout the country, and each can be used as an independent database. Each of these databases can be updated independently and on a regular basis—and can even be deferred to off hours.

How Does Replication Work?

Replication is quite straightforward. The data to be replicated is defined by a defining query, which determines the data that is to be replicated. After the query is defined, the data is selected from the master and copied to the replicated site.

The defining query is set up so that each row in the replicated table corresponds to one row or part of one row in the master table. The defining query cannot contain an aggregate function or GROUP BY clause.

NEW TERM   After the defining query is set up, it will be executed on a regular basis and its result will be propagated to the replicate systems. This propagation of fresh replicated data is called the *snapshot refresh*. The snapshot refresh can operate in a couple different modes:

☐ Complete refresh—In this mode the master executes the snapshot's defining query and the result replaces the entire snapshot on the replicated system.

☐ Fast refresh—In this mode the master determines what changes have been made to the master and applies these changes to the snapshot. If only a few changes have occurred since the last snapshot, this method is much more efficient.

NEW TERM   If multiple tables are involved in the snapshot, you can use a *snapshot group*. When you define a snapshot group, several different tables can be linked together so that there is transaction consistency within the snapshot (that is, the tables are in sync).

The snapshot refresh can occur manually or automatically, depending on how you configure the master and the replicated site. With an automatic refresh, no operator intervention is required. The snapshots are automatically refreshed on a regular time interval. With manual refresh, the operator determines when the refresh should occur and manually initiates the refresh. If changes to the tables are rare, manual refresh might work for you.

Configuring Replication

Replication can be configured through Replication Manager or manually via SQL commands. What method you use is up to you.

Configuring Using Replication Manager

To configure replication using Replication Manager, you should first make sure the database was created with the advanced replication option. This option is available through the Oracle Database Assistant installation process.

NOTE

> If your database was not built with the advanced replication option, you must run the administrative SQL script \orant\rdbms80\admin\ catrep.sql to install the replication packages.

Replication Manager can be invoked from the Enterprise Manager toolbar or from the Oracle Replication Manager program group. After you invoke Replication Manager, you will see the main screen (shown in Figure 18.3).

Figure 18.3.

Oracle Replication Manager.

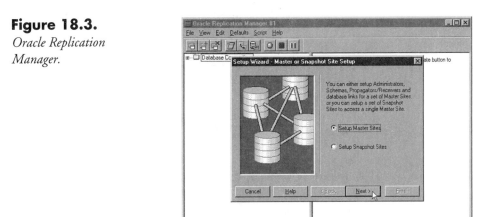

If you have never run Replication Manager, you might find yourself in the Setup wizard. From here you can create the master and snapshot sites. If you click the Cancel button, you will see that no database connections are set up, so no information can be displayed.

If you had specified advanced replication when you were building the database from the Database Assistant, this would already be set up for you. To invoke the Setup wizard, click Create (see Figure 18.4).

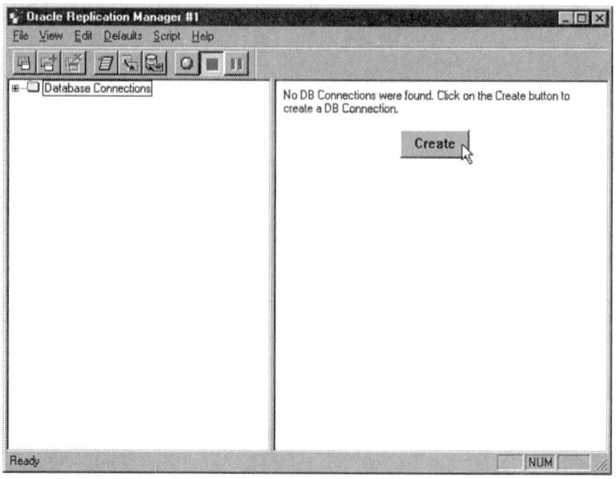

Figure 18.4.

Create the database connection.

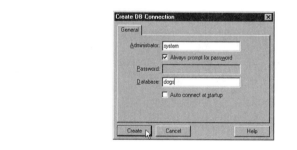

After you click Create, the Create DB Connection dialog (shown in Figure 18.5) prompts you to supply information to connect to a database.

Figure 18.5.

The Create DB Connection dialog.

You will also be prompted to set up a propagator. To do so, highlight the database connection from the Replication Manager main screen (system@dogs in this case) and pull down the Edit menu to select properties. To select a propagator, click the Propagator tab (see Figure 18.6). You can choose any of the users you have defined; DBSNMP is a good choice.

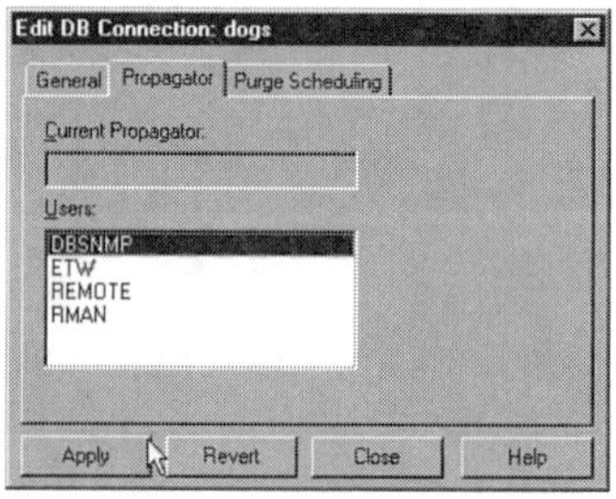

Figure 18.6.

The Edit DB Connection dialog.

The next step is to invoke the Setup wizard. Do so by selecting File | Setup Wizard. From here you will be led through a series of screens that will help you configure a replicated system. The first is the Master or Snapshot Site Setup screen, shown in Figure 18.7.

Figure 18.7.

The Master or Snapshot Site Setup screen of the Setup wizard.

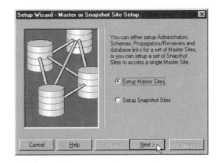

Here you can specify whether you are setting up a database as a master site or as a snapshot site. Both require initial setup.

Configuring the Master Site

Configuring the master site involves setting up a replication account and privileges as well as setting up scheduling for the snapshots. To do so, perform these steps:

1. First you'll see the Select Master Sites screen, shown in Figure 18.8. Here you set up the database that will serve as the master.

Figure 18.8.

The Select Master Sites screen of the Setup wizard.

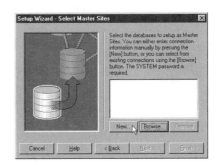

2. Clicking the New button invokes the New Master Site screen, shown in Figure 18.9. Enter the database connection name and the SYSTEM password on this screen.

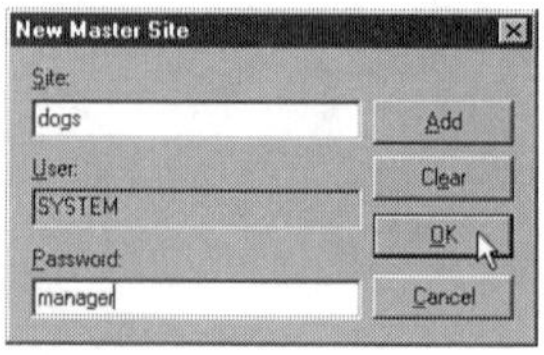

Figure 18.9.

*The New Master Site
screen of the Setup
wizard.*

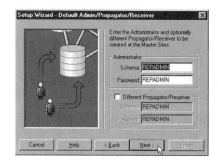

3. After you select the master site, you will be prompted for the default administrator and the propagator/receiver, as shown in Figure 18.10. I prefer to use the default settings in this case.

Figure 18.10.

*The Default Admin/
Propagator/Receiver
screen of the Setup
wizard.*

4. If a propagator already exists, you will be prompted for a password (see Figure 18.11). By default you will be prompted for the password for the default propagator DBSNMP. If you don't know the password, try DBSNMP.

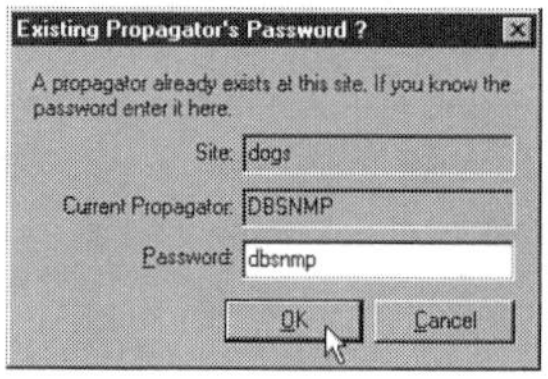

Figure 18.11.

*The Existing
Propagator's Password
screen of the Setup
wizard.*

5. In the New Replicated Object Schema screen, shown in Figure 18.12, you can choose to create a new schema to hold replicated objects. It is not necessary to choose any schemas at this point but this is a convenient place to do it.

Figure 18.12.

*The New Replicated
Object Schema screen
of the Setup wizard.*

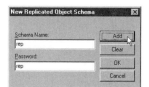

18

6. The next screen schedules the time for replication and a replication interval. You can leave the default to replicate once per day or change it, as shown in Figure 18.13.

NOTE

The values entered here represent the username and password of the account that does the replication. This account will be created by the Setup wizard.

Figure 18.13.

The Defaults for Scheduled Links screen of the Setup wizard.

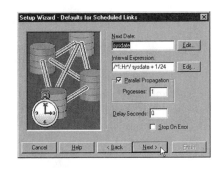

7. The next screen, which resembles the one shown in Figure 18.13, allows you to schedule default purging. The purge schedule lets you ordain what time the deferred transaction queues are purged.

8. The Master Site Customizations screen, shown in Figure 18.14, allows you to customize the master site as desired. Select a site and click the Customize button to modify users, the using clause, and so on.

Figure 18.14.

The Master Site Customizations screen of the Setup wizard.

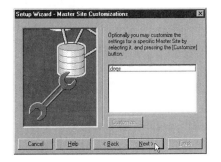

18

9. The Finish screen, shown in Figure 18.15, consists of an option to record the actions to be taken to a PL/SQL script. Enabling this option is a good idea if you want to be able to re-create these actions in the future.

Figure 18.15.

The Finish screen of the Setup wizard.

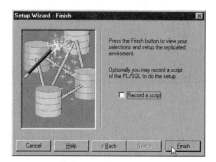

10. After you complete the Finish screen, you will be presented with a summary of the actions to be taken in the Setup Wizard Finish screen. If everything looks fine, click OK; the master setup will commence (see Figure 18.16).

Figure 18.16.

The Setup Wizard Finish screen of the Setup wizard.

Configuring the Snapshot Site

Configuring the snapshot site is similar to configuring the master site. The Setup wizard leads you through a series of screens to help you set up the snapshot site correctly:

1. First you'll see the Master Site Selection screen, where you select the site that will be the master for this snapshot site and provide the SYSTEM password.

2. After you have selected the master site, the Setup wizard connects to it to obtain information it needs for the configuration and to validate the connection.

3. Select the snapshot site via the Select Snapshot Sites screen, which resembles the Select Master Sites screen shown in Figure 18.8. From here you select one or more snapshot sites.

18

4. Clicking the New button invokes the New Snapshot Site screen, where you enter the site name and the SYSTEM password (see Figure 18.17).

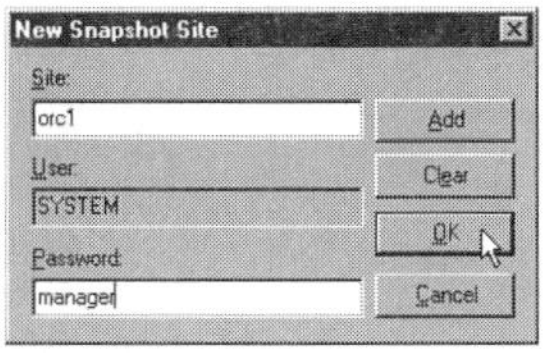

Figure 18.17.

The New Snapshot Site screen of the Setup wizard.

5. After you select the master and the snapshot site, you must set up the propagator and the replication administrator. This is done in the Snapshot Site Defaults screen, shown in Figure 18.18. The defaults usually work very well.

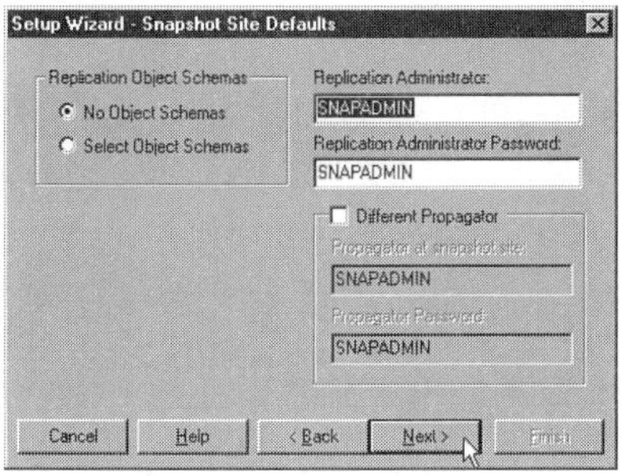

Figure 18.18.

The Snapshot Site Defaults screen of the Setup wizard.

6. You will be presented with the Defaults for Scheduled Links screen, which allows you to customize the update schedule just as you did in the previous section. Change this schedule to update at a faster or slower rate.

7. As with the master setup, you must also set the default purge schedule. This is done in the Default Purge Scheduling screen, which enables you to select an interval expression and rollback segment.

8. As with the master setup, you are given the opportunity to customize the snapshot site with the Snapshot Site Customizations screen, shown in Figure 18.19. Select a snapshot site and click the Customize button to modify users, the using clause, link scheduling, and the schema.

9. In the Finish screen, you have the option of running the setup or writing the steps to a script. If you write them to a script, you can get an idea of what steps are performed and you have a record of the operation.

10. After you finish the Setup wizard, you are presented with the Setup Wizard Finish screen (see Figure 18.20), which summarizes all the actions to be taken. When you are satisfied with the steps, click OK and the setup will begin.

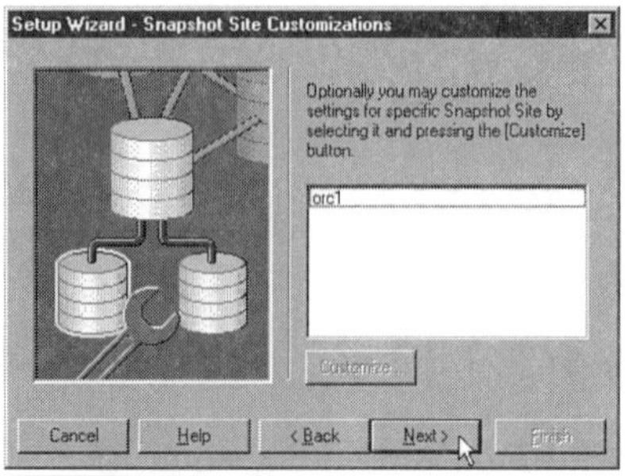

Figure 18.19.

*The Snapshot Site
Customizations screen
of the Setup wizard.*

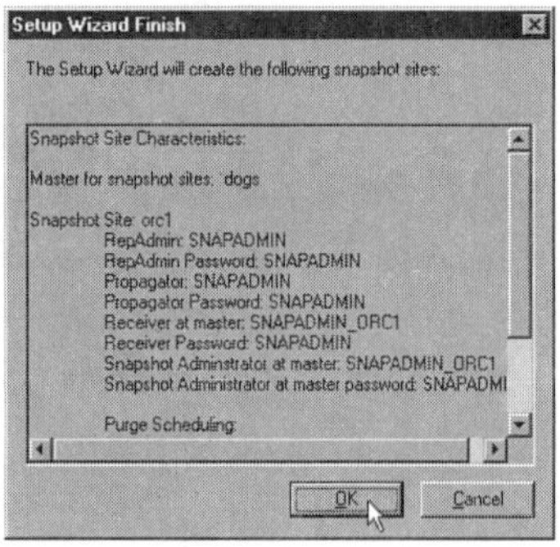

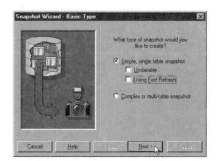

Figure 18.20.

*The Setup Wizard
Finish screen of the
Setup wizard.*

Both the master and snapshot setups offer a variety of different options. If you don't know which options to use, click the Help button for an explanation of the option. The online help is fairly complete and can be quite useful.

Creating the Snapshots Using Replication Manager

Now that you have set up the replication master (replicated from) and replication slave (replicated to), the final step is to set up the replication objects. To do so, follow these steps:

1. From the main screen of Replication Manager, select the master, then select File | Create New | Snapshot. This invokes the Snapshot wizard, where you can select what type of snapshot to create. I have chosen a simple snapshot, as shown in Figure 18.21.

Figure 18.21.

*The Basic Type screen
of the Snapshot
wizard.*

NOTE

Before you can create the snapshot, you must create a database link from the menu where you chose the Create Snapshot option. This link is scheduled between the master and the slave. It is also necessary to create a snapshot log on the database object on the master if you intend to do fast updates. This can be done through Replication Manager.

2. After you have selected the type of snapshot, you will be asked for the database link. Select the database link you scheduled from the Master Link screen shown in Figure 18.22.

Figure 18.22.

The Master Link screen of the Snapshot wizard.

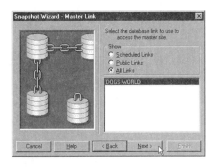

3. Select the master table on which to create the snapshot by selecting the schema and then the table, as shown in Figure 18.23.

Figure 18.23.

The Master Table screen of the Snapshot wizard.

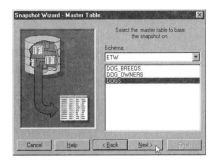

4. You are given the option of restricting the data in the snapshot via a WHERE clause. You can define this WHERE clause in the Where Clause screen, shown in Figure 18.24.

18

Figure 18.24.

The Where Clause screen of the Snapshot wizard.

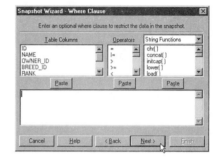

5. Define the refresh group in the Refresh Group screen, shown in Figure 18.25. If you do not yet have refresh groups, you can create one by clicking the Create New button.

Figure 18.25.

The Refresh Group screen of the Snapshot wizard.

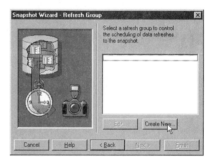

6. To create a refresh group, type the refresh group name in the Create Refresh Group screen, as shown in Figure 18.26.

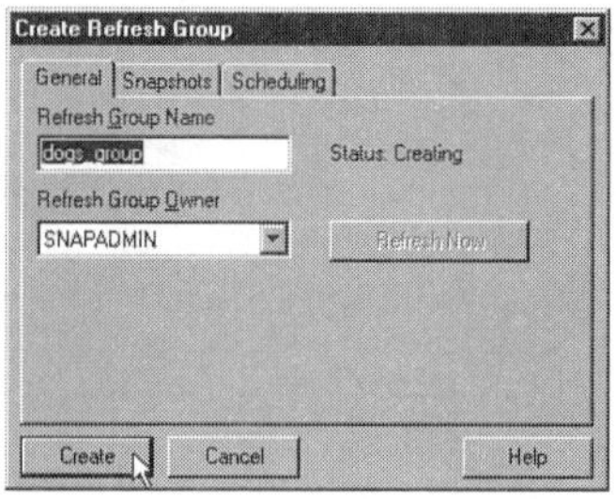

Figure 18.26.

The Create Refresh Group screen of the Snapshot wizard.

7. The Tablespace and Extent Characteristics screen, shown in Figure 18.27, allows you to change the tablespace and extent characteristics. Leave these at the default unless you have a reason to change them.

Figure 18.27.

The Tablespace and Extent Characteristics screen of the Snapshot wizard.

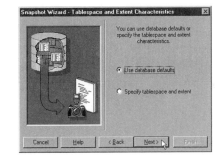

8. You have completed all the necessary steps and have reached the Finish screen. As with most Oracle wizards, you must click Finish on the final screen to proceed with the operation.

9. The Finish Snapshot Wizard screen (see Figure 18.28) summarizes all the operations to be performed. At this point you should review the snapshot-creation operation to determine whether all the options have been set up correctly. If you are satisfied, click OK.

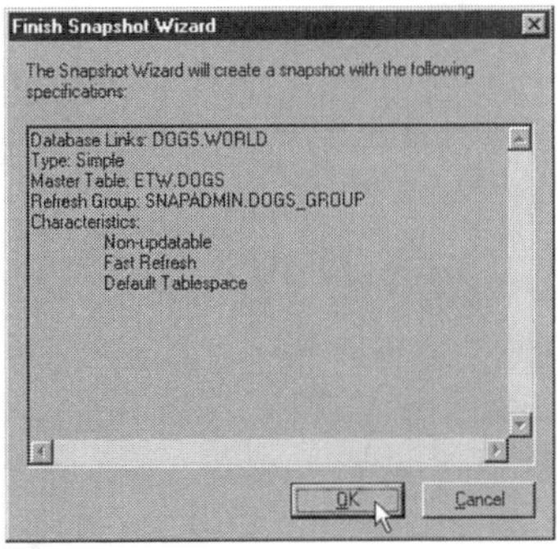

Figure 18.28.

The Finish Snapshot Wizard screen of the Snapshot wizard.

After the snapshot is configured, the database link refreshes the snapshot on a regular basis. You can set many small details and options; I have not gone into all of them here. Consult the Oracle documentation or the online help to better use all the options.

Configuring Using the CREATE SNAPSHOT Command

You can define a snapshot via the CREATE SNAPSHOT SQL statement, which is sometimes more useful if the query is complex. Use the CREATE SNAPSHOT command in conjunction with a query to create the snapshot-defining query. An example of a defining query is shown in Listing 18.1.

INPUT   **Listing 18.1. Creating a snapshot.**

```
CREATE SNAPSHOT etw.dogs AS
SELECT name, owner_name
FROM dogs, dog_owners
WHERE dogs.owner_id = dog_owner.id;
```

ANALYSIS   This creates a snapshot using a join between the dogs table and the dog_owners table. This snapshot can then be used to set up replicated sites.

Using Advanced Replication

Advanced replication can be used for a variety of different uses: for remote disconnected sites (portable computers), for distributing application loads, and to create failover sites in the event of system failure. Oracle's advanced replication option does not work in quite the same way as the snapshot-replication method. Because multiple sites might be modifying data, it would not work to simply copy the database on a regular basis. Instead, changes are saved and queued to be run on other replication sites.

NEW TERM   Oracle replicates changes on a row basis; this is known as *row-level replication.* These row changes are saved and queued to run at a later time on the replicated systems. I suggest that you read the Oracle documentation if you want a detailed description of the steps taken to perform advanced replication.

Using Advanced Replication for Disconnected Sites

Advanced replication can be used in a disconnected environment where some of the replicated systems are periodically disconnected and reconnected. For example, these systems can be used with portable computers where they are used on the road (disconnected) and reconnected to the network nightly via modem.

In this manner, the snapshot can be refreshed each night, causing the database to be resynced with other masters. The portable data and the data on the home system can be synced every night, providing the traveling user with regular updated access to corporate data.

Using Advanced Replication for Distributed Workloads

When your database's workload is spread across different areas of the country, it might be beneficial to use advanced replication to allow local access to your corporate data. If the replicated databases are local, access times will be reduced and the data will be available regardless of the state of the wide area network.

18

If you use advanced replication, each site can perform its own updates and the changes can be propagated nightly to the other systems. There are a few problems, however, if the same records are updated at multiple sites. You must address this when you configure the conflict-resolution setup for advanced replication.

If your database handles a large number of updates that typically involve the same records, replication might not be suitable for your configuration. But if you have only a few updates, and if they do not typically involve the same data, replication might be suitable.

Using Advanced Replication for Quick Recoverability

Advanced replication can serve a variety of different purposes, one of which is quick recovery in the event of a catastrophic system failure. If you use the advanced replication option, an entire database can be replicated. Not only can the database be used during normal operations, but if one of the systems should happen to fail, the users can use one of the available replicated sites.

Using a Standby Database

NEW TERM   Another method sometimes used for quick recovery is the Oracle standby database. A *standby database* is a complete copy of your primary database, but it is constantly in recovery mode. Each time a log switch occurs on your primary database, the archived log file is applied to the standby database, bringing it up to date.

In the event of a catastrophic system failure, the standby database can be used as the primary database. In the event of a failure on the primary system, you can archive the current log files using the ALTER SYSTEM ARCHIVE LOG CURRENT command. This creates an archive log file of the current redo log file. In this manner, the standby database can be made current with the primary database.

The standby database is designed to be used only as a recovery mechanism. After the standby database has been activated, it becomes the primary database. The original database can later be re-created as the standby database, but you cannot switch back to the original. More details on the standby database can be found in *Oracle8 Server Backup and Recovery Guide*.

Using Read-Only Tablespaces

By using read-only tablespaces in areas where updates are not necessary, you can reduce downtime spent in recovery. Because the RDBMS knows that a tablespace marked as read-only cannot be updated, the normal recovery process will be skipped. In the event of media failure on the volume containing the read-only tablespace, you must restore the damaged datafiles, but no instance recovery is necessary.

All tablespaces are created read-write and must be populated with data to be considered useful. After the data and indexes have been created to your specifications, the tablespace can be made read-only. This can happen in several ways. For example, Enterprise Manager or Storage Manager can be used to modify a tablespace to be read-only, as described in the previous section. Simply go to the Tablespace Modification screen, shown in Figure 18.29, and click the Read Only box. Invoke this screen by selecting the desired tablespace from the Storage Manager.

Figure 18.29.

Making a tablespace read-only.

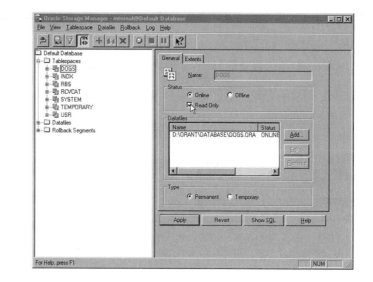

The tablespace can also be made read-only via the ALTER TABLESPACE command. The syntax will look something like this:

```
ALTER TABLESPACE DOGS READONLY;
```

There are several uses for the read-only tablespace, but they are fairly specific. Whether you can take advantage of it depends on your applications. If you have a large amount of static data that can be put on slower media, the read-only tablespace might be advantageous. Also, if you want to guarantee that archival data is not modified, a read-only tablespace might work.

Summary

Today you learned how Oracle replication works and how to configure it via Replication Manager. You also learned a few ways to reduce downtime by using replication and by using the standby database feature. You learned how using read-only tablespaces can reduce the amount of time it takes to recover a tablespace, because Oracle knows that no changes have been made to it.

Replication is a very specific option and is useful only in very specific cases. If you can take advantage of replication with your system, you will see very good results.

What's Next?

In tomorrow's lesson, "Advanced Oracle Options," you will learn about some of the advanced options available to Oracle, including the Oracle Parallel Server (OPS) and Oracle Parallel Query options.

The Oracle Parallel Server option, an add-on feature, allows more than one instance of Oracle to share the same database. This allows two or more systems to simultaneously access the same data, providing a performance boost and failover capabilities. This linking of systems to form one larger system has traditionally been called a *cluster*.

The Parallel Query option can provide a good-to-outstanding performance improvement over traditional query operations by splitting some operations into multiple processes or threads. Tomorrow you will learn how the Parallel Query option works and how to use it.

Q&A

Q What is replication?

A Replication is a feature that allows a database or schema object(s) to be copied to another system.

Q What types of replication does Oracle offer?

A Oracle offers several types of replication: read-only table snapshots, updateable snapshots, and realtime data replication.

Q What is a standby database?

A The standby database is a database that is constantly in recovery mode, recovering archived log files from the primary database. In the event of a failure, the standby database can immediately substitute for the primary database.

Q How does a read-only tablespace help speed up recovery?

A Because a tablespace is marked read-only, Oracle knows that no instance recovery is necessary. That tablespace can then be skipped.

Workshop

The workshop provides quiz questions to help you solidify your understanding of the material covered and exercises to provide you with experience in using what you've learned. Find answers to the quiz questions in Appendix A, "Answers."

18

Quiz

1. What is a read-only table snapshot?
2. What is an updateable snapshot?
3. What is realtime data replication?
4. What is a master site?
5. What is a snapshot site?
6. What are some uses of read-only table snapshots?
7. What are some uses of advanced replication?
8. What is the difference between a complete refresh and a fast refresh?
9. What is a standby database used for?
10. Why would you use a read-only tablespace?

Exercises

1. Use Replication Manager to set up a master site.
2. Use Replication Manager to set up a snapshot site.
3. Use Storage Manager to make a tablespace read-only.
4. Set that tablespace back to read-write.

Day 19

Advanced Oracle Options

Today you will learn about some of the advanced options available to Oracle, including the Oracle Parallel Server option (OPS) and the Oracle Parallel Query option. Although these options sound as though they would be similar to each other, they have no correlation.

NEW TERM The Oracle Parallel Server option, an add-on feature, allows more than one instance of Oracle to share the same database; two or more systems can simultaneously access the same data, providing a performance boost and failover capabilities where one node can take over for another in the event of a failure. This linking of systems to form one larger system has traditionally been called a *cluster*.

NOTE

> The term *cluster* has historically been used to identify a large system that performs a single task and is made up of two or more smaller systems working in tandem.
>
> Numerous vendors have recently introduced "clustering" systems that consist of an offline standby node or another node running a completely different application that can take over some tasks in the event the primary node fails. In my opinion, this is not a clustering solution. Because vendors are piggybacking on cluster terminology, the end-user is being deceived. Vendors such as Oracle, Tandem, DEC, and others have had true clusters for many years and are being cheated by these standby systems.
>
> My rule of thumb is that if you cannot access all data from all nodes all the time, it is not a cluster.

The Oracle parallel server cluster has been available for many years, but has recently been introduced on the NT platform. If you use the features of the Parallel Server option, both performance and system uptime can be improved.

The Oracle Parallel Query option is not a clustering option; it has nothing to do with clustering (except that you can use it on a cluster). This option allows certain SQL operations to be parallelized. By parallelizing these operations, you can improve performance by utilizing the time the system waits for I/O operations to complete.

The Parallel Query option can provide a good-to-outstanding performance improvement over traditional query operations. Today you will learn how to use the Parallel Query option as well as how to tune your application to better perform with the Parallel Query option.

The Parallel Server Option

The Parallel Server option is one of the most innovative and impressive options available from Oracle. With this option you can cluster several computers using a shared-disk subsystem and have multiple Oracle instances access the same database, as shown in Figure 19.1. If your application is suitable, you can see very good scalability by adding extra computers.

NEW TERM The Oracle Parallel Server option uses a sophisticated locking mechanism in conjunction with a shared-disk subsystem to allow multiple instances to access the same data. Communication between the computers occurs through a *server interconnect*, which usually consists of high-speed network accesses at a very low level. Using the traditional network stack does not provide the performance required for a server interconnect.

Figure 19.1.

A parallel-server configuration.

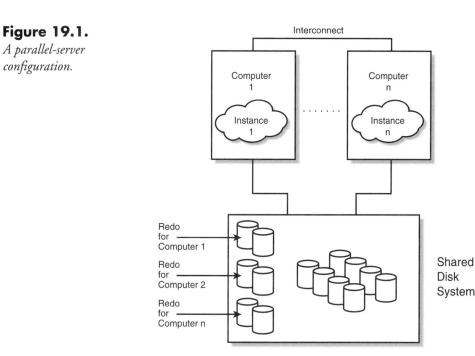

Server Interconnect

The server interconnect provides two functions: to communicate locking information and to act as a system heartbeat. The system heartbeat communicates to other systems in the cluster that the server is still operational. If the heartbeat message does not arrive, other servers in the cluster assume that the system is nonfunctional and roll back transactions that have not been committed.

The shared-disk subsystem allows all members of the cluster to access all shared data in the cluster. This disk subsystem must be shared and should be available at all times, regardless of the state of any particular server. This subsystem can use RAID and data caching as long as both operations are performed on the disk side of the shared channel rather than on the controller side. Because the release of a lock sometimes depends on data being written out to the shared disk, the more performance you have, the better off you are.

Locking

Locking is performed with a process called the Distributed Lock Manager (DLM). The DLM is responsible for locking data that is being modified so that the data cannot be modified in another instance. Locking ensures data integrity across the entire cluster. A data block or group of blocks is locked until another instance needs that data.

19

If you can partition your users so that users accessing data in a particular table all use the same instance to access that data, you will have reduced lock contention. You can enhance performance by carefully partitioning the data and the users. If you partition the data into update-intensive and read-intensive tables, you will also benefit.

At instance startup, a number of Parallel Cache Management (PCM) locks are created. PCM locks lock data blocks being accessed within each instance to guarantee that multiple instances do not alter the same data.

You can use PCM locks to lock data blocks for reading or for updating. If a PCM lock is used as a read-lock, other instances can acquire read-locks on the same data blocks. It is only when updating that an exclusive lock must be acquired.

PCM locks are allocated to datafiles; as such, they give you some flexibility over the configuration of the locks. A PCM lock locks one or more data blocks, depending on the number of PCM locks allocated to the datafile and the size of the datafile. Because an inherent overhead is associated with PCM locks, it is not beneficial to overconfigure the locks.

If you know your data-access patterns, you can configure your system based on these general rules:

- Partition work between servers. Try to balance the systems so that users accessing the same table reside on the same computer. This arrangement reduces lock contention between machines. By segmenting the work, you can reduce the amount of lock traffic. Remember that once a lock is acquired, it is released only when another system needs to lock that data.

- Put lots of PCM locks on tables with heavy update traffic. If you have lots of updates, you can benefit from lowering the blocks-per-lock ratio. By increasing the number of locks, you increase overhead—but by having fewer blocks per lock, you can cut down on the percentage of locks with contention.

- Use PCTFREE and PCTUSED to specify fewer rows per block on high-contention tables. By doing this and decreasing the number of blocks per lock, you reduce the lock contention—at the cost of more locks and more space required.

- Put fewer locks on read tables. If you have tables that are mostly read, use fewer PCM locks. Read locks are not exclusive; the reduction in locks cuts down on interconnect traffic.

- Partition indexes to separate tablespaces. Because indexes are mostly read, you can benefit by requiring fewer PCM locks. By segmenting the tables, you can put fewer PCM locks on the index tables and more on the data tables.

The dynamic performance tables VBH, VCACHE, and V$PING contain information about the frequency of PCM lock contention. By looking at the FREQUENCY column in these tables, you can get an idea of the number of times lock conversions took place because of contention between instances.

The dynamic performance table, V$LOCK_ACTIVITY, provides information about all types of PCM lock conversions. From this information you can determine whether a particular instance is seeing a dramatic change in lock activity. An increase in lock activity might indicate that you have an insufficient number of PCM locks on that instance. With this information, you can use the VBH, VCACHE, and V$PING tables to identify the problem area.

The Parallel Server option can be effective if your application is partitionable. If all the users in your system must access the same data, a parallel server might not be for you. But if you can partition your workload into divisions based on table access or if you need a fault-tolerant configuration, the Parallel Server option may work.

If you use the Parallel Server option, you must take special care to properly configure the system. By designing the system properly, you can take maximum advantage of the parallel server features.

The Parallel Query Option

The Oracle Parallel Query option makes it possible for some Oracle functions to be processed by multiple server processes. These functions are queries, index creation, data loading, and recovery. In each of these functions, the general principle is the same: Keep processing while Oracle waits for I/O.

For most queries, the time spent waiting for the data to be retrieved from disk usually overshadows the amount of time actually spent processing the results. With the Parallel Query option, you can compensate for this by using several server processes to execute the query. While one process is waiting for I/Os to complete, other processes can be executing. If you are running on a Symmetric Multiprocessor (SMP) computer, a cluster, or a Massively Parallel Processing (MPP) machine, you can take maximum advantage of the Parallel Query option.

Many different types of SQL functions can take advantage of the Parallel Query option, including

- Aggregatations
- The CREATE INDEX function
- The CREATE TABLE AS SELECT function
- The DELETE function
- The GROUP BY function
- Hash joins
- The instance recovery operation
- Nested loop joins

19

☐ The ORDER BY function
☐ Sort merge joins
☐ Table scans
☐ Union operations
☐ The UPDATE function

These operations and several others will automatically be parallelized based on the database-initialization parameters and table definitions.

Parallel Query Processing

Parallel query processing allows certain Oracle statements to be run in parallel by multiple server processes. The Oracle server can process the following statements in parallel:

☐ SELECT statements
☐ Subqueries in UPDATE and DELETE statements
☐ CREATE TABLE *tablename* AS SELECT statements
☐ CREATE INDEX statements

Parallel queries are effective on large operations such as table scans and sorts.

Parallel Query Operation

With traditional queries such as table scans, the server process reads the data sequentially, as shown in Figure 19.2. Much of the time spent in this query is spent waiting for I/Os to complete.

Figure 19.2.

A table scan per-formed without the use of the Parallel Query option.

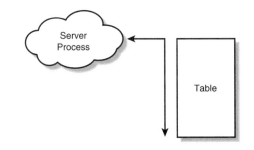

NEW TERM A parallel query splits the query into several pieces, each handled by a different server process. These processes, called *query servers*, are dispatched by a process known as the *query coordinator*. The query coordinator dispatches the query servers and coordinates the results from all the servers to send back to the user. The result of this arrangement is that many smaller table scans take place under the hood (transparent to the user). From the user's standpoint, it is simply a much faster table scan. Figure 19.3 shows a parallel query.

Figure 19.3.

*A table scan per-
formed with the use of
the Parallel Query
option.*

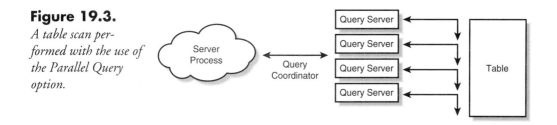

The query coordinator is given a SQL statement and a degree of parallelism, and is responsible for dividing the query among the query servers and integrating the individual results into one result. The degree of parallelism is the number of query servers assigned to the particular query.

The Oracle server can make parallel the following operations:

☐ Joins

☐ Sorts

☐ Table scans

Each of these operations has requirements that determine how the query is parallelized. The performance achieved by the parallel query is determined both by the size of the data to be accessed and the degree of parallelism achieved.

The query coordinator determines how the query is parallelized (if at all). The decision is made in this order:

1. The optimizer determines the execution plan of the statement.
2. The query coordinator determines which operations can be performed in parallel.
3. The query coordinator determines how many query servers to enlist.
4. The query coordinator enlists query servers that perform the query.
5. The query coordinator reassembles the resulting data and passes it back to the user.

The degree of parallelism is determined using the following precedence:

1. Query hints—User-defined hints included in the SQL statement have the highest precedence.
2. Table definition—The default degree of parallelism as defined for the table has second precedence.
3. Initialization parameters—Finally, the Oracle initialization parameters are used.

Regardless of what these values are set to, the number of query servers cannot exceed the number of query servers available in the query-server pool. This number is specified by the Oracle initialization parameter `PARALLEL_MAX_SERVERS`.

Hints for the degree of parallelism are set within a comment string in the SQL statement. The syntax of this comment is as follows:

```
PARALLEL (alias_or_tablename , [integer/DEFAULT] [, integer/DEFAULT])
```

The PARALLEL hint specifies the table or alias being scanned, followed by a value for the number of query servers to be used (or DEFAULT). The final optional value specifies how the table is to be split among different instances of a parallel server. Here is an example using the dogs table that you have seen throughout this book:

```
SELECT /*+ FULL(dogs) PARALLEL(dogs, 4) */
dogname
FROM dogs;
```

Because of the addition of the FULL and PARALLEL hints to this statement, the Oracle optimizer will create an execution plan that uses a full-table scan. Furthermore, this table scan will be executed with a parallel degree of 4 if the query servers are available. This statement overrides both the degree of parallelism specified in the table definition and the default Oracle initialization parameters.

The hint NOPARALLEL disables parallel scanning of a table and overrides the specified degree of parallelism. The NOPARALLEL hint has the following syntax:

```
NOPARALLEL (alias_or_tablename)
```

Parallel Query Tuning

Parallel query operations can be very effective on multiprocessor or parallel-processing computers; they can also be effective on uniprocessor systems where much of the time is spent waiting for I/O operations to complete. Systems with sufficient I/O bandwidth—and especially systems with disk arrays—benefit from parallel query operations.

If your system is typically processing at 100% of your CPU utilization and you have a small number of disk drives, you probably won't benefit from parallel query operations. The same is true if your system is extremely limited in memory.

The two areas that can be tuned for parallel queries are I/O and parallel servers. By properly configuring your datafiles, you can help parallel queries be more effective.

I/O Configuration

The function of a parallel query is to split up query operations so that they more effectively take advantage of the system. One of the ways a parallel query does this is by allowing the processing of the query to continue while pieces of the query operation are stalled, waiting for I/Os to complete. Parallel queries are not effective if the entire table is limited to one disk drive.

If you stripe the table across many drives, I/Os can be distributed and a higher level of parallelism can occur. Striping can be performed with OS striping, with Oracle striping, or (better yet) with a hardware disk array. See Day 20, "Effectively Tuning and Optimizing the Database," for more detailed information about tuning I/O.

Large contiguous extents can also help performance in parallel query operations. During scan operations, the query coordinator splits contiguous ranges of blocks into large, medium, and small groups of blocks. Each query server is given a large group of blocks to start with, and each server progressively works its way down to the small group of blocks until the scan is completed. This is done in an attempt to balance the load handled by each query server. If several large extents are in a table, the query coordinator can find blocks to dispatch to the query servers much more easily.

TIP

Remember, your temporary tablespace should consist of several large extents on a striped volume. This arrangement helps sorting performance.

Degree of Parallelism

The proper distribution of I/Os and the degree of parallelism are the two most important things to tune in the Parallel Query option. Tuning the degree of parallelism is partially trial and error and partially analysis. It is very important to take notes when you are experimenting with the degree of parallelism. Your first guess should be based on the following factors:

- [ ] The CPU capacity of your system—The number and capacity of CPUs affects the number of query processes you should run.
- [ ] The capacity of the system to handle large numbers of processes—Some operating systems can handle many simultaneous threads; others are more limited.
- [ ] The system load—If the system is already running at 100% capacity, the degree of parallelism doesn't have much effect. If you are running at 90%, too many query processes can overload the system.
- [ ] The amount of query processing on the system—If most operations are updates but there are a few critical queries, you might want many query processes.
- [ ] The I/O capacity of the system—If your disks are striped or if you are using a disk array, you should be able to handle a large number of parallel queries.
- [ ] The types of operations—Are you performing many full-table scans or sorts? These operations benefit greatly from parallel query servers.

All these parameters should have some influence on the degree of parallelism you set for your system. Remember that the preceding points are simply guidelines to help you guess a starting point. Here are a few other suggestions:

19

☐ CPU-intensive operations such as sorts should indicate a lower degree of parallelism. CPU-bound tasks are already taking advantage of the CPUs and tend not to be waiting for I/O.

☐ Disk-intensive operations such as full-table scans should indicate a higher degree of parallelism. The more operations waiting for I/O, the more the system can benefit from another query server.

☐ Many concurrent processes should indicate a lower degree of parallelism. Too many processes can overload the system.

Once you determine your starting point, you can monitor your system by querying the dynamic performance table, V$PQ_SYSSTAT. This can be performed with the query shown in Listing 19.1.

INPUT

Listing 19.1. Viewing parallel query performance data from V$PQ_SYSSTAT.

```
SQL> select * from v$pq_sysstat;
```

OUTPUT

```
STATISTIC                         VALUE
-------------------------------   ----------
Servers Busy                           0
Servers Idle                          12
Servers Highwater                     16
Server Sessions                      380
Servers Started                        4
Servers Shutdown                       4
Servers Cleaned Up                     0
Queries Initiated                     21
DFO Trees                             77
Local Msgs Sent                  2459361
Distr Msgs Sent                        0
Local Msgs Recv'd                2459318
Distr Msgs Recv'd                      0

13 rows selected.
```

ANALYSIS When looking at the output from this query, the following statistics are quite useful:

☐ Servers Busy—This indicates the number of servers busy at any one time. Check this statistic several times to get a good idea of the average value. If the value is equal to the initialization parameter PARALLEL_MIN_SERVERS, you have probably configured too many query servers.

☐ Servers Idle—This indicates the number of servers idle at any one time. If you always have many idle servers, consider reducing PARALLEL_MIN_SERVERS.

☐ Servers Started—This indicates the number of query servers that have started in this instance. If the value for Servers Busy is low but you see a large number for Servers Started, you might be using query servers sporadically.

☐ Servers Shutdown—This indicates the number of query servers that have been shut down because they are idle. This value is most likely similar to the Servers Started value.

After you determine your degree of parallelism, begin testing; evaluate the information you get from V$PQ_SYSSTAT and from your operating system's monitoring facilities. Keep an eye out for CPU usage and excessive waiting for I/O. If the CPU usage is too high, try reducing the degree of parallelism. If the CPU usage is too low and there is significant waiting for I/O, try increasing the degree of parallelism.

Remember that the degree of parallelism is determined by SQL hints, table definitions, and initialization parameters. The total number of query servers is determined by the initialization parameter PARALLEL_MAX_SERVERS; the number started initially is determined by the initialization parameter PARALLEL_MIN_SERVERS.

The total number of query servers in use is the number of queries executed in parallel multiplied by their degree of parallelism. If you try to use more than PARALLEL_MAX_SERVERS, you will not be able to parallelize your query.

Direct-Write Sorts

You can use the Direct Write Sort option with the Parallel Query option and have each query server perform its own direct writes.

As you saw earlier, using direct writes causes the server processes to write the output of sort operations directly to disk, bypassing the buffer cache. The effect of direct writes is that for sort operations, large amounts of block buffers are not ejected from the buffer cache. This leaves the buffer cache available for normal queries and updates. When you use direct-write sorts with the Parallel Query option, each query server gets its own set of direct-write buffers.

Remember, direct-write sorts require more memory than normal sorts. The amount of memory that these sorts use with the Parallel Query option can be determined with the following formula:

Direct write sort memory = (number of query servers) *
SORT_WRITE_BUFFERS * SORT_WRITE_BUFFER_SIZE

Use direct-write sorts only if you have sufficient memory and temporary disk space. The temporary disk space should have a sufficient I/O bandwidth to handle the load.

Parallel Index Creation

Another feature of the Parallel Query option is its ability to create indexes in parallel. With the parallel index creation feature, the time it takes to create an index can be greatly reduced.

As with parallel query processing, a coordinator process dispatches two sets of query servers. One set of query servers scans the table to be indexed to obtain the ROWIDs and column values needed for the index. Another set performs the sorting on those values and passes the results to the coordinator process. The coordinator process then assembles the B*-tree index from these sorted items.

When creating an index, the degree of parallelism follows the same precedence as it does in parallel query processing. The first value used is an optional PARALLEL clause in the CREATE INDEX statement, followed by the table definition, and finally the initialization parameters.

Creating an index in parallel can be several times faster than creating an index by normal means. The same conditions apply for index creation as were given for parallel query processing. A system that has been configured to take advantage of parallel query processing will also see good performance from parallel index creation.

Parallel Loading

You can load in parallel by having multiple concurrent sessions perform a direct path load into the same table. Depending on the configuration of the system, you can see excellent load performance by loading in parallel. Because loading is both CPU and I/O intensive, you should see good results in an SMP or MPP environment with a high-bandwidth I/O subsystem.

Parallel loads are performed by multiple direct loader processes, each using the PARALLEL=TRUE and DIRECT=TRUE options. When you specify PARALLEL=TRUE, the loader does not place an exclusive lock on the table being loaded as it would otherwise. During the parallel load, the loader creates temporary segments for each of the concurrent processes and merges them on completion.

Although parallel loading performs best when each temporary file is located on a separate disk, the increased performance of the load does not usually justify the complexity of the manual striping needed to do this. I still recommend striping the tables on an OS level—or preferably on a hardware disk. You can improve performance by putting each of the input files on a separate volume to take advantage of the sequential nature of the reads.

Parallel loading can be beneficial, especially if load time is critical in your environment. By putting each of the input files on separate disk volumes, you can increase performance. Overall, the general tuning principles used in parallel query processing are also valid in parallel loading.

Parallel Recovery

Parallel recovery is probably my favorite feature of the Parallel Query option. When benchmarking Oracle and testing hardware and software, it is often necessary to intentionally crash the system to prove recoverability. With the Parallel Recovery option, the time it takes to perform an instance recovery can be dramatically reduced.

Recovery time is significantly reduced when the system being recovered has many disks and supports asynchronous I/O. For a small system that has few drives or for an operating system that does not support asynchronous I/O, it might not be wise to enable parallel recovery.

In traditional recovery, one process reads from the redo log files and applies changes to the datafiles, as shown in Figure 19.4. This operation can take a significant amount of time because the recovery process must wait for disk I/Os to complete.

Figure 19.4.

Traditional instance recovery without parallel query.

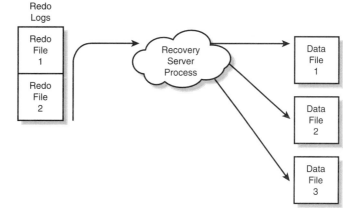

With the Parallel Recovery option, one process is responsible for reading and dispatching redo entries from the redo log files and passing those entries to the recovery processes that apply the changes to the datafiles, as shown in Figure 19.5.

Because the dispatcher process reads sequentially from the redo log files, the I/O performance is much higher than that of the recovery processes that are writing random data throughout the datafiles. Because writing the data is very seek intensive, it is a good idea to have one or two recovery processes for each data disk in the system.

By having more recovery processes, you can have more outstanding I/Os and thus use all the data drives simultaneously. Because recovery occurs at instance startup, this arrangement reduces dead time when no other database processing can be performed.

19

Figure 19.5.

Instance recovery with parallel recovery.

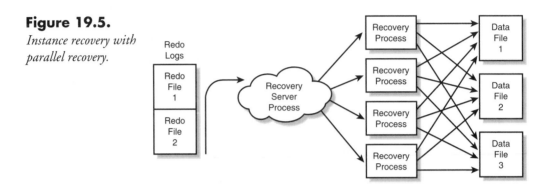

The number of concurrent recovery processes is set with the initialization parameter RECOVERY_PARALLEL. The value of this parameter cannot exceed the value specified in the initialization parameter PARALLEL_MAX_SERVERS.

If you specify a sufficient number of recovery servers, you will see an immediate improvement in instance recovery time. Do not use parallel recovery if your system does not support asynchronous I/O or if you are limited to a few disk drives. If your I/O subsystem is high bandwidth and your data is properly striped (either through software or hardware), you should see very good improvement.

In summary, the Parallel Query option is useful for distributing processing loads so that CPUs process while other processes wait for I/Os to complete. With multiprocessor machines, the Parallel Query option can be quite beneficial; this is not to say that the option is not beneficial on uniprocessor machines as well.

 NOTE

Probably the biggest performance problem I have come across is a lack of disk drives. As larger and larger disks are produced at lower and lower prices, many installations end up with I/O problems because a few large disks can provide the space of many smaller disks. The larger disks provide more disk space but not much more performance (per disk). The Parallel Query option can help only in systems where I/O is not a bottleneck. When I/O is not a problem, you will see significant gains from parallel queries.

If you have processes waiting for queries to complete and a sufficient number of disk drives, you will see an improvement with parallel queries, regardless of whether you are on a multiprocessor or uniprocessor system.

Summary

Today you learned about several features available to Oracle, including the Oracle Parallel Query and Oracle Parallel Server options. These features are quite different from each other and serve completely different purposes.

The Oracle Parallel Server option (OPS), a clustering option, can be used as a performance option and as a fault-tolerant option. Because multiple systems can access the same database, a significant performance enhancement can be seen in some situations.

 NOTE

> Under some conditions, the Oracle Parallel Server option can provide a significant performance increase. The performance improvement you see is very dependent on your application and data layout. Without careful planning, you might not see any performance improvement, and you might even see performance degradation.

The Oracle Parallel Query option allows certain SQL operations to be parallelized, thus reducing idle time waiting for I/Os to complete. If you take advantage of the Parallel Query option, you can see very good performance enhancements under the right conditions. The Parallel Query option is probably my favorite feature of the Oracle RDBMS because such incredible results can be seen from the right parallelism.

What's Next?

In tomorrow's lesson, "Effectively Tuning and Optimizing the Database," you will learn to tune the Oracle RDBMS, and how to use OS and RDBMS information to make changes that will improve your system's performance. You will learn how to use the Oracle administration scripts UTLBSTAT.SQL and UTLESTAT.SQL to obtain Oracle performance information, and you will learn how to interpret some of that information.

Q&A

Q What is the Oracle Parallel Server option?

A The Oracle Parallel Server option is a feature of Oracle that allows you to cluster two or more systems sharing the same database.

Q Does the Parallel Server option require any special hardware?

A Yes. The Parallel Server option requires a server interconnect that might be as simple as a fast network card and a shared-disk subsystem. The shared-disk subsystem is provided by your hardware vendor.

19

Q What is the Parallel Query option?

A The Parallel Query option allows certain SQL operations to be parallelized. If you parallelize the operation, time spent waiting for I/O by one thread of operation can be spent processing another thread of operation.

Q Do single-processor systems benefit from the Parallel Query option?

A Definitely. Because the greatest benefit of the Parallel Query option is to keep the system busy while it is waiting for I/Os to complete, this will work well even with a single-CPU system.

Workshop

The workshop provides quiz questions to help you solidify your understanding of the material covered and exercises to provide you with experience in using what you've learned. Find answers to the quiz questions in Appendix A, "Answers."

Quiz

1. What is the Oracle Parallel Server option used for?
2. What is the server interconnect for?
3. What is a shared-disk subsystem?
4. What does DLM stand for?
5. What does PCM stand for?
6. What is the Parallel Query option used for?
7. How does the Parallel Query option improve performance?
8. Name the primary way to set the degree of parallelism.
9. Name the secondary way to set the degree of parallelism.
10. Name some operations that can be parallelized.

Exercises

1. Run a query using traditional methods while timing it.
2. Run the same query using a parallel degree of 2 set in a hint. Compare the time.
3. Run the same query using a parallel degree of 4 set in a hint. Compare the time.
4. Run the same query using a parallel degree of 8 set in a hint. Compare the time.

Day **20**

Effectively Tuning and Optimizing the Database

Performance can be one of the most fun or most frustrating aspects of administering a database. It is almost always extremely challenging, and forces you to use all your experience to isolate the bottleneck and determine a response. I find performance tuning and system optimization to be extremely rewarding and challenging; I enjoy it, and I hope you do too.

I hate to refer to performance bottlenecks as *bugs* or *problems* because those terms suggest something is broken. Sometimes bottlenecks occur because you have reached the capacity of your system, and no tuning or changes can alter that fact; other solutions must be found. The capacity planner must try to anticipate both when the system will reach capacity and what new resources are needed before this happens.

NOTE

> Oracle instance and OS tuning should be performed in conjunction
> with application tuning. Because much of the instance tuning is based
> on the data-access patterns and memory usage of the application,
> changes to the application might result in the opportunity to retune
> the instance for greater optimization. A perfectly optimized Oracle
> instance cannot make up for a poorly tuned application. Unfortunately,
> this book does not cover application tuning in detail, but several good
> books on the subject are available. In fact, I have written just such a
> book: *Oracle Performance Tuning and Optimization* (Sams Publishing).

Performance tuning and capacity planning are closely related. They rely on and play off of
each other. The capacity-planning stage assumes that you have a well-tuned system, and bases
most of its recommendations on this. The system-tuning stage assumes you have a system that
can support the number of users and the number of tasks being performed. The capacity-
planning and system-performance engineers often work together to determine where the
bottleneck is and how to resolve it.

What Is a Bottleneck?

NEW TERM   The term *bottleneck* refers to the component or components that have a limiting
factor on the system. Some bottlenecks result from inherent limitations of your
system, but others can be fixed via parameter tuning. Many times, additional components
are needed to fix bottlenecks. System tuning typically involves finding system bottlenecks
and eliminating them. Examples of bottlenecks that are typically found in an Oracle system
include

- ☐ Disk drive bottleneck—A disk drive can handle only so many I/Os per second
  before latencies increase to unacceptable levels. The systemwide I/Os per second is
  fixed, so if your CPU and memory system requests I/Os more quickly than the I/O
  subsystem can deliver, a disk bottleneck will occur.

- ☐ Memory bottleneck—If you have inadequate memory, you won't have a good
  cache-hit rate. A high cache-hit rate indicates that most of the data you need is in
  the Oracle buffer cache. This reduces the number of needed I/Os.

- ☐ CPU bottleneck—In the case of a CPU bottleneck, you are running your system as
  quickly as the CPUs can run.

- ☐ Network bottleneck—A network bottleneck occurs when so much traffic is over
  the network, you can't transfer data any faster. This is important to backup and
  recovery.

☐ Bus bottleneck—A bus bottleneck occurs when your hardware cannot transfer data across the CPU to memory or I/O bus. This is a hardware limitation.

☐ Other bottlenecks—Numerous other bottlenecks, either hardware, software, or a combination of the two, can occur.

Some bottlenecks can be fixed easily, and others are difficult to overcome. Later today you will see how to determine the location of a bottleneck and receive some hints on how to fix bottlenecks.

NOTE

Every system is different. There is no magic diagnostic tool that can tell you how to tune your system. It is an acquired skill that you will develop with practice.

Performance Tuning Methodology

Determining what, if anything, is a bottleneck in your system can be difficult. I have found that following a tuning methodology or plan can help you to reach the correct conclusion in the shortest amount of time. By *tuning methodology,* I mean a way of looking at performance issues and determining of the root of those issues. Here is the performance tuning and optimization methodology I use:

1. Analyze the system—Determine whether a performance issue actually exists. You might determine this by running transactions and checking response times or by monitoring the system statistics. You should look at OS stats as well as Oracle stats.

2. Determine the cause—Here you form a hypothesis about where the bottleneck is by looking at the analysis from step 1.

3. Develop a solution or a test—If you are certain you have determined where the bottleneck is, develop a solution for it. If not, develop a test to verify your hypothesis. When you develop the test, you should know what the results of the test will tell you.

4. Run the test or implement the solution—If you have hit upon a solution, implement it. If not, run your test under carefully controlled conditions. This test will be used to determine whether you are right or wrong.

5. Analyze the results—After the test has been run, you must analyze the result. Always view your results with skepticism. If something is too good to be believed, perhaps you should not believe it.

20

NOTE

> You should know what you expect from the test you have developed. Many times a test result can provide good data if the result is positive, but no useful information if the result is negative. For example, adding another disk drive will tell you that you had a disk bottleneck if this addition increases performance, but does not tell you what the problem is if performance does not increase. These tests are still valuable, even though only one result gives you good data.

Although you don't need to use my system, it helps if you develop some system for troubleshooting.

Analyze the System

Analyzing the system gives you a good place to start. The first step in analyzing a system is to determine whether you have a problem. You should periodically monitor the following:

- ☐ Response times—Do users complain that the system seems slower? Periodically ask your user community how the performance of the system seems to them; sometimes end users are reluctant to tell you about prospective problems until they reach a critical state. It is a good idea to have a test query that you can run to compare current response times with previous response times. If your test query takes significantly longer to run than previously, you are seeing some kind of system slowdown.

- ☐ Throughput—Look at the system as a whole by examining the system performance monitor (perfmon for NT, sar for UNIX). Compare current and past results. Is your CPU utilization significantly higher than in previous samples? What about disk usage? You will look at these in more detail later today.

- ☐ Your intuition—Sometimes the system just feels wrong. If you think something isn't quite right, check it out. You know your system better than anyone.

After you analyze the system, you might determine that there are no performance issues, that everything is running fine. Great! But if you do come across performance problems, you can start determining the cause and possible solutions.

Determine the Cause

The next stage is to form a hypothesis of what you think the problem is. This should be based on analysis of the system and what you know of the system's design and capacity. For example, if you have a system with five 4.3GB SCSI disk drives for datafiles, the system should be able to support up to 350 I/Os per second before you see large disk latencies. If you are driving

20

those disk drives at 450 I/Os per second, you could hypothesize that you are having a disk I/O problem. This hypothesis should be specific enough to help lead you to a solution to the bottleneck.

Develop a Solution or a Test

Develop a solution to the bottleneck or some sort of test to confirm your hypothesis. Whether you need to develop a solution or a test depends on how certain you are about having discovered the bottleneck and how expensive the solution is. If you are certain you have a disk bottleneck and have more disk drives available, it is not necessary to test your theory. But if you are not certain or think that other issues might be involved, it is a good idea to develop a test. Be sure your test will give you meaningful information.

WARNING

> Remember the difference between *cause* and *effect*. You might see something that looks like a disk bottleneck when in fact a lack of memory is causing unnecessary I/O.

Anticipate Your Results

The test you devise to confirm or rule out a certain bottleneck should lead to expected results. If you are unsure what positive and negative results would indicate, the test is not worth running. I often run tests where a positive result is meaningful but a negative tells me nothing. This test is still worth running because that positive result might either solve the problem or rule out a cause. Some examples of the kinds of testing you can do are shown later today.

Run the Test or Implement the Solution

Either run a test that will give you valuable information about the bottleneck or try to fix the problem. Carefully monitor the system in both cases. Even if it seems that the performance of the system has immediately and dramatically improved, you should still monitor the system and collect some data. If you run into a performance bottleneck in the future, this data can be valuable.

Analyze the Results

Monitor the system after a change has been made or a test has been run to determine whether the bottleneck has been eliminated. In the case of a capacity issue, the bottleneck might appear to have been eliminated, but the fix might be only temporary. Carefully analyze your system so you can anticipate when you will run out of capacity again.

You will sometimes find that the results of your test prove that your hypothesis was incorrect. If this is the case, return to step 2 to determine the cause of the bottleneck.

20

Question Your Results

Sometimes testing does not afford a valid result. This typically occurs when you make a change that you expect to either increase or decrease performance, and neither occurs. This indicates that one of two things has occurred:

☐ The bottleneck is somewhere else—If you have a bus bandwidth problem and add more memory, there will be no improvement because you are limited by the speed of the bus.

☐ The test was flawed—This could occur for any number of reasons. Perhaps you modified the wrong parameter file, or perhaps the change requires a system reboot.

If your results are flawed, be skeptical. Check the results. It's okay if you don't believe the results and want to try another test. Only rarely does a test turn out to be flawed or do other problems occur.

Operating System Overview

If you understand the basic concepts of how the operating system works, you will have a better feel for how to monitor and tune the operating system.

Windows NT

Microsoft Windows NT, a relatively new operating system, has quickly gained popularity. Windows NT has file and print services similar to those offered by NetWare, but Windows NT is used primarily as an application server or client operating system. Windows NT comes in two varieties:

☐ NT Workstation—NT Workstation is designed for the client users and does not contain many of the management pieces that come standard with NT Server.

☐ NT Server—NT Server includes the management tools necessary for maintaining a server.

Windows NT, a multiprocessor operating system, can take advantage of scaleable performance increases via the addition of CPUs. Windows NT is also a server operating system; there is no facility within Windows NT to provide login functionality from terminals. From the beginning, Windows NT was designed to support clients over network connections. The Windows NT operating system provides functionality such as 16-bit Windows application support and a GUI, but because of this functionality, some overhead is associated with Windows NT.

Architectural Overview of Windows NT

NEW TERM — Windows NT is based on a microkernel architecture. In a *microkernel architecture*, the core kernel is small because most of the OS functionality is removed from the

20

kernel. Because of this, the system is modular; large pieces of the OS can be easily replaced. Although a microkernel does not provide additional performance, it does provide a flexibility that OS and device-driver developers can exploit. Because of the flexible subsystem architecture, OS changes such as file systems, hardware architecture, and memory subsystems can easily be replaced.

In Windows NT, hardware support is provided through the Hardware Abstraction Layer (HAL). The HAL is employed by hardware vendors to support their systems' base architectures and to provide device-driver support. Because of the microkernel and HAL, Windows NT can support different architectures such as Intel, DEC Alpha, MIPS, PowerPC, and so on. The microkernel is the common code base in which each of these architectures is rooted.

Most 16-bit applications written for Windows can run on non-Intel architectures through the use of a compatibility mode driver. Applications written specifically for Windows NT can be ported to non-Intel platforms with minimal effort. However, applications that have not been written to take advantage of a particular architecture might not run optimally. Oracle is currently supported only on the Intel architecture. As with all Oracle ports, Oracle has been optimized for Windows NT and specifically optimized for Windows NT on Intel platforms.

The Windows NT architecture provides for the use of *threads*, sometimes known as *lightweight processes*. Through the use of threads instead of processes, much of the overhead associated with process switching is reduced. Threads are automatically created when the Oracle instance is started (see Table 20.1).

Table 20.1. Oracle service threads.

Thread number	Oracle process
0, 1	Oracle Service
2	PMON
3	DBWR
4	LGWR
5	SMON
6	RECO

A shadow thread is created on behalf of each user accessing the Oracle database. Remember, The shadow processes communicate with the user and interact with Oracle to carry out the user's requests. For example, if the user process requests a piece of data not already in the SGA, the shadow process is responsible for reading the data blocks from the datafiles into the SGA. Under Windows NT, these processes are invoked as kernel threads. Each of these threads has its own thread number.

UNIX

UNIX, born in 1969, predates NetWare, Windows NT, and OS/2 by many years. UNIX is different from NetWare, Windows NT, and OS/2 in that it was not designed as a client/ server operating system. That is not to say that UNIX is not now used as a network server, but that network service was not the original intent of the operating system.

Even though UNIX is fairly standard, a divergence in UNIX has occurred over the years. Because almost every major computer company develops and sells a version of UNIX, there are differences in the UNIX offerings from the different vendors.

The PC server market boasts three main UNIX versions: SCO UNIX, SCO UnixWare, and Solaris from SunSoft. IBM calls its UNIX offering AIX. Hewlett-Packard has a UNIX operating system called HP-UX; AT&T Global Information Solutions simply calls its product UNIX System V. SunSoft produces versions of UNIX for both Intel and Sun SPARC processors; its products are called Solaris and Solaris X86. Currently, most vendors (with the exception of SCO) base their versions of UNIX on one common core: UNIX System V Release 4, which is sometimes referred to as UNIX SVR4.

In many cases, applications are binarily compatible between operating systems on the same platform, but it is not uncommon for the vendor to add special enhancements in the operating system for performance. Oracle always takes advantage of OS-specific features, even though it would be simpler to ship just one binary.

Architectural Overview of UNIX

UNIX consists of a core piece called the kernel surrounded by applications and tools. The kernel contains all hardware support, device drivers, scheduling routines, and the network stack. Unlike the microkernel architecture used in Windows NT, the UNIX kernel contains all the core operating system functionality.

UNIX is a virtual-memory operating system but is very configurable. In the UNIX operating system, not all memory is allocated and used in the same manner. Shared memory used for the Oracle SGA is treated differently from normal memory. Shared memory is allocated at boot time, is not available to general user processes, and must be allocated through shared memory system calls in the operating system.

The fact that shared memory is treated differently allows certain functions to occur. Some varieties of UNIX allow you to allocate shared memory using a 4MB memory page size. This arrangement cuts down on page entries that must be maintained by the operating system and guarantees larger chunks of contiguous memory. Shared memory is also unique in that it is nonpageable. This means that if you have enough shared memory to create the SGA at instance startup, you don't ever have to worry about the SGA being paged out.

Other features that have been added over the years to the UNIX operating system to improve database performance include realtime processing, high-speed semaphores, and asynchronous I/O. Not all these features are in every implementation of UNIX. Check with your OS vendor to see what is available for your environment.

Finding a Performance Bottleneck

Finding a performance bottleneck can be difficult. There is no proven formula or list of things to look for that immediately tells you what the problem is. Finding a performance bottleneck is an investigative task, and the more experience you get, the better at it you will be.

Knowing Your System's Limitations

To determine whether a system component is prompting a performance bottleneck, ascertain the limitations of that component when possible. Doing so allows you to determine whether you are exceeding that limitation. Unfortunately, these limitations are difficult to gauge in most cases, but it is possible to characterize the component in some cases. The limitations of the I/O subsystem and in the networking components are ascertainable.

The I/O Subsystem

Some pieces of the I/O subsystem, such as the disk drive, have been well tested and documented over the last few years; limitations of the controller and bus are not as well known. The disk drive is a physical piece of hardware that usually comes with a specification. This specification tells you certain things about the disk drive, such as

☐ Average seek time—This is the average time it takes for the disk arm to move from one location to another. This relates to the number of random I/Os per second that you can perform.

☐ Average track-to-track seek time—This is the time it takes to move to the next adjacent track on the disk drive. This relates to the number of sequential I/Os per second that you can perform.

☐ Transfer time—This is the time it takes to move the data from the disk to the system bus.

☐ Rotations per second—This is how quickly the disk spins. This relates to how quickly you can rotate to the next bit of data on the disk.

A typical disk drive might have an average seek time of 9 milliseconds; for random I/Os, it takes 9 milliseconds to move to the next data. Add 1 millisecond for data transfer to make 10 milliseconds per random I/O. Divide 1 second by 10 milliseconds to see how many times per second you can perform a random seek:

Seeks = 1 Sec / 0.01 Sec/Seek = 100 Seeks

20

On Day 4, "Properly Sizing Your Database and Planning for Growth," you saw the "knee of the curve" theory. According to that theory, you don't want to exceed 60–70% of your available capacity; otherwise, times increase. This is why you should not exceed 60–70 seeks per second for random I/O.

The Network Subsystem

The network subsystem is another area where you can compare your throughput against a known maximum. Ethernet networks are available in a number of different throughput levels. This is usually indicated in the name of the network hardware. A few of the network hardware specifications include

☐ 10BaseT—This is a 10Mb/second ethernet. With this hardware you can have a peak throughput of 10Mb, or approximately 1.25MB/second.

☐ 100BaseT—This is a 100Mb/second ethernet. With this hardware you can have a peak throughput of 100Mb, or approximately 12.5MB/second.

Monitor your system to you determine whether you are close to meeting or exceeding the available throughput. Remember that smaller packets are not as efficient, so if you send many small requests (common in database applications), you might not realize the full potential of the network.

A good way to determine how much network bandwidth you are using is by employing a network monitor. Network monitors can be hardware or software devices. Most operating systems do not provide any way to monitor the network from your system because your network card normally passes only packets addressed to that machine. Other packets are ignored.

Memory

Memory problems sometimes manifest themselves as other problems. For example, a lack of memory might cause excessive I/O, which will appear as an I/O problem. Of prime importance is the fact that the system is not paging or swapping. Paging and swapping occur when no physical memory is available for code processing. The CPU pages, or moves data out of memory, onto a paging area on disk. This operation can be quite expensive. If you are seeing significant paging, add more memory to the system or reduce the Oracle DB block buffer cache to free more memory.

WARNING

If your system is paging or swapping, you have a severe performance problem. No amount of tuning will make up for the performance degradation caused by this paging or swapping. If you are seeing excessive paging, get more memory. If you are at the limit of memory that your system can support, start looking for a new system.

20

Monitoring the System

After you know your limitations, you can determine whether you are exceeding them by monitoring the system. There are several ways to monitor the system; one of the best ways under Windows NT is with the Performance Monitor, or *perfmon*. On a UNIX system, you can monitor many objects with the sar utility. Most operating systems also offer a graphical monitoring tool. These tools are good, but are specific to the brand of hardware you purchase. Look in your OS documentation for instructions on how to use these tools.

Oracle provides a set of useful scripts for monitoring the performance of the RDBMS. These scripts are called UTLBSTAT (begin) and UTLESTAT (end). UTLBSTAT should be run first, followed shortly thereafter by UTLESTAT. UTLESTAT displays a large number of statistic and counter values based on the time since UTLBSTAT was run.

Using perfmon

Select Programs | Administrative Tools (Common) | Performance Monitor to invoke perfmon. The Performance Monitor appears in chart mode, which is fine for small numbers of items (such as a trend over an extended period of time). If you are looking at a large amount of data, use report mode; in this mode, values are displayed onscreen as numerical values. Invoke report mode by selecting it via the View drop-down menu or by clicking the Report button.

WARNING

perfmon adds some CPU overhead to the system. If you extend the report inverval, perfmon will run less often, thus reducing CPU overhead. Increasing the report interval also increases the accuracy of the report. I recommend setting the report interval to 15 or 30 seconds.

Looking for I/O Bottlenecks with perfmon

To use perfmon to view events in the system, you must select counters. Each of these counters represents a different event that is monitored. To view counter information, do the following:

1. Click the + button to add a new counter.
2. From the Add to Report screen, choose the PhysicalDisk object from the Object drop-down menu, as shown in Figure 20.1.

20

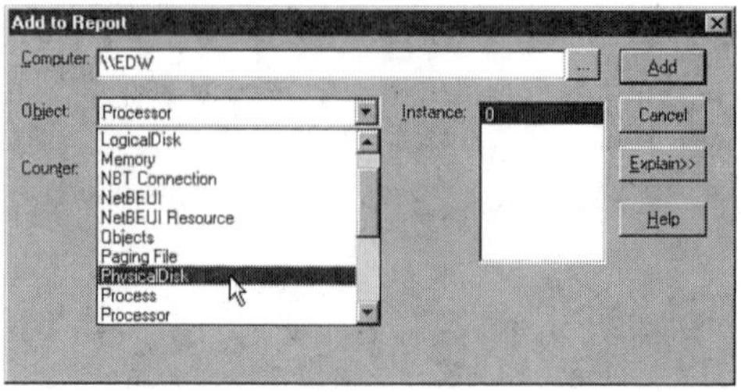

Figure 20.1.

Choose the
PhysicalDisk object.

3. You are presented with a number of objects from which you can select. You can monitor many useful objects, but my opinion is that the following items are most important in monitoring the disk I/O subsystem:

☐ Disk Reads/Sec—The number of reads per second to that disk or volume.

☐ Disk Writes/Sec—The number of writes per second to that disk or volume.

☐ Disk Transfers/Sec—The total number of reads and writes per second to that disk or volume.

☐ Avg. Disk Sec/Read—The average time it takes for the read operation to occur.

☐ Avg. Disk Sec/Write—The average time it takes for the read operation to occur.

☐ Avg. Disk Sec/Transfer—The average time it takes for the read and write operations to occur.

☐ Avg. Disk Queue Length—The average number of I/Os in the disk I/O subsystem.

NOTE

A hardware disk array will appear to the NT system as a single disk. Divide the number of I/Os per second by the number of disk drives to get the I/Os per second per disk drive. This is not 100% accurate because the I/O balance may not be perfect, but it is the best that you can do.

Of particular note should be the number of I/Os per second per disk drive and the disk latency. A typical disk drive or disk array should complete I/Os in 20–30 milliseconds (0.020–0.030 seconds). If any volume is much higher than that (more than 0.060 seconds), you are probably seeing some sort of disk bottleneck. Consider adding more disk drives.

If you are running on UNIX, you can get this information using sar or other monitoring tools.

20

Looking for Memory Bottlenecks with perfmon

In Windows NT, the Pages/Sec counter under the Memory objects can be used to indicate that the system is paging. If you see significant activity with this counter, you are using too much memory. If you cannot add more memory, you should reduce the memory used by Oracle and other processes or reduce the number of users on the system.

Using UTLBSTAT and UTLESTAT

Within the directory \ORANT\RDBMS80\ADMIN are a number of scripts used internally within Oracle. You ran CATPROC.ORA and CATALOG.ORA from this directory when you created a database. UTLBSTAT and UTLESTAT are also run from here.

UTLBSTAT sets up some internal tables and takes a snapshot of some of the internal Oracle counters. After you run under load for a time, UTLESTAT takes another snapshot and compares the results. UTLESTAT displays a large number of statistic and counter values based on the time since UTLBSTAT was run.

NOTE

The UTLBSTAT.SQL and UTLESTAT.SQL scripts each have a CONNECT INTERNAL string at the top. Most likely, this will not work under NT. Simply comment out this line and run the script from the INTERNAL user account. Place the word Rem at the beginning of those lines.

The UTLBSTAT and UTLESTAT scripts can be run from the SVRMGR30 utility. After you connect in as INTERNAL or SYS, you can run the UTLBSTAT script with the following syntax:

```
@D:\ORANT\RDBMS80\ADMIN\UTLBSTAT;
```

After you run for a while under load, you can finish monitoring Oracle and view the results by running the UTLESTAT script with the following syntax:

```
@D:\ORANT\RDBMS80\ADMIN\UTLESTAT;
```

NOTE

The usefulness of the data retrieved from UTLBSTAT and UTLESTAT might depend on the length of time for which the data is collected. When looking at specific events, five minutes might be enough. When looking at long-term performance, you might need to run for hours or more. If you are interested in a specific event such as a long-running query, the runtime of the event will be sufficient.

20

The result of UTLESTAT is, in its entirety, quite long. Following is the resulting data from UTLESTAT only; the echo of the SQL statements has been removed:

OUTPUT

LIBRARY	GETS	GETHITRATI	PINS	PINHITRATI	RELOADS	INVALIDATI
BODY	0	1	0	1	0	0
CLUSTER	97	1	50	1	0	0
INDEX	0	1	0	1	0	0
OBJECT	0	1	0	1	0	0
PIPE	0	1	0	1	0	0
SQL AREA	120	.808	364	.874	0	0
TABLE/PROCED	235	.923	265	.879	0	0
TRIGGER	0	1	0	1	0	0

Statistic	Total	Per Transact	Per Logon	Per Second
DBWR buffers scanned	601	601	150.25	2.86
DBWR free buffers found	581	581	145.25	2.77
DBWR lru scans	35	35	8.75	.17
DBWR make free requests	35	35	8.75	.17
DBWR summed scan depth	601	601	150.25	2.86
DBWR timeouts	68	68	17	.32
SQL*Net roundtrips to/from	129	129	32.25	.61
background timeouts	210	210	52.5	1
buffer is not pinned count	2175	2175	543.75	10.36
buffer is pinned count	6343	6343	1585.75	30.2
bytes received via SQL*Net	11212	11212	2803	53.39
bytes sent via SQL*Net to c	8270	8270	2067.5	39.38
calls to get snapshot scn:	145	145	36.25	.69
calls to kcmgas	1	1	.25	0
calls to kcmgcs	10	10	2.5	.05
calls to kcmgrs	181	181	45.25	.86
cleanouts only - consistent	5	5	1.25	.02
cluster key scan block gets	801	801	200.25	3.81
cluster key scans	506	506	126.5	2.41
commit cleanouts	16	16	4	.08
commit cleanouts successful	16	16	4	.08
consistent gets	4557	4557	1139.25	21.7
cursor authentications	6	6	1.5	.03
db block changes	104	104	26	.5
db block gets	141	141	35.25	.67
enqueue releases	26	26	6.5	.12
enqueue requests	20	20	5	.1
execute count	144	144	36	.69
free buffer inspected	7	7	1.75	.03
free buffer requested	1383	1383	345.75	6.59
immediate (CR) block cleano	5	5	1.25	.02
logons cumulative	4	4	1	.02
messages received	38	38	9.5	.18
messages sent	39	39	9.75	.19
no work - consistent read g	4063	4063	1015.75	19.35
opened cursors cumulative	109	109	27.25	.52

```
parse count (hard)              23           23        5.75         .11
parse count (total)            120          120          30         .57
physical reads                1369         1369      342.25        6.52
physical writes                 45           45       11.25         .21
recursive calls               2030         2030       507.5        9.67
redo blocks written             49           49       12.25         .23
redo entries                    67           67       16.75         .32
redo size                    25360        25360        6340      120.76
redo small copies               67           67       16.75         .32
redo synch writes                1            1         .25           0
redo wastage                   644          644         161        3.07
redo writes                      3            3         .75         .01
session logical reads         4698         4698      1174.5       22.37
session pga memory          645168       645168      161292     3072.23
session pga memory max      645168       645168      161292     3072.23
session uga memory           13772        13772        3443       65.58
session uga memory max      144296       144296       36074      687.12
sorts (memory)                  85           85       21.25          .4
sorts (rows)                   783          783      195.75        3.73
table fetch by rowid          2148         2148         537       10.23
table fetch continued row        2            2          .5         .01
table scan blocks gotten      1085         1085      271.25        5.17
table scan rows gotten         456          456         114        2.17
table scans (long tables)        2            2          .5         .01
table scans (short tables)      17           17        4.25         .08
total file opens                 5            5        1.25         .02
user calls                     139          139       34.75         .66
user commits                     1            1         .25           0
write requests                   6            6         1.5         .03
Average Write Queue Length
-------------------------
                                 0
Event Name            Count       Total Time    Avg Time
--------------------- ----------- ------------- -------------
SQL*Net message from client      150          0            0
SQL*Net message to client        150          0            0
control file sequential read      68          0            0
db file scattered read           137          0            0
db file sequential read          413          0            0
file identify                      3          0            0
file open                          9          0            0
log file sync                      1          0            0
Event Name            Count       Total Time    Avg Time
--------------------- ----------- ------------- -------------
control file parallel write        2          0            0
control file sequential read       2          0            0
db file parallel write             6          0            0
db file scattered read             1          0            0
db file sequential read            5          0            0
db file single write               2          0            0
log file parallel write            3          0            0
log file sync                      1          0            0
pmon timer                        70          0            0
rdbms ipc message                250          0            0
smon timer                         1          0            0
```

20

```
LATCH_NAME           GETS        MISSES       HIT_RATIO    SLEEPS       SLEEPS/MISS
-------------------  ----------  -----------  -----------  -----------  -----------
Active checkpoint            69            0            1            0            0
Checkpoint queue l         1488            0            1            0            0
Token Manager                22            0            1            0            0
cache buffer handl           43            0            1            0            0
cache buffers chai        10389            0            1            0            0
cache buffers lru          1451            0            1            0            0
dml lock allocatio           11            0            1            0            0
enqueue hash chain           24            0            1            0            0
enqueues                     62            0            1            0            0
ktm global data               1            0            1            0            0
library cache              3099            0            1            0            0
library cache load           64            0            1            0            0
list of block allo            1            0            1            0            0
messages                    536            0            1            0            0
modify parameter v            4            0            1            0            0
multiblock read ob          288            0            1            0            0
ncodef allocation             3            0            1            0            0
process allocation            1            0            1            0            0
redo allocation             115            0            1            0            0
row cache objects          1318            0            1            0            0
session allocation           56            0            1            0            0
session idle bit            288            0            1            0            0
session switching             3            0            1            0            0
shared pool                1063            0            1            0            0
sort extent pool              1            0            1            0            0
system commit numb          193            0            1            0            0
transaction alloca            7            0            1            0            0
undo global data            101            0            1            0            0
LATCH_NAME           NOWAIT_GETS     NOWAIT_MISSES     NOWAIT_HIT_RATIO
-------------------  ----------------  ----------------  -----------------
Token Manager                      3                 0                  1
cache buffers chai              8643                 0                  1
cache buffers lru               1465                 0                  1
library cache                      3                 0                  1
multiblock read ob                 1                 0                  1
process allocation                 1                 0                  1
row cache objects                  3                 0                  1
vecio buf des                      3                 0                  1
CLASS               COUNT            TIME
----------------    ----------------  ----------------
0 rows selected.
UNDO_SEGMENT        TRANS_TBL_GETS      TRANS_TBL_WAITS
➥UNDO_BYTES_WRITTEN  SEGMENT_SIZE_BYTES  XACTS
SHRINKS             WRAPS
----------------    ------------------   ------------------
➥----------------    ------------------   ------------------
- ----------------    ------------------
                                 0                 8
➥0                   2718            1226752
0                       0                 0
1 row selected.
```

```
NAME                              VALUE
---------------------------       -------------------------------------
background_dump_dest              %RDBMS80%\trace
compatible                        8.0.0.0.0
control_files                     D:\DATABASE\ctl1dogs.ora
db_block_size                     2048
db_files                          1024
db_name                           dogs
dml_locks                         100
log_buffer                        2048, 8192
log_checkpoint_interval           10000
max_dump_file_size                10240
processes                         20, 50
remote_login_passwordfile         SHARED
sequence_cache_hash_buckets       10
shared_pool_size                  3500000
snapshot_refresh_processes        1
user_dump_dest                    %RDBMS80%\trace
```

NAME	GET_REQS	GET_MISS	SCAN_REQ	SCAN_MIS	MOD_REQS	COUNT	CUR_USAG
dc_free_extents	9	9	0	0	0	27	10
dc_rollback_seg	2	0	0	0	0	7	2
dc_users	28	0	0	0	0	14	1
dc_objects	169	16	0	0	0	144	138
dc_synonyms	2	1	0	0	0	12	1
dc_usernames	128	0	0	0	0	20	2
dc_object_ids	108	5	0	0	0	104	97

```
TABLE_SPACE
➥READS       BLKS_READ   READ_TIME
WRITES       BLKS_WRT    WRITE_TIME MEGABYTES
-----------------------------------------------------------------------
➥ ---------- ---------- ---------- ----
---- ---------- ---------- ----------
DOGS
➥         0          0          0
0          0          0         10
SYSTEMB
➥       555       1378          0
53         53          0         26
TABLE_SPACE                      FILE_NAME
➥READS       BLKS_READ   READ_TIME
WRITES       BLKS_WRT    WRITE_TIME MEGABYTES
-----------------------------------------------------------------------
➥ ---------- ---------- ---------- ----
---- ---------- ---------- ----------
DOGS                             D:\DATABASE\DOGS1.DBF
➥         0          0          0
0          0          0         10
SYSTEMB                          D:\DATABASE\SYSDOGS.ORA
➥       555       1378          0
53         53          0         26
START_TIME               END_TIME
------------------------ ------------------------
15-jun-97 16:39:39       15-jun-97 16:43:09
```

20

```
BANNER
- - - - - - - - - - - - - - - - - - - - - - - - - - - - - - - - - - - - - - - - - - - -
Oracle8 Server Release 8.0.2.0.2 - Beta
PL/SQL Release 3.0.2.0.2 - Beta
CORE Version 4.0.2.0.1 - Production
TNS for 32-bit Windows: Version 3.0.2.0.0 - Beta
NLSRTL Version 3.3.0.0.1 - Beta
```

 As you can see, a wealth of data collected within Oracle can be retrieved via the UTLBSTAT and UTLESTAT SQL scripts. This data is retrieved mainly from the Oracle V$ views. These views are the window into the Oracle internal performance tables.

 NOTE

> When using a script such as UTLESTAT where the output data is useful, employ the spool option under SVRMGR30. This option copies the onscreen data into a file. If you specify a filename, that name will be used. Use the following syntax:
>
> ```
> SVRMGR> SPOOL stats;
> ```

System Tuning

I like to divide tuning into the following components:

- ☐ Software tuning—This involves both the OS and the RDBMS.
- ☐ Hardware tuning—This includes proper system design and disk layout.
- ☐ Application tuning—This involves properly designing the application and database to take advantage of performance features and planning.

Oracle Tuning

This section focuses on things that can be tuned in the Oracle RDBMS. A complete list of Oracle tuning parameters is given in Appendix B, "Oracle Tuning Parameters."

The SGA

The System Global Area (SGA) contains the shared pool, the redo log buffer, and the database block buffers.

The Shared Pool

The shared pool contains the library cache, the data-dictionary cache, and the shared session area (with the multithreaded server).

The Library Cache

The library cache contains the shared SQL and PL/SQL areas. You can improve performance by increasing the cache-hit rate in the library cache and by speeding access to the library cache by holding infrequently used SQL statements in cache longer.

The V$LIBRARYCACHE table contains statistics about how well you are using the library cache. The important columns to view in this table are PINS and RELOADS:

- ☐ PINS—The number of times the item in the library cache was executed.
- ☐ RELOADS—The number of times the library cache missed and the library object was reloaded.

A small number of reloads relative to the number of executions indicates a high cache-hit rate.

The Data-Dictionary Cache

The data-dictionary cache contains a set of tables and views that Oracle uses as a reference to the database. Here Oracle stores information about the logical and physical structure of the database.

To check the efficiency of the data-dictionary cache, check the cache-hit rate. Statistics for the data-dictionary cache are stored in the dynamic performance table V$ROWCACHE (the data-dictionary cache is sometimes known as the *row cache*). The important columns to view in this table are GETS and GETMISSES:

- ☐ GETS—The total number of requests for the particular item.
- ☐ GETMISSES—The total number of requests resulting in cache misses.

To determine your cache-hit ratio, use the following SQL statement or look at PINHITRATIO in the output of UTLESTAT:

```
SELECT SUM(reloads) "Cache Misses",
SUM(pints) "Executions",
100 * (SUM(reloads) / SUM(pins) ) "Cache Miss Percent"
FROMB V$librarycache;
```

This will show you the cache-miss percent:

```
Cache Hit % = 100% - Cache Miss %
```

A low number of cache misses is expected, especially during startup when the cache has not been populated.

Shared Session Information

In a multithreaded server configuration, the session information is also stored in the shared pool. This information includes the private SQL areas as well as sort areas. Ensure that you do not run out of memory for this shared session information.

20

To determine whether you need to increase space for these shared sessions, you can extract the sum of memory allocated for all sessions and the maximum amount of memory allocated for sessions from the dynamic performance table V$SESSTAT. If the maximum amount of memory used is high, it might be necessary to increase the size of the shared pool. Because the shared pool is used for other functions as well, such as the library cache and the data-dictionary cache, it is a good idea to increase the size of the shared pool to accommodate this additional memory usage. If you have enough memory in your system, increase the shared pool by the maximum amount of memory used by the shared server processes; if you have a limited amount of memory, use the sum of memory allocated to sessions that was obtained when an average number of users was connected and running as a basis for the amount of memory by which to increase the shared pool.

Database Block Buffer Cache

The most important Oracle cache in the system is probably the buffer cache. The buffer cache makes up the majority of the Oracle SGA and is used for every query and update in the system. The statistics for the buffer cache are kept in the dynamic performance table V$SYSSTAT and are included in the output from UTLESTAT. The important columns to view in this table are listed here:

☐ PHYSICAL READS—This indicates the total number of requests that result in a disk access. This is a cache miss.

☐ DB BLOCK GETS—This indicates the number of requests for blocks in current mode. Buffers are typically retrieved in current mode for INSERT, UPDATE, and DELETE statements.

☐ CONSISTENT GETS—This indicates the number of requests for blocks in consistent mode. Buffers are typically retrieved in consistent mode for queries.

The sum of the values in DB BLOCK GETS and CONSISTENT GETS represents the total number of requests for data. The cache-hit ratio is determined using this formula:

Cache-hit ratio = 1 − (PHYSICAL READS / (DB BLOCK GETS + CONSISTENT GETS))

The block buffers are the most important area of the SGA and must be tuned because of the large effect they have on the system and the number of resources they consume.

Performance Enhancements

I prefer to separate the performance-enhancement options from the general tuning of Oracle. Performance enhancements tend to be things that might or might not help your configuration and application; in fact, they might hurt. On the other hand, tuning parameters always help, based on the correct interpretation of Oracle statistics. The following sections review a few of the enhancements you have seen throughout the book.

20

Block Size

Depending on your configuration and data-access patterns, you might be able to benefit from using a larger block size. With a larger block size, you get the benefit of less wasted space and more efficient I/O in certain conditions. Here are a few guidelines that might help you decide whether changing the size of DB_BLOCK_SIZE can help you:

☐ OLTP systems benefit from smaller blocks—If your application is OLTP in nature, you will not benefit from larger blocks. OLTP data typically fits well in the default block size; larger blocks unnecessarily eject blocks from the SGA.

☐ DSS systems benefit from larger blocks—In the DSS system in which table scans are common, retrieving more data at a time results in a performance increase.

☐ Larger databases benefit from larger blocks—Larger databases see a space benefit from less wastage per block.

☐ Databases with large rows benefit from larger blocks—If your rows are extremely large (as is sometimes the case with images or text) and don't fit in the default block, you will see a definite benefit from a larger block size.

Because unnecessarily changing the block size increases I/O overhead, this change *does* carry some risk. Change the block size with caution.

Clusters

NEW TERM   A *cluster*, sometimes called an *index cluster*, is an optional method of storing tables in an Oracle database. Within a cluster, multiple related tables are stored together to improve access time to the related items. Clusters are useful in cases where related data is often accessed together. The existence of a cluster is transparent to users and applications; the cluster affects only how data is stored.

A cluster can be useful for tables in which data is primarily accessed together in a join. In such situations, the reduced I/O needed to bring the additional data into the SGA and the fact that the data is already cached can be a big advantage. However, for situations in which the tables have a large number of INSERT statements or the data is not frequently accessed together, a cluster is not useful and should not be used. Do not cluster tables if full-table scans are often performed on only one of the tables in the cluster. The additional space required by the cluster and the additional I/O reduces performance.

Reduction of Fragmentation

NEW TERM   *Fragmentation* occurs when pieces of the database are no longer contiguous. Fragmentation can consist of *disk fragmentation* or *tablespace fragmentation*. Both of these types of fragmentation usually affect performance. Disk fragmentation usually causes multiple I/Os to occur when one I/O would have been sufficient (for example, with chained or migrated rows). Disk fragmentation can occur when the extents that comprise the database segments are noncontiguous; this is sometimes caused by excessive dynamic growth.

20

Tablespace fragmentation is caused by the dropping and creating of segments. This can produce large free areas between segments, which results in the inefficient use of space and excessive disk seeks over the empty areas. Tablespace fragmentation can also prevent Oracle from taking advantage of multiblock reads.

One way to eliminate fragmentation is to export the table or tablespace data, remove and re-create the table or tablespace, and import the data. By eliminating fragmentation, you can reduce excessive I/Os and CPU usage, streamlining data access. Any overhead and unnecessary I/Os you can reduce will improve system performance.

Hash Clusters

New Term   A *hash cluster* is similar to a cluster except that it uses a hash function rather than an index to reference the cluster key. A hash cluster stores the data based on the result of a hash function. The hash function is a numeric function that determines the data block in the cluster based on the value of the cluster key. To achieve good performance from a hash cluster, you must meet the following criteria:

☐ The cluster key value must be unique.

☐ The majority of queries must be equality queries on the cluster key.

☐ The size of the table must be static (little growth occurs).

☐ The value of the cluster key must not change.

If you can take advantage of hashing by meeting this strict criteria, you will see good performance. Hashing is extremely efficient under the right conditions; however, having a hash cluster under the wrong conditions can degrade performance.

Indexes

New Term   An *index*, like the index in this book, is an optional structure designed to help you achieve faster access to your data. When optimally configured and used, indexes can significantly reduce I/O to the datafiles and greatly improve performance. You must first decide whether an index is appropriate for the data and access patterns in your particular system. Having decided to use an index, you must decide which columns to index. Indexing appropriately can greatly improve performance by reducing I/Os and speeding access times.

Careful planning and periodic testing with SQL Trace can lead to the effective use of indexes, with optimal performance being the outcome. Even though indexes have been built on tables in your database, they might not necessarily be used. If the SQL statement is not correctly formed, the index might be bypassed and a full-table scan might be the result. This is why the application developer and the system designer must communicate constantly throughout the development and deployment cycle. The application should be tested and the SQL statements analyzed to ensure that indexes are being used where intended. Indexes are covered in detail on Day 13, "Using Indexes and Sequences."

Multiblock Reads

When performing table scans, Oracle can read more than one block at a time, thus speeding I/Os. Consequently, a larger chunk of data can be read from the disk, thus eliminating some disk seeks. The reduction of disk seeks and the reading of larger blocks reduces both I/O and CPU overhead.

The amount of data read in a multiblock read is specified by the Oracle initialization parameter DB_FILE_MULTIBLOCK_READ_COUNT. The value for this parameter should always be set high because there is rarely any disadvantage in doing so. The size of the individual I/O requests depends on DB_FILE_MULTIBLOCK_READ_COUNT and DB_BLOCK_SIZE. A good value for multiblock reads is 64KB.

Multiblock Writes

Multiblock writes are similar to multiblock reads and have many of the same requirements. Multiblock writes are available through the direct path loader as well as through sorts and index creations. As with multiblock reads, the multiblock writes reduce I/O and CPU overhead by writing multiple database blocks in one larger I/O operation.

The amount of data written in a multiblock write is specified by the Oracle initialization parameter DB_FILE_MULTIBLOCK_WRITE_COUNT. The size of the individual I/O requests depends on both DB_FILE_MULTIBLOCK_WRITE_COUNT and DB_BLOCK_SIZE. As with multiblock reads, a good value is 64KB.

The Oracle Parallel Query Option

The Oracle Parallel Query option makes it possible for some Oracle functions to be processed by multiple server processes. The functions affected are queries, index creation, data loading, and recovery. For each of these functions, the general principle is the same: Keep processing while Oracle waits for I/O.

For most queries, the time spent waiting for the data to be retrieved from disk usually overshadows the amount of time actually spent processing the results. With the Parallel Query option, you can compensate for this wasted time by using several server processes to execute the query. While one process is waiting for I/Os to complete, other processes can execute. If you are running on a Symmetric Multiprocessor (SMP) computer, a cluster, or a Massively Parallel Processing (MPP) machine, you can take maximum advantage of the Parallel Query option. The amount of parallelism can be tuned with several of the Oracle initialization parameters:

☐ PARALLEL_DEFAULT_MAX_SCANS—This parameter specifies the maximum number of query servers to used by default for a query. This valued is used only if no value is specified in a PARALLEL hint or in the PARALLEL definition clause. This parameter limits the number of query servers used by default when the value of the PARALLEL_DEFAULT_SCANSIZE is used by the query coordinator.

20

- `PARALLEL_DEFAULT_SCANSIZE`—This parameter specifies the number of query servers to be used for a particular table. The size of the table divided by `PARALLEL_DEFAULT_SCANSIZE` determines the number of query servers, up to `PARALLEL_DEFAULT_MAX_SCANS`.

- `PARALLEL_MAX_SERVERS`—This parameter specifies the maximum number of query servers or parallel recovery processes available for this instance.

- `RECOVERY_PARALLELISM`—This parameter specifies the number of processes to be used for instance or media recovery. A large value can greatly reduce instance recovery time. A value of 0 or 1 indicates that parallel recovery will not be performed and that recovery will be serial. A good value for this parameter is in the range of the number of disks you have (up to 50).

I am a big fan of the Parallel Query option. I have seen great improvements from the use of parallel queries as well as dramatic reductions in recovery time when the parallel recovery feature is used. You saw this in yesterday's lesson, "Advanced Oracle Options."

The Oracle Parallel Server Option

The Oracle Parallel Server option is one of the most innovative and impressive options available from Oracle. With the Parallel Server option, you can cluster several computers using a shared-disk subsystem and have multiple Oracle instances access the same database. If your application is suitable, you can see good scalability from adding computers.

The Oracle Parallel Server option uses a sophisticated locking mechanism in conjunction with a shared-disk subsystem to allow multiple instances to access the same data. If you have an application that can take advantage of the Oracle parallel server architecture, you should see some good performance improvements.

The two areas that can most influence the performance of your parallel server system are data partitioning and PCM lock management. Both of these can make a huge difference in the performance of your system.

- Partitioning—By properly partitioning your data to reduce lock traffic and contention for blocks between servers, you can enhance performance. Try to balance your users so that the users accessing the same tables are on the same machine; doing so can reduce contention for locks.

- PCM locks—By carefully managing the number of locks on each table, you can enhance performance. Tables with a lot of traffic between nodes should have more locks than tables with less contention. By balancing the number of locks, you can reduce overhead.

TIP

By taking advantage of read-only tablespaces where applicable, you can reduce the number of PCM locks in your system. Because read-only tablespaces do not allow updates, no locking is necessary.

Spin Counts

Multiprocessor environments might benefit from tuning of the parameter SPIN_COUNT. Under normal circumstances, if a latch is not available, the process sleeps and then wakes up to try the latch again. If you are on a multiprocessor system, it is likely that the process holding the latch is currently processing on another CPU and will be finished in a short time. If you set SPIN_COUNT to a value greater than 0, the process spins while counting down from SPIN_COUNT to 0. If the latch is still not available, the process goes to sleep.

Setting SPIN_COUNT can hurt performance if you're not careful. This parameter should be set only for multiprocessor computers and should be monitored for effectiveness. A good value to try is 2,000. The value of SPIN_COUNT specifies how many times the process will spin before putting itself to sleep. Because the speed of processors varies, the time it takes to spin also varies; however, the speed of the process holding the desired resource will also vary with the speed of the processor.

OS Tuning

OS tuning is specific and depends on the OS you are running. I will present some of the basics on tuning Windows NT and UNIX here.

NT Tuning Considerations

With Windows NT, probably the most important tuning consideration is ensuring that sufficient physical memory is available to run Oracle and the required number of server processes. Windows NT uses virtual memory, which means that Oracle and user processes can allocate an almost unlimited amount of memory through paging. If you are not careful, you might overconfigure the amount of virtual memory that you are using and exceed the amount of physical memory in the system. If this occurs, the system will begin paging and performance will be severely degraded.

In addition to the concern about memory, other areas of importance in tuning the Windows NT system include the network and I/O subsystems and the reduction in OS overhead.

Memory

Windows NT uses only virtual memory. Because of this, all memory in the system is treated equally, limited only by the size of the paging file; you must be wary of user processes consuming large amounts of memory and causing paging out the SGA. In Windows NT, there are no limitations on memory used for user processes, disk caching, print caching, and so on; thus, it is best to dedicate the Windows NT server to either file and print services or to application services.

20

> **NOTE**
>
> The amount of virtual memory with Windows NT is limited by the size of the paging file. If the paging file is too small, you will get warning messages and be forced to resize it and reboot.
>
> The size of one process's virtual memory, also known as the working set size, is limited to 2GB under Windows NT 4.0 and earlier, and 3GB with the Windows NT Enterprise Edition.

If you use asynchronous I/O (AIO) and Oracle can lock down memory for AIO, the database block buffers are not swappable. Monitor the system on a regular basis to ensure that no paging is occurring in the system.

Reduce Unnecessary Memory Usage

You can take some measures to reduce the amount of memory used by Windows NT. Invoke the Control Panel's Network Settings screen and choose the Maximize Throughput for Network Applications option. This optimizes the server memory for network applications, reducing some of the file-system caching and overhead in memory management. Also remove any network protocols not needed by the system to cut down on system overhead and memory usage via the Control Panel.

Also use the Control Panel to turn off any services you are not using. Doing so reduces memory usage and CPU overhead. By reducing all the unnecessary services, you can increase the performance of the system.

SGA Tuning

To maximize performance, allocate as much memory as possible to the SGA. Use the techniques discussed on Days 9, "Managing Data," and 10, "Administering User Accounts," to determine whether the memory can best be used for the shared pool or for database block buffers. Because the SGA resides in virtual memory, it is important that you not allocate so much memory for the SGA that the system pages. The overhead of paging and swapping overshadows any benefit you might gain from a larger SGA. Remember to save memory for the user processes. You should frequently monitor your system to ensure that no paging occurs at any time.

User Capacity

You can easily determine the amount of memory necessary for your application on a per-user basis. Start Oracle and note the amount of available memory by using the Windows NT Performance Monitor. Monitor the Available Bytes option under Memory in the Performance Monitor. After users begin accessing the application in a typical manner, record the amount of memory again. Take the difference and divide this result by the number of users accessing the application. Multiply this per-user memory usage value by the maximum number of users who might be connected to the application to determine the amount of memory you must reserve for user connections. Be sure to add a little extra memory just in case. Be careful that a user's PGA does not consume too much system memory.

To increase the number of Oracle connections, you might also have to adjust the Oracle initialization parameter PROCESSES. This parameter should reflect the maximum number of user connections you expect to have plus the Oracle background processes. You should also include some extra processes for administrative tasks.

Network

Minimal network tuning is necessary with Windows NT. However, you can enhance performance by prioritizing the network bindings. Do so the with the Control Panel's Network Configuration utility. If you put the network protocol you use most frequently first on the list, that protocol gets highest priority. Place other network protocols in the list in the order in which you use them. Removing any protocols you do not use can also boost performance by reducing memory consumption and CPU overhead. Also be sure that the system is configured as a *server* in the Network Configuration screen.

I/O Subsystem

It is important that performance not be bound by physical I/O rates. If you ensure that the system disks are not driven past their limits, you can avoid this. This is covered in detail on Days 14, "Using Oracle Clusters, Stored Procedures, and Database Links," and 15, "Managing Job Queues and Using Oracle Auditing."

With Windows NT, asynchronous I/O (AIO) is always enabled. There is no need to adjust any tuning parameters to ensure that AIO is enabled.

The default block size for Oracle on Windows NT is 2,048. This might be sufficient. If you have a large database or if the data access is primarily sequential, you might want to increase DB_BLOCK_SIZE to 4,096. Although the data blocks take up more space in the SGA, the number of I/Os performed is significantly reduced. It doesn't take much more overhead and time to retrieve 4KB of data from the disks than it does to get 2KB of data.

If data access is primarily sequential, you might benefit by setting the DB_BLOCK_SIZE parameter to 8,192. Because sequential access to the database will read the next block anyway, larger block sizes will read that data into the SGA before you need it. If your data access is random, you will waste space in the SGA. The value you choose for the block size affects performance either for better or worse. If you are unsure, leave the parameter at the default of 2,048.

When creating Windows NT file systems, you have several choices:

- ☐ FAT
- ☐ HPFS
- ☐ NTFS

20

Although each of these performs well in certain situations, I recommend using NTFS. NTFS provides you with the best level of overall performance and is the file system that Microsoft endorses.

UNIX Tuning Considerations

As is true for NT and UNIX, the most important tuning consideration is ensuring that sufficient memory is available to run Oracle and the required number of server processes. Because UNIX is a virtual memory operating system, you can always start more server processes; but if you are not careful, you might begin paging.

Many varieties of UNIX have made available extended features such as the Post-Wait Semaphore and asynchronous I/O to enhance Oracle performance. Other areas of importance in tuning the UNIX system include the network and I/O subsystem.

Memory

Memory is important in the UNIX operating system. As you have seen in earlier lessons, the way to increase performance is to maximize the use of the SGA to avoid costly disk I/Os. In UNIX as in all operating systems, it is important to avoid paging. Because the SGA is in shared memory in UNIX, the SGA is guaranteed not to page—but the server processes can page if too much memory is being used.

It is important to allocate enough shared memory to accommodate the SGA. If you do not have enough memory to create the SGA, the instance does not start. If this happens, you must either configure the operating system to allow more shared memory or reduce the size of the SGA. If you are using enhanced 4MB shared memory pages, you can allocate the amount of shared memory only in 4MB units.

Be careful not to allocate so much shared memory for the SGA that user and server processes page. Be sure to periodically monitor the system to ensure that no paging is occurring. To maximize memory used by the SGA, reduce all unnecessary memory used by the operating system and limit the amount of memory that can be allocated by users.

Reduce Unnecessary Memory Usage

One of the best ways to free memory for Oracle is to siphon from memory used by the file-system buffers. These buffers are used by the OS to cache data. A significant performance increase can incur when files that have been cached are accessed. But Oracle uses a feature called *synchronous I/O* to ensure that writes to the disk are not returned until the data has actually been written. Because Oracle must guarantee that I/Os have been written to the disk to ensure data integrity, OS disk write caching cannot be performed.

By default, the number of file-system buffers is determined by the amount of memory in the system. Because Oracle bypasses the disk cache on writes and uses the SGA for reads, you don't really need a large number of file-system buffers. By reducing this number, you might see a slight performance decrease with OS operations, but any additional memory allocated to the SGA increases Oracle performance. The parameters used to tune the file-system buffers is fairly vendor dependent; this should be documented in your OS manuals.

If you reduce the unnecessary memory used for disk caching, more memory can be allocated to the SGA. Don't reduce the disk cache so far that it is difficult to run OS commands and access Oracle parameter files. Do not set the disk cache buffers to less than 600. These values represent the number of 512 byte blocks.

SGA Tuning

To maximize performance, allocate as much memory as possible to the SGA. Use the techniques discussed earlier today to determine whether memory is best used for the shared pool or for databases block buffers.

In UNIX, the shared memory area used by Oracle for the SGA is usually contiguous. However, if you have multiple instances of Oracle that have started and stopped several times, the shared memory area might no longer be contiguous. If you use 4MB pages, you are guaranteed to have at least 4MB of contiguous memory.

The amount of memory allocated for shared memory is the product of two OS-tunable parameters: SHMMAX and SHMSEG. SHMMAX specifies the maximum size of a shared memory segment; SHMSEG specifies the maximum number of shared memory segments available in the system. Applications are responsible for allocating only the amount of shared memory they need and so do not waste space. In SCO UNIX and UnixWare, the parameters SHMMAX and SHMSEG are located in the UNIX parameter file /ETC/CONF/CF.D/STUNE. In Solaris, the shared memory parameters are set in the file /ETC/SYSTEM. Your OS administrator's manual should have more information about setting system parameters.

NOTE	It is much more efficient for Oracle to have one large shared memory segment than several smaller ones. Therefore, SHMMAX should have a value larger than the size of the SGA.

Most varieties of UNIX that run on the Intel platform have a variety of 4MB pages. By referencing your OS vendor-specific documentation, you can determine how to tune this.

The use of 4MB pages can improve performance dramatically, especially if you are running on an Intel Pentium processor.

> **NOTE**
>
> In UNIX implementations that use 4MB pages, there is usually a threshold at which 4MB pages are used. This threshold is approximately 3MB. If you allocate a 2.5MB shared memory segment, you do not get a 4MB page.

The amount of memory allocated to a single user must also be tuned in the UNIX operating system. Because Oracle is treated the same as any other user, you must allocate enough memory for Oracle to use for the SGA and the server processes. By referencing your OS-specific documentation, you can see how to configure this.

Ensure that sufficient memory is available so that Oracle can allocate for the SGA. Remember to save memory for the user processes as well. You should frequently monitor your system to ensure that no paging is occurring at any time.

User Capacity

You can easily determine the amount of memory necessary for your application on a per-user basis. Start Oracle and note the amount of available memory available with the UNIX utility sar -r. The output from sar -r consists of freemem (free memory pages) and freeswp (free swap pages). The value given in the freemem column is the number of 4KB pages available. When users begin accessing the application in a typical manner, record the amount of memory again. Take the difference and divide this result by the number of users accessing the application. This value is the per-user memory usage. Multiply this value by the maximum number of users who might connect to the application to determine the amount of memory you must reserve for user connections. Be sure to leave a little extra memory just in case.

The size of a user's PGA is not bound by any initialization parameters. Because of this, be careful that a user's PGA does not consume too much system memory.

The UNIX operating system parameters MAXUP and NPROC must also be set to allow a sufficient number of users to connect. Remember that when users connect to Oracle, an Oracle shadow process is created under the Oracle user ID. Therefore, you must increase not only the number of processes systemwide, but also the per-user process limits.

The per-user process limit is set with the OS parameter MAXUP. The maximum number of processes systemwide is set by the OS parameter NPROC. Both values are in the stune file. NPROC should be at least 50 greater than MAXUP to account for OS processes.

To increase the number of Oracle connections, you might also have to adjust the Oracle initialization parameter PROCESSES. The PROCESSES parameter should reflect the maximum number of user connections you expect to have plus the Oracle background processes. You should also include some extra processes for administrative tasks.

Network

With UNIX, the amount of network tuning is usually minimal. Typically, no network tuning is required, and the network tuning that is required is vendor specific. Refer to your OS documentation for any networking tuning that is required.

I/O Subsystem

As with all other operating systems described today, it is important to ensure that performance is not bound by physical I/O rates. Be sure that random I/Os do not exceed the physical limitations of the disk drives. Refer to Days 14 and 15 for details.

With UNIX, you have the choice of using the UNIX file system for your data storage or the RAW device interface. This choice is not always an easy one. The RAW device interface is more difficult to manage but provides a higher level of performance. File-system files are much easier to use but have more overhead associated with them.

File System

Using the UNIX file system is easier than using RAW devices. Using file-system files, Oracle simply creates the file. However, when using the file system, Oracle must contend with the UNIX disk-caching system and use synchronous writes to ensure that the write request does not return to the DBWR or LGWR before it has actually written the data to disk. With the UNIX file system, there is also the overhead of the data being read into the UNIX disk cache and then being copied to the SGA. This arrangement causes additional overhead on reads. Finally, when you use the file system, you are not guaranteed to have contiguous blocks on the disk—in fact, you are almost guaranteed not to have contiguous blocks.

RAW Device Interface

The RAW device interface allows for the least amount of overhead you can achieve with UNIX I/Os. When using the RAW device interface, UNIX simply assigns a section of the disk to each RAW device. This portion of the disk is contiguous; accesses to it bypass all disk caching and file-system overhead.

RAW devices are not as easy to manage because each device is considered one big chunk of data for the operating system. Backup and recovery must be handled slightly differently because file copies do not work, and the size of the raw device cannot be changed after it is created. Backup operations must be done via the UNIX DD command or by a third-party backup utility that supports raw devices.

RAW devices give greater performance with less overhead and are fully supported by Oracle. Whether you use RAW devices is a decision you must make based on ease of use and increased performance.

20

Asynchronous I/O

With UNIX, AIO is not always enabled. It is necessary to enable AIO in both the OS and in Oracle. By using AIO, the DBWR can manage many I/Os at once, eliminating the need for multiple DBWR processes. List I/O allows the DBWR to pass to the OS a list of AIO commands, reducing the number of calls it must make.

NOTE

> If asynchronous I/O is not available to you, you can compensate by adding DBWR processes. You should have one or two DBWR processes per data disk. Use the parameter DB_WRITERS to increase the number of DBWR processes.

For some UNIX implementations, the following Oracle initialization parameters for asynchronous I/O should also be set:

- ☐ USE_ASYNC_IO—This parameter tells Oracle that the DBWR should use asynchronous I/O. Set it to TRUE.

- ☐ LGWR_USE_ASYNC_IO—This parameter tells Oracle that the LGWR should use asynchronous I/O. Set it to TRUE.

You should always use asynchronous I/O (if possible). When you use asynchronous I/O, you can keep the number of DBWR processes to one and therefore reduce process overhead.

Hardware Tuning

The I/O system should be designed and implemented with the following goals in mind:

- ☐ Isolate sequential I/O—By isolating sequential I/O so that it is purely sequential to the disk, you can greatly enhance throughput. Any random I/O to these disks degrades performance. Writes to the redo log are sequential.

- ☐ Spread out random I/O—Random I/O performance can be increased by adding more disk drives to the system and spreading out the I/Os among the disks. I/Os to the datafiles are typically random (especially in OLTP systems).

If you follow these guidelines and plan your system so that your disk drives can support the amount of disk I/O demanded of them, I/O should not be a problem.

Application Tuning

One of the most common areas that performance can be enhanced is in the application itself. SQL statements can often be redesigned to dramatically improve performance. I recently worked on a project where one of the engineers redesigned the SQL statements of a set of queries that took more than four hours to run to more effectively use indexes; after the engineer made the changes, the queries took less than 10 minutes to run.

Here are a few things that can be done to improve the application itself. My other book, *Oracle Performance Tuning and Optimization* (Sams Publishing) covers these topics in great detail.

☐ Use EXPLAIN PLAN—By using EXPLAIN PLAN, you can analyze the execution plan the optimizer has chosen for the SQL statement.

☐ Use SQL*Trace—By using SQL*Trace, you can analyze the execution of the SQL statement and determine any potential bottlenecks.

☐ Tune SQL statements—You can improve performance by configuring SQL statements to take advantage of such things as indexes, clusters, and hash clusters.

☐ Use the Oracle optimizer—Take advantage of the optimizer to improve performance.

☐ Use procedures and packages—Use procedures, functions, and packages to improve performance.

☐ Provide for data integrity—Consider the importance of data integrity and how to optimally provide for it.

☐ Use hints—Use hints to take advantage of information you know about the data and application.

If you tune the SQL statements and application to take advantage of indexes, clusters, and other features, you should see significant improvement in performance.

Summary

Today you looked at various ways of determining whether some sort of performance bottleneck exists, and if one does, how to isolate that bottleneck and provide solutions. The lesson began by defining the term *bottleneck*. You were also presented with my performance tuning methodology. If you follow these steps (or steps of your own), you should be able to find the bottleneck or at least find a way to work around it.

Today's lesson also provided a brief overview into the operation and function of your OS. Next, you saw a way of looking at the system in terms of performance. How you monitor the system was also shown today. Much can be learned from the NT Performance Monitor and sar, and much can be learned from Oracle itself using UTLBSTAT and UTLESTAT. With these tools, you can narrow the focus of your performance investigations and determine potential changes to your system.

What's Next?

Tomorrow's lesson is the last of the 21 days of instruction on the ins and outs of Oracle8. This book finishes up by teaching you the specifics of the Oracle8 networking system. You will learn how to configure SQL*Net and use the Oracle Name Server. Also, you will learn how to configure and use the Oracle Web server. Other miscellaneous topics will also be covered in the final lesson of the book.

Q&A

Q What is a bottleneck?

A The term *bottleneck* refers to a component in the system that is slowing down the whole system.

Q What type of operating systems are NT and UNIX?

A Windows NT and UNIX are virtual memory operating systems. This means that the memory used by a single process can be larger than the physical memory in the system. When more memory is needed than is available, some of the memory is paged out.

Q What sort of things are important when troubleshooting a performance bottleneck?

A There are many important things to keep in mind, but I feel that of primary importance is that you follow a methodology. By using some sort of method of troubleshooting, you can develop tests that can help you resolve the issues involved.

Q Should you always believe your results?

A No. Be skeptical. If something doesn't seem right, try another test.

Workshop

The workshop provides quiz questions to help you solidify your understanding of the material covered and exercises to provide you with experience in using what you've learned. The answers to the quiz questions can be found in Appendix A, "Answers."

Quiz

1. Name some areas that could be potential bottlenecks.

2. What is the best tool to use to look at the Oracle shared pool, cache-hit ratio?

3. How many random I/Os per second per disk drive are recommended before latencies start to increase?

4. How many sequential I/Os per second per disk drive are recommended before latencies start to increase?

5. What is disk latency?

6. How do you calculate the buffer cache-hit ratio?

7. How do you know whether the shared pool is large enough?

8. What two factors make an index effective?

9. Which is run first: `UTLBSTAT.SQL` or `UTLESTAT.SQL`?

10. Why might you use a large block size?

Exercises

1. Turn on diskperf and reboot your system. Use the Performance Monitor to look at physical disk statistics.

2. Use `UTLBSTAT.SQL` and `UTLESTAT.SQL` and analyze the results.

3. Check out your system's block buffer cache-hit ratio.

4. Determine the cache-hit ratio on your data-dictionary cache and your library cache.

20

Week 3

Day 21

Exploring the Web Publishing Assistant and Network Computing Architecture

In this final lesson of the book, I will teach you about the Oracle8 Web Publishing Assistant, a new product that provides a simple yet very effective method of publishing database information on the World Wide Web. You will learn how to use the Web Publishing Assistant to create Web pages. I'll also introduce you to the new and exciting world of the Oracle Network Computing Architecture (NCA). Finally, you will learn about some of Oracle's products, including the Web Commerce server, the Web Application server, and data cartridges.

The Web Publishing Assistant

The Web Publishing Assistant is a new product with Oracle8 for NT for publishing Web pages. Rather than being a sophisticated system for creating Web pages on the fly, the Web Publishing Assistant is a lightweight, easy-to-use utility for creating Web pages from database data. These Web pages are static but are re-created on a regular basis, so they remain up to date.

Perform the steps that follow to extract data from an Oracle database and create a static Web page. Later you will take steps to instigate the automatic re-creation of this Web page on a regular basis. This allows you to keep Web page information current without having to access that data online.

1. After you invoke the Web Publishing Assistant from the Oracle for Windows NT program group, you will be greeted by the screen shown in Figure 21.1. If you do not wish to see this screen every time you invoke the Web Publishing Assistant, deselect the checkbox at the bottom of the screen.

Figure 21.1.

The initial screen of the Oracle Web Publishing Assistant.

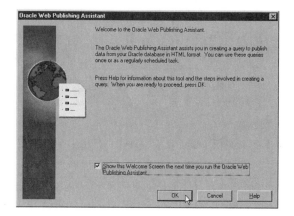

2. After you look at the welcome screen, click the OK button to invoke the main screen of the Web Publishing Assistant (shown in Figure 21.2). This screen shows you what active Web pages you have defined; in this case, you have defined no Web pages, so the screen is blank. After you create a Web page, information about the page and its update frequency will be displayed here. Each Web page created by and under the control of the Web Publishing Assistant will have a line of information here, as you will see later in this section.

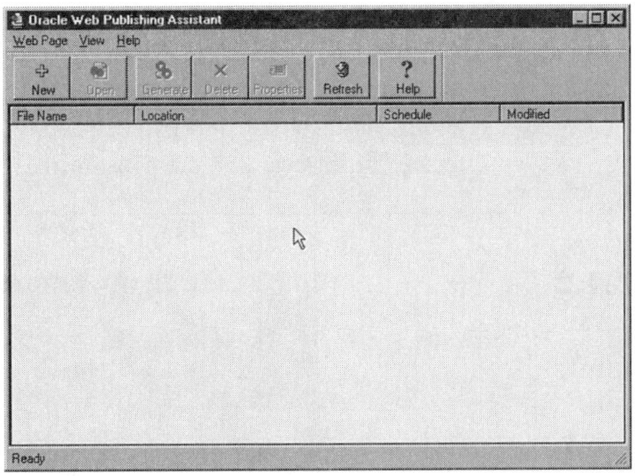

Figure 21.2.

The main screen of Web Publishing Assistant; no Web pages have been created, so none are defined.

3. To create a new Web page within the Web Publishing Assistant, you can use the Create Web Page wizard. This wizard steps you through the process of creating a new Web page. To invoke the wizard, select Web Page | New or click the New button.

4. Regardless of how you invoked the wizard, you will now see the wizard's first screen. Use this screen to define the database connection that will be used to retrieve the data. This screen requires you to enter the following data. These values will be used for the database connection (see Figure 21.3).

   ☐ Username—The username that will be used on all queries to access data for this Web page.

   ☐ Password—The password associated with that username.

   ☐ Database—The name of the database that will be accessed.

NOTE

Access into Oracle is based on username, password, and database (SID). This allows multiple users to create Web pages based on their own access into the Oracle database.

5. Use the second screen to define what data will be displayed on the Web page. This can be an entire table, as shown in Figure 21.4, or a query. Queries are useful if you want to use a join operation to display data from multiple tables. You can also accomplish this by accessing a previously created view. For simplicity, I chose the entire table here.

21

NOTE

> To simplify complex table accesses within the Web Publishing Assistant, you can use other means to create a view into these tables. After the view has been created you can use the Web Publishing Assistant and specify that view as the data source.

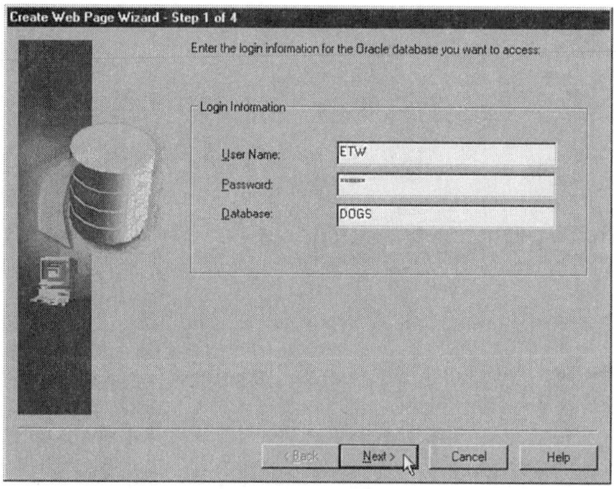

Figure 21.3.

The first screen of the Create Web Page wizard.

Figure 21.4.

The second screen of the Create Web Page wizard.

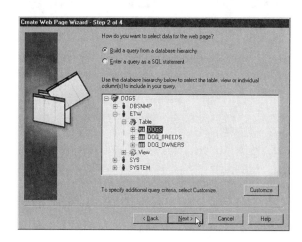

6. The third screen, shown in Figure 21.5, is crucial to the operation of the Web Publishing Assistant: This screen is used to define the schedule of the updates. The Web page will be refreshed from data in the database according to this schedule. The schedule that you choose for each Web page should be based upon the following criteria:

☐ How often the data changes—If the data does not change on a daily basis, it is not necessary to frequently update the Web page.

☐ The required accuracy of the data—If this data must always be up to date, the Web Publishing Assistant must refresh that data often. The Web page itself does not automatically identify its refresh time, but you can easily add that information.

Figure 21.5.

The third screen of the Create Web Page wizard.

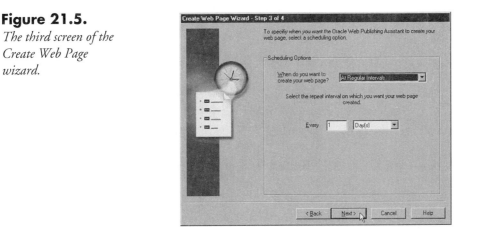

7. The final screen, shown in Figure 21.6, allows you to define the name of the Web page to be created as well as the formatting information. After you create a few pages, you might find you are dissatisfied with the default formatting and want to add your own. Feel free to customize the HTML code to meet your needs.

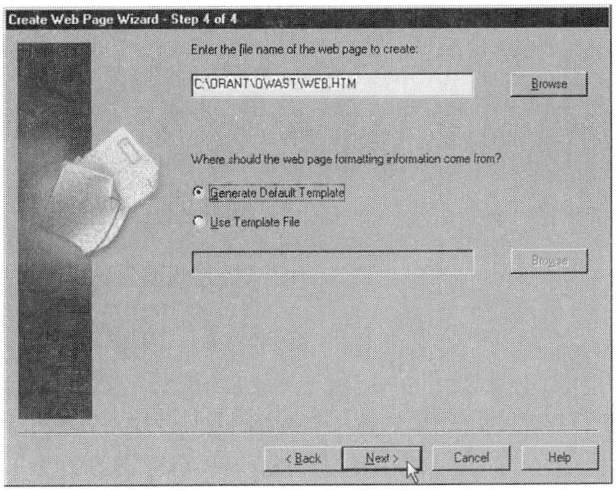

Figure 21.6.

The final screen of the Create Web Page wizard.

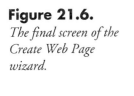

21

8. As with all of the Oracle tools, you are provided with a screen that summarizes the actions taken (see Figure 21.7). However, this step is redundant because scheduling has already occurred and the page has been created.

Figure 21.7.

Summary of the actions taken by the Create Web Page wizard.

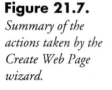

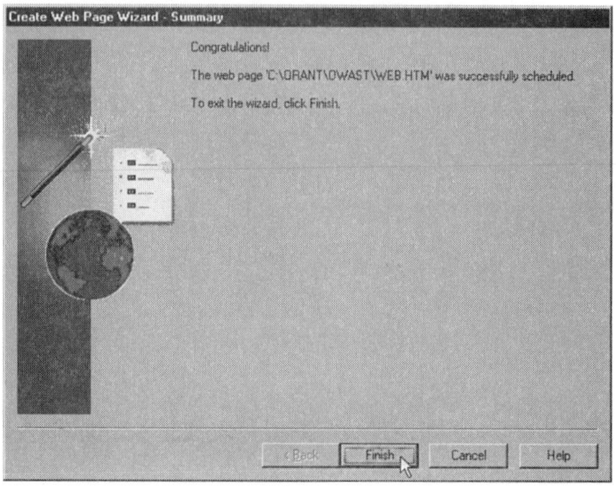

9. As shown in Figure 21.8, the main screen now shows information about the Web page that was created in the Create Web Page wizard. You can modify or delete this Web page from this screen. You can also refresh the Web page by clicking the Generate button.

Figure 21.8.

The main page of the Web Publishing Assistant; note that the new Web page appears on this screen.

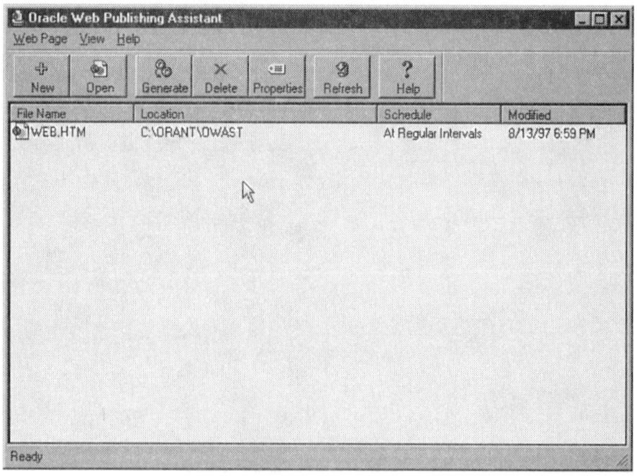

10. This new Web page can be added to the path that your Web server uses. You can even add graphics to the page, as shown in Figure 21.9.

Figure 21.9.

The Web page created by the Web Publishing Assistant. Note the added graphics.

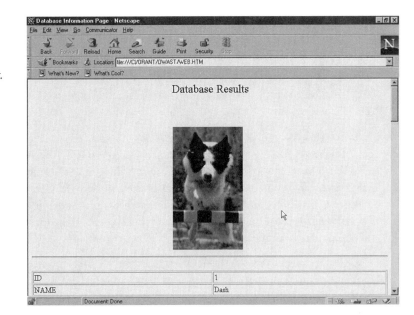

I think the Web Publishing Assistant is straightforward, easy to use, and quite effective. You simply rebuild a Web page on a regular basis from data in the database. You can modify the refresh rate and Web page template to suit your needs.

The Network Computing Architecture

The Network Computing Architecture (NCA) is a framework developed in part by Oracle for network computing. The NCA can be used to define applications that can be run either over the Internet or an intranet.

The NCA is a common set of technologies and products designed to help all systems work more closely together. The NCA's purpose is to join database servers, application servers, and Web servers under a common architecture, open to all vendors, that applications can use to communicate with each other.

The NCA consists of many different components, and in this lesson I provide brief overviews of several. Some of these components consist of the standards that make up the NCA such as CORBA 2.0 and HTTP/HTML. Other components consist programming languages such as Java. Still other components consist of distributed objects, data cartridges, thin clients, and so on.

21

NCA Standards

The NCA is based on open standards that are available to all vendors. These standards allow independent programs to work together and to fit into the architecture regardless of who developed them. The main standards that the NCA employs are CORBA 2.0 and HTTP/HTML. Due to the development of a standards-based architecture, all vendors have an equal chance of developing high-quality applications; no vendor receives special advantages.

CORBA 2.0

The Common Object Request Broker Architecture (CORBA) standard is a specification developed by a consortium called the Object Management Group (OMG), which is made up of over 600 companies from all areas of the computer industry. The CORBA standard defines a distributed architecture with an open communication channel between objects. When vendors program to this communication channel, their application can communicate and exchange information with other CORBA-compliant applications.

TCP/IP has been defined as the network-transport protocol for intersystem communication. For communication between different systems, an Internet Object Request Broker has been defined. This Internet Object Request Broker uses TCP/IP as its transport layer. If one adheres to these standards, intersystem and inter-OS communication is possible.

HTTP/HTML

The Hypertext Transport Protocol (HTTP) defines today's World Wide Web. This standard allows Web browsers to communicate with Web servers. This protocol, in conjunction with the Hypertext Markup Language (HTML), is what makes Web browsers work.

HTTP is the specification that defines the communication between servers and browsers. This specification is freely available to all vendors; indeed, it is freely available via the World Wide Web. Simply go to your favorite search engine and search for HTTP.

HTML is the language used to define Web pages. If you look at the source code of a Web page, you will see the HTML code that builds that page.

Web browsers use HTTP to communicate and HTML to define what they will be displaying on the Web page. It is necessary for both of these components to exist for you to properly receive and display World Wide Web information.

NCA Components

The NCA is made up of various components that work together to form the architecture. These components include

- [ ] NCA-compliant applications—These are what the end user sees, and include Web browsers, NCA cartridges, and the Oracle Universal Server.
- [ ] Cartridges—These pluggable objects provide specific extensible functionality.

☐ Protocols—These make up the core of the NCA and allow cartridges to exchange information via the Inter-Cartridge Exchange (ICX).

Applications

Applications are the most visible part of the NCA because they are what you, the end user or developer, will work with. The applications that comprise the NCA include but are not limited to the following:

☐ Application servers

☐ Database servers

☐ Extensible clients

These components have one goal: to deliver information to the user. This delivery of information can occur regardless of the operating system of the client or server, and regardless of the brand of Web browser you use, as long as these components meet the specification.

Application Servers

The application server is one of the NCA's key components. An application server is essentially a Web server that supports application cartridges for HTTP/HTML-based programs. You can think of application servers as controlling the application. Application servers, in conjunction with the database servers, provide the application code and data that end-users need and want.

Database Servers

The Oracle Universal Server provides the performance and scalable data storage that today's applications demand. With the advent of the NCA, the Universal Server has been extended to provide many new data types to accommodate the type of corporate data used today. These new data types include

☐ Video

☐ Audio

☐ Text

☐ Spatial data

These data types, in conjunction with traditional data types, provide a full spectrum of information to the user.

Clients

Web clients have become fairly standard, but tremendous competition remains as new technologies develop every day. What is important is that along with any proprietary components added to the Web browser, the core standards such as HTML and Java are available. In this way you can develop applications that adhere to these standards without worrying about whether they'll work on certain systems.

I prefer to program to the lowest common denominator by not using proprietary extensions. If you do the same, your application will work on a variety of platforms without requiring major rewriting of code.

The Network Computer

Oracle and others are working on a new type of system called the Network Computer (NC), which is essentially a thin client or Internet Web browser in a box. The NC is very inexpensive and has the advantage of no operating system and no disk drive. Having no OS and no disk drive means that there are fewer parts to break. The component of a computer system that is most likely to fail is the disk drive because disk drives are mechanical and will eventually wear out.

I think the NC will supplement, not supersede, the PC. There are many circumstances where a PC and its local storage are not required, and the NC will work well in those cases. For example, to provide Web access to guests in a hotel, you would not want to place PCs in every room. With a PC you would have to reformat the disk and reload the OS after each guest departed to guarantee that the he or she did not leave any information on the system. Other examples of circumstances where NCs would work nicely include any places where a traditional terminal is in use and more data access is necessary, such as

☐ Airline terminals—At ticket gates, most airlines still use terminals. Replacing them with NCs is practical because no local storage is needed and PCs would require a lot of maintenance. All application access is to the main server, not a local database, so an NC would be ideal.

☐ Phone booths—Replacing traditional phones with phones that allow Web access for e-mail or directory information would be great.

☐ Retail stores—You could replace traditional cash registers with NC registers. Information such as inventory in other stores and product descriptions (with graphics) could be added.

☐ Schools—Instead of placing expensive PCs in classrooms, NCs could be used. This would allow each student to access the Internet, which is a goal of Larry Ellison's "Dream for America."

☐ Large corporations—Many large corporations do not need each user to have his own personal data storage and an expensive PC. The use of NCs would provide low-cost access to all corporate applications and data.

Cartridges

Cartridges are plug-in applications that are typically specific to a single application. You can provide a wide range of applications by installing several different cartridges that can work together.

Think of a cartridge as an object that might serve one or more purposes. This object uses an Interface Definition Language (IDL) that allows it to identify itself to other objects in a distributed system. A cartridge can be written in a variety of languages, such as Java, Visual Basic, C++, SQL, and so on.

The cartridge itself also uses a software bus called the Inter-Cartridge Exchange (ICX). ICX allows cartridges that are part of a distributed system to communicate with each other. With ICX, a cartridge can communicate with other cartridges, clients, servers, database servers, and so on.

Protocols

Other key components of the NCA are the components and standards that comprise it, such as TCP/IP, HTML/HTTP, and CORBA 2.0. These were described earlier today in the section on NCA standards.

Summary

Today you learned about the Web Publishing Assistant and were introduced to the Oracle Network Computing Architecture (NCA). The Web Publishing Assistant is a new and innovative product that creates Web pages accessible by whatever Web server you use. These static Web pages are periodically updated by the Web Publishing Assistant. The NCA standard specification is designed to join database servers, application servers, and Web servers under a common architecture to allow common access over a network. This infrastructure is open to all vendors to promote a common architecture that applications can use to communicate with each other. In this lesson you were introduced to the NCA and the components that comprise it, such as CORBA, HTTP/HTML, and Java. The NCA is just getting started; you will hear more and more about it in the next few years.

As you have seen in the past 21 days, the Oracle Server product offers a tremendous amount of information and functionality. The purpose of this book has been to introduce the Oracle8 server. Nonetheless, I have tried to be thorough; there was so much information in many cases that I was required to speak at a more advanced level.

I hope these 21 days gave you the knowledge necessary to perform the functions of an Oracle DBA or an informed user, but book knowledge is no substitute for experience. Your next step is to practice and gain experience as an Oracle8 DBA or user.

What's Next?

Because you have finished reading the book, your next step is to practice what you have learned. I hope you have access to an Oracle8 system and can use Enterprise Manager to build databases, tablespaces, and tables. Try different things to see what new skills you can acquire.

21

If you have problems grasping a function or concept, don't give up. If you persevere, you will eventually understand. Fully understanding each component will serve you well in the long run; most aspects of the Oracle RDBMS build on each other.

Database technology is an exciting field that changes every day; new products and new technologies generate tremendous excitement. So above all, *enjoy.*

Q&A

Q **What is the Web Publishing Assistant used for?**

A The Web Publishing Assistant is used to create static Web pages from database data on a regular basis.

Q **What is the difference between the Web Publishing Assistant and the Oracle Web Application Server?**

A The Oracle Web Publishing Assistant creates static Web pages from database data whereas the Web Application Server dynamically creates Web pages based on database data.

Q **What is the NCA?**

A The NCA, or Network Computing Architecture, is a set of standards that defines how computing over the Internet or an intranet will be conducted in the future.

Q **What is the NC (Network Computer)?**

A The NC is a thin client or computer that is designed to run network applications without using local disk storage or an operating system.

Workshop

The workshop provides quiz questions to help you solidify your understanding of the material covered and exercises to provide you with experience in using what you've learned. For answers to quiz questions, see Appendix A, "Answers."

Quiz

1. What does NCA stand for?
2. What does CORBA stand for?
3. What is HTTP?
4. What is HTML?
5. What is a cartridge?
6. What is a static Web page?

7. What kind of Web pages can you create with the Web Publishing Assistant?

8. What is an NC?

9. What new types of data can the Oracle Universal Server handle?

10. What types of applications would be suitable for an NC?

Exercises

1. Invoke the Web Publishing Assistant.

2. Using the Create Web Page wizard, create a simple Web page.

3. Modify this Web page from the Web Publishing Assistant.

4. Delete the Web page using the Web Publishing Assistant.

21

WEEK 3

15
16
17
18
19
20
21

In Review

During week 3, you learned more about the tasks required of the Oracle administrator and finished learning about the structure of the data itself. You learned about the management of user accounts, Oracle processes, security, backup and recovery, and tuning.

Oracle Security

Day 15 covers various topics relating to Oracle security matters. One of the most common tasks of the Oracle DBA is the administration of users and security. Also covered here is the use of Oracle auditing.

Backup and Recovery

Days 16–18 cover the most important responsibility that the Oracle DBA has: the development and implementation of a backup plan. An effective backup and recovery plan can save your company millions of dollars in the event of a system failure. Also covered in this section are other methods of quick recovery such as the Oracle standby database, the use of replication for quick recovery, and the use of backup images.

Advanced Topics

Days 19–21 cover more advanced topics such as the use of the Oracle parallel server. Also included is a lesson on Oracle optimization and performance tuning. The book concludes with a lesson about using the Oracle Web Publishing Assistant and an overview of the Oracle Network Computing Architecture (NCA).

I hope these 21 days gave you the knowledge you need to perform the functions of an Oracle database administrator or an informed user. Any amount of knowledge is no substitute for experience. Your next step is to practice and gain experience as an Oracle8 DBA or user. Welcome to the exciting and demanding world of the Oracle database administrator!

APPENDIX A

Answers

Day 1: "Starting Out with Oracle"

1. A DBMS (Database Management System) consists of the program and utilities used to manage your data. The database is the actual data. A DBMS is used to control and manipulate a database.

2. A DDL (Data Definition Language) statement is used to manipulate or define the storage in the database. These statements are used to create and destroy tables, tablespaces, datafiles, and so on.

3. A DML (Data Manipulation Language) statement is used to manipulate the actual data that is stored in the database. These statements are used to input, change, delete, or retrieve data that is being stored in the database.

4. An OLTP (Online Transaction Processing) system is used to service online users who are inputting, changing, or deleting data from the database. An OLTP system is typically characterized by large numbers of online users.

5. A DSS, or Decision Support System, is used to retrieve valuable decision-making information from a database. The DSS is characterized primarily by read-only queries. The DSS typically has very few users but long-running operations.

6. Duties of a DBA might include software and hardware installation, configuration of new hardware and software, security, performance tuning, backup and recovery, routine maintenance, troubleshooting, and failure recovery.

7. The most important duty of an Oracle DBA is to maintain the integrity and reliability of the user's data. This means keeping the system running and properly backed up.

Day 2: "Exploring the Oracle Architecture"

1. The three types of files that make up an Oracle database are datafiles, control files, and redo log files.

2. The Oracle instance consists of the user processes, the Oracle background processes, and the shared memory that they use.

3. Memory is much faster than disk—sometimes 50 times faster.

4. New features of Oracle8 include partitioned tables, index-only tables, and improved parallelism.

Day 3: "Installing Oracle Software"

1. The Oracle8 RDBMS is the main component of Oracle8 server.
2. Intelligent agents allow the Oracle Enterprise Manager to communicate with the Oracle RDBMS.
3. Oracle utilities include the SQL*Loader, the Export utility, and the Import utility.
4. TCP/IP, SPX/IPX, named pipes, and DECNet are all protocols supported by SQL*Net.

Day 4: "Properly Sizing Your Database and Planning for Growth"

1. You should set aside 500,000 bytes of memory per concurrent user.
2. The individuals you need at a sizing effort are the database designer, the application designer, and a management-staff representative.
3. A good database block size for an OLTP application would be 2,048 bytes.
4. Any cache-hit percentage above 90%. A cache-hit percentage above 90% means that 90% or more of the reads are found in memory. Logical (memory) reads are much faster than physical (disk) reads.
5. RAID 1 would use a factor of two times the number of writes and RAID 5 would use a factor of two times the number of writes to calculate the additional reads and two times the number of writes to calculate writes.
6. You need to know the database size, the I/Os per second, and the RAID type that you will be using.
7. None. There will always be some page faulting, but you can minimize it.
8. The maximum CPU utilization in a steady-state situation is 75%.
9. The maximum disk utilization in a steady-state situation is 85%.
10. You should allocate 5.5MB for the Oracle8 executable.

Day 5: "Managing the Oracle RDBMS"

1. When a database is created, the SYS and SYSTEM accounts are automatically created.
2. Installing software; creating databases, tablespaces, tables, views, indexes, and accounts; monitoring space and performance; and maintaining the integrity of the data in the database are all duties of the DBA.
3. Implementing a sound backup and recovery strategy.

4. OSDBA and OSOPER are two OS roles created when the database is created.

5. This is the instance that is created under NT with the NT Instance Manager or with ORADIM80.EXE. This service allows you to start and stop the Oracle instance via the Oracle tools.

6. The TNSNAMES.ORA file is where information is kept about what Oracle services you can connect to. It also allows aliasing to occur.

7. The TNSNAMES.ORA file can be administered through the Oracle Network Configuration wizard.

8. The system state can be modified via the ALTER SYSTEM command.

Day 6: "Administering Databases and Datafiles"

1. You should not run more than 60–70 I/Os per disk drive on a standard SCSI disk drive. Pushing more I/Os than this can cause disk latencies to increase beyond recommended limits.

2. The SID is the system identifier. This environment variable is used to determine which database to connect to.

3. No, you can create or alter a data file to autoextend. This is a new feature in Oracle.

4. Yes, the Oracle RDBMS supports more than one instance running on a server.

5. Each SID uniquely identifies one database; therefore you can only create one database per SID. With the Oracle Parallel Server option, you can have multiple instances (and SIDs) accessing the same database, but for each system it appears as though there is a one-to-one relationship between the SID and the database.

6. There is no firm limit to the number of databases that can be created on one system. The system resources that each database consumes will be the limiting factor.

Day 7: "Administering Tablespaces"

1. An extent is the unit of space that a schema object allocates when it is created or grows. As a table increases in size and fills up all its space, another extent is allocated. An extent is a contiguous group of blocks.

2. The limits on the tablespace are OS dependent. A tablespace can consist of 1,022 datafiles. Under Windows NT, a datafile can be 8GB with a 2KB block size or 32GB with a 8KB block size, making the maximum size of a tablespace 32TB.

3. You can create more datafiles or alter a datafile to autoextend. This is a new feature in Oracle.

4. A tablespace can be online or offline.

5. You can have any number of tablespaces in a database. Tablespaces are usually split by function. Accounting might have a different tablespace from finance, and so on.

6. The four types of segments are data, index, rollback, and temporary.

Day 8: "Administering Redo Logs, Control Files, and Rollback Segments"

1. Oracle requires at least two redo log files. This allows the log switch to occur and archiving to happen while logging is also happening.

2. A log file group is a set of identical redo log files. This provides redundancy to protect against media failure.

3. The control file is used to keep information about the structure of the database. When the instance is started, the control file is used to identify the database files.

4. Yes. In fact, it is a good idea to have more than one control file in case of media failure.

5. Without the control file, Oracle will not know which datafiles to open. Oracle cannot start without a control file.

6. The ALTER DATABASE *database* BACKUP CONTROLFILE command is used to back up the control file. Using the TO TRACE qualifier generates the SQL statements necessary to reproduce the control file.

7. Yes, a log switch forces a checkpoint.

8. No, a checkpoint does not cause a log switch.

9. Just as the name indicates, a rollback segment is used to store change information that can be used in the event of a rollback. It is also used for read consistency.

10. The rollback segment dynamically allocates and deallocates space. If the OPTIMAL value is set, the rollback segment will try to stay that size.

Day 9: "Managing Data"

1. Export is used to place a database's content and structure information into a binary export file.

2. Import is used to take data from an export file and use that data to re-create the database's content and structure.

3. SQL*Loader is a very flexible tool that is used to load ASCII or *flat-file* data into an Oracle database.

4. Only the Import utility can load export files.

5. Export/Import can be used to back up and reorganize the database, and to transfer data between systems.

6. The Windows NT version of the Export program is called EXP80.

7. The Windows NT version of the Import program is called IMP80.

8. The Windows NT version of the SQL*Loader program is called SQLLDR80.

9. The fixed record load file has data in columns where the same column in each record has the same length. The variable record datafile has different records where the same column may be a different length.

10. The parameter file is a file that contains additional command-line parameters.

Day 10: "Administering User Accounts"

1. No, the user accounts are individual. Sometimes the DBA might be auditing the system and will be able to tell what users have been active and when. If many people use the same account, the DBA cannot tell who is using the system.

2. Each user should have only one account. In cases where a user is serving dual duties, you might want to assign individual accounts for each duty.

3. System resources are assigned through profiles. You would set the CPU per session through a profile.

4. Permissions to access certain utilities or tables are assigned through system privileges. This may be assigned through a role also.

5. The Admin option allows you (as the grantee) to grant a role or system privilege to other users or roles.

6. Roles are removed via Enterprise Manager, Security Manager, or the DROP ROLE command.

7. Privileges are removed from roles via either Security Manager or the REVOKE command.

8. No. Quotas are assigned to a user directly. A quota is given to a user based on tablespaces.

9. Temporary tablespaces as well as default tablespaces are assigned to a user. These values can be modified via Enterprise Manager, Security Manager, or the ALTER USER command.

10. CREATE LIKE is a shortcut that copies a user's properties to a blank user. This lets you copy users as templates. It is a very nice feature to use.

Day 11: "Managing Processes"

1. The DBWR (database writer) process is used to handle all the writes to disk. Whereas the shadow processes can actually read directly from the datafiles if necessary, only the DBWR can write to the datafiles.

2. The LGWR (log writer) process is used to handle all the log writes. The server processes log write information into the log buffer, and the log writer reads from the log buffer and writes to disk.

3. The CKPT (checkpoint) process is used to help the DBWR process when enabled.

4. If you are running with the Oracle Parallel Server option, you'll have LCK*n* processes running in your system.

5. A three-tier system includes a middleware piece. This middleware piece is typically a transaction monitor (TM).

6. The I/O subsystem is typically the limiting factor in your system.

7. The order of precedence is as follows: Hints are used first, then table definitions, and finally, if none of those are used, the parameter file is used.

8. No, even if you have only one CPU, you'll see a benefit from using the Parallel Query option. Without the parallel query, your CPU might be mostly idle, waiting for I/Os to complete.

9. Under Windows NT, the Oracle server uses threads. In most of this book, however, the term *process* refers to both processes and threads.

10. The multithreaded server takes most of its memory from the shared pool.

Day 12: "Working with Tables, Views, and Synonyms"

1. A table column represents the order and type of data that is in an Oracle record. The column is the placeholder of data types for each record.

2. A row in a table is an individual record. A row is the specific data that has been added to the database.

3. A row piece consists of a row header and the row data.

4. An object consists of an attribute and a method.

5. A nested table is a table that appears as a column in another table.

6. A partitioned table is a table where the data is divided into smaller pieces based on the data itself.

7. Oracle8 supports range partitioning. The data is divided into various chunks based on ranges of data in one or more columns.

8. A view is a logical representation of a subset or superset of information in schema objects.

9. When creating a table, the STORAGE clause is used to define how the table will grow. Because tables are made of extents, the STORAGE clause defines the extent growth parameters.

10. A synonym is simply an alias to another object in the database. This object can be a table, view, sequence, or program unit.

Day 13: "Using Indexes and Sequences"

1. There are no limits to the number of columns or combinations of columns that can be indexed. However, the more indexes you have, the more overhead there is in maintaining them.

2. Yes, the parallel-index creation facility can greatly enhance the performance of the index-creation operation.

3. A B*-tree index is a binary tree structure that can be used to find data quickly. A binary comparison is made and the tree is traversed based on that selection.

4. Yes. In fact, there are two ways to partition an index. A local partitioned index is an individual index that resides on a partition and indexes the data on that partition, whereas a global partitioned index is a single index over all of the partitioned data. A global partitioned index can in turn be partitioned itself.

5. An index-only table is an index where the column data resides in the leaf block of the index. This schema can be very useful under certain conditions.

6. A bitmap index is an index where the index values are kept in a bitmap. A 1 indicates that the key value is present; a 0 indicates that the key value is not present.

7. A sequence can be used to provide new account numbers, order numbers, invoice numbers, and so on. Any number that must be unique is a good candidate for a sequence.

8. A sequence can be as many as 38 digits in length—bigger than you will ever need.

9. An index does not need to be unique, but it can be.

10. An index can be used to enforce uniqueness on a column or set of columns.

Day 14: "Using Oracle Clusters, Stored Procedures, and Database Links"

1. If two or more tables are always accessed via a join operation, these tables are ideal candidates for clustering.

2. Criterion 1: The cluster key value is unique. Criterion 2: The majority of queries are equality queries on the cluster key.

3. By using a cluster on a set of tables that are primarily accessed via a join operation, the data from all the tables that will be used together is read into the SGA together, thus reducing I/O and improving performance.

4. Clustering is not a good idea if you are doing a lot of inserts. Because the data is stored together inserts cause more overhead than an insert to a standard table. Also, if you do not usually access the data with joins on the cluster key in the cluster, you will see no benefit from clustering.

5. A stored procedure is a set of SQL statements that are pre-parsed and stored in the database. When the stored procedure is invoked, only the input and output data is passed; the SQL statements are not transferred or parsed.

6. By having the SQL pre-parsed and stored in the database, less data needs to be transmitted, less work is done by Oracle, and a better library cache hit rate is achieved, all resulting in better performance.

7. Stored procedures typically perform more than just database operations; conditionals and logical operations are usually a big part of stored procedures.

8. Database links are used to simplify access to a remote database and to hide network details from the user. When you have provided a link, users can easily select data from a database on another server elsewhere in the network.

Day 15: "Managing Job Queues and Using Oracle Auditing"

1. The job queues are used to defer the execution of database activity. This can be done in order to schedule repeating activities or to defer activities until off-hours.

2. Various operations such as backups, exports, imports, and SQL statements can be scheduled.

3. OS operations can also be scheduled using the job queue.

4. It is not necessary for a new account to be created, but it is not a bad idea.

5. The NT user right "login as a batch job" must be enabled for the user who will be running the batch queue.

6. Yes, queued jobs can run on any system that is properly configured for the Enterprise Manager.

7. Jobs can be scheduled to run once, or at a regular interval that can be daily, weekly, or monthly.

8. You need to make sure that the preferred credentials (account information) are properly set up in the Enterprise Manager in order for job queuing to work.

9. Auditing might need to be enabled if you suspect some suspicious behavior on your system.

10. Auditing can consume a lot of system resources. Be careful what you audit and for how long.

Day 16: "Understanding Effective Backup Techniques"

1. An instance recovery is when Oracle recovers from an unorderly shutdown. Instance recovery is automatic as long as no datafiles are damaged.

2. Log file losses cannot be recovered from but do not cause system failure. If a log file is damaged and the datafiles are okay, you should shut down your system and perform an immediate backup.

3. Yes, if a datafile is damaged it can be restored from a backup, and the changes can be restored from the redo log files and archive log files.

4. If you are not running in ARCHIVELOG mode, you can perform an instance recovery but you cannot recover any changes that are older than the online redo log files. If a datafile is damaged, you cannot recover to this point, only to the last full backup.

5. The different types of backups that can be done are full backups, tablespace backups, archive log backups, control file backups, and datafile backups.

6. To completely back up your system, you must back up the datafiles and the control files. If you are running in ARCHIVELOG mode, you should also back up the archive log files.

7. RAID stands for Redundant Array of Inexpensive Disks. This hardware or software allows you to stripe, mirror, or provide other fault-tolerant striping to your disks.

8. No, the NT Backup Manager can only back up the local system.

9. The archive log files are essentially a copy of the redo log file after a log switch. When a log switch occurs, the old redo log file is copied to an archive log file.

10. An offline backup occurs when the Oracle instance is shut down. An online backup occurs when the instance is running.

Day 17: "Recovering the Database"

1. Types of recovery operations include instance recovery, media recovery, and point-in-time recovery.

2. All committed transactions can be recovered from an instance failure.

3. All committed transactions can be recovered from a media failure if you are running in ARCHIVELOG mode.

4. ARCHIVELOG mode causes all redo log files to be saved whenever a log switch occurs. These archived log files can be used to restore the database if necessary.

5. A dirty buffer is a buffer in the SGA that has been modified but has not been written to disk.

6. A checkpoint is a process that periodically causes all dirty buffers to be written to disk.

7. The database and online redo log files are necessary for instance recovery.

8. The database, the online redo log files, the backup files, and the archive log files are all necessary for media recovery.

9. A point-in-time recovery operation recovers only up to a specified point in time. This time can be specified as a time or a system change number (SCN).

10. A point-in-time recovery is used to recover up to a time just before a software or operator problem corrupted the database. This prevents the recovery process from running the command that corrupted the database in the first place.

Day 18: "Administering Oracle Replication"

1. A read-only table snapshot is a picture of a database or table that is copied to another system. The system from which the copy is made is called the master. The replicated system has the table or database available only in read-only mode.

2. An updateable snapshot is a replication method where both the master and the replication systems are updateable. The replicated systems synchronize themselves on a regular basis.

3. Realtime data replication causes all systems to be updated immediately after the change is made. This replication method needs all systems to be up and running for it to work effectively.

4. The master site is the system from which the data is replicated. Because it is updateable and holds the original data, it is considered the master.

5. The snapshot site is the system that receives the snapshots. If the snapshot site is read-only, no updates are allowed and the site is considered a slave site.

6. Read-only table snapshots can be used in a variety of applications: retail price lists, lookup tables, and so on.

7. Advanced replication can be used for sites that need remote updateable databases and as a failover system.

8. With a complete refresh, the entire snapshot is updated. With a fast refresh, only the changes are updated.

9. A standby database is a database that is constantly in recovery mode, recovering archive log files from the primary database. In the event of a failure, the standby database can immediately substitute for the primary database. The standby database is used to provide immediate restoration of service in the event of a primary system failure. In a matter of minutes or even seconds, this system can be operational.

10. A read-only tablespace can be used to prevent users from updating critical data as well as to reduce recovery time, because no instance recovery is needed on a read-only tablespace.

Day 19: "Advanced Oracle Options"

1. The Oracle Parallel Server option can be used as a fault-tolerant RDBMS solution, a performance-enhancement option, or both.

2. The server interconnect provides two functions: to communicate locking information and to act as a system heartbeat.

3. The shared-disk subsystem is what allows OPS to work. Each member of the cluster must be able to access all datafiles and redo log files at all times. Thus, the disk subsystem is shared.

4. *DLM* stands for Distributed Lock Manager. The DLM passes lock information between members of the cluster.

5. PCM stands for Parallel Cache Management. This term is used primarily to describe the Parallel Cache Management (PCM) locks. These locks are used to keep the various nodes in the cluster from overwriting each other by locking data that is being modified.

6. The Parallel Query option is used to parallelize certain SQL operations in order to improve performance.

7. The Parallel Query option improves performance by allowing multiple threads of execution to perform one task. Because the operation is split, the CPU(s) can continue processing while the system waits for I/Os to complete.

8. The best way to set the degree of parallelism is via a hint in the SQL statement.

9. The secondary way to set the degree of parallelism is to set the parallelism on the table with the ALTER TABLE command.

10. Parallelizable operations include table scans, joins, and the recovery operation.

Day 20: "Effectively Tuning and Optimizing the Database"

1. System memory, CPU, and the I/O subsystem are all potential areas of bottlenecks.

2. You can either query the V$ tables directly or use the UTLBSTAT and UTLESTAT tools to determine the shared pool cache-hit ratio.

3. I recommend that a disk drive doing random I/Os should not be pushed harder than 60–70 I/Os per second.

4. I recommend that a disk drive doing sequential I/Os should not be pushed harder than 90–100 I/Os per second.

5. Latency refers to the length of the response time. Disk latency refers to how long it takes for an I/O to complete. Remember the knee of the curve theory from Day 4.

6. The buffer cache-hit ratio is determined from this equation:

   Cache hit ratio = 1 − (PHYSICAL READS / (DB BLOCKB GETS + CONSISTENT GETS))

7. You can determine whether the shared pool is large enough by examining both the data dictionary cache-hit ratio and the library cache-hit ratio.

8. The effectiveness of an index depends on the index being present and the application forming SQL statements that can take advantage of that index.

9. Always run UTLBSTAT.SQL first. This script sets the system up to calculate data with UTLESTAT.SQL.

10. If you have a system that is performing DSS-type queries and large table scans, you could benefit from a large block size. Also, if you have large rows, you might benefit from a larger block size.

Day 21: "Exploring the Web Publishing Assistant and Network Computing Architecture"

1. NCA stands for the Network Computing Architecture and is a standard for computing over the network. The NCA was developed in conjunction with Oracle.

2. CORBA stands for the Common Object Request Broker Architecture and is a specification for object communications.

3. HTTP, or Hypertext Transport Protocol, is the protocol used in order for Web browsers to communicate with Web servers.

4. HTML, or Hypertext Markup Language, is the language used to define Web pages.

5. A cartridge is a plug-in object that performs an application function. Cartridges usually serve one function but work together with other cartridges to serve many functions.

6. A static Web page is one that does not dynamically change. It only changes when it is replaced.

7. The Web Publishing Assistant can create only static Web pages.

8. NC stands for *Network Computer*. This computer is designed to access the World Wide Web and run network applications.

9. The Oracle Universal server is designed to handle all traditional data types and new data types such as video, audio, text, and spatial data.

10. Any type of application that requires access to a central server would be suitable for running on an NC because no local data storage is required.

APPENDIX
B

Oracle Tuning Parameters

This appendix lists the Oracle tuning parameters, grouping them into general areas of use and then sorting them alphabetically within the group. The section headings are the syntax for the parameters. The syntax contains information in the following format:

```
PARAMETER [option1, option2, option3, etc..] <DEFAULT VALUE>
```

A value that is *italicized* indicates that the value should be replaced with one of your own. A value that is *italicized* and in *CAPS* indicates a choice of this keyword. The / character indicates an OR condition. A value enclosed in brackets (<>) indicates the default value for that parameter.

These parameters are divided into sections based on whether the parameter affects performance, enables system analysis, is a general parameter, and so on. There might be some overlap, so if a parameter is not in the section you expected, keep looking.

Performance

These parameters change the performance characteristics of the system.

ALWAYS_ANTI_JOIN [*NESTED_LOOPS*/*MERGE*/ *HASH*] <NESTED_LOOPS>
This parameter sets the type of anti-join that the Oracle server uses. This specifies the algorithm chosen for the anti-join.

B_TREE_BITMAP_PLANS [*TRUE*/*FALSE*] <FALSE>
When set to TRUE, the optimizer considers a bitmap access path even though a table might have only a regular B*-tree index.

BITMAP_MERGE_AREA_SIZE [*System Dependent*] <1MB>
This parameter specifies the amount of memory used to merge bitmaps retrieved from a range scan of the index. Larger values typically improve performance.

CLOSE_CACHED_OPEN_CURSORS [*TRUE*/*FALSE*] <FALSE>
This parameter specifies whether cursors opened and cached in memory are automatically closed at each commit. If you frequently use cursors, this should be set to FALSE.

CPU_COUNT [*0-unlimited*] <Automatic>
This parameter specifies the number of CPUs used by Oracle. This parameter is set automatically and should not be changed.

CREATE_BITMAP_AREA_SIZE [*OS Dependent*] <8MB>
This parameter specifies the amount of memory to be used for bitmap creation. A larger value might provide greater bitmap-creation performance. If the cardinality is small, this number can be small.

CURSOR_SPACE_FOR_TIME [*TRUE/FALSE*] <FALSE>

CURSOR_SPACE_FOR_TIME causes the system to use more space for cursors, thus increasing performance. This parameter affects both the shared SQL areas and the user's private SQL area. This parameter speeds performance but uses more memory.

If CURSOR_SPACE_FOR_TIME is TRUE, the shared SQL areas remain pinned in the shared pool as long as an open cursor references them. This parameter should be used only if you have a sufficiently large shared pool to simultaneously hold all the processes' cursors.

The user's private SQL area is also retained during cursor execution, thus saving time and I/Os at the expense of memory.

DB_BLOCK_BUFFERS [*4..65535*] <32 buffers>

This parameter controls the number of database block buffers in the SGA. DB_BLOCK_BUFFERS is probably the most significant instance tuning parameter because the majority of I/Os in the system are generated by database blocks. Increasing DB_BLOCK_BUFFERS increases performance at the expense of memory. You can calculate the amount of memory that will be consumed with the following formula:

Buffer size = DB_BLOCK_BUFFERS * DB_BLOCK_SIZE

A larger number of database block buffers in the system creates a higher cache-hit rate, thus reducing the amount of utilized I/O and CPU and improving performance.

DB_BLOCK_CHECKPOINT_BATCH [*0..derived*] <8>

This parameter specifies the number of blocks that the DBWR writes in one batch when performing a checkpoint. Setting this value too high causes the system to flood the I/O devices during the checkpoint, severely degrades performance, and increases response times—maybe to unacceptable levels.

You should set DB_BLOCK_CHECKPOINT_BATCH to a level that allows a checkpoint to finish before the next checkpoint occurs. Setting DB_BLOCK_CHECKPOINT_BATCH to 0 causes the default value of 8 to be used.

DB_BLOCK_SIZE [*1024..8192 (OS dependent)*] <OS dependent>

This parameter specifies in bytes the size of the Oracle database blocks. The typical values are 2048 and 4096. If you set the block size relative to the size of the rows in a database, you can reduce I/O. In some types of applications in which large amounts of sequential accesses are performed, a larger database block size can be beneficial. This value is useful only at database-creation time.

DB_FILE_MULTIBLOCK_READ_COUNT [*number (OS dependent)*] <OS dependent>

DB_FILE_MULTIBLOCK_READ_COUNT specifies the maximum number of blocks read in one I/O during a sequential scan. The default is a function of DB_BLOCK_BUFFERS and PROCESSES. Reasonable values are 4, 16, or 32. The maximum allowed values are OS dependent.

This parameter can be especially useful if you perform a large number of table scans, such as in a DSS system.

DB_FILE_SIMULTANEOUS_WRITES [1..24] <4>

This parameter specifies the number of simultaneous writes for each database file when written by the DBWR. For disk arrays that handle large numbers of requests in the hardware simultaneously, it is advantageous to set DB_FILE_SIMULTANEOUS_WRITES to its maximum.

DISCRETE_TRANSACTIONS_ENABLED [TRUE/FALSE] <FALSE>

This parameter implements a simpler, faster rollback mechanism that, under certain conditions, can improve performance. You can obtain greater efficiency in this mode, but the qualification criteria for what kind of transactions can take advantage of discrete transactions are quite strict.

DISK_ASYNCH_IO [TRUE/FALSE] <TRUE>

This parameter specifies that I/O to datafiles, control files, and log files are asynchronous. This should be left enabled and not altered.

DML_LOCKS [20..unlimited,0] <4 * TRANSACTIONS>

This parameter specifies the maximum number of DML locks. A DML lock is used for each table-modification transaction. DML locks are used in the DROP TABLE, CREATE INDEX, and LOCK TABLE IN EXCLUSIVE MODE statements. If the value is set to 0, enqueues (Oracle locking mechanisms) are disabled, which improves performance slightly.

DBWR_IO_SLAVES [0..OS Dependent] <0>

This parameter specifies the number of I/O slaves used by the DBWR process.

HASH_AREA_SIZE [0..OS Dependent] <2*SORT_AREA_SIZE>

This parameter specifies the maximum amount of memory to be used for hash joins.

HASH_MULTIBLOCK_IO_COUNT [OS Dependent] <1>

This parameter specifies how many sequential blocks a hash join reads and writes in one I/O.

LARGE_POOL_MIN_ALLOC [16K-64KB] <16KB>

This parameter specifies the minimum allocation size from the large pool.

LARGE_POOL_SIZE [300K or LARGE_POOL_MIN_ALLOC, whichever is larger] <0>

This parameter specifies the size of the large pool allocation heap.

LGWR_IO_SLAVES [0..OS Dependent] <0>

This parameter specifies the number of I/O slaves used by the LGWR process.

LOG_ARCHIVE_BUFFER_SIZE [1..OS Dependent] <OS dependent>

When running in ARCHIVELOG mode, this parameter specifies the size of each archival buffer in redo log blocks. This parameter can be used in conjunction with the LOG_ARCHIVE_BUFFERS parameter to make the archiving speed faster or slower to affect overall system performance.

LOG_ARCHIVE_BUFFERS [1..OS Dependent] <OS dependent>
When running in ARCHIVELOG mode, this parameter specifies the number of buffers to allocate to archiving. This parameter is used with the LOG_ARCHIVE_BUFFER_SIZE parameter to control the speed of archiving.

LOG_BUFFER [OS Dependent] <OS dependent>
LOG_BUFFER specifies the number of bytes allocated to the redo log buffer. Larger values reduce I/Os to the redo log by writing fewer blocks of a larger size. This might help performance, particularly in a heavily used system.

LOG_CHECKPOINT_INTERVAL [2..unlimited] <OS dependent>
This parameter specifies the number of redo log file blocks to be filled to cause a checkpoint to occur. Remember that a checkpoint always happens when a log switch occurs. This parameter can be used to cause checkpoints to occur more frequently. Sometimes, frequent checkpoints have less effect on the system than one large checkpoint when the log switch occurs.

LOG_CHECKPOINT_TIMEOUT [0..unlimited] <OS dependent>
This parameter specifies the maximum amount of time that can pass before another checkpoint must occur. This parameter can also be used to increase the frequency of the checkpoint process, thus changing the overall system effect.

LOG_SIMULTANEOUS_COPIES [0..unlimited] <CPU_COUNT>
LOG_SIMULTANEOUS_COPIES specifies the number of redo buffer copy latches simultaneously available to write log entries. You can have up to two redo copy latches per CPU. This helps the LGWR process keep up with the extra load generated by multiple CPUs.

If this parameter is 0, redo copy latches are turned off and all log entries are copied on the redo allocation latch.

LOG_SMALL_ENTRY_MAX_SIZE [number (OS dependent)] <OS dependent>
This parameter specifies the size in bytes of the largest copy to the log buffers that can occur under the redo allocation latch without obtaining the redo buffer copy latch. If LOG_SIMULTANEOUS_COPIES is zero, this parameter is ignored.

OPTIMIZER_MODE [RULE/COST/FIRST_ROWS/ALL_ROWS] COST
When set to RULE, this parameter causes rule-based optimization to be used, unless hints are supplied in the query. When set to COST, this parameter causes a cost-based approach for the SQL statement, providing that there are any statistics in the data dictionary. When set to FIRST_ROWS, the optimizer chooses execution plans that minimize response time. When set to ALL_ROWS, the optimizer chooses execution plans that minimize total execution time.

OPTIMIZER_PERCENT_PARALLEL [0..100] <0>
This parameter specifies the amount of parallelism the optimizer uses in its cost functions.

OPTIMIZER_SEARCH_LIMIT <5>

This parameter specifies the search limit for the optimizer.

PRE_PAGE_SGA [*TRUE*/*FALSE*] <FALSE>

When set to TRUE, this parameter specifies that at instance startup all pages of the SGA are touched, causing them to be allocated in memory. This increases startup time but reduces page faults during runtime. This is useful if you have a large number of processes starting at once. This parameter can increase the system performance in that case by avoiding memory-allocation overhead.

ROLLBACK_SEGMENTS [*Any rollback segment names*] <NULL>

ROLLBACK_SEGMENTS specifies one or more rollback-segment names to be allocated to this instance. If ROLLBACK_SEGMENTS is not specified, the public rollback segments are used. If you want to move your rollback segments to a different disk device, you must specify it here. The parameter is specified as follows:

```
ROLLBACK_SEGMENTS = (roll1, roll2, roll3)
```

If you use the Oracle Parallel Server option, you must name different rollback segments for each instance.

ROW_CACHE_CURSORS [*10..3300*] <10>

This parameter specifies the number of cached recursive cursors used by the row cache manager for selecting rows from the data dictionary. The default is usually sufficient unless you have particularly high access to the data dictionary.

ROW_LOCKING [*ALWAYS*/*INTENT*] <ALWAYS>

The value ALWAYS specifies that only row locks are acquired when a table is updated. If you set this value to INTENT, row locks are acquired on a SELECT FOR UPDATE, but when the update occurs, a table lock is acquired.

SEQUENCE_CACHE_ENTRIES [*10..32000*] <10>

This parameter specifies the number of sequences that can be cached in the SGA. By caching the sequences, an immediate response is achieved for sequences. Set a large value for SEQUENCE_CACHE_ENTRIES if you have a high concurrency of processes requesting sequences.

SEQUENCE_CACHE_HASH_BUCKETS [*1..32000 (prime number)*] <7>

This parameter specifies the number of buckets to speed up access to sequences in the cache. The cache is arranged as a hash table.

SERIAL_REUSE [*DISABLE*/*SELECT*/*DML*/*PLSQL*/*ALL*/*NULL*] <NULL>

This parameter specifies which type of SQL cursors should make use of serial-reusable memory.

SERIALIZABLE [*TRUE/FALSE*] <FALSE>

If this value is set to TRUE, queries obtain table-level read locks, which prohibits other transactions from modifying that table until the transaction has committed or rolled back the transaction. This mode provides repeatable reads and ensures that within the transactions multiple queries to the same data achieve the same result.

With SERIALIZABLE set to TRUE, degree-three consistency is provided. You pay a performance penalty when you run in this mode. Running in this mode is usually not necessary.

SESSION_CACHED_CURSORS [*0..OS dependent*] <0>

This parameter specifies the number of session cursors to cache. If parse calls of the same SQL statement are repeated, this can cause the session cursor for that statement to be moved into the session cursor cache. Subsequent calls need not reopen the cursor.

SESSION_MAX_OPEN_FILES [*1..MAX_OPEN_FILES*] <10>

This parameter specifies the maximum number of BFILEs that can be opened by any given session. The BFILE stores unstructured binary data in OS files outside the database.

SHARED_POOL_RESERVED_MIN_ALLOC [*5000..SHARED_POOL_RESERVE_SIZE*] <5000>

Memory allocations larger than this value cannot allocate space from the reserved list.

SHARED_POOL_RESERVE_SIZE [*SHARED_POOL_RESERVE_MIN_ALLOC..*
(*SHARED_POOL_SIZE/2*)] <5% of SHARED_POOL_SIZE>

This parameter specifies the shared pool space that is reserved for large contiguous requests for shared-pool memory.

SHARED_POOL_SIZE [*300KB..OS dependent*] <3.5MB>

This parameter specifies the size of the shared pool in bytes. The shared pool contains the data dictionary cache (row cache) and the library cache as well as session information. Increasing the size of the shared pool should help performance, but at the cost of memory.

SMALL_TABLE_THRESHOLD [*0..OS dependent*] <4>

This parameter specifies the number of buffers available in the SGA for table scans. A small table might be read entirely into cache if it fits in SMALL_TABLE_THRESHOLD number of buffers. When scanning a table larger than this, these buffers are reused immediately. This provides a mechanism to prohibit a single-table scan from taking over the buffer cache.

SORT_AREA_RETAINED_SIZE [*0..SORT_AREA_SIZE*] <SORT_AREA_SIZE>

SORT_AREA_RETAINED_SIZE defines the maximum amount of session memory in bytes that can be used for an in-memory sort. The memory is released when the last row is fetched from the sort area.

If the sort does not fit in SORT_AREA_RETAINED_SIZE bytes, a temporary segment is allocated and the sort is performed in this temporary table. This is called an *external (disk) sort.* This value is important if sort performance is critical.

SORT_AREA_SIZE [*number of bytes*] <OS dependent>

This value specifies the maximum amount of PGA memory to use for an external sort. This memory is released when the sorted rows are written to disk. Increasing this value increases the performance of large sorts.

Remember that each user process has its own PGA. You can calculate the potential memory usage if all the users are doing a large sort with the following formula:

Potential memory usage = SORT_AREA_SIZE * (number of users doing a large sort)

If very large indexes are being created, you might want to increase the value of this parameter.

SORT_SPACEMAP_SIZE [*bytes*] <OS dependent>

This parameter specifies the size in bytes of the sort spacemap in the context area. If you have very large indexes, increase the value of this parameter. Optimal performance is achieved when this parameter has the following value:

SORT_SPACEMAP_SIZE = (total-sort-bytes / sort-area-size) + 64

In this formula, total-sort-bytes has the following value:

total-sort-bytes = record-count * (sum-of-average-column-sizes + (2 * number-of-columns))

number-of-columns includes the SELECT list for ORDER BY, GROUP BY, and the key list for the CREATE INDEX. You should also add 10 or 20 extra bytes for overhead.

SORT_WRITE_BUFFER_SIZE [32KB/64KB] <32768>

This parameter specifies the size of the sort I/O buffer when SORT_DIRECT_WRITES is set to TRUE.

SORT_WRITE_BUFFERS [2..8] <1>

This parameter specifies the number of sort buffers when SORT_DIRECT_WRITES is set to TRUE.

SPIN_COUNT [*1..1,000,000*] <1>

This parameter specifies the number of times to spin on a latch before sleeping.

STAR_TRANSFORMATION_ENABLED [*TRUE/FALSE*] <FALSE>

This parameter specifies whether a cost-based query transformation will be applied to star queries.

USE_ISM [*TRUE/FALSE*] <TRUE>

This parameter specifies that the shared page table is enabled.

Parallel Query Option

The following parameters affect the operation of the Parallel Query option, which has been available in Oracle since version 7.1. The Parallel Query option can dramatically affect the performance of certain operations.

PARALLEL_DEFAULT_MAX_SCANS [0..unlimited] <OS dependent>
This value specifies the maximum number of query servers to be used by default for a query. This valued is used only if there are no values specified in a PARALLEL hint or in the PARALLEL definition clause. This limits the number of query servers used by default when the value of PARALLEL_DEFAULT_SCANSIZE is used by the query coordinator.

PARALLEL_DEFAULT_SCANSIZE [0..OS Dependent] <OS dependent>
This parameter is used to determine the number of query servers to be used for a particular table. The size of the table divided by PARALLEL_DEFAULT_SCANSIZE determines the number of query servers, up to PARALLEL_DEFAULT_MAX_SCANS.

PARALLEL_MAX_SERVERS [0..100] <OS dependent>
This parameter specifies the maximum number of query servers or parallel recovery processes available for this instance.

PARALLEL_MIN_MESSAGE_POOL [0..(SHARED_POOLSIZE*.9)] <equation>
This parameter specifies the minimum permanent amount of memory that will be allocated from the shared pool for messages in parallel execution.

PARALLEL_MIN_PERCENT [0..100] <0>
This parameter specifies the minimum percent of threads required for parallel query.

PARALLEL_MIN_SERVERS [0..PARALLEL_MAX_SERVERS] <0>
This parameter determines the minimum number of query servers for an instance. It is also the number of query servers started at instance startup.

PARALLEL_SERVER_IDLE_TIME [0..unlimited] <OS dependent>
This parameter specifies the number of minutes before Oracle terminates an idle query server process.

RECOVERY_PARALLELISM [0..PARALLEL_MAX_SERVERS] <OS dependent>
This parameter specifies the number of processes to be used for instance or media recovery. A large value can greatly reduce instance recovery time. A value of 0 or 1 indicates that parallel recovery will not be performed and that recovery will be serial.

Analysis Tools

These parameters turn on special features in Oracle for detailed analysis and debugging.

DB_BLOCK_CHECKSUM *[TRUE/FALSE]* *<FALSE>*
Setting this parameter to TRUE causes the DBWR and direct loader to calculate a checksum for every block they write to disk. This checksum is written into the header of each block.

DB_LOG_CHECKSUM *[TRUE/FALSE]* *<FALSE>*
Setting this parameter to TRUE causes the LGWR to calculate a checksum for every block it writes to disk. The checksum is written into the header of the redo block.

DB_BLOCK_LRU_EXTENDED_STATISTICS *[0..unlimited]* *<0>*
This parameter enables statistics in the X$KCBRBH table to be gathered. These statistics estimate the increased number of database block buffer cache hits for each additional buffer. Any value over zero specifies the number of buffers to estimate the cache hits for. If you are interested in estimating the cache hits for an additional 100 buffers, set this parameter to 100.

This parameter affects performance and should be turned off during normal operation.

DB_BLOCK_LRU_LATCHES *[1.. number of CPUs]* *<CPU_COUNT/2>*
This parameter specifies the upper bound of the number of LRU latch sets. This is the number of LRU latch sets that you want. Oracle decides whether to use this number or a smaller one.

DB_BLOCK_LRU_STATISTICS *[TRUE/FALSE]* *<FALSE>*
This parameter specifies whether statistics are gathered for database block buffer cache hit estimates as specified in DB_BLOCK_LRU_EXTENDED_STATISTICS. Set this parameter to TRUE when you want to gather these statistics.

DB_BLOCK_MAX_DIRTY_TARGET *[100..all buffers or 0]* *<all buffers>*
This parameter specifies the number of buffers that can be dirty. If the number of dirty buffers exceeds this, the DBWR writes out buffers to reduce the number of dirty buffers.

EVENT *<NULL>*
The EVENT parameter modifies the scope of ALTER SESSION SET EVENTS commands so that they pertain to the entire instance rather than just the session. This is an Oracle internal parameter and should be changed only at the direction of Oracle support.

FIXED_DATE *[date string]* *<NULL>*
FIXED_DATE allows you to set as a constant the Oracle function SYSDATE in the format *YYYY-MM-DD-HH24:MI:SS*. Use this parameter for debug only. This parameter allows you to test your application's functionality with certain dates, such as the turn of the century.

ORACLE_TRACE_COLLECTION_NAME *[valid name]* *<NULL>*
This parameter specifies the Oracle Trace collection name.

ORACLE_TRACE_COLLECTION_PATH [*valid path*] <NULL>

This parameter specifies the directory where Oracle Trace collection definition and datafiles are located.

ORACLE_TRACE_COLLECTION_SIZE [*0..4294967295*] <5242880>

The maximum size in bytes of the Oracle Trace collection file.

ORACLE_TRACE_ENABLE [*TRUE/FALSE*] <FALSE>

Enables Oracle Trace collections for the server.

ORACLE_TRACE_FACILITY_NAME [*valid name*] <OS Specific>

This parameter specifies the name of the Oracle Trace product definition file.

ORACLE_TRACE_FACILITY_PATH [*valid directory name*] <OS Specific>

This parameter specifies the directory where the Oracle Trace facility definition files are located.

SQL_TRACE [*TRUE/FALSE*] <FALSE>

This parameter specifies whether the SQL*Trace facility is enabled. The SQL*Trace facility can provide valuable information but at the price of some overhead. Use SQL*Trace only when you are tracking down a specific problem.

SORT_READ_FAC [*integer*] <OS Dependent>

SORT_READ_FAC defines a unitless ratio that describes the amount of time to read a single database block divided by the block transfer rate.

TIMED_OS_STATISTICS [*OFF/CALL/LOGOFF*] <OFF>

This parameter allows the system administrator to gather OS statistics when calls are pushed or popped or when a user logs off.

TIMED_STATISTICS [*TRUE/FALSE*] <FALSE>

When TIMED_STATISTICS is set to TRUE, the time-related statistics in the dynamic performance tables are enabled. This information can be quite useful, but there is considerable overhead involved. Only enable TIMED_STATISTICS when you are analyzing the system.

General

These parameters are of a general nature; they typically set limits and do not significantly affect performance—except that they might take up space in the SGA.

AQ_TM_PROCESS [*0/1*] <0>

This parameter specifies whether a time manager is created. If AQ_TM_PROCESS is set to 1, a time-manager process is created to monitor the messages.

ARCH_IO_SLAVES [0-15] <0>

The number of I/O slaves to be used by the ARCH process. This should be adjusted if archiving is running into an I/O bottleneck.

BACKGROUND_CORE_DUMP [FULL/PARTIAL] <FULL>

This parameter specifies whether the SGA is dumped as part of the generated core file.

BACKGROUND_DUMP_DEST [pathname] <OS dependent>

This parameter specifies the destination directory where the debugging trace files for the background processes are written. The background processes log all startup and shutdown messages and errors to these files, as well as any other error logs. A log of all CREATE, ALTER, or DROP statements is also stored here.

BLANK_TRIMMING [TRUE/FALSE] <FALSE>

If the value of BLANK_TRIMMING is TRUE, this allows a data assignment of a string variable to a column value that is smaller (assuming that the truncated characters are blank).

CHECKPOINT_PROCESS [TRUE/FALSE] <FALSE>

This parameter determines whether the CKPT background process is enabled. During a checkpoint, the headers of all the datafiles must be updated. This task is usually performed by the LGWR process. Writing the blocks to disk is the job of the DBWR process. If you notice that the LGWR is slowing down during checkpoints, it might be necessary to enable CKPT to eliminate the extra work that LGWR is doing.

CLEANUP_ROLLBACK_ENTRIES [number] <20>

This parameter specifies the number of undo records processed at a time when a rollback occurs. This breaks up the rollback and limits a large rollback from locking out smaller rollbacks.

CLOSE_CACHED_OPEN_CURSORS [TRUE/FALSE] <FALSE>

This parameter specifies whether cursors that have been opened and cached by PL/SQL are automatically closed at COMMIT. A value of FALSE allows these cursors to remain open for further use. If cursors are rarely reused, you can save space in the SGA by setting this value to TRUE. If cursors are reused, you can improve performance by leaving this parameter at the default value of FALSE.

COMPATIBLE [variable] <release dependent>

Setting this variable guarantees that the DBMS will remain compatible with the specified release. Some features might have to be limited for the compatibility to be maintained.

COMPATIBLE_NO_RECOVERY [variable] <release dependent>

This parameter works like the COMPATIBLE parameter except that the earlier version (specified as the parameter) might not work on the current database if recovery is necessary.

CONTROL_FILE_RECORD_KEEP_TIME [0-365] <7>
This parameter specifies the minimum age (in days) that a record in the control file must be kept before it can be reused.

CONTROL_FILES [1..8 filenames] <OS dependent>
This parameter specifies the path names of one to eight control files. It is recommended that there always be more than one control file and that they exist on different physical devices.

CORE_DUMP_DEST [directory name] <ORACLE_HOME/DBS/>
This parameter specifies the directory where core files are dumped.

DB_DOMAIN [extension components of a global db name] <WORLD>
This parameter specifies the extension components of the global database name consisting of valid identifiers separated by periods (for example, texas.us.widgets.com). This allows multiple divisions to each have an ACCOUNTING database that is uniquely identified by the addition of the domain.

DBLINK_ENCRYPT_LOGIN [TRUE/FALSE] <FALSE>
When you connect to another server, Oracle encrypts the password. If the value of DBLINK_ENCRYPT_LOGIN is FALSE and the connection fails, Oracle tries to connect again with a nonencrypted password. If DBLINK_ENCRYPT_LOGIN is TRUE and the connection fails, Oracle does not attempt to reconnect.

DB_FILES [min: MAXDATAFILES, max OS dependent] <OS dependent>
This parameter specifies the maximum number of database files that can be open. This value can be reduced if you want to reclaim space in the SGA. No performance degradation is incurred by leaving this value high, just additional memory usage in the SGA.

DB_FILE_DIRECT_IO_COUNT [OS Dependent] <64>
This parameter specifies the number of blocks to be used for I/O operations done by backup, restore, or direct path read/write functions.

DB_NAME [valid name] <NULL>
This parameter provides a string of up to eight characters in length that specifies the name of the database. The following characters are valid:

- ☐ Alphabetic characters
- ☐ Numbers
- ☐ Underscore (_)
- ☐ Pound sign (#)
- ☐ Dollar sign ($)

No other characters can be used. Double quotation marks are removed and cannot be part of the name. The characters used in the DB_NAME parameter are case insensitive, so SALES, Sales, and sales are equal.

ENQUEUE_RESOURCES [10..65535] <derived>

This parameter specifies the number of resources that can be locked by the lock manager. The default value is derived from PROCESSES and is usually sufficient. The value is derived from this formula:

PROCESSES <= 3; default values = 20
PROCESSES 4-10; default value = ((PROCESSES - 3) * 5) + 20
PROCESSES > 10; default value = ((PROCESSES - 10) * 2) + 55

If you use a large number of tables, you might have to increase this value. This value should never exceed DML_LOCKS + DDL_LOCKS + 20 (overhead).

GLOBAL_NAMES [TRUE/FALSE] <FALSE>

This parameter determines whether a database link is required to have the same name as the database to which it connects. Oracle recommends setting this parameter to TRUE to ensure the use of consistent naming conventions for databases and links.

IFILE [parameter filename] <NULL>

This parameter embeds another parameter file into the current parameter file. This can be very useful to separate specific changes from the general changes that you often make. The parameter also allows you to separate different types of parameters such as parallel options.

INIT_SQL_FILES [SQL filename] <NULL>

This parameter lists the names of SQL files that should be run immediately after database creation. This parameter can be used to automatically create the data dictionary.

JOB_QUEUE_INTERVAL [1..3600] <60>

This parameter specifies, in seconds, the interval between wake-ups of the SNP background process. The processes run jobs that have been queued.

JOB_QUEUE_KEEP_CONNECTIONS [1..10] <0>

This parameter specifies the number of SNP background processes per instance.

JOB_QUEUE_PROCESSES [TRUE/FALSE] <FALSE>

This parameter specifies whether remote connections should be shut down after remote jobs have finished executing.

LICENSE_MAX_SESSIONS [0..number of session licenses] <0>

LICENSE_MAX_USERS sets the maximum number of concurrent user sessions allowed. When this limit is reached, only users with RESTRICTED SESSION privilege can connect to the server. A zero value indicates that this constraint is not enforced. Either LICENSE_MAX_USERS or LICENSE_MAX_SESSIONS should be set, not both.

LICENSE_MAX_USERS [0..number of user licenses] <0>

LICENSE_MAX_USERS sets the maximum number of concurrent users that can simultaneously access the database. When this limit is reached, no more user sessions can be created. A zero value indicates that this constraint is not enforced. Either LICENSE_MAX_USERS or LICENSE_MAX_SESSIONS should be set, not both.

LICENSE_SESSIONS_WARNING [0..LICENSE_MAX_SESSIONS] <0>

Sets a warning limit so that the administrator can be aware that the LICENSE_MAX_SESSIONS limit might soon be reached. After LICENSE_SESSIONS_WARNING number of users have connected, a message is written to the alert log for each additional user connecting.

LOCAL_LISTENER [string] <Listener Identifier>

This parameter identifies local Net8 listeners.

LOG_ARCHIVE_DEST [valid path or device name] <OS dependent>

When running in ARCHIVELOG mode, this text value specifies the default location and root of the file or tape device to use when archiving redo log files. Archiving to tape is not supported under all operating systems.

LOG_ARCHIVE_DUPLEX_DEST [valid path] <NULL>

This parameter specifies a second archive destination for duplexed archiving.

LOG_ARCHIVE_FORMAT [valid filename] <OS dependent>

This parameter uses a text string and variables to specify the default filename format of the archive log files. This string is appended to the LOG_ARCHIVE_DEST parameter name. The following variables can be used in the string:

- %s—Log sequence number.
- %t—Thread number. Using uppercase letters (%S, %T) causes the value to be fixed length, padded to the left with zeros. A good value is similar to the following:

```
LOG_ARCHIVE_FORMAT = 'log%S_%T.arc'
```

LOG_ARCHIVE_MIN_SUCCEED_DEST [1..2] <1>

This parameter specifies the minimum number of archive log destinations that must succeed.

LOG_ARCHIVE_START [TRUE/FALSE] <FALSE>

When running in ARCHIVELOG mode, LOG_ARCHIVE_START specifies whether archiving should be started up automatically at instance startup. A setting of TRUE indicates that archiving is automatic; FALSE indicates that archiving is manual.

LOG_BLOCK_CHECKSUM [TRUE/FALSE] <FALSE>

Setting this parameter to TRUE causes each log block to be given a checksum. This checksum is written into the header of each block.

LOG_CHECKPOINTS_TO_ALERT [TRUE/FALSE] <FALSE>

This parameter specifies whether you want to log the checkpoints to the alert log. This can be useful in verifying the frequency of checkpoints.

LOG_FILES [2..255] <255>
This parameter specifies the maximum number of redo log files that can be opened at instance startup. Reducing this value can save some space in the SGA. If this value is set higher than the value of MAXLOGFILES used at database creation, it does not override MAXLOGFILES.

MAX_DUMP_FILE_SIZE [0..unlimited] <500 blocks>
This parameter specifies the maximum size in OS blocks of any trace file written. Set this if you are worried that trace files might consume too much space.

MAX_ENABLED_ROLES [0..48] <20>
This parameter specifies the maximum number of database roles (including subroles) that a user can enable.

MAX_ROLLBACK_SEGMENTS [1..65536] <30>
This parameter specifies the maximum number of rollback segments that can be online for one instance.

OBJECT_CACHE_MAX_SIZE_PERCENT [0%..OS Dependent] <10%>
This parameter specifies the percentage of the optimal cache size beyond which the Session object cache size can grow.

OBJECT_CACHE_OPTIMAL_PERCENT [10KB..OS Dependent] <100KB>
This parameter specifies the optimal size of the Session object cache.

OPEN_CURSORS [1..OS limit] <50>
This parameter specifies the maximum number of open cursors that a single user process can have open at once.

OPEN_LINKS [0..255] <4>
This parameter specifies the maximum number of concurrent open connections to remote database processes per user process. This value should exceed the maximum number of remote systems accessed within any single SQL statement.

PARTITION_VIEW_ENABLED [TRUE/FALSE] <FALSE>
If set to TRUE, the optimizer skips unnecessary table accesses in a partition view.

PLSQL_V2_COMPATIBILITY [TRUE/FALSE] <FALSE>
This parameter sets the compatibility level for PL/SQL.

PROCESSES [6 to OS dependent] <50>
This parameter specifies the maximum number of OS user processes that connect to the Oracle instance. This number must take into account the background processes and the login process that started the instance. Be sure to add an extra six processes for the background processes.

REMOTE_DEPENDENCIES_MODE [*TIMESTAMP/SIGNATURE*] <TIMESTAMP>

This parameter specifies how dependencies on remote stored procedures are to be handled by the database.

REMOTE_LOGIN_PASSWORDFILE [*NONE/SHARED/EXCLUSIVE*] <NONE>

This parameter specifies whether Oracle checks for a password file. A value of NONE indicates that users are authenticated through the operating system. A value of EXCLUSIVE indicates that the password file can be used only by one database and can contain names other than SYS and INTERNAL. Setting this parameter to SHARED allows more than one database to use this password file, but only SYS and INTERNAL are recognized by this password file.

REPLICATION_DEPENDENCY_TRACKING [*TRUE/FALSE*] <TRUE>

This parameter specifies that dependency tracking for read/write operations to the database is turned on.

RESOURCE_LIMIT [*TRUE/FALSE*] <FALSE>

A value of FALSE disables the enforcement of resource limits such as sessions, CPU time, and so on. This disables the enforcement of those limits regardless of how they are set.

SESSIONS [*number*] <1.1 * PROCESSES>

This parameter specifies the total number of user and system sessions. Because recursive sessions might occur, this number should be set slightly higher than PROCESSES. DDL_LOCKS is derived from this parameter.

SHADOW_CORE_DUMP [*FULL/PARTIAL*] <FULL>

This parameter specifies whether the SGA is included in core dumps.

SNAPSHOT_REFRESH_INTERVAL [*1..3600*] <60>

This parameter specifies the number of seconds between wake-ups for the instance's snapshot refresh process.

SNAPSHOT_REFRESH_KEEP_CONNECTION [TRUE/FALSE] <FALSE>

This parameter specifies whether the snapshot refresh process should keep remote connections after the refresh. If set to FALSE, the remote database connections are closed after the refreshes occur.

SNAPSHOT_REFRESH_PROCESS [*0..10*] <0>

This parameter specifies the number of snapshot refresh processes per instance. You must set this value to 1 or higher for automatic refreshes. One snapshot refresh process is usually sufficient.

SINGLE_PROCESS [*TRUE/FALSE*] FALSE

If SINGLE_PROCESS is set to TRUE, the database instance is brought up in a single-user mode. A value of FALSE indicates that the database is brought up in a multiprocess mode.

TEMPORARY_TABLE_LOCKS [*0..OS dependent*] <SESSIONS>

TEMPORARY_TABLE_LOCKS specifies the number of temporary tables that can be created in the temporary segment space. A temporary table lock is required whenever a sort occurs that cannot be held in memory (that is, the sort exceeds SORT_AREA_RETAINED_SIZE). If your application contains a large number of ORDER BY clauses or if you perform a large number of index sorts, you might want to increase this number.

TRANSACTIONS [*number*] <1.1 * PROCESSES>

This parameter specifies the maximum number of concurrent transactions in the instance. The default value is greater than PROCESSES to provide for recursive transactions. A larger value increases the size of the SGA. If you increase the number of transactions allowed in the system, you might also want to increase the number of rollback segments available.

TRANSACTIONS_PER_ROLLBACK_SEGMENT [*1..OS dependent*] <30>

This value specifies the maximum number of concurrent transactions allowed per rollback segment. You can calculate the minimum number of rollback segments enabled at startup with this formula:

```
Rollback Segments = TRANSACTIONS / TRANSACTIONS_PER_ROLLBACK_SEGMENT
```

Performance can be improved if there is less contention on rollback segments. In a heavily used system, you might want to reduce TRANSACTIONS_PER_ROLLBACK_SEGMENT to decrease this contention.

USER_DUMP_DEST [*valid path name*] <OS dependent>

USER_DUMP_DEST specifies the path to where the debugging trace files are written.

UTL_FILE_DIR [*valid directory*]

This parameter specifies directories that are permitted for PL/SQL file I/O.

Recovery Manager

These parameters are used in conjunction with the Recovery Manager.

BACKUP_DISK_IO_SLAVES [*0..15*] <0>

This parameter defines the number of I/O slaves used by the Recovery Manager to back up, copy, or restore.

BACKUP_TAPE_IO_SLAVES [*TRUE/FALSE*] <FALSE>

This parameter specifies whether I/O slaves are used by the Recovery Manager for tape operations.

DB_FILE_NAME_CONVERT [*string*]

This parameter converts the filename of a new datafile on the primary database to a filename on the standby database.

LOG_FILE_NAME_CONVERT [*string*]

This parameter converts the filename of a new log file on the primary database to a filename on the standby database.

TAPE_ASYNCH_IO [*TRUE/FALSE*] <TRUE>

This parameter specifies that I/O to sequential devices are asynchronous. This should be left enabled and not altered.

Multithreaded Server

These parameters are used if you are using the multithreaded server process.

MTS_DISPATCHERS ["*protocol, number*"] <NULL>

This parameter specifies the configuration of the dispatcher process(es) created at startup time. The value of this parameter is a quoted string of two values separated by a comma. The values are the network protocol and the number of dispatchers. Each protocol requires a separate specification. This parameter can be specified multiple times. Here is an example of two dispatcher definitions:

```
MTS_DISPATCHERS = "tcp, 2"

MTS_DISPATCHERS = "ipx, 1"
```

MTS_LISTENER_ADDRESS [*configuration*] <NULL>

This parameter specifies the configuration of the listener process addresses. There must be a listener process address for each protocol used in the system. Addresses are specified as the SQL*Net description of the connection address.

Because each connection is required to have its own address, this parameter might be specified several times. Here is an example:

```
MTS_LISTENER_ADDRESS = "(ADDRESS=(PROTOCOL=tcp)(HOST=hostname)(PORT=7002))"
MTS_LISTENER_ADDRESS = "(ADDRESS=(PROTOCOL=ipx)()())"
```

MTS_MAX_DISPATCHERS [*OS dependent*] <5>

This parameter specifies the maximum number of dispatcher processes allowed to run simultaneously.

MTS_MAX_SERVERS [*OS dependent*] <20>

This parameter specifies the maximum number of shared server processes allowed to run simultaneously.

MTS_MULTIPLE_LISTENERS [*TRUE/FALSE*] <FALSE>

This parameter is obsolete.

MTS_RATE_LOG_SIZE [DEFAULTS/EVENT_LOOPS/MESSAGES/SERVER_BUFFERS/ CLIENT_BUFFERS/TOTAL_BUFFERS/IN_CONNECTS/OUT_CONNECTS/RECONNECTS] <10>
This parameter specifies the sample size used to calculate dispatcher-rate statistics.

MTS_RATE_SCALE [DEFAULTS/EVENT_LOOPS/MESSAGES/SERVER_BUFFERS/ CLIENT_BUFFERS/TOTAL_BUFFERS/IN_CONNECTS/OUT_CONNECTS/RECONNECTS] <misc>
This parameter specifies the scale at which dispatcher-rate statistics are reported.

MTS_SERVERS [*OS dependent*] <0>
This parameter specifies the number of server processes created at instance startup.

MTS_SERVICE [*name*] <DB_NAME>
This parameter specifies the name of the service to be associated with the dispatcher. Using this name in the CONNECT string allows users to connect using the dispatcher. The name should be unique. Do not specify this name in quotes. It is usually a good idea to make this name the same as the instance name. Because the dispatcher is tried first, if it is not available, the CONNECT string can still connect the user into the database through a normal database connection.

Distributed Option

These parameters are meaningful only when you use the distributed option.

COMMIT_POINT_STRENGTH [*0..255*] <OS dependent>
This value is used to determine the commit point site when executing a distributed transaction. The site with the highest value for COMMIT_POINT_STRENGTH is the commit point site. The site with the largest amount of critical data should be the commit point site.

DISTRIBUTED_LOCK_TIMEOUT [*1..unlimited*] <60 seconds>
DISTRIBUTED_LOCK_TIMEOUT specifies, in seconds, how long distributed transactions should wait for locked resources.

DISTRIBUTED_RECOVERY_CONNECTION_HOLD_TIME [*1..1800*] <200 seconds>
DISTRIBUTED_RECOVERY_CONNECTION_HOLD_TIME specifies, in seconds, how long to hold a remote connection open after a distributed transaction fails. A larger value holds the connection longer but also continues to use local resources even though the connection might have been severed. Any value larger than 1,800 seconds interferes with the reconnection and recovery background processes and will never drop a failed connection.

DISTRIBUTED_TRANSACTIONS [*0..TRANSACTIONS*] <OS dependent>
DISTRIBUTED_TRANSACTIONS specifies the maximum number of distributed transactions that the database can process concurrently. This value cannot exceed the value of TRANSACTIONS. If you are having problems with distributed transactions because network failures are causing many in-doubt transactions, you might want to limit the number of distributed transactions.

If `DISTRIBUTED_TRANSACTIONS` is set to 0, no distributed transactions are allowed and the RECO process does not start at instance startup.

MAX_TRANSACTION_BRANCHES [1..32] <8>
This parameter controls the number of branches in a distributed transaction.

REMOTE_OS_AUTHENT [*TRUE*/*FALSE*] <FALSE>
If this parameter is set to TRUE, it allows authentication to remote systems with the value of OS_AUTHENT_PREFIX.

REMOTE_OS_ROLES [*TRUE*/*FALSE*] <FALSE>
If this parameter is set to TRUE, it allows remote clients to have their roles managed by the OS. If REMOTE_OS_ROLES is FALSE, roles are managed and identified by the database for the remote system.

Parallel Server Parameters

These parameters are used only in conjunction with the Oracle Parallel Server option.

ALLOW_PARTIAL_SN_RESULTS [*TRUE*/*FALSE*] <FALSE>
This parameter allows partial results to be returned on queries to global performance tables even if a slave could not be allocated.

CACHE_SIZE_THRESHOLD [*number*] <0.1 * DB_BLOCK_BUFFERS>
This parameter specifies the maximum size of a cached partition table split among the caches of multiple instances. If the partition is larger than this value, the table is not split among the caches.

DELAYED_LOGGING_BLOCK_CLEANOUTS [*TRUE*/*FALSE*] <TRUE>
This parameter enables the delayed block cleanout feature. This can reduce OPS pinging.

FREEZE_DB_FOR_FAST_INSTANCE_RECOVERY [*TRUE*/*FALSE*]
This parameter specifies that the entire database freeze in order to speed recovery.

GC_DEFER_TIME [*integer*] <0>
This parameter specifies the time the server waits (in hundredths of a second) before responding to a forced-write request for hot blocks.

GC_DB_LOCKS [*0..unlimited*] <0>
This parameter specifies the number of PCM locks allocated. The value of GC_DB_LOCKS should be at least one greater than the sum of the locks specified with the parameter GC_FILES_TO_LOCKS.

GC_FILES_TO_LOCKS [*file_number=locks:filename=locks*] <NULL>
This parameter supplies a list of filenames, each specifying how many locks should be allocated for that file. Optionally, the number of blocks and the value EACH can be added to further specify the allocation of the locks.

GC_LCK_PROCS [0..10] <1>
This parameter specifies the number of lock processes (LCK0 to LCK9) to create for the instance. The default value of 1 is usually sufficient unless an unusually high number of locks are occurring.

GC_RELEASABLE_LOCKS [0..DB_BLOCK_BUFFERS] <DB_BLOCK_BUFFERS>
This parameter allocates space for fine-grain locking.

GC_ROLLBACK_LOCKS [number] <20>
This parameter specifies the number of distributed locks available for each rollback segment. The default value is usually sufficient.

GC_ROLLBACK_SEGMENTS [number] <20>
GC_ROLLBACK_SEGMENTS specifies the maximum number of rollback segments systemwide. This includes all instances in the parallel server system, including the SYSTEM rollback segment.

GC_SAVE_ROLLBACK_LOCKS [number] <20>
This parameter specifies the number of distributed locks reserved for deferred rollback segments. These deferred rollback segments contain rollback entries for segments taken offline.

GC_SEGMENTS [number] <10>
This parameter specifies the maximum number of segments that might have space-management activities simultaneously performed by different instances.

GC_TABLESPACES [number] <5>
This parameter specifies the maximum number of tablespaces that can be simultaneously brought online or offline.

INSTANCE_GROUPS [string]
This parameter assigns the current instance to this instance group.

INSTANCE_NUMBER [1..OS dependent] <Lowest Available Number>
This parameter specifies a unique number that maps the instance to a group of free space lists.

LM_LOCKS [512..Limited by Instance Size] <12000>
This parameter specifies the number of locks that are configured for the lock manager.

LM_PROCS [36..PROCESSES+instances+safety factor] <64+instances>
This parameter represents the number of the PROCESSES parameter plus the number of instances.

LM_RESS [256..Limited by Instance Size] <6000>
This parameter controls the number of resources that can be locked by each lock-manager process.

LOCK_NAME_SPACE [*string*]
This parameter specifies the name space that the distributed lock manager (DLM) uses to generate lock names.

MAX_COMMIT_PROPAGATION_DELAY [0..90000] <90000>
This parameter specifies the maximum amount of time that can pass before the SCN (System Change Number) is changed by the DBWR. This value helps in certain conditions where the SCN might not be refreshed often enough because of a high load from multiple instances.

OPEN_LINKS_PER_INSTANCE [*0..UB4MAXVAL*] <4>
This parameter specifies the maximum number of migratable open connections.

OPS_ADMIN_GROUP [*group name*] <all instances>
This parameter allows instances to be grouped for monitoring and administration.

PARALLEL_DEFAULT_MAX_INSTANCES [*0..instances*] <OS dependent>
This parameter specifies the default number of instances to spit a table among for parallel query processing. This value is used if the INSTANCES DEFAULT is specified in the table/cluster definition.

PARALLEL_INSTANCE_GROUP [*string*] <group>
This parameter specifies the parallel instance group to be used for spawning parallel query slaves.

PARALLEL_SERVER [*TRUE/FALSE*] <FALSE>
Setting this to TRUE enables the Parallel Server option.

PARALLEL_TRANSACTION_RESOURCE_TIMEOUT [*0..OS Dependent*] <300>
This parameter specifies the maximum amount of time (seconds) that can pass before a session executing a parallel operation will time-out while waiting on a resource held by another session.

THREAD [*0..max threads*] <0>
This parameter specifies the number of the redo thread to be used by this instance. Any number can be used, but the value must be unique within the cluster.

Security

These parameters help set up system security; manipulate them to obtain the best mix of efficiency and security.

AUDIT_FILE_DEST [*dir_name*] <$ORACLE_HOME/RDBMS/AUDIT>
This parameter specifies the directory where audit files are stored.

AUDIT_TRAIL [*NONE,DB,OS*]

The AUDIT_TRAIL parameter enables auditing to the table SYSAUD. Auditing causes a record of database and user activity to be logged. Because auditing causes overhead, it limits performance. The amount of overhead and the effect on performance is determined by what and how much is audited. Once AUDIT_TRAIL is enabled, auditing is turned on by the Oracle command AUDIT.

O7_DICTIONARY_ACCESSIBILITY [*TRUE/FALSE*] <TRUE>

If set to TRUE (default), access to the SYS schema is allowed. This is Oracle7 behavior.

OS_AUTHENT_PREFIX [] <OPS$>

This is the value concatenated to the beginning of the user's OS login account to give a default Oracle account name. The default value of OPS$ is OS dependent and is provided for backward compatibility with previous Oracle versions. Typically, you use the default or set the value to " " (NULL) to eliminate prefixes altogether.

OS_ROLES [*TRUE/FALSE*] <FALSE>

Setting this parameter to TRUE allows the OS to have control over the username's roles. If set to FALSE, the username's roles are controlled by the database.

SQL92_SECURITY [*TRUE/FALSE*] <FALSE>

This parameter specifies whether the table-level SELECT privileges are needed to execute an update or delete that reference's table-column values.

TRANSACTION_AUDITING [*TRUE/FALSE*] <TRUE>

This parameter specifies that additional transaction information is included in a special redo record.

Trusted Oracle7

The following parameters apply to the Trusted Oracle7 option.

AUTO_MOUNTING [*TRUE/FALSE*] <TRUE>

When set to TRUE, this parameter specifies that a secondary database is mounted by the primary database whenever a user connected to the primary database requests data from the secondary database.

DB_MOUNT_MODE [*NORMAL/READ_COMPATIBLE*] <NORMAL>

This parameter specifies the access mode to which the database is mounted at instance startup. A value of NORMAL starts the database in normal read-write mode; READ_COMPATIBLE starts the database in read-write mode with the added feature of supporting concurrent mounting by one or more read-secure instances.

LABEL_CACHE_SIZE [*number> 50*] <50>
This parameter specifies the cache size for dynamic comparison of labels. This number should be greater than the label-category combinations in the OS and should never be less than 50.

MLS_LABEL_FORMAT [*valid label format*] <sen>
This parameter specifies the format used to display labels. The default value sen specifies sensitive.

OPEN_MOUNTS [*0..255*] <5>
This parameter specifies the maximum number of databases that an instance can simultaneously mount in OS MAC mode. This value should be large enough to handle all the primary and secondary databases you might mount.

National Language Support

The following parameters are used in the configuration of National Language Support features.

NLS_CURRENCY [*character string*] <derived from NLS_TERRITORY>
This parameter specifies the string to use as the local currency symbol for the L number format element.

NLS_DATE_FORMAT [*format mask*] <derived from NLS_TERRITORY>
This parameter defines the default date format to use with the TO_CHAR and TO_DATE functions. The value of this parameter is any valid date format mask. Here is an example:

```
NLS_DATE_FORMAT = 'DD/MM/YYYY'
```

NLS_DATE_LANGUAGE [*NLS_LANGUAGE value*] <value for NLS_LANGUAGE>
This parameter determines the language to use for the day and month names and date abbreviations (AM, PM, AD, BC).

NLS_ISO_CURRENCY [*valid NLS_TERRITORY value*] <derived from NLS_TERRITORY>
This parameter defines the string to use as the international currency symbol for the C number format element.

NLS_LANGUAGE [*NLS_LANGUAGE value*] <OS dependent>
This parameter defines the default language of the database. This specifies the language to use for messages, the language of day and month names, symbols to be used for AD, BC, A.M. and P.M., and the default sorting mechanisms.

NLS_NUMERIC_CHARACTERS [*two characters*] <derived from NLS_TERRITORY>
This parameter defines the characters to be used as the group separator and decimal. The group separator is used to separate the integer groups (that is, hundreds, thousands, millions, and so on). The decimal separator is used to distinguish between the integer and decimal

portion of the number. Any two characters can be used but they must be different. The parameter is specified by two characters within single quotes. To set the group separator to , (comma) and the decimal separator to . (period), use the following statement:

```
NLS_NUMERIC_CHARACTERS = ',.'
```

NLS_SORT [*BINARY or named linguistic sort*] <derived from NLS_LANGUAGE>
If this parameter is set to BINARY, the collating sequence for ORDER_BY is based on the numeric values of the characters. A linguistic sort decides the order based on the defined linguistic sort. A binary sort is much more efficient and uses much less overhead.

NLS_TERRITORY [*territory name*] <OS dependent>
This parameter specifies the name of the territory whose conventions are used for day and week numbering. The parameter also provides defaults for other NLS parameters.

APPENDIX

C

Oracle Roles and Privileges

This appendix lists the Oracle default roles and system privileges. Table C.1 lists the Oracle commands and the privileges necessary to run them. Table C.2 lists the default Oracle roles and the system privileges they contain.

Table C.1. Oracle commands and required privileges.

Command	Required system privilege
ALTER CLUSTER	ALTER ANY CLUSTER.
ALTER DATABASE	ALTER DATABASE.
ALTER FUNCTION	ALTER ANY PROCEDURE.
ALTER INDEX	ALTER ANY INDEX.
ALTER PACKAGE	ALTER ANY PROCEDURE.
ALTER PROCEDURE	ALTER ANY PROCEDURE.
ALTER PROFILE	To change profile resource limits, the ALTER PROFILE system privilege is required. To modify password limits and protection, the ALTER PROFILE and ALTER USER system privileges are required.
ALTER RESOURCE COST	ALTER RESOURCE COST.
ALTER ROLE	The ALTER ANY ROLE system privilege is required, or you must have been granted ROLE with ADMIN OPTION.
ALTER ROLLBACK SEGMENT	ALTER ROLLBACK SEGMENT.
ALTER SEQUENCE	The ALTER ANY SEQUENCE system privilege is required, you must have the ALTER system privilege on the sequence, or the sequence must be in your own schema.
ALTER SESSION	The ALTER SESSION system privilege is required to enable and disable the SQL Trace facility or change the default label format.
ALTER SNAPSHOT	The ALTER ANY SNAPSHOT system privilege is required, or a snapshot must be contained in your own schema.
ALTER SNAPSHOT LOG	Only the owner of a master table or a user with the SELECT system privilege for the master table can use this command.
ALTER SYSTEM	ALTER SYSTEM.
ALTER TABLE	The ALTER ANY TABLE system privilege is required, the table must be contained in your own schema, or you must have the ALTER system privilege on the table.
ALTER TABLESPACE	The ALTER TABLESPACE system privilege is required or, using MANAGE TABLESPACE, you can take the system offline or

Command	Required system privilege
	online, begin or end a backup, and make the system read-only or read-write.
ALTER TRIGGER	The ALTER ANY TRIGGER system privilege is required, or the trigger must be in your own schema.
ALTER TYPE	The ALTER ANY TYPE system privilege is required, or the object type must be in your schema and you must have CREATE TYPE or CREATE ANY TYPE system privileges.
ALTER USER	The ALTER USER system privilege is required. You can change your own password without this privilege.
ALTER VIEW	The ALTER ANY TABLE system privilege is required, or the view must be in your own schema.
ALTER CLUSTER	ALTER ANY TABLE.
ANALYZE	The ANALYZE ANY system privilege is required, or the schema object to be analyzed must be in your own schema.
AUDIT (SQL Statements)	AUDIT SYSTEM.
AUDIT (Schema Objects)	The AUDIT ANY system privilege is required, or the object you choose for auditing must be in your own schema.
COMMENT	The COMMENT ANY TABLE system privilege is required, or the view, snapshot, or table must be in your own schema.
COMMIT	No privileges are required.
CREATE CLUSTER	The CREATE CLUSTER system privilege is required for your own schema; for another user's schema, you need CREATE ANY CLUSTER plus either a space quota on the tablespace containing the cluster or the UNLIMITED TABLESPACE system privilege.
CREATE CONTROLFILE	The OSDBA role must be enabled.
CREATE DATABASE	The OSDBA role must be enabled.
CREATE DATABASE LINK	For a private link, CREATE DATABASE LINK is required. For a public link, CREATE PUBLIC DATABASE LINK is required along with the CREATE SESSION privilege on the remote database.
CREATE DIRECTORY	CREATE ANY DIRECTORY.
CREATE FUNCTION	The CREATE ANY PROCEDURE system privilege is required, or CREATE PROCEDURE is required if the function is in your own schema.

continues

Table C.1. continued

Command	Required system privilege
CREATE INDEX	The owner of the schema must have the space quota on the tablespace or the UNLIMITED TABLESPACE system privilege. For your own schema, either the table or the cluster must be in the schema, you must have the INDEX privilege on the table, or you must have the CREATE ANY INDEX system privilege. To create an index in another schema, you must have the CREATE ANY INDEX system privilege.
CREATE LIBRARY	The CREATE ANY LIBRARY system privilege is required. To use the library, you must have the EXECUTE object system privilege for the library.
CREATE PACKAGE	The CREATE ANY PROCEDURE system privilege is required. The CREATE PROCEDURE system privilege is required if the package is in your own schema.
CREATE PACKAGE BODY	The CREATE ANY PROCEDURE system privilege is required. The CREATE PROCEDURE system privilege is required if the package is in your own schema.
CREATE PROCEDURE	The CREATE ANY PROCEDURE system privilege is required with the CREATE PROCEDURE system privilege if the procedure is in your own schema, or the ALTER ANY PROCEDURE system privilege to replace a procedure.
CREATE PROFILE	CREATE PROFILE.
CREATE ROLE	CREATE ROLE.
CREATE ROLLBACK SEGMENT	The CREATE ROLLBACK SEGMENT system privilege is required, and you must have either the UNLIMITED TABLESPACE system privilege or the space quota on the tablespace.
CREATE SCHEMA	You must have the necessary privileges for included statements, if any.
CREATE SEQUENCE	For your own schema, the CREATE SEQUENCE system privilege is required. The CREATE ANY SEQUENCE system privilege is required for another user's schema.
CREATE SNAPSHOT	The CREATE SNAPSHOT, CREATE TABLE, and CREATE VIEW system privileges are required in your own schema; the CREATE ANY SNAPSHOT system privilege is required in another schema and you must have a sufficient quota in the tablespace or UNLIMITED TABLESPACE.

Command	Required system privilege
CREATE SNAPSHOT LOG	The CREATE TABLE system privilege is required if you own the master table, the CREATE ANY TABLE system privilege is required in another schema, and the COMMENT ANY TABLE and SELECT system privileges are required on the master table.
CREATE SYNONYM	The CREATE SYNONYM system privilege is required for your own schema. For another user's schema, the CREATE ANY SYNONYM system privilege is required. For public schemas, the CREATE PUBLIC SYNONYM system privilege is required.
CREATE TABLE	The CREATE TABLE system privilege is required to create a table in your own schema. The CREATE ANY TABLE system privilege is required to create a table in other schemas and requires either a sufficient quota on the tablespace or UNLIMITED TABLESPACE.
CREATE TABLESPACE	The CREATE TABLESPACE system privilege is required, and the SYSTEM tablespace must contain at least two rollback segments, including the SYSTEM rollback segment.
CREATE TRIGGER	The CREATE TRIGGER system privilege is required for your own schema. The CREATE ANY TRIGGER system privilege is required for other schemas.
CREATE TYPE	The CREATE TYPE system privilege is required for your own schema. The CREATE ANY TYPE system privilege is required for other schemas.
CREATE TYPE BODY	The CREATE TYPE system privilege is required for your own schema. The CREATE ANY TYPE system privilege is required for other schemas.
CREATE USER	CREATE USER.
CREATE VIEW	The CREATE VIEW system privilege is required for your own schema. The CREATE ANY VIEW system privilege is required for other schemas.
DELETE	DELETE.
DROP CLUSTER	The DROP ANY CLUSTER system privilege is required, or the cluster must be in your own schema.
DROP DATABASE LINK	To drop your own database link, it must be in your own schema. To drop a public database link, you must have the DROP PUBLIC DATABASE LINK system privilege.

continues

Table C.1. continued

Command	Required system privilege
DROP DIRECTORY	DROP ANY DIRECTORY.
DROP FUNCTION	DROP ANY PROCEDURE.
DROP INDEX	The DROP ANY INDEX system privilege is required, or the index must be in your own schema.
DROP LIBRARY	DROP LIBRARY.
DROP PACKAGE	DROP ANY PROCEDURE.
DROP PROCEDURE	DROP ANY PROCEDURE.
DROP PROFILE	DROP PROFILE.
DROP ROLE	The DROP ANY ROLE system privilege is required, or you must have been granted the role with the ADMIN option.
DROP ROLLBACK SEGMENT	DROP ROLLBACK SEGMENT.
DROP SEQUENCE	The DROP ANY SEQUENCE system privilege is required, or the sequence must be in your own schema.
DROP SNAPSHOT	The snapshot must be in your own schema, or the DROP ANY SNAPSHOT system privilege is required.
DROP SNAPSHOT LOG	The DROP ANY TABLE system privilege is required, or the table must be in your own schema.
DROP SYNONYM (PRIVATE)	SYNONYM must be in your own schema, or you must have the DROP ANY SYNONYM system privilege.
DROP SYNONYM (PUBLIC)	SYNONYM must be in your own schema, or you must have the DROP ANY PUBLIC SYNONYM system privilege.
DROP TABLE	The DROP ANY TABLE system privilege is required, or the table must be in your own schema.
DROP TABLESPACE	DROP TABLESPACE.
DROP TRIGGER	The DROP ANY TRIGGER system privilege is required, or the trigger must be in your own schema.
DROP TYPE	The DROP ANY TYPE system privilege is required, or you must be in your own schema.
DROP TYPE BODY	The object TYPE BODY must be in your own schema and you must have the CREATE TYPE or CREATE ANY TYPE system privilege or the DROP ANY TYPE system privilege.
DROP USER	DROP USER.
DROP VIEW	The DROP ANY VIEW system privilege is required, or the view must be in your own schema.

Command	Required system privilege
GRANT (SYSTEM PRIVILEGES and ROLES)	To grant a system privilege you must have GRANT ANY PRIVILEGE system privilege or you must have been granted the system privilege with the ADMIN OPTION. To grant a role you must have GRANT ANY ROLE system privileges, you must have been granted the role with the ADMIN OPTION, or you must have created the role.
INSERT	This must be in your own schema, or you must have the INSERT system privilege on the table. To insert into any table, you must have the INSERT ANY TABLE system privilege.
LOCK TABLE	The LOCK ANY TABLE system privilege is required, the table or view must be in your own schema, or you must have any object privilege on the table or view.
NOAUDIT (SQL Statements)	AUDIT SYSTEM.
NOAUDIT (Schema Objects)	The AUDIT ANY system privilege is required or you must be in your own schema.
RENAME	The object must be in your own schema.
REVOKE (SYSTEM PRIVILEGES and ROLES)	To revoke a system privilege, you must have been granted the system privilege or role with the ADMIN OPTION. To revoke a role, you must have GRANT ANY ROLE system privileges. To revoke a schema object privilege, you must have previously granted the object privileges to each user and role.
ROLLBACK	To roll back the current transaction, no privileges are necessary. To roll back an in-doubt distributed transaction, the FORCE TRANSACTION system privilege is required. To roll back an in-doubt distributed transaction originally committed by another user, the FORCE ANY TRANSACTION system privilege is required.
SAVEPOINT	None necessary.
SELECT	This command requires that you have the SELECT system privilege on the appropriate table or snapshot or that you have the SELECT ANY TABLE system privilege for any table or snapshot.
SET CONSTRAINT(S)	The SELECT system privilege on the table is required, or you must be in your own schema.

continues

Table C.1. continued

Command	Required system privilege
SET ROLE	You must have already been granted the roles that you name in the SET ROLE statement.
SET TRANSACTION	This must be the first statement in your transaction.
TRUNCATE	The DELETE TABLE system privilege is required or the table or cluster must be in your schema.
UPDATE	You must have UPDATE privileges on the appropriate table or base table or view.

Table C.2. Roles and their system privileges.

Role	System privileges
CONNECT	ALTER SESSION, CREATE CLUSTER, CREATE DATABASE LINK, CREATE SEQUENCE, CREATE SESSION, CREATE SYNONYM, CREATE TABLE, CREATE VIEW.
DBA	All system privileges with ADMIN OPTION.
DELETE_CATALOG_ROLE	DELETE privileges on all dictionary packages for this role.
EXECUTE_CATALOG_ROLE	EXECUTE privileges on all dictionary packages for this role.
EXP_FULL_DATABASE	SELECT ANY TABLE, BACKUP ANY TABLE.
IMP_FULL_DATABASE	BECOME USER.
RESOURCE	CREATE CLUSTER, CREATE PROCEDURE, CREATE SEQUENCE, CREATE TABLE, CREATE TRIGGER.
SELECT_CATALOG_ROLE	SELECT privileges on all catalog tables and views for this role.

APPENDIX
D

Glossary

A

aggregate functions—Functions that operate on the collection of values in a certain column. These operations include such things as SUM, COUNT, AVG, MAX, and so on.

asynchronous I/O (AIO)—Asynchronous I/O allows a process to submit an I/O and not have to wait for the response. Later, when the I/O is completed, an interrupt occurs or the process can check to see whether the I/O has completed. By using asynchronous I/Os, the DBWR can manage multiple writes at once so that it is not starved waiting for I/Os to complete.

B

bandwidth—A term often associated with networks or computer buses. The bandwidth is the throughput capacity. The bandwidth of the bus is the maximum rate at which data can be transferred across the bus.

batch processing system—Used to perform large background jobs, usually within a specified time window.

Binary Large Data—*See* **BLOB**.

BLOB (Binary Large Data)—A large amount of binary data stored within an Oracle database. BLOB data can consist of audio, video, images, documents, and so on; it is usually stored as LONG data.

block—The smallest unit of storage in an Oracle database. The database block contains header information concerning the block itself as well as the data.

buffer—An amount of memory used to store data. A buffer stores data that is about to be used or that has just been used. In many cases, buffers are in-memory copies of data that is also on disk. Buffers can be used as a copy of data for quick read access, they can be modified and written to disk, or they can be created in memory as temporary storage.

In Oracle, the database buffers of the SGA store the most recently used blocks of database data. The set of database block buffers is known as the **database buffer cache**. The buffers used to temporarily store redo entries until they can be written to disk are known as the **redo log buffers**.

A **clean buffer** is a buffer that has not been modified. Because this buffer has not been changed, it is not necessary for the DBWR to write this buffer to disk. A **dirty buffer** is a buffer that has been modified. It is the job of the DBWR to eventually write all dirty block buffers out to disk.

C

cache—A storage area used to provide fast access to data. In hardware terms, the cache is a small (relative to main RAM) amount of memory that is much faster than main memory. This memory is used to reduce the time it takes to reload frequently used data or instructions into the CPU. CPU chips themselves contain small amounts of memory built in as a cache.

In Oracle, the block buffers and shared pool are considered caches because they are used to store data and instructions for quick access. Caching is very effective in reducing the time it takes to retrieve frequently used data.

Caching usually works using a **least recently used algorithm**. Data that has not been used for a while is eventually released from the cache to make room for new data. If data is requested and is in the cache (a phenomenon called a **cache hit**), the data is retrieved from the cache, which means it does not have to be retrieved from disk. After the data has been accessed again, it is marked as recently used and put on the top of the cache list.

Cartesian products—The result of a join with no join condition. Each row in a table is matched with every row of another table.

checksum—A number calculated from the contents of a storage unit such as a file or data block. Using a mathematical formula, the checksum number is generated from data. Because it is highly unlikely that data corruption can occur in such a way that the checksum would remain the same, checksums are used to verify data integrity. From Oracle version 7.2 onward, checksums can be enabled on data blocks and redo blocks.

cluster (machine)—A group of computers that together form a larger logical machine. Oracle clusters computers with the Oracle Parallel Server option.

cluster (table)—A set of independent tables with a common column stored together. A cluster can improve performance by reducing I/Os and by preloading related data into the SGA before it is needed.

cluster index—The index on the cluster key. Each cluster key must have an index before data can be entered into the cluster.

cluster key—The common column in the set of tables built into a cluster. The cluster key must be indexed.

cold data—This term typically refers to infrequently used data. Cold data is rarely in cache because it is infrequently accessed.

cold database—This term typically refers to a database that is currently closed and not mounted. No users can connect to the database and no datafiles can be accessed.

D

collision—Typically refers to a network collision. A network collision occurs when two or more NICs try to use the network at the same time. When this happens, all the NICs must resend their data.

Common Object Response Broker Architecture—*See* **CORBA**.

complex statements—A SQL statement that contains a subquery. A **subquery** is a query within the SQL statement used to determine values in the main statement, or **parent statement**.

compound query—A query in which the set operators (UNION, UNION ALL, INTERSECT, and MINUS) are used to join two or more simple or complex statements. The individual statements in the compound query are referred to as **component queries**.

concurrency—The capability to perform many functions at the same time. Oracle provides for concurrency by allowing many users to access the database simultaneously.

consistent mode—In this mode, Oracle provides a consistent view of data from a certain point in time for the duration of the transaction. Until the transaction is complete, the data cannot change.

consistent read—A data access that causes a read from the rollback segment, thus keeping data consistent.

constraint—The mechanism that ensures that certain conditions relating columns and tables are maintained.

contention—A term usually used to describe a condition that occurs when two or more processes or threads attempt to obtain the same resource. The results of contention can vary depending on the resource in question.

CORBA—CORBA stands for the Common Object Request Broker Architecture, and is a specification for object communications.

cost-based optimizer—The Oracle optimizer that chooses an execution plan based on information and statistics that it has for tables, indexes, and clusters.

current mode—The mode in which Oracle provides a view as the data exists at this moment. Queries typically use **consistent mode**.

current read—A read in current mode; typically used for UPDATE, INSERT, and DELETE statements.

cursor—A handle to a specific private SQL area. Think of a cursor as a pointer to or a name of a particular private SQL area.

D

database administrator—*See* **DBA**.

Data Definition Language commands—*See* **DDL commands**.

data dictionary—A set of tables Oracle uses to maintain information about the database. The data dictionary contains information about tables, indexes, clusters, and so on.

Data Manipulation Language commands—*See* **DML commands**.

data warehouse—An extremely large database consisting of data from many sources to provide an information pool for business queries.

DBA—Database Administrator. The person responsible for the operation and configuration of the database. The DBA is responsible for the performance of the database, and is charged with keeping the database operating smoothly, ensuring that backups are performed on a regular basis (and that the backups work), and installing new software. Other responsibilities might include planning for future expansion and disk space needs, creating databases and tablespaces, adding users and maintaining security, and monitoring the database and retuning it as necessary. Large installations might have teams of DBAs to keep the system running smoothly; alternatively, the tasks might be segmented among the DBAs.

DDL commands—Data Definition Language commands. The commands used in the creation and modification of schema objects. These commands include the ability to create, alter, and drop objects; grant and revoke privileges and roles; establish auditing options; and add comments to the data dictionary. These commands are related to the management and administration of the Oracle database. Before and after each DDL statement, Oracle implicitly commits the current transaction.

deadlock—Deadlocks occur when two or more processes hold a resource that the other one needs. Neither of the processes will release its resource until it has received the other's resource; therefore, neither process can proceed.

Decision Support System—*See* **DSS**.

deferred frame—A network frame delayed from transferring because the network is busy.

DELETE—The SQL statement used to delete a row or rows from a table.

device driver—The piece of software, supplied by the OS or hardware vendor, that provides support for a piece of hardware such as a disk array controller or a NIC.

disk array—A set of two or more disks that might appear to the system as one large disk. A disk array can be a software or hardware device.

DML commands—Data Manipulation Language commands. The commands that allow you to query and modify data within existing schema objects. Unlike the DDL commands, a commit is not implicit. DML statements consist of DELETE, INSERT, SELECT, and UPDATE statements; EXPLAIN PLAN statements; and LOCK TABLE statements.

DSS—Decision Support System. A DSS is characterized by large business queries designed to provide valuable data that is used to make sound business decisions.

dynamic performance tables—Tables created at instance startup and used to store information about the performance of the instance. This information includes connection information, I/Os, initialization parameter values, and so on.

E

Ethernet—A network hardware standard. Ethernet is probably the most-used network type in the world.

equijoin—A join statement that uses an equivalency operation. The converse of this is the **nonequijoin** operation.

extent—A group of contiguous data blocks allocated for a table, index, or cluster. Extents are added dynamically as needed.

F

foreign key—An attribute requiring that a value must exist in another object, if not NULL, and be its primary key.

frame—*See* **network frame**.

function—A set of SQL or PL/SQL statements used together to execute a particular function. Procedures and functions are identical except that functions always return a value (procedures do not). By processing the SQL code on the database server, you can reduce the number of instructions sent across the network and returned from the SQL statements.

H

HAL—Hardware Abstraction Layer. A software layer closest to the hardware that performs all hardware-specific functions. The HAL includes the device drivers.

Hardware Abstraction Layer—*See* **HAL**.

hot data—This term typically refers to frequently accessed data. Hot data typically gets a good cache-hit rate.

hot database—This term typically refers to a database that is currently mounted, open, and servicing transactions. The instance is up and users are accessing data.

I

index—A device designed to give you faster access to your data. An index lets you avoid sequentially reading through data to find the item you are seeking.

initialization parameter—A parameter read by Oracle at instance startup. These parameters affect the Oracle configuration.

INSERT—The SQL statement used to insert a row into a table.

instance—The Oracle instance consists of the SGA, the Oracle background processes, and the datafiles that make up your database.

I/O (Input and Output [of data])—This term can be used to describe any type of data transfer but is typically associated with accesses to disk drives.

J

join—A query that selects data from more than one table. The data selected from the different tables is determined by conditions specified within the FROM clause of the statement. These conditions are called **join conditions**.

join condition—The specification within the WHERE clause of a query join that specifies the manner in which the rows in the different tables are paired.

L

LAN—A local, high-speed network that uses network hardware such as Ethernet or Token Ring and protocols such as TCP/IP and SPX/IPX.

lightweight process—Sometimes known as a **thread**. Similar to a process but shares the process context with other lightweight processes. A lightweight process has much less overhead associated with it than does a normal process. A **thread switch** (change between threads) has much less overhead than a process switch.

Local Area Network—*See* **LAN**.

logical disk—A term used to describe a disk that is in reality two or more disks in a hardware or software disk array. It appears to the user as one large disk when, in reality, it is two or more striped physical disks.

M

main memory—A term often used to describe RAM (Random Access Memory). This is the part of the computer system used to store data being processed or data that has recently been accessed. RAM is volatile and is not saved when the system is powered off.

Massively Parallel Processor system—*See* **MPP system**.

microkernel—The core component of a microkernel operating system. The microkernel contains the base components of the operating system. In a microkernel architecture, OS functions usually done in the kernel (such as I/O and device-driver support) are moved out of the kernel.

MPP system—Massively Parallel Processor system. A multiprocessor computer consisting of many independent processors that communicate through a complex, high-speed bus.

multiprocessor system—A computer that has two or more CPUs. A multiprocessor can be an SMP (Symmetric Multiprocessor) or an MPP (Massively Parallel Processor) system.

N

NCA—The Network Computing Architecture (NCA) is a standard for computing over the network. The NCA was developed in conjunction with Oracle.

Network Computing Architecture—*See* **NCA**.

network frame—The structure sent across the network that contains user data as well as network control information. The terms **network frame** and **network packet** are sometimes interchangeable.

Network Interface Card—*See* **NIC**.

network packet—The structure built by the Network Protocol layer. This structure includes user data as well as network and routing information.

NIC—Network Interface Card. A piece of hardware used to network computers together. A NIC can be one of several varieties including Ethernet, Token Ring, or fiber optic.

nonequijoin—A join statement that does not use an equality operation. The converse of this is the **equijoin** operation.

O

OCI—Oracle Call Interface. The standard set of calls used to access the Oracle database.

offline—This term typically refers to a database that is currently closed and not mounted. No users can connect to the database and no datafiles can be accessed.

OLTP—Online Transaction Processing. An OLTP system is characterized by large numbers of users inserting and retrieving data in a somewhat unstructured manner.

online—This term typically refers to a database that is currently mounted, open, and servicing transactions. The instance is up and users are accessing data.

Online Transaction Processing—*See* **OLTP**.

optimizer—A component of the Oracle RDBMS used to select SQL execution plans in the most efficient and cost-effective manner. There are two optimizers: a cost-based optimizer and a rules-based optimizer. Each determines the best execution plan based on different criteria.

Oracle Call Interface—*See* **OCI**.

outer join—A join operation that uses the outer join operator (+) in one of the join statements. The output of an outer join is the rows that satisfy the join condition and those rows in the first table for which no rows in the second table satisfy the join condition.

P

package—A collection of related, stored procedures or functions grouped together.

packet—*See* **network packet**.

paging—An operating system function used to copy virtual memory between physical memory and the paging file (*see* **virtual memory**). Paging is used when the amount of virtual memory in use has exceeded the amount of physical memory available. Paging is an expensive task in terms of performance and should be avoided if possible.

Parallel Query option—An add-on package to the Oracle RDBMS that allows for concurrent processing of some functions.

Parallel Server option—An add-on package to the Oracle RDBMS that allows for multiple systems to share a common database. Each system has its own instance but the database tables are shared. Data consistency is guaranteed by means of a sophisticated locking mechanism.

physical memory—The actual hardware RAM (Random Access Memory) available in the computer for use by the operating system and applications.

PL/SQL—A set of procedural language extensions that Oracle has added to standard SQL. Procedures, functions, packages, and triggers are written in the PL/SQL language.

primary key—Attributes used to uniquely identify a row in a table.

procedure—A set of SQL or PL/SQL statements used together to execute a particular function. Procedures and functions are identical except that functions always return a value (procedures do not). By processing the SQL code on the database server, you can reduce the number of instructions sent across the network and returned from the SQL statements.

program unit—In Oracle, the term used to describe a package, a stored procedure, or a sequence.

Q

query—A question. A SELECT statement is considered a query because it requests information from the database. Any read-only SQL statement can be thought of as a query.

R

random I/O—Occurs when data is accessed on a disk drive in no specific order. Random I/O typically creates significant disk-head movement.

read consistency—An attribute used to ensure that, during a SQL statement, data returned from Oracle is consistent. Oracle uses the rollback segments to ensure read consistency.

recursive call—A set of SQL statements generated by Oracle in response to some action or event.

redo log file—The file that contains a copy of all data blocks that have been modified as the result of a database transaction. In the event of a system failure, any transaction can be recovered with these redo blocks. Oracle requires at least two redo log files that are written to in a round-robin fashion.

referential integrity—A constraint on a column in a table that references another column. The constraint can be used to guarantee that the referenced value exists.

replication—The creation of an image of a database or table on another computer system. A **replicated database** is a copy of another database.

rollback—The act of undoing changes that have been made by a transaction.

rollback segment—The place in the database where undo information is kept and can be obtained if a rollback is needed.

rules-based optimizer—The Oracle optimizer that chooses an execution plan based on a table of costs associated with various operations.

S

scalability—Typically used in association with multiprocessor or cluster configurations. The scalability of the additional component refers to the performance gain obtained by adding that component. A perfectly scalable solution gives double the performance when you add a second component.

For example, if you have an SMP machine with a measured performance of 1.0 (normalized), add a second CPU, and get a performance of 1.9, the scalability of adding the second CPU is 1.9, or 90%. This term is used quite frequently in hardware and software manufacturers' literature when marketing multiprocessor or clustered solutions.

schema—A collection of objects associated with the database.

schema objects—Abstractions or logical structures that refer to database objects or structures. Schema objects consist of such things as clusters, indexes, packages, sequences, stored procedures, synonyms, tables, views, and so on.

SCN—System Change Number. The SCN is a number that identifies each change to the database. The SCNs are used during the checkpoint process, recovery process, and during point-in-time recovery.

segment—The set of extents that have been allocated to a specific object. Segment types consist of data, index, cluster, hash, and rollback.

self join—A join in which a table is joined with itself.

sequences—A convenience feature of Oracle that allows unique sequential numbers to be automatically generated for you.

sequential I/O—Occurs when data is accessed on a disk drive in order. Sequential I/O typically causes very little disk-head movement.

Server Manager—Oracle's GUI database administration tool. Server Manager is used to replace SQL*DBA.

session—The set of events that occurs from when a user connects to the Oracle RDBMS to when that user disconnects.

SGA—System Global Area. The SGA is a shared memory region Oracle uses to store data and control information for one Oracle instance. The SGA is allocated when the Oracle instance starts; it is deallocated when the Oracle instance shuts down. Each Oracle instance that starts has its own SGA. The information in the SGA is made up of the database buffers, the redo log buffer, and the shared pool; each has a fixed size and is created at instance startup.

shared pool—The area in the SGA that contains the data dictionary cache and shared parsed SQL statements.

simple statement—A SQL statement that involves only one INSERT, UPDATE, or DELETE statement.

SMP—Symmetric Multiprocessor. An SMP system is a multiprocessor computer that uses a shared-memory architecture. SMP systems are usually either a tightly coupled or a loosely coupled architecture.

D

snapshot—A copy of a database or table. This term is used in relation to database replication.

SPX/IPX—A network protocol developed for the NetWare operating system. Today, SPX/IPX runs on many operating systems.

SQL*DBA—The Oracle database administration tool. SQL*DBA is being made obsolete by Server Manager.

SQL*Loader—The Oracle database loading tool.

SQL*Net—The Oracle component that allows connections from a network into the Oracle RDBMS. SQL*Net supports many protocols; SQL*Net on any architecture can talk to SQL*Net on any other supported architecture.

SQL*Plus—An Oracle-supplied tool that allows users to run SQL statements directly.

streaming—Usually associated with a tape device. Tapes perform best when the tape is continually in motion, or streaming. If the data is not fed to the tape quickly enough, the tape drive must reposition the tape to wherever it last stopped recording data (to reposition the tape, the drive must stop the tape and rewind it). This action severely degrades performance.

stored function—*See* **function**.

stored procedure—*See* **procedure**.

subquery—A SELECT statement referenced in an UPDATE, INSERT, or DELETE statement.

swapping—An operating system function similar to paging; used to copy virtual memory between physical memory and the paging file (*see* **virtual memory**). Swapping is almost identical to paging except that swapping is done on a process basis and paging is done on a memory-page basis. Swapping is used when the amount of virtual memory in use has exceeded the amount of physical memory available. Swapping is quite expensive in terms of performance and should be avoided if possible.

Symmetric Multiprocessor—*See* **SMP**.

synonym—An alias for a table, view, sequence, or program unit.

System Change Number—*See* **SCN**.

System Global Area—*See* **SGA**.

T

table—The basic unit of storage in the Oracle database. Users store their data in tables.

tablespace—A logical structure that consists of one or more datafiles. A tablespace is used to logically contain tables, clusters, and indexes.

TCP/IP (Transmission Control Protocol/Internet Protocol)—A network protocol. TCP/IP is probably the most used network protocol in the world.

thread—Sometimes know as a **lightweight process**. Similar to a process but shares the process context with other threads. A thread has much less overhead associated with it than does a normal process. A **thread switch** (change between threads) has much less overhead than a process switch.

Token Ring—A hardware network standard. Token Ring networks use a token-passing mechanism for arbitration. Only the NIC with the token can use the network.

transaction—A set of database statements that represents a logical unit of work or function. A database transaction starts when the first SQL statement is submitted and ends when the COMMIT or ROLLBACK has occurred. Performance measurements often use the number of transactions per second as the performance metric.

trigger—A mechanism that allows you to write procedures that are automatically executed whenever an INSERT, UPDATE, or DELETE statement is executed on a table or view. Triggers can be used to enforce integrity constraints or automate some other custom function.

two-phase commit—The process by which distributed transactions occur. In a two-phase commit, each node commits its changes and signals that it has completed. When all nodes have successfully committed, the distributed transaction has committed.

U

UPDATE—The SQL statement used to change rows in a table.

V

view—A window into a table or set of tables. A view is a way for a table or set of tables to be seen. A view, like a table, can be queried, updated, inserted into, and deleted from. The data, however, is actually stored in the tables to which the view refers.

virtual memory—The memory that can be used for programs in the operating system. To overcome the limitations associated with insufficient physical memory, virtual memory allows programs to run that are larger than the amount of physical memory in the system. When there is not enough physical memory in the system, these programs are copied from RAM to a disk file called a **paging file** or **swap file**. This arrangement allows small systems to run many programs. You pay a performance penalty when the computer pages or swaps.

INDEX

MACMILLAN COMPUTER PUBLISHING USA

A VIACOM COMPANY

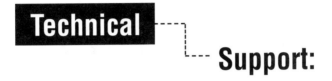

Technical ---- Support:

If you need assistance with the information in this book or with a CD/Disk
accompanying the book, please access the Knowledge Base on our Web
site at **http://www.superlibrary.com/general/support**. Our most
Frequently Asked Questions are answered there. If you do not find the
answer to your questions on our Web site, you may contact Macmillan
Technical Support **(317) 581-3833** or e-mail us at **support@mcp.com**.

Teach Yourself Oracle8 Database Development in 21 Days

David Lockman

Teach Yourself Oracle8 Database Development in 21 Days is a hands-on tutorial that will quickly teach you the basics of developing Oracle database applications. This book focuses on teaching the concepts behind logical and physical database design, a working knowledge of SQL and PL/SQL, the basics of Developer/2000, and Oracle Power Objects. This is the first and only beginning-level book devoted entirely to Oracle development.

Price: $49.99 USA/$70.95 CAN   User Level: Beginning–Intermediate

ISBN: 0-672-31078-3   600 pages

Teach Yourself SQL in 21 Days, Second Edition

Ryan K. Stephens, Ronald R. Plew, Bryan Morgan, and Jeff Perkins

Fully updated and revised to include coverage of PL/SQL and TransactSQL, this easy-to-understand guide teaches you everything you need to know from database concepts and processes to implementing security and constructing and optimizing queries. This book, which includes Q&A sections, step-by-step instructions, and review sections to make learning easy and fun, illustrates how to create tables, modify data, incorporate security features, and tune the database for optimum performance. This book emphasizes common database concepts, including SQL functions and queries.

Price: $39.99 USA/$56.95 CAN   User Level: New–Casual

ISBN: 0-672-31110-0   624 pages

Access 97 Programming Unleashed

Scott Billings, Joe Rhemann, et al

Access 97 solves all the development problems within Access 95, meaning that more developers will adopt Access 97 as their preferred database application development environment. Using hands-on, real-world examples, this book teaches key programming and development concepts and provides extensive coverage of the most widely used topics in database programming. This book covers key topics including VBA, ADO, OLE DB, ODBCDirect, jet replication, code libraries, performance optimization, security, Visual SourceSafe, and Web connectivity. The book's CD-ROM is loaded with sample database applications and source code that can be adapted to your everyday, real-world programs.

Price: $49.99 USA/$70.95 CAN   User Level: Accomplished–Expert

ISBN: 0-672-31049-X   1,000 pages

Peter Norton's Guide to Access 97 Programming

Peter Norton and Virginia Andersen

With the release of Access 97 and its use of Visual Basic for Applications, more users will be looking for a straightforward book that leads them through the basics of programming in Access 97—while still covering the more advanced topics. Following the success of the best-selling *Peter Norton Premier* series, this complete reference takes a user-friendly approach to allow beginners to learn at their own pace, while advanced users can quickly access the techniques and information they need. This book covers key development areas including VBA, ActiveX, ADO, OLE DB, ODBCDirect, replication, code libraries, reports, switchboards, toolbar objects, wizards, and more. Real-world programming techniques and the step-by-step format make learning easy. The CD-ROM contains source code and sample database applications.

Price: $35.00 USA/$49.95 CAN   User Level: Casual–Accomplished

ISBN: 0-672-31050-3   700 pages

Add to Your Sams Library Today with the Best Books for Programming, Operating Systems, and New Technologies

The easiest way to order is to pick up the phone and call

1-800-428-5331

between 9:00 a.m. and 5:00 p.m. EST.
For faster service, please have your credit card available.

ISBN	Quantity	Description of Item	Unit Cost	Total Cost
0-672-31078-3		Teach Yourself Oracle8 Database Development in 21 Days	$49.99	
0-672-31110-0		Teach Yourself SQL in 21 Days, Second Edition	$39.99	
0-672-31049-X		Access 97 Programming Unleashed	$49.99	
0-672-31050-3		Peter Norton's Guide to Access 97 Programming	$35.00	
		Shipping and Handling: See information below.		
		TOTAL		

Shipping and Handling: $4.00 for the first book and $1.75 for each additional book. If you need to have it NOW, we can ship product to you in 24 hours for an additional charge of approximately $18.00, and you will receive your item overnight or in two days. Overseas shipping and handling adds $2.00. Prices subject to change. Call between 9:00 a.m. and 5:00 p.m. EST for availability and pricing information on latest editions.

201 W. 103rd Street, Indianapolis, Indiana 46290

1-800-428-5331 — Orders   1-800-835-3202 — Fax   1-800-858-7674 — Customer Service